L'Europe[f]
0 50 100 200 300 400 500 MILLES
0 100 200 300 400 500 600 700 800 KILOMÈTRES
m = masculin f = féminin
Le français est la langue maternelle majoritaire
Le français est une des langues officielles
Le français est la langue administrative
Présence de la langue française sans statut particulier
Reykjavik
L'ISLANDE[f]
LA SUÈDE
LA FINLANDE
LA NORVÈGE
Helsinki
St-Pétersbourg
LA RUSSIE
Oslo
Tallinn
Stockholm
L'ESTONIE[f]
Moscou
L'ÉCOSSE[f]
LA MER DU NORD
Riga
LA LETTONIE
L'IRLANDE[f] DU NORD
LA GRANDE-BRETAGNE
LE DANEMARK
LA MER BALTIQUE
Copenhague
LA LITUANIE
L'IRLANDE[f]
Dublin
Vilnius
Tver
Minsk
LE PAYS DE GALLES
L'ANGLETERRE[f]
LA BIÉLORUSSIE
Amsterdam
Berlin
Varsovie
Londres
LES PAYS-BAS[m]
L'ALLEMAGNE[f]
LA POLOGNE
LA BELGIQUE
Bruxelles
Bonn
Kyev
Jersey
Luxembourg
Prague
L'UKRAINE[f]
LE LUXEMBOURG
LA RÉPUBLIQUE TCHÈQUE
Paris
LA SLOVAQUIE
L'OCÉAN[m] ATLANTIQUE
Bratislava
Vienne
LA MOLDAVIE
LA FRANCE
Budapest
Chisinau
Berne
Lausanne
LA SUISSE
L'AUTRICHE[f]
LA HONGRIE
Genève
Ljubljana
Zagreb
LA ROUMANIE
le Val d'Aoste
LA SLOVÉNIE
LA CROATIE
Belgrade
L'ITALIE[f]
LA BOSNIE-HERZÉGOVINE
Bucarest
LA MER NOIRE
LA MER ADRIATIQUE
Sarajevo
LA SERBIE
LA BULGARIE
LE PORTUGAL
L'ANDORRE[f]
LE MONTÉNÉGRO
Sofia
Madrid
La Corse
Istanbul
Lisbonne
Ajaccio
Rome
Titograd
Skopje
L'ESPAGNE[f]
Tirana
LA MACÉDOINE
L'ALBANIE[f]
LA TURQUIE
LA GRÈCE
LA MER ÉGÉE
LA MER MÉDITERRANÉE
Athènes
L'AFRIQUE[f]
LA CRÈTE

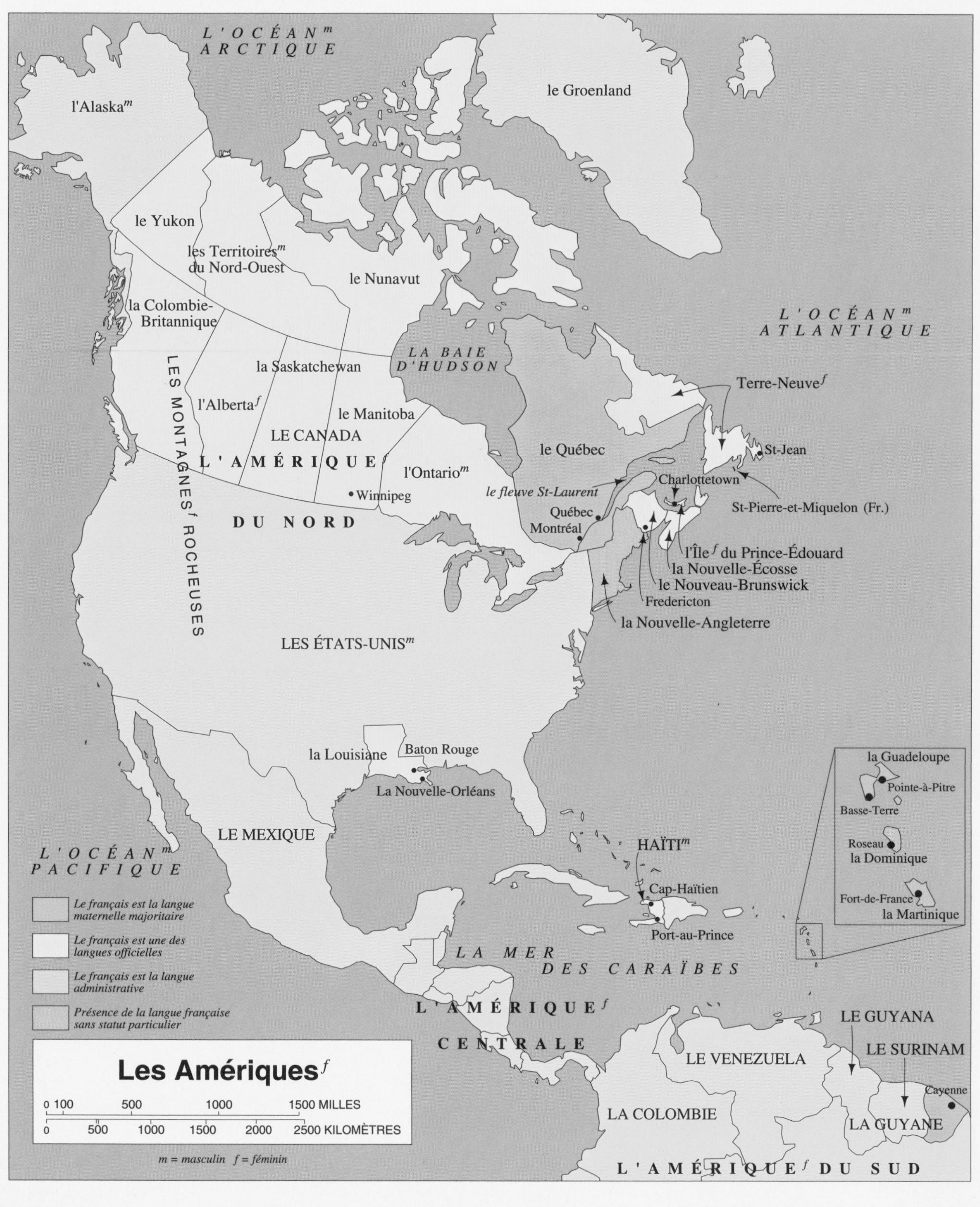
L'OCÉAN[m] ARCTIQUE
le Groenland
l'Alaska[m]
le Yukon
les Territoires[m] du Nord-Ouest
le Nunavut
la Colombie-Britannique
L'OCÉAN[m] ATLANTIQUE
LA BAIE D'HUDSON
LES MONTAGNES[f] ROCHEUSES
la Saskatchewan
Terre-Neuve[f]
l'Alberta[f]
le Manitoba
LE CANADA
le Québec
St-Jean
L'AMÉRIQUE[f]
l'Ontario[m]
Charlottetown
le fleuve St-Laurent
Winnipeg
St-Pierre-et-Miquelon (Fr.)
Québec
DU NORD
Montréal
l'Île[f] du Prince-Édouard
la Nouvelle-Écosse
le Nouveau-Brunswick
Fredericton
la Nouvelle-Angleterre
LES ÉTATS-UNIS[m]
la Guadeloupe
Baton Rouge
la Louisiane
Pointe-à-Pitre
La Nouvelle-Orléans
Basse-Terre
Roseau
la Dominique
LE MEXIQUE
HAÏTI[m]
L'OCÉAN[m] PACIFIQUE
Cap-Haïtien
Fort-de-France
la Martinique
Port-au-Prince
Le français est la langue maternelle majoritaire
Le français est une des langues officielles
LA MER DES CARAÏBES
Le français est la langue administrative
Présence de la langue française sans statut particulier
L'AMÉRIQUE[f] CENTRALE
LE GUYANA
LE SURINAM
LE VENEZUELA
Les Amériques[f]
0 100 500 1000 1500 MILLES
0 500 1000 1500 2000 2500 KILOMÈTRES
Cayenne
LA COLOMBIE
LA GUYANE
m = masculin f = féminin
L'AMÉRIQUE[f] DU SUD

IMPORTANT

HERE IS YOUR REGISTRATION CODE TO ACCESS MCGRAW-HILL PREMIUM CONTENT AND MCGRAW-HILL ONLINE RESOURCES

For key premium online resources you need THIS CODE to gain access. Once the code is entered, you will be able to use the web resources for the length of your course.

Access is provided only if you have purchased a new book.

If the registration code is missing from this book, the registration screen on our website, and within your WebCT or Blackboard course will tell you how to obtain your new code. Your registration code can be used only once to establish access. It is not transferable

To gain access to these online resources

1. USE your web browser to go to: **www.mhhe.com/debuts2**
2. CLICK on "First Time User"
3. ENTER the Registration Code printed on the tear-off bookmark on the right
4. After you have entered your registration code, click on "Register"
5. FOLLOW the instructions to setup your personal UserID and Password
6. WRITE your UserID and Password down for future reference. Keep it in a safe place.

If your course is using WebCT or Blackboard, you'll be able to use this code to access the McGraw-Hill content within your instructor's online course.

To gain access to the McGraw-Hill content in your instructor's WebCT or Blackboard course simply log into the course with the user ID and Password provided by your instructor. Enter the registration code exactly as it appears to the right when prompted by the system. You will only need to use this code the first time you click on McGraw-Hill content.

These instructions are specifically for student access. Instructors are not required to register via the above instructions.

The McGraw-Hill Companies

Thank you, and welcome to your McGraw-Hill Online Resources.

ISBN-13: 978-0-07-321921-9
ISBN-10: 0-07-321921-5 t/a
t/a
Siskin,Debuts, 2/e

NDQK-3NXG-3GUK-DRQP-4TFY

REGISTRATION CODE

REGISTRATION CODE

The McGraw-Hill Companies

Mc Graw Hill Higher Education

Débuts

An Introduction to French

Second Edition

H. Jay Siskin
Cabrillo College

Ann Williams
Metropolitan State College, Denver

Thomas T. Field
University of Maryland, Baltimore County

Boston Burr Ridge, IL Dubuque, IA Madison, WI New York San Francisco St. Louis
Bangkok Bogotá Caracas Kuala Lumpur Lisbon London Madrid Mexico City
Milan Montreal New Delhi Santiago Seoul Singapore Sydney Taipei Toronto

This is an EBI book.

Published by McGraw-Hill, an imprint of The McGraw-Hill Companies, Inc., 1221 Avenue of the Americas, New York, NY 10020.

This book is printed on acid-free paper.

2 3 4 5 6 7 8 9 0 DOW/DOW 0 9 8 7 6

ISBN 10: 0-07-312544-X (Student's Edition)
ISBN 13: 978-0-07-312544-2
ISBN 10: 0-07-321910-X (Instructor's Edition)
ISBN 13: 978-0-07-321910-3

Editor-in-chief: *Emily Barrosse*
Publisher: *William R. Glass*
Sponsoring editor: *William R. Glass*
Director of development: *Susan Blatty*
Development editor: *Peggy Potter*
Marketing manager: *Nick Agnew*
Project manager: *Anne Fuzellier*
Production supervisor: *Richard DeVitto*
Design manager: *Violeta Díaz*
Freelance interior and cover designer: *Maureen McCutcheon/McCutcheon Design*
Art editor: *Emma Ghiselli*
Supplements producer: *Louis Swaim*
Photo research coordinator: *Nora Agbayani*
Photo researcher: *PhotoSearch, Inc.*
Compositor: *TechBooks/GTS, York, PA*
Printer and binder: *RR Donnelley & Sons*
Typeface: *10/12 Legacy Serif Book*

Library of Congress Cataloging-in-Publication Data

Siskin, H. Jay.
Débuts : an introduction to French / H. Jay Siskin, Ann Williams, Thomas T. Field.—2nd ed.
p. cm.
Includes index.
ISBN 0-07-312544-X
1. French language—Textbooks for foreign speakers—English. I. Williams, Ann. II. Field, Thomas T. III. Title.

PC2129.E5 S546 2005
448.2'421—dc22

2005052269

The Internet addresses listed in the text were accurate at the time of publication. The inclusion of a Web site does not indicate an endorsement by the authors or McGraw-Hill, and McGraw-Hill does not guarantee the accuracy of the information presented at these sites.

http://www.mhhe.com

I dedicate this book to my partner, Gregory P. Trauth (1958–1999), whose life taught me the importance of generosity, integrity, and most of all, love. "Good night, sweet prince, / And flights of angels sing thee to thy rest!"

And to my family, David, Frances, and Jan Siskin, for their encouragement and support during the course of the project.

H. Jay Siskin

I dedicate this project to my son, Benjamin, a constant reminder that language opens all doors.

Ann Williams

Thank you once again, Marie-Hélène, for your support and help.

Thomas T. Field

About the Authors

H. Jay Siskin Dr. Siskin received his Ph.D. in French and Romance linguistics from Cornell University, and has taught at Wayne State University, Northwestern University, the University of Oregon, and Brandeis University. He is currently a professor of French at Cabrillo College. He has coauthored five college-level French textbooks.

Ann Williams Dr. Williams received her Ph.D. from Northwestern University and also has a Diplôme d'Études Approfondies from the Université de Lyon II. She is currently professor of French at Metropolitan State College of Denver, where she teaches courses in language, literature, and culture. She regularly presents conference papers and writes on contemporary culture, and she has coauthored three other college-level French textbooks. Dr. Williams was the recipient of a McGraw-Hill/Glencoe Teacher of the Year award in 2001, the Excellence in Teaching Award (Golden Key Honor Society) in 1994, and Young Educator of the Year in 1991 (Colorado Congress of Foreign Language Teachers).

Thomas T. Field Dr. Field received his Ph.D. in linguistics from Cornell University. He is currently professor of Linguistics and French and Director of the Center for the Humanities at the University of Maryland, Baltimore County. Dr. Field's research is focused on Occitan sociolinguistics and the teaching of French and Francophone culture. In 1996, he was named Maryland Professor of the Year by the Carnegie Foundation for the Advancement of Teaching.

Contents

Vocabulaire

Structures

Culture / Synthèse

Vocabulaire

Chapitre

Une nouvelle vie à Paris 83

Chapitre

Secrets 107

Chapitre

Bonjour, grand-père! 129

Structures	Culture / Synthèse
12. Les adjectifs possessifs; la possession avec **de** 91 13. Le verbe **avoir**; **il y a** et **il n'y a pas de**; expressions avec **avoir** 94 14. Questions avec inversion et avec **où**, **quand**, **pourquoi**, **comment**, **combien de** 98	*Regards sur la culture:* La diversité de la France 97 *Synthèse—Lecture:* La famille française du XXIe siècle (adapté du *Nouveau Guide France*) 103
15. Le verbe **faire**; des expressions avec **faire** 116 16. L'adjectif interrogatif **quel** et l'adjectif démonstratif **ce** 118 17. Le genre de certains substantifs et quelques pluriels spéciaux 122	*Regards sur la culture:* La famille 121 *Synthèse—Culture:* La famille, source de culture 126
18. Les verbes **pouvoir** et **vouloir** 136 19. Les verbes avec changement d'orthographe 139 20. Les pronoms interrogatifs 143	*Regards sur la culture:* Les habits et la mode 142 *Synthèse—Lecture:* Quelques grandes tendances de la mode française (adapté de l'Encyclopédie Microsoft® Encarta® en ligne) 145

Vocabulaire

Structures	Culture / Synthèse
21. L'article partitif et les expressions de quantité 156 22. Le complément d'objet indirect 161 23. Les verbes **prendre**, **mettre**, **boire** 165	*Regards sur la culture:* Le marché et la cuisine 164 *Synthèse—Culture:* Cuisines du monde francophone 170
24. Les verbes réguliers en **-re** 181 25. L'impératif 184 26. Quelques verbes comme **sortir** 188	*Regards sur la culture:* Principes de conversation 187 *Synthèse—Lecture:* «Familiale» (Jacques Prévert) 191
27. Le complément d'objet direct 202 28. Les verbes pronominaux 206 29. Le verbe **devoir** 211	*Regards sur la culture:* La santé en France 205 *Synthèse—Culture:* La médecine et la culture 213

Vocabulaire

Structures	Culture / Synthèse
30. Le passé composé (I) 224 31. Le passé composé (II) 227 32. Les verbes **voir, croire** et **recevoir** 231	*Regards sur la culture:* Les cafés et les restaurants 229 *Synthèse—Lecture:* La Deuxième Guerre mondiale, les Français et l'Occupation 235
33. Le passé composé avec l'auxiliaire **être** 248 34. Le passé composé des verbes pronominaux 250 35. Les verbes réguliers en **-ir** 253	*Regards sur la culture:* Le couple 252 *Synthèse—Culture:* L'histoire et le mythe 257
36. L'imparfait (I) 267 37. L'imparfait (II) 269 38. Les verbes **dire, lire** et **écrire** 273	*Regards sur la culture:* Les étapes de la vie 271 *Synthèse—Lecture:* «Mon amant de Saint-Jean» (Carrara et Agel) 275

Vocabulaire

Structures

Culture / Synthèse

Vocabulaire

Structures

Culture / Synthèse

Vocabulaire

Structures

Culture / Synthèse

Structures

Culture / Synthèse

Appendices

Lexiques

Preface

How often have you tried to integrate French films into your first-year French course and found the language too difficult for your students to comprehend? How many times have you been disappointed by the French videos offered with other textbooks? Would you like your students to watch a French film that they can actually understand, and one that will help them learn about French language and culture? If so, this program is for you!

The *Débuts* / *Le Chemin du retour* Program: What Is It?

The textbook, *Débuts,* and the film, *Le Chemin du retour,* are a completely integrated film-based introductory course for learning French language and culture.

A two-hour feature-length film, *Le Chemin du retour* is the story of a young television journalist, Camille Leclair, and her pursuit of the truth about her grandfather's mysterious past. Through Camille's quest, students learn language and culture in the functional context provided by the story.

Unlike other textbook/video programs in which the video component is thematically, functionally, or grammatically driven, and thus self-consciously pedagogical, this program has been developed so that the textbook is a complement to the film. The film narrative is what drives the scope and sequence of vocabulary and grammar, the presentation of culture, and the development of reading and writing. This does not mean, however, that these items are presented in a random fashion. Rather, the screenwriter worked within the authors' pedagogical framework *but did not let it limit* his creative expression. He did a wonderful job of writing a good story while still honoring the major steps in learning the French language.

The textbook/film package grew out of the authors' conviction that language learning is more than just learning skills: it is also a process in which understanding of culture must surely occupy a central position. Therefore, *Débuts* and *Le Chemin du retour* emphasize the importance of cultural awareness and understanding, not only of the French culture, but also of the student's own culture.

Equally important, the authors strongly believe in the principles of communicative competence. *Débuts* gives students a solid foundation in the structure of the language, stressing acquisition of high-frequency grammar, vocabulary, and functional language. In addition, students come to view listening, reading, and writing as active tasks, requiring meaningful interaction as well as high-order cognitive processing.

The Goals of the Program

The overall goal in *Débuts* is to move students toward communicative competence while guiding them toward intercultural sophistication. Included in this framework are the following student objectives:

- to communicate orally and in writing in natural-sounding French and in culturally appropriate ways
- to read with comprehension both informational and literary texts taken from authentic French sources
- to understand French when spoken by a variety of people using authentic speech patterns and rates of speed
- to increase awareness and understanding of cultural institutions and culturally determined patterns of behavior
- to develop critical-thinking skills as they apply to language learning
- to link language study to broader and complementary discipline areas

Cultural Competence

Débuts had its origins in the desire to provide students with a stimulating, culturally rich set of tools for the acquisition of French. Cultural content was thus a central concern in the devising of the plot of *Le Chemin du retour,* and it has been integrated into every section of the text. Through the film, students have the opportunity for intensive exposure not only to the language and communicative habits of French speakers, but also to the visual culture of objects and nonverbal communication and to the auditory culture of music and the sounds of everyday life.

The approach to culture in *Débuts* is content-based. Themes treated in the sections specifically devoted to culture derive from the film but consistently move students toward the big questions of culture, stimulating them to consider matters that are of concern to all people, whether or not they ever travel to the French-speaking world. The authors have made culture a "hook" in this program, to generate interest in longer-term language study and to place the study of language and culture within the larger context of a humanistic education. The cultural content of *Débuts* aims to be thought-provoking and to expand students' horizons beyond simple "travelogue" facts toward understanding the roots of cultural differences.

The National Standards

With its integrated, multifaceted approach to culture, *Débuts* exemplifies the spirit of the National Standards* of foreign language education. By watching the characters in the film perform routine tasks and interactions and by grappling with complex issues of history and identity, students are exposed to a multiplicity of products, processes, and perspectives.

Through the presentation of functional language, role-play activities, and personalized activities, as well as an emphasis on listening comprehension, *Débuts* emphasizes **communication**. Documents, readings, and other exploratory activities help students make **connections** between their study of French, other discipline areas, and their own lives. As for **culture**, the *Regards sur la culture* and *Synthèse* sections in the textbook provide sustained opportunities for hypothesis and analysis, inviting students to make connections between beliefs, behaviors, and cultural artifacts. Ample opportunities are also provided for cross-cultural **comparisons** in the follow-up activities to the *Regards sur la culture* and *Synthèse* sections. Finally, web-based and experiential activities allow students to explore the many types of **communities** inherent in the French-speaking world.

New to the Second Edition

Student Edition

- **New chapter openers:** The design of the book has been lightly modified to give it a fresh, appealing look. This redesign includes a new chapter opener feature incorporating the actual call sheet used by the film company during the shooting of *Le Chemin du retour*. This call sheet was used to inform the cast and crew of all the particulars of the filming of each scene—locations, dates, times, actors, and story line. It may be used in class in conjunction with the chapter opener photo as a previewing tool for each episode.
- **Vocabulary and grammar activities** have been reworked throughout to provide more opportunities for personalization.

**Standards for Foreign Language Learning: Preparing for the 21st Century* (1996, National Standards in Foreign Language Education Project). The standards outlined in this publication were established by a collaboration of the American Council on the Teaching of Foreign Languages (ACTFL), the American Association of Teachers of French (AATF), the American Association of Teachers of Spanish and Portuguese (AATSP), and the American Association of Teachers of German (AATG).

- **Revised grammar scope and sequence:** The sequencing of the grammar has been significantly revised for this edition, primarily in Chapters 10–22. These changes include the following:
  - More challenging grammar points such as the **passé composé** with **avoir** and **être**, the **passé composé** of pronominal verbs, and the **imparfait** have been split into five points to allow for easier comprehension and retention and to provide more opportunities for practice.
  - New structure points have been created to review difficult concepts before the introduction of a more sophisticated point. These include an object pronoun review before introduction of double object pronouns and a review of the **passé composé vs. imparfait** before the introduction of the **plus-que-parfait**.
  - Certain grammar points have been moved to earlier or later chapters where they are more appropriate. For example, adverbs of time, **il est vs. c'est** + profession, and **tout** have been moved from Chapters 10, 11, and 14 to the first third of the book. **Depuis/pendant** and the formation and position of adverbs formerly in Chapters 11 and 12 respectively have been moved to Chapter 14.
  - Certain structure points more appropriate for an intermediate-level program have been eliminated. These include possessive pronouns, the present participle, and **aucun ne...** .
- **New readings:** There are three new readings in this edition. The Chapter 6 reading is now an overview of the history of French fashion design. Chapter 11's reading treats **Le Grand Dérangement**, the history of the Acadian expulsion of the French and their move to Louisiana. Chapter 13 treats the recent trend toward text messaging (SMS) in France.

Changes to the Instructor's Edition

- The **Vocabulaire relatif à l'épisode** notes found in **Visionnement 1** have been reworked to present the key vocabulary in context in full sentences.
- Helpful teaching suggestions have been added to the *Annotated Instructor's Edition* that reflect valuable input from our users and reviewers.

Structure of *Le Chemin du retour*

Le Chemin du retour is available in a Director's Cut version that is the uninterrupted, full-length feature film. The Instructional Version of the film, however, divides the story into a preliminary episode, twenty-two story episodes, and an epilogue. Except for the **Épisode préliminaire**, which introduces students to the concept of learning French through film, each episode of *Le Chemin du retour* follows the same three-step format.

1. Students watch and participate in on-screen pre-viewing activities.
   - **Vous avez vu...** Scenes from previous episodes are used to remind students about main events in the story that will help them understand the new episode.
   - **Vous allez voir...** Scenes previewing the upcoming episode set up the context for what students will see and hear in the episode.
   - **Paroles et images** This section, which occurs through Episode 11, introduces and practices a particular viewing strategy that students can apply to help them understand the language and events of the film.
2. Students view the complete episode.

3. Students watch and participate in on-screen postviewing activities.
   - **Vous avez compris?** Scenes from the episode are used in a variety of multiple-choice and true-false activities to help students verify their comprehension of the main ideas and the plot of the episode they've just viewed. Students who didn't understand an important point as they viewed the episode will find they understand more after doing these activities.
   - **Langue en contexte** A transition back to the textbook, this section identifies for students the language functions and structures they will learn about in the textbook. Appropriate scenes from the film are subtitled in French and the targeted grammar and vocabulary are highlighted in yellow.

Using *Le Chemin du retour* in a Classroom Setting

The film, *Le Chemin du retour,* can be used as the foundation for a classroom-based beginning French course at the college level. As such, it offers several options for implementation. For example, an instructor may

- use the textbook, *Débuts,* and the film in class, assign most of the material in the *Workbook / Laboratory Manual* for homework, and follow up selected homework activities with discussions in class.
- use only the textbook in class, and have students view the film episodes at home, in the media center, or in the language laboratory.
- use the Student Viewer's Handbook with the film either by itself or to accompany other print materials.

Options for Using *Le Chemin du retour*

The film, *Le Chemin du retour,* can also be used

- in a distance learning course.
- as an offering for adult or continuing education students.
- as the foundation for French courses at the high school level.
- as a supplement to beginning, intermediate, or advanced courses, at all levels of instruction.
- as a resource for informal learning.
- as training materials for French-language classes in business and industry.
- as a significant addition to library movie collections.

Cast of Characters

Camille Leclair

A young television journalist who searches for the truth about her grandfather's past.

Mado Leclair

Camille's mother, who fears the truth and wants to keep her father's history hidden forever.

Bruno Gall

Camille's cohost on the morning television show "Bonjour!"

Rachid Bouhazid

A new reporter at "Bonjour!" who, with his family, must adjust to a new life in Paris.

Louise Leclair

Camille's grandmother, who encourages her granddaughter to pursue her quest for the truth.

Martine Valloton

Producer of "Bonjour!" who has to risk her job to support Camille's determination to find out about her grandfather.

Hélène Thibaut

A journalist from Quebec, and friend of Bruno and Camille.

David Girard

Historian, friend of Bruno, who researches information about Camille's grandfather.

Alex Béraud

A musician who plays in the Mouffetard Market. Friend of Louise, Mado, and Camille.

Sonia Bouhazid

Wife of Rachid and mother of their daughter, Yasmine.

Jeanne Leblanc

A woman who knew Camille's grandfather during the time of the German occupation of France.

Roland Fergus

A man who worked with Camille's grandfather during the German occupation and who holds the key to the truth.

A Guided Tour of the Textbook

Débuts, the textbook, is clearly organized and easy to use. The chapters are coordinated with the individual episodes of the film. Each of the twenty-two main chapters consists of the following self-contained teaching modules, which maximize flexibility in course design. The preliminary chapter, containing a slightly different structure, introduces students to basic vocabulary and provides an overall framework for using the film.

Chapter Opener

Chapter learning goals prepare students for what is to come in the chapter and in the accompanying movie episode.

Vocabulaire en contexte

Thematically grouped vocabulary is presented in culturally informative contexts with drawings and scenes from the movie. It is accompanied by activities that promote vocabulary development.

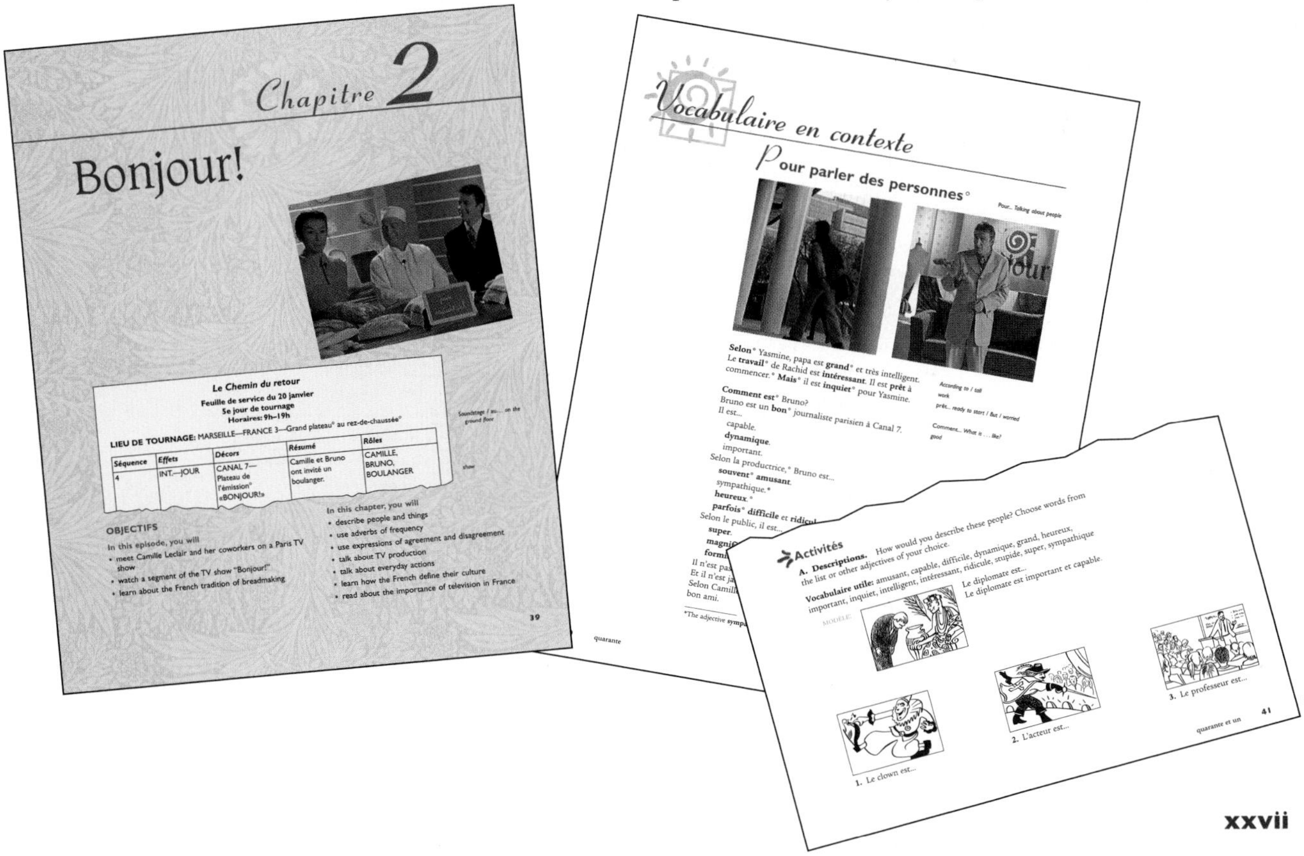

Visionnement 1

This section provides pre- and postviewing activities that supplement those found on-screen in the movie episode, as well as vocabulary needed for comprehension and questions that focus students' attention on what to watch and listen for in the story.

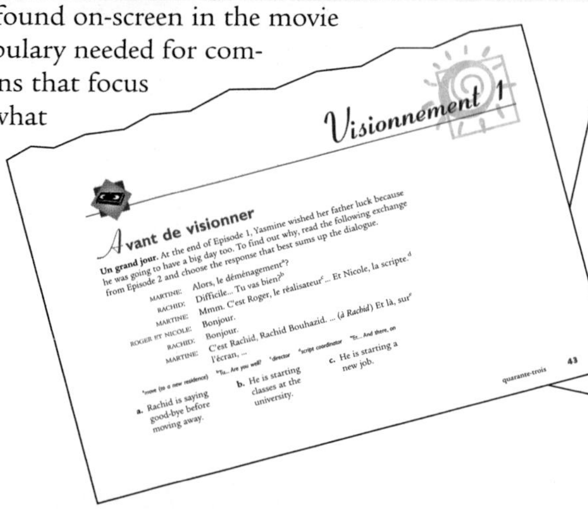

Structure

Three grammar points per chapter are introduced through clear and concise explanations and examples from the movie. Grammar points are accompanied by a wide range of practice, from controlled and form-focused to open-ended and creative communicative activities.

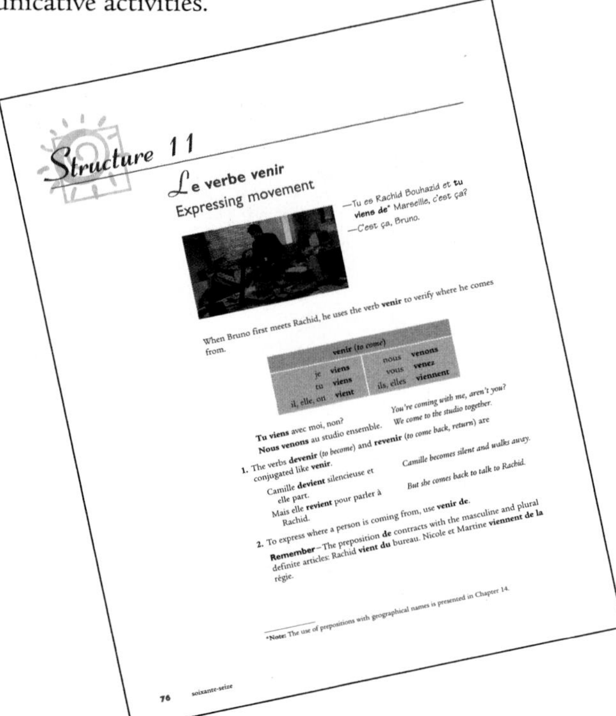

Structure 11

Le verbe venir

Expressing movement

—Tu es Rachid Bouhazid et tu viens de* Marseille, c'est ça?
—C'est ça, Bruno.

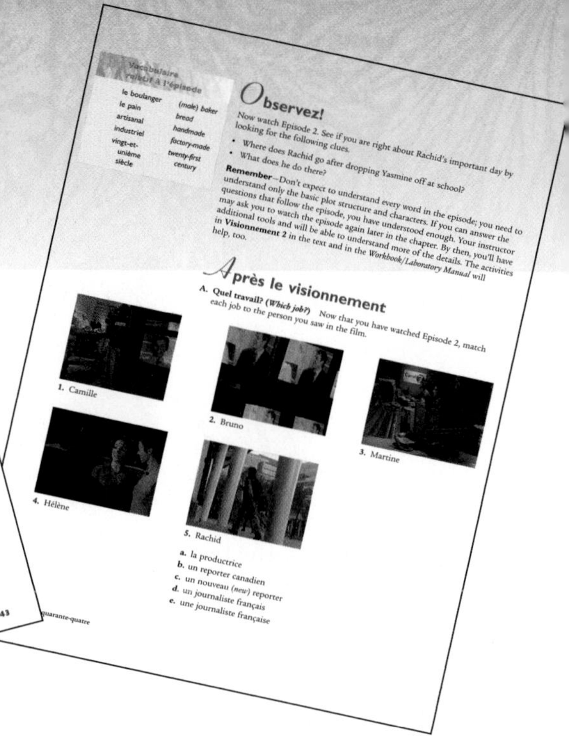

When Bruno first meets Rachid, he uses the verb **venir** to verify where he comes from.

venir (to come)	
je **viens**	nous **venons**
tu **viens**	vous **venez**
il, elle, on **vient**	ils, elles **viennent**

Tu viens avec moi, non? *You're coming with me, aren't you?*
Nous venons au studio ensemble. *We come to the studio together.*

1. The verbs **devenir** (*to become*) and **revenir** (*to come back, return*) are conjugated like **venir**.

Camille **devient** silencieuse et elle part. *Camille becomes silent and walks away.*
Mais elle **revient** pour parler à Rachid. *But she comes back to talk to Rachid.*

2. To express where a person is coming from, use **venir de**.

Remember—The preposition **de** contracts with the masculine and plural definite articles: Rachid **vient du** bureau. Nicole et Martine **viennent de la** régie.

*Note: The use of prepositions with geographical names is presented in Chapter 14.

76 soixante-seize

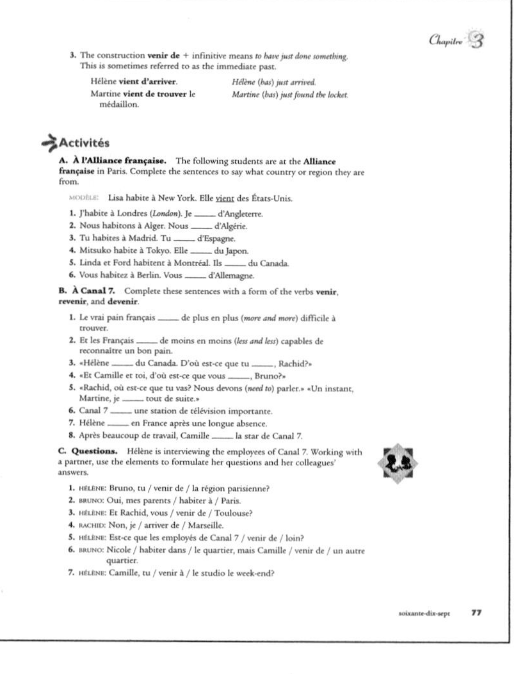

Chapitre 3

3. The construction **venir de** + infinitive means *to have just done something*. This is sometimes referred to as the immediate past.

Hélène **vient d'arriver**. *Hélène (has) just arrived.*
Martine **vient de trouver** le médaillon. *Martine (has) just found the locket.*

Activités

A. À l'Alliance française. The following students are at the **Alliance française** in Paris. Complete the sentences to say what country or region they are from.

MODÈLE: Lisa habite à New York. Elle vient des États-Unis.

1. J'habite à Londres (*London*). Je ____ d'Angleterre.
2. Nous habitons à Alger. Nous ____ d'Algérie.
3. Tu habites à Madrid. Tu ____ d'Espagne.
4. Mitsuko habite à Tokyo. Elle ____ du Japon.
5. Linda et Ford habitent à Montréal. Ils ____ du Canada.
6. Vous habitez à Berlin. Vous ____ d'Allemagne.

B. À Canal 7. Complete these sentences with a form of the verbs **venir**, **revenir**, and **devenir**.

1. Le vrai pain français ____ de plus en plus (*more and more*) difficile à trouver.
2. Et les Français ____ de moins en moins (*less and less*) capables de reconnaître un bon pain.
3. «Hélène ____ du Canada. D'où est-ce que tu ____, Rachid?»
4. «Et Camille et toi, d'où est-ce que vous ____, Bruno?»
5. «Rachid, où est-ce que tu vas? Nous devons (*need to*) parler.» «Un instant, Martine, je ____ tout de suite.»
6. Canal 7 ____ une station de télévision importante.
7. Hélène ____ en France après une longue absence.
8. Après beaucoup de travail, Camille ____ la star de Canal 7.

C. Questions. Hélène is interviewing the employees of Canal 7. Working with a partner, use the elements to formulate her questions and her colleagues' answers.

1. HÉLÈNE: Bruno, tu / venir de / la région parisienne?
2. BRUNO: Oui, mes parents / habiter à / Paris.
3. HÉLÈNE: Et Rachid, vous / venir de / Toulouse?
4. RACHID: Non, je / arriver de / Marseille.
5. HÉLÈNE: Est-ce que les employés de Canal 7 / venir de / loin?
6. BRUNO: Nicole / habiter dans / le quartier, mais Camille / venir de / un autre quartier.
7. HÉLÈNE: Camille, tu / venir à / le studio le week-end?

soixante-dix-sept 77

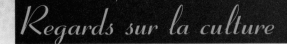

Regards sur la culture

A cultural note and its accompanying critical-thinking question deepen students' awareness and understanding of cultural issues raised in the movie episode or chapter vocabulary.

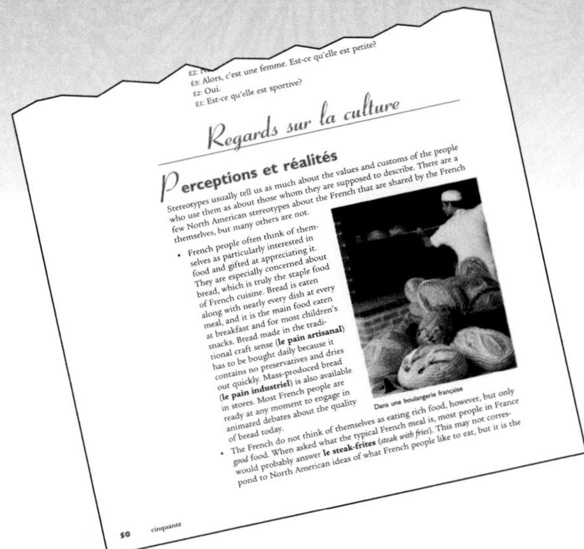

É2: N...
É3: Alors, c'est une femme. Est-ce qu'elle est petite?
É2: Oui.
É1: Est-ce qu'elle est sportive?

Regards sur la culture

Perceptions et réalités

Stereotypes usually tell us as much about the values and customs of the people who use them as about those whom they are supposed to describe. There are a few North American stereotypes about the French that are shared by the French themselves, but many others are not.

- French people often think of themselves as particularly interested in food and gifted at appreciating it. They are especially concerned about bread, which is truly the staple food of French cuisine. Bread is eaten along with nearly every dish at every meal, and it is the main food eaten at breakfast and for most children's snacks. Bread made in the traditional craft sense (**le pain artisanal**) has to be bought daily because it contains no preservatives and dries out quickly. Mass-produced bread (**le pain industriel**) is also available in stores. Most French people are ready at any moment to engage in animated debates about the quality of bread today.

Dans une boulangerie française

- The French do not think of themselves as eating rich food, however, but only *good* food. When asked what the typical French meal is, most people in France would probably answer **le steak-frites** (*steak with fries*). This may not correspond to North American ideas of what French people like to eat, but it is the

50 cinquante

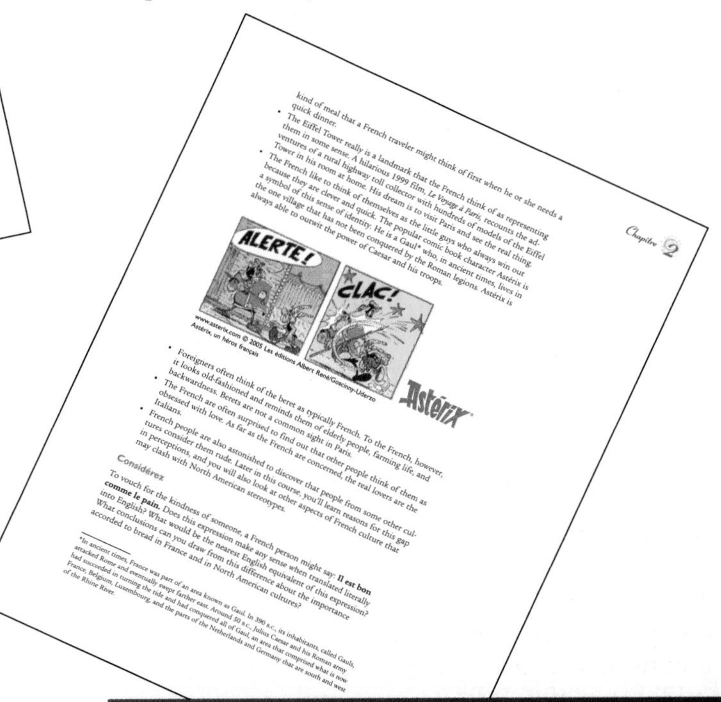

Chapitre 2

kind of meal that a French traveler might think of first when he or she needs a quick dinner.

- The Eiffel Tower really is a landmark that the French think of as representing them in some sense. A hilarious 1999 film, *Le Voyage à Paris*, recounts the adventures of a rural highway toll collector with hundreds of models of the Eiffel Tower in his room at home. His dream is to visit Paris and see the real thing.
- The French like to think of themselves as the little guys who always win out because they are clever and quick. The popular comic book character Astérix is a symbol of this sense of identity. He is a Gaul* who, in ancient times, lives in the one village that has not been conquered by the Roman legions. Astérix is always able to outwit the power of Caesar and his troops.

www.asterix.com © 2005 Les éditions Albert René/Goscinny-Uderzo
Astérix, un héros français

- Foreigners often think of the beret as typically French. To the French, however, it looks old-fashioned and reminds them of elderly people, farming life, and backwardness. Berets are not a common sight in Paris.
- The French are often surprised to find out that other people think of them as obsessed with love. As far as the French are concerned, the real lovers are the Italians.
- French people are also astonished to discover that people from some other cultures consider them rude. Later in this course, you'll learn reasons for this gap in perceptions, and you will also look at other aspects of French culture that may clash with North American stereotypes.

Considérez

To vouch for the kindness of someone, a French person might say: **Il est bon comme le pain.** Does this expression make any sense when translated literally into English? What would be the nearest English equivalent of this expression? What conclusions can you draw from this difference about the importance accorded to bread in France and in North American cultures?

*In ancient times, France was part of an area known as Gaul. In 390 B.C., its inhabitants, called Gauls, attacked Rome and eventually swept farther east. Around 50 B.C., Julius Caesar and his Roman army had succeeded in turning the tide and had conquered all of Gaul, an area that comprised what is now France, Belgium, Luxembourg, and the parts of the Netherlands and Germany that are south and west of the Rhine River.

Visionnement 2

An optional second viewing section encourages students to watch the episode again, this time to concentrate on cultural information.

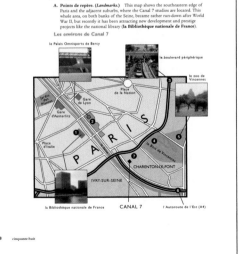

Visionnement 2

Avant de visionner

A. Points de repère. (*Landmarks.*) This map shows the southeastern edge of Paris and the adjacent suburbs, where the Canal 7 studios are located. This whole area, on both banks of the Seine, became rather run-down after World War II, but recently it has been attracting new development and prestige projects like the national library (**la Bibliothèque nationale de France**).

Les environs de Canal 7

le Palais Omnisports de Bercy
le boulevard périphérique
le zoo de Vincennes
Place de la Nation
Jardin des Plantes
Gare de Lyon
Gare d'Austerlitz
Place d'Italie
PARIS
le Bois de Vincennes
CHARENTON-LE-PONT
IVRY-SUR-SEINE
la Bibliothèque nationale de France
CANAL 7
l'Autoroute de l'Est (A4)

58 cinquante-huit

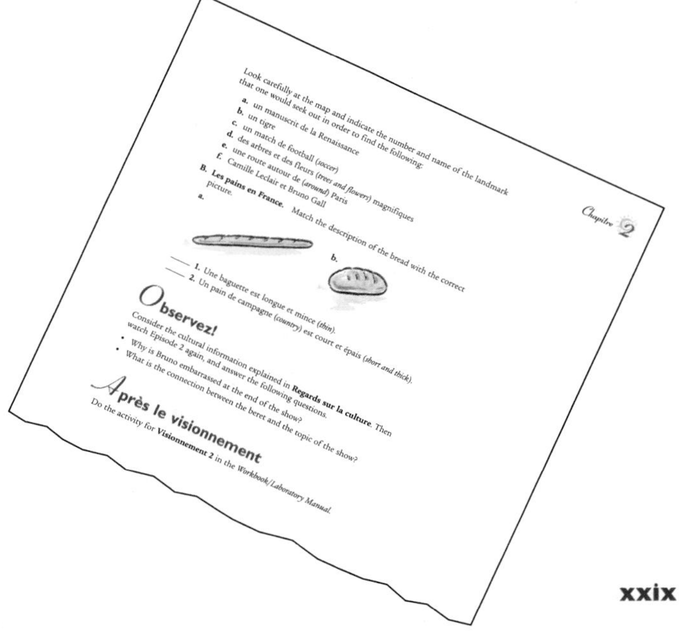

Chapitre 2

Look carefully at the map and indicate the number and name of the landmark that one would seek out in order to find the following:

a. un manuscrit de la Renaissance
b. un tigre
c. un match de football (*soccer*)
d. des arbres et des fleurs (*trees and flowers*) magnifiques
e. une route autour de (*around*) Paris
f. Camille Leclair et Bruno Gall

B. Les pains en France. Match the description of the bread with the correct picture.

a.
b.

___ 1. Une baguette est longue et mince (*thin*).
___ 2. Un pain de campagne (*country*) est court et épais (*short and thick*).

Observez!

Consider the cultural information explained in **Regards sur la culture**. Then watch Episode 2 again, and answer the following questions.

- Why is Bruno embarrassed at the end of the show?
- What is the connection between the beret and the topic of the show?

Après le visionnement

Do the activity for **Visionnement 2** in the *Workbook/Laboratory Manual*.

Synthèse

The chapter culminates in a synthesis section, which alternates between cultural presentations and readings, many of which are literary selections. Prereading strategies and postreading comprehension activities help students develop reading skills. A writing activity (**À écrire**) follows in the *Workbook / Laboratory Manual.*

La famille française du XXIe siècle°

°La... *The French family in the 21st century*

Introduction

La famille française se caractérise par la tradition et la nouveauté.[1] Elle reste la cellule[2] de la vie[3] sociale et on continue à célébrer la famille (fête des mères, fête des pères). Mais on aurait tort[4] de généraliser.

Réflexion de la société

La famille française reflète la diversité des conditions socio-économiques de la société entière. Sous l'influence des conditions de vie, elle se transforme. Il y a des crises internes et les conflits entre générations. La femme a une vie plus indépendante qu'autrefois;[5] les enfants s'émancipent de plus en plus tôt.[6]

Un déjeuner en plein air en famille

La transformation récente

Depuis[7] trente ans, le nombre des mariages diminue. Parallèlement, le nombre des divorces augmente. Autre phénomène récent: le développement de l'union libre ou cohabitation. Ce sont près de 17% des couples qui cohabitent. Conséquence de ce phénomène: 30% des naissances sont des naissances hors[8] mariage. Il faut ajouter[9] aussi la multiplication des familles monoparentales. Ces développements révèlent la coexistence de conceptions très différentes de la vie familiale.

Adapté du *Nouveau Guide France*

[1]*change* [2]*nucleus* [3]*life* [4]*on... one would be mistaken* [5]*than before* [6]*de... earlier and earlier* [7]*For* [8]*outside of* [9]*Il... One must add*

Après la lecture

A. Confirmation. Now that you have read the selection, go back to the prereading strategy activity and see if you would still choose the same

C. Expliquez. Name three factors that explain the evolution of the French family.

D. Jugements. What is the author's attitude toward the evolution of the French family? Does he/she approve of the "new" family, disapprove, or remain neutral? Explain.

À écrire

Do **À écrire** for Chapter 4 in the *Workbook/Laboratory Manual.*

Chapitre 4

Vocabulaire

Les parents

le beau-frère (les beaux-frères) stepbrother; brother-in-law
le beau-père (les beaux-pères) stepfather; father-in-law
la belle-mère (les belles-mères) stepmother; mother-in-law
la belle-sœur (les belles-sœurs) stepsister; sister-in-law
la femme wife
la fille daughter
le fils son
le frère brother
la grand-mère (les grands-mères) grandmother
le grand-père (les grands-pères) grandfather
le mari husband
la mère mother
le neveu nephew
la nièce niece
l'oncle *(m.)* uncle
les parents *(m. pl.)* parents; relatives
le père father
la petite-fille (les petites-filles) granddaughter
le petit-fils (les petits-fils) grandson
la sœur sister
la tante aunt

MOTS APPARENTÉS: **le cousin, la cousine, les grands-parents** *(m. pl.)*
À REVOIR: **les enfants** *(m., f.)*

L'état civil

célibataire single
Ils vivent en union libre. They are living together (without marriage).
veuf (veuve) widowed

MOTS APPARENTÉS: **marié(e), divorcé(e)**

Les nombres à partir de 60

soixante, soixante-dix, quatre-vingts, quatre-vingt-dix, cent, mille, un million, un milliard

cent cinq 105

Other features

Langage fonctionnel
This feature provides useful phrases for carrying on conversations in particular situations.

Vocabulaire relatif à l'épisode
Unfamiliar vocabulary items needed for comprehension of the episode are provided in **Visionnement 1.**

Notez bien!
These marginal notes highlight important details about grammar and vocabulary that students are expected to learn.

Pour en savoir plus
These marginal notes contain optional information about culture, vocabulary, and grammar.

Program Components

As a full-service publisher of quality educational products, McGraw-Hill does much more than just sell textbooks to students; we create and publish an extensive array of print, video, and digital supplements to support instruction on your campus. Orders of new (versus used) textbooks help us to defray the substantial cost of developing such supplements. Please consult your local McGraw-Hill representative to learn about the availability of the supplements that accompany *Débuts.*

Books and Multimedia Materials Available to Adopters and to Students

Student Edition
The *Débuts* textbook is correlated with the individual episodes in the film, *Le Chemin du retour,* and contains vocabulary presentations and activities; pre- and postviewing activities; grammar explanations and practice activities; cultural, historical, and literary readings; and pre- and postreading activities.

Le Chemin du retour

- **Director's Cut:** The full length, uninterrupted two-hour film is available on DVD and in VHS. For the second edition, the **Director's Cut DVD** version has been remastered and has a new, user-friendly interface. The VHS version is available without subtitles, with French subtitles, or with English subtitles.
- **Instructional Version:** This version, available in VHS and **now on DVD,** divides the film into 24 episodes and includes onscreen pre- and postviewing activities. From the main menu of the new DVD, instructors may choose to watch the episode with or without the pre- and postviewing activities.

Workbook / Laboratory Manual, Parts 1 and 2

The *Workbook / Laboratory Manual* Part 1 (Chapters P–11) and Part 2 (Chapters 12–Épilogue) accompany the textbook. Each chapter is divided into sections that follow the organization of the main textbook. Each section, as appropriate, may contain both workbook and laboratory activities. All chapters provide practice in global listening comprehension, pronunciation, speaking, vocabulary, grammar, reading, writing, and culture.

Student Audio Program

For use with the laboratory activities in the *Workbook / Laboratory Manual,* the audio CDs offer 13 hours of listening, oral communication, and pronunciation practice. Part A includes Chapters 1–11 and Part B includes Chapters 12–22. The Audio Program also contains the Vocabulary Audio CD, which is the recorded version of the end vocabulary for each chapter. The complete Audio Program can also be accessed on the *Débuts* website. (See **Premium Content on the Online Learning Center Website,** in the next column.)

Online Workbook / Laboratory Manual

McGraw-Hill is proud to partner with Quia™ in the development of a new digital version of the print *Workbook / Laboratory Manual.* This web version is easy for students to use and ideal for instructors who want to manage students' course work online. Identical in practice material to the print version, the online *Workbook / Laboratory Manual* also contains the full audio program. The Quia™ *Workbook / Laboratory Manual* provides students with automatic feedback and scoring of their work. The Instructor's Workstation contains an easy-to-use gradebook and class roster system that facilitate course management.

Student CD-ROM

This multimedia CD-ROM allows students to work with film clips to practice vocabulary and grammar skills, listening comprehension, and reading skills. Also included on the CD-ROM are Tetris games, sentence scrambles, and other interactive games to engage students in their language learning. A link to the *Débuts* website from each chapter of the CD-ROM gives students access to additional practice, cultural readings, and activities.

Online Learning Center

A complete learning and teaching resource center for both students and instructors, this website includes additional practice for each vocabulary and grammar section of each chapter and offers supplementary cultural readings and web-based activities that extend students' knowledge of the cultural topics introduced in the textbook. Instructors' resources include an online version of the Instructor's Manual, the Film Script, and Audioscript.

Premium Content on the Online Learning Center Website

Students who purchase a *new* copy of *Débuts* have access free of charge to Premium Content on the Online Learning Center website at www.mhhe.com/debuts2. This includes the complete Audio Program that accompanies the *Workbook / Laboratory Manual.* The card bound inside the front cover of this book provides a registration code to access the Premium Content. This code is unique to each individual user. Other study resources may be added to the Premium Content during the life of the edition of the book.

If students purchase a used copy of *Débuts* but would like access to the Premium Content, they may purchase a registration code for a nominal fee. Please visit the Online Learning Center website for more information.

If you are an instructor, you do not need a special registration code for Premium Content. Instructors have full access to all levels of content via the Instructor's Edition link on the home page of the Online Learning Center website. Please contact your local McGraw-Hill sales representative for your password.

Student Viewer's Handbook

Ideal for those courses in which *Le Chemin du retour* is used to supplement textbooks other than *Débuts,* the Handbook offers a variety of pre- and postviewing activities for use with the film.

Books and Multimedia Materials Available to Adopters Only

Instructor's Edition

The Instructor's Edition is identical to the Student Edition except that it contains annotated suggestions, cultural information, additional vocabulary, activity extensions and variations, and so on.

Instructor's Manual

The Instructor's Manual provides additional background information on the film, a tour of the Paris and Marseille locations from the film with neighborhood maps as well as sample lessons, syllabus planning, and scheduling suggestions. It also includes general teaching suggestions, helpful suggestions for using the film, chapter-by-chapter notes, and additional activities. In addition, a Distance Learning Guide and an Answer Key for the Student Edition activities are provided.

Testing Program

The Testing Program consists of two sets of tests for each chapter of *Débuts,* as well as quarter and semester exams. An audioscript is provided for the Listening Comprehension section of each test.

Instructor's Audio Program

The Instructor's Audio Program, available on CD, contains the same material as the Student Audio Program. The Audioscript, which contains the complete recording script of the Audio Program, can be downloaded from the Instructor's Edition of the Online Learning Center or from the Instructor's Resource CD.

Picture File

The Picture File contains fifty color photographs from the film and textbook and is designed to stimulate conversation in the classroom.

Instructor's Resource CD

The Instructor's Resource CD contains the Instructor's Manual, Audioscript, Film Script, and Testing Program.

Acknowledgments

The authors and the publisher would like to acknowledge the instructors across the country whose classroom experience with the program provided us with such valuable feedback for the preparation of the second edition. The appearance of their names in this list does not necessarily constitute their endorsement of the text or its methodology.

Reviewers for *Débuts,* Second Edition

User Diarists

Cynthia Bautista, University of New Mexico
Joan Debrah, University of Hawaii at Manoa
Kaye Murdock, University of Utah
Jennifer Shonk, University of Colorado, Boulder

Reviewers

Brian Arganbright, Transylvania University
Machteld De Poortere, State University of New York, Albany
Brigitte Debord, Lake Forest College
Dr. Béatrice Dupuy, University of Arizona
Audrey Gaquin, United States Naval Academy
Joseph E. Garreau, University of Massachusetts, Lowell
Solène A. Halabi, Mount San Antonio College
Dr. Bette G. Hirsch, Cabrillo College
Martine K. Howard, Camden County College
Kathryn Jospé, Monroe Community College
Sister Mary Helen Kashuba, Chestnut Hill College
Martine Motard-Noar, McDaniel College
Dr. Marina Peters-Newell, University of New Mexico, Albuquerque
William Ryall, State University College, Oneonta
Elizabeth A. Smith, Southwest Virginia Community College
Marisa Smurthwaithe, University of Utah, Salt Lake City
Joy Stalnaker, University of Colorado, Boulder
Larry Wineland, Messiah College
Yvonne Wittels, Albright College
Holly York, Emory University

Reviewers for *Débuts*, First Edition

The authors and the publisher would like to express their gratitude to the following instructors and students across the country whose valuable suggestions contributed to the preparation of the first edition of this program. The appearance of their names in this list does not necessarily constitute their endorsement of the text or its methodology.

Reviewers

Elizabeth Brereton Allen, Washington University
Eileen M. Angelini, Philadelphia University
Miguel Aparicio, Santa Monica College
Daniela Elena Ascavelli, Drexel University
Patricia Eileen Black, California State University, Chico
Ruth L. Bradshaw, Truman State University
Ruth L. Caldwell, Luther College
Judith Jean Chapman, Worcester State College
Simone Clay, University of California, Davis
Dennis Conrad, Clarke College
Suzanne E. Cook, United States Air Force Academy
Véronique F. Courtois, Tufts University
Diane Griffin Crowder, Cornell College
Susan L. Dorff, Boston University
Nicole Dufresne, University of California, Los Angeles
Richard Durán, Baylor University
Karin Egloff, Western Kentucky University
Helen Gant Guillory, St. Edward's University
Hollie Harder, Brandeis University
Shawn Huffman, SUNY Plattsburgh
Madeleine Kernen, Southwest Missouri State University
Elizabeth M. Knutson, United States Naval Academy
Carolyn Gascoigne Lally, University of Nebraska at Omaha
Marc Lony, Loyola Marymount University
Amy Lorenz-Ianke, Loras College
Domenico Maceri, Allan Hancock College
Sayeeda H. Mamoon, University of South Dakota
Alain Martinossi, University of Michigan
Hassan Melehy, University of Connecticut
Mary Jo Muratore, University of Missouri, Columbia
June Hall McCash, Middle Tennessee State University
George J. McCool, Towson University
Kay Riddle McLean, Volunteer State Community College
Juliette Parnell-Smith, University of Nebraska at Omaha
Marina Peters-Newell, University of New Mexico
Denis Rochat, Smith College
Sini Prosper Sanou, University of Arizona
Joanne Schmidt, California State University, Bakersfield
Mary Ellen Scullen, University of Maryland
Dianne Elizabeth Sears, University of Massachusetts, Amherst
Elizabeth Ann Smith, Southwest Virginia Community College
Stuart Smith, Austin Community College
Karen Rhea Sorsby, California State University, Chico
Beverly Turner, Truckee Meadows Community College
Patricia Ann Umfress, Western Carolina University
Guy H. Wagener, University of Nevada, Reno
Alexandra K. Wettlaufer, University of Texas at Austin
Susan L. Wolf, University of Massachusetts, Boston

Focus Group Participants

Ali Alalou, University of Delaware
Eileen M. Angelini, Philadelphia University
Theresa A. Antes, University of Florida
Anne-Marie Bourbon, Queensborough Community College, CUNY
Véronique F. Courtois, Tufts University
Robert Davis, University of Oregon
Hilary Fisher, University of Oregon
Janet Fisher-McPeak, University of Notre Dame
Jeffrey H. Fox, College of DuPage
Mary Jane Highfield, Cornell University
John J. Janc, Minnesota State University, Mankato
Elizabeth Knutson, United States Naval Academy
Philip A. Lee, Macalester College
Kathryn M. Lorenz, University of Cincinnati
George McCool, Towson University
Pary Pezechkian, Augsburg College
Debra Popkin, Baruch College, CUNY
Laurie Postlewate, Barnard College
Pam Renna, Delta College
Sylvie Richards, Queens College, CUNY
Gail L. Riley, American University
Jean Luc Robin, University of Oregon
Arlene J. Russell, Purdue University, Calumet
Gloria Sawicki, Brooklyn College, CUNY
Mary Ellen Scullen, University of Maryland
Christina Vander Vorst, University of Oregon
Catherine Wiebe, University of Oregon
Yvette A. Guillemin Young, University of Wisconsin, Oshkosh

Student Focus Group Participants

Cabrillo College
Brian Honeywell
Megan S. Marietti
Patrick Tanner
Michelle Wonnacott
Benjamin Worden

Metropolitan State College, Denver
Tom Bustinduy
Marina Hudgens
Marie-Meredith Mangum
Ana Bel Marquez
Devin Scheinberg
Bonni Stewart
Brian Stiller
Jennifer Suihlik
Jaime Vargas

University of Maryland, Baltimore County
Dawn Brautlacht
Katie Collins
Michael Cooper
LaTonya R. Howard
Christina Lee
Justina J. Lee
Alejandro Magadán
Omorola Oluponmile
Farah Philippe
John R. Scott
John Thomas

Tufts University
Jacqueline A. Fields
Daniel Kramer
Nannette Martinez
Reid Palmer

University of Oregon
Sara Anoushirvani
John Archetro
Mark Boloens
Hadley Brown
Erin Dawson
Connor Dudley
Amy Horgan
Kelsey Kopra
Abolade Majekobaje
Larissa Rhodes
Andrea Wilcox

The authors would also like to extend very special thanks to the following organizations and individuals:

- David Murray and Ginger Cassell for their tireless work on the creation, direction, production, and final editing of *Le Chemin du retour.*
- SAME Films in France for their efforts in producing this film.
- David Lang, for a beautiful script.
- Karine Adrover, Denis Cherer, and the whole cast and crew for a highly professional production.
- Edge Productions for taking chances and for providing support to get the filming started.
- Cherie Mitschke, Austin Community College, for her endless enthusiasm and creativity in writing the on-screen pre- and postviewing activities.

Additional thanks to Catherine Coste, Claudette Pelletier Deschesnes, Marie-Hélène Le Tuan, Jean-Michel Margot, and Lise Nathan, who provided materials and consultation during the development process.

Finally, the authors wish to thank the editorial, design, and production staff at McGraw-Hill and their associates, especially Peggy Potter, Leslie Oberhuber, and our former editor-in-chief, Thalia Dorwick, for their guidance and inspiration during the creation of the first edition. For this second edition we would like to express our appreciation once again to Peggy Potter for her sharp editorial work, to William R. Glass, our publisher, Susan Blatty, Nicole Dicop-Hineline, Veronica Oliva, Letizia Rossi, Allison Hawco, Nick Agnew, Rachel Dornan, and our terrific marketing team. We would also like to express our gratitude to the production team: David Staloch, Anne Fuzellier, Violeta Díaz, Nora Agbayani, Emma Ghiselli, Diane Renda, Rich DeVitto, Louis Swaim, Elizabeth Stroud, and Melissa Gruzs for all their dedication and hard work on this project.

Chapitre préliminaire

Ça tourne!°

Ça... *Action!*

Le Chemin du retour

Feuille de service° du 22 janvier
7e jour de tournage°
Horaires:° 7 h–17 h

LIEU° DE TOURNAGE: PARIS

Séquence	*Effets*	*Décors*	*Résumé*	*Rôles*
1A	EXT.—JOUR	PARIS—DIVERS PLANS°	Paris s'éveille.°	—

Feuille... *Call sheet*
jour... *day of filming*
Schedule
Place
awakens
divers... *various scenes*

OBJECTIFS

In the film, you will

- see a preview of *Le Chemin du retour*
- find out how the on-screen activities and episodes are organized

In this chapter, you will

- learn how to use this film to study French
- greet others, introduce yourself, and say good-bye in French
- count from 0 to 59 in French
- identify classroom objects and people in the classroom
- learn about French words that look or sound similar to English words
- identify people
- identify and specify people and things

Visionnement

Avant de visionner

Le film

The textbook, *Débuts,* is based on the film *Le Chemin du retour.* The film tells the story of Camille Leclair, a young TV journalist in Paris who risks her career to search for the truth about her grandfather. By following Camille's attempts to unravel the mystery surrounding her grandfather, you will learn about the culture of contemporary France and other French-speaking areas of the world, as well as historical information about France during the Second World War. *Le Chemin du retour* provides a natural, authentic context for learning to understand, speak, read, and write French.

Pour utiliser le film°

Pour... *Using the film*

To use the film to its full advantage as a learning tool, you'll want to remember a few important pieces of advice.

a
b
c
1
Dans le studio, Martine présente de nouveaux collègues à Rachid.
(new)

- Always participate fully in the activities that precede and follow your viewing of the film. These activities are specially designed to help you understand what you see and hear on-screen.
- As a beginning student of French, don't worry about understanding every word as you watch the film. Instead, just try to understand the gist (the main idea) of what is happening. You'll discover that you can figure out quite a lot by watching the action. Watch for body language and other visual clues that may clarify what is happening. Keep an ear tuned not only for vocabulary that you already know, but also for the tone people use as they speak. If you relax and don't worry about understanding every word, you'll find that you can still understand the story. As the course progresses, you will gradually understand more and more of what you hear.
- Watch, too, for similarities and differences between French culture and that of your own country. You may be surprised at some of the ways in which people

interact, and you may see objects that you do not recognize. Think of the film as an immersion experience, like actually going to France, and pay attention to the place and to details of behavior just as carefully as you do to the plot. Many of the cultural features that you notice will be discussed in this book, but you may want to ask your instructor about others.

Pour parler du film°

Pour… *Talking about the film*

To help you talk about the film, you will learn vocabulary in each chapter of the textbook. The following activity will teach you a few terms that you may need in class discussions and in your writing. See if you can find the French equivalent of each English term. Note: The words **un** and **une** mean *a.*

1. film	**a.** un acteur
2. studio	**b.** une actrice
3. scene	**c.** un cinéma
4. actress	**d.** une femme
5. actor	**e.** un film
6. story	**f.** une histoire
7. person	**g.** un homme
8. character	**h.** un personnage
9. movie theater	**i.** une personne
10. man	**j.** une scène
11. woman	**k.** un studio

How many of these words are similar in both English and French?

Visionnez!°

Watch!

Every chapter in the textbook contains previewing activities that you will do before watching the new episode of the story. In fact, you just did a previewing activity in the **Pour parler du film** section. In addition to the activities in the textbook, there are on-screen previewing and postviewing activities to help you understand what you see and hear in the story. Go ahead and do the on-screen lesson for this chapter now. It will introduce you to the story of *Le Chemin du retour* and show you how the on-screen activities in the episodes work.

Vocabulaire en contexte

Les salutations°

Les... *Greetings*

When you address a person you don't know well, include the word **monsieur** (*sir*), **madame** (*madam*), or **mademoiselle** (*miss*) in your greeting. In French, the use of these words is considered part of everyday polite conversation. Here is a very simple conversation that shows what people might say when meeting for the first time.

—**Bonjour**, monsieur. Vous êtes Monsieur* Le Roy?	*Hello. Are you Mr. Le Roy?*
—**Oui**, madame. **Et vous?**	*Yes. And you?*
Comment vous appelez-vous?	*What is your name?*
—**Je m'appelle** Chantal Lépine.	*My name is Chantal Lépine.*
—**Enchanté**, madame.	*Nice to meet you.*
—**Comment allez-vous**, monsieur?	*How are you?*
—**Très bien, merci.** Et vous?	*Very well, thank you. And you?*
—Très bien. **Au revoir**, monsieur.	*Very well. Good-bye.*
—Au revoir, madame.	*Good-bye.*

Note: If a woman wants to say *Nice to meet you,* she says **Enchantée**. This form is spelled with an extra **e**, but the word sounds the same as **Enchanté** when spoken.

Here is another conversation that includes greetings, introductions, and good-byes.

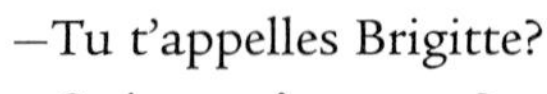

—Tu t'appelles Brigitte?	*Is your name Brigitte?*
—Oui, **et toi**, tu es... ?	*Yes, and you, you are . . . ?*
—Je suis Benoît.	*I'm Benoît.*
—**Salut**, Benoît.	*Hi, Benoît!*
—Salut, Brigitte, **ça va**?	*Hi, Brigitte, how's it going?*
—**Ça va bien.** Et toi, **comment vas-tu**?	*Fine. And how are you?*
—**Je vais bien aussi.**	*I'm fine, too.*
—**Salut**, Benoît. **À bientôt!**	*'Bye, Benoît. See you soon!*
—Oui, **à demain**! Salut, Brigitte!	*Yeah, see you tomorrow. 'Bye, Brigitte!*

What similarities do you notice between these two conversations? What differences? Can you guess why these differences occur? How do you think a child and an adult would interact? You probably noticed that two adults who don't know each other use **vous** and the titles **monsieur**, **madame**, **mademoiselle**. Children use **tu** among themselves. When a child and an adult (other than a parent or close relative) speak, the adult uses **tu** and the child uses **vous**.

---

*In writing, the words **Monsieur**, **Madame**, and **Mademoiselle** are capitalized only when used before a name or title. In addition, **Monsieur** is often abbreviated before a name as **M.** (with a period). **Madame** is abbreviated as **Mme** (without a period) and **Mademoiselle** as **Mlle** (without a period).

Activités

A. Que dire? (*What should they say?*) Complete each dialogue using one of the following expressions: **Au revoir, madame. / Au revoir, monsieur. / Bonjour, madame. / Salut!**

1. MME LÉPINE: Bonjour, monsieur. Je m'appelle Chantal Lépine.
   M. LE ROY: ______
2. BRIGITTE: Salut, Benoît.
   BENOÎT: ______
3. M. LE ROY: Au revoir, madame.
   MME LÉPINE: ______
4. MME LÉPINE: Au revoir, Brigitte.
   BRIGITTE: ______

B. Dans votre classe. (*In your class.*) With three other people in your classroom (one could be your instructor), greet each other, introduce yourself, and say good-bye. Depending on whom you speak to, use expressions from the appropriate column as a sort of script. Add names or the words **monsieur**, **madame**, **mademoiselle** after some phrases, as appropriate.

WITH OTHER STUDENTS	WITH YOUR INSTRUCTOR
—Bonjour.	—Bonjour,...
—Salut. Comment t'appelles-tu?	—Bonjour,... Comment vous appelez-vous?
—Je m'appelle... Et toi?	—Je m'appelle...
—Je m'appelle...	—Enchanté (Enchantée)... Et je m'appelle...
—Ça va?	—Comment allez-vous,... ?
—Oui, ça va bien, merci.	—Très bien, merci. Au revoir,...
—À bientôt...	—Au revoir,...
—Salut...	

Les nombres de 0 à 59

0	**zéro**	10	**dix**	20	**vingt**	30	**trente**
1	**un**	11	**onze**	21	**vingt et un**	31	**trente et un**
2	**deux**	12	**douze**	22	**vingt-deux**	32	**trente-deux**
3	**trois**	13	**treize**	23	**vingt-trois**	33	**trente-trois**
4	**quatre**	14	**quatorze**	24	**vingt-quatre**	34	**trente-quatre**
5	**cinq**	15	**quinze**	25	**vingt-cinq**	35	**trente-cinq**
6	**six**	16	**seize**	26	**vingt-six**	36	**trente-six**
7	**sept**	17	**dix-sept**	27	**vingt-sept**	37	**trente-sept**
8	**huit**	18	**dix-huit**	28	**vingt-huit**	38	**trente-huit**
9	**neuf**	19	**dix-neuf**	29	**vingt-neuf**	39	**trente-neuf**

1, 2, 3, j'irai dans les bois
4, 5, 6, cueillir des cerises
7, 8, 9, dans un panier neuf.
10, 11, 12, elles seront toutes rouges,
à Toulouse.*

40 **quarante**
41 **quarante et un**
42 **quarante-deux (...)**
49 **quarante-neuf**

50 **cinquante**
51 **cinquante et un**
52 **cinquante-deux (...)**
59 **cinquante-neuf**

Activités

A. Dans la papeterie. (*In the stationery store.*) What are the prices of the following items that you're thinking of buying in the stationery store? Use the expression **Ça coûte** (*That costs*) in your answers.

MODÈLE: → Ça coûte cinq euros.

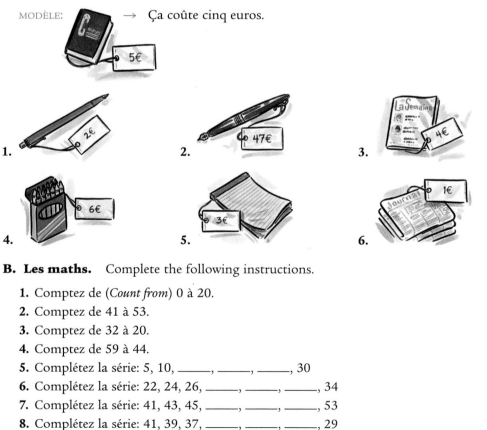

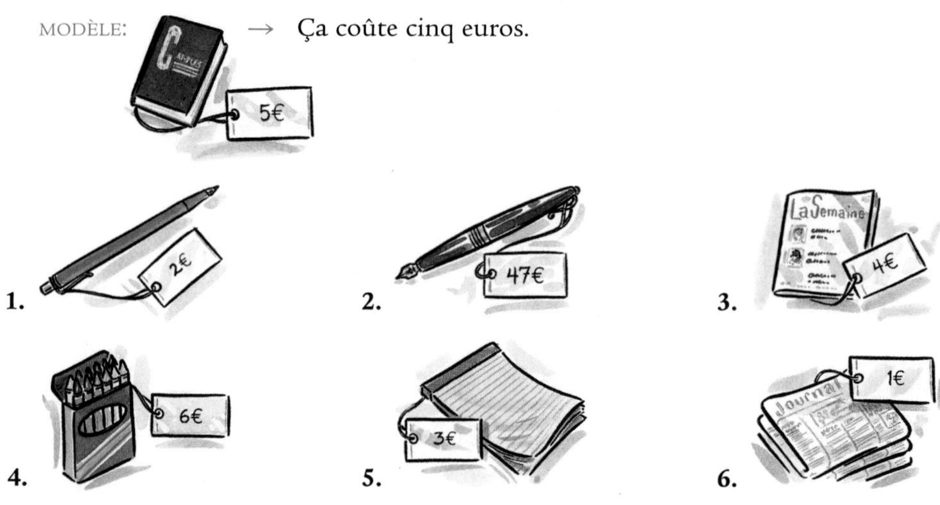

B. Les maths. Complete the following instructions.

1. Comptez de (*Count from*) 0 à 20.
2. Comptez de 41 à 53.
3. Comptez de 32 à 20.
4. Comptez de 59 à 44.
5. Complétez la série: 5, 10, _____, _____, _____, 30
6. Complétez la série: 22, 24, 26, _____, _____, _____, 34
7. Complétez la série: 41, 43, 45, _____, _____, _____, 53
8. Complétez la série: 41, 39, 37, _____, _____, _____, 29

*1, 2, 3... *1, 2, 3, I'll go into the woods 4, 5, 6, to pick cherries 7, 8, 9, in a new basket. 10, 11, 12, they'll all be red, in Toulouse.*

C. La température. Read the average high Celsius temperatures in January and July for the following French-speaking cities. For temperatures below zero, use the word **moins** (for example: −8 degrees = **moins huit**).

Température maximale moyenne pour le mois de...°		
	janvier	**juillet**
Abidjan	27	25
Casablanca	12	22
Genève	0	19
Marseille	6	23
Montréal	−10	21
Paris	4	19

°Température... *Average high temperature for the month of . . .*

1. Montréal
2. Abidjan
3. Paris
4. Casablanca
5. Genève
6. Marseille

Dans la salle de classe°

Dans... *In the classroom*

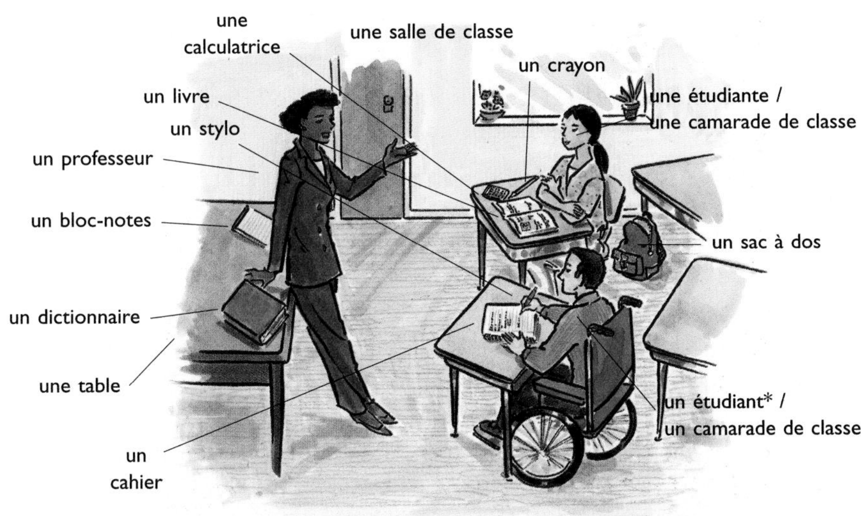

Autres mots utiles

un ami	(*male*) friend
une amie	(*female*) friend
une classe	class
un laboratoire	laboratory
une université	university, college

*__Un étudiant__ is a male student; **une étudiante** is a female student. You will learn more about differences in nouns for males and females later in the chapter.

Activités

A. Combien? (*How many?*) Say how many objects you see in each drawing. Use the phrase **Il y a...** (*There is/are . . .*).

MODÈLE:  crayons → Il y a six crayons.

1. étudiants

2. étudiantes

3. salle de classe

4. livres

5. stylos

6. laboratoire

7. enfants

8. calculatrices

B. Trouvez les différences. (*Find the differences.*) With a partner, compare the two drawings and tell what the differences are.

MODÈLE: É1: Dans le dessin 1, il y a un professeur.
É2: Et dans le dessin 2, il y a deux professeurs.

1.

2.

C. Dans votre salle de classe. (*In your classroom.*) With a partner, decide how many of the following people and things there are in your classroom. Use the expression **Il y a...** .

MODÈLE: cahiers →
É1: Il y a vingt-trois cahiers dans la salle de classe.
É2: Oui, vingt-trois. (*ou** Non, il y a vingt-cinq cahiers dans la salle de classe.)
É1: Voilà. (*ou* OK. Vingt-cinq.)

1. professeurs **2.** livres de français **3.** étudiants **4.** sacs à dos **5.** tables **6.** étudiantes

Les mots apparentés et les faux amis°†

Les... *Cognates and false cognates*

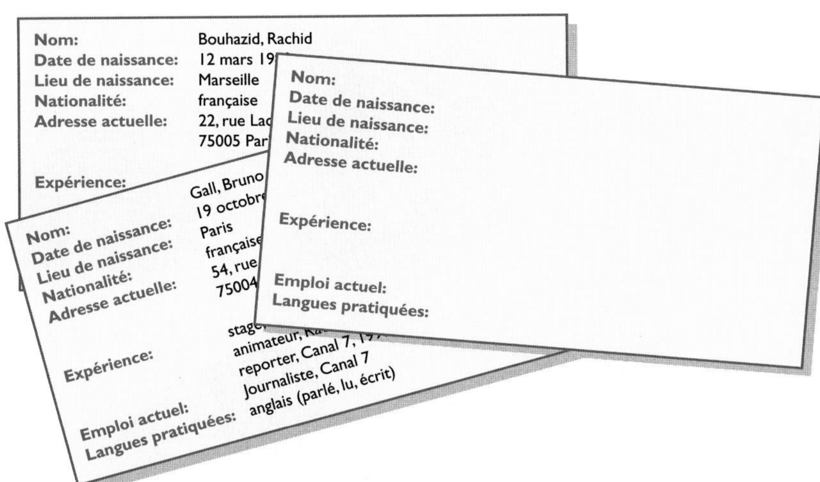

Nom: Bouhazid, Rachid
Date de naissance: 12 mars 19
Lieu de naissance: Marseille
Nationalité: française
Adresse actuelle: 22, rue Lac
75005 Par
Expérience:

Nom: Gall, Bruno
Date de naissance: 19 octobr
Lieu de naissance: Paris
Nationalité: française
Adresse actuelle: 54, rue
75004
Expérience: stage
animateur,
reporter, Canal 7, 19
Journaliste, Canal 7
Emploi actuel:
Langues pratiquées: anglais (parlé, lu, écrit)

Nom:
Date de naissance:
Lieu de naissance:
Nationalité:
Adresse actuelle:
Expérience:
Emploi actuel:
Langues pratiquées:

---

*The word **ou** means *or.* Here it shows a possible alternative answer.

†**Les faux amis** are words that have a different meaning from the English words they resemble. Examples are **actuel(le)** (*present, current*), **crayon** (*pencil*), and **conférence** (*lecture*).

Reading in French is made easier by the large number of French and English words that are related. Thousands of French words have been borrowed into English over the past millennium (10,000 in the 12th and 13th centuries alone). These words are called "cognates." The meanings are usually very similar, if not exactly the same, in both languages, although the spellings and pronunciations may sometimes differ slightly. Ask your instructor to pronounce the following French words and contrast the sound with the sound of the corresponding English word.

FRENCH	ENGLISH
date	*date*
expérience	*experience*

In *Débuts,* unfamiliar words that are true cognates, like the preceding examples, are not translated for you. False cognates will be translated until they have been presented for active use.

Activités

A. Que veut dire... ? (*What is the meaning of . . . ?*) For each French word, say what you think the English equivalent is.

1. visite
2. lampe
3. carottes
4. téléphone
5. appartement
6. microphone
7. adresse
8. géographie
9. groupe
10. drame
11. enthousiaste
12. calme

B. Écoutez bien. (*Listen well.*) Repeat the cognates after your instructor. The second time you hear them, match them to the appropriate drawing.

1. 

2. 

3. 

4. 

5. 

6. 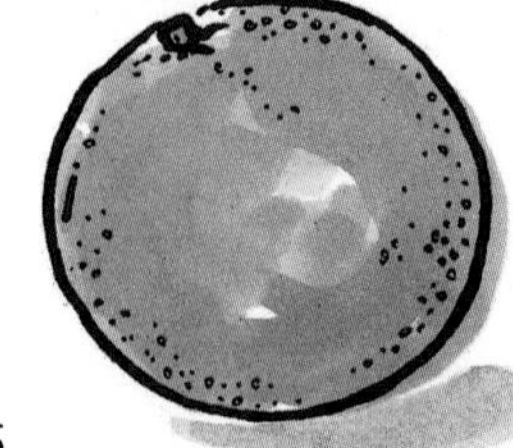

7. 

Structure 1

Qui est-ce? C'est... , Ce sont...

Identifying people

—**Qui est-ce?**	*Who is it?*
—**C'est** Suzanne.	*It is Suzanne.*
—Et là, **qui est-ce?**	*And who is that over there?*
—*Là,* **ce sont** Paul Lemieux et Diane Coste.	*They are Paul Lemieux and Diane Coste.*
—Et **qui est-ce** à la table?	*And who is that at the table?*
—**Je ne sais pas.**	*I don't know.*

1. To ask who a person is, use **Qui est-ce?**

Qui est-ce?	*Who is that?*

2. Use the phrase **c'est** to make an identification. The plural of **c'est** is **ce sont**.

C'est Paris.	*This is Paris.*
Ce sont Serge et Chantal.	*They are Serge and Chantal.*

3. In the negative, **c'est** and **ce sont** become **ce n'est pas** and **ce ne sont pas**.

Ce n'est pas Paul.	*This is not Paul.*
Ce ne sont pas Suzanne et Diane.	*They are not Suzanne and Diane.*

4. To indicate that you don't know the answer, say **Je ne sais pas.**

—Qui est-ce? Est-ce Chantal?	*Who is that? Is it Chantal?*
—**Je ne sais pas.**	*I don't know.*

Activités

A. Qui est-ce? Ask your partner **Qui est-ce?** Your partner will answer.

MODÈLE:

Yasmine →
É1: Qui est-ce?
É2: C'est Yasmine.

1. Camille

2. Rachid

3. Bruno et Camille

4. Rachid et Yasmine

5. Mado

6. ?

B. Négations. Look at the drawing and answer the question according to the model. Choose from the following cities: New York, Paris, Pise, Rome, San Francisco, St. Louis, Tokyo.

MODÈLE:

C'est San Francisco? →
Non, ce n'est pas San Francisco. C'est St. Louis.

1. C'est Paris?

2. C'est St. Louis?

3. C'est New York?

4. C'est Boston?

C. Qui est dans la classe de français? In groups of three to five students, introduce yourselves using **je m'appelle**. Then have conversations in which you check how well each of you remembers each name. Follow the model.

MODÈLE: É1: (*pointing to É3*) Qui est-ce?
É2: C'est Paul.
É3: Oui, je m'appelle Paul. (Non, je m'appelle Carlos.)

Now use the expressions **Qui est-ce?**, **C'est...** , **Ce sont...** to check whom your group members know in the whole class. If you don't know who someone is when you are asked, answer with **Je ne sais pas**.

Structure 2

Qu'est-ce que c'est?, les articles indéfinis et définis et les substantifs

Identifying and specifying people and things

—**Qu'est-ce que c'est?**	*What is this?*
—C'est **un** studio de télévision. Il y a **des** techniciens dans **la** salle. Il y a **une** caméra. **Les** acteurs regardent **le** chien.	*It's a television studio. There are technicians in the room. There is a camera. The actors are watching the dog.*

In French, nouns▲ are divided into two broad categories, masculine and feminine. Gender▲ in French is a grammatical category used to classify nouns that share certain patterns. You should learn the gender of each noun as you learn the noun itself. To do this, you will need to know the articles.▲

▲Terms followed by ▲ are explained in the *Glossary of Grammatical Terms* in Appendix A.

L'article indéfini

The **indefinite article**▲ means *a* (*an*) or *some*. **Un** is used before masculine nouns, **une** before feminine nouns, and **des** before plural nouns of either gender.

	SINGULIER	PLURIEL
masculin	**un** personnage	**des** personnages
féminin	**une** caméra	**des** caméras

C'est **un** film américain. — *It is an American film.*
C'est **une** photo de Louise. — *This is a photo of Louise.*
Ce ne sont pas **des** photos d'Antoine. — *These are not photos of Antoine.*

Notez bien!

Marginal notes called **Notez bien!** (*Note well!*) appear throughout your textbook. You should study and learn the material in all **Notez bien!** notes.

Many words that refer to people have only one gender. For example, **personne** is feminine, even when it designates a man. **Personnage** and **professeur** are masculine, even when they refer to women. In Canada, however, a distinction is made between **le professeur** and **la professeure**. In both France and Canada, the informal **le/la prof** is acceptable.

L'article défini

The **definite article**▲ means *the*. **Le** is used before masculine nouns, **la** before feminine nouns, and **les** in the plural. Note that before a noun beginning with a vowel sound, **le** and **la** become **l'**.

	SINGULIER	PLURIEL
masculin	**le** studio **l'**acteur **l'**hôtel	**les** studios **les** acteurs **les** hôtels
féminin	**la** personne **l'**actrice **l'**histoire	**les** personnes **les** actrices **les** histoires

Voilà **le** film. — *Here's the film.*
C'est **l'**histoire de Camille Leclair. — *It is the story of Camille Leclair.*
C'est **la** vérité. — *That's the truth.*
Voilà **les** acteurs! — *There are the actors!*

Le pluriel des substantifs

1. Noun plurals are usually formed by adding an **s** to the written singular form. See the examples in the preceding article charts. This plural **-s** ending is usually silent.

   le film
   les films

   Note the following plurals of compound nouns.

un sac à dos	deux sac**s** à dos
un bloc-notes	deux bloc**s**-notes
une salle de classe	deux salle**s** de classe

2. To ask for identification of a thing, use **Qu'est-ce que c'est?**

—**Qu'est-ce que c'est?**	*What is that? (this? it?)*
—C'est un sac à dos.	*It's a backpack.*

Activités

A. Quels articles? (*Which articles?*) Place the correct form of the indefinite and then the definite article before the following nouns.

MODÈLE: cahier → un cahier, le cahier

1. étudiante	4. professeur	7. calculatrice	10. amie
2. stylo	5. salle de classe	8. classe	11. personnage
3. livre	6. crayon	9. ami	12. personne

B. Transformez. Convert the singular to the plural or vice versa.

MODÈLES: les étudiantes → l'étudiante
un professeur → des professeurs

1. des crayons	5. des dictionnaires
2. le livre	6. la salle de classe
3. les étudiants	7. les amies
4. un sac à dos	8. une personne

C. Personnes et objets. Working with a small group, look around the room and point out at least five objects or people, asking **Qu'est-ce que c'est?** or **Qui est-ce?** Your partners will tell you what they think you're referring to, using definite and indefinite articles in the singular or plural.

MODÈLE: É1: [*Points to several female students.*] Qui est-ce?
É2: Ce sont des étudiantes.

D. Les étudiants et les professeurs. Working with a partner and using what you have learned in this chapter, use the following guidelines to play the roles of a professor and a student in French class.

1. Say hello to each other and introduce yourselves.
2. Ask each other how you are.
3. Professor: Tell the student to count from zero to ten. Use the expression **Comptez de 0 à 10.**
4. Student: Tell how many students are in the class today. Use **il y a**.
5. Student: Tell how many professors are in class.
6. Student: Ask what certain objects in the classroom are. Professor: Tell him/her what they are.
7. Discuss how many books and other things are in the classroom.
8. Talk about who other people in the class are, using **Qui est-ce?**, **C'est...** , and **Je ne sais pas.**
9. Say good-bye to each other.

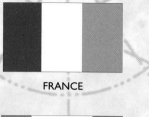

FRANCE

CANADA

MAROC

ALGÉRIE

SÉNÉGAL

HAÏTI

Le français dans le monde[1]

Félicitations! You are among the 100 to 110 million people outside of the Francophone world who are studying French. Not only is French one of the six official languages of the United Nations, but it is important in many ways in places all around the world. French ranks tenth worldwide in terms of the number of native speakers—70 million—and, impressively, it ranks sixth in the world in the number of people for whom it is an official language—220 million. In fact, French ranks *second* in the world, after English and before Spanish, in the number of countries where it is an official language—28 countries, located on five continents. Take a look at the maps in the front and back of your textbook to see its distribution throughout the world.

The ten countries with the largest numbers of French speakers are France, Algeria, Canada, Morocco, Belgium, Cote d'Ivoire, Tunisia, Cameroon, the Democratic Republic of the Congo, and Switzerland. However, the official status of French varies from country to country. French is one of two or more official languages in Canada, Belgium, Cameroon, and Switzerland, and although it is spoken by many in Algeria, Morocco, and Tunisia it is not an official language at all in those countries. In Cote d'Ivoire, however, French is the only official language and is used in some aspects of day-to-day life because there is no common African language that is used by all the people of the nation. In fact, Cote d'Ivoire is one place in Africa where local innovations in French are giving birth to a new dialect of the language. In other countries, such as Senegal, French is again the only official language, but it is used almost exclusively in an administrative or educational context. As you can imagine, these two contexts mean a significant use of the French language there.

Numbers of speakers and status as an official language tell only part of the story of the importance of French in the world, however. Other factors must also be considered in order to appreciate fully the role of French in the community of nations. French is one of the world's major languages, not only because of the geographic spread of its speakers, but more importantly, because of the many contributions of French-speaking nations to the advancement of knowledge and artistic creation throughout the international community. France and the French language have had a profound influence on international culture in such areas as science, sociology, political theory, literature, the arts, fashion, and gastronomy. Furthermore, in the realm of international relations, France has had long historical ties with both the United States and Canada. You will explore some of these many influences in more detail throughout *Débuts*.

[1]Le... *French in the world*

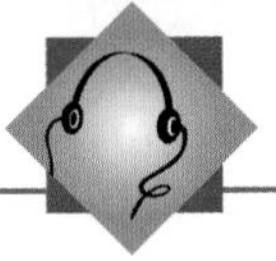

Vocabulaire

Pour parler du film

un(e) acteur/actrice actor, actress
un cinéma movie theater
une femme woman
une histoire story
un homme man
un personnage character

MOTS APPARENTÉS: **un film, une personne, une scène, un studio**

Dans la salle de classe

un(e) ami(e) (*male/female*) friend
un bloc-notes (des blocs-notes) pad of paper
un cahier notebook; workbook
une calculatrice calculator
un(e) camarade de classe (des camarades de classe) (*male/female*) classmate
un crayon pencil
un(e) étudiant(e) (*male/female*) university student
un livre book
un sac à dos (des sacs à dos) backpack
une salle de classe (des salles de classe) classroom
un stylo pen

MOTS APPARENTÉS: **une classe, un dictionnaire, un laboratoire, un professeur, une table, une université**

Articles

des some
le, la, les the
un, une a (an)

Les nombres de 0 à 59

zéro, un, deux, trois, quatre, cinq, six, sept, huit, neuf, dix, onze, douze, treize, quatorze, quinze, seize, dix-sept, dix-huit, dix-neuf, vingt, vingt et un, vingt-deux, trente, quarante, cinquante

Pour identifier

Qui est-ce? Who is this/that/it?
Qu'est-ce que c'est? What is this/that/it?
c'est this/that/it is
ce sont these/those/they are
ce n'est pas this/that/it is not
ce ne sont pas these/those/they are not
je ne sais pas I don't know

Salutations

À bientôt.	See you soon.	**Enchanté(e).**	Nice to meet you., It's a pleasure.
À demain.	See you tomorrow.	**Et toi?**	And you? (*fam. sing.*)
Au revoir.	Good-bye.	**Et vous?**	And you? (*fam. pl.; formal sing. and pl.*)
Bonjour.	Hello.	**Je m'appelle...**	I am . . . , My name is . . .
Ça va?	How's it going?	**Je vais bien.**	I'm fine.
Ça va bien.	I'm fine., I'm well.	**madame (Mme)**	madam, ma'am; Mrs.
Comment allez-vous?	How are you?	**mademoiselle (Mlle)**	miss; Miss
Comment t'appelles-tu?	What is your name? (*fam. sing.*)	**merci**	thank you
Comment vas-tu?	How are you? (*fam. sing.*)	**monsieur (M.)**	sir; Mr.
Comment vous appelez-vous?	What is your name? (*fam. pl.; formal sing. and pl.*)	**Salut.**	Hi.; 'Bye.
		très bien	very well

Autres expressions utiles

aussi	also	**là**	there; here
bien	well	**non**	no
dans	in	**ou**	or
de	of; from	**oui**	yes
et	and	**très**	very
il y a	there is, there are (*for counting*)		

Chapitre 1

Un grand jour°

Un... *A big day*

Le Chemin du retour

Feuille de service du 12 octobre
2e jour de tournage
Horaires: 9h–19h

LIEU DE TOURNAGE: PARIS—ÉCOLE° SAINT VICTOR—37 rue Jussieu, 5e

school

Séquence	*Effets*	*Décors*	*Résumé*	*Rôles*
3	EXT.—JOUR	ÉCOLE YASMINE—Cour° intérieure	Rachid emmène° sa fille° à sa nouvelle école.	RACHID, YASMINE, INSTITUTRICE°

takes
courtyard / daughter
teacher

OBJECTIFS

In this episode, you will

- meet Rachid Bouhazid and his daughter, Yasmine, as they begin a new life in Paris
- learn cultural information about Paris and about French customs

In this chapter, you will

- spell words in French
- identify more classroom objects
- talk about your studies
- talk about yourselves and others
- express negative ideas
- ask simple yes/no questions
- learn about the school system in France
- learn about education in other French-speaking countries

Vocabulaire en contexte

L'alphabet français

a	a	j	ji	s	esse
b	bé	k	ka	t	té
c	cé	l	elle	u	u
d	dé	m	emme	v	vé
e	e	n	enne	w	double vé
f	effe	o	o	x	iks
g	gé	p	pé	y	i grec
h	hache	q	ku	z	zède
i	i	r	erre		

1. Spelling a word correctly in French requires using written accents, which are part of the spelling of some words. They may not be omitted.

ACCENT	NOM	EXEMPLE
´	accent aigu	éléphant
`	accent grave	scène
^	accent circonflexe	dîner
ç	cé cédille	français
¨	tréma	Noël

2. You will also need these additional terms when spelling a word aloud.

majuscule	*uppercase*	apostrophe	*apostrophe*
minuscule	*lowercase*	trait d'union	*hyphen*

3. To ask how to spell a French word, say **Comment s'écrit le mot... ?** (*How do you spell the word . . . ?*).

—Comment s'écrit le mot **Eiffel**?

—Le mot **Eiffel** s'écrit «e majuscule-i-deux effes-e-elle»*.

—Comment s'écrit le mot **s'aider**?

—Le mot **s'aider** s'écrit «esse apostrophe-a-i-dé-e-erre».

Activités

A. Qui sont ces personnes? (*Who are these people?*) Here are the names of some of the characters in the film. Taking turns with a partner, spell their names aloud.

*Note that double consonants are spelled using the expression **deux...** (*two. . .*): **ss** = **deux esses**.

1. Camille Leclair
2. Bruno Gall
3. Hélène Thibaut
4. Rachid Bouhazid
5. Yasmine Bouhazid

B. Informations personnelles. Spell out the following personal information. Your partner will write it down. Then change roles.

1. votre nom (*your name*)
2. le nom de votre professeur
3. le nom d'un ami / d'une amie
4. votre ville (*city*) favorite
5. votre actrice favorite

La rentrée°

La... *Back-to-school day*

C'est **un** grand **jour**° **pour**° Brigitte.
Elle est **à l'école**°* **avec**° des amis.
Elle dit° bonjour à la maîtresse et aux élèves.
L'institutrice est très **sympa**.°
C'est **une leçon** de sciences naturelles, **alors**° la maîtresse montre une fleur **à**° la classe.

un... *a big (important) day* / *for*
à... *at school* / *with*
Elle... *She says*
nice
so
montre... *is showing a flower to*

Pour en savoir plus...

Marginal notes called **Pour en savoir plus...** (*To know more . . .*) appear throughout your textbook. The information in these notes is for general interest and understanding, but you are not required to memorize it.

In one sense, **la rentrée** designates the period when students return to school—mid-September for students ages 6 to 18 and October for universities. It also implies "back-to-work" for parents, who may have been on the traditional long (four-to-five-week) summer vacation, and in general a return to the everyday rhythms of life.

*__Une école__ is an elementary school, and the pupils are referred to as **élèves**. A secondary school is **un lycée**, and its students are also called **élèves**, or they can be called **lycéen(ne)s**. Students at colleges and universities are called **étudiant(e)s**.

1. The plural forms of **le tableau** and **le bureau** are **les tableaux** and **les bureaux**, ending with **-x** instead of **-s**.
2. The words **élève** (*pupil*) and **enfant** (*child*) can be either masculine or feminine, depending on the sex of the child.
3. A male primary school teacher is called **un maître** or **un instituteur**.*

Activités

A. Trouvez l'intrus! (*Find the intruder!*) Tell which item doesn't belong to the group.

1. une table, une chaise, un bureau, une horloge
2. un tableau, un ordinateur, une craie, une éponge
3. un mur, une fenêtre, une porte, une leçon
4. un étudiant, une maîtresse, un professeur, une institutrice
5. un élève, un tableau, un étudiant, un camarade de classe

B. Combien? (*How many?*) How many of each object are there? Use the expression **Il y a...**

MODÈLE:  → Il y a deux maîtresses. (Il y a deux institutrices.)

1. 

2. 

3. 

4. 

5.  

6. 

*To reinforce the status of elementary school teachers, the official term is now **un professeur des écoles**. Children, however, still do not talk about their **prof** but use the older expressions instead.

C. Qu'est-ce que c'est que ça? (*What is that?*) Your partner will tell you to point out an object in the classroom. Point to the object and say that it is there. Take turns telling each other what to point out. Don't forget that you can use vocabulary you learned in the preliminary chapter as well. Use the expressions **Montre-moi** (*Show me*), **Voilà** (*There is/are*), and **Voici** (*Here is/are*).

MODÈLE: É1: Montre-moi un tableau.
É2: [*pointing*] Voilà un tableau. Montre-moi une étudiante.

Les leçons / Les études / Les cours°

Les... Lessons / Studies / Courses

À l'école, Yasmine apprend° (*is learning*)

- **la lecture**° (*reading*)
- **l'écriture**° (*f.*) (*penmanship, writing*)
- **le français**
- **les mathématiques (les maths)** (*f. pl.*)
- **les sciences** naturelles (*f. pl.*)
- **la géographie** (*f.*)
- **l'histoire** (*f.*)

D'autres° élèves dans l'école apprennent aussi° (*Other / apprennent... also learn*)

- **l'anglais**° (*m.*) (*English*)
- **l'informatique**° (*f.*) (*computer science*)

Activités

A. Qu'est-ce qu'il faut? (*What's needed?*) For each lesson, name two useful classroom objects. There may be several appropriate answers. Follow the model, and vary your choices, using words from the list and other words you know.

Vocabulaire utile: un bloc-notes, un cahier, un crayon, un dictionnaire, un livre, un microscope, un ordinateur, un stylo, une calculatrice

MODÈLE: pour une leçon de géographie →
Pour une leçon de géographie? Un livre de géographie et aussi un atlas.

1. pour une leçon de maths
2. pour une leçon d'anglais
3. pour une leçon de sciences naturelles
4. pour une leçon d'histoire
5. pour une leçon d'informatique
6. pour une leçon de français

B. Associations. With which class or course do you associate the following? Answer with a complete sentence according to the model.

MODÈLE: les problèmes et les formules →
J'associe les problèmes et les formules avec les maths.

1. les continents, les océans et les nations
2. les dates, les événements du passé (*events of the past*)
3. les codes et les programmes

4. les mots (*words*) et les livres simples
5. les lettres majuscules et minuscules
6. les plantes et les animaux (*animals*)

Visionnement 1

Before you watch each new episode of *Le Chemin du retour*, you will do several activities that prepare you to understand what you will see and hear.

Avant de visionner

A. La tour Eiffel a quatre pieds. (*The Eiffel Tower has four feet.*) The film opens with children singing a **comptine**, a song somewhat like a nursery rhyme. A **comptine** often has an instructional purpose, for example, to help children learn months of the year, holidays, or telling time. **Comptines** are also used in school to help pupils improve their pronunciation. Read the following **comptine**. Later, as you hear it in the film, you can follow along.

La tour Eiffel a quatre pieds; Il en faut deux pour y monter (bis)
Et pour s'aider, on peut chanter (bis)
A...B...C...D...E...F...G...H...I...J...K...L...M...N... (bis)

The Eiffel Tower has four feet; You need two feet to climb it (repeat)
And to help, you can sing (repeat)
A...B...C...D...E...F...G...H...I...J...K...L...M...N... (repeat)

B. Moments importants. Here is a look at two important moments in Episode 1. Read the exchanges and answer the questions.

1. In this scene, a little girl named Yasmine and her father, Rachid, are arriving at school. How do you think she feels about being there?

YASMINE: C'est ma nouvelle[a] école?
PAPA: Mmm-hmm. La maîtresse est là. Elle est très sympa. Regarde![b]
YASMINE: Non, papa, je ne veux pas.[c] On repart à la maison![d]

[a]*ma... my new* [b]*Look!* [c]*je... I don't want to (look at her)* [d]*On... Let's go home!*

a. Yasmine est contente.
b. Yasmine est nerveuse.

2. What is the relationship between the people in this dialogue?

ISABELLE: Vous êtes Monsieur Bouhazid?
RACHID: Oui. Bonjour, madame.
ISABELLE: Monsieur. Et toi, tu es Yasmine. Je m'appelle Isabelle.

a. Isabelle et Rachid sont amis.
b. Isabelle ne connaît pas (*doesn't know*) Rachid et Yasmine.

Observez!

Now watch Episode 1. You already know that Yasmine is going to school. As you watch the film, see if you can answer these questions.

- What is Yasmine worried about?
- Why does she wish her father luck?

Remember—Don't expect to understand every word in the episode; you need to understand only the basic plot structure and characters. If you can answer the questions that follow the episode, you have understood enough. Your instructor may ask you to watch the episode again later. By then, you'll have additional tools and will be able to understand more of the details. The activities in **Visionnement 2** in the text and in the *Workbook/Laboratory Manual* will help, too.

Vocabulaire relatif à l'épisode

Here are a few more expressions from the film. Don't worry if you miss them as you are watching. You don't need to hear every word to understand the main idea of what is happening.

Qu'est-ce qu'il y a, ma puce?	*What's wrong, sweetheart?*
Pourquoi... ?	*Why . . . ?*
Où est... ?	*Where is . . . ?*
fatiguée	*tired*
le déménagement	*move (to a new residence)*
bonne chance	*good luck*

Après le visionnement

In this section of each chapter, you will review important information from the episode you have just watched.

A. Identifiez. Who makes the following statements to whom in Episode 1? Choose among Rachid, Yasmine, and the teacher (**l'institutrice**).

MODÈLE: La maîtresse est là. Elle est très sympa. →
Rachid parle à (*is speaking to*) Yasmine.

1. C'est ma nouvelle école?
2. Mais (*But*) où est-elle? Où est maman?
3. Au Jardin des Plantes (*To the Botanical Garden*), pour une leçon de sciences naturelles.
4. Au revoir, madame. Salut, ma chérie (*honey*)!
5. Pour toi aussi, c'est un grand jour, non?

B. Réfléchissez. (*Think.*) Read the following dialogue exchanges and answer the questions.

1. In this episode, Yasmine asks where her mother is, but Rachid seems uncomfortable discussing her.

YASMINE: Pourquoi maman n'est pas là[a]?

RACHID: C'est, euh, maman est fatiguée à cause du déménagement. Alors, elle se repose.[b]

YASMINE: Mais où est-elle? Où est maman?

RACHID: Allez viens,[c] ma chérie. Regarde les enfants.

[a]n'est... *isn't here* [b]elle... *she's resting* [c]Allez... *Come on*

Why might Rachid feel so uncomfortable? What does this scene tell you about his relationship with his wife?

2. As Yasmine begins her first day at her new school, she wishes her father luck.

YASMINE: Bonne chance, papa! Pour toi aussi, c'est un grand jour, non?
RACHID: Oui. Salut, ma chérie.

Why might Rachid have a big day ahead of him, too?

Structure 3

Les pronoms sujets et le verbe *être*

Talking about ourselves and others

—**Vous êtes** Monsieur Bouhazid?

—Oui. Bonjour, madame.

—Monsieur. Et toi, **tu es** Yasmine.

Les pronoms sujets

Just as in English, every French verb▲ has a subject,▲ the person or thing that performs the action of the verb. Subjects are singular or plural, as well as masculine or feminine. Sometimes the subject is not named specifically but is identified by a pronoun.▲

▲Terms followed by ▲ are explained in the *Glossary of Grammatical Terms* in Appendix A.

je	I	**nous**	we
tu	you (*fam. sing.*)	**vous**	you (*fam. pl.; formal sing. and pl.*)
il	he; it (*m.*)	**ils**	they (*m.* or *m.* + *f.*)
elle	she; it (*f.*)	**elles**	they (*f.*)
on	one; you; people; we; they		

1. **Je** becomes **j'** before a verb form beginning with a vowel sound.

   J'adore Paris! — *I love Paris!*

2. French has two pronouns meaning *you*; the distinction is mostly one of politeness. **Tu** is familiar and informal. It is used with animals, young children, family, friends, and contemporaries in age and status. The plural of **tu** is **vous**.

   Tu es Yasmine? — *Are you Yasmine?*
   Vous êtes Yasmine et Benoît? — *Are you Yasmine and Benoît?*

   Vous is also used in more formal situations, to address a person with whom you are not well acquainted, who is older, or who possesses greater status (for example, a superior at work). The plural form is also **vous**.

   Vous êtes M. Bouhazid? — *Are you Mr. Bouhazid?*
   Vous êtes M. et Mme Bouhazid? — *Are you Mr. and Mrs. Bouhazid?*

   These guidelines are general and may vary according to situation, region, or social class. If you are in doubt, it is best to address a person using **vous**.

3. **Il**, **elle**, **ils**, and **elles** may refer to both people and things. (Note that French has no single equivalent of the pronoun *it*.) Use **il** or **ils** to replace masculine nouns; use **elle** or **elles** to replace feminine nouns.

   —**Le livre** est sur la table? — *Is the book on the table?*
   —Oui, **il** est sur la table. — *Yes, it is on the table.*

   —**Les comptines** sont utiles? — *Are comptines useful?*
   —Oui, **elles** sont très utiles. — *Yes, they are very useful.*

   If you need to refer to both masculine and feminine nouns at once, use the pronoun **ils.**

   Rachid, Yasmine et Isabelle sont à l'école. **Ils** parlent ensemble. — *Rachid, Yasmine, and Isabelle are at school. They are talking.*

4. The meaning of the pronoun **on** depends on the context: *one, you, people, we, they.*

   En France, **on** aime le pain. — *In France, people like bread.*
   On va où? — *Where are we going?*

5. **Tout le monde** is a singular expression meaning *everybody.* It takes the same verb form as **il**, **elle**, **on**.

   Tout le monde est là? — *Is everybody here?*

Le verbe être

In French, the form of a verb changes depending on its subject.

Je suis Isabelle.	*I am Isabelle.*
Tu es Yasmine?	*Are you Yasmine?*
Vous êtes M. Bouhazid?	*Are you Mr. Bouhazid?*

être (*to be*)			
je	**suis**	nous	**sommes**
tu	**es**	vous	**êtes**
il, elle, on	**est**	ils, elles	**sont**

1. The verb **être** can be followed by a name, a noun,▲ an adjective,▲ and many other kinds of phrases.

Je **suis** Yasmine!	*I am Yasmine!*
C'**est*** une éponge.	*That is an eraser.*
Il **est** intelligent.	*He is intelligent.*
C'**est** vrai.	*That's true.*
Vous **êtes** dans la classe?	*Are you in the class?*

2. When expressing someone's job or profession in French, the indefinite article is not used after the verb **être**.

Je suis institutrice.	*I am a school teacher.*
Il est professeur.	*He is a professor.*

Activités

A. Complétez. Here are some things people might have said on Yasmine's first day at her new school. Complete the sentences with the correct form of **être**.

1. Voilà! Nous _____ à l'école Bullier.
2. Vous _____ Monsieur Bouhazid?
3. Je _____ Isabelle.
4. Tu _____ inquiète (*worried*), Yasmine?
5. Marie et Claire, elles _____ dans ta (*your*) classe.
6. Tout le monde _____ là?
7. On _____ maintenant (*now*) au Jardin des Plantes!
8. C' _____ vrai? Super!

B. *Tu* ou *vous*? Which pronoun would you use to address the following people: **vous** or **tu**?

1. un étudiant ou une étudiante dans la classe
2. deux étudiants dans la classe

*You already know the expressions **c'est** and **ce sont**, which are combinations of the verb **être** with the pronoun **ce** (*this, that, it, these, those, they*).

3. le professeur de français
4. un homme et une femme
5. une enfant

C. Questions. A friend asks you to tell about the following people. Answer each question using the appropriate subject pronoun and form of **être** with the information in parentheses.

MODÈLE: Paul et toi (*you*)? (étudiants) →
Nous sommes étudiants.

1. Charles et Robert? (à l'université)
2. Christine? (dans la salle de classe)
3. Jeanne-Marie et toi? (amis/amies)
4. Le professeur? (fantastique)
5. Toi? (sympa)
6. Moi? (sociable)

Now with a partner, talk about the people you know.

Structure 4

Ne... pas et d'autres négations

Expressing negatives

—Non, papa, je **ne** veux **pas**.

You have already learned the negative forms of **c'est** and **ce sont**.

Ce n'est pas vrai.	*It's not true.*
Ce ne sont pas mes parents.	*They are not my parents.*

To negate a verb in French, insert **ne** before the verb and **pas** after it.

Je suis content.	*I am happy.*
Je **ne** suis **pas** content.	*I am not happy.*

Pour en savoir plus...

When you hear rapid spoken French, you may notice that the **ne** or **n'** of the negative is sometimes not pronounced. The presence of the term **pas** identifies the sentence as negative.

CAREFUL FRENCH

Ce n'est pas Yasmine.
Ce n'est pas vrai!

RAPID, SPOKEN FRENCH

C'est pas Yasmine.
C'est pas vrai!

Remember that in writing, the **ne** or **n'** must always be included.

1. There are other negations, with special meanings, that work exactly like **ne... pas**.

ne... pas du tout	*not at all, absolutely not*
ne... pas encore	*not yet*
ne... plus	*not anymore, no longer*
ne... jamais	*never, not ever*

Yasmine **n'**est **pas du tout** fatiguée.*	*Yasmine is not tired at all.*
La maman de Yasmine **n'**est **pas encore** là.	*Yasmine's mother is not there yet.*
Yasmine et Rachid **ne** sont **plus** à Marseille.	*Yasmine and Rachid are not in Marseille anymore.*
Vous **n'**êtes **jamais** calme.	*You are never calm.*

2. Note that **ne** becomes **n'** before a verb form beginning with a vowel sound.

Isabelle **n'**est pas la maman de Yasmine.	*Isabelle is not Yasmine's mother.*

Activités

A. Mais non! (*No!*) Here are some incorrect statements made by Yasmine's classmate. Compose a negative response to each sentence using the cues provided.

MODÈLE: C'est une leçon de sciences naturelles. (maths)
Mais non, ce n'est pas une leçon de sciences naturelles. C'est une leçon de maths.

1. La Terre est plate (*flat*). (ronde)
2. Les serpents sont des amphibiens. (reptiles)
3. C'est un cercle. (triangle)
4. L'instituteur est sévère. (indulgent)
5. Nous sommes des élèves médiocres. (exceptionnels)
6. L'hydrogène est un gaz stable. (volatil)
7. Les premières (*first*) lettres de l'alphabet sont d, e, f. (a, b, c)

*The position of **du tout** is flexible. This same sentence might be expressed as **Yasmine n'est pas fatiguée du tout**.

B. On n'est pas comme ça. (*We're not like that.*) Working with a partner, take turns asking and answering the following questions. Use a variety of these expressions in your answers: **ne... pas, ne... pas du tout, ne... pas encore, ne... plus, ne... jamais.**

MODÈLE: É1: Tes (*Your*) amis sont calmes avant (*before*) les examens?
É2: Mes (*My*) amis ne sont jamais calmes avant les examens.
(Mes amis ne sont pas du tout calmes avant les examens.)

1. Tu es professeur? **2.** Tu es un(e) enfant? **3.** Tes amis sont dans la classe de français? (Mes amis...) **4.** Le cours de français est terminé (*finished*)? **5.** Les professeurs d'université sont toujours sympas? **6.** Les cours d'anglais sont difficiles?

Regards sur la culture

L'enseignement° en France

°Education

Here are some basic facts about the public school program in France.

Les enfants à l'école primaire

- Discipline, memorization, and the imitation of good models are the fundamental principles of early education in French schools. Students do a lot of very careful copying of language (the teacher's notes on the board) and of images (the teacher's model of the umbrella indicating the day's weather, for example*). They also spend quite a bit of time memorizing and reciting poetry and **comptines**.
- The French educational system is very centralized. School programs and the requirements for diplomas are usually determined by the Ministry of Education so that all citizens, no matter where they live or what their social status, have the same educational opportunities.
- Nearly all French children enter elementary school having already been in public preschools for several years. Thirty-six percent of French children are in **l'école maternelle** (preschool) at age 2, and by age 3, 99.8% of all children attend. **L'école maternelle** is free and available to all.
- When they enter elementary school (**l'école primaire**), French children usually know how to copy cursive handwriting, but not how to read. "Printing" is never learned. The first year of elementary school in France is called **le cours préparatoire**. Children enter this class around age 6. In **le cours préparatoire**, they begin to learn to read.

*Every morning in the early primary grades, many teachers draw a symbol on the board to indicate the day's weather—a sun for sunny weather, an umbrella for rain, a snowflake for snow, and so on.

Âge	Écoles	Classes
17	Lycée	Terminale
16		1
15		2
14	Collège	3
13		4
12		5
11		6
10	École primaire	Cours moyen
9		
8		Cours élémentaire
7		
6		Cours préparatoire
5	École maternelle	
4		
3		
2		

Considérez

Education in the United States is controlled locally and may vary greatly from county to county and from state to state. In Canada, education is the responsibility of each province and territory. What advantages and disadvantages do you see in local control of education? Are there advantages to a centralized system like the one in France? What about a compromise like the Canadian system?

Structure 5

L'intonation et *est-ce que*...

Asking yes/no questions

—Elle m'aime toujours? C'est promis?

—Ben, bien sûr! Viens, ma puce.

There are two very common ways to ask yes/no questions in French.

1. The simplest way to form a question in French is to raise the pitch of your voice at the end of the sentence. A sentence ending in a period (a declarative statement) always ends in a falling tone, whereas the same sentence used as a question ends in a rising tone.

STATEMENT: C'est l'école de Yasmine. *This is Yasmine's school.*

QUESTION: C'est l'école de Yasmine? *Is this Yasmine's school?*

2. A statement can also be turned into a yes/no question by placing **est-ce que** at the beginning. A rising tone is used in **est-ce que** questions.

STATEMENT: Rachid est reporter. *Rachid is a reporter.*

QUESTION: Est-ce que Rachid est reporter? *Is Rachid a reporter?*

Note that **est-ce que** becomes **est-ce qu'** before a subject that begins with a vowel sound: **est-ce qu'il...** , **est-ce qu'elle...** , etc.

Activités

A. Questions sur le film. Some of these statements about the film are true and some are false. Make each one into a question. Vary the way you express the questions, using rising intonation and **est-ce que**.

1. Les enfants chantent (*sing*) une comptine. 2. La classe est à la tour Eiffel.
3. La maîtresse de Yasmine est sympa. 4. La maman de Yasmine est là.
5. C'est un grand jour pour Rachid.

Now work with a partner. When your partner asks the question again, answer either **oui** or **non**. If your answer is **oui**, restate the sentence. If it is **non**, rephrase the sentence in the negative.

B. Les professions. Working with a partner, take turns asking and answering questions about each person's profession. Follow the model.

MODÈLE: Pierre / athlète / garagiste →
É1: Est-ce que Pierre est athlète?
É2: Non, il n'est pas athlète. Il est garagiste.

1. Michel / chauffeur de taxi / journaliste
2. Midori (*f.*) / accordéoniste / violoniste
3. Jean-Paul / violoniste / accordéoniste
4. Barbara / actrice / athlète
5. Chantal / institutrice / reporter
6. Isabelle / reporter / institutrice
7. Marcel / acteur / mime
8. David / journaliste / instituteur

C. Conversation. Carry on a conversation with a partner following the guidelines.

1. Greet your partner and find out how he/she is feeling.
2. Give your name and say that you are a student.
3. Find out if your partner is a teacher.

4. Ask whether the students in the class are friends.
5. Say good-bye to each other and that you'll see each other soon.

Visionnement 2

Avant de visionner

A. Quelle classe? (*Which class?*) The public school system in France is described earlier in this chapter in **Regards sur la culture**. Considering Yasmine's age, the type of field trip the class is about to take, and the song the class is singing as they line up, what level do you think Yasmine is entering? Choose the best answer.

   a. Elle est à l'école maternelle.
   b. Elle est au cours préparatoire.
   c. Elle est au collège.

Les environs de l'appartement des Bouhazid

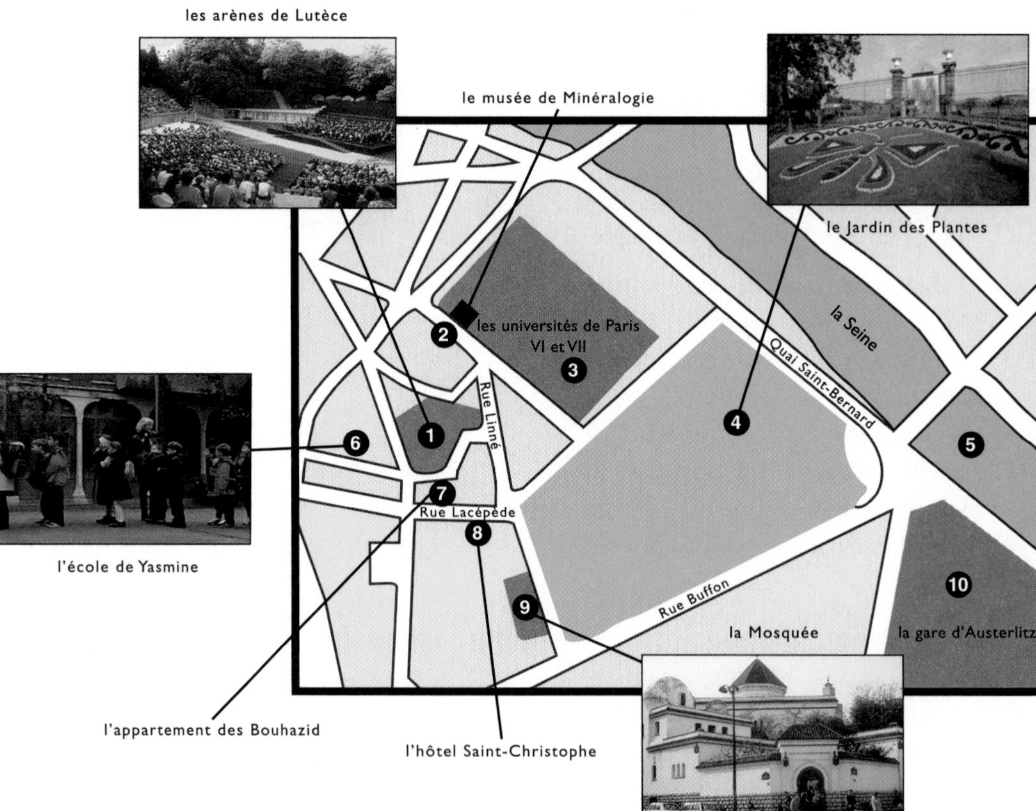

B. Points de repère. (*Landmarks.*) Look at this map showing the part of Paris where the action in this episode takes place. It is part of the **Quartier latin** (*Latin quarter*), so named because hundreds of years ago, Latin was the language of instruction at the university there. Rachid and Yasmine also live near the **Jardin des Plantes**, a botanical garden. The area around the **Jardin des Plantes** has always been a place where groups mixed: university students, wine merchants, and, since the 18th century, the scientists who have directed the **Jardin des Plantes**. Look carefully at the map and indicate the number and the name that correspond to the following landmarks in the neighborhood near Yasmine's school.

a. un édifice (*building*) religieux **b.** une résidence **c.** des ruines romaines **d.** un fleuve (*large river*) **e.** une école

Observez!

Rachid and the teacher greet each other in a typical French manner for people who don't know each other. Watch and listen to answer the following questions.

- Would you use a similar gesture when meeting a teacher for the first time?
- What level of language (formal, informal) does Rachid use when he speaks with the teacher? when he speaks with Yasmine? How do you know?

Après le visionnement

Do the activity for **Visionnement 2** in the *Workbook/Laboratory Manual.*

Synthèse: Culture

L'école dans le monde francophone°

°L'école… *School in the French-speaking world*

Yasmine's school uses the standard curriculum prescribed by the French Ministry of Education, and French is the language of instruction. But in most places in the French-speaking world, the decision about which language should be used in education is a difficult one. In fact, elementary school is one of the most important places in which "the politics of language" are played out.

Quebec

Faced with a massive language shift to English in Montreal, the Quebec government has passed several laws that restrict access to public English-language elementary schools. Today, only those children with at least one parent who studied in an English elementary school somewhere in Canada can attend Montreal's English-language school system. This means that immigrants from other countries (including the United States) are required to enter the French system. Many feel that this is an important factor in preventing the disappearance of French in North America and that the rights of the French community to maintain its integrity occasionally have to outweigh the freedom of individual choice.

New Caledonia

In the colonial period, the entire French Empire used the same school curriculum. The children of Africa and those in New Caledonia in the south Pacific were all schooled in French, not in their native language. They studied the history of France and the building of the French nation, just as children in Paris or Marseille did. Not until the late 1980s, after violent confrontations between the French police and the native Melanesian population in New Caledonia, did local elements become a systematic part of the teaching of geography, history, and civics there. It was only then that Melanesian languages could be used in primary school. Today, about 20% of the curriculum in this French territory is devoted to learning about New Caledonia.

Louisiana

Many generations of children in Louisiana were punished for speaking French at school.* In 1968, the Council for the Development of French in Louisiana (CODOFIL) was established to change this situation and to promote the use of the language. But what form of French was to be taught in the schools? CODOFIL did not want to teach the Cajun French dialect, which it considered to be substandard, so teachers of standard European French were brought in from France. The results were not successful at first. The debates over the "Louisianification" of French teaching in Cajun country are still going on, but the use of teachers from Quebec, whose language is closer to that of the Cajuns, has improved the situation.

*Louisiana was a French colony until 1803. In the mid-1700s, the use of French was intensified there by the arrival of thousands of Acadians, who were deported from Nova Scotia by the British. These are the people who came to be called "Cajuns." You will learn more about this expulsion and the evolution of Cajun culture in the **Synthèse: Culture** in Chapter 11.

À vous

A. Which is more important in your family: the preservation of ethnic tradition or complete assimilation to your country's culture? In your opinion, should children of immigrants or those that are not native speakers of English be schooled in English, in their native language, or in both languages? Whose history and culture should they learn in school?

B. Imagine that you are developing the educational policy for a town in northern Quebec where most of the population speaks Cree.* In a small group, decide what language or languages you would use in the classroom and at what points in the child's development. Keep in mind that French is the official language of the province of Quebec and that English is the other official language of Canada. Would you aim to make the children bilingual or trilingual? Organize your plan using the grid below.

Age	Language of instruction	Other language(s) studied

À écrire

Do **À écrire** for Chapter 1 in the *Workbook/Laboratory Manual.*

*Cree is a Native American (Amerindian) language of the Algonquian family. Algonquian is one of the largest of Native American language groups, which also includes Ojibwa, Cheyenne, and many others.

Vocabulaire

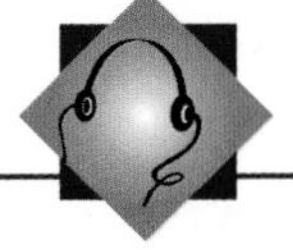

La rentrée

un bureau (des bureaux)	desk
une chaise	chair
une craie	chalk
une école	(elementary) school
un(e) élève	pupil
un(e) enfant	child
une éponge	sponge; blackboard eraser
les études (*f. pl.*)	studies
une fenêtre	window
une horloge	clock

un(e) instituteur/ institutrice	elementary school teacher	**un ordinateur**	computer
un jour	day	**une porte**	door
un lycée	secondary school	**un tableau (des tableaux)**	blackboard
un(e) lycéen(ne)	high school student		
un(e) maître/ maîtresse	elementary school teacher		
un mur	wall		

MOTS APPARENTÉS: **un cours, une leçon**

Les leçons / Les études / Les cours

l'anglais (*m.*)	English	**la lecture**	reading
l'écriture (*f.*)	penmanship; writing		
le français	French		
l'informatique (*f.*)	computer science		

MOTS APPARENTÉS: **la géographie, l'histoire** (*f.*), **les mathématiques** (*fam.* **les maths**) (*f. pl.*), **les sciences (naturelles)** (*f. pl.*)

Les pronoms sujets

je	I	**tout le monde**	everyone
tu	you (*fam. sing.*)	**nous**	we
il	he; it (*m.*)	**vous**	you (*fam. pl.; formal sing. and pl.*)
elle	she; it (*f.*)	**ils**	they (*m.*)
on	one; you; people; we; they	**elles**	they (*f.*)

Verbe, question et négations

être	to be	**ne... pas encore**	not yet
est-ce que... ?	is it (*true*) that . . . ?	**ne... plus**	not anymore
ne... pas	not	**ne... jamais**	never, not ever
ne... pas du tout	not at all, absolutely not		

Prépositions

à	to; at	**pour**	for
avec	with		

Autres expressions utiles

alors	so, therefore; then, in that case	**voici**	here is/are
sympathique (*fam.* **sympa**)	nice	**voilà**	there is/are; here is/are (*for pointing out*)

Chapitre 2

Bonjour!

Le Chemin du retour

Feuille de service du 20 janvier
5e jour de tournage
Horaires: 9h–19h

LIEU DE TOURNAGE: MARSEILLE—FRANCE 3—Grand plateau° au rez-de-chaussée°

Soundstage / au... on the ground floor

Séquence	*Effets*	*Décors*	*Résumé*	*Rôles*
4	INT.—JOUR	CANAL 7—Plateau de l'émission° «BONJOUR!»	Camille et Bruno ont invité un boulanger.	CAMILLE, BRUNO, BOULANGER

show

OBJECTIFS

In this episode, you will

- meet Camille Leclair and her coworkers on a Paris TV show
- watch a segment of the TV show "Bonjour!"
- learn about the French tradition of breadmaking

In this chapter, you will

- describe people and things
- use adverbs of frequency
- use expressions of agreement and disagreement
- talk about TV production
- talk about everyday actions
- learn how the French define their culture
- read about the importance of television in France

Vocabulaire en contexte

Pour parler des personnes°

Pour... *Talking about people*

Selon° Yasmine, papa est **grand**° et très intelligent. Le **travail**° de Rachid est **intéressant**. Il est **prêt** à commencer.° **Mais**° il est **inquiet**° pour Yasmine.

According to / tall
work
prêt... *ready to start / But / worried*

Comment est° Bruno?
Bruno est un **bon**° journaliste parisien à Canal 7.
Il est...

- capable.
- **dynamique**.
- important.

Selon la productrice,° Bruno est...

- **souvent**° **amusant**.
- sympathique.*
- **heureux**.°
- **parfois**° **difficile** et **ridicule**.

Selon le public, il est...

- **super**.
- **magnifique**.
- **formidable**.°

Il n'est pas **sans**° charme.
Et il n'est jamais **ennuyeux**.°
Selon Camille, Bruno est un **vrai** Français° et un bon ami.

Comment... *What is . . . like?*
good
producer
often
happy
sometimes
terrific
without
boring
vrai... *true Frenchman*

---

*The adjective **sympa**, which you learned in Chapter 1, is a shortened form of **sympathique**.

Langage fonctionnel

Pour exprimer l'accord / le désaccord°

Pour... *Expressing agreement/disagreement*

The following expressions can be used to express agreement or disagreement.

Pour exprimer l'accord

Bien sûr! (Bien sûr que oui!)	*Of course! (Yes, of course!)*
D'accord! (Je suis d'accord!)	*Okay! (I agree!)*
C'est vrai!	*That's true!*
Sans doute!	*Probably! No doubt!*

Pour exprimer le désaccord

Bien sûr que non!	*Of course not! Certainly not!*
Je ne suis pas d'accord.	*I don't agree.*
Ce n'est pas vrai! (Pas vrai!)	*That's not true! (Not true!)*
C'est faux.	*That's false.*

—Bruno est ridicule. *Bruno is ridiculous.*
—Non, **c'est faux**! Il est amusant. *No, that's wrong! He's funny.*

Activités

A. Descriptions. How would you describe these people? Choose words from the list or other adjectives of your choice.

Vocabulaire utile: amusant, capable, difficile, dynamique, grand, heureux, important, inquiet, intelligent, intéressant, ridicule, stupide, super, sympathique

MODÈLE:

Le diplomate est...
Le diplomate est important et capable.

1. Le clown est...

2. L'acteur est...

3. Le professeur est...

B. Un portrait. Think of a famous male sports figure, entertainer, or politician, and describe him by completing the following sentences.

1. J'admire (Je déteste) ______.
2. Il est...
3. Il est toujours...
4. Il est souvent...
5. Il est parfois...
6. Il est rarement...
7. Il n'est pas du tout...
8. Il n'est jamais...

Notez bien!

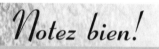

To make your descriptions more accurate, use these five useful adverbs▲:

toujours	always
souvent	often
parfois	sometimes
rarement	rarely
ne... jamais	never

These adverbs usually precede the adjectives they modify.*

Bruno est **souvent** amusant, mais **rarement** ridicule.
Rachid est **toujours** capable et il **n'**est **jamais** ridicule.

C. D'accord ou pas d'accord? Use one of the expressions of agreement or disagreement to give your opinion regarding these statements about television.

MODÈLE: Les films à la télé† sont souvent violents. →
C'est vrai! Les films à la télé sont très souvent violents. (*ou* Je ne suis pas d'accord. Les films à la télé ne sont pas violents du tout. *ou* Ce n'est pas vrai. Les films à la télé sont rarement violents.)

1. Les Américains sont très influencés par la télé.
2. La télé est un élément important de ma vie (*my life*).
3. Le travail d'un reporter à la télé est super.
4. Les reporters à la télé sont toujours objectifs.
5. Les documentaires à la télé sont rarement éducatifs.

Notez bien!

To say someone has a certain profession, use **je suis (tu es, il est**, etc.) + profession (with no article).

Je suis productrice.
I am a producer.
Vous êtes journaliste.
You are a journalist.
Elle est professeur.
She is an instructor.
Ils sont étudiants.
They are students.

For the third person (**il, elle, ils, elles**), you can also use **c'est (ce sont)** + indefinite article + profession.

C'est un professeur.
She is an instructor.
Ce sont des étudiants.
They are students.

Les locaux et les employés de Canal 7

La régie

la productrice (Martine)

Le plateau

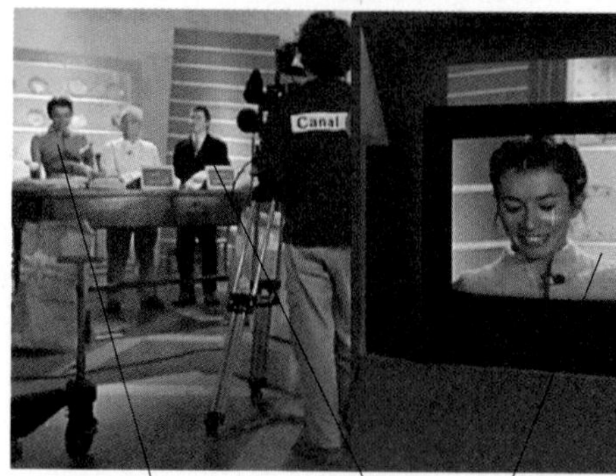

la journaliste (Camille)
le journaliste‡ (Bruno)
l'écran (*m.*)

▲Terms followed by ▲ are explained in the *Glossary of Grammatical Terms* in Appendix A.
*Remember also that **ne... jamais** follows the pattern of **ne... pas** for its placement with the verb.
†**La télé** is a short form of **la télévision**. It is often used in conversation.
‡Depending on the gender of the person, a job title may vary slightly: for example, **le/la journaliste, le producteur / la productrice**. A few job titles have only one grammatical gender even if the person doing the job is not of that gender: **Bruno est *la star* de l'émission. Hélène est *un reporter* canadien.**

Autres mots utiles

une émission	program
un reporter	reporter
la télévision (télé)	television

Activité

À Canal 7. Fill in the blanks with the appropriate word from the list of useful vocabulary. Look at the preceding photos if you need to verify who has which job.

Vocabulaire utile: écran, émission, journalistes, productrice, reporter, public, télévision, studio

«Bonjour!» est une ______[1] diffusée[a] à la ______[2] sur Canal 7. Les ______[3] de «Bonjour!» sont Camille Leclair et Bruno Gall. Martine est la ______[4].

À Canal 7, l'émission est filmée dans le ______[5] sur le plateau. Martine est en régie pendant[b] l'émission, et elle peut voir[c] Bruno et Camille sur l'______[6]. «Bonjour!» est une émission populaire. Le ______[7] adore Camille et Bruno.

[a]*broadcast* [b]*during* [c]*peut... can see*

Visionnement 1

Avant de visionner

Un grand jour. At the end of Episode 1, Yasmine wished her father luck because he was going to have a big day too. To find out why, read the following exchange from Episode 2 and choose the response that best sums up the dialogue.

MARTINE: Alors, le déménagement[a]?
RACHID: Difficile... Tu vas bien?[b]
MARTINE: Mmm. C'est Roger, le réalisateur[c]... Et Nicole, la scripte.[d]
ROGER ET NICOLE: Bonjour.
RACHID: Bonjour.
MARTINE: C'est Rachid, Rachid Bouhazid. ... (*à Rachid*) Et là, sur[e] l'écran, ...

[a]*move (to a new residence)* [b]*Tu... Are you well?* [c]*director* [d]*script coordinator* [e]*Et... And there, on*

a. Rachid is saying good-bye before moving away.
b. He is starting classes at the university.
c. He is starting a new job.

Vocabulaire relatif à l'épisode

le boulanger	*(male) baker*
le pain	*bread*
artisanal	*handmade*
industriel	*factory-made*
vingt-et-unième siècle	*twenty-first century*

Observez!

Now watch Episode 2. See if you are right about Rachid's important day by looking for the following clues.

- Where does Rachid go after dropping Yasmine off at school?
- What does he do there?

Remember—Don't expect to understand every word in the episode; you need to understand only the basic plot structure and characters. If you can answer the questions that follow the episode, you have understood enough. Your instructor may ask you to watch the episode again later in the chapter. By then, you'll have additional tools and will be able to understand more of the details. The activities in **Visionnement 2** in the text and in the *Workbook/Laboratory Manual* will help, too.

Après le visionnement

A. **Quel travail? (*Which job?*)** Now that you have watched Episode 2, match each job to the person you saw in the film.

1. Camille

2. Bruno

3. Martine

4. Hélène

5. Rachid

a. la productrice
b. un reporter canadien
c. un nouveau (*new*) reporter
d. un journaliste français
e. une journaliste française

B. Qu'est-ce qui se passe? (*What's happening?*) Complete the summary of Episode 2 by filling in the blanks with the appropriate word from the list of useful vocabulary.

Vocabulaire utile: béret, Camille, Canal 7, content, émission, médaillon, Montréal, pain, présente, prêt, test

Rachid arrive à ______[1]. Martine, la productrice, ______[2] ses nouveaux[a] collègues. Rachid va travailler[b] avec ______[3] et Bruno.

Aujourd'hui,[c] pendant[d] l'émission «Bonjour!», Camille et Bruno interviewent un boulanger parisien. Il y a un ______[4] sur le pain: pain artisanal ou pain industriel? Bruno est ______[5] pour le test. Il identifie le ______[6] artisanal, et il gagne[e] le ______[7] de la semaine[f]... mais il n'est pas ______[8].

Hélène, une amie de Bruno, arrive de ______[9]. Bruno est très content de la revoir.[g] Plus tard,[h] Camille cherche son[i] ______[10]. Où[j] est-il?

[a]*ses... his new* [b]*va... will be working* [c]*Today* [d]*during* [e]*wins* [f]*week* [g]*de... to see her again* [h]*Plus... Later* [i]*her* [j]*Where*

C. Réfléchissez. (*Think.*) Answer the following questions based on what you saw and heard in Episode 2.

1. Bruno and Camille work together as hosts of "Bonjour!" From what you have seen, would you guess that they are friends or simply coworkers? Or is it too early to tell?
2. Camille seems to have lost something. What do you think she has lost? What could its significance be?

Structure 6

Les adjectifs

Describing people and things

—Les Français sont **formidables**! Au XXIe siècle, vous êtes encore **inquiets** pour le pain.

Hélène uses two adjectives▲ to describe the character and preoccupation of the French: **formidables** and **inquiets**. French adjectives agree in gender (feminine or masculine) and number (singular or plural) with the noun being described. That is, an adjective used to describe a noun will be

- masculine if the noun is masculine: **Le reporter est *intelligent.***
- feminine if the noun is feminine: **La productrice est *intelligente.***
- masculine plural if the noun is masculine plural: **Les reporters sont *intelligents.***
- feminine plural if the noun is feminine plural: **Les productrices sont *intelligentes.***

Le genre des adjectifs

Adjectives can be grouped according to the sound and spelling of their masculine and feminine singular forms.

1. Many adjectives have masculine and feminine forms that sound alike and are spelled alike.*

difficile	*difficult*	**magnifique**	*magnificent*
facile	*easy*	**ridicule**	*ridiculous, silly*
formidable	*terrific*	**sympathique**	*nice*
jeune	*young*	**triste**	*sad*

*Adjectives in this group are often cognates or near-cognates to English words: **dynamique**, **stupide**, and so on.

La rentrée n'est pas **facile** pour Yasmine.	*The first day of school is not easy for Yasmine.*
Bruno n'est probablement jamais **triste**.	*Bruno is probably never sad.*

2. Some adjectives have masculine and feminine forms that sound alike but have different spellings. The feminine form usually ends in **-e** whereas the masculine does not.

fatigué(e) *tired* **joli(e)** *pretty* **vrai(e)** *true* **fâché(e)** *angry*

Rachid n'est pas **fatigué**.	*Rachid is not tired.*
Sonia est **fatiguée**.	*Sonia is tired.*
Le médaillon de Camille est **joli**.	*Camille's locket is pretty.*
Yasmine est **jolie**.	*Yasmine is pretty.*

Note that the feminine forms of adjectives like **cher** and **intellectuel** have additional changes: **chère**, **intellectuelle**.

Chère maman,...	*Dear Mom, . . .*
Est-ce qu'Hélène est **intellectuelle**?	*Is Hélène intellectual?*

3. Many adjectives have masculine and feminine forms that are pronounced and spelled differently. A large number of these have a silent final consonant in the masculine but a pronounced final consonant in the feminine. There are several types in this group.

- Those that form the feminine by adding **-e** to the masculine are common.

amusant(e)	*amusing*	**laid(e)**	*ugly*
français(e)	*French*	**mauvais(e)**	*bad*
grand(e)	*big; tall*	**petit(e)**	*little*
intéressant(e)	*interesting*	**prêt(e)**	*ready*

Benoît n'est pas **laid**.	*Benoît isn't ugly.*
Yasmine n'est pas **laide**.	*Yasmine isn't ugly.*
Benoît est **petit**.	*Benoît is little.*
Yasmine est **petite**.	*Yasmine is little.*
Benoît est **mauvais** en arithmétique.	*Benoît is bad in arithmetic.*
Yasmine n'est pas **mauvaise** en arithmétique.	*Yasmine isn't bad in arithmetic.*

- Those with masculine forms ending in **-x** form the feminine by dropping the **-x** and adding **-se**.

heureux → **heureuse**	*happy*
ennuyeux → **ennuyeuse**	*boring*
malheureux → **malheureuse**	*unhappy*

Bruno est **heureux**.	*Bruno is happy.*
Yasmine est **malheureuse**?	*Is Yasmine unhappy?*

- Those with masculine forms ending in a nasal vowel make the feminine by denasalizing the vowel and pronouncing the final consonant. The feminine of this type ends with either **-e** or a doubled final consonant plus an **-e.** Learn each feminine spelling when you learn the adjective.

américain(e)	*American*
canadien(ne)	*Canadian*
bon(ne)	*good*
parisien(ne)	*Parisian*

Bruno est **parisien**.	*Bruno is Parisian.*
Martine est **parisienne**.	*Martine is Parisian.*

- Other adjectives have masculine and feminine forms that are spelled various ways. Learn both forms when you learn the adjective.

inquiet/inquiète	*anxious, worried*
gentil(le)	*nice; kind; well behaved*

Bruno est **gentil**.	*Bruno is nice.*
Camille est **gentille** aussi.	*Camille is also nice.*

4. Some adjectives end in one consonant sound in the masculine and another in the feminine.

actif/active	*active*
sportif/sportive	*athletic*

Rachid est **sportif**.	*Rachid is athletic.*
Est-ce que Camille est **sportive**?	*Is Camille athletic?*

Le pluriel des adjectifs

1. To form the plural of adjectives, add an **-s** to the singular, except where the singular already ends in an **-s** or an **-x**.

	Il est **sportif**.	Ils sont **sportifs**.
but	Il est **mauvais** en maths.	Ils sont **mauvais** en maths.
	Il est **ennuyeux**.	Ils sont **ennuyeux**.

2. **Sympa** is invariable for masculine and feminine, meaning its ending doesn't change for feminine nouns. It does take a plural ending. **Super** is completely invariable; its ending never changes for feminine or plural nouns.

Les institutrices sont **sympas**!	*The teachers are nice!*
Elles sont **super** aussi!	*They are also super!*

3. When describing a group of which at least one member is masculine, the masculine plural form of the adjective is used.

   Yasmine, Carmen et Benoît sont **sportifs**.

Activités

A. Descriptions. Create complete statements about Episodes 1 and 2.

MODÈLE: Camille / être / heureux / aujourd'hui →
Camille est heureuse aujourd'hui.

1. l'institutrice / être / patient / et / sympathique
2. Yasmine et les autres enfants / être / petit
3. la démonstration / être / intéressant
4. les baguettes* (*f.*) / être / bon
5. Bruno / ne pas être / content
6. le béret / être / ridicule
7. Camille / être / parfois / impatient
8. l'émission «Bonjour!» / ne jamais être / ennuyeux

B. Vrai ou faux? (*True or false?*) Take turns with your partner using **est-ce que** to change the following statements about Episodes 1 and 2 into questions. The person who answers the question should use one of the expressions of agreement or disagreement.

MODÈLE: L'institutrice est inquiète. →
É1: Est-ce que l'institutrice est inquiète?
É2: Bien sûr que non! Elle est contente.

1. Camille est triste aujourd'hui.
2. Yasmine est gentille.
3. Camille est laide.
4. L'émission «Bonjour!» est intéressante.
5. Les collègues de Rachid sont sympathiques.
6. Rachid est malheureux à Canal 7.
7. Hélène est heureuse.
8. Bruno est prêt pour le test.

C. Comment sont-ils? (*What are they like?*) Take turns with a partner describing the following people. Use the correct forms of the adjectives in the list, and create both affirmative and negative sentences when possible.

Vocabulaire utile: amusant, calme, ennuyeux, fâché, fatigué, gentil, intellectuel, intelligent, joli, laid, malheureux, riche, ridicule, sportif, stupide, triste

MODÈLE: les hommes politiques →
É1: Les hommes politiques sont intelligents.
É2: Oui, mais parfois ils ne sont pas gentils.

1. Arnold Schwarzenegger
2. Julia Roberts
3. les stars (*f.*) de cinéma
4. les journalistes
5. un clown

***Baguettes** are long, thin loaves of French bread.

D. Célébrités mystérieuses. Your teacher will show you pictures of eight celebrities. Work in groups of three. One member of the group chooses a celebrity, without telling the others. The other group members ask yes/no questions to try to guess the identity of the chosen celebrity. When the first celebrity is identified, another group member chooses a different celebrity, and the activity continues until each member of the group has had an opportunity to choose a "mystery celebrity."

Vocabulaire utile: cher, difficile, ennuyeux, fâché, facile, fatigué, grand, intéressant, laid, malheureux, mauvais, petit, ridicule, sportif, super, sympa

MODÈLE: É1: Est-ce que c'est un homme?
É2: Non.
É3: Alors, c'est une femme. Est-ce qu'elle est petite?
É2: Oui.
É1: Est-ce qu'elle est sportive?

Regards sur la culture

Perceptions et réalités

Stereotypes usually tell us as much about the values and customs of the people who use them as about those whom they are supposed to describe. There are a few North American stereotypes about the French that are shared by the French themselves, but many others are not.

- French people often think of themselves as particularly interested in food and gifted at appreciating it. They are especially concerned about bread, which is truly the staple food of French cuisine. Bread is eaten along with nearly every dish at every meal, and it is the main food eaten at breakfast and for most children's snacks. Bread made in the traditional craft sense (**le pain artisanal**) has to be bought daily because it contains no preservatives and dries out quickly. Mass-produced bread (**le pain industriel**) is also available in stores. Most French people are ready at any moment to engage in animated debates about the quality of bread today.

Dans une boulangerie française

- The French do not think of themselves as eating rich food, however, but only *good* food. When asked what the typical French meal is, most people in France would probably answer **le steak-frites** (*steak with fries*). This may not correspond to North American ideas of what French people like to eat, but it is the kind of meal that a French traveler might think of first when he or she needs a quick dinner.

- The Eiffel Tower really is a landmark that the French think of as representing them in some sense. A hilarious 1999 film, *Le Voyage à Paris,* recounts the adventures of a rural highway toll collector with hundreds of models of the Eiffel Tower in his room at home. His dream is to visit Paris and see the real thing.
- The French like to think of themselves as the little guys who always win out because they are clever and quick. The popular comic book character Astérix is a symbol of this sense of identity. He is a Gaul* who, in ancient times, lives in the one village that has not been conquered by the Roman legions. Astérix is always able to outwit the power of Caesar and his troops.

www.asterix.com © 2005 Les éditions Albert René/Goscinny-Uderzo
Astérix, un héros français

- Foreigners often think of the beret as typically French. To the French, however, it looks old-fashioned and reminds them of elderly people, farming life, and backwardness. Berets are not a common sight in Paris.
- The French are often surprised to find out that other people think of them as obsessed with love. As far as the French are concerned, the real lovers are the Italians.
- French people are also astonished to discover that people from some other cultures consider them rude. Later in this course, you'll learn reasons for this gap in perceptions, and you will also look at other aspects of French culture that may clash with North American stereotypes.

Considérez

To vouch for the kindness of someone, a French person might say: **Il est bon comme le pain.** Does this expression make any sense when translated literally into English? What would be the nearest English equivalent of this expression? What conclusions can you draw from this difference about the importance accorded to bread in France and in North American cultures?

*In ancient times, France was part of an area known as Gaul. In 390 B.C., its inhabitants, called Gauls, attacked Rome and eventually swept farther east. Around 50 B.C., Julius Caesar and his Roman army had succeeded in turning the tide and had conquered all of Gaul, an area that comprised what is now France, Belgium, Luxembourg, and the parts of the Netherlands and Germany that are south and west of the Rhine River.

Structure 7

Les verbes réguliers en *-er* et la construction *verbe + infinitif*

Talking about everyday actions

—Tu **arrives*** de Montréal?

—Oui. Je **lance** une série de reportages sur la vie au Québec.

When Bruno and Hélène exchange remarks about her visit to Paris, they use the verbs **arriver** and **lancer** (*to launch*). These infinitives▲ end in **-er**. Many French verb forms are created, or conjugated,▲ like **arriver** and **lancer**.

Les verbes réguliers en *-er*

1. To use regular **-er** verbs, drop the **-er** and add these endings: **-e**, **-es**, **-e**, **-ons**, **-ez**, **-ent**.

chercher (*to look for*)			
je	cherch **e**	nous	cherch **ons**
tu	cherch **es**	vous	cherch **ez**
il, elle, on	cherch **e**	ils, elles	cherch **ent**

aimer (*to like*)			
j'	aim **e**	nous	aim **ons**
tu	aim **es**	vous	aim **ez**
il, elle, on	aim **e**	ils, elles	aim **ent**

*In the film, Bruno runs the subject and verb together, saying **T'arrives...** . This is a common occurrence in everyday French conversation when the pronoun **tu** precedes a verb that begins with a vowel sound.

2. Here is a list of some common regular **-er** verbs.

aimer *to like; to love*	**habiter** *to live (in a place), reside*
aimer mieux *to prefer*	**parler** *to speak; to talk*
chercher *to look for*	**penser** *to think*
dîner *to eat dinner, dine*	**porter** *to wear*
donner *to give*	**regarder** *to watch; to look at*
écouter *to listen (to)*	**travailler** *to work*
étudier *to study*	**trouver** *to find; to consider*

As you continue your study of French, you'll recognize other regular **-er** verbs, many of which are cognates. Before doing the activities, be sure you know the meaning of the following cognate verbs: **commencer**, **identifier**, **inviter**, **présenter**, **respecter**, **visiter**.

3. The present tense verb forms in French can express three different meanings in English.

j'étudie { *I study* / *I am studying* / *I do study*

nous travaillons { *we work* / *we are working* / *we do work*

4. Useful expressions are **penser que** (*to think that*), **penser à** (*to think about*), and **penser de** (*to have an opinion about*).

Qu'est-ce que Bruno **pense du** béret?	*What does Bruno think of (What is Bruno's opinion of) the beret?*
Bruno **pense que** le béret est ridicule.	*Bruno thinks that the beret is ridiculous.*
Il **pense aux** personnes âgées à la campagne quand il voit un béret!	*He thinks about old people in the countryside when he sees a beret!*

Verbe + infinitif

When two verbs are used together to express an idea, the first verb is conjugated and the second remains in the infinitive form. Some verbs that can be followed by an infinitive are **adorer**, **aimer**, **désirer**, and **détester**.

Rachid **aime habiter** à Paris.	*Rachid likes to live in Paris.*
Je **désire trouver** un emploi.	*I want to find a job.*

Activités

A. Résumons. (*Let's summarize.*) Retell the story of *Le Chemin du retour* by filling in the blank with the appropriate form of the verb in parentheses.

Aujourd'hui, Rachid ____[1] (commencer) un travail à Canal 7. Les employés de Canal 7 ____[2] (être) très sympathiques. Bruno Gall et Camille Leclair ____[3] (présenter) l'émission «Bonjour!». Un boulanger ____[4] (parler) de deux sortes de pain. Bruno ____[5] (identifier) le bon pain.

Bruno gagne° le béret d'honneur, mais il _____[6] (trouver) le béret ridicule. Nous, les Américains et les Canadiens, nous _____[7] (penser) que le béret est typiquement français. Mais en France, on ne porte pas très souvent le béret.

°*wins*

B. La vie d'un journaliste. Create complete sentences from the following cues. Then state whether the statements accurately describe the life and reputation of a journalist.

MODÈLE: nous / respecter / l'opinion des journalistes →
É1: Nous respectons l'opinion des journalistes.
É2: C'est vrai, nous respectons l'opinion des journalistes. *ou*
Non, c'est faux, nous ne respectons pas l'opinion des journalistes.

1. je / penser / que le journalisme est une bonne carrière
2. les journalistes / adorer / leur (*their*) travail
3. ils / dîner / dans des restaurants chers
4. ils / parler / avec des personnes intéressantes
5. tout le monde / écouter et respecter / les journalistes
6. nous / trouver / la vie (*life*) d'un journaliste facile
7. les journalistes / travailler / beaucoup (*a lot*)

C. Préférences. Work in groups of three or four to describe your own preferences and those of your group or other people you know. You can create sentences using words from each column or other words that you know.

MODÈLE: Je n'aime pas préparer (*to study for*) les examens. J'aime mieux regarder la télévision.

je/j'	adorer	dîner à la cafétéria
tu	(ne pas) aimer	écouter de la musique classique
vous	aimer mieux	être étudiant(e)
nous	(ne pas) désirer	étudier à la bibliothèque (*library*)
le professeur	détester	habiter à la résidence universitaire
maman		parler en classe
mon (*my*) ami(e)		préparer les examens
?		regarder la télévision
		travailler
		?

D. Sondage. (*Survey.*) Interview as many classmates as you can to find out who shares your interests and habits. Jot down what you learn.

MODÈLE: regarder les comédies à la télévision →
É1: Tu regardes les comédies à la télévision?
É2: Oui, je regarde souvent les comédies. (Non, je ne regarde jamais les comédies.)

1. étudier très tard (*late*)
2. habiter à la résidence universitaire
3. chercher les salles de classe
4. détester les films d'horreur
5. trouver [*nom d'une star de cinéma*] formidable
6. inviter le professeur à dîner
7. aimer le fast-food
8. visiter souvent des musées (*museums*)
9. écouter la radio
10. penser que la politique est fascinante ou ennuyeuse

Now share your findings with the class by telling at least one thing you learned.

MODÈLE: Jon, Ashley et Greg n'habitent pas à la résidence universitaire. Ils habitent dans un appartement.

Structure 8

La place des adjectifs

Describing people and things

—Le pain, en France, est très **important**! Alors, voilà des baguettes, du pain de campagne...

—Et avec nous, aujourd'hui, un **grand** boulanger **parisien**. Bonjour, Monsieur Liégeois!

—Bonjour!

You already know that adjectives may follow the verb **être**. Remember that they must always agree in gender and number with the noun or pronoun they modify.

Maman est **fatiguée**.	*Mom is tired.*
Le **pain**, en France, est très **important**.	*Bread, in France, is very important.*
Je suis Bruno et **je** suis **prêt**.	*I'm Bruno and I'm ready.*
Vous êtes **sûrs**, Camille et Bruno?	*Are you sure, Camille and Bruno?*

Notez bien!

Three common adjectives have irregular forms: **beau** (*beautiful, good-looking*), **nouveau** (*new*), and **vieux** (*old*).

m. s.	**beau**	**nouveau**	**vieux**
	(bel)	**(nouvel)**	**(vieil)**
f. s.	**belle**	**nouvelle**	**vieille**
m. pl.	**beaux**	**nouveaux**	**vieux**
f. pl.	**belles**	**nouvelles**	**vieilles**

Rachid est assez **beau.** *Rachid is rather handsome.*

C'est ma **nouvelle** école? *Is this my new school?*

Louise est **vieille.** *Louise is old.*

Notice that these three adjectives precede the noun. The special masculine singular forms are used when the adjective precedes a noun that begins with a vowel sound.

un **bel** homme *a good-looking man*

un **nouvel** emploi *a new job*

un **vieil** ordinateur *an old computer*

1. When placed next to the noun they are describing, most adjectives follow the noun.

C'est une leçon de **sciences naturelles**.	*It's a natural science lesson.*
D'un côté, le **pain industriel**. De l'autre, le **pain artisanal**.	*On one hand, factory-made bread. On the other, handmade bread.*

2. A few adjectives usually precede the noun they describe. You already know some of these: **bon**, **cher**, **grand**, **joli**, **mauvais**, **petit**, **vrai**. Another useful one is **autre** (*other*).

Bonne chance, papa! Pour toi aussi, c'est un **grand jour**, non?	*Good luck, Daddy! It's a big day for you, too, isn't it?*
Bruno! Encore de **mauvaise humeur**?!	*Bruno! In a bad mood again?!*
Bruno adore l'**autre pain**—le pain artisanal.	*Bruno loves the other bread—the handmade bread.*

3. If two or more adjectives describe the same noun, they should be placed where they would normally go. If two are the type that follows the noun, the word **et** is usually placed between them.

Yasmine est une **jolie petite** enfant.	*Yasmine is a pretty little child.*
Et avec nous, aujourd'hui, un **grand** boulanger **parisien**.	*And with us, today, an important Parisian baker.*
C'est un pain **doux et moelleux**.	*This is a soft and velvety bread.*

Activités

A. Un nouveau travail. (***A new job.***) Here is a job announcement for positions at Canal 7. Fill in each blank with the correct form of the appropriate adjective in parentheses.

Canal 7 cherche un scripte et une assistante pour la productrice. Les candidats doivent avoir[a] de ______[1] (patient, bon) qualifications et une ______[2] (excellent, mauvais) formation.[b] Le travail du scripte n'est pas ______[3] (vrai, difficile), mais il est ______[4] (intéressant, autre). Nous désirons une ______[5] (bon, laid) assistante ______[6] (ennuyeux, sympathique) et ______[7] (patient, impatient).

[a]doivent... *must have* [b]*education*

B. Canal 7. Rachid is describing his new workplace to Yasmine. Put the correct form of the adjective in the appropriate place.

MODÈLE: Martine, la productrice, est une professionnelle. (vrai) →
Martine, la productrice, est une vraie professionnelle.

1. Je travaille dans un bureau. (petit)
2. Camille et Bruno sont des journalistes. (formidable)
3. Camille n'est pas une femme. (triste)
4. Camille et Bruno travaillent dans un studio. (grand)
5. Il y a un reporter. (canadien) C'est Hélène.
6. C'est une amie de Bruno. (vieux)
7. «Bonjour!» est une émission. (amusant, intéressant)
8. Hélène lance une émission sur le Québec. (autre, intéressant)
9. Elle apprécie beaucoup la province de Québec. (beau)
10. Elle va parler d'un artiste. (nouveau, québécois) 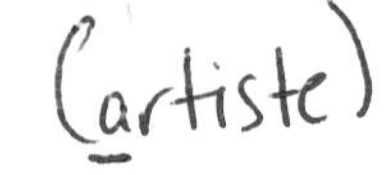

C. Une petite annonce. Jean and Jeanne have been looking for a partner without success. Make their personal ads more interesting by adding adjectives from the list or others of your choice.

Vocabulaire utile: beau, dynamique, exotique, français, généreux, jeune, joli, luxueux, nouveau, professionnel, responsable, riche, sérieux, sincère, vieux

1. Homme, 35 ans, cherche une femme. Je suis cadre (*executive*). J'habite dans une maison.
2. Femme, 28 ans, cherche un homme. Je suis journaliste. J'aime les films et les voyages.

D. En général. With a partner, talk about your likes and dislikes by using elements from the three columns. How similar are you?

MODÈLE: É1: J'aime les grandes universités.
É2: Moi (*Me*), j'aime mieux les petites universités. (*ou* Moi aussi, j'aime les grandes universités.)

J'adore	amusant	les automobiles (*f.*)
J'aime	bon	les cours
Je déteste	cher	les écoles
J'aime mieux	difficile	les émissions de télévision
	ennuyeux	les films
	facile	les histoires
	grand	les livres
	mauvais	les professeurs
	petit	les salles de classe
	vieux	les universités
	?	?

Visionnement 2

Avant de visionner

A. Points de repère. (*Landmarks.*) This map shows the southeastern edge of Paris and the adjacent suburbs, where the Canal 7 studios are located. This whole area, on both banks of the Seine, became rather run-down after World War II, but recently it has been attracting new development and prestige projects like the national library (**la Bibliothèque nationale de France**).

Les environs de Canal 7

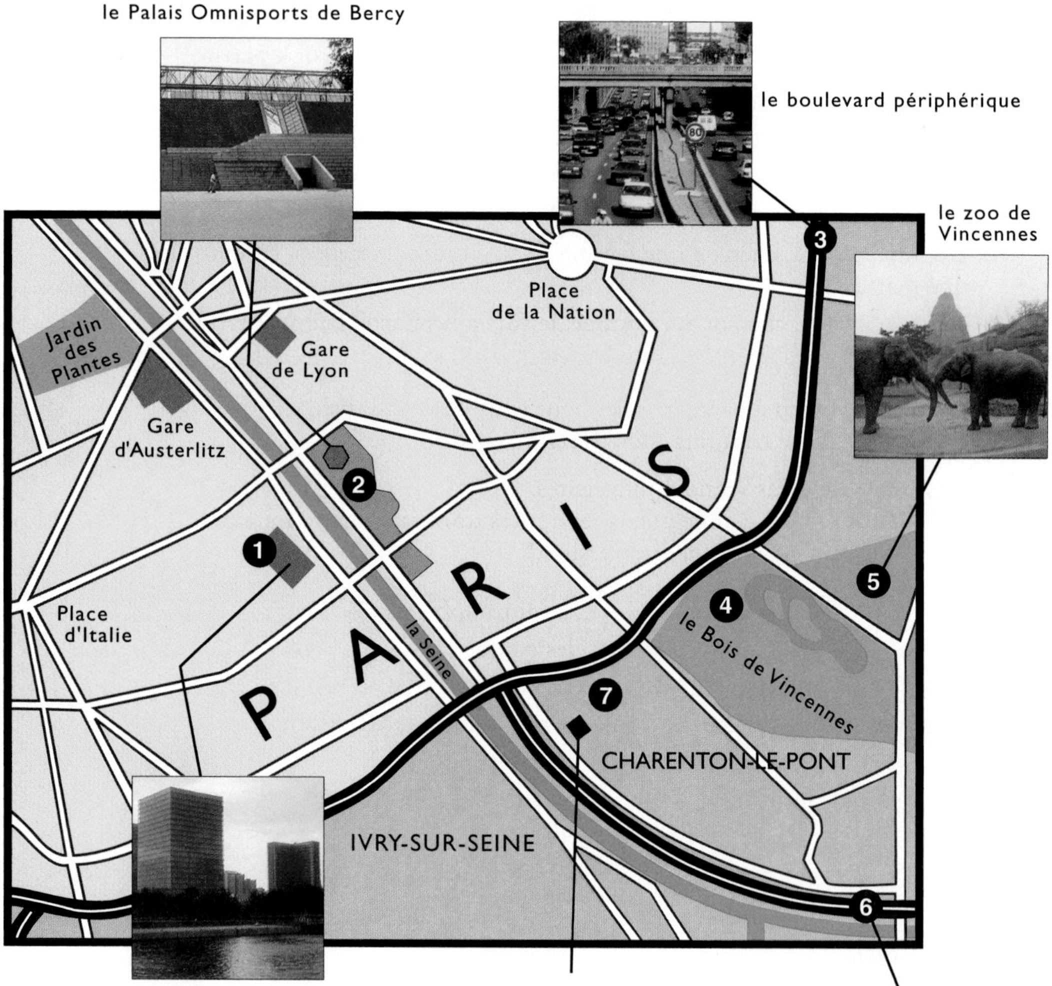

le Palais Omnisports de Bercy

le boulevard périphérique

le zoo de Vincennes

Place de la Nation

Jardin des Plantes

Gare de Lyon

Gare d'Austerlitz

PARIS

Place d'Italie

la Seine

le Bois de Vincennes

CHARENTON-LE-PONT

IVRY-SUR-SEINE

1 2 3 4 5 6 7

la Bibliothèque nationale de France

CANAL 7

l'Autoroute de l'Est (A4)

Look carefully at the map and indicate the number and name of the landmark that one would seek out in order to find the following:

a. un manuscrit de la Renaissance
b. un tigre
c. un match de football (*soccer*)
d. des arbres et des fleurs (*trees and flowers*) magnifiques
e. une route autour de (*around*) Paris
f. Camille Leclair et Bruno Gall

B. Les pains en France. Match the description of the bread with the correct picture.

a.

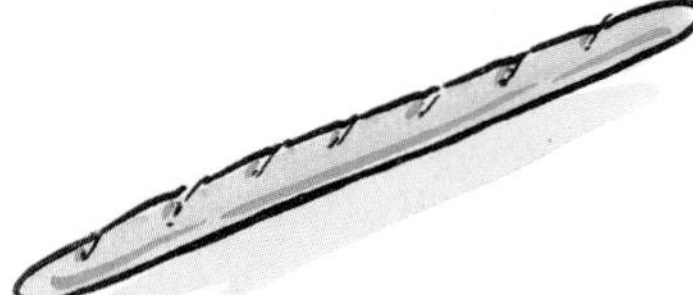

b.

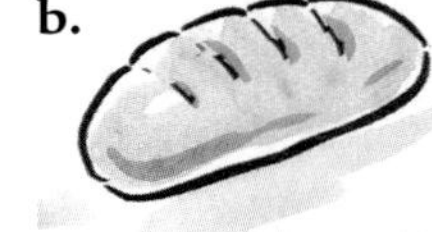

_____ **1.** Une baguette est longue et mince (*thin*).
_____ **2.** Un pain de campagne (*country*) est court et épais (*short and thick*).

Observez!

Consider the cultural information explained in **Regards sur la culture**. Then watch Episode 2 again, and answer the following questions.

- Why is Bruno embarrassed at the end of the show?
- What is the connection between the beret and the topic of the show?

Après le visionnement

Do the activity for **Visionnement 2** in the *Workbook/Laboratory Manual.*

Synthèse: Lecture

Mise en contexte

Public television in France is supported by an annual tax of about $100 that must be paid by every household having at least one television set.* This method of funding public television is found in most European countries. About half of French television broadcast stations (not cable) are state owned.

Commercials rarely interrupt shows in France. Rather, they are grouped at the beginning and end of programs. French television commercials have long been known as very creative and entertaining, and their style has been imitated over recent years in many North American television commercials.

Both public and private channels in France show a large number of foreign programs, usually from the United States, but also from Australia, Japan, Germany, and elsewhere. The heavy presence of American programming is of concern to some French people.

Here are statistics about the viewing audience (age 15 or older) for some of the major television channels that can be viewed nationally.

		Audience
Chaînes[a] publiques	France 2	25,0 %
	France 3 (télévision régionale)	17,0 %
	France 5 (mission éducative)	1,8 %
	Arte (mission européenne)	1,6 %
Chaînes privées	TF1 (jeux,[b] sports, variétés, films)	34,0 %
	M6 (accent sur la musique)	12,0 %
Chaîne privée payante[c]	Canal + (films, sports)	4,6 %

[a]*Networks* [b]*games* [c]Chaîne... *Private subscription channel*

Stratégie pour mieux lire
Recognizing related words

Remember—You have already learned about cognates, French words that look or sound similar to English words and that have similar meanings. Even when you can't understand every detail of a French text, you can often get a good idea of the reading's content by paying attention to cognates.

Scan the entire text that follows, and locate at least five cognates in the opening paragraphs and five more in the list. Choose the best title for this selection. Then read the whole text through and see whether your choice of title is a good one.

*This law does not apply to people over 65 years old or to handicapped people.

Des inventions importantes du XXe siècle*

Les Français aiment la télévision

La télévision et la violence

Pour les Français, les deux inventions les plus[1] importantes du XXe siècle sont la télévision et l'ordinateur. Viennent ensuite[2] la greffe du cœur,[3] les antibiotiques, le lave-linge,[4] la pilule contraceptive, le scanner (pour l'ordinateur), la pénicilline, le réfrigérateur, la carte bancaire,[5] le TGV[6] et le laser.

Au cours de sa vie,[7] un Français passe environ[8] neuf années devant[9] la télévision, mais six années au travail. Les enfants passent environ huit cents heures par an[10] à l'école—et huit cents heures devant le petit écran.

Les émissions les plus populaires, par ordre décroissant,[11] sont:

les émissions de fiction
les magazines et documentaires
les journaux télévisés[12]
la publicité[13]
les jeux
les films
les variétés
les sports
les émissions pour la jeunesse[14]
le théâtre et la musique classique

Adapté de *Francoscopie: Comment vivent les Français*

[1]les... *most* [2]Viennent... *Next come* [3]greffe... *heart transplant* [4]*washing machine* [5]carte... *bank card* [6]*high-speed train* [7]Au... *In his lifetime* [8]*about* [9]années... *years in front of* [10]huit... *800 hours per year* [11]*descending* [12]journaux... *TV news programs* [13]la... *commercials* [14]*youth*

***XXe** means *twentieth* and is written **vingtième**. **Siècle** means *century*.

Après la lecture

A. Votre titre. (*Your title.*) Now that you've read the text, do you think you chose the most appropriate title? If not, which title might be better? If you did choose correctly the first time around, which words guided you in your choice?

B. Et vous? Compare yourself to the French after studying the statistics in the article.

1. Pour les Français, les deux inventions les plus importantes du XXe siècle sont _____ et _____. Pour moi, les deux inventions les plus importantes sont _____ et _____.
2. Au cours de sa vie, un Français passe _____ années devant le petit écran. Au cours d'une journée typique (*typical day*), je passe _____ heures devant le petit écran.
3. Au cours de sa vie, un Français passe _____ années à travailler. Au cours d'une journée typique, je passe _____ heures à travailler et à étudier.
4. Les émissions favorites des Français sont _____ et _____. Moi, j'aime _____ et _____.

À écrire

Do **À écrire** for Chapter 2 in the *Workbook/Laboratory Manual.*

Vocabulaire

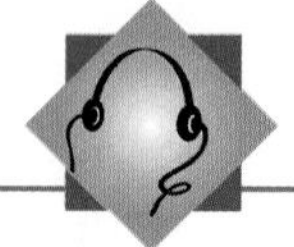

Les locaux et les employés de Canal 7

un écran	screen
une émission	program
un plateau (des plateaux)	set
un(e) producteur/trice	producer
la régie	control room
le travail	work; job

MOTS APPARENTÉS: **un(e) journaliste, un reporter, la télévision** (*fam.* **la télé**)

Verbes réguliers en *-er*

aimer	to like; to love
aimer mieux	to prefer
chercher	to look for
dîner	to eat dinner, dine
donner	to give
écouter	to listen (to)
étudier	to study
habiter	to live (*in a place*), reside
lancer	to launch
parler	to speak; to talk
penser	to think
porter	to wear
regarder	to watch; to look at
travailler	to work
trouver	to find; to consider

MOTS APPARENTÉS: **adorer, arriver, désirer, détester**

Adjectifs pour parler des personnes

autre	other
beau (bel, belle)	beautiful, good-looking
bon(ne)	good
cher (chère)	dear; expensive
ennuyeux/euse	boring
fâché(e)	angry
facile	easy
fatigué(e)	tired
faux (fausse)	false
formidable	terrific, wonderful
gentil(le)	nice; kind; well behaved
grand(e)	big; tall
heureux/euse	happy
inquiet/ète	anxious, worried
jeune	young
joli(e)	pretty
laid(e)	ugly
malheureux/euse	unhappy, miserable
mauvais(e)	bad
nouveau (nouvel, nouvelle)	new
petit(e)	small
prêt(e)	ready
sportif/ive	athletic
triste	sad
vieux (vieil, vieille)	old
vrai(e)	true

MOTS APPARENTÉS: **actif/ive, amusant(e), difficile, dynamique, intellectuel(le), intéressant(e), magnifique, ridicule, super**

À REVOIR: **sympathique** (*fam.* **sympa**)

Adverbes

parfois	sometimes
rarement	rarely
souvent	often
toujours	always

Conjonction

mais	but

Pour exprimer l'accord / le désaccord

Bien sûr! (Bien sûr que oui!)	Of course! (Yes, of course!)
Bien sûr que non!	Of course not!
C'est faux.	That's/It's false.
C'est vrai.	That's/It's true.
D'accord! (Je suis d'accord.)	Okay! (I agree.)
Je ne suis pas d'accord.	I don't agree.
Sans doute!	Probably! No doubt!

Autres expressions utiles

C'est un(e) (journaliste).	He/She is a (journalist).
Comment est/sont... ?	What is/are . . . like?
Il/Elle est (journaliste).	He/She is a (journalist).
sans	without
selon	according to

Chapitre 3

Le médaillon

Le Chemin du retour

Feuille de service du 25 janvier
9e jour de tournage
Horaires: 13h–23h

LIEU DE TOURNAGE: MARSEILLE—FRANCE 3—corridor, rez-de-chaussée° *ground floor*

Séquence	***Effets***	***Décors***	***Résumé***	***Rôles***
9	INT.—JOUR	CANAL 7—corridor	Camille récupère° son médaillon.	CAMILLE, RACHID, PRODUCTRICE

gets back

OBJECTIFS

In this episode, you will

- see Camille's reaction when her locket is found
- discover new sides to Bruno's personality
- learn more about Rachid's background

In this chapter, you will

- talk about places people go
- talk about where things are located
- discuss nationalities
- express movement from place to place
- talk about what will happen soon
- ask questions using tag phrases
- talk about things people just did
- learn about nonverbal communication in France
- learn about communication customs in different cultures

Vocabulaire en contexte

Les environs de Canal 7°

Les... The area around Channel 7

Le bureau de Rachid et de Bruno est dans **le bâtiment** de Canal 7, situé dans **un quartier** de **banlieue** (*f.*). Regardez bien le plan.

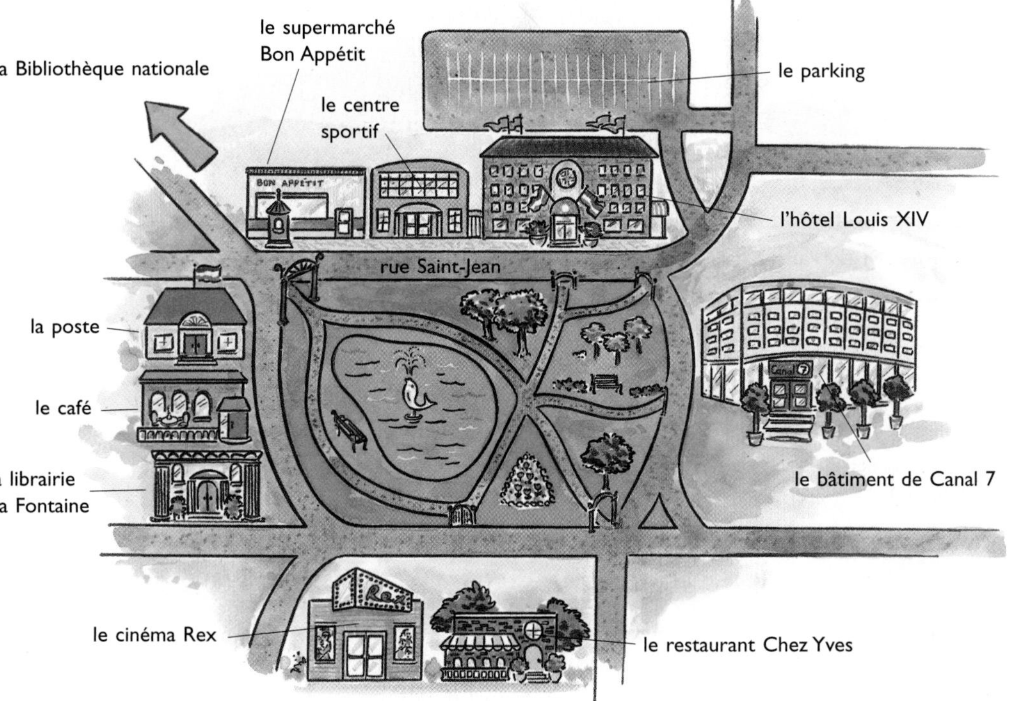

—Où° est le bâtiment de Canal 7? *Where*
—Le bâtiment de Canal 7 est **en face du** parc.

—**Où se trouve**° le restaurant Chez Yves? *Où... Where is . . . located?*
—Il est **à côté du** cinéma.

Un autre restaurant se trouve **dans** le bâtiment de Canal 7.
Le centre sportif est là, **dans la rue** Saint-Jean.
Il y a un kiosque **devant** le supermarché.
Le parking est **derrière** le centre sportif et l'hôtel.
Un café est **entre** la librairie et la poste.
La Bibliothèque nationale n'est pas **loin d'ici**.° *loin... far from here*
Le supermarché est **près de** la poste.

Autres prépositions de lieu° (*m.*) *place*

au-dessous de*	below	**chez**	at the home (business) of		
au-dessus de†	above, over	**sous**	under	**sur**	on

*The expression **en dessous de** may also be used.
†The expression **en dessus de** may also be used.

Notez bien!

Whenever **de** is used with **le** and **les**, it forms a contraction. No contraction is made with **la** or **l'**.

de + le → **du**
de + la → **de la**
de + l' → **de l'**
de + les → **des**

Le parking de Canal 7 se trouve en dessous **du** bâtiment.

Le supermarché est près **de la** poste.

Le restaurant **de l'**hôtel Louis XIV est excellent!

Le bâtiment de Canal 7 est loin **des** monuments de Paris.

Activités

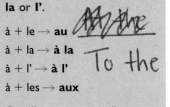

Notez bien!

Whenever **à** is used with **le** and **les**, it forms a contraction. No contraction is made with **la** or **l'**.

à + le → **au**

à + la → **à la**

à + l' → **à l'**

à + les → **aux**

Camille est **au** maquillage (*in make-up*)?

Nous allons **à la** cantine.

Yasmine va **à** l'école.

Il parle **aux** reporters.

A. Où? (*Where?*) Where might people be when they do the following activities?

MODÈLE: On filme l'émission «Bonjour!»... →
On filme l'émission «Bonjour!» dans le bâtiment de Canal 7.

1. On dîne bien...
2. Rachid regarde les carottes...
3. Bruno pratique des sports...
4. Roger gare sa moto (*parks his motorbike*)...
5. Les studios du Canal 7 se trouvent...
6. Camille envoie (*sends*) une lettre...
7. Martine regarde un film...
8. Rachid travaille...
9. Un touriste dort (*sleeps*)...

a. au cinéma
b. à la poste
c. au restaurant
d. dans son (*his*) bureau
e. à l'hôtel
f. au parking
g. au supermarché
h. au centre sportif
i. dans une banlieue de Paris

B. Où se trouve... ? Fill in each blank with a preposition to give information about classroom and student life.

1. Le bureau du professeur est _____ la classe.
2. Les livres de français sont _____ les bureaux.
3. Les sacs à dos des étudiants sont normalement _____ les bureaux ou les chaises.
4. Les lumières (*lights*) sont en général _____ bureaux.
5. Il y a souvent un(e) camarade de classe _____ moi (*me*).
6. Les étudiants habitent parfois _____ leurs (*their*) parents.

C. Où habitent-ils? Indicate where these people live, using the expressions **au-dessous de**, **au-dessus de**, **à côté de**, **dans la rue Pajol**. Use at least two expressions to situate the residents.

MODÈLE: M. Nathan habite au-dessus de M. Abdul-Hassan dans la rue Pajol.

1. Rachid et Sonia Bouhazid
2. Catherine Lapointe
3. Mohammed Abdul-Hassan
4. Isabelle Coste
5. Laurent Nathan

D. Vrai ou faux? Look at the drawing of the neighborhood of Canal 7 on page 65, and indicate whether the following statements are true or false. If the statement is true, say **C'est vrai!** and repeat the sentence. If it is false, say **C'est faux!** and correct the statement.

MODÈLES: Le bâtiment de Canal 7 est près de l'hôtel. →
C'est vrai. Le bâtiment de Canal 7 est près de l'hôtel.

Le restaurant Chez Yves est loin du cinéma. →
C'est faux. Le restaurant Chez Yves est à côté du cinéma. (C'est faux. Le restaurant Chez Yves est près du cinéma.)

1. Le parking est derrière le centre sportif.
2. Le bâtiment de Canal 7 est en face du supermarché.
3. La Bibliothèque nationale est loin de ce quartier.
4. Le centre sportif est à côté de la librairie.
5. Le restaurant Chez Yves est entre le cinéma et la librairie.

E. Sur votre campus. A new student on your campus asks you where certain buildings are. Play the roles with a partner. Then switch roles.

MODÈLE: la faculté des sciences (*school of sciences*) →
É1: Excuse-moi, où se trouve la faculté des sciences?
É2: C'est le bâtiment là-bas (*over there*), devant la bibliothèque. (Il se trouve là-bas, devant la bibliothèque.)
É1: Merci.

1. le laboratoire de langues (*languages*)
2. la faculté des langues étrangères (*foreign*)
3. une résidence universitaire
4. le bureau de l'administration de l'université
5. la bibliothèque
6. le restaurant universitaire
7. la librairie universitaire

Les nationalités, les origines régionales et les langues

Camille et M. Liégeois sont de Paris. Ils sont **français**.

Rachid est de Marseille. Il est **français**, mais son papa est **algérien**.

Hélène est de Montréal. Elle est **canadienne**.

To talk about where people come from, you'll need to know the names of countries or regions of the world, as well as the adjectives used for those places. Take a look at the maps in the front and back of your textbook to find out in which countries French is spoken (**les pays** (*m.*) **francophones**).

PAYS EUROPÉENS	ADJECTIFS	LANGUES OFFICIELLES
l'Allemagne° (*f.*)	allemand(e)	l'allemand (*m.*)
l'Angleterre (*f.*)	anglais(e)	l'anglais (*m.*)
l'Espagne (*f.*)	espagnol(e)	l'espagnol (*m.*)
la France	français(e)	le français
PAYS AFRICAINS		
l'Algérie (*f.*)	algérien(ne)	l'arabe (*m.*)
le Maroc	marocain(e)	l'arabe
PAYS ET RÉGIONS NORD-AMÉRICAINS		
le Canada	canadien(ne)	l'anglais, le français
les États-Unis (*m.*)	américain(e)	l'anglais
le Mexique	mexicain(e)	l'espagnol
le Québec*	québécois(e)	le français
PAYS ASIATIQUES		
la Chine	chinois(e)	le (chinois) mandarin
le Japon	japonais(e)	le japonais
le Viêtnam	vietnamien(ne)	le vietnamien

°*Germany*

1. The names of languages are masculine and are often formed from an adjective of nationality or regional origin. The article is omitted when the language follows **parler**, but it is otherwise required.

   On parle **mandarin** et d'autres langues chinoises en Chine.
   L'anglais est la langue officielle en Angleterre et aux États-Unis.

2. The noun referring to a person from a particular country is formed from the appropriate adjective with the first letter capitalized.

   Mais quoi, tu es magnifique comme ça! **Un** vrai **Français**.
   Les Français sont formidables!
   Hélène? C'est **une Canadienne**.

Activités

A. Nationalités et langues. Give the nationalities of the following people and say what language(s) they might speak.

MODÈLE: Ana María Ordoñez / Mexique →
Ana María Ordoñez est mexicaine.
Elle parle probablement espagnol.

*__Le Québec__ refers to the province of Quebec in Canada. Quebec City is known in French as **Québec**. **J'aime le Québec** means *I like Quebec* (the province). **J'aime Québec** means *I like Quebec City.*

1. Noriko Matsushita (*f.*) / Japon
2. Mao He (*m.*) / Chine
3. Mohammed Ibn-Da'ud / Algérie
4. María Losada / Espagne
5. Nick Brown / Angleterre
6. Lise Nathan / France
7. Anne Nguyen / Viêtnam
8. Monique Tremblay / Canada (Québec)
9. Ahmed el-Diah / Maroc

B. Quel pays? Identify the country being described.

MODÈLE: C'est un pays anglophone au nord (*north*) de l'Europe. La capitale est Londres. →
C'est l'Angleterre.

C'est...

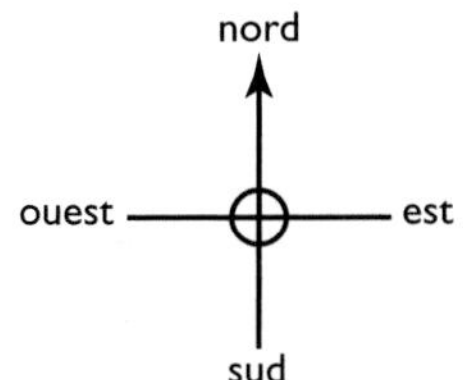

1. un grand pays près du Maroc en Afrique du Nord. La capitale est Alger.
2. un pays à l'est de la France. L'allemand est la langue officielle.
3. une ancienne (*former*) colonie française. La capitale est Ho Chi Minh Ville.
4. le pays au sud des États-Unis. L'espagnol est la langue officielle.
5. une province francophone au Canada. Un port important est Montréal.
6. le pays situé entre le Canada et le Mexique. Un président est le chef du gouvernement. (Ce sont...)

Visionnement 1

Avant de visionner

Précisez. (*Specify.*) Which sentence best describes the dialogue? Choose from among the statements that follow the dialogue.

PRODUCTRICE: Attends,[a] Camille. Je te présente Rachid Bouhazid. C'est notre[b] nouveau reporter.

RACHID: Très heureux.

CAMILLE: Enchantée.

RACHID: «Bonjour!» est une émission très sympa. Vous êtes forts,[c] Bruno et vous!

CAMILLE: Merci.

[a]*Wait* [b]*our* [c]*strong (a good team)*

a. Rachid critique l'émission.
b. Rachid admire l'émission.
c. Rachid préfère Bruno à Camille.

Pour en savoir plus...

"Stressed" pronouns are used after **c'est**, after prepositions, and to add emphasis.

je → **moi**	nous → **nous**
tu → **toi**	vous → **vous**
il → **lui**	ils → **eux**
elle → **elle**	elles → **elles**
on → **soi**	

Tu vas travailler avec **eux**.
You'll be working with them.

Vocabulaire relatif à l'épisode

C'est à toi?	*Is this yours?*
Tu viens de Marseille, c'est ça?	*You come from Marseille, right?*
Tu as faim?	*Are you hungry?*

Observez!

Martine, the producer, makes an important discovery in Episode 3: she finds the locket Camille has lost. As you watch, try to answer the following questions.

- How does Camille react when Martine asks **Qui est-ce?**
- What is missing from the locket?

Après le visionnement

A. Qu'est-ce qui se passe? (*What's happening?*) Tell what happens in Episode 3 by choosing words from the list to fill in the blanks in the summary of the story.

Vocabulaire utile: le bureau, chez, l'émission, invite, jolie, pense, une photo, présente, propose, «Qui est-ce?», trouve

Martine, la productrice, _____[1] le médaillon de Camille, et il y a _____[2] dedans.[a] Martine demande _____[3], mais Camille ne répond pas.[b] Ensuite,[c] Martine _____[4] Rachid à Camille. Il aime _____[5] «Bonjour!» et _____[6] que Camille et Bruno sont forts. Bruno _____[7] à Hélène de se marier avec lui,[d] mais c'est une plaisanterie.[e] Finalement, Bruno entre dans _____[8] et rencontre[f] Rachid. Il regarde une photo de la femme[g] de Rachid et pense qu'elle est _____[9], mais Rachid ne répond pas. Pour être sociable, Bruno _____[10] Rachid à déjeuner.[h]

[a]*in it* [b]*ne… doesn't answer* [c]*Then* [d]*de… to marry him* [e]*joke* [f]*meets* [g]*wife* [h]*have lunch*

B. Les personnalités. In this episode, several characters revealed a little more of their personalities. Read these exchanges and choose which sentence best describes each person's character.

1. Quel est le caractère de Bruno?

   BRUNO: Hélène?... On se marie, toi et moi?
   HÉLÈNE: Eh! Quelle bonne idée! D'abord, je divorce avec Tom Cruise, OK?

   a. Il aime flirter.
   b. C'est un menteur (*liar*).
   c. C'est un intellectuel.

2. Quel est le caractère de Camille?

   MARTINE: C'est à toi... ? Le médaillon est ravissant. Qui est-ce?
   CAMILLE: ... Merci, Martine. (Elle referme[a] le médaillon et part.[b])

[a]*closes* [b]*walks away*

a. Camille est heureuse.
b. Camille est réservée (*reserved*).
c. Camille est bavarde (*talkative*).

3. Quel est le caractère de Rachid?

BRUNO: Euh, excuse-moi, c'est mon[c] bureau, ici. Ton[d] bureau, il est là.
RACHID: Ah! Bon ben, pas de problème!

[c]*my* [d]*Your*

a. Rachid est ridicule.
b. Rachid n'est pas gentil.
c. Rachid est sympathique.

Structure 9

Le verbe *aller* et le futur proche

Expressing movement and intention

—On **va** où?

—Au Jardin des Plantes, pour une leçon de sciences naturelles.

Le verbe *aller*

1. The verb **aller** means *to go.* In the preceding example, Yasmine used the verb **aller** to ask where her class was going.

aller (*to go*)			
je	**vais**	nous	**allons**
tu	**vas**	vous	**allez**
il, elle, on	**va**	ils, elles	**vont**

Rachid **va** à la cantine avec ses collègues. — *Rachid goes to the cafeteria with his coworkers.*

Nicole et Hélène **vont** à la régie. — *Nicole and Hélène are going to the control room.*

Because **aller** expresses movement *to* a place, it is often used with the preposition **à**.

Est-ce que Yasmine **va à** la maison maintenant?	*Is Yasmine going home (to the house) now?*
Oui, elle **va** tout de suite **à** la maison.	*Yes, she's going home right away.*

2. You have already learned another use of **aller**—to ask and answer questions about how a person is feeling or doing.

Comment **allez-vous**, monsieur?	*How are you?*
Tu vas bien, Hélène?	*Are you well, Hélène?*
Oui, **ça va** très bien.	*Yes, everything's fine.*

Le futur proche: *Aller* + infinitif

1. To talk about what someone is going to do, you can use a conjugated form of **aller** followed by an infinitive. This is often called the "near future."

Tu **vas travailler** avec eux.	*You are going to work with them.*
Est-ce que Bruno **va identifier** le pain artisanal?	*Is Bruno going to identify the handmade bread?*

2. To make a negative statement with the near future, **ne... pas** surrounds the conjugated verb **aller**. The infinitive follows.

Je **ne vais pas porter** le béret.	*I am not going to wear the beret.*

Activités

A. Après le cours. Two students are talking about where they and others are going after class. Play the roles with a partner, following the model.

MODELE: tu / la résidence universitaire / la bibliothèque →
É1: Est-ce que tu vas à la résidence universitaire?
É2: Non, je vais à la bibliothèque.

1. Michèle / le restaurant universitaire / le cours d'histoire
2. Paul et Marc / le bureau du prof / la librairie
3. vous / le centre sportif / la bibliothèque
4. Murielle / le supermarché / le bureau de l'administration
5. le professeur / la poste / le parking
6. les autres étudiants / le laboratoire / le cinéma

B. Où est-ce qu'on va? Say where each of the following people is going, based on what is told about them.

Vocabulaire utile: bibliothèque, centre sportif, cinéma, parking, poste, restaurant, supermarché

1. Je n'aime pas dîner chez moi. Je...
2. Michel cherche un livre d'histoire. Il...
3. Vous désirez regarder un bon film. Vous...

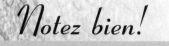

Notez bien!

Many adverbs can be used to talk about the time when things are happening or will happen. The following adverbs can be used at the beginning or end of a sentence.

aujourd'hui	*today*
bientôt	*soon*
demain	*tomorrow*
maintenant	*now*

Aujourd'hui Rachid va à Canal 7.

Hélène arrive **bientôt**.

Some other adverbs of time usually follow the conjugated verb. Notice that **jusqu'à** must be followed by a time or an event.

encore	*again; still*
jusqu'à	*until*
tard	*late*
tôt	*early*
toujours	*still; always*
tout de suite	*right away*

Bruno travaille **jusqu'à** 14 h.

Il dîne **tôt** aujourd'hui.

4. Nous cherchons notre (*our*) automobile. Nous...
5. Tu aimes jouer (*to play*) au tennis. Tu...
6. Les Robidoux vont préparer un bon dîner chez eux. Ils...

C. Et après? (*And later?*) What are the following people going to do later on? Choose phrases that seem appropriate for the characters, and use **aller** + infinitive to explain.

MODÈLE: Rachid va chercher la maman de Yasmine.

1. Rachid		travailler avec Rachid
2. Bruno et Camille		trouver son (*her*) papa après (*after*) l'école
3. Hélène	aller	lancer une série de reportages sur le Québec
4. Yasmine		regarder son médaillon
5. Camille		habiter à Paris
6. Yasmine et Rachid		chercher la maman de Yasmine

D. Et vous? Carry on a conversation with a partner, following the instructions.

Vocabulaire utile: chercher un livre, dîner, écouter la radio, étudier, parler avec des amis, regarder la télévision, travailler, visiter un musée, ?

1. Greet each other. **2.** Find out how your partner is feeling today. **3.** Tell your partner where you are going after class (**après le cours**). **4.** Explain what you will do there and what you will not do there. **5.** Say good-bye to each other.

Structure 10

Les questions avec *n'est-ce pas? non? c'est ça? je suppose? d'accord? OK?*

Asking questions with tag phrases

—Pour toi aussi, c'est un grand jour, **non**?

—Oui. Salut, ma chérie!

You have already seen two ways of asking yes/no questions.

Rising intonation:	Tu vas bien?
Est-ce que:	Est-ce que tu vas bien?

1. A third way of formulating a yes/no question is by adding a tag at the end of the statement. Common tags are highlighted in the following examples.

Dans votre famille, on est boulanger de père en fils, **n'est-ce pas?**	*In your family, you've been bakers for generations, haven't you?* (*lit. ... you are bakers from father to son, isn't that so?*)
Pour toi aussi, c'est un grand jour, **non?**	*This is a big day for you too, right?* (*no?*)
Tu viens de Marseille, **c'est ça?**	*You come from Marseille, right?* (*is that so?*)
Tu es musulman, **je suppose**.	*You're Muslim, I take it.* (*I suppose.*)
On va à la cantine, **d'accord?**	*Let's go to the cafeteria, okay?* (*agreed?*)
D'abord, je divorce avec Tom Cruise, **OK?**	*First, I'll divorce Tom Cruise, okay?*

2. **N'est-ce pas? non? c'est ça?** and **je suppose** have similar functions: They simply ask for a confirmation (yes or no) of the statement that precedes the tag. **C'est ça** can be used as an answer meaning *That's right.*

—Tu viens de Marseille, **c'est ça?**	*You come from Marseille, right?*
—**C'est ça**, Bruno.	*That's right, Bruno.*

3. The function of **d'accord?** and **OK?** is to ask for agreement to do something. **D'accord** and **OK** can also be used to answer these questions.

—On va à la cantine, **OK?**	*We'll go to the cafeteria, okay?*
—**D'accord.** Pas de problème.	*Sure. No problem.*

Activité

D'accord ou pas d'accord? Change the following sentences into questions using a tag. Your partner will respond by using appropriate expressions of agreement or disagreement. Follow the model.

MODÈLE: Nous allons à la bibliothèque. →
É1: Nous allons à la bibliothèque, OK?
É2: Oui. D'accord.

ou É1: Nous allons à la bibliothèque, je suppose.
É2: Bien sûr que non! Nous allons au restaurant!

1. Tu aimes les cours ce (*this*) semestre.
2. Tu vas travailler après le cours.
3. Tout le monde adore travailler.
4. Les étudiants adorent les week-ends.
5. Nous dînons au restaurant ce soir.
6. Le professeur est québécois.
7. Les émissions de télévision sont intéressantes.
8. Vous êtes d'origine marocaine.

Regards sur la culture

La communication non-verbale

Notice how close Martine, Rachid, and Camille stand when they are speaking. This illustrates one aspect of nonverbal communication that poses problems for many Americans and Canadians. Because we are not usually aware of our own gestures and needs for communication space, nonverbal communication can be one of the most difficult areas of adjustment when we visit another culture. Here are two examples.

Rachid fait la connaissance de (*meets*) Camille

- The handshake, often consisting of a single quick up-and-down movement, is an obligatory greeting in France for all colleagues and friends the first time they meet each day. It can be replaced with a quick kiss on the cheeks (two or three or four times depending on the region) between two women or between men and women, when the people involved know each other well.
- Cultures differ in how they set interpersonal distances. In English-speaking North America, the distance people maintain in day-to-day business conversations with strangers and acquaintances (sometimes called "social" distance) starts at around 4 feet. In France, social distance tends to be smaller, starting at around 0.6 meters (2 feet). When English-speaking North Americans encounter French social distances, they may back up in an attempt to reset the situation with American spacing. The French person will normally move closer so as to reestablish the space with which he or she is comfortable. More than one American or Canadian has backed all the way across a room before the end of a French conversation.

Considérez

Many people have commented that it is extremely easy to spot North Americans in France just by the way they walk and stand. If you were studying abroad, would you want to try to adjust to the nonverbal habits of the culture in which you were living, or would that be unnecessary? How hard would it be?

Structure 11

Le verbe venir

Expressing movement

—Tu es Rachid Bouhazid et **tu viens de*** Marseille, c'est ça?

—C'est ça, Bruno.

When Bruno first meets Rachid, he uses the verb **venir** to verify where he comes from.

venir (*to come*)			
je	**viens**	nous	**venons**
tu	**viens**	vous	**venez**
il, elle, on	**vient**	ils, elles	**viennent**

Tu viens avec moi, non? — *You're coming with me, aren't you?*

Nous venons au studio ensemble. — *We come to the studio together.*

1. The verbs **devenir** (*to become*) and **revenir** (*to come back, return*) are conjugated like **venir**.

   Camille **devient** silencieuse et elle part. — *Camille becomes silent and walks away.*

   Mais elle **revient** pour parler à Rachid. — *But she comes back to talk to Rachid.*

2. To express where a person is coming from, use **venir de**.

   Remember—The preposition **de** contracts with the masculine and plural definite articles: Rachid **vient du** bureau. Nicole et Martine **viennent de la** régie.

---

*__Note:__ The use of prepositions with geographical names is presented in Chapter 14.

3. The construction **venir de** + infinitive means *to have just done something.* This is sometimes referred to as the immediate past.

Hélène **vient d'arriver**.	*Hélène (has) just arrived.*
Martine **vient de trouver** le médaillon.	*Martine (has) just found the locket.*

Activités

A. À l'Alliance française. The following students are at the **Alliance française** in Paris. Complete the sentences to say what country or region they are from.

MODÈLE: Lisa habite à New York. Elle <u>vient</u> des États-Unis.

1. J'habite à Londres (*London*). Je _____ d'Angleterre.
2. Nous habitons à Alger. Nous _____ d'Algérie.
3. Tu habites à Madrid. Tu _____ d'Espagne.
4. Mitsuko habite à Tokyo. Elle _____ du Japon.
5. Linda et Ford habitent à Montréal. Ils _____ du Canada.
6. Vous habitez à Berlin. Vous _____ d'Allemagne.

B. À Canal 7. Complete these sentences with a form of the verbs **venir**, **revenir**, and **devenir**.

1. Le vrai pain français _____ de plus en plus (*more and more*) difficile à trouver.
2. Et les Français _____ de moins en moins (*less and less*) capables de reconnaître un bon pain.
3. «Hélène _____ du Canada. D'où est-ce que tu _____, Rachid?»
4. «Et Camille et toi, d'où est-ce que vous _____, Bruno?»
5. «Rachid, où est-ce que tu vas? Nous devons (*need to*) parler.» «Un instant, Martine, je _____ tout de suite.»
6. Canal 7 _____ une station de télévision importante.
7. Hélène _____ en France après une longue absence.
8. Après beaucoup de travail, Camille _____ la star de Canal 7.

C. Questions. Hélène is interviewing the employees of Canal 7. Working with a partner, use the elements to formulate her questions and her colleagues' answers.

1. HÉLÈNE: Bruno, tu / venir de / la région parisienne?
2. BRUNO: Oui, mes parents / habiter à / Paris.
3. HÉLÈNE: Et Rachid, vous / venir de / Toulouse?
4. RACHID: Non, je / arriver de / Marseille.
5. HÉLÈNE: Est-ce que les employés de Canal 7 / venir de / loin?
6. BRUNO: Nicole / habiter dans / le quartier, mais Camille / venir de / un autre quartier.
7. HÉLÈNE: Camille, tu / venir à / le studio le week-end?

8. CAMILLE: Oui, mais je / aller à / le centre sportif après.
9. HÉLÈNE: Nous / venir tous (*all*) de / un pays francophone?

D. Devinez. Try to guess what your classmates have just done and are going to do.

MODÈLE: É1: Tu viens de regarder la télé, c'est ça?
É2: Non, je viens de dîner. (*ou* Oui, c'est ça.)

É1: Et tu vas commencer à étudier maintenant?
É2: Oui, c'est ça. (*ou* Non, je vais aller au cinéma.)

Visionnement 2

Avant de visionner

Pour en savoir plus...

Some people, because of their personality or training, are slow to switch from **vous** to **tu**, but others switch relatively quickly. In professions such as advertising and television, **tu** is used much more freely among coworkers. You may have noticed that Camille and Bruno use **tu** most of the time but switch to **vous** on the set to portray a more formal working relationship to the viewers.

***Tu* ou *vous*?** Read the following dialogues and choose the correct explanation(s) for why the highlighted pronoun **tu** or **vous** is used in that context.

1. RACHID: «Bonjour!» est une émission très sympa. **Vous** êtes forts, Bruno et vous.
   CAMILLE: Merci.

   a. C'est normal d'employer **vous** pour parler de deux personnes.
   b. Rachid vient de faire la connaissance de (*just met*) Camille.
   c. Rachid est un bon ami de Camille et de Bruno.

2. BRUNO: **Tu** es Rachid Bouhazid et **tu** viens de Marseille, c'est ça?
   RACHID: C'est ça, Bruno.

   a. Bruno vient de faire la connaissance de Rachid.
   b. Bruno accueille (*welcomes*) Rachid avec amitié (*friendship*).
   c. Bruno est beaucoup plus âgé que (*much older than*) Rachid.

Observez!

Consider the cultural information explained in **Regards sur la culture**. Then watch Episode 3 again, and answer the following questions.

- What gesture do Rachid and Bruno use when they first greet each other?
- What differences in behavior do you notice between how people greet each other in the film and how they greet each other in your country?

Après le visionnement

Do the activity for **Visionnement 2** in the *Workbook/Laboratory Manual.*

Synthèse: Culture

La communication interculturelle

La communication non-verbale

When we think about communicating with the people of another culture, we tend to focus on language. However, some researchers claim that as much as 65% of what is communicated in human interactions is not accomplished with language. This means that entering a new culture requires you to reset your expectations in dozens of areas.

Use of space

People in North African countries such as Algeria maintain social distances that are even smaller than those of the French. North Americans who have stood in line with Algerians have often remarked that "everyone was pushing."

Conceptions of time

In Togo, friends and family make regular visits to each other unannounced. It is expected that visitors will be made welcome for as long as they care to stay.

Gestures and body language

To indicate a direction in French Polynesia, people signal with their head or eyes; pointing with a finger would be considered rude.

Rules of politeness

In France, when you are at a café, it is polite to offer to pay for everyone at the table. It would be impolite, however, to let someone else pay without protesting a bit, and the expectation is that you would pay the next time.

Social attitudes

In Morocco, "white lies" are an accepted way of saving face in many circumstances; absolute truth and frankness are not as important as social connection and respect.

Facial displays of emotion

One of the most important areas of intercultural communication is the expression of emotion in the face. Certain emotions, such as happiness, universally produce particular facial displays, a smile for example. But culture complicates things. Every culture establishes its own set of "display rules" that regulate the actual production of these facial signals. For example, there are many occasions in North American culture where one is expected to amplify the smile, suggesting more pleasure than one actually feels. Take the case of Americans and Canadians greeting guests, compared to the way the French greet them. Americans and Canadians amplify their smile when greeting others; the French do not amplify the smile and, in fact, may not smile at all in this situation.

In other words, a smile does not always mean the same thing. When Rachid enters the control room in Episode 2, Martine does not really smile. In Episode 3, when Rachid and Camille meet, there are not a lot of big smiles. In France, the smile is not used as a sign of civility. Neither cashiers nor strangers of any kind will normally smile at you in France. To the North American, the French lack of a smile, in many circumstances, feels like a snub. To a French person, what seems like the eternal smile of a North American connotes hypocrisy or naïveté.

À vous

A. Choose someone in class whom you do not know well. Position yourself about two feet away from this person (the normal French distance for strangers) and carry on a short conversation in French: Start with a handshake, greet the other person, ask how he or she is doing, ask where she or he is from, and so on. Then move a step closer together to simulate the Algerian distance and repeat the experiment. Discuss your comfort level in each of these experiences with the class.

B. With your partner, think of a situation in your own culture in which you are expected to amplify the facial expression of an emotion (happiness, sadness, disgust, anger) and a situation in which you are supposed to play down the emotional display. How might someone from another culture have problems interpreting what is going on? Put together a 30-second skit and perform it for the class.

À écrire

Do **À écrire** for Chapter 3 in the *Workbook/Laboratory Manual.*

Vocabulaire

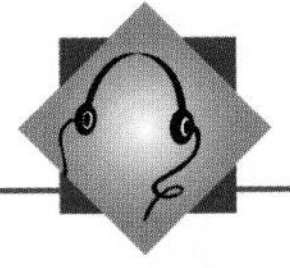

Les environs de Canal 7

une banlieue	suburb	**la poste**	post office
un bâtiment	building	**un quartier**	neighborhood
une bibliothèque	library		
un bureau (des bureaux)	office		
une librairie	bookstore		
un lieu (des lieux)	place, location		

MOTS APPARENTÉS: **un café, un centre sportif, un hôtel, un parking, un restaurant, un supermarché**

À REVOIR: **un cinéma**

Pays et régions

l'Allemagne (*f.*)	Germany	**le Maroc**	Morocco
l'Angleterre (*f.*)	England	**un pays**	country
l'Espagne (*f.*)	Spain		
les États-Unis (*m.*)	United States		

MOTS APPARENTÉS: **l'Algérie** (*f.*), **le Canada, la Chine, la France, le Japon, le Mexique, le Québec, le Viêtnam**

Verbes

aller	to go	**revenir**	to come back, return
devenir	to become	**venir**	to come

Nationalités et origines régionales

allemand(e)	German	**chinois(e)**	Chinese
anglais(e)	English	**espagnol(e)**	Spanish

français(e)	French	**québécois(e)**	from Quebec
francophone	French-speaking	**vietnamien(ne)**	Vietnamese
japonais(e)	Japanese		
marocain(e)	Moroccan		

MOTS APPARENTÉS: **algérien(ne), américain(e), canadien(ne), mexicain(e)**

Adverbes et expressions de temps

aujourd'hui	today	**maintenant**	now
bientôt	soon	**tard**	late
demain	tomorrow	**tôt**	early
encore	again; still	**toujours**	still; always
jusqu'à	until	**tout de suite**	right away

Prépositions de lieu

à côté de	beside	**entre**	between
au-dessous de	below	**loin (de)**	far (from)
au-dessus de	above, over	**près (de)**	near
chez	at the home (business) of	**sous**	under
derrière	in back of, behind	**sur**	on
devant	in front of		
en face de	facing		

À REVOIR: **à, dans, de**

Questions

c'est ça?	right?, is that so?	**non?**	right?, no?
d'accord?	agreed?, okay?	**OK?**	okay?
je suppose?	I suppose?, I take it?		
n'est-ce pas?	right?, isn't that so?, aren't you?, etc.		

À REVOIR: **est-ce que... ?**

Autres expressions utiles

dans la rue [Pajol]	on [Pajol] Street	**Où se trouve... ?**	Where is . . . located?
ici	here		

À REVOIR: **là**

Chapitre 4

Une nouvelle vie à Paris

Le Chemin du retour

Feuille de service du 22 janvier
7e jour de tournage
Horaires: 9h–19h

LIEU DE TOURNAGE: MARSEILLE—FRANCE 3—Self-service, 2e étage° *floor*

Séquence	*Effets*	*Décors*	*Résumé*	*Rôles*
14	INT.—JOUR	CANAL 7—Cantine	La productrice rejoint Rachid et Bruno. Elle avertit° Rachid que sa femme a téléphoné.	BRUNO, RACHID, PRODUCTRICE, CUISINIER

tells

OBJECTIFS

In this episode, you will

- listen as Bruno and Rachid order lunch
- learn about Rachid's background and family

In this chapter, you will

- talk about family, marriage, and age
- use large numbers
- talk about days, months, and dates
- talk about possession
- express feelings and sensations
- practice another way to ask yes/no questions
- ask questions about where, when, why, how, how much, and how many
- learn about the diversity of France
- read about the notion of family in France

Vocabulaire en contexte

La famille de Bruno Gall (le côté paternel)°

La... *Bruno Gall's family (on his father's side)*

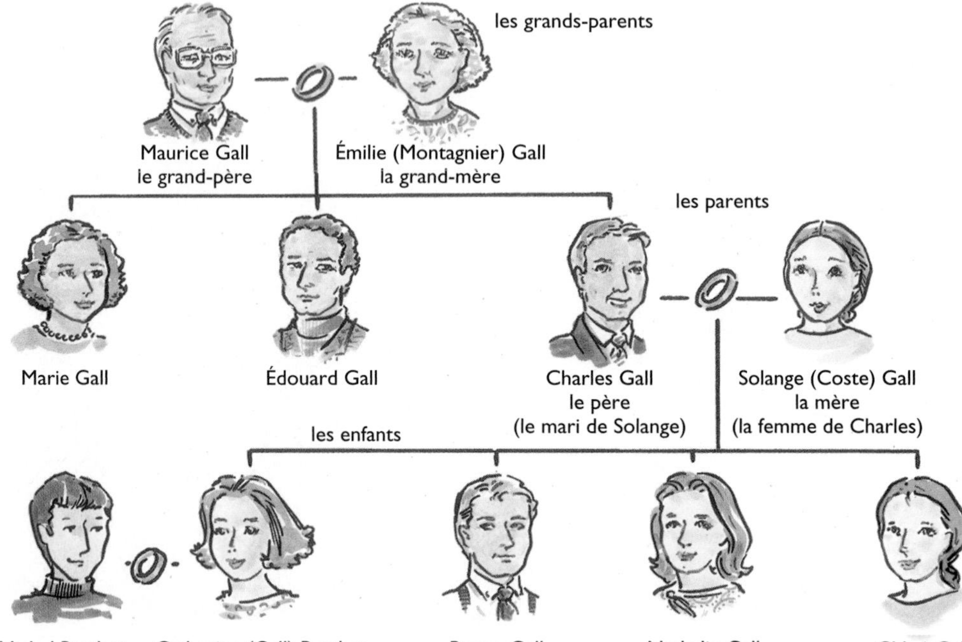

Pour en savoir plus...

Other family words you may find useful are:

l'enfant unique	*only child*
le fils unique	*only son*
la fille unique	*only daughter*
le gendre	*son-in-law*
la belle-fille	*daughter-in-law*
le demi-frère	*half-brother*
la demi-sœur	*half-sister*

Bruno est **le petit-fils** de Maurice et d'Émilie. Catherine, Nathalie et Chloé sont **les petites-filles** de Maurice et d'Émilie.
Bruno est **le neveu** de Marie et d'Édouard. Ses sœurs sont **les nièces** de Marie et d'Édouard.
Marie est **la tante** de Bruno. Édouard est **l'oncle** de Bruno.
Bruno a (*has*) **une cousine**; elle **s'appelle** Chantal. Il n'a pas de **cousin**.

Les beaux-parents

le beau-père	stepfather; father-in-law
la belle-mère	stepmother; mother-in-law
le beau-frère	stepbrother; brother-in-law
la belle-sœur	stepsister; sister-in-law

L'état civil

célibataire single **divorcé(e)** divorced
marié(e) married **veuf (veuve)** widowed
Ils vivent en union libre. They are living together (without marriage).

The adjectives **célibataire**, **marié(e)**, **divorcé(e)**, and **veuf (veuve)** may also be used as nouns.

La veuve parle souvent de son mari. *The widow often speaks of her husband.*

Activités

A. Quelle parenté? (*What's the relationship?*) Now look at the maternal side of Bruno's family tree and explain the relationships.

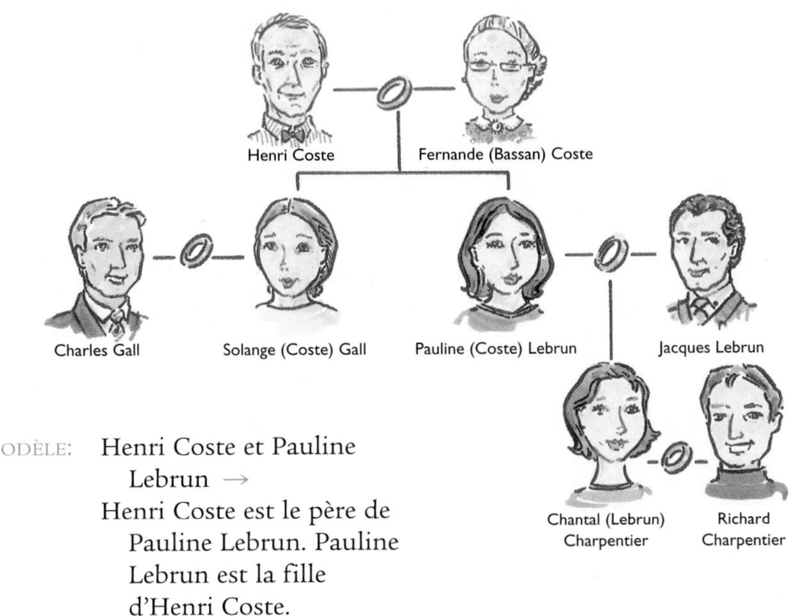

MODÈLE: Henri Coste et Pauline Lebrun →
Henri Coste est le père de Pauline Lebrun. Pauline Lebrun est la fille d'Henri Coste.

1. Solange Gall et Pauline Lebrun **2.** Chantal Charpentier et Richard Charpentier **3.** Chantal Charpentier et Fernande Coste **4.** Henri Coste et Jacques Lebrun **5.** Henri Coste et Solange Gall

Pour en savoir plus...

Weddings in churches and synagogues are still important for some French families, but the official ceremony recognized by the French government takes place in the mayor's office. Many couples, however, choose to live together without being married, and an increasing number have children. According to INSEE (l'Institut National de la Statistique et des Études Économiques), there are now around 12 million married couples in France, whereas almost 2.4 million couples prefer a less traditional relationship. The gap has been narrowing since the late 1970s.

B. Marié ou non? Give the marital status of these individuals.

1. un homme dont (*whose*) la femme est morte (*dead*): C'est un...
2. un homme dont le mariage est terminé: Il est...
3. une femme qui (*who*) n'est pas encore mariée: C'est une...
4. un couple qui vit ensemble (*lives together*) mais qui n'est pas marié: Ils vivent...

C. Une famille. Show a photo of your family or one that you invent using a picture from a magazine. Identify several family members to your partner, giving their names and relationships. Then your partner will ask you follow-up questions.

MODÈLE: É1: Voilà Charles. Charles est le frère de John et le fils de David.
É2: Et qui est cette (*this*) personne?
É1: Cette personne s'appelle Monique. C'est la sœur de David.
É2: Comment est-elle?
É1: Elle est petite et un peu (*a little*) bizarre, mais très sympathique.

Les nombres à partir de 60°

° à… *from 60 on*

60	**soixante**	80	**quatre-vingts**
61	**soixante et un**	81	**quatre-vingt-un**
62	**soixante-deux**	82	**quatre-vingt-deux**
63	**soixante-trois**	83	**quatre-vingt-trois**
70	**soixante-dix**	90	**quatre-vingt-dix**
71	**soixante et onze**	91	**quatre-vingt-onze**
72	**soixante-douze**	92	**quatre-vingt-douze**
73	**soixante-treize**	93	**quatre-vingt-treize**

100	**cent**	200	**deux cents**	300	**trois cents**
101	**cent un**	201	**deux cent un**	301	**trois cent un**
102	**cent deux**	202	**deux cent deux**	302	**trois cent deux**

999	**neuf cent quatre-vingt-dix-neuf**
1.000	**mille**
1.001	**mille un**
2.000	**deux mille**
1.000.000	**un million**
1.000.000.000	**un milliard**

1. In **quatre-vingts** and in the plural form **cents**, the **s** is dropped when immediately followed by another number.

   quatre-vingt**s** — deux cent**s**

   but quatre-vingt-un — *but* deux cent un

2. **Mille** is invariable. It does not add **s** in the plural.

   trois mille — onze mille

3. French uses a period for writing larger numbers, where a comma is used in English.

   French: **1.000.000** English: 1,000,000

   Conversely, French uses a comma for decimals, where English uses a period.

   French: **10,5 % (dix virgule cinq pour cent)** English: 10.5%

4. Larger numbers are written out and spoken as shown in the following examples. In dates, the spelling **mil** is used rather than **mille**.

1789	mil sept cent quatre-vingt-neuf
1954	mil neuf cent cinquante-quatre
2007	deux mil sept
815.100	huit cent quinze mille cent
2.113.000	deux millions cent treize mille

Pour en savoir plus…

In this episode, Bruno asks Rachid if he is **musulman** (*Muslim*). Here is a list of some world religions and the corresponding adjectives.

le bouddhisme	bouddhiste
le catholicisme	catholique
l'islam (*m.*)	musulman(e)
le judaïsme	juif (juive)
le protestantisme	protestant(e)

Here are the most prevalent religions in France today.

Environ (*About*)
46.600.000 des Français sont catholiques baptisés.
5.980.000 sont musulmans.
1.700.000 sont protestants.
600.000 sont bouddhistes.
510.800 sont juifs.

Pour en savoir plus…

The French use the metric system for measurement. Here are some equivalencies that might be useful for talking about lengths or distances in France.

un millimètre = *.04 inch*
un centimètre = *.4 inch*
un mètre = *3.3 feet*
un kilomètre = *.62 mile*

Activités

A. Dans un guide touristique. A well-known tourist guide tells how far each city is from certain other cities. Here are the listings for Marseille and for Alès, a town in the Cévennes region. Tell how many kilometers there are between these cities and the others listed.

MODÈLE: Marseille—Paris: 773 km →
Marseille est à sept cent soixante-treize kilomètres de Paris.

MARSEILLE

1. Lyon: 314 km
2. Nice: 191 km
3. Lille: 1.008 km
4. Toulon: 64 km
5. Toulouse: 405 km

ALÈS

6. Paris: 708 km
7. Albi: 227 km
8. Avignon: 72 km
9. Montpellier: 70 km
10. Nîmes: 46 km

B. Lisez. (*Read.*) According to *Quid* (2005), these are the average readership figures for certain French newspapers and magazines. Read each title and number aloud.

1. *Paris Match:* 4.536.000
2. *Le Figaro:* 367.100
3. *Femme actuelle:* 7.654.000
4. *Le Monde:* 408.000
5. *Pariscope:* 675.000
6. *Le Nouvel Observateur:* 2.571.000

Les jours de la semaine, les mois de l'année et les dates°

°Les... *Days of the week, months of the year, and dates*

Les jours (*m.*) de la semaine

mai 2007						
lundi	**mardi**	**mercredi**	**jeudi**	**vendredi**	**samedi**	**dimanche**
	1	2	3	4	5	6
7	8	9	10	11	12	13
14	15	16	17	18	19	20
21	22	23	24	25	26	27
28	29	30	31			

1. On a French calendar, the week begins with Monday (**lundi**) and ends with Saturday and Sunday, which together are referred to as **le week-end**. The word for *today* is **aujourd'hui**.
2. The days of the week begin with a lowercase letter in French.
3. To talk about an event that takes place regularly on the same day each week, use the definite article.

J'ai cours de français **le** lundi. — *I have French class on Mondays.*

Le week-end, je ne travaille pas. — *I don't work on the weekend (on weekends).*

Notez bien!

You already know the expression **tout le monde** (*everyone, everybody*). The meaning of the adjective **tout** varies depending on the context: *all, every, each, the whole, the entire.*

Here are the forms of **tout**.

tout (*m. s.*)	tous (*m. pl.*)
toute (*f. s.*)	toutes (*f. pl.*)

Tout is often used with expressions about days, weeks, months, and seasons.

tout le printemps *all spring*

toute une semaine *a whole week, an entire week*

tous les lundis *every Monday, each Monday*

Notice that **tout** is usually followed by an article (**le**, **un**, etc.).* Both **tout** and the word that follows it agree in gender and number with the noun they modify.

Tout can also be used in expressions that are not related to time.

Est-ce que Bruno est sur le plateau pendant **toute** l'émission?

J'aime passer **toutes les** vacances à la campagne.

Tous les personnages dans le film ont une histoire intéressante à raconter.

*__Tout__ can also be followed by other words that stand in the place of an article. You will learn about such words later in this chapter and subsequent chapters.

Les mois (*m.*) de l'année

Months, like days of the week, begin with a lowercase letter in French.

janvier	**avril**	**juillet**	**octobre**
février	**mai**	**août**	**novembre**
mars	**juin**	**septembre**	**décembre**

You may have noticed there are two words for *year* in French: **l'an** (*m.*) and **l'année** (*f.*). **An** emphasizes discrete units of time (**deux ans**), whereas **année** emphasizes the duration of time. (**Il passe** [*is spending*] **l'année en France**.) For now, just use examples in the textbook as your guide.

Les dates (*f.*)

Dates in French are expressed with the number first, then the month. Use **le premier** (*the first*) for the first day of a month. Other dates are expressed with the cardinal number.

C'est **le premier janvier**! — *It's the first of January!*
Mon anniversaire, c'est **le deux avril**. — *My birthday is on April second.*

Notez bien!

To say that something happens in a particular month, use **en**.

Je commence mes études **en septembre**. *I begin my studies in September.*

Langage fonctionnel

Pour parler du jour et de la date

Pour parler du jour

Quel jour sommes-nous aujourd'hui?	*What day is it today?*
Aujourd'hui, c'est (lundi).	*Today is (Monday).*
Nous sommes (lundi).	*Today is (Monday).*

Pour parler de la date

Quelle est la date (aujourd'hui, de ton anniversaire, etc.)?	*What is the date (today, of your birthday, etc.)?*
Aujourd'hui, c'est le (deux février).	*Today is (February 2nd).*
La date (de mon anniversaire), c'est le (dix-neuf octobre).	*The date (of my birthday) is (October 19th).*
Nous sommes le (quinze juin) aujourd'hui.	*Today is (June 15th).*

To talk about when a person was born, say **Il est né (Elle est née)** and add the date. To talk about when a person died, say **Il est mort (Elle est morte)** and add the date.

Le grand-père **est mort** en 1999.	*The grandfather died in 1999.*
Sa femme **est morte** le 5 juin 2000.	*His wife died on June 5, 2000.*
Brigitte **est née** le 7 juillet 2000.	*Brigitte was born on July 7, 2000.*

Activités

A. Identifiez. Identify the dates.

MODÈLE: your birthday →
C'est le 2 avril 1985.

1. your birthday
2. tomorrow
3. the date of your next exam
4. the beginning and ending dates of your next school vacation
5. an important date in your life

B. Quelle date? On what date and day of the week do the following events fall this year? Use a calendar for this school year, and work with a partner. Follow the model.

MODÈLE: É1: Quelle est la date de la fête nationale des États-Unis?
É2: C'est le 4 juillet. Ça tombe (*It falls on*) un mardi.

Quelle est la date

1. de votre anniversaire (*birthday*)?
2. de la fin (*end*) du semestre ou du trimestre?
3. de l'anniversaire d'un ami / d'une amie?
4. de l'anniversaire de Martin Luther King, Jr.?
5. du nouvel an (*New Year*)?
6. aujourd'hui?

C. Détails biographiques. Here are the birth and death dates for some famous French figures. Read the dates. Follow the model.

MODÈLE: Claude Debussy: 22.8.1862–25.3.1918 →
Claude Debussy est né le vingt-deux août mil huit cent soixante-deux. Il est mort le vingt-cinq mars mil neuf cent dix-huit.

1. Marie Curie: 7.11.1867–4.7.1934
2. Louis Pasteur: 27.12.1822–28.9.1895
3. Voltaire: 21.11.1694–30.5.1778
4. Charles de Gaulle: 22.11.1890–9.11.1970
5. René Descartes: 31.3.1596–11.2.1650

D. Obligations et activités. (***Obligations and activities.***) Ask your partner questions to find out the following information.

1. what day of the week it is today
2. whether he/she goes to any other classes today
3. if he/she goes to French class on Tuesdays
4. if he/she is usually busy (**occupé[e]**) on Saturdays
5. whether he/she studies on Friday nights

Visionnement 1

Avant de visionner

Qu'est-ce que cela veut dire? (*What does it mean?*) In Episode 4, Rachid has the following conversation with Martine. Read the dialogue and then choose the meaning of each of the sentences containing the word **appeler**, which means *to call*.

MARTINE: Ta femme vient d'appeler.
RACHID: Ma femme?
MARTINE: Oui... Il y a un problème?
RACHID: Sonia n'aime pas Paris. ...
MARTINE: (*donne son téléphone portable à Rachid*) Appelle ta femme.

1. Ta femme vient d'appeler.

a. Your wife is going to call.
b. Your wife just called.
c. Your wife is coming to the studio.

2. Appelle ta femme.

a. Are you going to call your wife?
b. Your wife is calling.
c. Call your wife.

Observez!

Now watch Episode 4. As you watch, try to fill in more details about Rachid.

- Where do Rachid's parents come from?
- What is Rachid's father's religion? What might Rachid's mother's religion be?

Vocabulaire relatif à l'épisode

le jarret de porc aux lentilles	*ham hocks with lentils*
l'alcool	*alcohol*
le cochon	*pig; pork*
le jambon	*ham*
des nouvelles	*news*
tu l'attends	*you'll wait for her*

Après le visionnement

A. Un résumé. Fill in the blanks to finish the summary of events in Episode 4.

Vocabulaire utile: arrive, la cafétéria, l'école, la femme, un hamburger, le mari, n'aime pas, séparés

Rachid et Bruno sont à ______1. Le chef de cuisine recommande le jarret de porc, mais Rachid commande[a] ______2. Martine ______3 et annonce que ______4 de Rachid vient d'appeler. Rachid explique que[b] Sonia ______5 Paris. Rachid et

[a]*orders* [b]explique... *explains that*

Sonia sont ______[6]. À la fin de la journée,[c] Rachid va chercher Yasmine à

______[7]. Camille va avec lui.

[c]À... *At the end of the day*

B. Réfléchissez. (*Think.*) What type of relationship exists between Martine and Rachid? Is it professional (**un rapport professionnel**) or personal (**un rapport personnel**)? Explain your answer in French, using examples from the episode. Combine appropriate sentence fragments to form your examples.

MODÈLE: Martine et Rachid ont un rapport...
Par exemple, Martine...

	donne un conseil (*gives advice*) à	
	est la productrice de l'émission	
	montre (*shows*) son intérêt pour	«Bonjour!»
Martine	parle de sa (*his*) famille avec	Camille
Rachid	parle de soucis (*worries*) personnels à	Martine
	pose (*asks*) des questions à	Rachid
	présente le nouveau reporter, Rachid, à	
	travaille pour	

Structure 12

Les adjectifs possessifs; la possession avec de

Expressing possession

—Tu es musulman, je suppose? Pas d'alcool, pas de cochon...

—**Mon** père est algérien et musulman. Et **ma** mère est bretonne et elle adore le jambon! Comme ça, il y a les deux côtés.

When Rachid describes his family, he uses possessive adjectives▲ to designate his father and his mother.

Pour en savoir plus...

France is divided into a number of provinces that represent administrative divisions and that each have their own distinct history and traditions. Some provinces you may have heard of are **l'Alsace** (*f.*), **la Bretagne**, **la Normandie**, and **la Provence**. The corresponding adjectives are **alsacien(ne)**, **breton(ne)**, **normand(e)**, and **provençal(e)**.

Les adjectifs possessifs

mon père		**ma** mère		**mes** parents		*my*
ton père		**ta** mère		**tes** parents		*your*
son père		**sa** mère		**ses** parents		*his/her/its/one's*
notre père		**notre** mère		**nos** parents		*our*
votre père		**votre** mère		**vos** parents		*your*
leur père		**leur** mère		**leurs** parents		*their*

1. The form of the possessive adjective (**mon** or **ma**, for example) depends on the gender and number of the noun it modifies. When Rachid says *my father*, he uses **mon** (because he is referring to **le père**, a masculine noun); when he says *my mother*, he uses **ma** (because **la mère** is a feminine noun).

Appelle **ta** femme.	*Call your wife.*
Je vais chercher **ma** fille à l'école Bullier.	*I'm going to pick up my daughter at the Bullier School.*
Ton bureau, il est là.	*Your desk is over there.*

2. Before a feminine noun beginning with a vowel sound, the forms **mon**, **ton**, **son** are used.

C'est **mon** amie Yasmine.	*This is my friend Yasmine.*
Est-ce que c'est **ton** école?	*Is that your school?*
Jeanne raconte **son** histoire et Fergus raconte **son** histoire.	*Jeanne tells her story and Fergus tells his story.*

La possession avec *de*

Another way of expressing possession is by joining two nouns with **de**.

le bureau **de** Bruno	*Bruno's desk* (literally, *the desk of Bruno*)
le médaillon **de** Camille	*Camille's locket*
la régie **du** studio	*the studio's control room*

Activités

A. Précisions sur l'Épisode 4. Tell about Rachid's day at Canal 7 using possessive adjectives to complete the sentences.

Bruno regarde la photo sur ______[1] bureau. C'est la photo de la femme de Rachid et de ______[2] enfant. ______[3] famille est petite. À la cafétéria, Rachid dit[a] à Bruno: « ______[4] père est algérien et musulman. Et ______[5] mère est bretonne... » À table, Martine dit à Rachid: « ______[6] femme vient d'appeler.» Rachid est surpris. Il explique que Sonia n'aime pas Paris. ______[7] ville préférée est Marseille parce que[b] ______[8] amis et ______[9] famille habitent à Marseille. Après, Camille invite Rachid à rentrer[c] à Paris dans ______[10] auto (*f.*).

[a]*says* [b]parce... *because* [c]*return*

B. Possessions. Answer the following questions according to the model.

MODÈLE: Est-ce que tes cousines aiment tes livres? Non, elles... →
Non, elles aiment leurs livres.

1. Est-ce que vous regardez la télévision de vos cousins?
   Non, nous...
2. Est-ce que tu écoutes les CD de tes parents?
   Non, j'...
3. Est-ce que j'emploie l'ordinateur de mon oncle?
   Non, tu...
4. Est-ce que nous aimons le livre de notre grand-mère?
   Non, vous...
5. Est-ce que vous cherchez les calculatrices du professeur?
   Non, nous...
6. Est-ce que les étudiants aiment le professeur d'une autre classe?
   Non, ils...

C. Satisfait ou mécontent? Find out whether your partner is generally satisfied or unhappy with his/her current living and working situation by asking him/her the following questions. Ask if he/she is . . .

1. happy with (**content/contente de**) his/her job
2. satisfied with (**satisfait/satisfaite de**) his/her house or apartment or dorm room
3. proud of (**fier/fière de**) his/her university
4. satisfied with his/her friends
5. happy with his/her car
6. proud of his/her achievements (**accomplissements**)

Now, make some suggestions as to how your partner might improve his/her situation.

MODÈLE: Tu n'es pas content de ton emploi? Alors, il faut (*it is necessary*) trouver un autre emploi!

Structure 13

Le verbe *avoir*; *il y a* et *il n'y a pas de*; expressions avec *avoir*

Expressing possession and physical conditions

—Sonia n'aime pas Paris. Elle **a** froid. Elle n'**a** pas sa famille…

In this episode, Rachid explains why his wife, Sonia, doesn't like Paris. The highlighted words in what he says are a form of the verb **avoir**, which means *to have*. It is also used in idiomatic expressions, for example, **avoir froid** (*to be cold*).

Le verbe *avoir*

avoir (*to have*)			
j'	**ai**	nous	**avons**
tu	**as**	vous	**avez**
il, elle, on	**a**	ils, elles	**ont**

1. The most common use of **avoir** means *to have*.

   Vous **avez** un ordinateur? — *Do you have a computer?*

2. After a negative form of **avoir**, the indefinite articles **un**, **une**, **des** all become **de** (**d'** before a vowel sound).

   Sonia **n'a pas de** famille à Paris. — *Sonia doesn't have any family in Paris.*

   Désolé! Nous **n'avons pas d'**ordinateur. — *Sorry! We don't have a computer.*

Pour en savoir plus...

In rapid, spoken French, **il y a** becomes **i' y a**; **il n'y a pas** may be heard as **i' y a pas** or even **y a pas**.

Il y a et *il n'y a pas de*

1. You already know that the expression **il y a** means *there is, there are*.

   Il y a des studios et une cantine à Canal 7. — *There are studios and a cafeteria at Channel 7.*

   Est-ce qu'**il y a** des salles de répétition aussi? — *Are there also rehearsal rooms?*

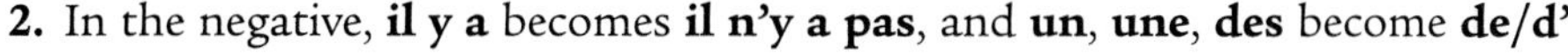

2. In the negative, **il y a** becomes **il n'y a pas**, and **un**, **une**, **des** become **de/d'**.

Non, **il n'y a pas de** salles de répétition à Canal 7.	*No, there are no rehearsal rooms at Channel 7.*
Il **n'y a pas de** boutique non plus.	*There is no small store either.*
Il **n'y a pas d'**ordinateur ici?	*There's no computer here?*

Expressions avec *avoir*

1. Some common idiomatic expressions with **avoir** are the following.

avoir chaud	*to be hot*	On **a** souvent **chaud** en juillet.
avoir froid	*to be cold*	Hélène **a froid** à Montréal en janvier.
avoir faim	*to be hungry*	Camille **a faim**, alors (*so*) elle va dans un restaurant.
avoir soif	*to be thirsty*	Rachid **a soif**. Il désire de l'eau (*water*).
avoir honte (de)	*to be ashamed (of)*	Est-ce que Camille **a honte** de sa famille?
avoir peur (de)	*to be afraid (of)*	Yasmine **a peur** d'aller à l'école.
avoir besoin de	*to need*	Rachid **a besoin** d'un téléphone pour appeler sa femme.
avoir envie de	*to feel like, want*	Yasmine **a envie de** rentrer à la maison.
avoir l'air	*to look, seem*	La maîtresse **a l'air** sympa.
avoir... ans	*to be . . . years old*	Yasmine **a six ans**.

2. **Avoir besoin de** and **avoir envie de** can be followed by either an infinitive or a noun. **Avoir honte** and **avoir peur** can be used either alone or with **de** + infinitive or **de** + noun.

Bruno **n'a pas envie de travailler**.	*Bruno doesn't feel like working.*
Il **a besoin de vacances**.	*He needs a vacation.*
Il va avec sa cousine parce qu'**elle a peur de voyager** seule.	*He's going with his cousin because she's afraid of traveling alone.*

3. To ask for someone's age in French, use the question **Quel âge avez-vous?** (**a-t-il? ont-elles?**, etc.).

Quel âge a Camille?	*How old is Camille?*
Elle **a vingt-sept ans**.	*She's twenty-seven years old.*

Activités

A. On a... et on n'a pas... ! Tell what the following people have and don't have using the correct forms of **avoir**.

MODÈLE: Yasmine / sac à dos / ordinateur →
Yasmine a un sac à dos. Elle n'a pas d'ordinateur.

1. Camille et Bruno / table / chaises
2. Bruno / béret / livres

Notez bien!

To describe someone's eye and hair color, you can use **avoir** + definite article + noun + color.

Elle a **les** yeux marron (noisette, bleus). *She has brown (hazel, blue) eyes. (Her eyes are . . .)*

J'ai **les** cheveux blonds (châtain, noirs, roux, blancs). *I have blond (brown, black, red, white) hair. (My hair is . . .)*

Notice that even though English sometimes uses a possessive adjective (*My hair is . . .*), this is not true of French, which always uses the definite article.

Also notice that the adjectives **marron**, **noisette**, and **châtain** are invariable. That is, they do not change form for feminine or plural nouns.

Pour en savoir plus...

To talk about a person's age in comparison to his or her brothers and sisters, you can use the following nouns.

l'aîné(e)	*eldest*
le cadet / la cadette	*youngest*
le jumeau / la jumelle	*twin*

Catherine est **l'aînée** et Chloé est **la cadette**. Bruno et Natalie sont **jumeaux**. *Catherine is the eldest and Chloé is the youngest. Bruno and Natalie are twins.*

3. Camille / microphone / médaillon
4. Rachid / ordinateur / crayon

B. Des photos. Two students are looking at a photo album. With a partner, create their dialogue by making complete sentences with the elements given. Follow the model.

MODÈLE: —Sur cette photo, il y / avoir / nos cousins. Ils / avoir / seize ans et douze ans.
—Est-ce que vous / avoir / des cousines aussi? →
É1: Sur cette photo, il y a nos cousins. Ils ont seize ans et douze ans.
É2: Est-ce que vous avez des cousines aussi?

1. —Sur cette photo, je / avoir / peur.
   —Pourquoi? Est-ce qu'il y / avoir / un serpent?
2. —Ma mère / avoir / deux sœurs.
   —Est-ce que ses sœurs / avoir / des enfants aussi?
3. —Voici mon grand-père. Il / avoir / 86 ans.
   —Est-ce que tu / avoir / encore (*still*) ta grand-mère?
4. —Sur cette photo, nous / avoir / chaud.
   —Je suppose que vous / avoir / envie de nager (*to swim*).

C. La vie des étudiants. (*Students' lives.*) Use one of the **avoir** expressions to talk about the following situations. There is often more than one possible answer.

MODÈLE: Melissa a une mauvaise note (*grade*) en géographie. →
Elle a honte. (Elle a besoin d'étudier.)

1. Paul cherche un coca.
2. Cinquante étudiants sont dans une petite salle de classe en août.
3. Nous allons à la bibliothèque.
4. Carole étudie le français.
5. Anne et Isabelle ne sont pas de bonnes étudiantes.
6. Vous étudiez au Canada en janvier.
7. Les étudiants vont au restaurant universitaire.
8. Un homme demande l'âge d'un enfant. Il dit...

Pour en savoir plus...

A number of adjectives that end in **-eux/-euse** are cognates of English adjectives that end in *-ous*.

généreux/euse	*generous*
nerveux/euse	*nervous*
sérieux/euse	*serious*

D. Vos familles. Work with a partner to share information about yourself and two other members of your family. Describe each person, but also use as many **avoir** expressions as you can to talk about their age, appearance, needs, wants, what they have and don't have, and so on. Take notes about your partner's family.

MODÈLE: Mon frère, Mike, a vingt-trois ans. Il est sympa, mais il n'est pas généreux. Il a honte de travailler dans un petit restaurant, mais c'est un bon job pour lui, parce qu'il a toujours faim. Il a envie d'aller à l'université, mais il a peur des professeurs et il n'a pas d'argent (*money*)!

When you have finished taking notes on your partner's family, describe them to another pair of students.

Regards sur la culture

La diversité de la France

Foreigners often have a view of France and French culture that doesn't actually match the truth; for them, Paris tends to represent the whole of France. In fact, the great diversity of the country makes it rather difficult to generalize about any aspect of culture.

- Geographically, France is one of the most diverse countries in Europe. It has warm Mediterranean coasts, the highest mountains on the continent, a range of extinct volcanoes, vast plains, deep canyons, and even landscapes that look like Arizona. Paris has a damp climate that is influenced by the Atlantic Ocean, whereas Marseille, located on the Mediterranean, in some ways is more like southern California than it is like Paris.

Cirque de Gavarnie, Pyrénées

Pointe du Raz, Bretagne

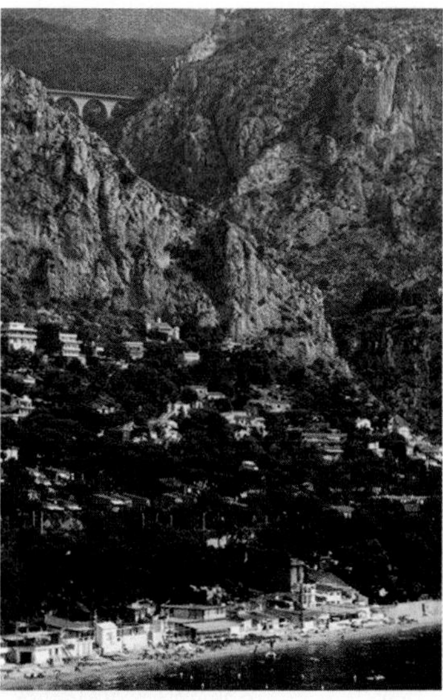

Èze-sur-Mer, Côte d'Azur

- This geographical diversity helps to explain the cultural diversity of France. Agriculture, architecture, and local traditions vary along with the landscapes. It is often clear when one has traveled from one province to the next, because the structure of the farm buildings, the layout of the villages, and the shapes of the fields have changed.

La Beauce

Le Périgord

L'Alsace

- The cuisine of the different regions of France varies, too. In the Southwest of France, food is traditionally cooked with goose fat, whereas in Normandy, butter is the essential cooking ingredient, and in Provence, it is olive oil.
- Recent immigration to France has added another level of diversity. The largest groups to arrive in France over the past fifty years have been the Spanish, the Portuguese, and, most recently, people from the Maghreb, which are the former French colonies of Morocco, Algeria, and Tunisia. Although these North Africans are Muslims, many of them have begun to assimilate into French society just as earlier groups did.

Considérez

Try to explain why the two farms pictured in this section would probably not be located in the regions that are represented in the photographs of the Pyrenees, Brittany, and the Riviera. Think about building materials, the layout of the farms, and the kind of agriculture that is possible in these places.

Structure 14

Questions avec inversion et avec où, *quand, pourquoi, comment, combien de*

Asking for specific information

—Les Français aujourd'hui **sont-ils** capables de reconnaître un bon pain?

—**Pourquoi** maman n'est pas là?

—C'est, euh, maman est fatiguée à cause du déménagement. Alors, elle se repose.

—Mais **où est-elle? Où est maman?**

Questions avec inversion

In a French declarative sentence, as in English, the subject is placed before the verb. The verb may or may not be followed by a complement.

SUJET	VERBE	COMPLÉMENT
Elle	vient.	
Tu	aimes	ta fille.

This word order is maintained in the three types of yes/no questions you have studied.

		SUJET	VERBE	COMPLÉMENT	
Rising intonation		Elle	vient?		
		Tu	aimes	ta fille?	
Est-ce que	Est-ce qu'	elle	vient?		
	Est-ce que	tu	aimes	ta fille?	
Tag		Elle	vient,		n'est-ce pas?
		Tu	aimes	ta fille,	je suppose?

1. Another way of asking yes/no questions is to place the verb before the subject, joined by a hyphen. This change in word order is known as *inversion*.

VERBE	SUJET	COMPLÉMENT
Vient-	elle?	
Aimes-	tu	ta fille?
Parlez-	vous	de Sonia?

Notez bien!

C'est... when inverted becomes **Est-ce...** ?

C'est Sonia. *That's Sonia.*
Est-ce Sonia? *Is that Sonia?*

2. In the **il/elle/on** form, when the verb ends in a vowel, **-t-** is inserted between the verb and the subject. This also applies to the expression **il y a.**

   Parle-t-il français? *Does he speak French?*
   Va-t-elle au cinéma? *Is she going to the movies?*
   Y a-t-il un film français ce soir? *Is there a French film tonight?*

3. Inversion is not made with a proper noun.▲ Instead, it is made with the pronoun that corresponds to the name. Thus, the subject is mentioned twice, once as a noun before the verb, and then as a pronoun after the verb.

   Camille **regarde-t-elle** les spectateurs? *Is Camille watching the spectators?*
   Bruno et Rachid **ont-ils** le même bureau? *Do Bruno and Rachid have the same office?*

4. For yes/no questions with verb + infinitive constructions, inversion is performed on the first verb and the infinitive follows.

Aimez-vous habiter à Marseille?	*Do you like living in Marseille?*
Déteste-t-il porter un béret?	*Does he hate wearing a beret?*
Va-t-il identifier le pain artisanal?	*Will he identify the handmade bread?*
Vient-elle d'arriver?	*Did she just arrive?*

Questions avec *où, quand, pourquoi, comment, combien de*

Up until now, you have studied yes/no questions. Another type of question asks for information.

où	*where*
quand	*when*
pourquoi	*why*
comment	*how*
combien de	*how much; how many*

Information questions are normally formed with either **est-ce que** or inversion. Study the word order in these model sentences.

1. Information questions with **est-ce que**

MOT(S) INTERROGATIF(S)		SUJET	VERBE	COMPLÉMENT
Où	est-ce que	tu	vas?	
Quand	est-ce que	tu	invites	ton ami à dîner?
Pourquoi	est-ce qu'	elle	vient?	
Comment	est-ce que	tu	viens?	
Combien d'étudiants	est-ce qu'	il	y a	dans la classe?

2. Information questions with inversion

MOT(S) INTERROGATIF(S)	VERBE	SUJET	COMPLÉMENT
Où	vas-	tu?	
Quand	invites-	tu	ton ami à dîner?
Pourquoi	vient-	elle?	
Comment	viens-	tu?	
Combien d'étudiants	y a-t-	il	dans la classe?

Pour en savoir plus...

Information questions with rising intonation are characteristic of informal spoken French. It is recommended that you not use this form, but you have heard the following examples in the film.

On va où? *Where are we going?*

Elle est où? *Where is she?*

Note that with information questions (except with **pourquoi**), inversion may be made with a noun subject.

Où est la mère de Yasmine?	*Where's Yasmine's mother?*
Comment va Bruno?	*How is Bruno doing?*

Activités

A. À la cantine. (*In the cafeteria.*) Using inversion, transform the following statements about the cafeteria scene in Episode 4 into yes/no questions.

MODÈLE: Bruno parle au chef de cuisine. →
Bruno parle-t-il au chef de cuisine?

1. Rachid et Bruno sont devant le chef de cuisine. **2.** Rachid a soif. **3.** Martine vient d'arriver. **4.** Martine a un petit pain. **5.** Sonia regarde son téléphone. **6.** Camille et Rachid vont chercher Yasmine à l'école.

B. La bonne question. (*The right question.*) Use **où**, **quand**, **pourquoi**, **comment**, or **combien de** to form a question that would prompt the italicized part of each given answer. Be careful about changing pronouns where necessary.

MODÈLE: Notre professeur est *au restaurant* maintenant. →
Où est votre professeur maintenant?

1. Les cours commencent *en septembre*. **2.** Je viens à l'université *en autobus*. **3.** Il y a *vingt étudiants* dans notre classe. **4.** Nous aimons parler en classe *parce que le sujet est intéressant*. **5.** J'aime ce (*this*) cours *parce que les étudiants sont sympathiques*. **6.** Nous avons cinq grandes tables *dans la salle de classe*. **7.** *Le lundi*, nous allons au cinéma. **8.** Les étudiants travaillent *à la bibliothèque*.

Notez bien!

The answer to a question asking **pourquoi** often includes the expression **parce que** (*because*).

—Pourquoi est-ce que tu viens en autobus?	*Why do you come by bus?*
—**Parce que** je n'ai pas de voiture.	*Because I don't have a car.*

C. Questions. Ask your partner questions based on the illustrations.

1. 

2. 

3.

4. 

D. Un étudiant / Une étudiante typique? Use question words and inversion to interview your partner.

1. Find out why he/she is studying French.
2. Find out how many courses he/she has.
3. Find out when (which days) he/she goes to class.
4. Find out how he/she likes to spend weekends (**passer le week-end**).
5. Find out where he/she works and when.
6. Find out whether he/she likes horror movies (**les films d'horreur**).
7. Find out if he/she is afraid of spiders (**les araignées**).
8. What else can you find out?

When you have finished interviewing, present your partner to the class. Tally the information. What are the most typical responses? Are you typical?

Visionnement 2

Avant de visionner

A. J'ai faim! Bruno and Rachid decide to have lunch in the cafeteria. Here is their conversation with the chef. Stage directions are included to portray the chef's reactions. Read the dialogue and then answer the question.

CUISINIER: Alors, pour aujourd'hui, en plat principal,[a] du jarret de porc aux lentilles! Vachement[b] bon, hein!

BRUNO: Ah bien, bien. Ça marche![c]

RACHID: Un hamburger, c'est possible?

CUISINIER (*se rembrunit*[d]): Oh. D'accord! (*Il grommelle en s'éloignant.*[e])

[a]en... *as a main course* [b]*Very* [c]Ça... *That works (for me)* [d]se... *frowning* [e]Il... *He grumbles as he walks off.*

Pourquoi le cuisinier se rembrunit-il et grommelle-t-il? Il y a deux ou trois raisons.

a. Préparer un hamburger, c'est beaucoup (*a lot*) de travail.
b. Il pense que Rachid n'apprécie pas ses efforts culinaires.
c. Il est toujours de mauvaise humeur (*in a bad mood*).
d. Il pense que Rachid préfère un plat américain à un plat français.
e. Certains Français sont parfois impatients avec les gens (*people*) d'origine étrangère.

B. La culture musulmane? After ordering, Rachid and Bruno discuss their food preferences. Read their exchange and reflect on the cultural information it contains. Then answer the questions.

RACHID: Bonjour. Un verre d'eau,[a] s'il vous plaît. Merci.

BRUNO: Tu es musulman, je suppose? Pas d'alcool, pas de cochon...

RACHID: Mon père est algérien et musulman. Et ma mère est bretonne[b] et elle adore le jambon... ![c]

[a]Un... *A glass of water* [b]*Breton, from Brittany (a region in the northwestern part of France)* [c]*ham*

1. Pourquoi Bruno pense-t-il que Rachid est musulman?
2. Quelles viandes et boissons (*Which meats and drinks*) ne sont probablement pas permises (*permitted*) pour une personne musulmane?

Observez!

Consider the cultural information explained in **Regards sur la culture**. Then watch Episode 4 again, and answer the following questions.

- Why does Sonia not like Paris? What difference(s) between Marseille and Paris are implied by this explanation?

- Listen for the name and location of Yasmine's school. Locate the neighborhood on a map of Paris or on the map in **Visionnement 2** in Chapter 1. Which monuments and institutions are found near the school?

Après le visionnement

Do the activity for **Visionnement 2** in the *Workbook/Laboratory Manual.*

Synthèse: Lecture

Mise en contexte

The notion of family in France has for centuries been the traditional dual-parent household and a closely knit extended family. In this tradition, husbands support the family, wives stay at home and raise the children, the whole family sits down to meals together, the children cooperate rather than compete, and so on. Marriage, children, and family are almost synonymous in this tradition, and it is, of course, a generalization.

Stratégie pour mieux lire
Recognizing cognates

Scientific texts tend to use a vocabulary that is high in cognate forms. This text draws on sociological terminology that may be familiar to you because of its similarity to English. Skim the passage, paying particular attention to familiar words and cognates. Then predict which of the following sentences will best summarize the gist of the entire text.

1. L'institution de la famille reste (*remains*) très importante pour la majorité des Français.
2. La diversité de la famille française résulte en une déstabilisation de la société.
3. La famille française assume (*takes on*) une multiplicité de configurations.

Now read the whole text through and see if your prediction is correct.

La famille française du XXIe siècle°

La... The French family in the 21st century

Introduction

La famille française se caractérise par la tradition et la nouveauté.[1] Elle reste la cellule[2] de la vie[3] sociale et on continue à célébrer la famille (fête des mères, fête des pères). Mais on aurait tort[4] de généraliser.

Réflexion de la société

La famille française reflète la diversité des conditions socio-économiques de la société entière. Sous l'influence des conditions de vie, elle se transforme. Il y a des crises internes et les conflits entre générations. La femme a une vie plus indépendante qu'autrefois;[5] les enfants s'émancipent de plus en plus tôt.[6]

Un déjeuner en plein air en famille

La transformation récente

Depuis[7] trente ans, le nombre des mariages diminue. Parallèlement, le nombre des divorces augmente. Autre phénomène récent: le développement de l'union libre ou cohabitation. Ce sont près de 17% des couples qui cohabitent. Conséquence de ce phénomène: 30% des naissances sont des naissances hors[8] mariage. Il faut ajouter[9] aussi la multiplication des familles monoparentales. Ces développements révèlent la coexistence de conceptions très différentes de la vie familiale.

Adapté du *Nouveau Guide France*

[1]*change* [2]*nucleus* [3]*life* [4]*on... one would be mistaken* [5]*than before* [6]*de... earlier and earlier* [7]*For* [8]*outside of* [9]*Il... One must add*

Après la lecture

A. Confirmation. Now that you have read the selection, go back to the prereading strategy activity and see if you would still choose the same paraphrase to summarize the gist of the article. How much did it help you to check for cognates before reading the entire passage? What new cognates did you notice as you read the whole article?

B. Tradition ou nouveauté? Tell whether each sentence describes the traditional family (**C'est la famille traditionnelle**), the "new" family (**C'est la nouvelle famille**), or both (**Ce sont les deux**).

1. La femme reste à la maison. **2.** Les enfants s'émancipent plus tôt. **3.** L'union libre est fréquente. **4.** Les fêtes familiales sont célébrées. **5.** La famille monoparentale est ordinaire. **6.** La famille est la cellule de la vie sociale.

C. Expliquez. Name three factors that explain the evolution of the French family.

D. Jugements. What is the author's attitude toward the evolution of the French family? Does he/she approve of the "new" family, disapprove, or remain neutral? Explain.

À écrire

Do **À écrire** for Chapter 4 in the *Workbook/Laboratory Manual.*

Vocabulaire

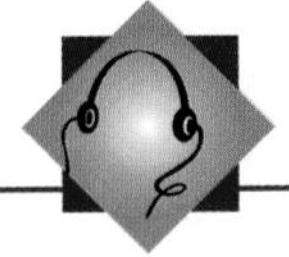

Les parents

le beau-frère (les beaux-frères)	stepbrother; brother-in-law
le beau-père (les beaux-pères)	stepfather; father-in-law
la belle-mère (les belles-mères)	stepmother; mother-in-law
la belle-sœur (les belles-sœurs)	stepsister; sister-in-law
la femme	wife
la fille	daughter
le fils	son
le frère	brother
la grand-mère (les grands-mères)	grandmother
le grand-père (les grands-pères)	grandfather
le mari	husband
la mère	mother
le neveu	nephew
la nièce	niece
l'oncle (*m.*)	uncle
les parents (*m. pl.*)	parents; relatives
le père	father
la petite-fille (les petites-filles)	granddaughter
le petit-fils (les petits-fils)	grandson
la sœur	sister
la tante	aunt

MOTS APPARENTÉS: **le cousin, la cousine, les grands-parents** (*m. pl.*)

À REVOIR: **les enfants** (*m., f.*)

L'état civil

célibataire	single
Ils vivent en union libre.	They are living together (without marriage).
veuf (veuve)	widowed

MOTS APPARENTÉS: **marié(e), divorcé(e)**

Les nombres à partir de 60

soixante, soixante-dix, quatre-vingts, quatre-vingt-dix, cent, mille, un million, un milliard

L'année

janvier, février, mars, avril, mai, juin, juillet, août, septembre, octobre, novembre, décembre

un an	year	**un anniversaire**	birthday
une année	year	**un mois**	month

La semaine

lundi, mardi, mercredi, jeudi, vendredi, samedi, dimanche

aujourd'hui	today	**la semaine**	week

MOT APPARENTÉ: **le week-end**

Les adjectifs possessifs

mon, ma, mes	my	**notre, notre, nos**	our
ton, ta, tes	your	**votre, votre, vos**	your
son, sa, ses	his; her; its; one's	**leur, leur, leurs**	their

Verbes

avoir	to have
avoir... ans	to be . . . years old
avoir besoin de	to need
avoir chaud	to be hot
avoir envie de	to feel like, want
avoir faim	to be hungry
avoir froid	to be cold
avoir honte (de)	to be ashamed (of)
avoir l'air	to look, seem
avoir les cheveux blonds (chataîn, noirs, roux, blancs)	to have blond (brown, black, red, white) hair
avoir les yeux marron (noisette, bleus)	to have brown (hazel, blue) eyes
avoir peur (de)	to be afraid (of)
avoir soif	to be thirsty
il n'y a pas de	there is/are not any
Quel âge avez-vous (a-t-il, etc.)?	How old are you (is he, etc.)?

À REVOIR: **il y a**

Questions

combien de	how many; how much	**pourquoi**	why
comment	how	**quand**	when
où	where		

À REVOIR: **Est-ce que... ?, je suppose?, n'est-ce pas?**

Autres expressions utiles

est-ce... ?	is that/this . . . ?
il/elle s'appelle	his/her name is
parce que	because
le premier	first (*of a month*)
tout (le), toute (la), tous (les), toutes (les)	all (the), every
Y a-t-il... ?	Is there . . . ?/Are there . . . ?

Chapitre 5

Secrets

Le Chemin du retour

Feuille de service du 15 octobre
5e jour de tournage
Horaires: 7h–17h

LIEU DE TOURNAGE: PARIS—31, rue Coquillère, 1er

Séquence	*Effets*	*Décors*	*Résumé*	*Rôles*
22	INT.—FIN DU JOUR	APPARTEMENT CAMILLE—Séjour	Rachid regarde un livre sur les Cévennes et des photos de la grand-mère de Camille.	CAMILLE, RACHID

OBJECTIFS

In this episode, you will

- meet Camille's mother
- learn more about Camille's family

In this chapter, you will

- describe houses, rooms, and furnishings
- tell time
- express and respond to apologies
- talk about everyday activities
- ask about and identify specific people and things
- learn more about the gender of nouns and how to form the plural of some nouns
- learn about common French family customs and their diversity from region to region

Vocabulaire en contexte

La maison: les pièces et les meubles°

La... *The house: Rooms and furniture*

Voici **l'appartement** (*m.*) de Camille.

la salle de séjour
le canapé
le tapis
la chaîne stéréo
le portable
le fauteuil
la chambre
la radio
le lit
l'armoire (*f.*)
le miroir
la commode
le lavabo
la salle de bains
le frigo (le réfrigérateur)
le four à micro-ondes
la cuisinière
la cuisine
le buffet
la salle à manger
la chaise
la table

Pour en savoir plus...

To gain access to a French apartment building, you often need to enter a code into an electronic security keypad. When guests are invited, they must be given the code in order to enter on their own. When you enter a French building, you are on the ground floor, **le rez-de-chaussée.** The next floor up is **le premier étage** (*the first floor*), the next is **le deuxième étage** (*the second floor*), and so on.*

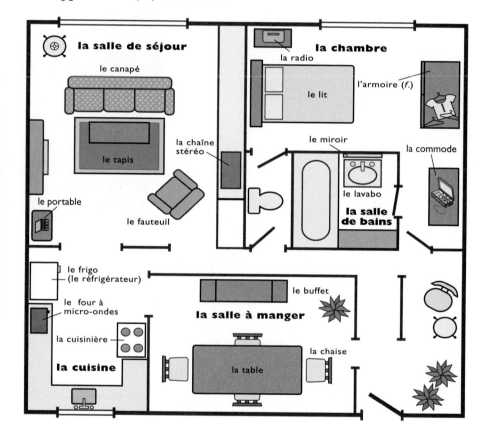

L'appartement de Camille se trouve au **rez-de-chaussée** d'**un immeuble** parisien. C'est un deux-pièces.[†] Sa mère habite au premier **étage.**

Activités

A. Identifiez. Identify two or three pieces of furniture or other objects you have in different rooms. If your residence doesn't have one of those rooms, use your imagination.

MODÈLE: salle de bains →
Dans la salle de bains, j'ai un lavabo et un miroir.

*You will learn ordinal numbers (first, second, and so on) in Chapter 11.

†Apartments are identified by the number of bedrooms they have in addition to a living area. **Un studio** has no bedroom, **un deux-pièces** has a living area and one bedroom, and so on.

1. salle de séjour
2. chambre
3. cuisine
4. salle à manger
5. sous-sol (*m.*) (*basement*): Au sous-sol...

B. Où? Complete the following sentences with the name of the appropriate location, based on the drawing of Camille's apartment.

MODÈLE: Camille écoute la radio... →
Camille écoute la radio dans la chambre.

1. Elle parle avec ses amis...
2. Elle prépare des spaghettis...
3. Elle dîne...
4. Ses vêtements (*clothes*) sont...
5. Elle se lave (*washes up*)...

C. Un château en Espagne. Describe your ideal dwelling to your partner. Tell what type of living space it is, where it is located, how many rooms it has, and what type of furniture is in each room.

Vocabulaire utile: à la campagne (*in the country*), en ville, une cheminée (*fireplace*), un lave-vaisselle (*dishwasher*), une piscine (*swimming pool*)

MODÈLE: Ma maison idéale est à la campagne. C'est une maison à deux pièces. Il y a une chambre avec un grand (*double*) lit et deux fenêtres et une salle de séjour avec une cheminée, un canapé et trois fauteuils confortables. En plus, il y a une salle à manger avec une grande table et douze chaises et une grande cuisine avec un frigo, une cuisinière et une table.

Le studio de Chloé Gall

Voici l'appartement de Chloé Gall, la sœur de Bruno. Elle habite **un studio**. Tous **les meubles** (*m.*) sont dans **la même**° **pièce**.

° same

Chloé a un vélo, mais elle a aussi **une voiture** dans le garage. C'est une Citroën.*

†Another word for cell phone is **un mobile**.

*A Citroën is a French-made automobile.

Activités

A. Quel appareil? Identify the object that Chloé uses to perform the following activities.

MODÈLE: pour parler à ses amis →
Chloé utilise (*uses*) le téléphone pour parler à ses amis.

1. pour écouter de la musique
2. pour regarder une cassette vidéo
3. pour regarder un DVD
4. pour aller au bureau
5. pour prendre (*to take*) des photos

B. Objets personnels. What objects might be in the apartments of the following people? Name at least two or three items, using vocabulary from this or earlier chapters.

MODÈLE: Mme Renée est actrice. →
Dans son appartement, il y a une grande affiche et des cassettes vidéo avec son nom dessus (*with her name on them*).

1. M. Rodriguez est musicien.
2. M. Armstrong est cycliste.
3. Mme Lumière est photographe.
4. M. Plume est écrivain (*writer*).
5. Mlle Nathan est étudiante.

C. Êtes-vous matérialiste? Tell your partner what you must have in your home to be comfortable and what you can do without. Who is the more materialistic?

MODÈLE: Pour être bien chez moi, j'ai absolument besoin d'un magnétoscope, d'un téléphone et d'un ordinateur. Un appareil photo n'est pas essentiel.

Quelle heure est-il?°

La journée° typique de Camille et Bruno commence.

Quelle... *What time is it?*
day

Il est sept heures:
Camille au maquillage°

Il est **sept heures dix**:
Bruno au maquillage

Il est **sept heures et quart**:
Techniciens sur le plateau

make-up

Il est **sept heures et demie**:
Productrice à la régie

Il est **huit heures moins le quart**:
Bruno exerce sa voix°

exerce... *does voice exercises*

Il est **huit heures moins cinq**:
Bruno et Camille sur le plateau

Il est **huit heures**:
Début° de «Bonjour!»

° Beginning

—**À quelle heure** Camille arrive-t-elle sur le plateau?
—Elle arrive sur le plateau **à huit heures moins cinq**.

Il est dix heures **du matin**.

Il est **midi**.

Il est cinq heures **de l'après-midi**.

Il est dix heures **du soir**.

Il est **minuit**.

1. To tell someone the time, add minutes to the hour for the first half hour. After the half hour, deduct minutes from the next hour.

Il est **une heure vingt-quatre**.	*It's 1:24 (twenty-four minutes past one).*
Il est **deux heures moins vingt**.	*It's 1:40 (twenty minutes to two).*

2. Special expressions are often used for the quarter hour and half hour.

Il est midi **et demi**.	*It's half past noon.*
Il est une heure **moins le quart**.	*It's a quarter to one.*
Il est une heure **et quart**.	*It's a quarter past one.*

3. The spelling **et demie** is used in most time-related expressions because the word **heure** is feminine. The masculine spelling **et demi** is used for **midi** and **minuit**.

Il est cinq heures **et demie**.	*It's five thirty.*
Il est midi **et demi**.	*It's twelve thirty.*

4. Whereas English uses a colon to show hours and minutes, French uses the abbreviation **h**, standing for **heure(s)**.

8 **h** 20 *8:20*   9 **h** *9:00*

Notez bien!

Three words in French can mean *time.* They are used in different ways.

L'heure (*f.*) is used for the time of day and punctuality.

Quelle **heure** est-il? *What time is it?*

Le train arrive toujours **à l'heure**. *The train always arrives on time.*

La fois is used for how many times something happens.

Je mange trois **fois** par jour. *I eat three times a day.*

Le temps is used for the broader concept of time or the availability of time.

Je n'ai pas **le temps** de parler maintenant. *I don't have time to talk now.*

5. French uses the twenty-four hour clock for train schedules, event times, and appointments. Hours are counted consecutively from 0 h (= **minuit** = *12:00 A.M.*) to 23 h 59 (= 11 h 59 **du soir** = *11:59 P.M.*). Thus, because no ambiguity is possible, the expressions **du matin**, **de l'après-midi**, **du soir**, **midi**, and **minuit** are not necessary.

onze heures du matin	=	11 h	*11:00 A.M.*
onze heures du soir	=	23 h	*11:00 P.M.*

In the 24-hour system, minutes are added to the hour up to the following hour. The quarter hours and half hours are expressed in minutes as well.

3 h 08	trois heures huit	3 h 40	trois heures quarante
3 h 15	trois heures quinze	3 h 45	trois heures quarante-cinq
3 h 30	trois heures trente	3 h 59	trois heures cinquante-neuf

6. To say an event occurs between two times, use **de... à...** .

Le musée est ouvert **de** 10 h **à** 20 h. — *The museum is open from 10:00 A.M. till 8:00 P.M.*

7. Three expressions are used to talk about punctuality.

en avance *early* **à l'heure** *on time* **en retard** *late*

Pierre est **en retard**. — *Pierre is late.*

Langage fonctionnel

Pour exprimer le regret et s'excuser°

°Pour... *Expressing regret and apologizing*

Here are some common ways of expressing regret and excusing yourself.

Expressions de regret ou d'excuse

Excusez-moi. / Excuse-moi.	*Excuse me.*
Pardon.	*Pardon (me).*
(Je suis) désolé(e).	*(I'm) sorry.*

Réponses possibles

Ce n'est pas grave.	*It's okay.*
Ne vous inquiétez pas. / Ne t'inquiète pas.	*Don't worry. Forget it.*
Pas de problème.	*No problem.*

—**Désolé** d'être en retard. *Sorry for being late.*
—**Ne t'inquiète pas.** *Don't worry about it.*

Activités

A. Quelle heure est-il? The following times are shown in English. Your partner will ask you what time it is, using the word **maintenant** (*now*). Answer by saying the time in French.

MODÈLE: 3:20 P.M. →
É1: Quelle heure est-il maintenant?
É2: Il est trois heures vingt de l'après-midi.

1. 8:45 P.M.
2. 6:15 A.M.
3. 12:30 P.M.
4. 4:55 P.M.
5. 12:00 midnight
6. 12:00 noon
7. 11:30 A.M.
8. 1:20 P.M.

B. Les musées. Read aloud the opening and closing times of the following museums for the days indicated. Use the chart to find the correct information.

MODÈLE: le Louvre / lundi →
Le Louvre est ouvert (*open*) le lundi de 9 heures à 18 heures.

1. le Mémorial du Martyr Juif Inconnu / mardi
2. le Musée de l'Homme / jeudi
3. le Musée d'Orsay / vendredi
4. l'Institut du Monde Arabe / dimanche
5. le Musée du Vin / samedi
6. le Centre national d'art et de culture Georges Pompidou / mercredi

	L	M	M	J	V	S	D
Louvre	9 h–18 h	–	9 h–21 h 45	9 h–18 h	9 h–18 h	9 h–18 h	9 h–18 h
Mémorial du Martyr Juif Inconnu	10 h–13 h, 14 h–18 h	10 h–13 h, 14 h–18 h	10 h–13 h, 14 h–18 h	10 h–13 h, 14 h–18 h	10 h–13 h, 14 h–16 h 30	–	10 h–13 h, 14 h–18 h
Musée de l'Homme	9 h 45–17 h 15	–	9 h 45–17 h 15	9 h 45–17 h 15	9 h 45–17 h 15	9 h 45–17 h 15	9 h 45–17 h 15
Musée d'Orsay	–	10 h–18 h	10 h–18 h	10 h–21 h 45	10 h–18 h	10 h–18 h	9 h–18 h
Institut du Monde Arabe	–	10 h–18 h	10 h–18 h	10 h–18 h	10 h–18 h	10 h–18 h	10 h–18 h
Musée du Vin	–	10 h–18 h	10 h–18 h	10 h–18 h	10 h–18 h	10 h–18 h	10 h–18 h
Centre... Georges Pompidou	12 h–22 h	–	12 h–22 h	12 h–22 h	12 h–22 h	10 h–22 h	10 h–22 h

C. Fois? Temps? Heure? Fill in the blanks in a logical manner. Use **fois**, **temps**, or **heure(s)**.

1. Neuf heures! Les enfants, c'est l' _____ d'aller au lit!
2. Je suis en avance, alors j'ai le _____ de lire un magazine.
3. Paul regarde toujours deux _____ ses films préférés.
4. À quelle _____ dînez-vous d'habitude?
5. Notre _____ est précieux!
6. C'est la première _____ que je mange des escargots!

D. Questions personnelles. Ask your partner questions about what time he/she does things.

Demandez à (*Ask*) votre partenaire à quelle heure il/elle...

1. vient à l'université
2. dîne
3. travaille
4. regarde la télévision
5. va en boîte (*goes to a club*)

Demandez-lui aussi s'il / si elle arrive généralement aux rendez-vous à l'heure, en retard ou en avance. Combien de minutes de retard sont acceptables?

E. Allons au cinéma! Using the movie schedule, ask a partner if he/she would like to go to a particular film. Your partner will accept or refuse, and may also use an expression of regret. If your partner refuses and/or apologizes, respond appropriately and try to negotiate another film, time, or date.

MODÈLE: É1: Tu as envie d'aller au cinéma aujourd'hui? Il y a «Cités de la plaine» qui passe au MK2-Beaubourg.
É2: C'est vrai? À quelle heure y a-t-il des séances (*showings*)?
É1: Il y a une séance à dix-neuf heures cinquante.
É2: Désolé. Ce n'est pas possible.
É1: Pas de problème. Demain, c'est possible? etc.

FILM	DESCRIPTION	OÙ ET QUAND?
Les âmes perdues (***Lost Souls***)	Film fantastique[a] américain avec Winona Ryder, Ben Chaplin, John Hurt	Georges-V (en VO [version originale])—Tlj[b] à 10 h 35, 12 h 45, 15 h, 19 h 40, 22 h
Cités de la plaine	Drame français avec Ben, Bernard Trolet	MK2 Beaubourg—Tlj à 11 h 30, 13 h 30, 15 h 35, 17 h 15, 19 h 50, 22 h 05
Duos d'un jour (***Duets***)	Comédie américaine avec Gwyneth Paltrow, Andre Braugher	Megarama (en VF)—Sam, Dim à 11 h 30; Tlj à 14 h, 16 h 30, 19 h 15, 22 h
Esperanza et ses saints	Comédie mexicaine avec Dolores Heredia	Latina (en VO)—Mer, Ven, Sam, Dim, Lun à 14 h; Tlj à 16 h, 18 h, 20 h, 22 h
Selon Matthieu	Comédie dramatique française avec Benoît Magimel, Natalie Baye, Jeanne Moreau	UGC-Ciné Cité des Halles—Tlj à 11 h 30, 13 h 40, 15 h 50, 18 h, 20 h 10, 22 h 20

[a] *fantasy* [b] Tlj = Tous les jours *every day*

Visionnement 1

Avant de visionner

Qu'est-ce que cela veut dire? (*What does that mean?*) In this episode, Rachid admires something in Camille's apartment. Read the following exchange and then answer the questions.

RACHID: Écoute, ce livre est vraiment,[a] euh... Il est vraiment magnifique!
CAMILLE: C'est un cadeau[b] de ma grand-mère... Tu aimes les Cévennes?
RACHID: Ah oui, beaucoup[c]... beaucoup.

[a]*truly* [b]*gift* [c]*a lot*

1. Qu'est-ce que Rachid admire? **2.** Qui a donné cette chose (*Who gave this thing*) à Camille? **3.** Est-ce que Rachid aime les Cévennes?

Pour en savoir plus...

The **Cévennes,** a mountainous area in the southeast of France, is known for its magnificent scenery and its biodiversity. The region is quite isolated and relatively empty of young people, because many have moved away to find work. Lately, however, a diversified economic base, an influx of population, and the establishment of a national park in 1970 have brought more prosperity to the area.

Observez!

In Episode 5, Rachid goes to Yasmine's school and finds his wife there. Later on he meets Camille's mother. As you watch, answer the following questions.

- What does Rachid say to Yasmine's mother? What is her reaction?
- How does the attitude of Camille's mother, Mado, change during the episode?

Vocabulaire relatif à l'épisode

Je ne me rappelle jamais.	*I never remember (it).*
J'apporte tout ce qu'il faut.	*I'll bring everything that's needed.*
Je peux t'emprunter le livre?	*May I borrow the book from you?*
De quoi se mêle-t-il?	*What business is it of his?*

Après le visionnement

A. Moments clés. (*Key moments.*) Here are some key moments from Episode 5. Fill in the blanks with the name of the appropriate person or thing.

1. Rachid retrouve (*meets*) _____ dans la cour (*courtyard*) de son école. **2.** _____ demande pardon à Sonia. **3.** _____ invite Rachid et Camille à dîner. **4.** Rachid admire _____ sur les Cévennes. **5.** Il examine _____ de la grand-mère de Camille. **6.** Mado ne veut pas parler de _____. **7.** _____ se méfie de (*distrusts*) Rachid.

B. Réfléchissez. (*Think.*) Answer the following questions about Camille's mother, Mado, according to your impressions from the episode.

1. Comment l'attitude de Mado change-t-elle envers (*toward*) Rachid dans cet épisode?

Vocabulaire utile: aimable, content(e), cynique, horrifié(e), hostile, méfiant(e) (*suspicious*)

- Au début (*At the beginning*)...
- Pendant (*During*) la visite de Rachid...
- À la fin (*At the end*)...

2. Pourquoi son attitude change-t-elle, à votre avis (*in your opinion*)? Choisissez (*Choose*) **a**, **b** ou **c**.

   a. Rachid n'accepte pas son invitation à dîner et part vite (*leaves quickly*).
   b. Mado a un secret de famille et Rachid pose trop de (*too many*) questions.
   c. Rachid est impoli avec Camille et Mado n'aime pas cela.

Structure 15

Le verbe *faire*; des expressions avec *faire*

Talking about everyday activities

—Mais qu'est-ce que **tu fais** là?

Le verbe *faire*

faire (*to do; to make*)			
je	**fais**	nous	**faisons**
tu	**fais**	vous	**faites**
il, elle, on	**fait**	ils, elles	**font**

Because **faire** has the general meaning of *to do* or *to make*, when you are asked a question with **faire**, you may need to use a different verb in your answer.

—Qu'est-ce que **tu fais**? *What are you doing?*
—**Je vais chercher** ma fille à l'école. *I'm going to pick up my daughter at school.*

Expressions avec *faire*

Faire is a high-frequency verb found in many common expressions that describe everyday activities.

faire attention (à) *to pay attention (to)*
faire la connaissance de *to make the acquaintance of*
faire les courses *to do errands*
faire la cuisine *to cook, make a meal*
faire les devoirs *to do homework*
faire la fête *to have a party*
faire la lessive *to do the laundry*

faire le lit *to make the bed*
faire le ménage *to do housework*
faire une promenade *to take a walk*
faire la queue *to stand in line*
faire du shopping *to go shopping*
faire du sport *to play/do a sport*
faire la vaisselle *to do the dishes*
faire un voyage *to take a trip*

Activités

A. Des activités agréables, désagreables ou obligatoires. Form complete sentences from the cues. After you say each one, tell whether it is a pleasant, unpleasant, or required activity.

MODÈLE: tu / faire une promenade dans le parc →
Tu fais une promenade dans le parc. C'est une activité agréable.

1. Anne / faire la lessive pour sa famille
2. vous / faire les courses au marché
3. nous / faire la cuisine pour notre soirée (*party*)
4. je / faire un voyage au Japon
5. tu / faire la queue au cinéma
6. Christelle et Brigitte / faire du shopping
7. mon frère et moi / faire la connaissance d'un nouvel étudiant
8. les étudiants / faire attention en classe
9. mes amis et moi / faire la fête

B. Activités de tous les jours. (*Everyday activities.*) Your partner will ask you what the people in the illustrations are doing. Answer, using expressions with **faire**, remembering to change the pronoun as necessary.

MODÈLE:

vous →
É1: Qu'est-ce que vous faites?
É2: Nous faisons la vaisselle.

1. tu

2. Robert et Ahmed

3. vous

4. les Truffaut

5. Chantal

6. Émilie / Magalie

C. Vos activités de tous les jours. Using the expressions with **faire**, interview a partner to find out when he/she usually does those activities.

MODÈLE: É1: À quelle heure fais-tu tes devoirs généralement?
É2: Je fais mes devoirs à 9 h du soir.
É1: Quand fais-tu le ménage généralement?
É2: Je fais le ménage le samedi matin.

Structure 16

L'adjectif interrogatif *quel* et l'adjectif démonstratif ce

Asking and identifying which person or thing

—Alors, **quel** est le plat du jour?

—Écoute, ***ce*** livre est vraiment, euh... Il est vraiment magnifique!

L'adjectif interrogatif *quel*

	SINGULIER	PLURIEL
masculin	**quel**	**quels**
féminin	**quelle**	**quelles**

1. You have already seen forms of the interrogative adjective▲ **quel** in several common questions.

Quel âge avez-vous?	*How old are you?*
Quelle est la date aujourd'hui?	*What is today's date?*
Quel jour sommes-nous?	*Which day of the week is it?*
Quelle heure est-il?	*What time is it?*

2. **Quel** (or a preposition + **quel**) can be placed directly before the noun. **Quel** can also be separated from the noun by the verb **être**. In either case, because it is an adjective, it must agree in gender and number with the noun it modifies.

Quel est **le nom** de cette émission? — *What is the name of this show?*

Quelle émission regardez-vous à 8 h du matin? — *Which show do you watch at 8:00 in the morning?*

Quels journalistes sont les animateurs de «Bonjour!»? — *Which journalists are the hosts of "Bonjour!"?*

Quelles sont **les émissions** diffusées sur Canal 7? — *Which shows are broadcast on Channel 7?*

À **quelle heure** viens-tu? — *(At) what time are you coming?*

Dans **quel immeuble** habitez-vous? — *In which building do you live?*

Pour en savoir plus...

Quel is also often used in exclamations and compliments.

Quelle chance! — *What luck!*

Quel joli médaillon! — *What a pretty locket!*

L'adjectif démonstratif ce

	SINGULIER	PLURIEL
masculin	**ce (cet)**	**ces**
féminin	**cette**	**ces**

1. To point out or designate things, use a form of the demonstrative adjective▲ **ce** (*this, that, these, those*). Because it is an adjective, the form of **ce** must agree in gender and number with the noun it modifies. The plural is the same for both masculine and feminine.

   Écoute, **ce** livre est vraiment... magnifique. — *Hey, this book is really . . . wonderful.*

   Cette photo est de la grand-mère de Camille. — *That photo is of Camille's grandmother.*

   Mado ne parle pas de **ces** secrets. — *Mado doesn't talk about those secrets.*

   ...pourquoi s'intéresse-t-il à **ces** photos? — *. . . why is he interested in these photos?*

2. The form **cet** is used before a masculine singular noun beginning with a vowel sound.

   Mado habite dans **cet** immeuble. — *Mado lives in this apartment building.*

   Comment s'appelle **cet** homme? — *What is that man's name?*

Pour en savoir plus...

The forms of **ce** mean either *this* (*these*) or *that* (*those*). To make this distinction explicit, **-ci** (indicating nearness) and **-là** (indicating remoteness) can be attached to the noun.

ce livre-**ci** — *this book (= the one here)*

cette photo-**là** — *that photo (= the one over there)*

ces femmes-**là** — *those women (= those over there)*

Activités

A. Un bon choix? (*A good choice?*) Paulette is thinking of moving into her friend's apartment. What does she think of it? Choose the correct form of **ce** to complete the sentences.

1. **Dans sa chambre:** J'adore _____ tapis, mais _____ lit est petit. _____ armoire est fantastique, mais _____ bureau est trop petit pour mon ordinateur.
2. **Dans la salle de séjour:** Je n'aime pas _____ énorme canapé. _____ affiche est jolie, mais je trouve _____ petits miroirs sur le mur ridicules. _____ fauteuils ne sont pas confortables.
3. **Dans la cuisine:** _____ frigo est grand et _____ table est parfaite. J'aime _____ cuisine.

Now talk with a partner and decide whether or not Paulette likes the apartment. Is she going to live there? Why (not)?

B. Un client indécis. M. Martin is looking for a gift for his boss. His indecision leads him to ask his wife her opinion about each gift idea. Choose the correct form of **quel** or **ce** to complete their conversation.

MODÈLE: Chérie, quelle vidéo (*f.*) est-ce qu'il aimerait (*would he like*)? Ce film classique ou ce concert (*m.*)?

1. Chérie, _____ livre est-ce qu'il aimerait? _____ album (*m.*) de photos ou _____ collection (*f.*) d'essais?
2. Et _____ stylo est-ce qu'il aimerait? _____ beau stylo Waterman ou _____ élégant stylo Mont Blanc?
3. _____ affiches (*f.*) est-ce qu'il aimerait? _____ affiches de Paris et Nice ou _____ affiche de Londres?
4. _____ CD (*m.*) est-ce qu'il aimerait? _____ CD de musique populaire française ou _____ collection (*f.*) de raï?
5. Finalement, _____ gadget (*m.*) est-ce qu'il aimerait? _____ micro-ordinateur ou _____ calculatrice?

C. *Le Chemin du retour.* What questions with **quel** must you ask to find out the italicized information about *Le Chemin du retour*? Use a preposition before **quel** when necessary.

MODÈLE: La profession de Martine, c'est «*productrice*». →
Quelle est la profession de Martine? (*ou* Quelle profession Martine a-t-elle? *ou* Quelle profession a Martine?)

1. Le nom de la chaîne de télévision est *Canal 7.*
2. «Bonjour!» commence à *08 h 00.*
3. Bruno aime le pain *artisanal.*
4. Yasmine va à l'école *Bullier.*
5. Le code de l'immeuble de Mado est *A456.*
6. La photo *du grand-père* n'est pas dans le médaillon de Camille.

D. Pour faire connaissance. Interview a classmate to find out what he/she prefers in the following categories. Also say whether or not you like the same thing. Then switch roles.

MODÈLE: livre →
É1: Quel est ton livre préféré?
É2: *Les Misérables* est mon livre préféré.
É1: Je n'aime pas ce livre. (*ou* J'aime ce livre.)

1. possession
2. cours
3. film
4. émissions de télévision
5. acteurs
6. professeur
7. actrice
8. jour
9. pièce (de la maison)

Regards sur la culture

La famille

As you noticed in this segment, Mado tries to discourage Camille from talking about family matters with Rachid. Although there is a very particular reason for this in the film (one that has not yet been made clear), it is also true that the family and its affairs are generally felt to be very private matters for French people.

- Unless the friendship is strong and well established, it is rather unusual for a visitor to France to be invited as a guest to the home of a French family. The home is a private domain, and even when one does enter a home in France, the visit is normally limited to the living room and dining room. One would almost never visit the entire house the way people do in North America. In addition, a French home is generally closed to the outside by a fence or wall and by shutters on the windows.
- French people often feel that they need to know something about a person's family in order to evaluate him/her. They sometimes judge an individual in part on the basis of the family's reputation or social standing within the community. Of course, because reputations are based partly on hearsay, the French know that such evaluations are only approximate.
- Meals are extremely important family affairs in France. It would be very unusual for a French person to schedule an event that would interfere with the family mealtime.

Un grand repas familial

- Competition between siblings is very strongly discouraged in France. North Americans tend to be surprised at how well French siblings appear to get along.
- To a greater extent than in North America, French children are discouraged from engaging in activities that would take them away from their families. Except in large urban areas, it is often expected that they will eventually find a job that will allow them to settle down relatively close to their parents.
- In France, it is traditionally considered shameful to the family if an elderly person ends his/her life in a retirement home or a hospital, rather than at home with the family.

Considérez

Why might a newcomer to a small town initially have a more difficult time assimilating in France than in Canada or the United States? Can you explain the origins of this difference?

Structure 17

Le genre de certains substantifs et quelques pluriels spéciaux

Guessing genders and spellings

—C'est **un cadeau** de ma grand-mère.

Le genre de certains substantifs

It is sometimes possible to identify the gender of a noun by its ending. Although this is not a foolproof system—you should always memorize the gender along with each noun you learn—the following chart will give you some hints.

IF A NOUN ENDS IN...	IT IS PROBABLY...	EXAMPLES	IMPORTANT EXCEPTIONS
-eau	masculine	bureau, cadeau, jumeau, tableau	eau (*water*)
-isme	masculine	catholicisme, impressionnisme	
-ment	masculine	appartement, bâtiment, visionnement	
-sion	feminine	émission, télévision	
-tion	feminine	attention, gratification	
-ie	feminine	Algérie, géographie, librairie	
-té	feminine	université, liberté, égalité, fraternité	côté

Quelques pluriels spéciaux

Some nouns form the plural in special ways. Check the following chart for a few general rules for vocabulary you've already seen.

IF A NOUN ENDS IN...	ITS PLURAL PROBABLY ENDS IN...	EXAMPLES
-al -ail	-aux	hôpital → hôpitaux travail → travaux
-eu -eau	-x	neveu → neveux tableau → tableaux
-s	-s	fils → fils
-x	-x	époux (*husband*) → époux
-z	-z	nez (*nose*) → nez

You already know that the plurals of some compound nouns (**des salle*s* de classe**, **des sac*s* à dos**) are formed by making the first noun in the compound plural. In compound words for family members, because one part is an adjective and the other is a noun, the plural ending is added to both parts: **grand*s*-mère*s***, **grand*s*-père*s***, **petit*s*-fils**, **petite*s*-fille*s***, **belle*s*-mère*s***, **beau*x*-père*s***, **belle*s*-sœur*s***, **beau*x*-frère*s***.

Activités

A. Est-ce important? Indicate whether or not you think each of the following is important. Follow the model. Then compare your answers with those of a partner.

MODÈLE: géographie →
La géographie est importante. (La géographie n'est pas importante.)

1. réalisme **2.** télévision **3.** liberté **4.** tableau de la salle de classe **5.** sentiments **6.** université **7.** cadeaux d'anniversaire (*birthday presents*) **8.** biologie **9.** beauté

B. Quelle chance! Sophie is a very rich woman with lots of family and possessions. Marie, who always wants to seem better, says she has more. What does each woman say?

MODÈLE: voiture de sport (*sports car*) →
SOPHIE: J'ai une voiture de sport.
MARIE: Moi, j'ai deux voitures de sport.

1. grand-père généreux **2.** bureau Louis XV **3.** cheval (*horse*) **4.** fils brillant **5.** neveu **6.** tableau impressionniste **7.** château **8.** ex-époux (*ex-husband*) riche **9.** travail

C. Signez, s'il vous plaît. Copy the chart on page 124, then find a person who has more than one of the objects or relations listed. Write the person's name and how many he/she has.

MODÈLE: É1: As-tu plus d'un cheval?
É2: Oui. J'ai deux chevaux.
É1: Comment t'appelles-tu?
É2: Deborah.

Trouvez quelqu'un qui a plus d'un (*more than one . . .*)	Nom	Combien?
1. cheval	*Deborah*	*2*
2. neveu		
3. bureau		
4. tableau		
5. fils		
6. sac à dos		

Visionnement 2

Avant de visionner

Les environs de l'appartement de Camille

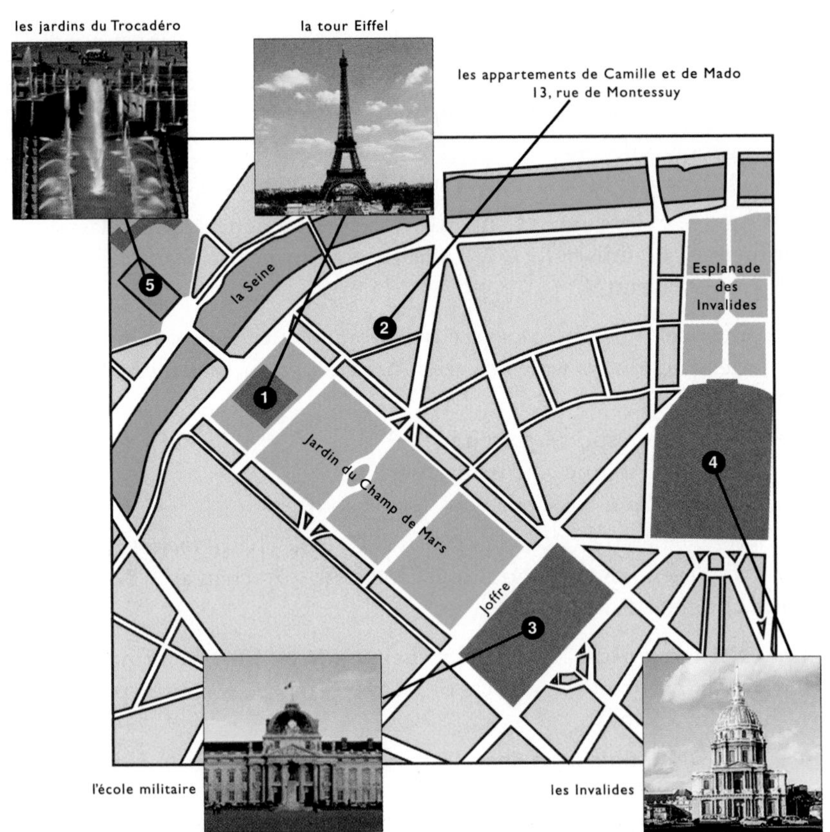

A. Visites dans le quartier. This map shows the elegant area of Paris in which Mado and Camille live. It wasn't until the time of Louis XIV, the Sun King, in the late 1600s, that this part of Paris began to be built. Louis XIV constructed **les Invalides**, an enormous complex of buildings, as a hospital and retirement home for the veterans of his many wars. Napoleon studied at the **École militaire**, and in 1840, nearly twenty years after his death, his remains were buried in the **Église du Dôme** at **les Invalides**. The **Champ de Mars** was the site of important ceremonies during the Revolutionary period in the late eighteenth century. But most of the buildings in this area date from the late nineteenth century, when the **tour Eiffel** was built. The **jardins du Trocadéro** are a reminder of the 1937 World's Fair.

Mado likes taking historical walks in her neighborhood. Indicate the number and name of the landmark that corresponds to each description.

a. un ensemble architectural de 1676
b. un bâtiment de 1773
c. un tombeau (*tomb*) de 1840
d. une construction de 1889
e. des fontaines de 1937

B. Les relations familiales. What do you remember about Episode 5?

1. Comment est la relation entre Camille et sa mère, Mado?
   a. Mado traite (*treats*) sa fille comme une enfant.
   b. Camille s'occupe de (*takes care of*) sa mère.
   c. Mado et Camille ont une vie (*life*) indépendante l'une de l'autre (*from one another*).
2. Selon les observations de **Regards sur la culture** dans ce chapitre, est-ce qu'il est normal que Mado invite Rachid à dîner? Expliquez.

Observez!

Consider the cultural information explained in **Regards sur la culture**. Then watch Episode 5 again, and answer the following questions.

- What does Mado do to make Rachid feel welcome?
- What behaviors exhibited by Rachid might not conform to Mado's cultural expectations of a guest?

Après le visionnement

Do the activity for **Visionnement 2** in the *Workbook/Laboratory Manual.*

Synthèse: Culture

La famille, source de culture

Family relationships are the first and most important sources of culture. The kinds of interactions one has with one's parents, grandparents, and siblings are very closely related to the values and behaviors that one carries through life. Thus, different ways of raising children, or of treating the elderly, for example, determine different cultures in a very real sense.

Quelques générations d'une famille à l'occasion d'un mariage dans les années 40.

You saw in Chapter 4 that even within France there is enormous cultural variety. This diversity carries over into the realm of family structures. Of course, the many immigrant groups in France have widely varying kinds of families. For example, Jewish families of Algerian origin, most of whom arrived in France over the second half of the twentieth century, are more likely to live as extended families (grandparents, parents, and children together) than many other groups.

Even the traditional rural French family is not the same in the various French provinces. De Gaulle is famous for having said that it is impossible to govern a country that makes as many cheeses as days in the year. The differences in traditional family structures are a very real difficulty hinted at by de Gaulle's comment.

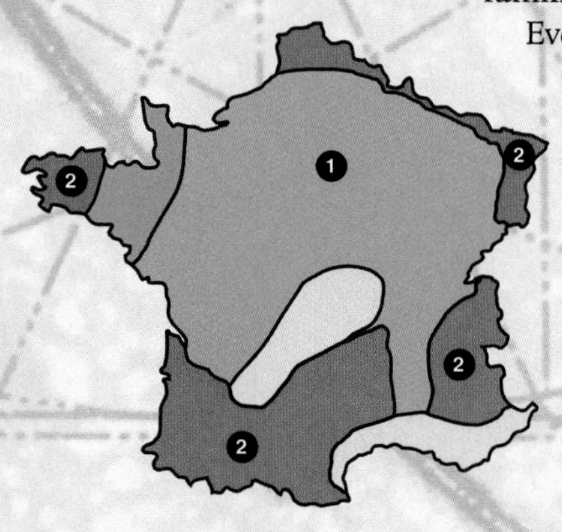

The two most important traditional rural family types are

Type 1: Each child marries and founds a separate, independent household. The parents' property is divided up equally, either before or after the death of the parents.

Type 2: One child marries and inherits the parents' property, remaining under the authority of the father as long as he lives. The others leave home and find work elsewhere or remain unmarried as "uncles" or "aunts" on the farm.

Although these traditions of family structure play no role in urban environments and are disappearing even in the countryside, their presence over the centuries has left traces in the attitudes and mind-sets of the different regions of France. In type 1 families, the values of equality and independence are fundamental. In type 2, family cohesion is most important, and values such as authority and inequality are basic.

À vous

In groups, discuss the values upon which your own family relationships are based. Consider the following factors: degree of equality, independence vs. community, strong vs. weak authority, and cooperation vs. individualism. In what ways has your family structure determined your values and attitudes?

À écrire

Do **À écrire** for Chapter 5 in the *Workbook/Laboratory Manual.*

Vocabulaire

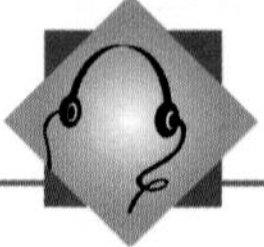

Résidences

un appartement	apartment	**une maison**	house
un étage	floor, level	**le rez-de-chaussée**	ground floor
un immeuble	apartment building		

Pièces d'une maison

une chambre	bedroom	**une salle à manger**	dining room
une cuisine	kitchen	**une salle de bains**	bathroom
une pièce	room	**une salle de séjour**	living room

Meubles et possessions

une affiche	poster	**une chaîne stéréo**	stereo
un appareil photo	camera	**une cuisinière**	stove
une armoire	armoire, wardrobe (*furniture*)	**un fauteuil**	armchair
un canapé	sofa	**un four (à micro-ondes)**	(microwave) oven
une commode	dresser		

un lavabo	bathroom basin
un lecteur de CD/DVD	CD/DVD player
un lit	bed
un magnétoscope	videocassette recorder (VCR)
un meuble	(piece of) furniture
un miroir	mirror
un portable	laptop computer; cell phone
un réfrigérateur (*fam.* **un frigo**)	refrigerator
un tapis	rug
une télévision	television set
un vélo	bicycle
une voiture	automobile

MOTS APPARENTÉS: **un buffet, une guitare, un piano, une radio, un téléphone**

À REVOIR: **une chaise, un ordinateur, une table**

L'heure

l'heure (*f.*)	hour; (clock) time
Quelle heure est-il?	What time is it?
il est... heure(s)	it's . . . o'clock
midi (*m.*)	noon
minuit (*m.*)	midnight
et quart	quarter past
et demi(e)	half past
moins	before (the hour); less; minus
moins le quart	quarter to
à quelle heure... ?	at what time . . . ?
à... heure(s)	at . . . o'clock
de... à...	from . . . to . . .
du matin	in the morning
de l'après-midi	in the afternoon
du soir	in the evening
à l'heure	on time
en avance	early
en retard	late
une fois	one time, occasion
le temps	time

Verbes

faire	to do; to make
faire attention	to pay attention
faire la connaissance de	to make the acquaintance of
faire les courses	to do errands
faire la cuisine	to cook, make a meal
faire les devoirs	to do homework
faire la fête	to have a party
faire la lessive	to do the laundry
faire le lit	to make the bed
faire le ménage	to do housework
faire une promenade	to take a walk
faire la queue	to stand in line
faire du shopping	to go shopping
faire du sport	to play/do a sport
faire la vaisselle	to do the dishes
faire un voyage	to take a trip

Autres expressions utiles

ce (cet, cette)	this; that
même	same
quel (quelle)	which

À REVOIR: **maintenant**

Chapitre 6

Bonjour, grand-père!

Le Chemin du retour

Feuille de service du 24 janvier
8e jour de tournage
Horaires: 9h–19h

LIEU DE TOURNAGE: MARSEILLE—FRANCE 3—Photocopieuse à l'inter-étage° — *mezzanine*

Séquence	*Effets*	*Décors*	*Résumé*	*Rôles*
30	INT.—JOUR	CANAL 7—Couloir° photocopieuse	En faisant° des photocopies du livre sur les Cévennes, Rachid découvre° une photo.	RACHID

En... *While making*
Corridor
discovers

OBJECTIFS

In this episode, you will

- watch a segment of "Bonjour!" on the subject of fashion
- find out how Camille feels about a discovery Rachid makes

In this chapter, you will

- describe types and colors of clothing
- use shopping terminology
- express your abilities and say what you want
- talk about everyday activities
- ask questions about people and things
- learn about French clothing and fashion
- read about the history of French fashion

Vocabulaire en contexte

La mode°

La... *Fashion*

Paris est toujours la capitale de la mode. Et la mode, c'est l'image éternelle de la France…

Et n'**oublions** pas° **les vêtements** (*m.*) de sport et les accessoires de sport.

n'oublions... let's not forget

un tee-shirt
un short
des chaussettes (*f.*)

Activités

A. Décrivez. (*Describe.*) What clothing are people wearing in this episode? What else are they probably wearing that is not shown in the picture? Name one thing each is not wearing.

1. 

2. 

3. 

B. Qu'est-ce que tu portes? (*What do you wear?*) Using the verb **porter**, ask your partner ten questions about his/her clothing habits. For negative answers, your partner should provide the correct information.

MODÈLE: É1: D'habitude, est-ce que tu portes une veste en cours?
É2: Non, d'habitude, je porte un tee-shirt.

des bottes et un chapeau	au centre sportif
une écharpe	à un concert de rock
un jean	en cours
des lunettes de soleil	à l'opéra
un maillot de bain	à la piscine (*swimming pool*)
un short	au sauna
un sweatshirt	au théâtre
un tailleur	au centre commercial
une veste	à une soirée habillée (*dressy*)
?	?

Les couleurs

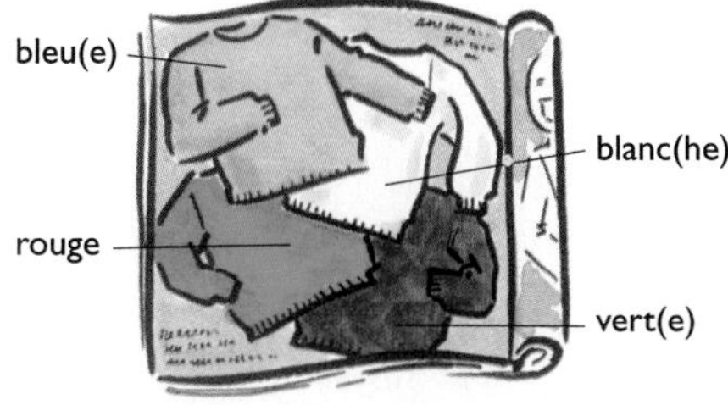

Le nouveau pull-over Maxichaud. 80% laine,[a] 20% cachemire.[b]

Des foulards en soie.[c] Coloris fantaisie.

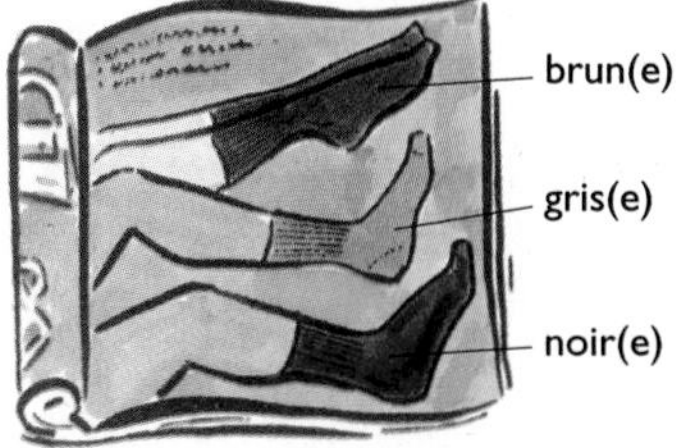

Nos chaussettes en coton et acrylique.

[a]*wool* [b]*cashmere* [c]*silk*

When colors are used as adjectives, most follow the standard rules for feminine and plural forms. The feminine forms of **violet** and **blanc** are **violette** and **blanche**.

Ce pantalon est **brun** et **violet**. Ces chapeaux sont **gris** et **blancs**.

Cette cravate est **brune** et **violette**. Ces chaussettes sont **grises** et **blanches**.

Pour en savoir plus...

Popular fabrics for clothing include **le coton** (*cotton*), **le cuir** (*leather*), **la laine** (*wool*), and **la soie** (*silk*). To say something is made of one of these fabrics, you may use either **en** or **de**.

J'aime mon écharpe **en laine** rouge. *I like my red wool scarf.*

C'est une ceinture **de cuir** noir. *It is a black leather belt.*

The colors **marron** (*chestnut*) and **orange** are invariable.

des yeux **marron**	*chestnut eyes*
des cravates **orange**	*orange ties*

Langage fonctionnel

Pour parler de la mode

Pour demander une opinion sur la mode

Ça me va?	*Does it look good on me?*
Vous l'aimez? (Tu l'aimes?)	*Do you like it?*

Pour faire des compliments

Quel beau… ! / Quelle belle… !	*What a beautiful . . . !*
Ce/Cette… vous (te) va bien.	*This . . . suits you.*
Vous êtes (Tu es) très chic.*	*You look very stylish.*

Pour exprimer des réservations

Je n'aime pas l'imprimé.	*I don't like the pattern.*
C'est un peu trop serré.	*It's a little too tight.*
C'est un peu trop large.	*It's a little too big.*

—**Quelle belle** jupe! *What a pretty skirt!*

—Moi, je pense qu'elle est **un peu trop large**. *I think it's a little too big.*

Activités

A. Un ensemble bien assorti. Use colors to create well-matched outfits.

MODÈLE: un jean / bleu / une chemise →
Un jean bleu va bien avec une chemise blanche.

1. une chemise / orange / un pull-over
2. un pantalon / noir / une veste
3. une jupe / violet / un chemisier
4. un costume / bleu / des chaussures
5. une robe / marron / un foulard
6. des chaussettes / gris / un costume
7. un tailleur / brun / des chaussures
8. un pantalon / vert / une ceinture
9. un manteau / rouge / des bottes
10. un maillot de bain / rose / des lunettes de soleil

*L'adjectif **chic** est invariable: **Elles sont très chic.**

B. Qui est-ce? Think of a student in your class. Your partner will ask questions about the student's clothing to try to find out who it is. A maximum of five questions is allowed.

MODÈLE: É1: Je pense à un étudiant dans la classe.
É2: Est-ce qu'il porte un pantalon gris?
É1: Oui. Il porte un pantalon gris.
É2: Est-ce qu'il porte une ceinture noire?
É1: Non. Pas de ceinture noire.
É2: Porte-t-il une chemise bleue?
É1: Oui.
É2: Alors, c'est Jacques, n'est-ce pas?
É1: C'est ça! C'est Jacques.

Dans un grand magasin°

Dans... *In a department store*

Quand on a de **l'argent**° (*m.*), on fait parfois du shopping. On achète° des vêtements dans une boutique ou dans **un grand magasin**. Voici un grand magasin.

money / buys

Pour en savoir plus...

Customers buying clothes in France often request the services of the clerk before trying anything on, particularly in small shops or boutiques. In many small shops, if a person expresses interest in an item, there is an underlying assumption that he/she will probably buy it. But in French department and discount stores, the shopping behavior more closely resembles that of North America.

Le client paie **en espèces**?°
Non, il paie **par chèque**.

La cliente paie **par carte de crédit**?
Non, elle paie **par carte bancaire**.°

en... *in cash*
carte... *debit card*

Activités

A. Dans un grand magasin. Fill in the blanks with an appropriate word.

1. Aujourd'hui, j'ai de l'_____ dans ma poche (*pocket*).
2. Je fais des achats (*make purchases*) dans un grand magasin. Je suis _____.

3. Pour acheter (*To buy*) un costume, je vais au _____ mode homme.
4. J'ai une question, alors je demande (*so I ask*) au _____ ou à la _____.
5. Je paie à _____.
6. Le magasin n'accepte ni (*neither*) cartes de crédit ni (*nor*) chèques, alors je paie en _____.

B. Interview. Find out about your partner's shopping habits by asking him/her the following questions.

Demandez-lui s'il / si elle...

1. aime faire du shopping.
2. préfère aller dans des grands magasins ou des petites boutiques.
3. pose beaucoup de (*asks a lot of*) questions au vendeur / à la vendeuse.
4. accepte souvent les conseils (*advice*) du vendeur / de la vendeuse.
5. paie en général par carte de crédit ou par carte bancaire.

Visionnement 1

Avant de visionner

Vocabulaire relatif à l'épisode

Du calme.	*Stay calm.*
coupée	*cut*
le marié	*bridegroom*
de l'autre côté	*on the other side*
vivante	*alive, living*

Qu'est-ce que cela veut dire? (*What does that mean?*) In this episode, Rachid tries to learn more about Camille's family. After two or three questions, Camille responds with the following remark.

Rachid, tu es gentil, tu me poses des questions, tu t'intéresses à ma famille... Mais, tu as peut-être autre chose à faire? Ton reportage, par exemple?

Match each of Camille's phrases to the most appropriate interpretation.

1. ...tu me poses des questions...
2. ...tu t'intéresses à ma famille...
3. ...tu as peut-être autre chose à faire...

a. ...tu dois (*must*) faire ton travail...
b. ...tu trouves ma grand-mère et mon grand-père intéressants...
c. ...tu es indiscret...

Observez!

Two photographs are important to the story in Episode 6. As you watch, see if you can answer the following questions.

- Where does Rachid find a picture of Camille's grandmother?
- What is unusual about the picture?
- What other photograph is important?

Après le visionnement

A. Vous avez compris? (*Did you understand?*) Summarize the episode by completing the paragraph with the correct word from the parentheses.

Au début de l'épisode, Camille est au _____[1] (plateau, maquillage) et Bruno devient _____[2] (triste, impatient). Aujourd'hui, le sujet de l'émission «Bonjour!» est _____[3] (la mode, la cuisine). Rachid trouve _____[4] (une photo, une carte) dans le livre sur les Cévennes. Selon[a] Camille, c'est une photo de Louise, le jour de _____[5] (ses fiançailles,[b] son mariage). La photo n'est pas entière. Elle est _____[6] (coupée, floue[c]). À la fin de l'épisode, Camille utilise _____[7] (un ordinateur, un rétroprojecteur) pour agrandir[d] une autre photo de sa grand-mère. Elle trouve son _____[8] (père, grand-père) sur cette photo.

[a]*According to* [b]*engagement* [c]*blurry* [d]*enlarge*

B. Réfléchissez. (*Think.*) Choose what you think might be the most likely answer to each question. Explain your choice (in French).

1. Pourquoi Rachid pose-t-il beaucoup de (*many*) questions?
   - **a.** Il aime bavarder (*to gossip*).
   - **b.** Il s'intéresse à la famille de Camille et désire aider Camille.
   - **c.** Il aime les mystères comme la photo coupée.
2. Qu'est-ce qui explique (*What explains*) la réponse de Camille quand Rachid pose des questions sur la photo?
   - **a.** Camille désire parler de sa famille, mais l'histoire est trop (*too*) longue.
   - **b.** Rachid pose des questions troublantes pour Camille.
   - **c.** Camille s'impatiente parce que Rachid néglige (*is neglecting*) son travail.

C. Imaginez. In your opinion, what link might there be between the book on the Cévennes and the picture that Rachid finds in it? Use the expressions in two or three columns to form possible answers.

MODÈLE: Louise s'est mariée dans les Cévennes, peut-être.

Camille	aime voyager	dans les Cévennes
le grand-père de Camille	est mort(e) (*died*)	de noces (*wedding*)
le livre	est né(e) (*was born*)	des Cévennes
Louise	est un cadeau (*gift*)	du mari de Louise
Mado	est un ensemble de photos	
	habite	
	s'est mariée (*got married*)	
	vient	

Pour en savoir plus...

Learn to recognize the following adverbs.▲ They occur frequently in *Le Chemin du retour* and in your textbook.

TIME: aujourd'hui, demain (*tomorrow*), plus tard (*later*)

FREQUENCY: encore (*again; still*), parfois, rarement, souvent, toujours

MANNER: bien, franchement (*frankly*), peut-être (*perhaps*), très, vachement (*very*), vite (*quickly, fast*)

PLACE: ici, là

Structure 18

Les verbes *pouvoir* et *vouloir*

Expressing ability and what you want

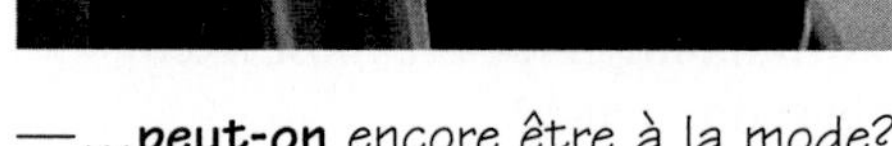

—...**peut-on** encore être à la mode?

—Non, papa, **je ne veux pas**. On repart à la maison!

Bruno uses the verb **pouvoir** to ask whether people *are able* to be stylish anymore. Yasmine uses the verb **vouloir** to tell her father she doesn't *want* to look at the teacher and children at school.

Le verbe *pouvoir*

pouvoir (*to be able, can; to be allowed*)			
je	**peux**	nous	**pouvons**
tu	**peux**	vous	**pouvez**
il, elle, on	**peut**	ils, elles	**peuvent**

Je **peux** t'emprunter le livre sur les Cévennes? — *May I borrow your book about the Cévennes?*

Est-ce que vous **pouvez** venir chez moi ce soir? — *Can you come to my house tonight?*

Pouvoir is usually followed by an infinitive.

Où **peut-on acheter** au meilleur marché? — *Where can we buy (clothing) at bargain prices?*

Le verbe *vouloir*

vouloir (*to want*)			
je	**veux**	nous	**voulons**
tu	**veux**	vous	**voulez**
il, elle, on	**veut**	ils, elles	**veulent**

Vous voulez autre chose? | *Do you want anything else?*

1. **Vouloir** can be followed by a noun or by an infinitive.

   Je veux **un hamburger**. — *I want a hamburger.*
   Voulez-vous **venir**? — *Do you want to come?*

2. When making a request, it is more polite to use the expression **je voudrais**.

   Je voudrais le jarret de porc aux lentilles, s'il vous plaît. — *I would like the ham hocks with lentils, please.*

3. Two useful expressions are **vouloir dire** (*to mean*) and **vouloir bien** (*to be glad/willing* [*to do something*]).

   Que **voulez-vous dire**? — *What do you mean?*
   Camille **veut bien** prêter son livre à Rachid. — *Camille is glad to lend her book to Rachid.*

Vous voulez
louer une voiture.
Nous aussi.

La location de voitures, c'est simple comme : "Bonjour, je voudrais louer une voiture." Alors, nous avons mis tout en œuvre pour vous simplifier la location. Nombreux forfaits, tous types de voitures. Nous sommes présents dans plus de 75 pays à travers le monde (dont 40 pays européens) et nous avons plus de 250 points de vente en France.

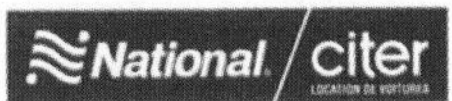
National / citer

Nous ne sommes pas là pour vous compliquer la vie

Activités

A. Mini-dialogues. Complete the following mini-dialogues by replacing the blanks with the correct form of either **pouvoir** or **vouloir**.

HÔTESSE: Vous _____[1] une coupe de champagne?
INVITÉ 1: Oui. Je _____[2] bien!
INVITÉ 2: Désolé, je ne _____[3] pas. Ma famille m'attend (*is waiting for me*).

TOURISTES: Pardon, monsieur. Nous _____[4] acheter une robe française pour notre fille. Où est-ce qu'on _____[5] faire de bonnes affaires (*find bargains*) dans cette ville?
HABITANT: Ce n'est pas difficile. Les acheteurs malins (*clever shoppers*) _____[6] faire des affaires partout. Vous _____[7] commencer par demander à une vendeuse dans la petite boutique au coin (*on the corner*).

B. Situations. Complete the sentence for each situation by choosing from the phrases provided. Be sure to use the correct form of the verb.

Vocabulaire utile:

ne pas vouloir faire la vaisselle
ne plus pouvoir regarder la télévision
ne pas pouvoir écouter tes CD
pouvoir aller en Guadeloupe
pouvoir entrer
pouvoir parler français
pouvoir travailler pour Microsoft
vouloir bien
vouloir dîner avec moi
vouloir dire qu'il est bizarre
vouloir étudier à la bibliothèque
vouloir trouver mes chaussures
vouloir un sandwich
vouloir une robe bleue

MODÈLE: Deux enfants regardent trop de (*too much*) télévision. Leur mère dit (*says*): «Vous... » →
Vous ne pouvez plus regarder la télévision.

1. Une étudiante veut entrer dans la salle de classe. Un(e) camarade dit: «Oui, tu... »
2. La vaisselle est dans l'évier (*sink*). Les enfants disent (*say*): «Nous... »
3. Un homme invite une femme au restaurant. Il dit: «Est-ce que vous... »
4. Un étudiant a besoin d'étudier. Il...
5. Une jeune fille (*girl*) cherche ses chaussures. Elle dit: «Je... »
6. Trois femmes aiment l'informatique (*computer science*). Elles...
7. Une femme est dans un grand magasin au rayon mode femme. Elle...
8. Vous demandez à votre camarade de vous prêter (*lend*) son pull. Il dit: «Oui, d'accord, je... »
9. Un étudiant dit (*says*) que son professeur est excentrique. Son ami demande: «Tu... ?»
10. M. Untel menace (*threatens*) son fils: «Si tu ne fais pas tes devoirs, tu... »
11. Deux jeunes hommes ont très faim. Ils...
12. Un couple veut aller en vacances (*vacation*). Le mari suggère: «Nous... »

C. Journal universitaire. (*University newspaper.*) You are writing an article on student life for your school newspaper. Interview three classmates to find out about the coming week. Ask them one thing they want to do, one thing they don't want to do, one thing they can do, and one thing they cannot do. Follow the model.

MODÈLE: É1: Qu'est-ce que tu veux faire cette semaine?
É2: Je veux dîner dans un bon restaurant.
É1: Qu'est-ce que tu ne veux pas faire cette semaine?
É2: Je ne veux pas aller au supermarché.
É1: Qu'est-ce que tu peux faire cette semaine?
É2: Je peux étudier avec mes amis.
É1: Qu'est-ce que tu ne peux pas faire cette semaine?
É2: Je ne peux pas aller au cinéma.

Now summarize your findings for the class.

MODÈLE: Mark et Katie veulent aller au cinéma, mais Ann ne veut pas. Elle veut...

Les verbes avec changement d'orthographe°

changement... *spelling changes*

Talking about everyday activities

—...où peut-on **acheter** au meilleur marché?

Some **-er** verbs are called "spelling-change" (or stem-change) verbs because the stem from the infinitive changes its spelling slightly in certain persons of the conjugation.

Verbes comme *commencer* et *manger*

Verbs that end in **-cer** and **-ger** have a spelling change in the stem of the **nous** form.

commencer (*to begin*)	
je	commence
tu	commences
il, elle, on	commence
nous	commençons
vous	commencez
ils, elles	commencent

manger (*to eat*)	
je	mange
tu	manges
il, elle, on	mange
nous	mangeons
vous	mangez
ils, elles	mangent

Another verb like **commencer** is **lancer** (*to launch*).
Other verbs like **manger** are **changer** (*to change*), **encourager** (*to encourage*), **partager** (*to share*), and **voyager** (*to travel*).

L'émission **commence** dans trois minutes! — *The show starts in three minutes!*

Nous **voyageons** souvent en Europe. — *We often travel to Europe.*

Verbes comme *préférer*

Verbs like **préférer** change the **é** before the final consonant of the infinitive stem to **è** for all singular forms and for **ils/elles**.

préférer (*to prefer*)			
je	préfère	nous	préférons
tu	préfères	vous	préférez
il, elle, on	préfère	ils, elles	préfèrent

Other verbs like **préférer** are **espérer** (*to hope*) and **répéter** (*to repeat*).

J'espère reconnaître le bon pain. — *I hope to recognize the good bread.*

Est-ce que **vous préférez** la personnalité de Camille ou de Bruno? — *Do you prefer the personality of Camille or of Bruno?*

Verbes comme *payer*

Verbs like **payer** change **y** to **i** at the end of the infinitive stem for all singular forms and for **ils/elles**.

payer (*to pay*)			
je	paie	nous	payons
tu	paies	vous	payez
il, elle, on	paie	ils, elles	paient

Other verbs like **payer** are **employer** (*to use; to employ*), **envoyer** (*to send*), and **essayer** (*to try; to try on*).

Rachid **envoie** Yasmine vers le groupe d'enfants. — *Rachid sends Yasmine toward the group of children.*

Essayer is followed by **de** when used with an infinitive.

Rachid **essaie** toujours **de** rassurer Yasmine. — *Rachid always tries to reassure Yasmine.*

Verbes comme *appeler*

Verbs like **appeler** double the final consonant of the stem for all singular forms and for **ils/elles**.

appeler (*to call*)			
j'	appelle	nous	appelons
tu	appelles	vous	appelez
il, elle, on	appelle	ils, elles	appellent

Sonia **appelle** Rachid à Canal 7. — *Sonia calls Rachid at Channel 7.*

Verbes comme *acheter*

Verbs like **acheter** change the **e** before the final consonant of the infinitive stem to **è** for all singular forms and for **ils/elles**.

acheter (*to buy*)			
j'	achète	nous	achetons
tu	achètes	vous	achetez
il, elle, on	achète	ils, elles	achètent

Est-ce que Camille **achète** une robe? *Is Camille buying a dress?*

Activités

A. La vie de couple. (*Married life.*) A newlywed couple is talking about their married life. Complete each sentence with the correct form of the appropriate verb in parentheses.

1. Nous _____ tout le travail à la maison. (partager, acheter)
2. Tu _____ faire la cuisine, et je _____ faire la vaisselle. (préférer, encourager)
3. Je _____ mon nouveau travail bientôt. (appeler, commencer)
4. Tu _____ mon indépendance. (voyager, encourager)
5. Tu _____ tes parents tous les samedis. (essayer, appeler)
6. J' _____ trop de (*too many*) chaussures. (acheter, espérer)
7. Nous _____ aussi trop de disques compacts. (payer, acheter)
8. Nous _____ changer nos mauvais traits de caractère. (essayer de, employer)
9. Mais en réalité, nous ne _____ jamais. (changer, employer)
10. Nous _____ pendant (*during*) les vacances. (voyager, répéter)
11. Tu _____ toujours les achats en espèces (partager, payer), mais moi, je _____ par carte bancaire. (payer, espérer)
12. Nos parents _____ parfois de petits cadeaux. (préférer, envoyer)
13. Tu ne _____ pas mes secrets à nos amis. (répéter, lancer)
14. Nous _____ passer le week-end ensemble. (espérer, payer)
15. Nous _____ à apprécier nos différences. (envoyer, commencer)

B. Le shopping. Find out about the clothing purchases and preferred styles of your partner and be prepared to report to the class. Use the **vocabulaire utile** or other verbs you know.

Vocabulaire utile: acheter, employer, espérer, essayer, partager, payer, préférer

Ask your partner

1. where he/she buys clothes and why
2. if he/she usually tries things on before buying (**avant d'acheter**)
3. what kinds of clothing he/she rarely buys
4. which colors he/she prefers
5. whether he/she uses a credit card, a check, or cash when buying things
6. whether he/she and his/her friends share their clothing from time to time
7. whether he/she hopes to be chic

Regards sur la culture

Les habits et la mode°

Les... *Clothing and fashion*

In this chapter, Bruno and Camille present a segment of "Bonjour!" devoted to fashion. The significance of clothing in French culture is very great and has been so for centuries. Clothing expresses a person's wealth and status, of course, and it may also serve as an indication of age group and ethnic origin. In addition, however, clothing expresses attitudes, including, in France, a concern for elegance and "good taste."

La mode «américaine» chez les enfants

- As a general rule, appearance is more overtly valued in France than in North America. In fact, most French children are taught that how they appear to other people (in clothing, in actions, in language) is extremely important.
- French people tend to comment explicitly on the way others dress. It would not be shocking or unusual for someone in France to say that so-and-so is attractive but badly dressed (**mal habillé[e]**).
- French people pay a lot of attention to how they dress, but may not actually own very large wardrobes. The care with which items of clothing are combined is more important than the variety of items worn.
- French children spend much of their time dressed in what North Americans might think is rather fancy clothing. They are expected not to get dirty when they are playing.
- In North America, French clothing is usually associated with elegance and high style: classic fashion like Chanel or modern styles like those of Jean-Paul Gaultier, for example. In France, however, young people love North American clothing for casual wear. In fact, there are several "imitation" American clothing companies in France. Chevignon, for example, was founded in 1979 and has created a very successful "American" style based on U.S. clothing of the 1950s.

La mode au masculin

Considérez

Someone who is passionately interested in clothing might be considered superficial by certain people in North America. This would not be the case in France. Do Americans or Canadians feel the same way about someone who has a passion for good food or for fancy cars? If not, what do you think is the difference?

Structure 20

Les pronoms interrogatifs

Asking questions

—**Qu'est-ce qu'**il y a, ma puce?

—**Qui** est-ce?

—**De quoi** se mêle-t-il?

There are two kinds of interrogative pronouns▲: those that ask questions about people and those that ask about things.

1. **Qui** (*who, whom*) asks questions about people. It can be the subject or object▲ of a verb or the object of a preposition.

Subject:	**Qui** parle?	*Who is talking?*
Object:	**Qui** est-ce que tu vois?	*Whom do you see?*
Object of a preposition:	À **qui** envoies-tu cette lettre?	*To whom are you sending that letter?*

2. **Que** (*what*) asks questions about things. For now, you will learn its use as the object of a verb. Two patterns are possible: **Que** + verb + subject (inversion) or **Qu'** + **est-ce que** + subject + verb. You already know the **Qu'est-ce que** form.

Object:	**Que** fais-tu? **Qu'est-ce que** tu fais?	*What are you doing?*

When *what* is the object of a preposition, it is expressed with the word **quoi**. It too can be used with inversion or with **est-ce que**.

Object of a preposition:	**De quoi** parlez-vous? **De quoi est-ce que** vous parlez?	*What are you talking about?*

Activités

A. Dans le film. Using an interrogative pronoun (and a preposition if necessary), ask the question that is answered by the word or phrase in parentheses. Follow the model.

MODÈLE: _____ est-ce un grand jour? (pour Yasmine et Rachid) →
Pour qui est-ce un grand jour?

1. _____ est-ce que Yasmine adore? (son père)
2. _____ veut sa maman? (Yasmine)
3. _____ Martine travaille-t-elle en régie? (avec Roger et Nicole)
4. _____ Martine trouve? (le médaillon de Camille)
5. _____ Martine présente-t-elle Camille? (à Rachid)
6. _____ fait le téléphone de Sonia? (Il sonne. [*It is ringing.*])
7. _____ Rachid s'intéresse-t-il? (aux Cévennes)
8. _____ Rachid emprunte (*borrows*) à Camille? (un livre sur les Cévennes)
9. _____ est la photo sur l'ordinateur de Camille? (du grand-père de Camille)

B. Mes amis. Give the question that would prompt the italicized part of each given answer.

MODÈLE: *Mon amie Jennie* aime danser.
Question: Qui aime danser?

1. Je préfère aller au restaurant *avec Thomas.*
2. Richard parle *de ses problèmes* avec ses parents.
3. Maggie cherche souvent *des livres* à la bibliothèque.
4. Mohua et Manoj envoient souvent des e-mails bizarres *à tout le monde.*
5. Je fais *mes devoirs* avec Catherine.

C. Interview. Working in pairs, use the cues to prepare a series of interview questions. Then imagine the answers that a famous person might give, and perform your interview for the class.

Demandez à cette personne...

1. d'identifier qui elle admire
2. en qui elle a confiance
3. ce qu'elle fait pendant son temps libre
4. de quoi elle a peur
5. de quoi elle a besoin pour être heureuse
6. ce qu'elle veut faire dans l'avenir (*the future*)
7. ?

D. Questions personnelles. Interview three classmates, asking the same questions you asked in Activity C. Write down their names and their answers. Then work in small groups to see which answers are the most or least common.

Visionnement 2

Avant de visionner

La culture de la mode. In his introduction to the fashion segment, Bruno says:

> ...Mais, pour beaucoup d'entre nous, la mode reste un rêve. Eh oui, c'est cher, très cher! Alors, aujourd'hui, la question que l'on se pose, c'est: peut-on encore être à la mode? Est-ce que c'est possible? Combien ça coûte? Et surtout, où peut-on acheter au meilleur marché?

Reflect on what you have read in **Regards sur la culture**. What cultural assumptions about the importance of appearance does Bruno express?

Observez!

Consider the cultural information explained in **Regards sur la culture**. Then watch Episode 6 again, and answer the following questions.

- What compliment does Bruno give to Camille?
- What is her response? How might an American respond to this compliment?

Après le visionnement

Do the activity for **Visionnement 2** in the *Workbook/Laboratory Manual.*

Synthèse: Lecture

Mise en contexte

For more than two centuries, Paris has been considered the world center for high fashion. This tradition began during the Second Empire,* when the Englishman Charles Frédéric Worth, official purveyor to the Empress Eugénie, introduced the hallmarks of **haute couture**: the identification of a designer with a brand; the annual fashion show with live models exhibiting exclusive styles that are sold at high prices; and the use of advertising.

*The reign of Napoleon III, 1852–1870.

Stratégie pour mieux lire
Using visuals to facilitate comprehension

Before reading a text, examining the accompanying photos, can facilitate your comprehension of the passage and allow you to anticipate content or predict meaning.

You are going to read a brief history of French fashion from World War I to the present adapted from the Encyclopédie Microsoft® Encarta® en ligne. Look at the photos and see if you can determine what period is being described in each quotation from the text. Your choices are

- les années folles (*the twenties*)
- l'avant-guerre (*the period before 1939, the outbreak of World War II*)
- pendant la guerre (*during World War II*)
- l'après-guerre (*after 1945*)
- l'époque contemporaine

1. [Cette époque voit] l'apparition de la robe cocktail, des talons aiguilles et la quasi-disparition du chapeau.
2. Les cheveux restent courts, mais ondulés.
3. [Cette génération] cherche dans le vêtement un moyen (*means*) d'affirmer ses choix et le désir de faire disparaître (*erase*) les différenciations sexuelles en adoptant la mode unisexe.
4. L'inspiration militaire confère aux modèles une allure martiale, accentuée par l'introduction de renforts dans les épaules (les « paddings »).
5. Les grands créateurs de l'époque... imposent une silhouette « à la garçonne ».

Quelques grandes tendances de la mode française

Les années folles: L'émancipation de la femme

La Première Guerre mondiale[1] a une influence considérable sur l'évolution de la mode: l'absence des hommes modifie la place des femmes dans la société. Les grands créateurs de l'époque—Jean Patou, Jeanne Lanvin, Henri Poirier—imposent une silhouette « à la garçonne ». Portant cheveux courts,[2] arborant[3] de longs fume-cigarettes, les femmes manifestent une volonté de libération par rapport aux années de l'avant-guerre. La pratique des sports impose la création de tenues[4] spéciales pour le tennis, le golf, le casino ou la montagne, comme celles[5] de Coco Chanel.

Les courants de l'avant-guerre

La crise économique de 1929, les inquiétudes internationales et les

Note: The dresses pictured in the photos were designed by Chanel.

[1]*La... The First World War* [2]*Portant... Wearing their hair short* [3]*sporting* [4]*outfits* [5]*those*

bouleversements[6] sociaux ont une profonde influence sur la mode. Dès la fin[7] des années vingt, la mode devient plus féminine. Les cheveux restent courts, mais ondulés.[8] En 1933, Hermès lance la mode des foulards (ou carrés) en soie imprimée.[9] Cette époque est dominée par Chanel, célèbre pour ses robes du soir en mousseline de soie.[10]

La mode pendant la guerre

La période de la Seconde Guerre mondiale, marquée par d'importantes restrictions de tissu, voit[11] aussi la fermeture d'un certain nombre de grandes maisons parisiennes, comme Chanel. L'inspiration militaire confère aux modèles une allure martiale, accentuée par l'introduction de renforts dans les épaules (les « paddings »). Les jupes très courtes coexistent avec de gigantesques chapeaux ou des turbans.

La mode de l'après-guerre: une nouvelle ligne

Contrastant avec cette extravagance, la mode de l'après-guerre se caractérise par un souci[12] du bon goût et de l'équilibre, qui permet rapidement à Paris de retrouver son statut de capitale de la mode. Période de transformations, les années cinquante voient[13]

l'apparition[14] de la robe cocktail, des talons aiguilles[15] et la quasi-disparition[16] du chapeau. Les années soixante voient aussi l'apparition, après Pierre Cardin, d'un certain nombre de nouveaux couturiers, dont[17] André Courrèges et Yves Saint Laurent, qui travaille d'abord chez Dior avant de[18] fonder sa propre maison. Saint Laurent, Cardin et Courrèges se lancent[19] significativement les premiers dans le prêt-à-porter féminin.

L'époque contemporaine: une mode pour la jeunesse

La jeunesse issue[20] du baby-boom cherche dans le vêtement le désir de faire disparaître[21] les différenciations sexuelles en adoptant la mode unisexe.

Les grandes tendances, de plus en plus[22] évidentes depuis les années soixante-dix, sont le style décontracté,[23] le style grunge, l'antimode et l'extrême simplicité des tenues urbaines (tailleur basique, tee-shirt et pantalon, souvent même dans le monde du travail).

Note: The outfits pictured here (from left to right) were designed by Chanel, Christian Dior, Guy Laroche, and Christian Dior.

[6]*upheavals, disruptions* [7]Dès... *From the end* [8]*wavy* [9]*printed* [10]mousseline... *chiffon* [11]*sees* [12]*concern* [13]*see* [14]*appearance* [15]talons... *stiletto heels* [16]*near disappearance* [17]*including* [18]avant... *before* [19]se... *launch* [20]*coming from* [21]faire... *erase, eliminate* [22]de... *more and more* [23]*casual*

Après la lecture

A. Les vêtements. Identify which period each of these articles of clothing belongs to.

1. les turbans
2. le tee-shirt et pantalon
3. la robe cocktail
4. les robes du soir en mousseline de soie
5. les jupes très courtes
6. les foulards

B. Quel facteur? Which historical or cultural factors influenced the development of the following fashion trends?

Tendance

1. l'allure martiale
2. la mode unisexe
3. le style décontracté
4. une remise en valeur de la forme du corps
5. une silhouette « à la garçonne »

Facteur

a. le désir de se démarquer (*dissociate themselves*) du monde des adultes
b. la Seconde Guerre mondiale
c. l'émancipation de la femme
d. réaction à la mode androgyne
e. le désir de faire disparaître les différenciations sexuelles

C. Et vous? Quel look est-ce que vous préférez—**BCBG** (*preppy*), **grunge**, **unisexe**, **goth**, **hip-hop**, **décontracté**, **élégant**? Expliquez quels vêtements vous portez pour réaliser (*achieve*) ce look. Comment est-ce que votre look varie selon l'occasion?

À écrire

Do **À écrire** for Chapter 6 in the *Workbook/Laboratory Manual.*

Vocabulaire

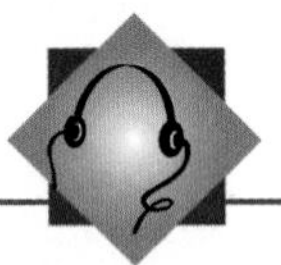

Les vêtements

une botte	boot	**un chemisier**	blouse
une ceinture	belt	**un costume**	(man's) suit
un chapeau	hat	**une cravate**	tie
une chaussette	sock	**une écharpe**	scarf
une chaussure	shoe	**un foulard**	lightweight scarf
une chemise	shirt	**une jupe**	skirt

des lunettes (*f. pl.*) **de soleil**	sunglasses	**un tailleur**	(woman's) suit
un maillot de bain	bathing suit	**une veste**	sports coat, jacket
un manteau	overcoat	**un vêtement**	(article of) clothing
un pantalon	pants, trousers		
une robe	dress		

MOTS APPARENTÉS: **un jean, un pull-over** (*fam.* **un pull**), **un short, un sweatshirt** (*fam.* **un sweat**), **un tee-shirt**

Dans un grand magasin

l'argent (*m.*)	money	**un rayon**	department (*in a store*)
la caisse	checkout	**un(e) vendeur/euse**	salesclerk
une carte bancaire	bank (*debit*) card		
en espèces (*f. pl.*)	in cash		
un (grand) magasin	(department) store		

MOTS APPARENTÉS: **une carte de crédit, un chèque, un(e) client(e)**

Les couleurs

blanc(he)	white	**noir(e)**	black
brun(e)	brown	**rose**	pink
gris(e)	gray	**rouge**	red
jaune	yellow	**vert(e)**	green
marron	chestnut brown		

MOTS APPARENTÉS: **bleu(e), orange, violet(te)**

Verbes

acheter	to buy	**partager**	to share
appeler	to call	**pouvoir**	to be able, can; to be allowed
employer	to use; to employ	**vouloir**	to want
envoyer	to send	**vouloir bien**	to be glad, willing (*to do something*)
espérer	to hope	**vouloir dire**	to mean
essayer	to try; to try on		
lancer	to launch		
manger	to eat		
oublier	to forget		

MOTS APPARENTÉS: **changer, commencer, encourager, payer, préférer, répéter, voyager**

Pronoms interrogatifs

que	what	**qui**	who; whom
qu'est-ce que	what	**quoi**	what

Autres expressions utiles

je voudrais	I would like	**par**	by; per

Chapitre 7

Préparatifs°

°Preparations

Le Chemin du retour

Feuille de service du 16 octobre
6e jour de tournage
Horaires: 9h–19h

LIEU DE TOURNAGE: PARIS—QUARTIER MOUFFETARD

Séquence	*Effets*	*Décors*	*Résumé*	*Rôles*
35	EXT.—JOUR	MARCHÉ, RUE MOUFFETARD	Divers plans dans le marché (3 plans)	CAMILLE

OBJECTIFS

In this episode, you will

- watch Camille as she shops for food in an outdoor market
- learn more about Camille's family

In this chapter, you will

- learn the names of food merchants, their stores, and their merchandise
- learn how to express quantities
- learn to avoid repetition by using indirect object pronouns
- talk about everyday actions
- learn about how French people buy and prepare food
- read about common foods in France and other French-speaking countries

Vocabulaire en contexte

Au marché Mouffetard°

Au… *At the Mouffetard market*

Camille fait des courses au **marché** Mouffetard.
Elle va **chez le boucher** pour acheter un kilo de **bœuf** (*m.*).
Elle va **chez la marchande** de légumes pour acheter des **carottes** (*f.*), des **oignons** (*m.*) et des **pommes* de terre** (*f.*).
Elle va **chez le marchand** de fruits pour acheter des **pommes** (*f.*), des **cerises** (*f.*), des **citrons** (*m.*) et du† **raisin**.
Elle va chez le marchand de vin pour acheter du **vin rouge** (un Côtes-du-Rhône) et du **champagne**.

Autres mots utiles

un aliment	food
les haricots‡ (*m.*) **verts**	green beans
le maïs	corn
les petits pois (*m.*)	peas
une tomate	tomato
le vin (rouge, blanc, rosé)	(red, white, rosé) wine

*Compound nouns (nouns made from more than one word) often form their plurals by adding **s** to the main noun in the compound. You can tell which is the main noun because it usually comes first and because the rest of the compound describes it in some way: ***pomme(s)* de terre**, ***sac(s)* à dos**.
†Nouns preceded by **du** are masculine; those preceded by **de la** are feminine. The genders of plural nouns are shown in parentheses.
‡There are two kinds of **h** in French. The **h muet** (*mute h*) is not pronounced and allows liaison and elision before it: **l'histoire, les/z/histoires**. The **h aspiré** (*aspirate h*) is not pronounced either, but liaison and elision are not used before it: **le haricot**, **les haricots**.

Pour en savoir plus…

Although more and more French people now shop in supermarkets, which have become quite common, many also continue to shop at outdoor markets, particularly for fresh fruit and vegetables. By talking to the merchants, they can learn more about the quality of a product, its origin, and how to prepare it. Many larger towns also have enclosed markets (**les halles**), where individual vendors set up their merchandise.

Pour en savoir plus…

The French use the metric system for weights. Here are some equivalencies that might be useful if you're buying food in France.

un kilo (1000 grammes)
= about $2\frac{1}{4}$ pounds

un demi-kilo
(500 grammes)
= about 1 pound

250 grammes
= about $\frac{1}{2}$ pound

Activités

A. Vrai ou faux. Dites si les phrases suivantes sont vraies (**C'est vrai.**) ou fausses (**C'est faux.**). Corrigez les phrases fausses. (*Say whether the following sentences are true or false. Correct the false sentences.*)

MODÈLE: Les cerises sont vertes. →
C'est faux. Les cerises sont rouges. (Les petits pois sont verts.)

1. On peut acheter de la viande au marché en plein air (*open air*).
2. On va chez le boucher pour acheter des cerises.
3. Une pomme est un fruit acide (*sour*).
4. Une pomme de terre est un fruit sucré (*sweet*).
5. On trouve souvent des tomates et des carottes dans une salade.
6. Pour acheter du champagne, on peut aller chez la marchande de légumes.
7. On emploie des petits pois pour faire du vin.
8. Le maïs est populaire dans les repas (*meals*) américains.

B. Descriptions. Identifiez...

MODÈLE: un légume orange → Une carotte est un légume orange.

1. un fruit sucré
2. un fruit jaune
3. un vin pétillant (*sparkling*)
4. un légume vert
5. un légume qui a une odeur forte
6. un légume jaune

C. Interview. Demandez (*Ask*) à votre partenaire...

1. s'il / si elle est végétarien(ne) ou s'il / si elle mange de la viande
2. combien de fois par jour il/elle mange des fruits
3. quel légume et quel fruit il/elle préfère
4. s'il / si elle aime les haricots verts ou les brocolis
5. s'il / si elle préfère les fruits ou le chocolat

Les environs de la rue Mouffetard

Il y a des magasins dans les environs de la rue Mouffetard. **Chaque**° magasin a sa spécialité. On va à **la boulangerie**° pour acheter du **pain** et des croissants, mais on va à **la pâtisserie**° pour des **pâtisseries** (*f.*) et des **tartes** (*f.*), par exemple.

Each / (bread) bakery
pastry shop

À **la boucherie**,° on peut acheter du bœuf et du **poulet**.° À **la charcuterie**, on achète du **jambon**,° du **porc**, des **saucisses**° (*f.*) et du pâté. On va à **la poissonnerie**° pour acheter du **poisson** et des **fruits de mer**:° du **saumon**, de la sole et des **crevettes**° (*f.*).

butcher shop / chicken
ham / sausages
fish store
fruits... seafood / shrimp

On va à **la crémerie**° pour acheter de **la crème**, du **beurre**° et du **fromage**:° du camembert, du brie et du chèvre, par exemple. À **l'épicerie** (*f.*), on achète du **sucre**,° de **l'eau**° (*f.*) **minérale gazeuse** et **plate**, de **la confiture**,° des boîtes de **thon**° (*m.*), etc.

dairy shop / butter
cheese
sugar / water
jam
tuna

Notez bien!

To say you are at or going to one of these shops, you may use **à** before the name of a shop (**je vais à la boucherie**) or **chez** before the title of the shopkeeper (**je vais chez le boucher**).

Autres mots utiles

un(e) boucher/ère	butcher
un(e) boulanger/ère	(bread) baker
un(e) charcutier/ière	(pork) butcher
un(e) crémier/ière	dairyman/woman
un(e) épicier/ière	grocer
un(e) pâtissier/ière	(pastry) baker
un(e) poissonnier/ière	fishmonger

Langage fonctionnel

Pour faire des achats°

Pour... *Making purchases*

Here are some expressions that are frequently used in making purchases.

Pour saluer le client / la cliente

Qu'est-ce que je vous sers, monsieur/madame/mademoiselle?	*What can I get you, sir/madam/miss?*
Vous désirez?	*What would you like?*

Pour demander un service

Je voudrais regarder... / acheter... / essayer..., s'il vous plaît.	*I would like to see . . . / buy . . . / try on (a piece of clothing), please.*

Pour parler du prix et pour payer

Combien est-ce que ça coûte?	*How much does it cost?*
C'est cher / raisonnable / bon marché / en solde.	*It's expensive / reasonable / inexpensive / on sale.*
Vous payez comment?	*How will you pay?*

Derniers° mots | | *Last*

Merci.	*Thank you.*
Bonne journée.	*Have a nice day.*

—Bonjour, madame. **Vous désirez**?
—**Je voudrais acheter** un kilo de bœuf, s'il vous plaît.
—Bien sûr, madame.
—**Combien est-ce que ça coûte**?
—15,09 euros, madame. **Vous payez comment**?
—Par chèque, s'il vous plaît.
—Très bien. Voilà. **Bonne journée**, madame.

Activités

A. Catégories. Indiquez à quelle catégorie correspond chacun (*each one*) des articles mentionnés.

1. la crème
2. l'eau
3. le fromage
4. le jambon
5. une pâtisserie
6. un poisson
7. le porc
8. le saumon
9. le sucre
10. le thon

a. des aliments sucrés
b. des produits laitiers (*dairy products*)
c. des produits de la mer
d. des produits à base de viande de porc
e. une boisson (*drink*) pure

B. Où va-t-on? Voici une liste de provisions. Dites où on va pour les acheter (*to buy them*).

MODÈLE: du jambon →
Pour acheter du jambon, on va à la charcuterie.

1. une tarte aux pommes
2. de la confiture
3. du pain
4. du poulet
5. des saucisses
6. des crevettes
7. du beurre

Maintenant, répétez l'activité, et utilisez les noms des marchands.

MODÈLE: du jambon →
Pour acheter du jambon, on va chez le charcutier.

C. Jeu de rôle. (*Role play.*) Vous passez l'année à Paris et vous décidez de préparer un repas typiquement américain pour votre famille d'accueil (*host family*). Vous passez au marché Mouffetard pour acheter les ingrédients. Demandez aux marchands si les ingrédients sont disponibles (*available*). Jouez la scène avec deux ou trois camarades de classe en utilisant les expressions de la note **Pour faire des achats**.

Visionnement 1

Avant de visionner

La réponse logique. Choisissez la phrase qui suit (*follows*) logiquement l'expression donnée.

1. LOUISE: Alex. Tu m'achètes du champagne? Une bonne bouteille,[a] s'il te plaît!

   ALEX: ______

   a. Oui, d'accord, mais chez moi!
   b. Tu fais la fête ce soir?
   c. Vous en prenez[b] un kilo?

2. MARCHANDE DE LÉGUMES: Qu'est-ce que je vous sers, mademoiselle?

   CAMILLE: ______

   a. Euh, des carottes, s'il vous plaît.
   b. Non, juste deux ou trois...
   c. Est-ce que vous pouvez me le couper en petits morceaux?[c]

[a]*bottle* [b]*take* [c]*Est-ce... Can you cut it into little pieces for me?*

Vocabulaire relatif à l'épisode

ensemble	*together*
Vous en prenez un kilo?	*Will you take a kilo (of them)?*
Je vais prendre...	*I'll take . . .*
du premier choix	*top quality*
Tu as l'air en forme.	*You seem to be doing well.*
Tu refermes... ?	*Will you close . . . ?*

Observez!

Dans l'Épisode 7, Camille va dîner avec quelqu'un (*someone*). Regardez l'épisode et essayez de trouver les réponses aux questions suivantes (*following*).

- Où va Camille et qu'est-ce qu'elle achète?
- Quel est l'état physique de la femme à qui Camille rend visite (*whom Camille visits*)?

Après le visionnement

Notez bien!

To talk about doing something with someone else, you can often use the word **ensemble** (*together*). Camille uses it to invite her grandmother to have dinner with her.

On dîne **ensemble** ce soir?
Shall we have dinner together tonight?

A. Identifiez. Qui dit (*says*) les phrases suivantes? Est-ce Camille, Louise (la grand-mère), Alex, le boucher ou la marchande de légumes?

MODÈLE: On dîne ensemble ce soir? →
C'est Camille.

1. Oui, d'accord, mais chez moi!
2. Je fais la cuisine!
3. Tu m'achètes du champagne? Une bonne bouteille, s'il te plaît!
4. D'accord, mais vous signez un autographe!
5. Qu'est-ce que je vous sers, mademoiselle?
6. Tu vas bien? Tu as l'air en forme!

Maintenant, racontez (*tell the story of*) l'Épisode 7. Commencez avec les phrases suivantes.

Camille invite sa grand-mère à dîner. La grand-mère invite Camille chez elle, et Camille propose de faire la cuisine...

B. Réfléchissez. (*Think.*) Répondez.

1. Faites une liste des produits que Camille achète. Qu'est-ce qu'elle prépare, probablement—une quiche lorraine? un poulet rôti (*roasted*)? un bœuf bourguignon? des crêpes?
2. Pourquoi est-ce que Camille invite Louise à dîner? Est-ce qu'il y a une raison particulière, à votre avis? Expliquez.

Structure 21

L'article partitif et les expressions de quantité

Talking about quantities

—Alex. Tu m'achètes **du champagne**? **Une** bonne **bouteille**, s'il te plaît!

Nouns can be divided into two classes: those you can count using cardinal numbers (*one* apple, *two* croissants, *ten* carrots, etc.) and those that cannot be counted (*some* beef, *too much* wine, *a glass of* water, etc.). Nouns in the second group are sometimes referred to as "mass" nouns.

You have already learned to use definite and indefinite articles with nouns.

le légume	*the vegetable*	**un** légume	*one/a vegetable*
la saucisse	*the sausage*	**une** saucisse	*one/a sausage*
les légumes	*the vegetables*	**des** légumes	*some vegetables*
les saucisses	*the sausages*	**des** saucisses	*some sausages*

The indefinite article **des** expresses an indefinite quantity of count nouns.

L'article partitif

The partitive article▲ indicates an indefinite amount of mass nouns. The forms are **du** and **de la**.

du vin (*m.*)	*(some) wine*
de la viande (*f.*)	*(some) meat*

1. If a noun begins with a vowel sound, **de l'** is used in place of both **du** and **de la**.

de l'argent (*m.*)	*(some) money*
de l'eau (*f.*)	*(some) water*

2. The partitive can be expressed in English as *some* or *any*, but it is often omitted. In French, however, the notion of indefinite quantity must always be expressed.

Avez-vous **de l'**eau?	*Do you have (some, any) water?*

3. In a negative statement, the partitive article becomes **de** (**d'**), unless it follows the verb **être**.

	Nous n'avons pas **de** champagne.	*We don't have any champagne.*
	Je ne veux pas **de** salade.	*I don't want any lettuce.*
but	Ce n'est pas **du** champagne.	*It's not champagne.*
	Ce n'est pas **de la** salade.	*It's not lettuce.*

4. In some contexts, such as when ordering in restaurants, nouns that are usually preceded by a partitive article may be preceded by a number instead.

Un vin et **deux** cafés, s'il vous plaît.	*One wine and two coffees, please.*

5. After verbs of preference (**adorer**, **aimer**, **détester**, **préférer**, etc.), the definite article is used because it expresses a generality about all of something.

Bruno aime **le** porc.	*Bruno likes pork.*
Rachid préfère **les** hamburgers.	*Rachid prefers hamburgers.*

Expressions de quantité

There are two kinds of expressions of quantity.

1. For *unspecified* quantities, the following expressions may be used with both singular and plural nouns.

trop (de)	*too much; too many*
beaucoup (de)	*much; many; a lot of*
assez (de)	*enough*
peu (de)	*little; few*

Bruno mange **beaucoup de** bœuf.	*Bruno eats a lot of beef.*
Camille achète **assez de** viande et de légumes.	*Camille buys enough meat and vegetables.*
Peut-on manger **trop de** crevettes?	*Can one (ever) eat too many shrimp?*

2. To *specify* quantities, expressions of measure such as the following can be used.

une boîte (de)	*a can (of); a box (of)*
une bouteille (de)	*a bottle (of)*
un demi-kilo (de)	*one-half kilogram (of)*
une douzaine (de)	*a dozen*
un kilo (de)	*a kilogram (of)*
une livre (de)*	*a pound (of); a half-kilogram (of)*
un morceau (de)	*a piece (of)*

Alex achète **une bouteille de** champagne à Louise.	*Alex buys a bottle of champagne for Louise.*
... et **une livre de** pommes de terre.	*. . . and a pound of potatoes.*

3. Expressions of quantity always include **de (d')** when they precede a noun.

beaucoup d'amis	*many friends*
un peu d'argent	*a little money*
une bouteille de vin	*a bottle of wine*
une boîte de thon	*a can of tuna*

4. **Peu de** is used to describe both singular and plural nouns. **Un peu de** (*a little*), however, may only be used to quantify singular mass nouns.

Bruno a **peu de** nourriture chez lui.	*Bruno has little food at home.*
Camille achète très **peu de** carottes et juste **un peu de** viande.	*Camille buys very few carrots and only a little meat.*

Pour en savoir plus...

Beaucoup and the other nonspecific expressions of quantity may be used without **de** to modify verbs.

Est-ce que Bruno flirte **trop** avec Camille et Hélène?

Rachid aime **beaucoup** les Cévennes.

*Selon les régions, on utilise les termes **un demi-kilo** ou **une livre** pour désigner un poids (*weight*) de cinq cents grammes. Dans les marchés en plein air, le terme **livre** est plus courant.

Activités

A. Faire les courses en France. Vous faites les courses pour la semaine au supermarché *Super-U.* Choisissez un produit de chaque rayon.

MODÈLE: Au rayon crémerie, j'achète du camembert.

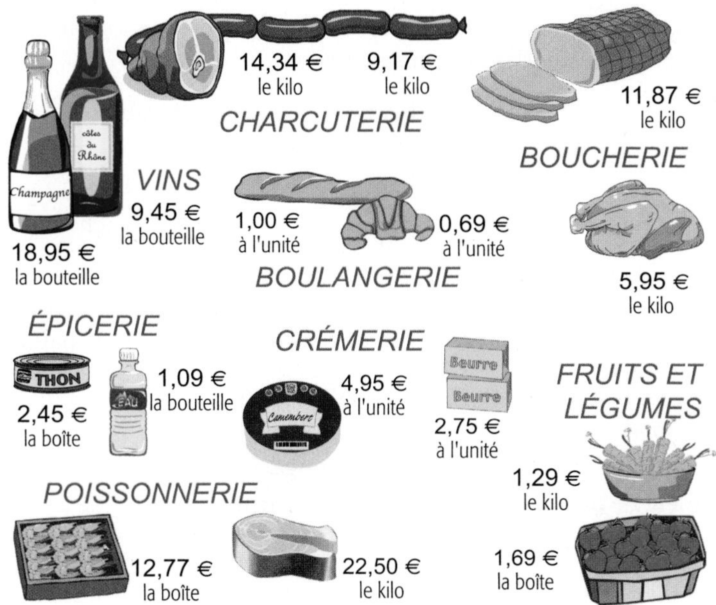

B. Un bon régime. (***A healthy diet.***) Nommez trois choses que ces personnes achètent ou n'achètent pas au marché.

MODÈLE: Un musulman pratiquant (*practicing Muslim*) achète du poulet et des tomates au marché. Il n'achète certainement pas de porc.

1. un végétarien
2. une personne qui n'aime pas le sucre
3. un athlète qui s'entraîne (*is in training*)
4. une personne allergique aux produits laitiers
5. une personne qui a trop de cholestérol

C. Souvenirs du film. (***Memories of the film.***) Mettez l'article indéfini (**un/une/des**), l'article défini (**le/la/les**), l'article partitif (**du/de la/de l'**) ou **de/d'**.

MODÈLE: Bruno prend (*has*) <u>de la</u> salade (*f.*) verte. Rachid ne prend pas <u>de</u> salade verte.

1. Le chef cuisinier propose _____ jarret (*m.*) de porc aux lentilles, mais Rachid veut _____ hamburger et _____ eau.
2. Le père de Rachid ne mange pas _____ porc, mais sa mère adore _____ jambon.
3. Martine va manger _____ pain.
4. Camille aime _____ champagne. Rachid ne veut pas _____ champagne.

5. Louise dit (*says*): «Alex. Tu m'achètes _____ champagne? _____ bonne bouteille, s'il te plaît.»
6. Camille dit: «J'aimerais _____ kilo _____ bœuf, s'il vous plaît.»
7. Camille dit: «Je vais prendre aussi _____ oignons et _____ livre de pommes de terre.»

D. Qu'est-ce qu'ils ont? Utilisez des expressions de quantité et les substantifs (*nouns*) de la liste pour parler des gens suivants.

argent	crevettes	livres	responsabilités
beurre	croissants	oranges	saumon
bœuf	enfants	pain	travail
champagne	légumes	problèmes	vêtements (chic, de sport)

MODÈLE: Une femme qui prépare une fête achète... →
Une femme qui prépare une fête achète un kilo de saumon, une livre de crevettes, un demi-kilo de beurre et beaucoup de pain.

1. Un étudiant qui fait des études de yoga achète...
2. Un journaliste qui parle à la télé a...
3. Un enfant qui n'aime pas la viande mange...
4. Une mère de douze enfants achète... pour le matin.
5. Un père de quinze enfants a...
6. Un jeune homme pauvre a...
7. Une femme riche a...
8. Un professeur a... dans son bureau.
9. Une femme qui prépare une fête achète...

E. Ressemblances. Regardez la liste suivante et notez en quelle quantité vous achetez toutes ces choses chaque mois. Ensuite (*Then*), interviewez des camarades de classe pour trouver quelqu'un (*someone*) qui achète les mêmes quantités que vous. Notez son nom.

Vocabulaire utile: du, de la, de l', un, une, des, de, d', beaucoup de, un peu de, peu de, trop de, une bouteille de, une boîte de, un demi-kilo de

MODÈLE: É1: J'achète peu de pain chaque mois.
É2: Moi aussi, j'achète peu de pain chaque mois. (*ou* Moi, j'achète trois kilos de pain chaque mois.; Moi, j'achète beaucoup de pain chaque mois.)

1. le pain
2. la viande
3. l'eau minérale
4. les pâtisseries
5. les crevettes
6. le vin
7. les petits pois
8. les pommes

Structure 22

Le complément d'objet indirect

Avoiding repetition

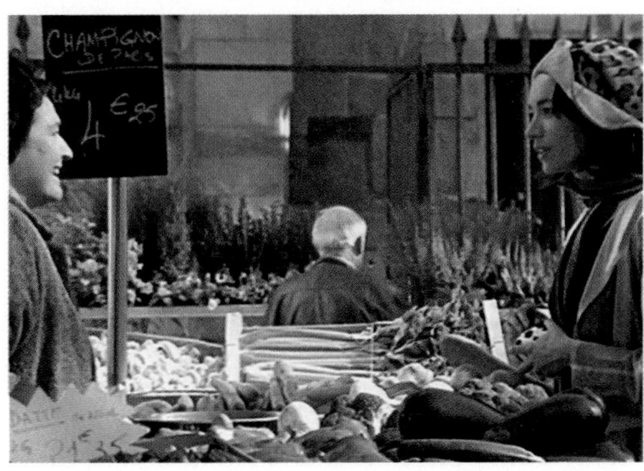

—Qu'est-ce que je **vous** sers, mademoiselle?

Le complément d'objet indirect

There are three broad grammatical functions in a sentence: the subject (the doer of the action); the verb (the action); and the complement (a word or phrase that "completes" what is said about another element of the sentence).

Martine	donne	le médaillon	à Camille.
sujet	**verbe**	**complément**	**complément**

In this sentence, the complement consists of two nouns. The first, **le médaillon**, is the thing that is given. It is called the direct object▲ (**le complément d'objet direct**) because the verb acts directly upon it. The second noun, **Camille**, is the person to whom the locket is given. She is the indirect object▲ (**le complément d'objet indirect**), the person for whom (or to whom) the action was done.

Les pronoms compléments d'objet indirect

Pronouns are words that stand in place of nouns in sentences so that the nouns themselves do not have to be constantly repeated. They make speech and writing flow more smoothly and sound more natural. In this lesson, you will learn the forms and uses of pronouns that serve as the indirect object.

me (m')	*to/for me*	**nous**	*to/for us*
te (t')	*to/for you*	**vous**	*to/for you*
lui	*to/for him/her*	**leur**	*to/for them*

1. Here are some verbs that are frequently used with an indirect object.

acheter (à quelqu'un)	*to buy (for someone)*
demander* (à quelqu'un) (**si**)	*to ask (someone) (if, whether)*
donner (à quelqu'un)	*to give (to someone)*
montrer (à quelqu'un)	*to show (to someone)*
parler (à quelqu'un)	*to speak (to someone)*
téléphoner* (à quelqu'un)	*to call (someone) on the telephone*

Camille téléphone **à Louise**. → Camille **lui** téléphone.
Camille calls her.

Rachid parle **à Bruno et Camille**. → Rachid **leur** parle.
Rachid talks to them.

2. The indirect object pronoun precedes the verb.

Louise dit: «Alex. Tu **m'**achètes du champagne?»
*Louise says, "Alex. Will you buy some champagne **for me**?"*
*Louise says, "Alex. Will you buy **me** some champagne?"*

Martine cherche Camille et **lui** montre le médaillon.
*Martine looks for Camille and shows the locket **to her**.*
*Martine looks for Camille and shows **her** the locket.*

3. Because **lui** and **leur** can refer to both masculine and feminine nouns, the context is important for understanding exact meaning.

Bruno? Je **lui** donne un cadeau. Et Camille... Je **lui** donne un cadeau aussi.	*Bruno? I'm giving **him** a present. And Camille . . . I'm giving **her** a present too.*

4. In the negative, the pronoun still directly precedes the verb.

Tu ne **me** donnes jamais de cadeaux.	*You never give me presents.*

5. In verb + infinitive constructions, the pronoun precedes the infinitive, even in the negative.

Je vais **lui** téléphoner aujourd'hui.	*I'm going to call him/her today.*
Je ne veux pas **lui** parler.	*I don't want to talk to him/her.*

Activités

A. La journée de Camille. Camille parle de sa journée. Complétez les phrases avec les pronoms compléments d'objet indirect qui conviennent (*are appropriate*).

Je vais au travail. Bruno et moi préparons l'émission de jeudi avec deux chefs de cuisine. Nous ____[1] (lui, leur) demandons de préparer un dessert délicieux.

*Les verbes **demander** et **téléphoner** sont accompagnés d'un complément d'objet indirect en français. *Je téléphone **à mes parents** toutes les semaines. Je demande **à mon ami** s'il veut venir avec moi.*

Ils _____[2] (nous, vous) proposent une mousse au chocolat, mais Bruno n'aime pas le chocolat. Les chefs _____[3] (lui, te) demandent ce qu'il préfère (*what he prefers*). Alors, ils vont _____[4] (vous, nous) préparer une tarte aux pommes américaine.

L'après-midi, je pense à ma grand-mère et je _____[5] (te, lui) téléphone. On va dîner ensemble ce soir. Au marché, le boucher _____[6] (me, lui) demande de signer un autographe. La marchande de légumes demande: «Qu'est-ce que je _____[7] (vous, te) sers, mademoiselle?» Quand j'arrive chez grand-mère, je _____[8] (me, nous) prépare un bœuf bourguignon. Après le dîner, je _____[9] (lui, leur) dit: «Je veux _____[10] (vous, te) montrer quelque chose. C'est une surprise.»

B. Questions et réponses. Votre partenaire va poser des questions. Utilisez des pronoms compléments d'objet indirect pour répondre.

MODÈLE: Est-ce que tu parles à tes parents (tes enfants) de tes problèmes? → Non, je ne leur parle jamais de mes problèmes. (Oui, je leur parle parfois de mes problèmes.)

1. Est-ce que tu téléphones souvent à tes amis d'enfance? **2.** Est-ce que tu achètes une vidéo à ton ami? **3.** Est-ce que tu donnes une pomme à ton professeur? **4.** Est-ce que tu nous montres ton livre? **5.** Est-ce que tu téléphones à tes parents (tes enfants) tous les jours? **6.** Est-ce que tu demandes de l'argent à tes amis? **7.** Est-ce que tu me parles?

C. Tu es de la police? Votre partenaire vous pose des questions personnelles en utilisant les éléments suivants. Répondez avec un pronom complément d'objet indirect.

MODÈLE: É1: Quand est-ce que tu achètes des fleurs à une amie?
É2: Je lui achète des fleurs quand elle n'est pas heureuse. (Je ne lui achète jamais de fleurs.)

	acheter des fleurs	des étudiants dans la classe
	acheter une carte	moi
	demander un rendez-vous	nous (les autres étudiants et moi)
	donner les devoirs	tes amis
Pourquoi	montrer des photos de vacances	tes parents
Quand	montrer un examen	toi
	parler	vous (les autres étudiants et toi)
	parler de politique	ton professeur
	parler de religion	un(e) camarade de classe
	téléphoner	une amie

Regards sur la culture

Le marché et la cuisine°

Le... *The market and cooking*

In this chapter, you have seen Camille pick up a few items at an outdoor market as she prepares to make dinner for her grandmother. Food has a very high priority in French culture, and many social relations are maintained around home-cooked meals.

Un marché en plein air

Un supermarché

- One advantage of the traditional market is its appeal to the various senses. The displays are set up to highlight color and aesthetic appeal, and the mix of sounds (vendors calling, boxes being stacked) and smells (flowers, fruit, meat, cheese, fish) contributes to the experience. But for many people, the most important part of shopping at the market is the socializing that goes on.
- Another advantage to the traditional market is that the vendor typically prepares the products to order for the customer, cutting the meat into particular sized pieces, for example, or slicing off just the right amount of cheese.
- In markets and in neighborhood grocery stores, customers do not pick out individual pieces of fruit or vegetables. They tell the vendor what they want, and the vendor picks out the produce. More than one North American has been thought to be shoplifting when picking out an apple from a market display.
- Most French shoppers are very concerned about the quality of the food they buy, and they are often careful to buy pesticide-free products. They may want to know where the vegetables and beef come from or what kind of feed the chicken ate.
- Meals at home play a crucial role in family relationships. In addition, it is almost obligatory to treat guests to a meal consisting of three or more courses. Thus, having a large dining room is relatively important for French families, and one of the first pieces of furniture that many young couples purchase is a large dining table so that they can entertain family and friends appropriately.
- A French meal without some kind of first course is unusual. Even the simplest meal usually begins with the **entrée**—a few slices of salami, a bowl of soup, or a serving of marinated mushrooms—before the main dish (**le plat principal**) arrives. The distinction between **une entrée** and **un hors-d'œuvre** is based mostly on how many courses are served with the meal and whether the dish is served as part of the meal or before it begins.

Considérez

In France, **bien manger** means to eat delicious, refined food. What does *to eat well* mean in North America? Why the difference?

Structure 23

Les verbes *prendre, mettre, boire*

Talking about everyday actions

—...**Vous** en **prenez** un kilo?

—Non, juste deux ou trois...

—D'accord. Et avec ça?

—Euh, je vais **prendre** aussi des oignons et une livre de pommes de terre.

Le verbe *prendre*

prendre (*to take*)			
je	**prends**	nous	**prenons**
tu	**prends**	vous	**prenez**
il, elle, on	**prend**	ils, elles	**prennent**

Vous en **prenez** un kilo? — *Will you take a kilo of them?*

1. **Prendre** is used in several idiomatic expressions: **prendre du temps** (*to take [a long] time*), **prendre un verre** (*to have a drink*), **prendre du jambon/du pain/etc**. (*to have some ham/some bread/etc.*), and **prendre une décision** (*to make a decision*).

   Ce travail **prend du temps**! — *This work takes a long time!*
   Tu **prends un verre** avec moi? — *Will you have a drink with me?*
   Je vais **prendre** du jambon. — *I'll have some ham.*

2. Other verbs conjugated like **prendre** are **apprendre** (*to learn*) and **comprendre** (*to understand*). To say you are learning to do something, the expression is **apprendre à** + infinitive.

   Nous **apprenons** le français. — *We are learning French.*
   Nous **apprenons à parler** français. — *We are learning to speak French.*
   Tu **comprends** la leçon? — *Do you understand the lesson?*

Le verbe *mettre*

mettre (*to put*)			
je	**mets**	nous	**mettons**
tu	**mets**	vous	**mettez**
il, elle, on	**met**	ils, elles	**mettent**

Vous mettez la bouteille dans le frigo? — *Are you putting the bottle in the refrigerator?*

1. Common expressions are **mettre un vêtement** (*to put on a piece of clothing*), **mettre la table** (*to set the table*), **mettre la radio/télé/lumière** (*to turn on the radio/TV/light*), and **mettre du temps à** (*to spend time on*).

   Pourquoi **tu mets ce béret** ridicule? — *Why are you putting on that ridiculous béret?*

   Tu **mets la table**, Camille? — *Are you setting the table, Camille?*

   Rachid **met la radio** pour écouter de la musique raï. — *Rachid turns on the radio to listen to raï music.*

   Ils **mettent du temps à** trouver la vérité. — *They spend time finding the truth.*

2. Other verbs like **mettre** are **permettre (à)** (*to permit, allow* [*someone*]) and **promettre (à)** (*to promise* [*someone*]). With an infinitive, you have to use **permettre de** + infinitive and **promettre de** + infinitive.

   Mado ne permet pas à Camille **de parler** de son grand-père. — *Mado doesn't let Camille talk about her grandfather.*

   Je promets de te **téléphoner** demain. — *I promise to call you tomorrow.*

Le verbe *boire*

boire (*to drink*)			
je	**bois**	nous	**buvons**
tu	**bois**	vous	**buvez**
il, elle, on	**boit**	ils, elles	**boivent**

—Tu **bois** quelque chose, Rachid? — *Are you drinking anything, Rachid?*

—Non, les musulmans pratiquants ne **boivent** pas d'alcool. — *No, practicing Muslims don't drink alcohol.*

Activités

A. Habitudes. (*Habits.*) Complétez les phrases avec la forme correcte d'un des verbes indiqués.

PRENDRE, APPRENDRE, COMPRENDRE

1. Tu _____ un verre avec moi?
2. Est-ce que ton frère et toi, vous _____ le train pour aller au travail?
3. Nous _____ la leçon, mais nous ne pouvons pas l'expliquer (*explain it*) en français.
4. J' _____ à faire la cuisine.
5. Nos devoirs _____ du temps.
6. Est-ce que vous _____ cette décision importante?

METTRE, PERMETTRE, PROMETTRE

7. Pourquoi est-ce que tu _____ un pantalon vert et une chemise rose?
8. Est-ce que vous _____ de revenir?
9. Je _____ la télé pour regarder un débat politique.
10. Nous ne _____ pas à nos enfants de mettre la télé avant le dîner.
11. Tu _____ la table pour le dîner, s'il te plaît?

BOIRE

12. Tu _____ trop de coca.
13. Je _____ de l'eau minérale.
14. Nous ne _____ pas d'alcool parce que nous sommes musulmans.
15. Les étudiants _____ beaucoup de café avant les examens.

Apprendre une langue étrangère: Les méthodes les plus efficaces!

B. Enquête. (*Survey.*) Demandez à trois camarades de classe ce qu'ils (*what they*) boivent et ce qu'ils mangent normalement au dîner. Ensuite, demandez ce qu'ils ne boivent pas et ce qu'ils ne mangent pas. Prenez des notes et présentez les résultats de votre enquête à la classe en utilisant les verbes **prendre** et **boire**. Quelles boissons et quels repas sont populaires?

C. Que font-ils? Décrivez (*Describe*) chaque photo. Utilisez des éléments de chaque colonne.

		la photo sur le bureau
Rachid		le portable dans son sac
Sonia	(ne... pas) prendre	de l'eau / d'eau
Rachid et Camille	(ne... pas) mettre	le portable de Martine
Camille	(ne... pas) boire	la photo de la main (*hand*) de Bruno
		du vin / de vin
		le bus

MODÈLE: Rachid prend la photo de la main de Bruno.

1. 

2.  

3. 

4. 

5. 

6. 

Visionnement 2

Le Quartier latin. (***The Latin Quarter.***) The area represented on the map is the southern part of the **Quartier latin**, which was first built up in the 12th and 13th centuries as the home of the great Parisian schools, renowned across all of Europe. **La Sorbonne**, originally a center of theological studies, today is just one part of the University of Paris. Many of the students who attend the numerous schools and universities of the Latin Quarter spend evenings in the restaurants and bars of the **rue Mouffetard**. **Le jardin du Luxembourg** is a large public park. The building that houses the French Senate, **le palais du Luxembourg**, is located within it. **Le Panthéon**, completed in 1789, honors great men and women of France. Among those buried there are Voltaire, Rousseau, Victor Hugo, Marie Curie, Louis Braille, and Jean Moulin, one of the most famous heroes of the Resistance. **L'Institut national des Jeunes Sourds**, founded in 1760, was a pioneering institution in the education of the deaf and is closely connected with the origins of American Sign Language.

Les environs de l'appartement de Louise

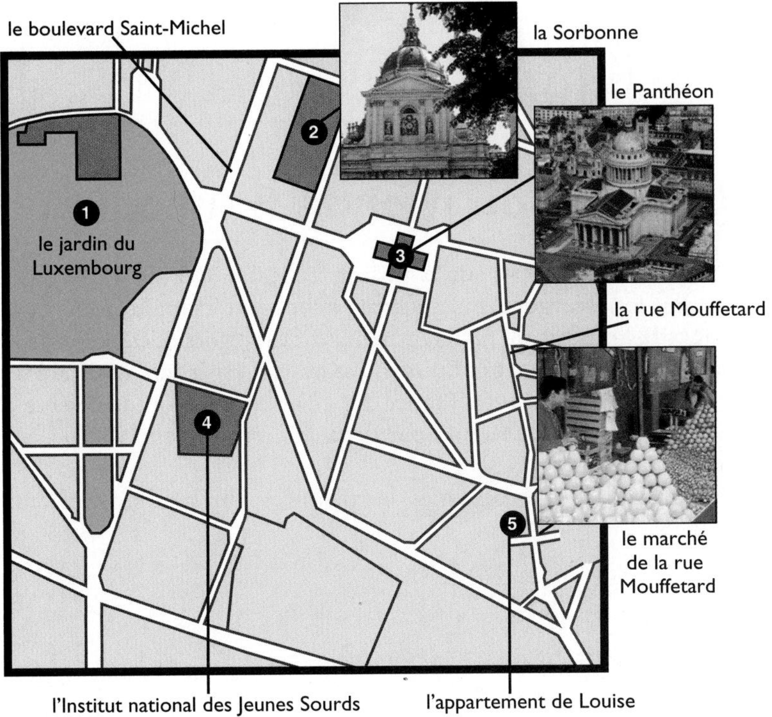

Un étudiant parle de sa journée. Complétez chaque phrase avec le nom de l'endroit qui convient.

1. Ce matin j'ai un cours (*class*) d'anthropologie à...
2. Après, j'ai un cours de langue des signes française à...
3. À midi, je vais manger un sandwich en plein air (*outdoors*) au...
4. Avec mon cousin, qui s'intéresse à l'histoire, je vais visiter...
5. Le soir, nous allons chercher un bon petit restaurant dans la...

Observez!

Considérez les aspects culturels expliqués dans **Regards sur la culture**. Ensuite, regardez l'Épisode 7 encore une fois, et répondez aux questions suivantes.

- Quelles expressions Camille et les marchands emploient-ils pour montrer leur souci (*concern*) pour la qualité des produits?
- Que fait et que dit Camille au marché Mouffetard? Comparez ce marché avec un marché près de chez vous.

Après le visionnement

Faites l'activité pour le **Visionnement 2** dans le cahier.

Synthèse: Culture

Cuisines du monde francophone

Il y a beaucoup de stéréotypes sur la cuisine française. On dit souvent que les Français aiment les escargots[1] et les sauces riches, par exemple. Mais la vérité est que beaucoup de Français ne mangent jamais d'escargots. L'élément de base de la cuisine française est le blé,[2] et la boisson essentielle est le vin, mais à part cela[3] on mange des choses très variées en France. De région en région, la cuisine change: en Normandie, on cuisine avec du beurre, par exemple, et en Provence avec de l'huile[4] d'olive.

Dans les autres pays francophones, la cuisine est différente. Voici deux exemples.

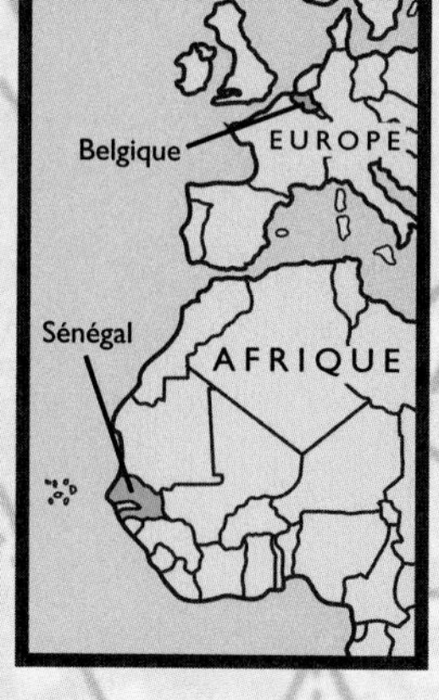

La Belgique

L'élément de base de la cuisine = la pomme de terre
La boisson essentielle = la bière

La Belgique est située à la frontière des cultures germanique et latine. Certains éléments de sa cuisine sont d'origine allemande, d'autres sont d'origine française. Les Belges mangent beaucoup de moules[5] et de frites.[6] Le chocolat est une autre grande spécialité de la Belgique.

Des aliments typiquement belges

Un repas belge

Le jambon des Ardennes

•••

La carbonnade flamande

du bœuf, des pommes de terre et des oignons cuisinés dans une sauce à la bière

Les choux de Bruxelles

•••

La tarte à la rhubarbe

[1]*snails* [2]*wheat* [3]**à…** *besides that* [4]*oil* [5]*mussels* [6]*fries*

Le Sénégal

L'élément de base traditionnel = le mil[7]; aujourd'hui = le riz[8]
La boisson essentielle = le thé à la menthe

Le Sénégal est situé sur l'Atlantique, dans l'ouest de l'Afrique. Son climat est influencé par le Sahara. Dans la cuisine sénégalaise, il y a aujourd'hui des influences françaises. Par exemple, en ville, les Sénégalais mangent du pain comme en France. Et le riz, introduit au Sénégal par la France, est maintenant un aliment[9] essentiel.

Un repas typiquement sénégalais

Un repas sénégalais

Le poulet au yassa
du poulet mariné
avec des citrons verts[10] et des piments,[11]
cuisiné avec des oignons
dans de l'huile de cacahuète[12]
Le riz
•••
Le lakh
du mil bouilli[13] servi avec du lait caillé[14] et du sucre

[7]*millet (a grain that thrives in dry climates)* [8]*rice* [9]*food* [10]citrons… *limes* [11]*hot peppers* [12]*peanut* [13]*boiled* [14]lait… *a dairy product like sour cream*

À vous

Un repas francophone. In groups of three or four, plan a meal that would illustrate the diversity of cooking in the Francophone world. It should be designed to be appetizing as well as to educate someone who knows nothing about the countries where French is spoken. Choose from among the dishes just mentioned and others presented in this book or that you know about (from Louisiana, for example). Once you have established the menu for your meal, have one person present it to the class, along with an explanation of why each of the dishes was chosen and what the overall menu communicates.

À écrire

Faites **À écrire** pour le Chapitre 7 dans le cahier.

Vocabulaire

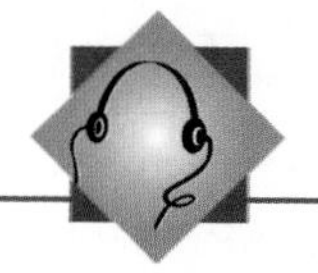

Vendeurs

un(e) boucher/ère	butcher
un(e) boulanger/ère	(bread) baker
un(e) charcutier/ière	(pork) butcher
un(e) crémier/ière	dairyman/woman
un(e) épicier/ière	grocer
un(e) marchand(e)	merchant
un(e) pâtissier/ière	(pastry) baker
un(e) poissonnier/ière	fishmonger

Magasins

une boucherie	butcher shop
une boulangerie	(bread) bakery
une charcuterie	pork butcher shop; delicatessen
une crémerie	dairy product store
une épicerie	grocery store
une pâtisserie	(pastry) bakery
une poissonnerie	fish store

MOT APPARENTÉ: **un marché**

À REVOIR: **un magasin**

Provisions

un aliment	food
le beurre	butter
le bœuf	beef
une cerise	cherry
un citron	lemon
la confiture	jam
des crevettes (*f.*)	shrimp
l'eau (*f.*) **(minérale, gazeuse, plate)**	(mineral, carbonated, noncarbonated) water
le fromage	cheese
des fruits (*m.*) **de mer**	seafood
des haricots (*m.*) **verts**	green beans
le jambon	ham
un légume	vegetable
le maïs	corn
le pain	bread
une pâtisserie	pastry
des petits pois (*m.*)	peas
un poisson	fish
une pomme	apple
une pomme de terre	potato
le poulet	chicken
du raisin (des raisins)	grapes
une saucisse	(link) sausage
le saumon	salmon
le sucre	sugar
une tarte	pie
le thon	tuna
la viande	meat
le vin (rouge, blanc, rosé)	(red, white, rosé) wine

MOTS APPARENTÉS: **une carotte, le champagne, la crème, un fruit, un oignon, le porc, une tomate**

L'article partitif

du, de la	some

Expressions de quantité

une boîte (de)	can (of); box (of)
une bouteille (de)	bottle (of)
une livre (de)	pound (of)
un morceau (de)	piece (of)
(un) peu (de)	(a) little; (a) few
assez (de)	enough
beaucoup (de)	much; many; a lot of
trop (de)	too much; too many

MOTS APPARENTÉS: **un demi-kilo (de), une douzaine (de), un kilo (de)**

Pronoms compléments d'objet indirect

me	to/for me
te	to/for you
lui	to/for him/her
nous	to/for us
vous	to/for you
leur	to/for them

Verbes

apprendre	to learn
boire	to drink
comprendre	to understand
demander (si)	to ask (if, whether)
mettre	to put
mettre du temps à	to spend time on
mettre la radio/télé/lumière	to turn on the radio/TV/light
mettre la table	to set the table
mettre un vêtement	to put on a piece of clothing
montrer	to show
permettre	to permit, allow
prendre	to take
prendre du temps	to take (a long) time
prendre du jambon (du pain, etc.)	to have (to eat) some ham (some bread, etc.)
prendre une décision	to make a decision
prendre un verre	to have a drink
promettre	to promise

MOT APPARENTÉ: **téléphoner**

À REVOIR: **acheter, donner, parler**

Autres expressions utiles

chaque	each
ensemble	together
si	if, whether

À REVOIR: **chez**

Chapitre 8

C'est loin, tout ça.°

C'est… *All that was long ago.*

Le Chemin du retour

Feuille de service du 14 octobre
4e jour du tournage
Horaires: 9h–19h

LIEU DE TOURNAGE: PARIS—3, square Rapp, 7e

Séquence	*Effets*	*Décors*	*Résumé*	*Rôles*
39	INT.—SOIR	APPARTEMENT LOUISE—Séjour	Camille montre la photo de son grandpère à Louise. Louise lui parle d'une lettre d'Antoine envoyée quand il était° dans les Cévennes.	CAMILLE, LOUISE

°was

OBJECTIFS

In this episode, you will

- witness the Leclair family's reluctance to talk about past events
- learn more about Camille's relationship with Mado

In this chapter, you will

- talk about meals and dining habits
- talk about everyday activities
- give commands and make suggestions
- learn how the French conduct conversations
- read the poem "Familiale," by Jacques Prévert

Vocabulaire en contexte

Les repas en France°

Les... *Meals in France*

Le matin, on prend **le petit déjeuner**. On peut manger et boire

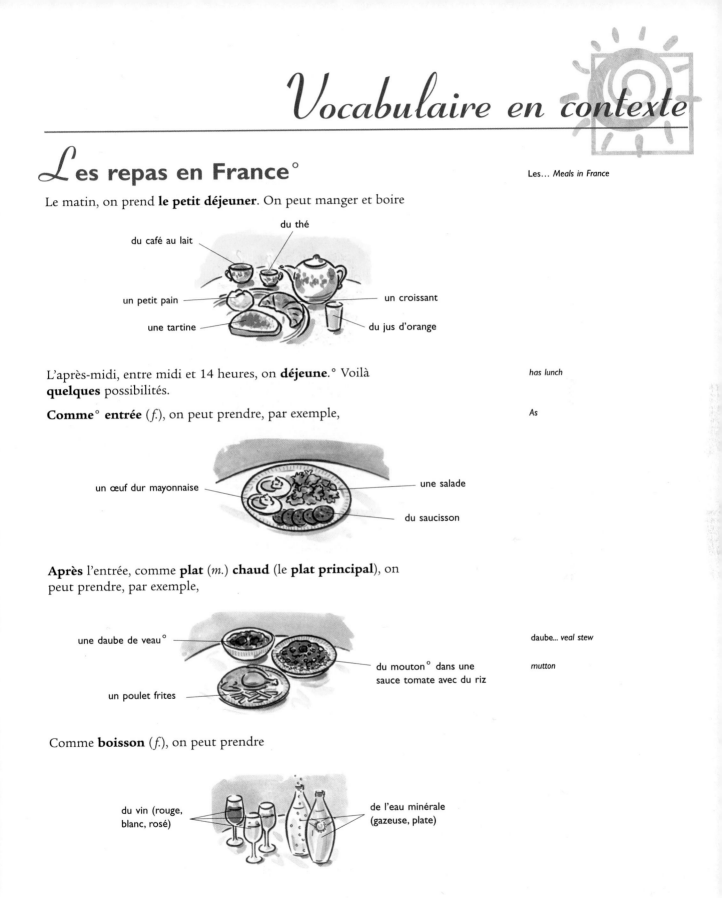

L'après-midi, entre midi et 14 heures, on **déjeune**.° Voilà **quelques** possibilités.

has lunch

Comme° **entrée** (*f.*), on peut prendre, par exemple,

As

Après l'entrée, comme **plat** (*m.*) **chaud** (le **plat principal**), on peut prendre, par exemple,

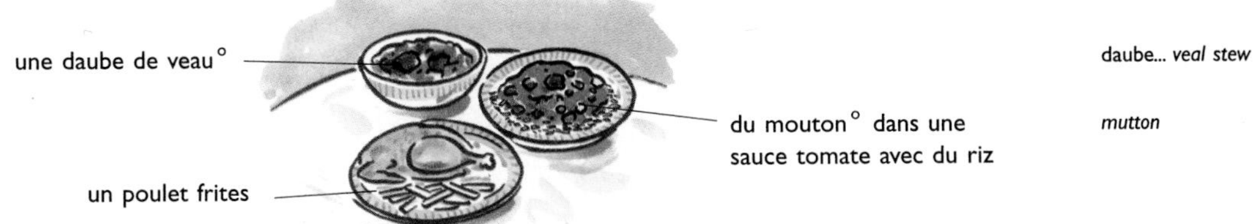

daube... *veal stew*

mutton

Comme **boisson** (*f.*), on peut prendre

On prend du pain avec le plat chaud, et du fromage **avant le dessert**. Comme dessert, on peut prendre quelque chose° de **sucré**.

quelque... *something*

Il y a aussi des gens° qui mangent **du fast-food**: **un hamburger** et **un coca**, par exemple. D'autres prennent **une pizza** ou **un sandwich**.

people

Pour en savoir plus...

Eating habits are gradually changing in France. Although lunch typically remains the day's heaviest meal, involving a warm dish, vegetables, and a salad, some people are now taking lighter noon meals and heavier evening meals. The French are also consuming less bread and wine than in the past. Drinking orange juice at breakfast has recently begun to gain popularity.

Le soir, entre 19 heures et 21 heures, on dîne. En général, c'est un repas **léger**. Voici quelques possibilités. On peut manger et boire

Après, on peut prendre du fromage ou un dessert.

Qu'est-ce que vous aimez manger? Quelles **choses**° est-ce que vous trouvez particulièrement délicieuses?

things

Autres mots utiles

le déjeuner	lunch
le dîner	dinner
le poivre	pepper
le sel	salt
la salade	lettuce

Activités

A. Quelle catégorie? Classez les aliments dans les catégories suivantes: **une entrée**, **un plat chaud**, **une boisson**, **un dessert**, **du fast-food**.

1. une daube de veau
2. une mousse au chocolat
3. du thé
4. du saucisson
5. du fromage
6. du jus d'orange

7. du coca
8. un fruit
9. de la charcuterie
10. du mouton
11. de la glace
12. un hamburger

B. Quel repas? Dites (*Say*) à quel repas on mange probablement ces choses en France.

MODÈLE: du pain →
On mange du pain au petit déjeuner, au déjeuner ou au dîner.

1. de la soupe
2. de l'eau minérale
3. du café au lait
4. du mouton
5. du riz
6. un croissant
7. de la tarte
8. un petit pain
9. un poulet frites
10. un sandwich
11. un verre de vin rouge
12. une omelette
13. une pizza
14. une salade
15. une tartine

Maintenant, dites si on mange ou boit ces choses avant, après ou avec d'autres parties (*parts*) du repas.

MODÈLE: du pain →
On mange du pain avec le plat principal.

C. Correspondances. Identifiez un plat qui correspond aux descriptions suivantes.

1. une boisson caféinée
2. un plat riche en calories et en cholestérol
3. un plat léger
4. un plat sucré
5. deux condiments
6. un plat que vous avez envie d'essayer
7. un plat que vous n'avez pas envie d'essayer

D. Sondage. (*Survey.*) Demandez à votre partenaire

1. ce qu'il/elle prend comme petit déjeuner.
2. ce qu'il/elle mange pour le déjeuner.
3. ce qu'il/elle mange pour le dîner.
4. combien de fois par semaine il/elle mange de la viande.
5. quelles sortes de légumes il/elle mange et combien de fois par semaine.
6. s'il / si elle mange beaucoup de pâtes (*pasta*) ou de pommes de terre.
7. combien de boîtes de coca il/elle boit par semaine.
8. s'il / si elle prend un dessert tous les jours (*every day*).
9. ce qu'il/elle mange entre les repas.

Maintenant, présentez vos résultats à la classe. En général, est-ce que les étudiants de la classe ont un régime alimentaire sain (*healthy diet*)? Est-ce qu'ils consomment trop de matières grasses (*fat*)? de calories? de sucreries (*sweets*)?

À table

Pour mettre la table, on y° met les choses suivantes. *there*

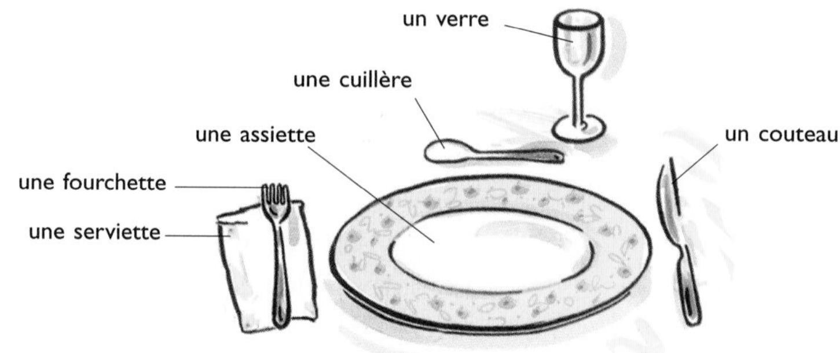

Autres mots utiles

une nappe	tablecloth
une tasse	cup

Quelques conseils° *advice*

- Tenez° le couteau dans la main droite° pour couper° la viande; tenez la fourchette dans la main gauche° pour porter le morceau à la bouche.° *Hold / la… the right hand / cut / left / mouth*
- Rompez° votre morceau de pain; ne coupez pas le pain! *Break*
- Mettez votre pain sur la table à côté de votre assiette.
- Ne mangez pas le pain avant le repas. Mangez le pain avec le repas.
- Pliez les feuilles° de la salade. Ne les coupez pas. *Fold the leaves*
- Ne parlez pas la bouche pleine!° *full*

Langage fonctionnel

Pour parler du repas

The following expressions are often used at meals.

Pour souhaiter un bon repas

Bon appétit.	*Enjoy your meal.*
À votre santé! (À ta santé!) / Et à la vôtre! (À la tienne!)	*To your health! / And to yours!*

Pour demander quelque chose

Est-ce que vous pourriez (tu pourrais) me passer… ?	*Could you please pass . . . ?*

Pour offrir encore quelque chose

Encore du (de la, des)... ?	*(Would you like) more . . . ?*
Je vous (te) ressers de... ?	*May I serve you more . . . ?*
Vous pouvez (Tu peux) en reprendre un peu.	*You could have a little more.*

Pour accepter ou refuser une offre

Avec plaisir!	*With pleasure!*
Merci. (Non, merci.)	*No, thank you.*
Volontiers!	*Gladly!*

Pour faire un compliment

C'est (C'était) délicieux.	*It is (was) delicious.*
J'ai très bien mangé.	*I've had a very good meal.*

—**Je te ressers** du rôti? *May I serve you more roast?*
—**Merci. C'était délicieux.** *No, thank you. I've had a very good meal.*

Activités

A. Qu'est-ce qui ne va pas? (*What's wrong?*) Quelles choses ne sont pas bien placées sur la table? Quels conseils ne sont pas suivis (*followed*) par les personnes à table?

B. À table. Vous êtes à table. Quelle expression pouvez-vous utiliser dans chaque (*each*) situation?

1. Tout le monde est à table. Votre hôtesse vous invite à manger. Vous dites...
2. Avant de manger, vous levez (*raise*) votre verre de vin et vous dites...
3. Vous voulez des carottes. Vous dites...
4. On vous demande si vous voulez encore du vin. Vous acceptez. Vous dites...
5. On vous offre encore du poulet. Vous refusez mais vous faites un compliment. Vous dites...

Visionnement 1

Avant de visionner

In this episode, you will hear examples of two new verb tenses: The **passé composé** (in **boldface** type) is used to talk about past events; the ***imparfait*** (in ***bold italic*** type) is used to talk about past conditions or states of mind, and ongoing action in the past. You will learn to form and use these tenses in Chapters 10, 11, and 12, but for now, just learn to recognize them so you can understand Episode 8.

Vous comprenez? Essayez de comprendre les deux extraits (*extracts*) du film.

Camille pose une question à sa grand-mère, Louise.

CAMILLE: C'***était***[a] quand, la dernière[b] fois qu'il t'**a contactée**[c]?

LOUISE: En 1943. Il ***était*** dans les Cévennes. Il m'**a envoyé** une lettre... pour l'anniversaire de ta maman. Elle ***avait*** quatre ans.

Plus tard,[d] Mado parle à Camille.

MADO: D'où sort-elle,[e] cette photo?! Pourquoi tu **as montré** ça à ta grand-mère?

[a]*It was* [b]*last* [c]*il... he contacted you* [d]Plus... *Later* [e]D'où... *Where does it come from*

Maintenant, indiquez si les phrases suivantes sont vraies ou fausses. Corrigez les phrases qui sont fausses.

1. Quelqu'un (*Someone*) contacte Louise pour la dernière fois en 1940.
2. Il est à Paris.
3. Il envoie une lettre pour l'anniversaire de Mado.
4. Mado a quarante ans à cette époque (*at that time*).
5. Mado demande pourquoi Camille montre une photo à sa grand-mère.

Notez bien!

Two new words are useful for talking about the film.

la guerre war

raconter to tell (about)

Camille uses them both when she asks her grandmother . . .

Tu me **racontes** son histoire pendant **la guerre**? *Will you tell me his story during the war?*

Vocabulaire relatif à l'épisode

La guerre, c'est moche!	*War is awful!*
En es-tu sûr(e)?	*Are you sure about that?*
Mais qu'est-ce que tu as?	*What's wrong with you?*
On ne réveille pas les morts.	*Nobody should disturb the dead.*
Tu mérites une gifle!	*You deserve a slap!*
Ça suffit!	*That's enough!*

Observez!

Dans cet épisode, Camille cherche des informations sur le rôle de son grand-père pendant (*during*) la Deuxième Guerre mondiale (*Second World War*).

- Comment Louise réagit-elle (*does Louise react*) à la demande de Camille?
- Comment réagit Mado? Pourquoi?

Après le visionnement

A. Vrai ou faux? Indiquez si les phrases suivantes sont vraies ou fausses. Corrigez les phrases fausses.

1. Camille montre une lettre d'Antoine à Louise.
2. Louise aime parler de son mari.

3. Louise raconte la visite de son mari dans les Cévennes.
4. Mado est furieuse parce que Camille a montré la photo à Louise.
5. Mado pense qu'on ne doit pas (*should not*) parler de son père.

B. Réfléchissez. (*Think.*) Répondez aux questions.

1. Quels mots et expressions montrent que Louise et Mado considèrent encore Camille comme une enfant?
2. Comment Camille essaie-t-elle de montrer son indépendance?

Structure 24

Les verbes réguliers en -re

Talking about everyday activities

—Tu **perds** la tête… !

—Et cesse de me **répondre**. Tu mérites une gifle!!

The verbs **perdre** (*to lose*) and **répondre** (*to answer*) are examples of a category of verbs that are all conjugated in the same way. They are sometimes referred to as regular **-re** verbs.

1. To use regular **-re** verbs in the present tense, drop the **-re** ending and add the endings **-s**, **-s**, —, **-ons**, **-ez**, **-ent**. Notice that no ending is added for the **il/elle/on** form.

répondre (*to answer*)			
je	répond**s**	nous	répond**ons**
tu	répond**s**	vous	répond**ez**
il, elle, on	répond	ils, elles	répond**ent**

Quand le prof pose une question, **nous répondons**. — *When the professor asks a question, we answer.*

Louise **répond** au téléphone. — *Louise answers the telephone.*

2. Here is a list of some common regular **-re** verbs.

attendre	*to wait (for)*	**rendre**	*to return (something); to render, make*
descendre	*to descend, go (get) down, get off*	**répondre**	*to answer*
entendre	*to hear*	**vendre**	*to sell*
perdre	*to lose*		

Tu descends du train.	*You get off the train.*
L'argent **rend-il** les gens heureux?	*Does money make people happy?*

3. **Attendre** does not take a preposition before an object as *wait* does in English.

Bruno **attend** Camille.	*Bruno waits for Camille.*

4. **Perdre** usually takes an article or a possessive adjective before the thing that is lost. The idiomatic expression **perdre la tête** (*to lose one's mind*) follows this pattern; the expression **perdre patience** (*to lose patience*) does not.

	Camille **perd son médaillon**.	*Camille loses her locket.*
	Tu **perds la tête**... !	*You're losing your mind . . . !*
but	Mado **perd patience** avec Camille.	*Mado loses patience with Camille.*

5. When **rendre** means *to return something*, it takes a direct object.▲ To talk about *returning something **to someone***, an indirect object pronoun or the preposition **à** + indirect object noun is needed.

choose either

Rachid **rend** le livre **à Camille**.	*Rachid returns the book to Camille.*
Il **lui rend** le livre.	*He returns the book to her.*

An idiomatic expression with **rendre** is **rendre visite à** (*to visit*). It is used only for visiting people, not places. Use **visiter** for visiting a place.

Camille **rend visite à** Louise.	*Camille visits Louise.*
Nous **visitons** Marseille.	*We're visiting Marseilles.*

6. **Répondre** can be used alone or with an indirect object (meaning *to answer something or someone*). If an object is required, use **répondre à**. Remember that for a person as object, you can use an indirect object pronoun.

Louise **répond au téléphone**.	*Louise answers the telephone.*
Yasmine **répond à Rachid**.	*Yasmine answers Rachid.*
Elle **lui répond**.	*She answers him.*

Activités

A. La journée typique de Nicole. Nicole, la scripte à Canal 7, décrit (*describes*) sa journée typique. Utilisez les éléments donnés pour compléter sa description. Attention: Il faut ajouter (*You have to add*) la préposition **à** dans deux des phrases.

MODÈLE: à 7 h 30, je / attendre / mon amie pour prendre un café →
À 7 h 30, j'attends mon amie pour prendre un café.

1. à 8 h, nous / entendre / les enfants dans l'appartement au-dessus
2. ils / descendre / les escaliers (*the stairs*) pour aller à l'école
3. on / nous / vendre / des tickets de bus dans la station de métro
4. à 8 h 30, nous / attendre / le bus
5. les gens / perdre / patience quand le bus est en retard
6. Roger et moi, nous / répondre / les questions de Martine
7. parfois nous / entendre / les discussions de Bruno ou de Camille
8. à midi, je / rendre visite / ma sœur dans le quartier
9. ma sœur / attendre / toujours ma visite avec impatience
10. je / perdre / parfois ma clé quand je rentre (*return*) à la maison

B. Pourquoi tout remettre au lendemain? (*Why put everything off until the next day?*) Votre partenaire fait-il/elle les choses à temps (*on time*) ou a-t-il/elle tendance à tout remettre au lendemain? Posez-lui ces questions pour analyser ses habitudes. Quelle est votre conclusion?

MODÈLE: Demandez-lui s'il / si elle répond immédiatement à ses e-mails →
É1: Est-ce que tu réponds immédiatement à tes e-mails?
É2: Non, je ne réponds pas immédiatement.

Demandez-lui s'il / si elle...

1. répond immédiatement à ses e-mails
2. rend ses livres à la bibliothèque à temps
3. attend le dernier (*last*) moment pour faire ses devoirs
4. descend le recyclage avant la collecte
5. vend ses livres immédiatement en juin
6. perd du temps sur le Web
7. répond promptement aux invitations
8. rend ses devoirs avant la date limite

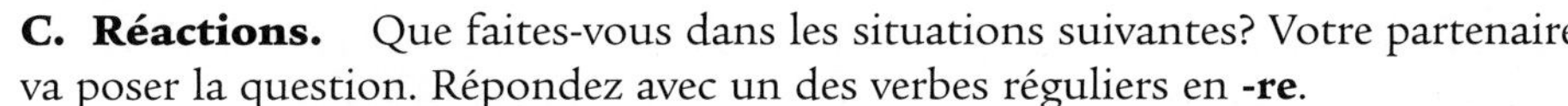

C. Réactions. Que faites-vous dans les situations suivantes? Votre partenaire va poser la question. Répondez avec un des verbes réguliers en **-re**.

MODÈLE: tu as besoin d'argent →
É1: Que fais-tu quand tu as besoin d'argent?
É2: Je vends mes disques compacts. (Je rends visite à ma grand-mère!)

1. le professeur pose une question
2. une amie est triste
3. ton/ta camarade de chambre (ton fils, ta fille) joue (*plays*) de la guitare à deux heures du matin
4. tu as envie d'une nouvelle voiture
5. un film commence en retard
6. le téléphone sonne (*rings*)
7. tu vas à un concert
8. tu n'as plus besoin d'une chose empruntée à (*borrowed from*) un ami

Structure 25

L'impératif

Giving commands and advice

—Ne **parle** jamais de lui à ta grand-mère!

The imperative is used for giving orders and advice and for making suggestions. There are three forms: **tu**, **vous**, and **nous**.

Pour en savoir plus...

Depending on the social context, the imperative may be considered too forceful and impolite in French. To "soften" a request or advice, use (1) **je voudrais**, (2) the present tense, and/or (3) **s'il te plaît** or **s'il vous plaît**.

Je voudrais parler à M. Gall, **s'il vous plaît**. *I would like to speak to Mr. Gall, please.*

Tu rentres chez toi et **tu** l'**attends**. *You should just go home and wait for her.*

Tu me **racontes** son voyage dans les Cévennes? **S'il te plaît?** *Will you tell me about his trip to the Cévennes? Please?*

1. The **tu** and **vous** imperatives are the **tu** or **vous** forms of the present tense, used without the pronoun. Note, however, that regular **-er** verbs and **aller** drop the final **s** of the **tu** form.

INFINITIF	(TU)	(VOUS)
regarder	Regarde... !	Regardez... !
répondre	Réponds... !	Répondez... !
aller	Va... !	Allez... !
boire	Bois... !	Buvez... !
faire	Fais... !	Faites... !
mettre	Mets... !	Mettez... !
prendre	Prends... !	Prenez... !
venir	Viens... !	Venez... !

Répondez à ma question! — *Answer my question!*
Et **cesse** de me répondre. — *And stop talking back to me.*
Viens, papa! **Viens**... — *Come on, Daddy! Come . . .*
Va me chercher du sucre, s'il te plaît. — *Go get me some sugar, please.*

The verbs **être** and **avoir** have irregular imperative forms.

INFINITIF	(TU)	(VOUS)
être	Sois... !	Soyez... !
avoir	Aie... !	Ayez... !

Sois prudent, Bruno. — *Be careful, Bruno.*
Ayez un peu de patience! — *Have a little patience!*

2. To make suggestions that include yourself, use the **nous** form of the imperative, which is, of course, the **nous** form of the present tense used without the pronoun. **Être** and **avoir** again have irregular forms: **soyons** and **ayons**.

Allons au marché.	*Let's go to the market.*
Prenons un café.	*Let's get some coffee.*
Soyons prudents.	*Let's be careful.*
Ayons un peu de patience!	*Let's have a little patience!*

3. To say not to do something in any of the three forms, place **ne** before the verb and **pas** after it.

Ne faites **pas** ça.	*Don't do that.*
Ne parle **jamais** de lui à ta grand-mère!	*Never speak of him to your grandmother!*
N'ayez **pas** peur!	*Don't be afraid!*
N'attendons **pas**. Je perds patience.	*Let's not wait. I'm getting impatient.*

4. To use an indirect object pronoun with a *negative* imperative, place the pronoun before the verb, just as in a declarative sentence.

DECLARATIVE	Tu ne lui rends pas visite.	*You don't visit him/her.*
IMPERATIVE	Ne **lui** rends pas visite!	*Don't visit him/her.*

For an *affirmative* imperative, however, place the pronoun after the verb, attached with a hyphen. The pronouns **me** and **te** become **moi** and **toi** in this situation.

Téléphone-**lui** immédiatement.	*Call him/her immediately!*
Réponds-**moi**!	*Answer me!*

Pour en savoir plus...

The imperative of **écouter** is often used as an interjection that in English might be translated as *Say!* or *Hey!* and sometimes as *Listen!* or *Look!*

Écoute, ce livre est vraiment, euh... Il est vraiment magnifique!

Écoute, Rachid... tu es gentil... Mais, tu as peut-être autre chose à faire?

Activités

A. De la régie. Martine parle aux membres de l'équipe (*team*) de «Bonjour!». Mettez l'infinitif à la forme impérative.

MODÈLE: (à Bruno) / regarder / la caméra
Regarde la caméra!

1. (à Camille) parler / lentement (*slowly*), s'il te plaît
2. (aux techniciens) attendre / un instant et / faire attention
3. (à l'équipe) commencer dans trois minutes
4. (à Roger et Nicole) être / perfectionnistes
5. (à Bruno) répéter ton texte (*rehearse your lines*) et / mettre / un beau costume
6. (à Camille et Bruno) venir / me parler après l'émission
7. (à Camille) prendre / un café ensemble

B. Conseils. Les personnages dans *Le Chemin du retour* donnent souvent des ordres et des suggestions. Utilisez le verbe entre parenthèses pour compléter leurs phrases.

MODÈLE: RACHID À YASMINE: «_____ les enfants!» (regarder) →
Regarde les enfants!

1. RACHID À YASMINE: «Ben, bien sûr! _____, ma puce.» (venir)
2. M. LIÉGEOIS À CAMILLE: «_____ (*Let's hope*) que les Français peuvent identifier un bon pain.» (espérer)
3. CAMILLE À BRUNO: «Eh bien, _____ un test ensemble.» (faire)
4. MARTINE À CAMILLE: «_____, Camille. Je te présente Rachid Bouhazid.» (attendre)
5. BRUNO À RACHID: «Euh, _____ -moi, c'est mon bureau ici. Ton bureau, il est là.» (excuser)
6. LOUISE À CAMILLE: «_____ me chercher du sucre, s'il te plaît.» (aller)
7. MADO À CAMILLE: «Ne _____ jamais de lui à ta grand-mère!» (parler)

C. Le week-end. Suggérez (*Suggest*) à votre partenaire une activité pour le week-end. Votre partenaire n'aime pas votre idée; il/elle va suggérer autre chose.

MODÈLE: dîner à la maison ce soir / manger au restaurant →
É1: Dînons à la maison ce soir.
É2: Non, ne dînons pas à la maison ce soir! Mangeons au restaurant.

1. étudier dans nos chambres / travailler à la bibliothèque
2. préparer une salade / partager cette pizza surgelée (*frozen*)
3. aller à un concert de rock / écouter la radio
4. regarder la télé / faire les courses
5. commencer à parler français / parler anglais
6. mettre des vêtements chic pour sortir (*go out*) avec des amis / porter des vêtements confortables

D. La politesse à table. Vous êtes un(e) expert(e) sur la politesse en France. Faites des phrases impératives (à l'affirmatif ou au négatif) pour donner des conseils. Soyez logique (et consultez les conseils à la page 178 si nécessaire).

MODÈLE: faire beaucoup de bruit (*noise*) →
Ne faites pas beaucoup de bruit.

1. mettre votre pain sur la table
2. prendre la place de votre hôtesse à table
3. manger un morceau de pain avant le repas
4. couper la salade avec un couteau
5. être toujours poli(e)
6. boire trop de vin

Maintenant, donnez d'autres conseils logiques en remplaçant les mots en italique par un pronom complément d'objet indirect et en utilisant la forme affirmative ou négative, selon le cas.

MODÈLE: acheter des fleurs *à l'hôtesse* →
Achetez-lui des fleurs.

7. téléphoner *à l'hôtesse* si vous êtes en retard d'une heure
8. parler *à vos voisins* la bouche pleine
9. répondre *à l'hôtesse* quand elle vous pose une question
10. montrer les photos de tous vos cousins et cousines *aux autres invités*
11. demander *à l'hôtesse* de vous donner du sel pour le plat principal

E. Situations difficiles. À l'aide de la liste, donnez une suggestion pour résoudre (*resolve*) les problèmes suivants.

Vocabulaire utile: attendre, ne pas avoir peur, boire du jus d'orange, écouter avec patience, étudier avec des camarades de classe, être patient(e), manger des hamburgers, mettre un manteau, prendre le bus, rendre visite à, téléphoner à, venir souvent

MODÈLE: Nous ne comprenons pas ce chapitre. →
Étudiez avec des camarades de classe.

1. J'ai froid. **2.** J'ai peur de parler en classe. **3.** Nous avons faim. **4.** J'apprends lentement (*slowly*). **5.** J'ai soif. **6.** Mon ami est en retard! **7.** Nos professeurs aiment beaucoup parler. **8.** Je n'ai pas de voiture.

Regards sur la culture

Principes de conversation

When people are angry with each other, they tend to use confrontational language, as Camille and Mado do in this episode. In this case, Mado is extremely angry, but in France, argument and debate can also be a normal part of any conversation. In fact, there are several aspects of French conversational practices that North Americans in France generally have to adjust to.

Une conversation animée

- A conversation between two French people may sometimes sound aggressive to North Americans. This impression is partly due to the lively tone of French dialogue, and it is partly because conversation in France is an art that requires some degree of expertise in argument and disagreement. This approach to conversation may surprise English-speaking North Americans who expect exchanges to sound calm even when disagreement is involved. Some North American conversations may feel spiritless and uninteresting to French people, who are accustomed to defending their own point of view in a lively way.
- In a French conversation, it may be more important for a participant to state his/her point of view and to defend it well than it is to come to an agreement or compromise on the subject being discussed.
- It is also typical in French conversation to be critical. Criticism of food and of people's physical appearance in France may seem especially striking to North Americans, who sometimes find such comments impolite. The French, on the other hand, think of criticism as something constructive and tend to find the

North American hesitation to be frank about these things insincere or even hypocritical.

- Being a conversational partner is serious business in France! A French child learns early to speak in a lively and interesting manner.
- In the English-speaking parts of North America, conversational etiquette requires a slight pause between speakers' turns. In France, such pauses would be unusual: One begins talking just as the preceding speaker is finishing his/her turn. The result is that some North Americans find it quite challenging to get a word in when they are communicating with a group of French people: They are waiting for a tiny pause so that they can politely begin to speak, and often, the pause never arrives!
- In public places, French people tend to talk more quietly than North Americans. In France, the ideal is to speak in such a way that conversations cannot be overheard by others. North American groups often stand out in France because they tend to talk more loudly than the French in restaurants and shops.
- Conversations between strangers are rather unusual in France. It would be quite normal to spend several hours on a train face to face with three or four French people and never exchange a word with them.*

Considérez

How would you react if you arrived in France for the first time and soon faced contradiction and opposition to your point of view from conversational partners? What do you think you could learn in order to cope with these new patterns of dialogue? Do you think you could learn to enjoy or appreciate these practices? How would these new practices help you improve the way you express your ideas?

Structure 26

Quelques verbes comme *sortir*

Talking about more everyday activities

—D'où **sort**-elle, cette photo?!

*Some European trains are different from North American trains in that travelers may be seated in compartments rather than rows. Each compartment is like a small room with two seats facing each other. Several people can fit on each seat and they face the people across from them for the duration of their trip.

Mado uses the verb **sortir** to ask Camille where she found the photograph of Antoine. Her use of **sortir** is slightly idiomatic; usually **sortir** means *to go out.*

1. **Sortir** uses one stem (**sor-**) for the singular forms and another stem (**sort-**) for the plural forms. The endings are **-s**, **-s**, **-t**, **-ons**, **-ez**, **-ent**.

sortir (*to go out*)			
je	sor**s**	nous	sort**ons**
tu	sor**s**	vous	sort**ez**
il, elle, on	sor**t**	ils, elles	sort**ent**

Bruno **sort** de Canal 7 avec Hélène. — *Bruno leaves Channel 7 with Hélène.*

2. Here is a list of verbs conjugated like **sortir**. Each one uses one stem for the singular and another for the plural.

dormir *to sleep* — **sentir** *to smell*
mentir *to lie* — **servir** *to serve*
partir *to leave (a place)*

Camille **part** pour le studio à 6 h 30. — *Camille leaves for the studio at 6:30 A.M.*
Je **sors** avec des amis ce soir. — *I'm going out with friends tonight.*
Nous **dormons** bien. — *We sleep well.*
Les serveurs **servent** les repas. — *The waiters serve the meals.*

3. The imperative is formed in the normal way.

Ne **mens** pas. Je sais la vérité. — *Don't lie. I know the truth.*
Partez. Elle ne veut pas vous parler! — *Leave. She doesn't want to talk to you!*
Sortons par cette porte. — *Let's go out by this door.*

Notez bien!

The verb **quitter** also means *to leave,* but it always requires a direct object.

Camille **part**. Elle **quitte** le studio à 15 h. *Camille leaves. She leaves the studio at 3:00 P.M.*

Activités

A. Légendes. (*Captions.*) Utilisez les verbes **dormir**, **partir**, **sentir**, **servir** et **sortir** pour expliquer les actions des personnages ou pour compléter les paroles des personnages.

MODÈLE: «D'où __sort__-elle, cette photo?»

1. Le pain _____ bon.

2. À la cafétéria, les cuisiniers _____ des salades.

3. Rachid et Martine _____ du bâtiment.

4. Mado _____ du champagne.

5. Rachid vient de partir. Mado dit: «Pourquoi _____ -il aussi vite?»

6. Louise _____.

B. Vérité ou mensonge? (*Truth or lie?*) Posez des questions à votre partenaire en utilisant les éléments ci-dessous. Votre partenaire va répondre avec la vérité ou avec un mensonge. Décidez alors si la réponse de votre partenaire est vraie ou fausse.

MODÈLE: tu / quitter toujours / la maison / à l'heure pour aller à l'université →
É1: Quittes-tu toujours la maison à l'heure pour aller à l'université?
É2: Oui, je quitte toujours la maison à l'heure.
É1: Je pense que c'est vrai. (*ou* Tu mens! Tu quittes parfois la maison en retard.)
É2: Non, c'est la vérité. (*ou* Tu as raison, je quitte parfois la maison en retard.)

1. tes parents / servir / des tartines au petit déjeuner
2. les repas à la caféteria / sentir / bon
3. tu / sortir / à la discothèque / le samedi soir
4. tu / dormir / dix heures par jour
5. tu / partir tôt / pour arriver aux rendez-vous (*appointments*) à l'heure
6. tu / mentir beaucoup / dans cet exercice

Maintenant, posez ces questions à un groupe d'étudiants ou à votre professeur en utilisant le pronom **vous**.

Visionnement 2

Observez!

Considérez les aspects culturels expliqués dans **Regards sur la culture**. Ensuite (*then*), regardez l'Épisode 8 encore une fois et répondez aux questions suivantes.

- Est-ce que la conversation entre Mado et Camille est un échange vif (*intense*) mais normal, ou est-ce que les deux femmes sont fâchées?
- Quelles expressions Mado emploie-t-elle pour indiquer son attitude?
- Est-ce que Camille répond à sa mère calmement ou avec colère (*with anger*)?

Après le visionnement

Faites l'activité pour le **Visionnement 2** dans le cahier.

Synthèse: Lecture

Mise en contexte

During his life, the poet Jacques Prévert (1900–1977) witnessed the horrors of two world wars that decimated Europe. The work of this prolific writer includes screenplays, short stories, and volumes of poetry, including *Paroles,* published in 1943, which contains the poem "Familiale" ("*Family Life*").

Stratégie pour mieux lire
Understanding syntax and punctuation

Poets often "play" with language to create special effects and to enrich expression. You are already familiar with techniques such as rhythm and rhyme.

In this poem, Prévert uses language creatively. One way is by changing the word order (syntax) that you have come to expect in declarative sentences (subject–verb–object). Read through the first four lines of the poem, and try to identify the subject of each sentence. How many times does it occur? In what form? In what position?

La mère fait du tricot
Le fils fait la guerre
Elle trouve ça tout naturel la mère
Et le père qu'est-ce qu'il fait le père?

The first two lines use the normal syntax, but in the third line, the subject occurs twice, once at the beginning of the line of verse, as **elle**, and again at the end as **la mère**. In the fourth line, the subject (**le père**) is mentioned twice in noun form and once as a pronoun.

As you read these lines of the poem, you probably also noticed that for the most part, the verses lack punctuation. Working with a partner, reread the stanza and punctuate it. Does the addition of punctuation help your understanding? How does punctuation change the flow of the verse?

Now, read the entire poem carefully. Pay particular attention to the syntax, and imagine punctuation where you think it will clarify meaning. What message has Prévert tried to convey?

Familiale

La mère fait du tricot[1]
Le fils fait la guerre
Elle trouve ça tout naturel la mère
Et le père qu'est-ce qu'il fait le père?
Il fait des affaires[2]
Sa femme fait du tricot
Son fils la guerre
Lui des affaires
Il trouve ça tout naturel le père
Et le fils et le fils
Qu'est-ce qu'il trouve le fils?
Il ne trouve rien[3] absolument rien le fils
Le fils sa mère fait du tricot son père des affaires lui la guerre
Quand il aura fini[4] la guerre
Il fera[5] des affaires avec son père
La guerre continue la mère continue elle tricote
Le père continue il fait des affaires
Le fils est tué[6] il ne continue plus
Le père et la mère vont au cimetière[7]
Ils trouvent ça naturel le père et la mère
La vie[8] continue la vie avec le tricot la guerre les affaires
Les affaires la guerre le tricot la guerre
Les affaires les affaires et les affaires
La vie avec le cimetière.

Jacques Prévert (*Paroles,* 1943)

[1]*knitting* [2]des... *business* [3]*nothing* [4]Quand... *When he has finished* [5]*will do* [6]*killed* [7]*cemetery* [8]*life*

Après la lecture

A. Vérifiez! En groupes de deux, comparez vos analyses de la syntaxe du poème. Où avez-vous mis des signes de ponctuation?

B. Les personnages. Décrivez les personnages en précisant leurs activités.

1. Que fait la mère?
2. Que fait le père?
3. Et le fils, qu'est-ce qu'il fait? Qu'est-ce qui lui arrive (*happens to him*)?

C. Le sens. (***The meaning.***) Répondez aux questions suivantes.

1. Quelle est l'attitude de cette famille face à la vie? Leurs journées sont-elles variées ou monotones?
2. Selon vous, les parents sont-ils conscients (*aware*) ou inconscients des événements (*events*) dans leur vie?
3. Quelle est la réaction du père et de la mère à la mort (*death*) de leur fils? Sont-ils surpris? fâchés? indifférents?
4. Quelle idée Prévert essaie-t-il de communiquer? Choisissez parmi (*Choose among*) les suggestions suivantes, ou donnez votre propre (*own*) interprétation.
   - **a.** Lutter (*To fight*) pour son pays, c'est un acte patriotique.
   - **b.** La guerre est devenue (*has become*) un événement banal.
   - **c.** En temps de guerre, la vie ne compte pas beaucoup.
   - **d.** Les parents devraient être fiers (*should be proud*) d'avoir un fils qui fait la guerre.
   - **e.** Il faut (*One must*) faire des sacrifices pendant une guerre.

À écrire

Faites **À écrire** pour le Chapitre 8 dans le cahier.

Vocabulaire

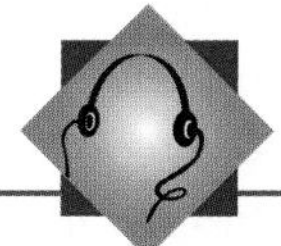

Les repas

une boisson	drink
le déjeuner	lunch
une entrée	first course
le petit déjeuner	breakfast
un plat (chaud, principal)	(hot, main) dish
un repas	meal

MOTS APPARENTÉS: **un dessert, le dîner**

Des provisions

le café (au lait)	coffee (with an equal amount of milk)	**le riz**	rice
la charcuterie	delicatessen (pork) products	**la salade; une salade**	lettuce; salad
une chose	thing	**le saucisson**	sausage
les frites (*f.*)	French fries	**le sel**	salt
la glace	ice cream	**une tartine**	*piece of French bread with butter and jam*
le jus (d'orange)	(orange) juice	**le thé**	tea
le lait	milk	**le veau**	veal
le mouton	mutton		
un œuf (dur mayonnaise) (des œufs)	egg (hard-boiled with mayonnaise)		
un petit pain	bread roll		
le poivre	pepper		
un poulet frites	chicken with fries		

MOTS APPARENTÉS: **le chocolat, un coca, un croissant, le fast-food, un hamburger, la mousse (au chocolat), une omelette, une pizza, un sandwich, une sauce, la soupe**

À REVOIR: **l'eau** (*f.*), **un fruit, un poulet, une tarte, une tomate, le vin**

À table

une assiette	plate	**une nappe**	tablecloth
un couteau	knife	**une serviette**	napkin
une cuillère	spoon	**une tasse**	cup
une fourchette	fork	**un verre**	glass

Pour parler de la guerre

la guerre	war

Verbes

attendre	to wait (for)	**raconter**	to tell (about)
déjeuner	to have lunch	**rendre**	to return (*something*); to render, to make
descendre	to descend; to go (get) down, to get off	**rendre visite à**	to visit (*a person*)
dormir	to sleep	**répondre**	to answer
entendre	to hear	**sentir**	to smell
mentir	to lie	**servir**	to serve
partir	to leave (a *place*)	**sortir**	to go out
perdre	to lose	**vendre**	to sell
perdre la tête	to lose one's mind	**visiter**	to visit (*a place*)
perdre patience	to lose one's patience		
quitter	to leave (*a place, someone*)		

Autres expressions utiles

après	after	**léger (légère)**	light
avant	before	**quelques**	several, some, a few
comme	as; like	**sucré(e)**	sweet

Chapitre 9

Inquiétudes°

Worries

Le Chemin du retour

Feuille de service du 16 octobre
6e jour du tournage
Horaires: 9h–19h

LIEU DE TOURNAGE: PARIS—QUARTIER MOUFFETARD—Placette face au n°134, rue Mouffetard

Séquence	*Effets*	*Décors*	*Résumé*	*Rôles*
48	EXT.—MATIN	PLACE APPARTEMENT LOUISE	Camille demande à Alex de jouer° «Mon amant° de Saint-Jean». Le médecin° est inquiet. Mado ne le dit pas à Camille.	CAMILLE, MADO, ALEX, MÉDECIN

play / lover

doctor

OBJECTIFS

In this episode, you will

- learn more about Louise, Camille's grandmother
- see Hélène interview Camille for her show in Montreal

In this chapter, you will

- talk about health and parts of the body
- use direct object pronouns to avoid repetition
- talk about daily routines and activities
- discuss duties and obligations
- learn about health care in France

Vocabulaire en contexte

Les parties du corps°

Les... *Parts of the body*

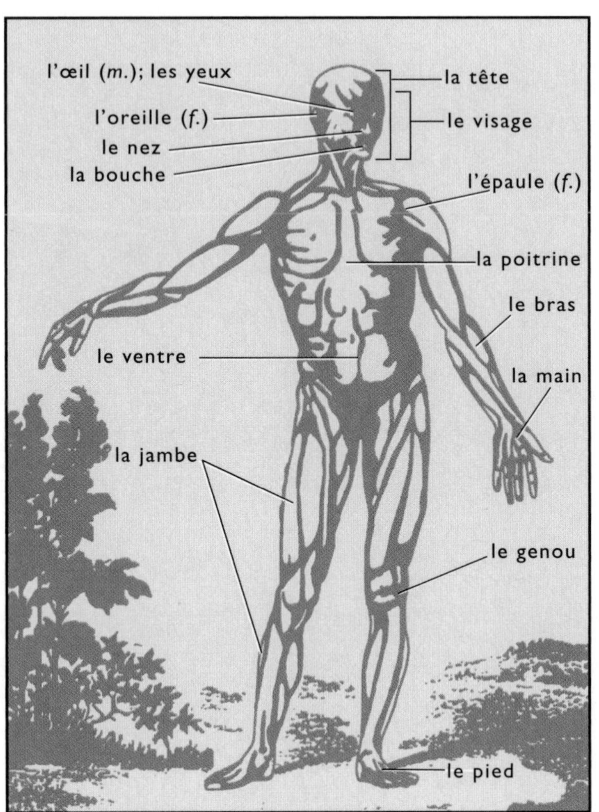

Le corps

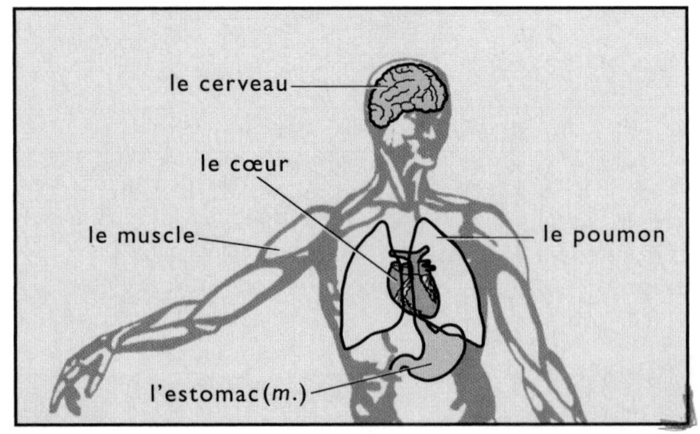

Pour en savoir plus...

The first anatomical drawing is based on the one in the 18th-century *Encyclopédie ou Dictionnaire raisonné des sciences, des arts et des métiers.* The goal of the *Encyclopédie* was to gather together the sum of human knowledge. This massive work, directed and in part written by the French philosopher and writer Denis Diderot, was published between 1751 and 1766. Other contributors included Montesquieu, Voltaire, and Rousseau, all very important writers and thinkers during that period.

Autres mots utiles

les cheveux (*m.*)	hair	**le dos**	back
la dent	tooth		

Activités

A. Identifiez. Identifiez la partie du corps.

MODÈLE: la partie du corps où se trouve le cerveau et où on trouve les cheveux, les oreilles et d'autres organes des sens →
C'est la tête.

1. les organes de la respiration
2. la partie arrière (*back*) du corps, du torse (*torso*) en particulier
3. l'organe central du système circulatoire
4. la partie de la tête où on trouve la bouche, le nez et les yeux
5. l'organe du système digestif
6. la partie du bras où il s'attache (*is attached*) au torse

B. Dans la salle de musculation. Faites-vous de la gymnastique? Combien de fois par semaine? Quels muscles sont développés par les machines et les exercices suivants?

MODÈLE: le rameur (*the rowing machine*) →
Le rameur développe les muscles du bras et des jambes.

1. les abdos (*sit-ups*)
2. le stepper
3. les flexions biceps
4. les squats
5. les pompes (*push-ups*)
6. les relevés (*lifts*) de jambes
7. les exercices aérobiques
8. les haltères (*free weights*)

C. Quelle partie du corps? Quelles parties du corps sont impliquées dans chacune (*each one*) des actions suivantes? Utilisez un verbe de la liste et une partie du corps pour chaque réponse.

Vocabulaire utile: boire, danser, écouter, entendre, essayer, faire, goûter (*to taste*), jouer (*to play*) au football américain, manger, montrer, parler, penser, porter, prendre, regarder, sentir, servir, tenir (*to hold*), toucher

MODÈLE: aller à un concert →
On écoute avec les oreilles. On regarde les musiciens avec les yeux. On montre son appréciation avec les mains.

1. apprécier un bon repas
2. aller en boîte (*to a nightclub*)
3. aller au cinéma
4. visiter un parc
5. acheter des vêtements
6. faire la cuisine avec des amis
7. aller à une conférence (*lecture*)

La santé°

La... *Health*

Michel est **malade**. Il a **un rhume**. Il **tousse** beaucoup et il **a mal à la gorge**.° C'est pourquoi il prend des **pastilles**. En plus, il a **le nez qui coule**, alors il a besoin de beaucoup de **mouchoirs en papier**.° Michel reste à la maison et boit des jus de fruits.

throat

mouchoirs... *tissues*

Nathalie n'est pas du tout **en bonne forme**; elle a **une grippe**. Elle a de **la fièvre**. Elle **a mal au** ventre et elle a des **douleurs**° musculaires. **Le médecin** lui conseille° de dormir et de prendre de **l'aspirine**. Il lui donne aussi **une ordonnance** pour **des comprimés**.

aches, pains

advises

Autres expressions utiles

une femme médecin	(*female*) doctor
un hôpital	hospital
un(e) infirmier/ière	nurse
un médicament	medicine, drug
avoir mal à	to have a pain/ache in; to have a sore . . .

avoir mal au cœur	to feel nauseated
avoir mal au ventre	to have a stomachache
être en (bonne, pleine) forme	to be in (good, great) shape
tomber malade	to become sick

Activités

A. Identifiez. Identifiez la personne ou la chose.

MODÈLE: l'endroit où vont les malades pour guérir (*to be cured*) →
C'est l'hôpital.

1. une personne qui a fait des études en médecine
2. un morceau de papier qu'on donne au pharmacien pour obtenir (*to obtain*) un médicament
3. une température élevée
4. un médicament qui réduit la douleur (*reduces pain*)
5. une maladie dont (*whose*) les symptômes sont la fièvre et des douleurs musculaires
6. une sorte de bonbon qui calme une gorge irritée

B. Maladies et remèdes. (*Illnesses and remedies.*) Pour les maladies ou conditions suivantes, décrivez (*describe*) les symptômes.

MODÈLE: Michel a un rhume. →
Il a le nez qui coule. Il tousse beaucoup. Il a mal à la gorge.

1. Brigitte a une migraine.
2. Thomas a mal au cœur.
3. Caroline a une bronchite (*bronchitis*).
4. David a une grippe.
5. Anne n'est pas en bonne forme.
6. Marguerite est stressée.

Maintenant, suggérez des remèdes possibles.

Vocabulaire utile: acheter des médicaments, aller voir le médecin, boire de l'eau, éviter (*to avoid*) l'alcool, faire du sport, prendre de l'aspirine, prendre des comprimés, prendre du repos, rester au lit

MODÈLE: Michel a un rhume. →
Restez au lit, Michel. Buvez beaucoup d'eau. Prenez de l'aspirine.

C. Une interview. Posez à votre partenaire des questions sur sa santé. Demandez-lui...

1. s'il / si elle a mal quelque part. Demandez-lui d'expliquer les symptômes.
2. ce qu'il/elle fait quand il/elle a un rhume.
3. s'il / si elle va régulièrement chez le médecin et avec quelle fréquence. Si sa réponse est négative, demandez-lui d'expliquer.
4. quelles maladies sont fréquentes chez les étudiants.
5. ce qu'on peut faire pour éviter ces maladies.
6. ce qu'il/elle pense des traitements comme l'homéopathie et l'acuponcture.

Visionnement 1

Avant de visionner

Qu'est-ce qui se passe? Voici des extraits du dialogue du film. Choisissez la réponse qui explique le dialogue.

1. LOUISE: Oh, chérie!

CAMILLE: Grand-mère, à quoi tu joues... ?° Tu veux me faire peur?

LOUISE: Je suis en pleine forme!

°à... *are you playing games?*

a. Camille est inquiète pour la santé de sa grand-mère.
b. Camille est fascinée par le jeu (*game*) de sa grand-mère.
c. Camille est contente de voir sa grand-mère.

2. HÉLÈNE: Bon ben, voilà, c'était[a] Hélène Thibaut, sur les bords[b] de la Seine, avec Camille Leclair à mes côtés. Avec un temps radieux,[c] mais un «Bientôt à Montréal» à tous.[d] Ciao!

[a]*I'm* (lit., *this was*) [b]sur... *on the banks* [c]Avec... *With great weather* [d]*everyone*

a. Hélène va quitter Paris pour rentrer (*return*) à Montréal.
b. Hélène aime Paris et ne rentre pas à Montréal.
c. Hélène fait un reportage sur les monuments du Québec.

3. CAMILLE: On va au restau? J'ai faim!

BRUNO: Tu as faim? Je ne le crois pas... !?[a] Eh! Eh oh! Appelez les photographes! Là, vite,[b] j'ai un scoop! Camille arrête son régime,[c] elle va faire un vrai repas! Ce n'est pas un scoop, ça?!

[a]Je... *I don't believe it . . . !?* [b]*quickly* [c]arrête... *is going off her diet*

a. Bruno ne veut pas aller au restaurant avec Camille.
b. Bruno taquine (*teases*) Camille, parce que d'habitude (*usually*) elle mange très peu.
c. Bruno est surpris parce que Camille préfère en général manger chez elle.

Vocabulaire relatif à l'épisode

un malaise	*weakness, fainting spell*
Vous devez	*You must*
Tu connais... ?	*Do you know . . . ?*
inutile	*useless*
au plus mal	*very ill*
Tout va bien.	*Everything's fine.*
Ne t'inquiète pas.	*Don't worry.*

Observez!

La grand-mère Louise figure dans l'Épisode 9. Regardez l'épisode et répondez à ces questions.

- À quel sujet Mado ment-elle à Camille? Qu'est-ce qu'elle dit (*say*)?
- Qu'est-ce que Louise suggère à Camille de faire avec elle?

Après le visionnement

A. Vous rappelez-vous? (*Do you remember?*) Complétez le paragraphe pour résumer l'Épisode 9 en choisissant une expression de la liste.

Vocabulaire utile:

à l'hôpital	en France	sa mère est au plus mal
à Montréal	ment	elle est en pleine forme
au lit	va bien	près de la cathédrale Notre-Dame
au restaurant	va mieux	
dans la chambre	ce n'est pas vrai	
dans la rue Mouffetard		
dans les Cévennes		

L'épisode commence _____[1] de Louise. Elle est _____[2], et le médecin l'examine.[a] Il encourage Louise à aller _____[3]. Elle refuse et dit[b] à Camille qu' _____[4]. Camille voit[c] que _____[5]. Louise demande à Camille si Alex est là, _____[6]. Camille dit oui et elle va dans la rue pour lui parler. Pendant ce temps, le médecin dit à Mado que _____[7]. Mais Mado _____[8] à Camille et dit que tout[d] _____[9].

Hélène interviewe Camille au bord de la Seine _____[10]. C'est pour une émission _____[11]. Camille dit qu'elle vit[e] bien _____[12], et que la famille est très importante pour elle.

Quand Louise _____[13], elle invite Camille à faire un voyage _____[14]. Camille est très heureuse et elle invite Bruno à venir avec elle _____[15].

[a]*is examining her* [b]*says* [c]*sees* [d]*everything* [e]*lives*

B. Réfléchissez. Répondez aux questions suivantes. Choisissez parmi les idées suggérées, ou formulez (*make up*) votre propre (*own*) hypothèse.

1. Pourquoi est-ce que Louise envoie Camille parler à Alex (l'homme avec l'accordéon)?
   a. Louise cherche un prétexte pour terminer sa conversation avec Camille.
   b. Louise veut entendre une chanson familière pour se réconforter (*comfort*).
   c. Camille et Alex sont comme frère et sœur.
2. Pourquoi Mado ment-elle quand Camille demande l'opinion du médecin?
   a. Mado et Camille n'ont pas une relation très ouverte.
   b. Mado ne veut pas faire peur à Camille.
   c. Mado a du mal à parler de la maladie et de la mort.

3. Pourquoi Louise veut-elle faire un voyage aux Cévennes?

   a. Elle cède (*gives in*) toujours aux demandes de Camille.
   b. Elle veut montrer la région à Camille, qui ne la connaît pas.
   c. Elle veut apprendre plus de détails sur l'histoire de son mari.

Structure 27

Le complément d'objet direct

Avoiding repetition

—Je **te** remercie beaucoup.

Le complément d'objet direct

You have already studied indirect objects as one type of verb complement. Another verb complement is the direct object.▲ A direct object is the person or thing that is affected by the action of the verb (that is, it answers the question *what?* or *whom?*). Direct object nouns are not preceded by a preposition.

Vous attendez le prince charmant?
Nous regardons l'émission «Bonjour!»
Martine donne le médaillon à Camille.
Bruno présente Rachid à Camille.

Les pronoms compléments d'objet direct

me (m')	*me*	**nous**	*us*
te (t')	*you*	**vous**	*you*
le (l')	*him/it*	**les**	*them (m., f.)*
la (l')	*her/it*		

1. Direct object pronouns refer to or replace direct object nouns in a sentence. Use of either **le** or **la** depends on whether the direct object is masculine or feminine. Use of **me**, **te**, **nous**, and **vous** depends on whether you are referring to yourself or to the person or people you are talking to.

Martine trouve le médaillon. Martine **le** trouve. *Martine finds it.*	Martine regarde la photo. Martine **la** regarde. *Martine looks at it.*
Je **t'**aime, grand-mère. Et tu **m'**aimes aussi, n'est-ce pas?	*I love you, Grandmother. And you love me too, don't you?*

2. Like indirect object pronouns, the direct object pronoun directly precedes the verb in both affirmative and negative sentences (except in the affirmative imperative).

Je **te** remercie beaucoup, Camille.	*I thank you very much, Camille.*
Tu as faim? Je ne **le** crois pas... !	*You're hungry? I don't believe it . . . !*

3. In the negative imperative, word order follows the normal rule (i.e., the pronoun precedes the verb), but in the affirmative imperative, the pronoun follows the verb and is attached with a hyphen. **Me** becomes **moi** and **te** becomes **toi**.

	Ne **la** regarde pas!	*Don't look at her/it!*
	Ne **m'**attendez pas!	*Don't wait for me!*
but	Regarde-**la**!	*Look at her/it!*
	Attendez-**moi**!	*Wait for me!*

4. In verb + infinitive constructions, the pronoun again directly precedes the verb for which it is the object (usually the infinitive). If the sentence is negative, the negation surrounds the conjugated verb, not the infinitive.

Elle va **l'**interviewer sur les bords de la Seine.	*She is going to interview her on the banks of the Seine.*
Elle **ne** va **pas l'**interviewer à Canal 7.	*She is not going to interview her at Channel 7.*
Nous voulons **vous** inviter.	*We want to invite you.*
Vous **ne** pouvez **pas m'**entendre?	*You can't hear me?*
Il **ne nous** invite **pas** à sortir.	*He doesn't ask us to go out.*

5. Some verbs that take a direct object in French take an indirect object in English. Among them are the following:

attendre *to wait for (someone, something)*
écouter *to listen to (someone, something)*
regarder *to look at (someone, something)*

Bruno **attend** Camille sur le plateau.	*Bruno waits for Camille on the set.*

Activités

A. Les personnages. Faites des questions avec les éléments donnés, puis (*then*) répondez aux questions à l'affirmatif ou au négatif avec un pronom sujet et un pronom complément d'objet direct.

MODÈLE: Yasmine / regarder / la télévision (non) →
É1: Est-ce que Yasmine regarde la télévision?
É2: Non, elle ne la regarde pas.

1. une employée de l'hôtel / apporter (*to bring*) / le dîner d'Hélène (non)
2. Bruno / manger / sa salade (oui)
3. la femme du boucher / regarder / l'émission (oui)
4. Camille / aller finir / son dessert (non)
5. Rachid / préparer / ses reportages (oui)
6. il / vouloir montrer / ses reportages à Martine (oui)
7. Yasmine / mettre / son pyjama (oui)
8. Rachid / mettre / sa cravate (non)
9. Hélène / aller quitter / l'hôtel (non)

B. Un(e) fiancé(e) complexé(e). Vous venez de vous fiancer, mais votre fiancé(e) a un complexe d'infériorité. Répondez à ses questions et rassurez-le/la.

MODÈLE: É1: Est-ce que tu veux me parler tous les jours?
É2: Bien sûr, je veux te parler tous les jours.

1. Est-ce que tu me trouves magnifique?
2. Est-ce que tes amis nous regardent avec jalousie?
3. Est-ce que tu me cherches quand tu es en ligne?
4. Est-ce que tes parents nous respectent?
5. Est-ce que tu m'aimes de tout ton cœur?

Maintenant, refaites cette activité et donnez des réponses négatives.

C. J'adore... Je déteste... Benoît, un camarade de classe de Yasmine, a des opinions arrêtées (*definite*). Imaginez les réponses de sa mère. Utilisez un impératif négatif ou affirmatif selon la logique de la situation.

Verbes utiles: acheter, attendre, écouter, finir, manger, mettre, prendre, regarder

MODÈLES: BENOÎT: Je déteste *cette émission.*
SA MÈRE: Ne la regarde pas, alors!

BENOÎT: J'adore *cette chanson* (*song*).
SA MÈRE: Alors écoute-la!

1. Je n'aime pas *ce poisson.*
2. J'aime *cette musique.*
3. Je n'aime pas *ce pantalon ridicule.*
4. Je déteste *ces chaussures.*
5. Je veux *ce CD de rock.*
6. Je ne veux pas *ce médicament.*
7. Je veux regarder *cette émission sur les dinosaures.*
8. Je ne veux pas *t'*attendre.

D. Questions et réponses. Posez des questions en utilisant les éléments des trois colonnes. Votre partenaire va vous répondre.

MODÈLE: É1: Est-ce que tes parents écoutent les concerts de rock?
É2: Non, ils ne les écoutent pas.

tu	aimer	le bus
tes amis	attendre	un café le matin
tes amis et toi	comprendre	les concerts de rock
tes parents	écouter	les devoirs avant la classe
ta classe	faire	la télé le week-end
nous	finir	me
	prendre	nous
	regarder	le professeur
		la radio

Regards sur la culture

La santé en France

The United Nations has consistently placed France at or near the top of its world ratings based on access to health care. We tend to think of health as a rather objective matter, but cultural attitudes and traditions always play a large role in people's sense of what is healthful and what is not and in the development of policies for health care delivery.

- In part, culture determines what we think makes us healthy or sick. North Americans think of apples as especially healthful. In France, apples are considered hard to digest. On the other hand, many French people consider nearly any moving air a draft (**un courant d'air**) and a threat to one's health.
- Many common digestive complaints are referred to in France as **une crise de foie** (literally, *a liver attack*). Doctors even use this term in their diagnoses. The **crise de foie**, from which so many French people suffer, does not correspond to any single Anglo-American illness.
- French doctors make house calls, even in the middle of the night when necessary. They tend to prescribe larger numbers of different medicines than do their counterparts in North America. In fact, the French consume more medicine than any other nationality in Europe, though the government is now urging doctors to prescribe less. French doctors are also relatively generous in prescribing long hospital stays and time off from work.

Le médecin examine Louise chez elle.

- The French system of **Sécurité sociale**, established in 1945, reimburses 75 percent of health care expenses, and about 70 percent of prescription medicine costs, although the average patient is expected to pay the doctor or pharmacist at time of service. However, many people in France take out additional insurance policies so that nearly all of their expenses are covered. Prenatal care, as prescribed by French Social Security, is virtually free and is considered a world-class model by most professionals.
- French pharmacists have a good deal of medical training and are often consulted for common health problems. They are also expected to be able to examine mushrooms collected in the woods to indicate if they are edible or not. The Health Code limits the number of pharmacies that may be opened, through a licensing process. In a city of over 30,000 people, for example, there may be only one pharmacy for every 3000 inhabitants. One of the functions of such limits is to protect the integrity and prestige of the profession.

Considérez

The French Social Security system was founded on the explicit need for maintaining "national solidarity." This is related to the notion of **fraternité** that was one of the founding principles of the French Revolution. In what ways do the health care systems in North America relate to general cultural and political principles?

Structure 28

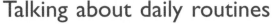

Les verbes pronominaux

Talking about daily routines

—Maman est fatiguée à cause du déménagement. Alors, **elle se repose.**

—Alors, qu'est-ce que vous attendez? **Vous vous embrassez?**

A set of French verbs, called pronominal verbs,▲ are conjugated with a personal pronoun in addition to the subject. You have already heard or seen a few pronominal verbs in *Le Chemin du retour* and in your textbook.

Je **m'appelle** Isabelle.

Où **se trouve** la bibliothèque?

1. In pronominal verbs, the pronoun corresponds to the subject. It directly precedes the verb in both affirmative and negative uses (except in the affirmative imperative). In negative sentences, the **ne** precedes the pronoun and **pas** (**jamais**, etc.) follows the verb.

se laver (*to wash*)			
je **me**	lave	nous **nous**	lavons
tu **te**	laves	vous **vous**	lavez
il, elle, on **se**	lave	ils, elles **se**	lavent

	Je ne me rappelle jamais.	*I never remember.*
	Pourquoi **s'intéresse-t-il** à ces photos?	*Why is he interested in these photos?*
	Ne *t*'inquiète pas.	*Don't worry.*
but	**Lavez-*vous*!**	*Get washed!*

Notice that when **me**, **te**, and **se** precede a verb that begins with a vowel sound, they become **m'**, **t'**, and **s'**.

2. Here are some common pronominal verbs.

s'amuser	*to have a good time*
s'appeler*	*to be named*
se brosser (les dents, les cheveux)	*to brush* (*one's teeth, one's hair*)
se casser	*to break* (*a limb*)
se coucher	*to go to bed*
se dépêcher	*to hurry*
se disputer	*to argue*
s'embrasser	*to kiss* (*each other*)
s'endormir	*to fall asleep*
s'entendre (bien/mal) (avec)	*to get along* (*well, poorly*) (*with*)
se fâcher (contre)	*to become angry* (*with*)
s'habiller (en)	*to get dressed* (*in*)
s'inquiéter† (de, pour)	*to worry* (*about*)
s'intéresser à	*to be interested in*
se laver	*to get washed, wash up*
se laver (les mains, les cheveux)	*to wash* (*one's hands, hair*)

*conjugated like **appeler: je m'appelle, nous nous appelons**

†conjugated like **préférer: je m'inquiète, nous nous inquiétons**

se lever*	*to get up (out of bed); to stand up*
se maquiller	*to put on makeup*
se passer	*to happen*
se peigner (les cheveux)	*to comb (one's hair)*
se promener*	*to take a walk*
se rappeler†	*to remember*
se raser	*to shave*
se rendre compte (de)	*to realize*
se reposer	*to rest*
se réveiller	*to wake up*
se souvenir‡ (de)	*to remember*
se tromper (de)	*to make a mistake, be mistaken (about)*

3. In the negative imperative, the word order follows the normal rule. However, in the affirmative imperative, the pronoun follows the verb and is attached with a hyphen. **Te** becomes **toi**.

	Ne **t'**inquiète pas.	*Don't worry.*
	Ne **nous** disputons pas.	*Let's not argue.*
but	Dépêchons-**nous**!	*Let's hurry up.*
	Réveille-**toi**!	*Wake up!*

4. In verb + infinitive constructions, where the pronominal verb is usually the infinitive, the pronoun precedes the infinitive. If the sentence is negative, the negation surrounds the conjugated verb, not the infinitive.

Yasmine et moi, **on va** *se* **promener** un petit peu.	*Yasmine and I are going to take a little walk.*
Mado ***ne* peut *pas* se rappeler** le code.	*Mado can't remember the code.*

5. When a pronominal verb is used to talk about actions that affect a part of the body, the definite article is used before the body part.

Camille se brosse **les** dents et **les** cheveux, et elle se maquille **les** yeux et **les** lèvres.	*Camille brushes her teeth and her hair, and she puts makeup on her eyes and lips.*

6. Pronominal verbs sometimes have a *reciprocal* sense: They describe an action that two or more people do for or to each other.

Camille et Louise **se téléphonent**.	*Camille and Louise call each other.*
Nous **nous parlons** le samedi.	*We speak to each other on Saturdays.*
On **se marie**, toi et moi?	*Want to get married?*

---

*conjugated like **acheter: je me lève, nous nous levons**

†conjugated like **appeler: je me rappelle, nous nous rappelons**

‡conjugated like **venir: je me souviens de, nous nous souvenons de**

Activités

A. Qu'est-ce qui se passe? Complétez chaque phrase avec la forme correcte d'un des deux verbes.

MODÈLE: Camille et Bruno ______. (s'embrasser, se regarder) → Camille et Bruno se regardent.

1. Le soleil (*sun*) ______ au début de «Bonjour!» (se lever, se passer)

2. Camille ______ bien pour l'émission sur la mode. (se disputer, s'habiller)

3. Louise ______ de son mari, Antoine. (se souvenir, se tromper)

4. Camille et Mado ______. (s'embrasser, se disputer)

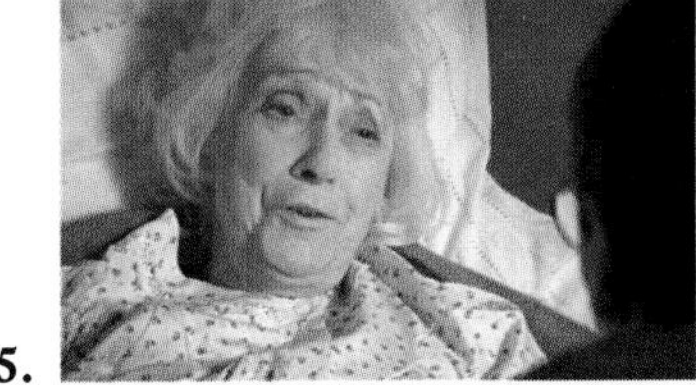

5. Selon le médecin, Louise a besoin de ______. (s'habiller, se reposer)

6. Mado et le médecin ______ de la santé de Louise. (se souvenir, s'inquiéter)

7. Yasmine (à ses parents): «Alors, qu'est-ce que vous attendez? Vous ______ ?» (se disputer, s'embrasser)

8. Camille: «Rachid, tu es gentil, tu me poses des questions, tu ______ à ma famille... » (se parler, s'intéresser)

9. Les deux enfants ______ au marché. (se coucher, s'amuser)

B. Ce qu'on fait. Utilisez un verbe pronominal pour exprimer la suite (*outcome*) logique des situations suivantes. Plusieurs réponses sont possibles, à l'affirmatif et au négatif.

MODÈLE: Nous sommes le couple parfait. Nous... →
Nous ne nous disputons pas. Nous nous embrassons. Nous nous entendons bien.

1. Marie Dupont prend le nom de son mari, Christian Martel. Maintenant, elle...
2. Il est 7 h du matin. Les étudiants...
3. Tu as les mains sales (*dirty*). Tu...
4. Paul et Virginie s'aiment. Ils...
5. Vous allez à une soirée élégante. Vous...
6. Mes parents n'ont pas assez d'argent. Ils...
7. Nous parlons des vacances (*vacations*) passées. Nous...
8. Magalie a envie d'aller au parc. Elle...
9. La classe commence à 8 h, mais tu es en retard et tu arrives à 8 h 30. Tu...
10. J'ai les cheveux en désordre. Je...
11. Pierre tombe quand il fait du ski. Il...
12. Je rends visite à ma grand-mère. Je...

C. Conseils. (*Advice.*) Utilisez la forme affirmative ou négative de l'impératif des verbes utilisés dans les phrases suivantes pour donner des conseils à ces personnes. Suivez le modèle.

MODÈLE: Paul se réveille à 11 h 30. →
Réveille-toi à 6 h 30! (Ne te réveille pas à 11 h 30!)

1. Christian et Anne s'embrassent souvent en public.
2. Monique se maquille au restaurant.
3. Carole et Jean-Pierre se disputent tout le temps.
4. Nicole se dépêche tous les matins.
5. Magalie se couche à 2 h du matin.
6. Chantal et François ne se parlent pas.
7. Myriam et David se promènent au centre-ville à minuit.

D. La routine. Parlez avec votre partenaire de votre routine quotidienne (*daily*). Comparez vos habitudes et préparez ensemble un résumé (*summary*) des similarités et des différences en utilisant au moins cinq verbes pronominaux. Présentez ce résumé à la classe.

MODÈLE: É1: À 6 h 30, je me réveille. Et toi?
É2: Moi, je me réveille à 6 h, mais je me lève à 6 h 30.

Structure 29

Le verbe devoir

Talking about duties and obligations

—Vous **devez** aller à l'hôpital.

devoir (*to have to, must; to owe*)			
je	**dois**	nous	**devons**
tu	**dois**	vous	**devez**
il, elle, on	**doit**	ils, elles	**doivent**

1. The verb **devoir** expresses obligation or probability when followed by an infinitive.

   Quelqu'un **doit** rester près d'elle. — *Someone must stay close to her.*
   Louise **doit** parler au médecin. — *Louise must (has to) speak to the doctor.*
   Alex **doit** avoir environ 20 ans. — *Alex must be about 20 years old.*

2. When used with a noun, **devoir** means *to owe.*

   Nous **devons** beaucoup de respect à nos collègues. — *We owe a lot of respect to our colleagues.*
   Je lui **dois** 500 euros. — *I owe him 500 euros.*

Activités

A. Quand ça ne va pas. (*When you're not feeling well.*) Complétez les phrases avec la forme correcte du verbe **devoir**.

1. Quand on a le bras cassé, on _____ aller chez le médecin.
2. Quand vous avez mal à la tête, vous _____ prendre de l'aspirine.
3. Quand j'ai une grippe, je _____ boire beaucoup d'eau.
4. Quand les enfants sont malades, ils ne _____ pas aller à l'école.
5. Quand nous consultons un spécialiste, nous lui _____ beaucoup d'argent.
6. Quand tu as mal aux yeux, tu _____ mettre des lunettes de soleil.

B. Obligations. Qu'est-ce que les personnes suivantes doivent faire dans les situations décrites?

MODÈLE: Vous comparaissez (*appear*) devant un tribunal. →
Je dois dire la vérité.

1. Vos amis ont trouvé un sac contenant (*containing*) mille dollars.
2. Vos parents et vous, vous vous disputez souvent.
3. Votre amie a trouvé un chat perdu (*lost cat*) dans la rue.
4. Vous allez arriver en retard pour un rendez-vous important.
5. Vous avez vu un de vos camarades de classe qui a triché (*cheated*) à un examen.

C. Responsabilités et désirs. Posez à votre partenaire des questions sur les responsabilités et les désirs des personnes suivantes. Essayez d'utiliser des verbes pronominaux après **devoir**, **vouloir**, **avoir envie de**, etc.

MODÈLE: É1: Est-ce que votre père doit se lever à 8 h du matin?
É2: Non, il doit se lever à 6 h.
É1: Qu'est-ce qu'il veut faire?
É2: Il veut se recoucher (*go back to bed*).

ta mère (tes enfants, etc.)	à 6 h (8 h, 10 h 30, etc.) du matin
ton/ta meilleur(e) (*best*) ami(e)	à midi
ton professeur	à 15 h (16 h 30, 17 h, etc.)
tu	le week-end
tes amis et toi	pendant la semaine
nous	pendant les vacances (*vacation*)

Visionnement 2

Observez!

Considérez les aspects culturels expliqués dans **Regards sur la culture**. Ensuite, regardez l'Épisode 9 encore une fois, et répondez aux questions suivantes.

- Quelle pratique particulière aux médecins français voit-on dans cet épisode?
- En parlant de la France avec Hélène, Camille dit: «C'est un pays que j'aime. On y vit bien.» Dans cet épisode et dans le film en général, qu'est-ce qui montre qu'on vit bien en France?

Après le visionnement

Faites l'activité pour le **Visionnement 2** dans le cahier.

Synthèse: Culture

La médecine et la culture

Dans le monde francophone, la médecine moderne est toujours présente. Au Canada et en Belgique, le gouvernement assure l'accès aux soins médicaux,[1] comme en France. Mais dans beaucoup de pays, il n'y a pas assez de médecins. Par exemple, au Maroc, il y a seulement[2] un médecin pour 5.000 personnes. Dans ces pays, la médecine moderne coexiste avec la médecine ancienne ou traditionnelle.

Les médecines douces[3]

En France et dans les autres pays francophones, il y a aussi des personnes qui guérissent[4] les malades avec des plantes, des mouvements de la main et d'autres méthodes anciennes. Ces «médecines traditionnelles» sont souvent très efficaces.[5] En 1999, l'Organisation Mondiale de la Santé[6] a recommandé l'intégration de la médecine traditionnelle dans les systèmes modernes de santé en Afrique.

En France, on appelle ces médecines «les médecines douces».

Le thermalisme

Le thermalisme, c'est l'utilisation de l'eau de source[7] dans la médecine. En Amérique du Nord, le thermalisme n'est pas très important dans la médecine aujourd'hui, mais en France, son rôle est considérable. Les médecins recommandent souvent des «cures». Faire une cure, c'est passer un certain nombre de jours dans une station thermale.

L'Auvergne est une région française particulièrement importante pour le thermalisme. Située dans le centre de la France, c'est une région volcanique. L'eau d'une station thermale contient[8] souvent beaucoup de minéraux. Elle est souvent chaude ou gazeuse. Et quelquefois elle est radioactive. Les stations thermales ont des spécialités. Voici quelques détails sur la station de Saint-Nectaire, en Auvergne.

La station thermale de Vichy

Saint-Nectaire

Agent thérapeutique

Il y a plus de 40 sources. L'eau de la station de Saint-Nectaire est chaude et gazeuse. Elle est riche en lithium et en autres minéraux.

Indications

- les maladies urinaires
- les maladies métaboliques (obésité, diabète, hypertension artérielle, etc.)
- le stress

[1]soins... *health care* [2]*only* [3]Les... *Alternative medicine* [4]*heal* [5]*effective* [6]Organisation... *World Health Organization* [7]l'eau... *spring water* [8]*contains*

Soins proposés	*Autres activités proposées*
• la cure de boisson • le bain thermal • le bain d'algues[9] • le bain de boue[10] • la douche au jet[11] • les massages • l'aquagym[12]	• le tennis • le mini-golf • la pêche[13] • les promenades dans la montagne • les promenades au lac Chambon • la visite des églises[14] médiévales • les concerts • le casino • la cuisine traditionnelle d'Auvergne

[9]*seaweed* [10]*mud* [11]douche… *high-pressure shower* [12]*pool gymnastics* [13]*fishing* [14]*churches*

À vous

Une cure. Imagine that you have won a free stay of one night and one day at the spa in Saint-Nectaire. This prize includes four treatment sessions, three meals, and free access to all other activities. You want to take advantage of this prize to reduce your stress level, and so you plan a program for the day. List your activities for the day, starting at 8 A.M. and ending at 9 P.M., when you return home.

À écrire

Faites **À écrire** pour le Chapitre 9 dans le cahier.

Vocabulaire

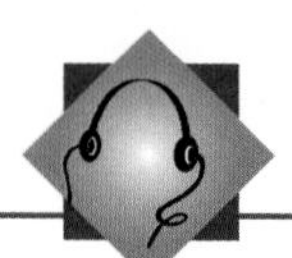

Les parties du corps

la bouche	mouth
le bras	arm
le cerveau	brain
les cheveux (*m. pl.*)	hair
le cœur	heart
le corps	body
la dent	tooth
le dos	back
l'épaule (*f.*)	shoulder
le genou	knee
la gorge	throat
la jambe	leg
la main	hand
le nez	nose
l'œil (*m.*) **(les yeux)**	eye
l'oreille (*f.*)	ear
le pied	foot
la poitrine	chest
le poumon	lung
la tête	head
le ventre	belly; abdomen
le visage	face

MOTS APPARENTÉS: **l'estomac** (*m.*), **le muscle**

La santé

un comprimé tablet
une douleur ache, pain
une grippe influenza (flu)
un(e) infirmier/ière nurse
un(e) médecin / femme médecin doctor
un médicament medicine, drug
un mouchoir en papier facial tissue
le nez qui coule runny nose
une ordonnance prescription
une pastille cough drop, lozenge
un rhume common cold
la santé health
avoir de la fièvre to have a fever
avoir mal à to have pain / an ache in; to have a sore . . .
avoir mal au cœur to feel nauseated
avoir mal au ventre to have a stomachache
être en (bonne, pleine) forme to be in (good, great) shape; to feel good
tomber malade to become sick
tousser to cough
malade sick

MOTS APPARENTÉS: **une aspirine, un hôpital**

Pronoms compléments d'objet direct

me me
te you
le, la him; her; it
nous us
vous you
les them

Verbes

s'amuser to have a good time
s'appeler to be named
se brosser (les dents, les cheveux) to brush (one's teeth, one's hair)
se casser to break (*a limb*)
se coucher to go to bed
se dépêcher to hurry
devoir to have to, must; to owe
se disputer to argue
s'embrasser to kiss (each other)
s'endormir to fall asleep
s'entendre (bien, mal) (avec) to get along (well, poorly) (with)
se fâcher (contre) to become angry (with)
s'habiller (en) to get dressed (in)
s'inquiéter (de, pour) to worry (about)
s'intéresser à to be interested in
se laver to get washed, wash up
se laver (les mains, les cheveux) to wash (one's hands, hair)
se lever to get up (*out of bed*); to stand up
se maquiller to put on makeup
se passer to happen
se peigner (les cheveux) to comb (one's hair)
se promener to take a walk
se rappeler to remember
se raser to shave
se rendre compte (de) to realize
se reposer to rest
se réveiller to wake up
se souvenir (de) to remember
se tromper (de) to make a mistake, be mistaken (about)

Autre expression utile

mal badly

Chapitre 10

Rendez-vous au restaurant

Le Chemin du retour

Feuille de service du 11 octobre
1er jour du tournage
Horaires: 7h–17h

LIEU DE TOURNAGE: PARIS—«À la Pomponette», 42, rue Lepic, 18e

Séquence	*Effets*	*Décors*	*Résumé*	*Rôles*
64	INT.—NUIT	RESTAURANT MOUFFETARD—Salle à manger	Camille et Bruno plaisantent° et passent leur commande°.	CAMILLE, BRUNO, PATRON RESTAURANT

joke
passent… *order*

OBJECTIFS

In this episode, you will

- watch Camille and Bruno order dinner
- listen to banter between the husband and wife who own the restaurant
- learn more about Camille's and Bruno's family life

In this chapter, you will

- talk about things to do in the city
- learn how to order a meal
- discuss the weather
- talk about past events and when they happened
- talk about what you see and what you believe
- learn about French cafés and restaurants
- read about World War II in France

Vocabulaire en contexte

Les distractions en ville°

La vie° **urbaine** offre beaucoup de **distractions** (*f.*), le jour et **la nuit**.°
On peut aller, par exemple,

Les... *Recreational activities in the city*

life / night

On peut aussi faire

Pour en savoir plus...

French cities often have free or inexpensive publications that list upcoming movies and cultural and sporting events. In Paris, two of the most popular are *Pariscope* and *L'Officiel des spectacles*. *Pariscope* has a site on the Web.

Tickets for major events may be purchased at the box office, at the FNAC (a chain of book, music, video, and electronics stores), or by Minitel.

The Minitel is a small computer terminal connected by phone to an online database. A user can obtain telephone numbers and schedules, as well as access to many other services.

Notez bien!

To say you play a sport or a game, use **jouer à** + sport or game.

Tu aimes **jouer au base-ball?** *Do you like playing baseball?*

To say you play a musical instrument, use **jouer de** + instrument.

Mon ami **joue du piano**. *My friend plays the piano.*

A more generic expression is **faire de** + sport, game, instrument.

Je **fais du jogging** tous les jours. *I jog every day.*

Il **fait du piano**. *He is playing the piano.*

Et on peut
jouer° au billard.
jouer au volley-ball.

play

Les fanatiques du sport aiment aussi aller aux **matchs** (*m.*) **de foot° (football)** ou à **des matchs de boxe**, par exemple. Le **football américain°** n'est pas très pratiqué en France, mais il est de plus en plus° populaire grâce à° la télévision.

soccer
football... *football*
de... *more and more* / grâce... *thanks to*

Autres mots utiles

un jeu (**des jeux**)	game
une ville	city
assister à	to attend (*an event*)

Langage fonctionnel

Pour commander un repas°

Pour... *Ordering a meal*

Here are some expressions that are useful when dining in a restaurant in France.

Le serveur / La serveuse

Vous prenez un apéritif?	*Would you like an aperitif?*
Vous avez choisi?	*Have you decided?*
Qu'est-ce que vous désirez comme entrée?	*What would you like for the first course?*
Et comme plat principal?	*And as a main dish?*
Et à boire?	*And to drink?*
C'est terminé?	*Will that be all?*
Bon appétit.	*Enjoy your meal.*
Tout va comme vous voulez?	*Is everything to your liking?*

Vous

Je voudrais... / Je vais prendre...	*I'd like . . . / I'll take . . .*
le menu à [20] euros	*the [20] euro meal*
L'addition, s'il vous plaît.	*May I have the check, please?*

—**Vous avez choisi**, madame?
—Oui. **Je vais prendre** le menu à 12 euros.

Activités

A. Loisirs. (***Leisure.***) Qu'est-ce que ces personnes vont faire aujourd'hui? Basez vos réponses sur leurs personnalités.

MODÈLE: M. Coste: Il adore les Impressionnistes.
M. Coste va aller au musée.

1. Mlle Matt: Le soir, elle adore sortir et danser avec d'autres jeunes.
2. Mlle Regolo: Elle apprécie beaucoup la musique classique.

3. Mme Senty: Elle aime essayer les cuisines exotiques.
4. M. Sollier: Il attend avec impatience le prochain (*next*) film de Bruce Willis.
5. M. Albe: C'est un fanatique de football.

B. Une soirée au restaurant. Vous allez au restaurant avec un ami / une amie. En groupes de trois, jouez les rôles des clients et du serveur.

1. Le serveur / La serveuse vous accueille (*welcomes*) et vous annonce les spécialités de la maison.
2. Vous consultez le menu à 20 euros. N'oubliez pas de poser des questions au serveur / à la serveuse si vous voulez des détails sur la préparation d'un plat ou si vous n'êtes pas certain(e) de la boisson à choisir.
3. Vous choisissez et le serveur / la serveuse répond.
4. Pendant le repas, le serveur / la serveuse vous demande si tout va comme vous voulez. Quand il/elle part, vous dites à votre ami(e) pourquoi vous aimez ce restaurant.
5. À la fin du repas, vous demandez l'addition.

Restaurant Chez Paul

Menu à 20 €

Les Entrées
Assiette anglaise (jambon cru,[a] jambon cuit,[b] saucisson[c])
Le pâté du chef
Tomates et mozzarella
Quiche

Les Plats principaux
Riz à l'espagnole (riz, porc, poivrons,[d] crevettes, tomates)
Couscous à l'agneau[e]
Poulet rôti[f] avec haricots verts
Cassoulet (haricots blancs, saucisses, sauce tomate)
Spaghettis bolognaises (spaghettis, sauce tomate à la viande)
Steak-frites
Côte[g] de porc avec purée de pommes de terre
Filets de sardine en marinade orientale

Le Plateau[h] de fromages

La Salade verte

Les Desserts
Tarte aux pommes
Crème caramel
Mousse au chocolat
Sorbet aux fruits
Bananes flambées[i] à la crème Chantilly[j]
Riz au lait maison

Les Boissons
Vin rouge, rosé ou blanc (carafe, bouteille, demi-bouteille)
Eau minérale
Bière[k]
Café, Thé

[a]*smoked* [b]*cooked* [c]*salami* [d]*sweet peppers* [e]*lamb* [f]*roasted* [g]*Cutlet* [h]*Platter* [i]*flaming* [j]*crème... whipped cream* [k]*Beer*

C. Distractions. Posez les questions suivantes à votre partenaire. Demandez-lui...

1. combien de fois par semaine il/elle va au restaurant.
2. s'il / si elle fait souvent de la musculation. Sinon (*If not*), avec quelle fréquence (parfois, rarement, jamais)?
3. s'il / si elle aime aller au musée. Si oui, quelle sorte de musée préfère-t-il/elle?
4. s'il / si elle est fanatique de sport. Si oui, quel(s) sport(s) aime-t-il/elle? Va-t-il/elle voir des matchs?
5. combien de fois par mois il/elle va au cinéma ou au théâtre.
6. s'il / si elle joue d'un instrument. De quel instrument? Joue-t-il/elle bien ou mal?
7. à quels sports ou jeux il/elle aime jouer.

Le temps et les saisons°

Le... *Weather and seasons*

Pour en savoir plus...

Temperature in France and Canada is measured in degrees Celsius. Compare some common Celsius temperatures to their close equivalents in the Fahrenheit scale used in the United States.

0°C is the same as 32°F and is the freezing point of water.

10°C is about 50°F.

20°C is about 68°F.

34°C is about 90°F.

100°C is the same as 212°F and is the boiling point of water.

Quel temps fait-il aujourd'hui? Quelles sont **les températures** (*f.*)? Consultons **la météo**.

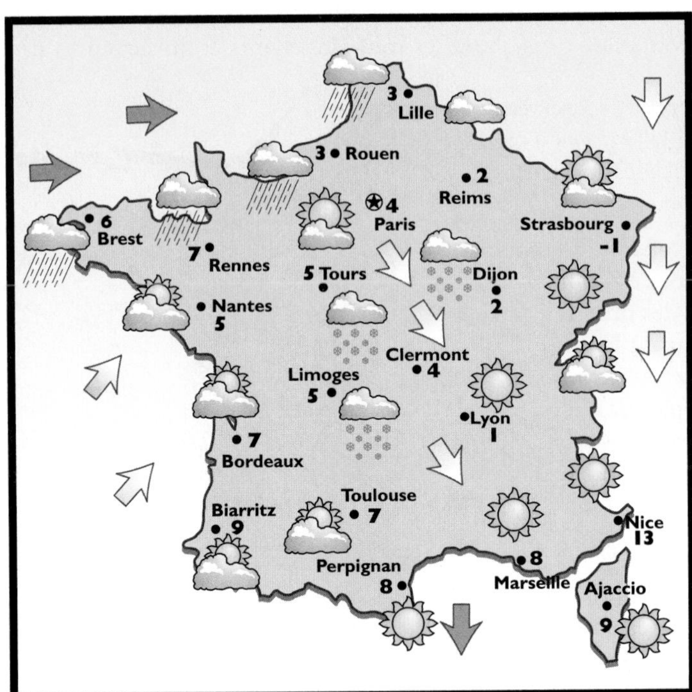

Le 16 janvier. **Le temps** est **nuageux** au nord de la Loire. **Le ciel est couvert** à Reims. **Il fait froid**. **Il neige** à l'intérieur des terres° et **il pleut** de la Bretagne à la Normandie. Il va **faire du vent** près des côtes. À Marseille, **le ciel est clair** et **il fait du soleil**.

intérieur... *center of the country*

Pour en savoir plus...

The islands of Guadeloupe and Martinique are overseas departments (like states) of France in the Caribbean Sea. They have two seasons.

- The dry season, from December to May, is known as **le carême antillais**.
- The rainy season is known as **l'hivernage**, which, despite its name, actually corresponds to summer, in the months from June to November. This is the season for hurricanes and cyclones.

Les quatre saisons (*f.*) de Paris

En hiver (*m.*), les nuits sont longues. Il fait souvent froid, il pleut souvent et parfois il neige.

Au printemps (*m.*), les jours sont plus longs.[a] **Il fait** plus **doux**.[b] Il pleut, mais **il fait** rarement **mauvais**.

[a]plus... *longer* [b]plus... *milder*

En été (*m.*), **il fait** souvent **beau** et **chaud**.[c] Il y a parfois **un orage**[d] en fin de journée.[e]

[c]*hot* [d]*thunderstorm* [e]en... *at the end of the day*

En automne (*m.*), **il fait frais**[f] et il pleut souvent.

[f]*cool*

Un seul printemps
dans l'année...,
et dans la vie
une seule jeunesse.

Simone de Beauvoir

Activités

A. Des cartes postales. Voici des cartes postales de diverses régions de la France. Quel temps fait-il dans ces scènes? De quelle saison s'agit-il?

1.

2.

3.

4.

B. La météo. Voici une carte météorologique du Canada. Parcourez (*Scan*) les températures maximales et minimales et regardez les dessins. De quelle saison s'agit-il? Faites des prévisions (*forecasts*) pour les villes données.

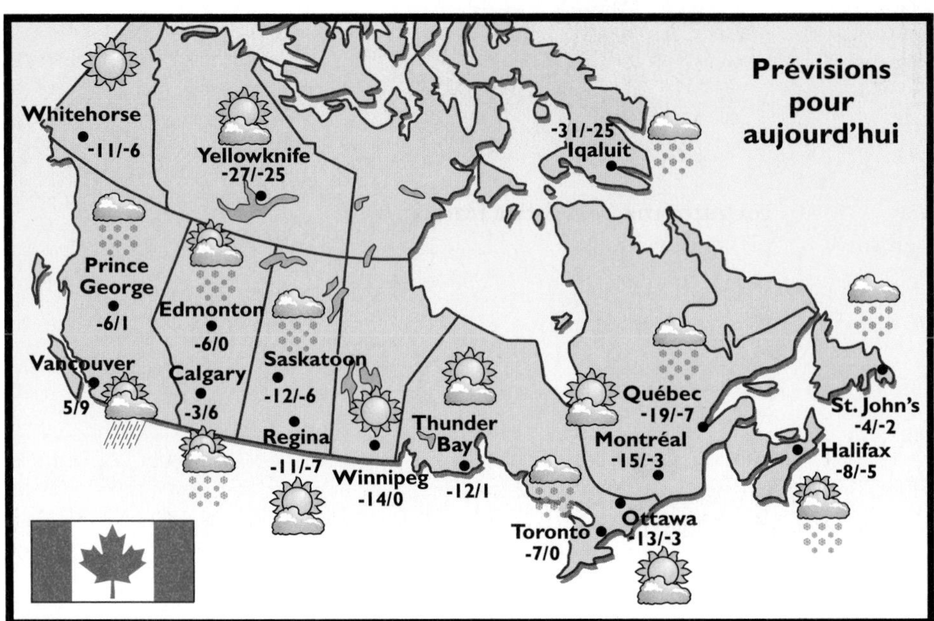

MODÈLE: À Whitehorse, il va faire très froid. On prévoit une température minimale de moins 11 et une température maximale de moins 6. Il va faire du soleil.

C. Les saisons. Décrivez (*Describe*) les saisons dans votre ville.

MODÈLE: J'habite à Miami. En été, il fait très chaud, mais en hiver, il fait doux. Ma saison préférée est le printemps parce que...

Visionnement 1

Avant de visionner

Histoire de couples. Dans cet épisode, vous allez voir Camille et Bruno et le patron et la patronne du restaurant, un couple marié. Lisez (*Read*) le dialogue entre ces deux derniers (*latter two*), et choisissez la phrase qui résume la scène.

1. PATRONNE: Tu as vu ça?[a] C'est étonnant![b]
PATRON: Quoi?
PATRONNE: Ils sont à nouveau ensemble,[c] ces deux-là?
PATRON: Ben, apparemment, oui. Il faut croire.[d]

[a]Tu... *Did you see that?* [b]*amazing* [c]à... *together again* [d]Il... *It looks like it.*

a. Le patron et la patronne connaissent déjà (*already know*) Bruno et Camille.
b. Le patron et la patronne n'aiment pas beaucoup Bruno et Camille.
c. C'est la première fois que Camille et Bruno viennent dans ce restaurant.

2. PATRONNE: Tu regardes trop de sitcoms à la télévision!
PATRON: Mais, je ne regarde que toi, mon amour!
PATRONNE: Regarde plutôt[a] ta sauce! Elle brûle![b]
PATRON: Oh, nom d'un chien![c]

[a]Regarde... *Better look at* [b]*is burning* [c]nom... *damn!*

a. La patronne critique son mari.
b. Le patron et la patronne se taquinent (*are teasing each other*).
c. Le patron et la patronne ne s'aiment plus.

Notez bien!

The phrase **ne... que** means *only*. The **ne** precedes the verb and **que** precedes the person or thing that is restricted or limited.

Je **ne regarde que** toi. *I look only at you.*

Camille **ne parle de son père qu'**à Bruno. *Camille speaks only to Bruno about her father.*

Observez!

Dans cet épisode, vous allez apprendre quelques détails supplémentaires sur la relation de Camille et Bruno. Ces deux personnages vont aussi révéler des détails sur leur famille.

- Est-ce que Bruno se considère comme un bon fils? Pourquoi ou pourquoi pas?
- Est-ce que Camille se considère comme une bonne fille? Pourquoi ou pourquoi pas?
- Quelle sorte de rapport Camille et Bruno avaient-ils (*did they have*) avant? Quelle sorte de rapport semblent-ils avoir (*do they seem to have*) maintenant?

Vocabulaire relatif à l'épisode

dragueur	*pick-up artist*
tellement	*quite, somewhat*
depuis quelque temps	*for some time*
comme d'habitude	*as usual*
à part la nôtre, évidemment	*except for ours, obviously*

Après le visionnement

A. Avez vous compris? (*Did you understand?*) Faites un résumé de l'épisode en complétant chacune (*each one*) des phrases suivantes avec une des options de la colonne de droite (*on the right*).

1. Le patron est étonné de voir Camille et Bruno...
2. Bruno n'est pas marié...
3. Camille n'est pas une bonne fille...
4. Bruno commande...
5. Comme vin, Bruno choisit...
6. Selon la patronne, son mari regarde trop de...
7. Mais il ne regarde pas...

a. parce qu'elle est nerveuse et impatiente.
b. des œufs en meurette.
c. sa sauce. Elle brûle.
d. parce qu'il ne les a pas vus (*hasn't seen them*) depuis quelque temps.
e. sitcoms à la télé.
f. parce qu'un bon fils ne devient pas toujours un bon mari.
g. du vin rouge.

B. Hypothèses. Réfléchissez aux questions suivantes.

1. Selon vous, est-ce que le patron et la patronne sont mariés depuis longtemps (*for a long time*)? Comment peut-on décrire leur relation?
2. Est-ce qu'on découvre un nouvel aspect de la personnalité de Bruno dans cet épisode? Expliquez.

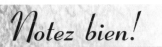

Structure 30

Le passé composé (I)

Talking about past events

—Le décor **n'a pas changé**, hein...

Notez bien!

The following expressions of sequence are useful in narration to describe a succession of events. All of them tend to come at the beginning of a clause.

d'abord	*first, first of all, at first*
ensuite	*next, then*
puis	*then*
enfin	*at last; finally*

D'abord, Camille trouve une photo, **puis** elle pose des questions à sa mère.

Other expressions of time are also useful in narration.

après	*afterward*
avant	*beforehand*
déjà	*already; ever; yet*
hier	*yesterday*
le lendemain	*the next day*
plus tard	*later*

Déjà usually comes after the conjugated verb, but the other expressions often come at the beginning of the sentence.

Camille a **déjà** fait des achats au marché. **Avant**, elle a téléphoné à sa grand-mère.

To talk about the past in French, you will need to learn several past tenses. You have already seen examples of two of these tenses. Here is an exchange from Episode 8 in the film.

Camille pose une question à sa grand-mère, Louise.

CAMILLE: C'*était* quand, la dernière fois qu'il t'**a contactée**?

LOUISE: En 1943. Il *était* dans les Cévennes. Il m'**a envoyé** une lettre... pour l'anniversaire de ta maman. Elle *avait* quatre ans.

Plus tard, Mado parle à Camille.

MADO: D'où sort-elle, cette photo?! Pourquoi tu **as montré** ça à ta grand-mère?

The verb forms in **bold type** are examples of the **passé composé**; you will learn the forms and uses of this tense in this chapter and the next. The *italicized* verbs in the dialogue are examples of the **imparfait**, another past tense, which is presented in Chapter 12.

1. The **passé composé** is used for talking about a completed past event or a sequence of completed past events.

D'abord, Mado **a invité** Camille et Rachid à dîner. Ensuite, elle **a servi** du champagne. Rachid n'**a** pas **bu** de champagne.	*First, Mado invited Camille and Rachid to have dinner with her. Then she served champagne. Rachid didn't drink any champagne.*

2. As you can see, the **passé composé** is a compound tense, consisting of two parts: (1) an auxiliary verb▲ in the present tense and (2) a past participle.▲ The auxiliary verb is usually **avoir**.

Bravo, Bruno! Vous **avez gagné** le béret de la semaine!	*Bravo, Bruno! You have won the beret of the week!*

3. The past participle of regular verbs is formed by dropping the infinitive ending and adding **é** (for **-er** verbs) or **u** (for **-re** verbs).

regard~~er~~ →	regard + **é** →	**regardé**
attend~~re~~ →	attend + **u** →	**attendu**

The past participles of **dormir**, **mentir**, **sentir**, and **servir** are formed by adding **i** to the infinitive stem.*

dormi **menti** **senti** **servi**

Some verbs have irregular past participles.

avoir	**eu**	être	**été**	pouvoir	**pu**
boire	**bu**	faire	**fait**	prendre	**pris**
devoir	**dû**	mettre	**mis**	vouloir	**voulu**

4. To make a **passé composé** form negative, place **ne** before the auxiliary and the second part of the negation (**pas**, **jamais**, etc.) after the auxiliary (and before the past participle).

Il **n'a pas contacté** sa femme? *He didn't contact his wife?*

Notez bien!

Adverbs that follow the verb in the present tense usually follow the auxiliary in the **passé composé**. The adverbs **jusqu'à, tard, tôt,** and **tout de suite**, however, follow the past participle.

Martine a **déjà** trouvé le médaillon.

but La patronne et le patron ont travaillé **tard.**

Activités

A. Vous souvenez-vous? Regardez la photo et complétez chaque phrase avec la forme affirmative ou négative du passé composé d'un des verbes donnés à droite.

MODÈLES: Martine *a donné* son téléphone à Rachid. Rachid *a téléphoné* à sa femme. Sonia *n'a pas répondu*.

donner
ne pas répondre
téléphoner

1. Bruno _____ le pain artisanal.
2. Camille _____ un béret qui était (*was*) derrière la table.
3. Elle a dit (*said*): «Vous _____ le béret de la semaine!»

gagner (*to win*)
identifier
prendre

4. Bruno _____ Camille avant l'émission.
5. Soudain, il _____ peur et il _____ «Où est Camille?»
6. Mais Camille _____ commencer à l'heure.

attendre
avoir
demander
pouvoir

7. Louise et Camille _____ ensemble.
8. Camille _____ la cuisine et elle _____ la table.
9. Elle _____ de la viande et des légumes.
10. Elles _____ du café après le dîner.

boire
dîner
faire
mettre
servir

*You will learn the **passé composé** of **partir** and **sortir** in Chapter 11.

11. Louise _____ un malaise.
12. Le médecin _____ expliquer à Mado que Louise était (*was*) au plus mal.
13. Mado _____ parler de la gravité de la maladie de Louise avec Camille.
14. Elle _____ à Camille.

avoir
devoir
mentir
ne pas vouloir

15. Bruno et Camille _____ de dîner ensemble.
16. Ils _____ longtemps (*a long time*) au restaurant avant de commander.
17. Camille a dit: «Le décor _____, hein... »

attendre
ne pas changer
décider

18. La patronne _____ Bruno et Camille par le judas (*peephole*).
19. Elle a dit: «Ils _____ fiancés (*They were engaged*), non?»
20. Son mari _____ que les histoires d'amour finissent (*love stories end*) toujours mal.

être
regarder
répondre

Notez bien!

Certain expressions that you already know can be used to negate particular expressions of time.

Ne... pas encore (*not yet*) is the negation of **déjà**.

Ne... plus (*no longer*) is the negation of **encore** and **toujours** (meaning *still*).

Ne... jamais (*never*) is the negation of the adverbs of frequency: **toujours** (*meaning always*), **souvent**, **parfois**, **quelquefois**, **de temps en temps**, and **rarement**.

Le père de Mado **n'est plus** en vie (*is no longer living*). Camille **n'a pas encore** trouvé la vérité sur lui, mais elle **ne** va **jamais** arrêter de la chercher.

B. Style de vie. Dites à votre partenaire si vous avez fait les activités suivantes le mois précédent. Ensuite, il/elle va analyser votre style de vie.

MODÈLE: Je n'ai pas fait régulièrement de la gymastique. J'ai regardé...

Dites si vous avez...

1. fait régulièrement de la gymnastique
2. regardé la television plus d'une (*more than one*) heure par jour
3. assisté à au moins (*attended at least*) deux expositions d'art
4. mangé plus de trois fois par semaine au restaurant
5. passé (*spent*) les week-ends à dormir
6. joué à un sport au moins deux fois par semaine
7. fréquenté la bibliothèque
8. pu aller au musée au moins deux fois

Analyse: En se basant sur vos réponses, votre partenaire va maintenant décider si vous êtes plutôt actif/active, sédentaire, sportif/sportive, ou intellectuel(le).

Structure 31

Le passé composé (II)

Talking about past events

—C'était quand, la dernière fois qu'il **t'**a contactée?

1. Yes/no questions can be asked in the **passé composé** using **est-ce que**, rising intonation, or inversion. Notice that inversion occurs with the auxiliary verb and the subject pronoun.

   Est-ce qu'elle a montré une photo à sa grand-mère?
   Elle a montré une photo à sa grand-mère?
   A-t-elle montré une photo à sa grand-mère?

   For information questions, the most common patterns are the following:

   - question word + **est-ce que** + subject + auxiliary + past participle

     Quand est-ce que Camille a trouvé la photo?
     Où est-ce qu'elle a trouvé la photo?

   - question word + inversion of auxiliary verb and subject pronoun + past participle

     Où a-t-elle trouvé la photo?

2. Object pronouns precede the auxiliary in the **passé composé**.

   DIRECT OBJECT: Camille a arrêté son régime. → Camille **l'**a arrêté.
   INDIRECT OBJECT: Tu as parlé à Bruno? → Tu **lui** as parlé?

Notez bien!

To express how long *ago* an action took place, you can use the **passé composé + il y a** + unit of time.

Camille a trouvé une photo de son grand-père **il y a** trois jours. *Camille found a photograph of her grandfather three days ago.*

To make a sentence with an object pronoun negative, place **ne** before the object pronoun.

NEGATION WITH OBJECT PRONOUN: Tu n'as pas parlé à Bruno? → Tu **ne** lui as **pas** parlé?

Attention—When a *direct* object—either a noun or a pronoun—precedes the past participle, the past participle agrees with it in gender and number. In the following example, **les** refers to a feminine plural direct object (**les photos**), therefore **-es** is added to the past participle **regardé** to make it agree in both gender and number.

Camille a regardé les photos. (*direct object follows the past participle*)
Camille **les** a regardé**es**. (*direct object precedes the past participle*)

In the next example, the direct object noun precedes the past participle, requiring agreement.

Les photos que Camille a regardé**es** sont intéressantes.

Activités

A. Une interview. Formulez des questions au passé composé en utilisant (*using*) les éléments ci-dessous pour interviewer Camille. Ensuite, imaginez ses réponses.

MODÈLE: téléphoner / à son agent / hier
É1: Est-ce que vous avez téléphoné à votre agent hier? *ou*
É2: Avez-vous téléphoné à votre agent hier?

1. bien étudier / le script avant l'émission
2. reparler / à sa mère de son grand-père
3. pouvoir / avancer dans ses recherches
4. faire / encore un repas pour sa grand-mère
5. plus tard / mettre / un jean / pour aller au restaurant
6. prendre / un apéritif / avant de manger
7. trop manger / au restaurant
8. poser des questions / à Bruno / sur sa vie sentimentale
9. jouer / avec les émotions de Bruno

B. Camarades de classe curieux. Posez les questions suivantes à votre partenaire. Il/Elle va répondre en utilisant un pronom complément d'objet. Demandez-lui...

MODÈLE: combien de fois il/elle a rendu des devoirs à son prof cette semaine. →
É1: Combien de fois as-tu rendu des devoirs à ton prof cette semaine?
É2: Je lui ai rendu des devoirs trois fois.

1. combien de fois il/elle a téléphoné à ses parents cette semaine.
2. s'il / si elle a donné un cadeau (*gift*) à un ami cette année.
3. s'il / si elle a attendu son professeur pendant plus de 20 minutes.

4. combien de fois il/elle a rendu visite à ses amis ce mois-ci.
5. s'il / si elle a perdu son livre de français aujourd'hui.
6. s'il / si elle a téléphoné au prof cette semaine.

C. Maman, maman! Les enfants Dufour posent beaucoup de questions à leur maman. Jouez le rôle des enfants, qui posent des questions, et de leur maman, qui répond en utilisant des pronoms compléments d'objet direct. Attention à l'accord du participe passé.

MODÈLE: prendre / ma guitare →
É1: Maman, as-tu pris ma guitare?
É2: Oui, je l'ai prise.

1. acheter / les pommes pour le pique-nique
2. mettre / ma veste dans la voiture
3. prendre / mes chaussures de sport
4. inviter / ma cousine à la maison
5. faire / la pizza pour ma soirée
6. laver / mes vêtements de sport

D. Trouvez quelqu'un qui... (*Find someone who . . .*) Faites une liste de cinq choses que vous avez faites la semaine dernière (*last week*). Transformez ces phrases en questions et posez-les à trois camarades de classe. Qui a fait les mêmes choses que vous?

MODÈLE: J'ai mangé au restaurant. (élément de la liste)
É1: As-tu mangé au restaurant?
É2: Non, je n'ai pas mangé au restaurant. (Oui, j'ai mangé au restaurant.)

Notez les réponses et préparez un petit compte rendu (*report*) pour la classe.

Regards sur la culture

Les cafés et les restaurants

In this episode, Camille and Bruno have dinner in what is a rather typical French restaurant. As we have already seen, food is very important in France, and the experience of eating out is somewhat different there from what we know in North America. Cafés, for example, have a different function in France from restaurants, even though it is possible to get something simple to eat in many of them.

Bruno et Camille dînent au restaurant.

- The average French restaurant is family-owned and operated. There are very few large chain restaurants in France. This means that the owners or chefs are likely to know some of their customers quite well and may come out to speak with them.

- When French people go to a restaurant, they are looking forward to real culinary pleasure: something unusual to eat, or something that is difficult to make at home. The notion of going to a place that serves "homestyle cooking" would not be appealing to the French. They often say that there is no point in going to a restaurant if you could eat just as well at home.
- Because the focus on the quality of the food is so strong, a restaurant's décor is less important in France than it is in North America. Although successful restaurants tend to be very comfortable, French people delight in finding a place **qui ne paie pas de mine** (that is not much to look at), but that serves wonderful food.
- Waiting on tables in France is a professional (and usually male-dominated) activity. Service is expected to be efficient and unobtrusive. No French waiter will ever introduce himself. Professionalism and courtesy are more important to the French than the "friendliness" of the service.
- French people spend lots of time looking for good restaurants, and comparing notes on restaurants is a big part of everyday conversation. The average French person judges an establishment on the basis of the cost and apparent quality of the "menus" that it serves. A **menu** in France is a fixed-price meal with at least two courses. These menus are always posted outside the restaurant door.
- In contrast to restaurants, the focus in cafés is not so much on the food or drink as it is on the social scene. Every café has its own particular clientele. In university towns, for example, law students might have a café where they meet and where students of philosophy, for example, would never go. Their gathering place would be another café where law students would not go.
- Because one can order just a simple drink at a café and then stay seated for quite a long time, people use the café as a meeting place. They may read, write, or study at a café table. They may simply want to watch people going by (staring at others is not nearly as impolite in France as it is in North America). They may sit down and order a coffee in order to rest in the middle of a long walk.
- The social functions of the café have declined somewhat over the past 30 years, particularly in the evening. Many French people feel that having a drink at a café has become too expensive. Probably more important is the fact that people tend to stay home at night and watch television, rather than go out to socialize at the café.

Un café à Paris

Considérez

Why do you think there aren't many establishments in North America that serve the functions cafés do in France? Where in North America does café-style socializing exist?

Structure 32

Les verbes *voir, croire* et *recevoir*

Talking about everyday activities

—Et vous, Bruno?

—Moi?... Oui, oui, oui! **Je crois.** Oui!

—Eh bien, faisons un test.

—Ah! Maman, pardon si je me trompe, hein? (*les yeux bandés*) Il y a une panne d'électricité, là? **Je** ne **vois** plus rien du tout.

Le verbe *voir*

voir (*to see*)			
je	**vois**	nous	**voyons**
tu	**vois**	vous	**voyez**
il, elle, on	**voit**	ils, elles	**voient**
passé composé: j'**ai vu**			

Je ne le **vois** pas depuis le divorce. — *I haven't seen him since the divorce.*

Another verb like **voir** is **revoir** (*to see again*).

Et je n'ai aucune envie de le **revoir**. — *And I don't have any desire to see him again.*

Le verbe *croire*

croire (*to believe*)			
je	**crois**	nous	**croyons**
tu	**crois**	vous	**croyez**
il, elle, on	**croit**	ils, elles	**croient**
passé composé: j'**ai cru**			

1. **Croire** can be accompanied by a direct object or by a clause beginning with **que**.

Vous me **croyez**, n'est-ce pas?	*You believe me, don't you?*
Tu as faim? Je ne le **crois** pas... !?	*You're hungry? I don't believe it.*
Mado **croit** que Camille est encore une enfant.	*Mado believes that Camille is still a child.*

2. **Croire à** means *to believe in.*

Je **crois au** Père Noël.	*I believe in Santa Claus.*

Le verbe *recevoir*

recevoir (*to receive; to entertain*)			
je	**reçois**	nous	**recevons**
tu	**reçois**	vous	**recevez**
il, elle, on	**reçoit**	ils, elles	**reçoivent**
passé composé: j'**ai reçu**			

Notice the use of **ç** in the **je**, **tu**, **il/elle/on**, and **ils/elles** forms and in the past participle: When **c** is followed by **a**, **o**, or **u**, it needs the cedilla to keep the sound of a soft *c*.

Camille **a reçu** le livre sur les Cévennes de sa grand-mère.	*Camille received the book about the Cévennes from her grandmother.*
Camille reçoit souvent des amis chez elle.	*Camille often entertains friends at home.*

Activités

A. Au présent. Faites des phrases au temps présent avec les expressions et les pronoms donnés.

MODÈLE: croire que le musée est ouvert (*open*) aujourd'hui (je) →
Je crois que le musée est ouvert aujourd'hui.

1. croire que cette boîte de nuit est fantastique (ils)
2. ne plus croire au Père Noël (tu)
3. croire que votre ami a fait du jogging ce matin (*this morning*) (vous)
4. ne pas voir de bonnes pièces de théâtre tous les jours (on)
5. ne pas revoir mes anciens (*former*) profs (je)
6. voir que vous aimez jouer au billard (nous)
7. ne jamais recevoir de bonnes notes (elles)
8. recevoir les billets pour le cirque (vous)

B. Les fêtes. L'arrivée des fêtes suscite un état d'anxiété chez beaucoup d'individus. Voici quelques problèmes constatés par les experts. Complétez les phrases suivantes avec la forme correcte du verbe approprié: **croire, voir, recevoir.**

1. Les gens _____ que les fêtes d'hiver sont trop commerciales.
2. On _____ l'arrivée des fêtes avec appréhension.
3. Nous _____ qu'il est nécessaire de dépenser beaucoup d'argent pour les fêtes.
4. Je _____ beaucoup trop d'invitations!
5. Certaines personnes _____ qu'il faut _____ leurs amis à la maison.
6. On n'a pas le temps de _____ tous ses parents et ses amis pendant cette période trop chargée d'activités.

Laquelle (Lesquelles) (*Which*) de ces phrases exprime(nt) vos inquiétudes (*worries*) pendant les fêtes d'hiver? Qu'est-ce que vous pouvez faire pour réduire votre niveau de stress?

MODÈLE: Moi aussi, je crois que les fêtes sont trop commerciales. La prochaine fois, je vais demander à mes amis de faire une donation à une charité.

C. La quatrième dimension. Posez ces questions à votre partenaire pour déterminer s'il / si elle croit à l'existence d'une quatrième dimension. Demandez-lui s'il / si elle...

1. a déjà vu un OVNI (objet volant non-identifié)
2. croit à l'existence des extraterrestres
3. reçoit la visite des fantômes
4. reçoit des messages mystérieux
5. voit des signes de l'avenir (*future*)

Visionnement 2

Le Quartier des Halles. Bruno and Camille have gone to dinner in another part of Paris, on the right bank of the Seine. This area housed the central market of Paris until 1969; it was both picturesque and run-down. The district was redeveloped in the 1970s and '80s. The **Centre Pompidou**,* completed in 1977, was built to house the National Museum of Modern Art and other cultural services. It has remained a controversial piece of architecture. **Le Forum des Halles** is a complex of shops, movie theaters, and restaurants, rising in tiers from a sunken patio. Much of the rest of the old market area is occupied by gardens. Nearby stands the **église Saint-Eustache**, where Richelieu* was baptized and

*__Le Centre national d'art et de culture Georges Pompidou__ porte le nom de Georges Pompidou (1911–1974), qui a été Premier ministre (1962–1968) sous le Président Charles de Gaulle et président de 1969 à 1974.

*Le cardinal Richelieu (1585–1642), grand homme d'État, ministre de Louis XIII. Il a fondé l'Académie française pour créer un dictionnaire de la langue française.

where Molière's* funeral was held. It is probably the best architectural example of a French Renaissance church in Paris. Near the Seine, the **Hôtel de Ville**, the city hall of Paris, is a replica of the 17th-century building that was burned down when the army put down a revolutionary government that had taken over Paris in 1871.

Les environs du restaurant préféré de Camille et Bruno

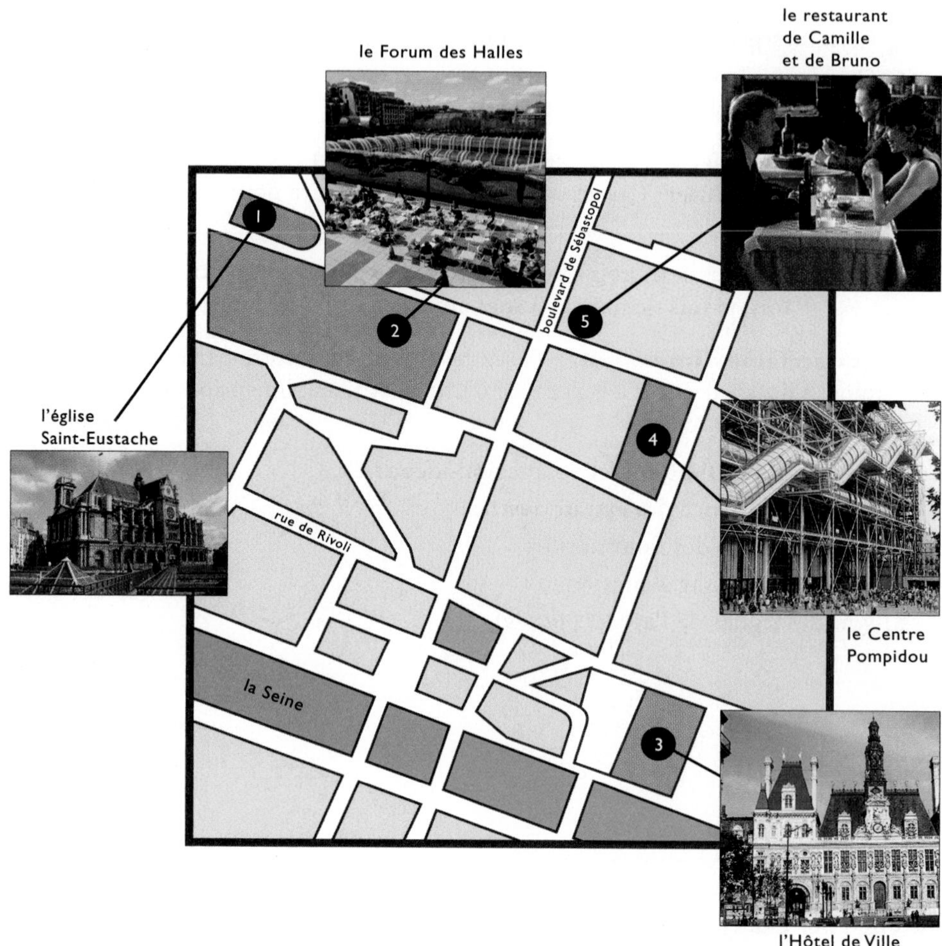

Vous recherchez une atmosphère particulière. Indiquez où vous voulez aller. Plusieurs (*Several*) réponses sont possibles.

MODÈLE: la tranquillité et les plaisirs gastronomiques
Je veux aller au restaurant où vont Camille et Bruno.

a. des souvenirs historiques
b. une ambiance esthétique
c. une atmosphère mouvementée
d. une ambiance de méditation
e. la solitude

*Molière (1622 - 1673), auteur célèbre de nombreuses pièces de théâtre comiques.

Observez!

Considérez les aspects culturels dans **Regards sur la culture**. Ensuite, regardez l'Épisode 10 encore une fois, et répondez aux questions suivantes.

- Comment est le décor du restaurant? Selon vous, quelle sorte de clientèle fréquente ce restaurant?
- Comment peut-on qualifier le rapport entre Bruno, Camille et le serveur? Le serveur est-il froid? réservé? respectueux? familier? trop familier? Expliquez son comportement (*behavior*).

Après le visionnement

Faites l'activité pour le **Visionnement 2** dans le cahier.

Synthèse: Lecture

Mise en contexte

The events of World War II form a backdrop to the story line of *Le Chemin du retour*. This destructive conflict is still an open wound for many in French society. The role and actions of the French during this period are being critically examined even today. The many stories of heroism, generosity, and self-sacrifice have been tempered by tales of collaboration and atrocities. In the reading for this chapter, you will learn about the war and its impact on France.

Stratégie pour mieux lire

Guessing meaning from context

You may be able to predict the meaning of an unknown word by using cues from the surrounding context. For example, read the following sentence and use it to figure out the meanings of the words in bold type.

1. Le gouvernement allemand prend des mesures d'exclusion **contre** les races **dites** «inférieures».

contre:	**a.** counter	**b.** against	**c.** with
dites:	**a.** that are	**b.** ditto	**c.** said to be

Did you correctly guess "b. against" and "c. said to be"? Try out this skill with some more sentences from the reading passage. Try to identify the meaning of the French words in **bold** type below.

2. Hitler lance un programme d'agression. L'Autriche est **envahie**.

   envahie: **a.** envisioned **b.** invaded **c.** afraid

3. Un **appel** à la résistance est lancé de Londres par le général Charles de Gaulle.

   appel: **a.** call **b.** criticism **c.** apple

4. La Résistance s'organise en divers groupes non centralisés. Elle publie des **journaux** clandestins, **cache** des Juifs, donne des **renseignements** aux Alliés, **exécute** des sabotages.

journaux:	**a.** magazines	**b.** newspapers	**c.** journals
cache:	**a.** hides	**b.** catches	**c.** searches for
renseignements:	**a.** help	**b.** reassigns	**c.** information
exécute:	**a.** stops	**b.** carries out	**c.** kills

Now read the whole text through. Be sure to make use of context to facilitate the reading task. If you didn't get all meanings from the context in items 2–4, you may still be able to figure them out with the help of the greater context of the full passage. Also, pay attention to which events are results of other conditions or events.

La Deuxième Guerre mondiale,[1] les Français et l'Occupation

• janvier 1933–1938

Hitler est nommé chancelier d'Allemagne après une crise économique et politique. Une dictature totalitaire s'établit en Allemagne. Le gouvernement allemand prend des mesures d'exclusion contre les races dites «inférieures».

• 1938–1940

Hitler lance un programme d'agression. L'Autriche est envahie, puis la Pologne. La France et l'Angleterre déclarent la guerre à l'Allemagne en 1939. L'armée française lutte[2] contre les forces allemandes en Europe. L'Allemagne envahit la France.

• juin 1940

Paris est occupée. La France cède. L'Allemagne contrôle les deux tiers[3] de la France. Un appel à la résistance est lancé de Londres par le général Charles de Gaulle. La Résistance est formée. Le maréchal Pétain, chef du gouvernement «libre»[4] à Vichy, signe l'armistice. La France est coupée en deux—la zone occupée, au nord, et la «zone libre», au sud, sur la façade atlantique.

[1]Deuxième... *Second World War* [2]*fights* [3]les... *two thirds* [4]*free*

• 1940–1942

Le régime autoritaire de Pétain collabore avec les Allemands. Les élections, les partis politiques et les syndicats[5] sont supprimés.[6] L'État français édicte «le statut des Juifs» et participe à leur arrestation et déportation. Deux millions de Français sont faits prisonniers et envoyés en Allemagne.

La Résistance s'organise en divers groupes non centralisés. Elle publie des journaux clandestins, cache des Juifs, donne des renseignements aux Alliés, exécute des sabotages. La milice[7] française lutte contre les résistants.

• 1942–1944

Les troupes allemandes envahissent la zone libre de la France. La Résistance s'accentue. Le régime de Vichy organise la «Révolution nationale» destinée à redresser la France. La main-d'œuvre française est au service de l'Allemagne. La devise du pays devient «Travail, Famille, Patrie».[8]

• juin–septembre 1944

Les Alliés débarquent en Normandie et avancent progressivement vers l'intérieur du pays. Après un second débarquement des Alliés en Provence, Paris est libéré. La retraite des troupes allemandes s'accompagne de massacres de civils. La majeure partie du territoire français est libérée.

• 1945

Les prisonniers des camps d'extermination en Allemagne sont libérés. Hitler se suicide. La guerre en Europe est finie.

[5]*unions* [6]*eliminated* [7]*militia* [8]*Fatherland*

Après la lecture

A. Avez-vous compris? (*Did you understand?*) Quelle est la signification de chaque mot en caractères **gras**?

1. Le régime de Vichy organise la «Révolution nationale» destinée à **redresser** la France.

   a. punish **b.** rebuild **c.** reconfirm

2. La **main-d'œuvre** française est au service de l'Allemagne.

   a. manpower **b.** main people **c.** handiwork

3. La **devise** du pays devient «Travail, Famille, Patrie».

   a. device **b.** loss **c.** motto

4. Les Alliés **débarquent** en Normandie.

   a. land **b.** debase **c.** attack

B. Cause et effet. Quelle est la conséquence des actes et des événements (*events*) suivants?

MODÈLE: Il y a une crise économique et politique en Allemagne. → Hitler est nommé chancelier.

1. Hitler lance un programme d'agression. Il envahit l'Autriche et la Pologne.
2. La France est attaquée.
3. Le général de Gaulle lance un appel à la résistance.
4. Le régime de Vichy organise la «Révolution nationale».

À écrire

Faites **À écrire** pour le Chapitre 10 dans le cahier.

Vocabulaire

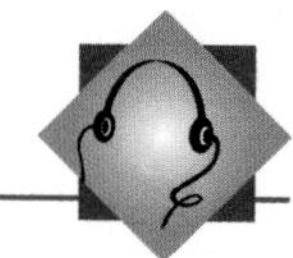

Les distractions en ville

une boîte de nuit	nightclub
le cirque	circus
la course à pied	running race
les distractions (*f.*)	leisure activities
une exposition d'art	art exhibit
un(e) fanatique de sport	sports fan
le football (*fam.* **le foot**)	soccer
le footing	running (*not in a race*)
un jeu (des jeux)	game
un match (de foot, de boxe)	(soccer, boxing) match
la musculation	weight training
un musée (d'art, de sciences naturelles)	museum (of art, of natural science)
la nuit	night
le roller	roller-skating
le skate	skateboarding
la vie (urbaine)	(urban, city) life
la ville	city

MOTS APPARENTÉS: **le base-ball, le billard, le bowling, le football américain, le jogging, le tennis, le théâtre, le volley-ball**

À REVOIR: **un restaurant, un cinéma**

Les saisons

en hiver (*m.*)	in winter
au printemps	in spring
en été (*m.*)	in summer
en automne (*m.*)	in autumn, in the fall

MOT APPARENTÉ: **la saison**

Le temps qu'il fait

la météo	weather report, forecast	**il fait du vent**	it's windy out
un orage	thunder and lightning storm	**il fait frais**	it's cool out
le temps	weather	**il fait froid**	it's cold out
le ciel (est couvert, clair)	sky (is cloudy, clear)	**il fait mauvais**	it's bad weather
Quel temps fait-il?	What's the weather like?	**il neige**	it's snowing
il fait beau	it's nice out	**il pleut**	it's raining
il fait chaud	it's hot out	**nuageux/euse**	cloudy
il fait doux	it's mild out		
il fait du soleil	it's sunny out		

MOT APPARENTÉ: **la température**

Verbes

assister à	to attend (*an event*)	**revoir**	to see again
croire	to believe	**voir**	to see
jouer (à, de)	to play		
recevoir	to receive; to entertain		

À REVOIR: **faire**

Des adverbes et des expressions de temps

d'abord	first, first of all, at first	**plus tard**	later
déjà	already; ever; yet	**puis**	then
enfin	at last, finally; well; in short		
ensuite	next, then		
hier	yesterday		
il y a (dix ans)	(ten years) ago		
le lendemain	the next day		

À REVOIR: **après, aujourd'hui, avant, d'habitude, encore, jusqu'à, maintenant, ne... jamais, ne... pas encore, ne... plus, parfois, rarement, souvent, tard, tôt, toujours, tout de suite**

Autre expression utile

ne... que	only

Chapitre 11

De quoi as-tu peur?

Le Chemin du retour

Feuille de service du 26 janvier
10e jour du tournage
Horaires: 13h–23h

LIEU DE TOURNAGE: FUVEAU—GARE DE FUVEAU

Séquence	***Effets***	***Décors***	***Résumé***	***Rôles***
71	INT.—SOIR	APPARTEMENT LOUISE 1940–Séjour	Flash-back 1940: Antoine a décidé de partir. Il donne un médaillon à Louise.	LOUISE 1940, ANTOINE 1940

OBJECTIFS

In this episode, you will

- learn more about Antoine's activities during the war
- find out how Bruno may be able to help Camille

In this chapter, you will

- discuss occupations
- talk about holidays, festivals, and celebrations
- use ordinal numbers (*first, second,* and so on)
- narrate events in the past
- talk about everyday actions
- read about the French concept of the couple and male-female relationships
- read about the period of the "Great Disturbance" in the history of Acadians and their expulsion to Louisiana

Vocabulaire en contexte

Les métiers° et les professions

Les... *Trades*

Comment trouver **un emploi**,° **un métier**, **une profession**? — *work, employment*

Pour un emploi **à mi-temps** ou à temps partiel, on peut regarder **le tableau d'affichage** à l'université. Là, on trouve **des postes**° (*m.*). Parfois **les gens**° recherchent... — *positions, jobs / people*

un(e) baby-sitter
un(e) garde-malade° — garde... *nurse's aide*
un(e) gardien(ne) d'immeuble

Pour un emploi à mi-temps ou **à plein temps**,° on peut consulter **les petites annonces**° dans le journal ou chercher **sur Internet**. Par ces intermédiaires, on recrute, par exemple,... — à... *full time* / petites... *classified ads*

un agent (de sécurité)
un(e) avocat(e)° — *lawyer*
un(e) cadre° — *executive*
un(e) comptable° — *accountant*
un(e) conservateur/trice (de musée)° — *(museum) curator*
un(e) cuisinier/ière° — *cook*
un(e) employé(e) de fast-food
un(e) fonctionnaire°* — *civil servant*
un(e) ingénieur° / **femme ingénieur** — *engineer*
un(e) interprète
un(e) ouvrier/ière° — *manual laborer*
un(e) patron(ne)° **(d'un bar, d'un restaurant)** — *owner; boss*
un(e) secrétaire

Famille cherche baby-sitter
3 enfants: 3, 5, 6 ans
Tél. 01.45.54.30.85

75 agents de sécurité
Débutants hommes/femmes.
Stage d'emploi. Gardiens d'immeuble Tél. 01.43.78.96.58

Jeune femme 25 ans recherche emploi stable à plein temps. Secrétaire 5 ans expérience. Word et Works
Tél. 01.26.82.64.47

Est-ce qu'on trouve les emplois suivants dans les petites annonces?

un(e) agriculteur/trice° — *farmer*
un(e) artisan(e)° — *craftsman, artisan*
un(e) écrivain° / **femme écrivain** — *writer*
un(e) musicien(ne)
un(e) peintre° / **femme peintre** — *painter*

On peut travailler dans...

les affaires° (*f. pl.*) — *business*
le commerce (international)
la gestion° — *management*
le marketing

Un étudiant peut faire **un stage**° dans **une société**° internationale ou nationale. — *internship / company*

---

*Le mot **fonctionnaire** est un terme générique pour les gens qui travaillent pour le gouvernement: les facteurs (*mail carriers*), les agents de police, les instituteurs et institutrices, etc.

Activités

A. Qui est-ce? Quel est le métier ou la profession de la personne décrite?

MODÈLE: Anne Leduc garde des enfants. →
C'est une baby-sitter.

1. Mme Robert défend des clients devant un juge (*judge*).
2. M. Fourny travaille pour l'État. Il passe toute la journée dans un bureau à la préfecture de police.
3. Mme Bassan vient de finir son chef-d'œuvre: un tableau qui s'appelle «Le soleil couchant à Roissy».
4. Jackie travaille chez Quick où il sert des hamburgers et des frites.
5. Le père de Jackie prépare des repas dans un restaurant élégant: la Tour d'Argent.
6. M. Gascon est doué (*talented*) pour les chiffres (*numbers*). Il est responsable des comptes (*accounting*) d'une grande société.
7. Mlle Corbet est l'assistante d'un cadre. Elle envoie des lettres, répond au téléphone, etc.

B. À la recherche d'un emploi. (*Job hunting.*) À quel emploi les personnes suivantes se préparent-elles?

MODÈLE: Serge étudie la gestion et le marketing. →
Il va travailler comme cadre. (Il va travailler dans le commerce.)

1. Claude fait un stage dans une société internationale.
2. Thomas va travailler dans la ferme (*farm*) familiale.
3. Laurence organise des expositions au musée.
4. Robert fait ses études de mathématiques.
5. Michel fait des études d'anglais et d'allemand.
6. Nicole lit (*reads*) beaucoup de livres par des auteurs célèbres.

C. Identifiez. Utilisez la liste pour identifier des emplois qui correspondent aux descriptions.

Vocabulaire utile: agent de sécurité, artisan, avocat, baby-sitter, écrivain, employé de fast-food, gardien d'immeuble, ingénieur, musicien, ouvrier, patron d'un bar, peintre

Un emploi qui exige (*requires*)...

1. une bonne connaissance (*knowledge*) d'un bâtiment ou d'un appartement
2. de la créativité
3. des connaissances techniques
4. de l'amour pour les enfants
5. une personnalité extravertie
6. de la logique
7. du rythme

Un emploi...

8. qui n'est pas très prestigieux
9. qui paie mal
10. pour quelqu'un qui aime la solitude
11. que vous trouvez ennuyeux (*boring*)
12. qui est idéal pour vous (expliquez pourquoi!)

D. Interview. Demandez à votre partenaire...

1. s'il / si elle a un emploi en ce moment et si c'est un travail à mi-temps ou à plein temps.
2. d'identifier son emploi.
3. à quelle profession il/elle se prépare à l'université et quelles qualités sont nécessaires pour exercer (*to practice*) cette profession.
4. s'il / si elle a déjà fait un stage et pour quelle entreprise.
5. ce qu'un candidat à un emploi doit porter ou ne pas porter pour un entretien (*interview*).
6. ce qu'on ne doit pas faire pendant (*during*) un entretien.
7. de faire le portrait du patron idéal.

Les jours fériés et les fêtes°

Les... *Legal holidays and festivals*

QUELQUES JOURS FÉRIÉS EN FRANCE

le nouvel an	C'est le premier janvier. On fête le réveillon le 31 décembre.	
la fête du Travail	C'est le premier mai. On organise des défilés.°	*parades*
la fête nationale	C'est le 14 juillet. On commémore la prise de la Bastille en 1789 avec des défilés et des feux d'artifice.°	feux... *fireworks*

QUELQUES FÊTES RELIGIEUSES

la Pâque	C'est une fête juive qui a lieu° en mars ou avril; la date exacte varie selon l'année. On fait un repas spécial avec du pain sans levain.°	a... *takes place*; *yeast*
Pâques* (*f. pl.*)	C'est une fête chrétienne qui a lieu un dimanche en mars ou avril. La date exacte varie selon l'année. On va à la messe.°	*mass*
le Ramadan	C'est le neuvième mois du calendrier musulman. On jeûne° pendant la journée.	*fasts*
la Toussaint	C'est une fête chrétienne qui a lieu le premier novembre. On va au cimetière.°	*cemetery*
Hanoukka	C'est une fête juive qui dure° huit jours en décembre. La date exacte varie selon l'année. On allume des bougies° et on donne des cadeaux° aux enfants.	*lasts*; *candles*; *gifts*
Noël (*m.*)	C'est une fête chrétienne qui a lieu le 25 décembre. On va à la messe et on offre des cadeaux à la famille et aux amis.	

DEUX FÊTES FAMILIALES

un anniversaire (de naissance) **un anniversaire de mariage**	Les dates varient selon les personnes.

*__Pâques__ (*Easter*) et **Noël** (*Christmas*) sont des fêtes nationales en France.

Activités

A. Identifiez. Identifiez une fête...

MODÈLE: qui a lieu en hiver. →
Le nouvel an a lieu en hiver.

1. qui a lieu au printemps.
2. qui commémore un événement (*event*) historique.
3. où on jeûne.
4. où on prépare un repas spécial.
5. où on offre des cadeaux.
6. qui a lieu en hiver.
7. où on fête le réveillon.
8. où on participe à un défilé.
9. où on va au cimetière.

B. Interview. Demandez à votre partenaire...

1. quelle est la date de son anniversaire.
2. comment il/elle aime fêter son anniversaire.
3. quels sont les jours fériés dans son pays et quelles sont les dates de ces jours fériés cette année.
4. quelle est sa fête préférée et pourquoi.
5. quelles fêtes religieuses il/elle observe.

Les nombres ordinaux°

Les... *Ordinal numbers*

You have already learned the cardinal numbers, which are used for counting. Ordinal numbers (*first, second, third,* etc.) are used for ordering and sequencing.

premier/ière	**troisième**	**cinquième**	**septième**	**neuvième**
deuxième	**quatrième**	**sixième**	**huitième**	**dixième**

1. **Premier** (*m.*) and **première** (*f.*) mean *first.*

   C'est la **première** fois que je mange du couscous. — *It's the first time I've eaten couscous.*

2. Most other ordinal numbers are formed by adding the suffix **-ième** after the final consonant of the cardinal number. Some ordinal numbers have a slightly irregular formation.

   quatre − **e** + ième → **quatrième**
   cinq + **u** + ième → **cinquième**
   neuf − **f** + **v** + ième → **neuvième**

3. Ordinal numbers can be made from compound numbers.

   le **dix-neuvième** siècle — *the nineteenth century*
   le **vingt et unième** siècle — *the twenty-first century*

4. Remember that except for **le premier**, ordinal numbers are *not* used when expressing a date in French.

   le **quatorze** juillet — *July fourteenth*
   le **vingt-cinq** décembre — *December twenty-fifth*

Pour en savoir plus...

Ordinal numbers can be abbreviated as follows.

1e 2e 3e 4e

Centuries are designated using roman numerals.

XXIe siècle — *21st century*

Royalty are designated using cardinal roman numerals.

Louis XIV (quatorze) — *Louis the fourteenth*

Activités

A. Dans quel quartier? Dans quel arrondissement de Paris se trouvent les monuments suivants (*following*)?

MODÈLE: la basilique (*basilica*) du Sacré-Cœur →
La basilique du Sacré-Cœur est dans le dix-huitième arrondissement.

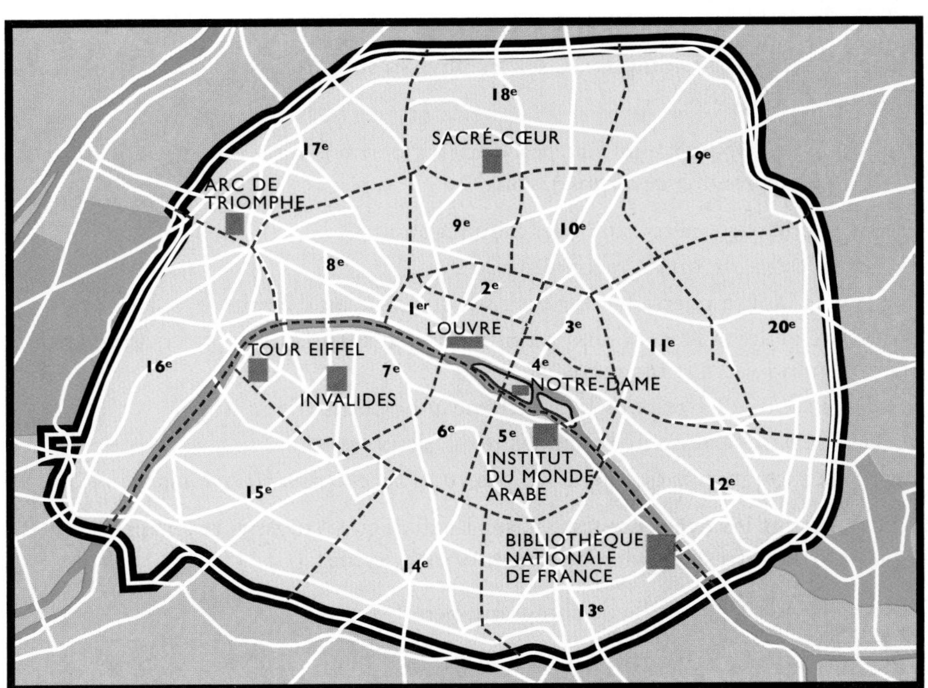

1. le Louvre
2. l'Arc de Triomphe
3. la Bibliothèque nationale de France
4. l'Institut du monde arabe
5. la cathédrale Notre-Dame de Paris
6. les Invalides

B. Personnages historiques. Quelles sont les dates de la naissance et de la mort des personnages suivants? En quel(s) siècle(s) ont-ils vécu (*lived*)?

MODÈLE: Louis XIV: 1638–1715 →
Louis quatorze est né (*was born*) en mil six cent trente-huit et il est mort (*died*) en mil sept cent quinze. Il a vécu aux dix-septième et dix-huitième siècles.

1. Edgar Degas: 1834–1917
2. Pierre de Ronsard: 1524–1585
3. Simone de Beauvoir: 1908–1986
4. Napoléon Ier: 1769–1821
5. Molière: 1622–1673

Pour en savoir plus...

Les Français célèbres qui sont nommés dans l'Activité B ont beaucoup contribué à l'histoire et à la culture françaises.

Louis XIV: roi de France de 1643 à 1715. Roi soleil (*sun*).

Edgar Degas: peintre, pastelliste, graveur et sculpteur impressionniste.

Pierre de Ronsard: poète, auteur de *Odes, Amours, Bocages, Hymnes*, etc.

Simone de Beauvoir: femme de lettres, auteur d'essais (*le Deuxième Sexe*), de romans, de pièces de théâtre et de mémoires.

Napoléon Ier: empereur. Il a établi (*established*) le Code civil, des universités, la Légion d'honneur, etc.

Molière: auteur de pièces de théâtre comiques—*Le Misanthrope, L'Avare, Le Bourgeois gentilhomme*, etc.

Visionnement 1

Avant de visionner

A. Révision du passé composé. Dans cet épisode, il y a beaucoup d'exemples de verbes au passé composé. Lisez les phrases suivantes et donnez l'infinitif de chaque (*each*) verbe.

Verbes utiles: disparaître (*to disappear*), écrire (*to write*), faire, pouvoir, raconter (*to tell*), revoir, surprendre (*to surprise*), voir

1. Et il a disparu de tous (*all*) les albums-photos?
2. Et qu'est-ce qu'on t'a raconté sur lui?
3. Et pendant la guerre (*during the war*), qu'est-ce qu'il a fait?
4. Toute petite, à l'âge de sept ou huit ans, j'ai surpris une conversation entre ma grand-mère et ma mère.
5. Il a écrit une lettre pour le quatrième anniversaire de sa fille.
6. Il a disparu. Louise ne l'a jamais revu. (deux verbes)
7. Ça fait longtemps que je ne l'ai pas vu. (*I haven't seen him for a long time.*)

B. Les dates et les événements. Lisez les dialogues suivants et ensuite, donnez la date qui correspond aux événements mentionnés.

Bruno parle avec Camille de son grand-père.

BRUNO: Et maintenant, Camille, raconte-moi ton histoire. Ton grand-père est toujours vivant?[a]

CAMILLE: Non, il est mort[b]... pendant la guerre, en 1943.

[a]*alive* [b]*il... he died*

Plus tard...

BRUNO: Ta grand-mère a toujours habité le quartier Mouffetard?

CAMILLE: Oui, à partir de[c] 1938, avec son mari.

BRUNO: Antoine? Et quel âge a-t-il à cette époque-là?[d]

CAMILLE: 20 ans.

BRUNO: Il a déjà son atelier d'ébéniste?[e]

CAMILLE: Oui, il en a hérité[f] de son père. Les affaires marchent[g] bien. Il a trois employés avec lui.

BRUNO: Et ta mère? Elle est déjà née?[h]

CAMILLE: Pas encore. Elle est venue au monde[i] en septembre 1939.

BRUNO: Oh. 1939? La déclaration de guerre contre les Allemands...

[c]*à... beginning in* [d]*à... at that time* [e]*atelier... cabinetmaker's workshop* [f]*il... he inherited it* [g]*are going* [h]*born* [i]*est... came into the world*

1. Louise et Antoine s'installent dans la rue Mouffetard.
2. date de naissance de Mado
3. date de la déclaration de guerre aux Allemands
4. date de la mort d'Antoine

Observez!

Dans l'Épisode 11, Camille parle à Bruno des expériences de ses grands-parents pendant la guerre. Pendant votre visionnement du film, essayez de trouver les réponses aux questions suivantes.

- Qui est Samuel Lévy? Où va-t-il et pourquoi?
- Que fait Antoine?
- De quoi est-ce qu'Antoine est accusé?
- Comment Bruno offre-t-il d'aider Camille?

Vocabulaire relatif à l'épisode

presque	*almost, practically*
non plus	*neither*
juif	*Jewish*
personne n'envoie	*nobody sends*
Que Dieu te protège	*May God protect you*
Prenez soin de vous	*Take care of yourself*
ce qui est juste	*what is right*
plus rien	*nothing more*
est-ce qu'il vit toujours	*is he still living*

Après le visionnement

A. Un résumé. Faites un résumé de l'histoire d'Antoine pendant la guerre en complétant le paragraphe suivant.

Vocabulaire utile: 1939, a trahi (*betrayed*), dans les Cévennes, la déclaration de guerre, ébéniste (*cabinetmaker*), en Amérique, un historien, juif, quatrième, dans la rue Mouffetard, trois, vingt

À partir de 1938, Antoine et Louise habitent _____[1]. À l'époque, Antoine a _____[2] ans. Il travaille comme _____[3] avec _____[4] employés. Sa fille, Mado, naît[a] en _____[5]. C'est une année importante, parce qu'elle marque _____[6] aux Allemands. Un des employés d'Antoine—Samuel Lévy—est _____[7]. Hitler veut exterminer les Juifs, alors, Samuel part _____[8] pour rejoindre[b] sa femme.

Antoine va _____[9]. Il écrit une carte pour le _____[10] anniversaire de sa fille. Ensuite, on perd sa trace. Le bruit court[c] qu'il _____[11] son pays. Bruno connaît _____[12] et espère qu'il peut aider Camille à découvrir la vérité.[d]

[a]*is born* [b]*join* [c]Le... *Rumor has it* [d]découvrir... *to discover the truth*

B. Questions. Faites une liste de questions dont (*whose*) les réponses peuvent éclaircir (*shed light on*) ce mystère familial. Utilisez les mots **où**, **quand**, **pourquoi**, **comment**, **combien de**, **qu'est-ce que**, etc.

MODÈLE: Pourquoi Antoine va-t-il dans les Cévennes?

Ensuite, essayez de répondre aux questions de vos camarades de classe. À quelles questions est-ce qu'on ne peut pas encore répondre?

Structure 33

Le passé composé avec l'auxiliaire être

Narrating in the past

—Ton grand-père est toujours vivant?

—Non, il **est mort**... pendant la guerre, en 1943.

Some verbs—generally those that express motion or a change of state—use the present tense of **être** as their auxiliary in the **passé composé**. When Camille says **Non, il est mort**, she is using the **passé composé** of the verb **mourir** (*to die*).

1. Verbs that use **être** as their auxiliary include

INFINITIVE		PAST PARTICIPLE
aller	*to go*	**allé**
arriver	*to arrive*	**arrivé**
descendre	*to go/get down (off)*	**descendu**
devenir	*to become*	**devenu**
entrer	*to enter*	**entré**
monter	*to go up, climb*	**monté**
mourir*	*to die*	**mort**
naître†	*to be born*	**né**
partir	*to leave*	**parti**
passer (par)	*to pass (by)*	**passé**
rentrer	*to come/go back (home)*	**rentré**
rester	*to stay*	**resté**
retourner	*to return*	**retourné**
revenir	*to come back*	**revenu**
sortir	*to go out*	**sorti**
tomber	*to fall*	**tombé**
venir	*to come*	**venu**

Où Antoine **est**-il **allé** pendant la guerre?	*Where did Antoine go during the war?*
Antoine **est parti** dans les Cévennes.	*Antoine left for the Cévennes.*
Antoine **n'est jamais revenu** à Paris.	*Antoine never returned to Paris.*

---

*La conjugaison du présent de **mourir** est: **je meurs, tu meurs, il/elle/on meurt, nous mourons, vous mourez, ils/elles meurent. Je meurs de faim/soif/peur.**

†La conjugaison du présent de **naître** est rarement utilisée et n'est pas présentée dans ce cours.

2. When a verb is conjugated with **être** in the **passé composé**, the past participle agrees in gender and number with the subject of the verb.

Bruno est **arrivé** à l'heure.	*Bruno arrived on time.*
Camille est **venue** en retard.	*Camille came late.*
Bruno et Rachid sont **allés** déjeuner.	*Bruno and Rachid went to eat lunch.*
Mado et Camille sont **parties**.	*Mado and Camille left.*

This agreement does not usually affect pronunciation, but feminine agreement of the past participle **mort** causes the pronunciation of the final **t**.

Antoine est **mort** en 1943.
but La mère de Louise est **morte** à l'âge de 85 ans.

Activités

A. Premiers jours. Comment sont les premiers jours après la naissance d'un enfant? Choisissez (*choose*) le verbe qui convient et mettez-le au passé composé.

MODÈLE: La mère _____ (sortir, aller) à l'hôpital. →
La mère est allée à l'hôpital.

1. Une petite fille _____ (naître, ne pas retourner).
2. Les parents et l'enfant _____ (arriver, partir) de l'hôpital.
3. La famille _____ (rentrer, devenir) à la maison.
4. Le papa _____ (ne pas retourner, naître) au travail.
5. La maman _____ (tomber, rester) à la maison aussi.
6. Une poupée (*doll*) du bébé _____ (venir, tomber) par terre.
7. La petite fille _____ (devenir, monter) très triste.
8. Les grands-parents _____ (sortir, arriver) pour garder le bébé.
9. Les parents _____ (sortir, rester) ensemble au restaurant, tout contents.
10. Après le départ des grands-parents, des amies _____ (venir, devenir) pour aider les parents.

B. La tragédie de l'Occupation. Samuel Lévy, l'ami et l'employé d'Antoine, parle de la situation à Paris en 1940. Mettez les verbes en italique au passé composé avec **avoir** ou **être**.

Les nazis *arrivent*[1] à Paris en 1940. Ils *viennent*[2] après la défaite de l'armée française où deux de mes amis de l'atelier *meurent.*[3] Ma femme *part*[4] tout de suite en Amérique. Mes amis *vont*[5] dans le sud de la France.

Un jour, je *descends*[6] du bus près de l'atelier d'Antoine. Antoine *arrive*[7] au même moment. «Qu'est-ce qui se passe?» je lui *demande*[8]. Il me *répond:*[9] «Tu dois quitter Paris. La vie *devient*[10] trop dangereuse pour les Juifs et mes autres amis juifs *partent.*[11]»

Alors Antoine *rentre*[12] chez lui. Je *reste*[13] dans la rue et je *deviens*[14] de plus en plus inquiet. Finalement, *j'entre*[15] dans son appartement. Nous *restons*[16] près de la porte pour parler. Puis, je lui *dis*[17] au revoir et je *sors.*[18]

Quand je *reviens*[19] chez moi, la gardienne de mon immeuble me *voit.*[20] Elle me *dit:*[21] «Heureusement vous *sortez*[22] de chez vous. Des policiers *viennent*[23] ici et *entrent*[24] dans votre appartement.» Je *fais*[25] une valise et je *pars*[26] de Paris pour toujours.

Structure 34

Le passé composé des verbes pronominaux

Narrating in the past

—Qu'est-ce qui **s'est passé** dans les Cévennes?

1. All pronominal verbs are conjugated with **être** in the **passé composé.**

   Qu'est-ce qui **s'est passé** dans les Cévennes? — *What happened in the Cévennes?*

2. The pronoun in a pronominal verb can function as a direct object or an indirect object. When the pronoun serves as a direct object, the past participle must agree with it. Remember that this is the normal rule for a preceding direct object. However, if the pronoun serves as an indirect object, the past participle does not agree with it.

   Camille **s'**est **lavée.**
   D.O.

   Camille **s'**est **lavé les cheveux**.
   I.O. D.O.

   Pourquoi **se** sont-ils **séparés**?
   D.O.

   Pourquoi **se** sont-ils **téléphoné**?
   I.O.

3. In order to determine whether the pronoun is a direct object or an indirect object, follow these guidelines:

a. If the sentence already contains a direct object after the verb, the pronoun is an indirect object.

Bruno s'est brossé **les cheveux**.	*Bruno brushed his hair.*

b. If the sentence has only one object, you need to determine whether the same verb takes a direct or indirect object when it is used in a nonpronominal sense.

Nonpronominal use:	Sonia a habillé Yasmine.	*Sonia dressed Yasmine.*
Pronominal use:	Yasmine s'est habillée.	*Yasmine got dressed.*
Nonpronominal use:	Rachid a parlé à Bruno.	*Rachid talked to Bruno.*
Pronominal use:	Ils se sont parlé.	*They talked to each other.*

Look at the examples above. In the nonpronominal construction, **habiller** is followed by a direct object (**Yasmine**). Therefore, in its pronominal use, the pronoun is a direct object, and the past participle agrees with that pronoun. In the nonpronominal construction, **parler** is followed by an indirect object (**à Bruno**). Therefore, in its pronominal use, the pronoun is an indirect object, and the past participle does *not* agree with that pronoun.

c. These rules of agreement usually do not affect the pronunciation of the past participle.

Activités

A. Championnat d'orthographe. Formulez cinq questions sur le dernier (*last*) week-end de votre partenaire. Utilisez les éléments ci-dessous. Ensuite, posez vos questions à votre partenaire. Il/Elle va écrire ses réponses. Changez ensuite de rôle. Qui, de vous deux, gagne le championnat d'orthographe?

MODÈLE: VOUS: Ta famille et toi, est-ce que vous vous êtes téléphoné plusieurs fois le week-end dernier?

VOTRE PARTENAIRE: Oui, nous nous sommes téléphoné plusieurs fois. *ou*
Non, nous ne nous sommes pas téléphoné.

	se parler	
	se promener	
tu	se téléphoner	plusieurs fois
ta famille	se brosser les dents	le matin
ta famille et toi	se réveiller	tôt
tes ami(e)s	se raser	tard
	se maquiller	avant de quitter la maison
	se coucher	
	se parler souvent	

B. Interview d'une personne célèbre. Avec votre partenaire, jouez les rôles. Un(e) journaliste formule (à l'écrit) six questions personnelles qu'il/elle aimerait (*would like*) poser à une célébrité sur la journée (*day*) qu'elle a passée hier. Ensuite, le/la journaliste pose ces questions (à l'oral). La «célébrité» va répondre. Utilisez des questions et des verbes de la liste ou d'autres que vous choisissez.

Questions utiles: à quelle heure, à qui, avec qui, combien de, comment, où, pourquoi, quand

Verbes utiles: s'amuser, se coucher, se disputer, s'entendre avec, se fâcher contre, s'inquiéter de, s'intéresser à, se laver, se lever, se maquiller, se passer, se promener, se raser, se reposer, se tromper

MODÈLE: É1: Nicole Kidman, à quelle heure est-ce que vous vous êtes levée hier?
É2: Je me suis levée à 7 h.
É1: Vous êtes-vous bien amusée avec vos enfants toute la journée?
É2: Non, je suis partie au studio pour tourner un nouveau film.

Regards sur la culture

Le couple

In this segment of the film, we see Louise and Antoine together as a young couple. The other important couple in the story, Camille and Bruno, is linked by a somewhat ambiguous relationship, although it is clear that the two Canal 7 reporters share very strong emotional ties. Their interactions illustrate some differences between France and North America in the relations between the sexes.

- French children are usually brought up to be very happy about their sex. Both males and females are taught that they have many advantages being the sex that they are.
- In adolescence, there is no such thing as "dating." Rather than engage in the kind of one-on-one formalized "trial" relationship that is common in North America, French young people usually go out in groups. If two people do become a couple, they still may prefer to go most places with friends, rather than by themselves.
- Adolescent boys in France sometimes utter exaggerated compliments or engage in mock boasting about their sex appeal in front of girls their own age. These girls learn very young how to appreciate the attention but to deflate the pretensions of the male. Some of this male-female sparring continues later in life. Young North American women who encounter it are often at a loss about how to react. An uncomfortable smile is often the result, just the opposite of the culturally appropriate reaction.
- Anthropologist Raymonde Carroll has stated that French couples tend to manifest their relationship through the kinds of verbal interactions they

have: They tease each other in front of friends and may argue, say, about politics or the choice of a restaurant. In fact, she claims that French people might be suspicious of a couple who is always in agreement, thinking that there is no "spark" in the relationship.

- The partners in a French couple tend to maintain more independence than do those in North America. They continue to frequent their own friends individually.
- Even when there is no question of a romantic or sexual relationship, French people enjoy trying to be attractive to the opposite sex. They do not find this demeaning. One might even speak of "the game between the sexes" in France, in opposition to the North American "war between the sexes."

Yves Montand et Simone Signoret, un couple célèbre

Considérez

What possible conflicts could emerge in an intercultural relationship between a mainstream North American and a French person?

Structure 35

Les verbes réguliers en *-ir*

Talking about everyday actions

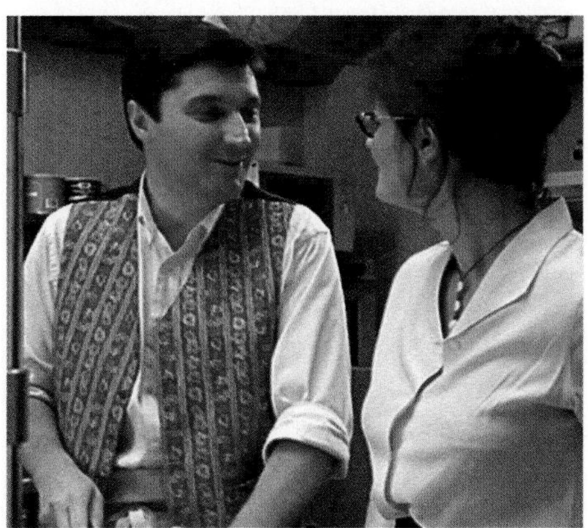

—Les histoires d'amour **finissent** toujours mal.

In earlier chapters, you learned how to conjugate two large classes of regular French verbs: those ending in **-er** and those ending in **-re**. The verb **finir** (*to finish, end*) is an example of another large category of verbs that are all conjugated the same way. They are usually referred to as regular **-ir** verbs.

1. To use regular **-ir** verbs in the present tense, drop the **-ir** ending and add the endings **-is**, **-is**, **-it**, **-issons**, **-issez**, **-issent**. To form the past participle, drop the **-ir** and add **i**.

finir (*to finish*)			
je	fin **is**	nous	fin **issons**
tu	fin **is**	vous	fin **issez**
il, elle, on	fin **it**	ils, elles	fin **issent**
passé composé: j'**ai fini**			

Bruno et Camille **finissent** l'émission à neuf heures.	*Bruno and Camille finish the show at nine o'clock.*
Ils **ont fini** leur soirée à vingt-trois heures.	*They finished their evening at eleven o'clock.*

2. Here is a list of some common regular **-ir** verbs and their past participles.

INFINITIVE		PAST PARTICIPLE
applaudir	*to applaud*	**applaudi**
choisir	*to choose*	**choisi**
finir	*to finish*	**fini**
obéir (à)	*to obey*	**obéi**
réfléchir (à)	*to reflect (on), think (about)*	**réfléchi**
réussir (à)	*to succeed; to pass (a course or exam)*	**réussi**

Yasmine **obéit** à ses parents.	*Yasmine obeys her parents.*
Les Français **choisissent** généralement le pain artisanal.	*French people usually choose handmade bread.*

3. When **choisir** and **finir** are used with an infinitive, they are followed by the preposition **de**. When **réfléchir** and **réussir** are used with an infinitive, they are followed by **à**.

Camille **choisit de** dîner avec Bruno.	*Camille chooses to eat dinner with Bruno.*
Martine **réussit à** trouver le médaillon.	*Martine succeeds in finding the locket.*

4. When **obéir**, **réfléchir**, and **réussir** are used with a noun, they are followed by **à**.

Camille **n'obéit pas à** sa mère.	*Camille doesn't obey her mother.*
Elle **réfléchit à** l'histoire de son grand-père.	*She thinks about her grandfather's story.*

Notez bien!

A question using **quel** with one of these verbs must begin with the preposition **à**.

À quel problème réfléchissez-vous? *What problem are you thinking about?*

À quels cours est-ce que vous réussissez? *In what courses are you doing well?*

Activités

A. Au travail. Faites des phrases complètes au temps présent avec les éléments donnés. Utilisez une préposition (**de** ou **à**) si nécessaire.

MODÈLE: Marc / réfléchir / questions financières. →
Marc réfléchit aux questions financières.

1. Jacques / choisir / aider les gens malades chez eux
2. Paul et René / obéir / juges quand ils travaillent à la cour (*in court*)
3. nous / réussir / parler trois langues pendant une journée normale à l'Organisation des Nations unies
4. nous / finir / la préparation d'une exposition dans un musée d'art
5. les gens / applaudir / après mes concerts
6. Patricia / réfléchir / problèmes de la ferme de son père
7. Danielle / choisir / travailler pour un cadre
8. tu / ne pas finir / le nouveau livre que tu écris (*are writing*)
9. vous / ne pas réussir / trouver un travail intéressant

Maintenant, avec un(e) partenaire, choisissez le métier ou la profession de la liste à la page 241 qui correspond aux intérêts ou aux problèmes des gens mentionnés dans cette activité.

B. Explications. (***Explanations.***) Deux anciens (*former*) étudiants parlent de la situation dans leurs universités respectives. Avec votre partenaire, complétez le dialogue en utilisant le passé composé des verbes indiqués.

finir

É1: Nous _____[1] nos cours en mai. Quand est-ce que vous _____[2]?

É2: Les étudiants de mon université _____[3] en juin.

choisir

É1: Est-ce que tout le monde _____[4] des cours faciles?

É2: Beaucoup d'étudiants _____[5] des cours difficiles. Moi, je (j') _____[6] des cours intéressants.

réussir

É1: À quels cours est-ce que tu ______[7]?

É2: Moi, je (j') ______[8] aux cours de maths et de sciences naturelles. Et toi?

É1: Mes amis et moi, nous aimions° les cours d'histoire. Alors, nous ______[9] à ces cours.

° *liked*

réfléchir

É2: Est-ce que tu ______[10] à ta future profession pendant tes années à l'université?

É1: Non. Je (J')______[11] aux examens et à mes études!

C. Les fêtes. Posez les questions suivantes à votre partenaire pour vous faire une idée du rôle des fêtes dans sa vie. Demandez-lui...

1. quelle est la fête la plus importante dans sa famille
2. s'il / si elle finit d'habitude toutes les préparations pour cette fête à temps (*in time*) (avec un exemple de son passé)
3. s'il / si elle réussit à se relaxer pendant (*during*) les fêtes de famille
4. s'il / si elle choisit des cadeaux pour ses amis en avance ou au dernier (*last*) moment
5. s'il / si elle obéit aux traditions pendant les fêtes
6. à quelles questions il/elle réfléchit le jour du nouvel an
7. s'il / si elle réussit à faire des changements (*changes*) dans sa vie après le nouvel an

Visionnement 2

Observez!

Regardez l'Épisode 11 encore une fois, et répondez aux questions suivantes.

- Pourquoi Samuel Lévy et sa femme ont-ils décidé de quitter la France?
- Est-ce que les Allemands sont les seuls à vouloir exterminer les Juifs?

Après le visionnement

Faites l'activité pour le **Visionnement 2** dans le cahier.

Synthèse: Culture

L'histoire et le mythe

Dans tous les pays, certains moments historiques prennent un aspect mythique. Ces moments sont souvent des épisodes très dramatiques qui ont déterminé un changement important dans l'histoire. Souvent aussi, ce sont des moments qui aident à expliquer des problèmes qui existent encore ou des tensions sociales qui persistent. C'est pour ces raisons que l'Occupation est encore une obsession pour beaucoup de Français et la Révolution française aussi. Dans d'autres pays de tradition francophone, il y a aussi des moments historiques mythiques.

RÉGIONS ACADIENNES DE L'ATLANTIQUE

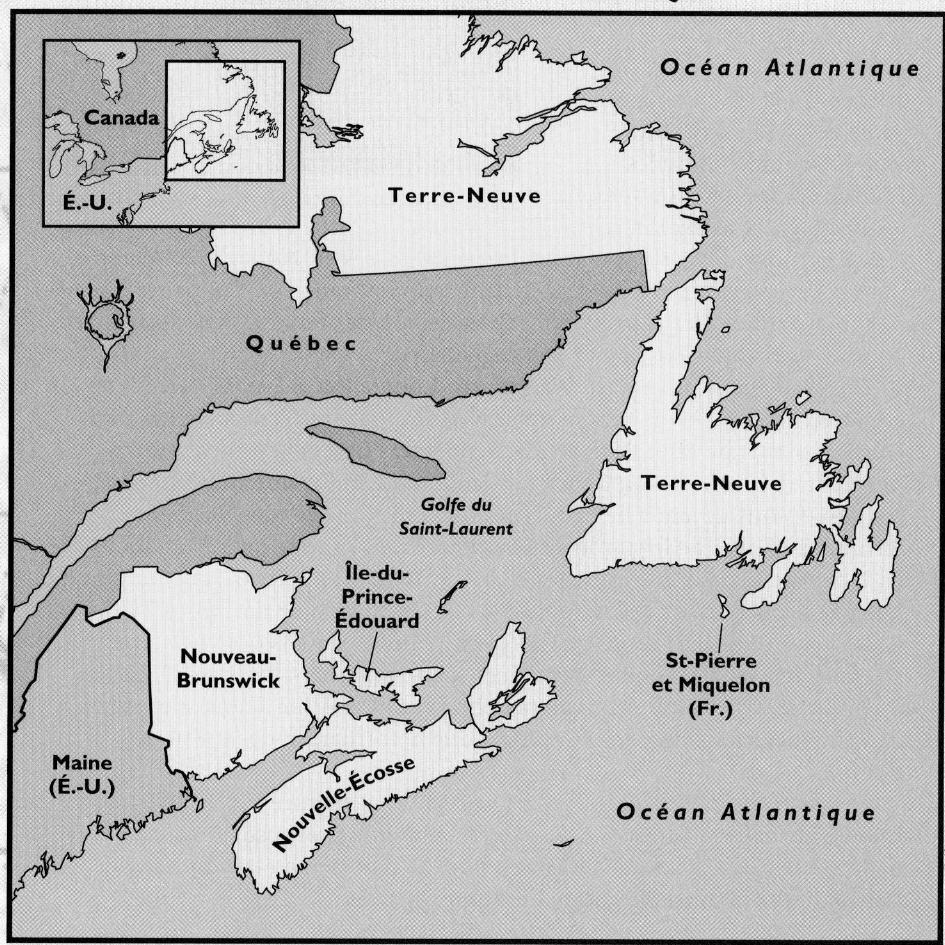

Régions acadiennes de l'Atlantique

L'Acadie: Le Grand Dérangement[1]

Au XVIe siècle, des pionniers français courageux viennent cultiver la terre et vivre en liberté dans les provinces canadiennes de la Nouvelle-Écosse et du Nouveau-Brunswick. Les pionniers sont acceptés par les Amérindiens et leur culture prend forme. Influencés par le Nouveau Monde,[2] ils gardent néanmoins[3] certaines de leurs traditions françaises et la religion catholique. En 1710, l'Acadie est conquise par les Britanniques, mais les 15 000 Acadiens refusent de prêter serment[4] à la Grande-Bretagne. Alors en 1755, après une violente bataille entre les Français et les Britanniques, les Acadiens sont expulsés. Certains[5] sont déportés vers les colonies anglaises en Nouvelle Angleterre, mais d'autres partent en Louisiane, une colonie française. Ces pauvres gens ont tout perdu et les Anglais ont même séparé des familles. On appelle cet épisode historique «Le Grand Dérangement».

Statue d'Évangéline à Grand-Pré, en Nouvelle-Écosse

Le poète américain Henry Wadsworth Longfellow a évoqué cette situation tragique dans son poème *Évangéline* presque cent ans plus tard. Une histoire vraie est à l'origine de ce poème: l'histoire d'une jeune Acadienne séparée de son fiancé par le Grand Dérangement. Évangéline et Gabriel sont devenus des symboles de la souffrance[6] des Acadiens. Aujourd'hui, une belle statue de l'héroïne Évangéline se dresse[7] à Grand-Pré en Nouvelle-Écosse, et c'est aussi ce prénom qu'on a retenu pour un grand journal acadien, *L'Évangéline,* publié en Nouvelle-Écosse de 1887 à 1982. Cette histoire a aussi contribué à l'identité des Acadiens qui vivent[8] aujourd'hui dans plusieurs[9] provinces canadiennes et aux États-Unis. Par exemple, on voit aujourd'hui cette culture acadienne en Louisiane, où les descendants s'appellent les «Cajuns» (une déformation de leur nom d'origine).

Des festivals de musique et d'art cajuns nous montrent une culture vivante et riche en Amérique du Nord. La langue française est soutenue[10] depuis 1971 par CODOFIL (Conseil pour le développement du français en Louisiane) et la musique cajun a un grand succès.

[1]Le… *The Great Disturbance* [2]Nouveau… *New World* [3]*nevertheless* [4]prêter… *to take an oath of allegiance* [5]*Some* [6]*suffering* [7]se… *stands* [8]*live* [9]*several* [10]*supported*

Les Acadiens n'ont pas oublié le Grand Dérangement. C'est d'ailleurs le nom d'un groupe de rock de la Nouvelle-Écosse. En 1755, les Acadiens ont tout perdu, mais au vingt et unième siècle, leur vitalité nous montre l'importance de l'histoire et de l'identité culturelle.

À vous

Un événement mythique. In groups of three or four people, create a list of five characteristics that often make a historical event "mythical." Choose from such things as heroism, insurmountable obstacles, fundamental values in conflict, and so on. Then select two events in your own people's history that have the kind of legendary status that we find in the Great Disturbance.

Faites **À écrire** pour le Chapitre 11 dans le cahier.

Vocabulaire

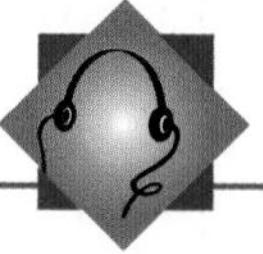

Le monde du travail

les affaires (*f. pl.*)	business
un emploi	work, employment
la gestion	management
un métier	trade
une petite annonce	classified ad
un poste	position, job
une société	company
un stage	internship
un tableau d'affichage	bulletin board

MOTS APPARENTÉS: **le commerce (international), le marketing, sur Internet, une profession**

Les métiers et les professions

un(e) agent(e) de sécurité	security guard
un(e) agriculteur/trice	farmer
un(e) artisan(e)	craftsman, artisan
un(e) avocat(e)	lawyer
un(e) cadre	executive
un(e) comptable	accountant
un(e) conservateur/trice (de musée)	curator (of a museum)

un(e) cuisinier/ière	cook
un(e) écrivain/ femme écrivain	writer
un(e) fonctionnaire	civil servant
un(e) garde-malade	nurse's aide
un(e) gardien(ne) d'immeuble	building superintendent
un(e) ingénieur/ femme ingénieur	engineer
un(e) interprète	interpreter
un(e) ouvrier/ière	manual laborer
un(e) patron(ne) (d'un bar, d'un restaurant)	owner; boss (of a bar, of a restaurant)
un(e) peintre/ femme peintre	painter

MOTS APPARENTÉS: **un(e) baby-sitter, un(e) employé(e) de fast-food, un(e) musicien(ne), un(e) secrétaire**

À REVOIR: **un(e) acteur/trice, un(e) boucher/ère, un(e) boulanger/ère, un(e) charcutier/ière, un(e) cremier/ière, un(e) épicier/ière, un(e) infirmier/ière, un(e) instituteur/trice, un(e) journaliste, un(e) maître/tresse, un(e) marchand(e), un(e) médecin / femme médecin, un(e) pâtissier/ière, un(e) producteur/trice, un professeur, un reporter, un(e) vendeur/euse**

Les jours fériés et les fêtes

un anniversaire de mariage	wedding anniversary
une fête	holiday; festival; party, celebration
la fête du Travail	Labor Day
la fête nationale	national holiday
un jour férié	legal holiday
Noël (m.)	Christmas
le nouvel an	New Year's Day
la Pâque	Passover
Pâques (*f. pl.*)	Easter
la Toussaint	All Saints' Day

MOTS APPARENTÉS: **le Ramadan, Hanoukka**

À REVOIR: **un anniversaire (de naissance)**

Les nombres ordinaux

premier/ière, deuxième, troisième, quatrième, cinquième, sixième, septième, huitième, neuvième, dixième, vingtième, vingt et unième

Verbes

choisir	to choose
finir	to finish
monter	to go up, climb
mourir	to die
naître	to be born
réfléchir (à)	to reflect (on), think (about)
rentrer	to come/go back (home)
rester	to stay
réussir (à)	to succeed; to pass (*a course or exam*)
tomber	to fall

MOTS APPARENTÉS: **applaudir, arriver, entrer, obéir (à), passer (par), retourner**

À REVOIR: **aller, descendre, devenir, partir, revenir, sortir, venir**

Autres expressions utiles

à mi-temps	half-time
à plein temps	full-time

Chapitre 12

C'est à propos de Louise.°

C'est... *It's about Louise.*

Le Chemin du retour

Feuille de service du 15 octobre
5e jour de tournage
Horaires: 7h–17h

LIEU DE TOURNAGE: PARIS—31, rue Coquillère, 1er

Séquence	*Effets*	*Décors*	*Résumé*	*Rôles*
74	INT.—AUBE°	APPARTEMENT CAMILLE—Séjour	Alex vient annoncer à Camille la mort° de Louise, sa grand-mère	CAMILLE, ALEX

dawn

death

OBJECTIFS

In this episode, you will

- find out more about Louise
- find out more about where Camille's grandfather was during World War II

In this chapter, you will

- discuss life's milestones
- talk about popular media
- describe things in the past
- tell about what you used to do
- discuss daily activities such as speaking, reading, and writing
- learn the lyrics to a French song that is mentioned in *Le Chemin du retour*

Vocabulaire en contexte

Les étapes de la vie°

Les... *Stages of life*

Voici une feuille d'un album de photos. Ce sont **les étapes** (*f.*) de la vie d'Adèle.

La naissance d'Adèle. C'est **un bébé** content.

Une jolie **jeune fille**, mais son **enfance** (*f.*) n'est pas heureuse. **La jeunesse**° n'est pas toujours facile. Qu'est-ce que **l'adolescence** (*f.*) lui réserve?

La... *Youth*

Le mariage d'Adèle et son mari. C'est un **événement joyeux**.

Adèle a cinquante ans. Elle **a divorcé** il y a dix ans.

Adèle à quatre-vingts ans. C'est maintenant une personne **du troisième âge**,° mais **la vieillesse** n'est pas un handicap!

du... *elderly*

Autres mots et expressions

un(e) adolescent(e) (*fam.* **un[e] ado**)	adolescent
un(e) adulte	adult
l'enterrement (*m.*)	burial
un garçon	boy
jeune	young
la mort	death
un(e) retraité(e)	retiree, retired person
prendre sa retraite	to retire

Activités

A. Qui est-ce? Complétez ces descriptions avec des termes appropriés.

1. Une personne qui (*who*) ne travaille plus est un(e)... **2.** Une fille de 15 ans est une... **3.** Je suis né il y a 6 ans. Je suis un petit... **4.** Le nouveau membre de la famille, âgé de 3 mois, est...

B. Quelle étape? Décidez à quelle étape de la vie on fait allusion dans chacune (*each one*) de ces descriptions.

1. C'est une période de rébellion. **2.** On commence à parler. **3.** On a eu beaucoup d'anniversaires, on se souvient du passé. **4.** On n'a pas encore 30 ans. **5.** On commence ses études au lycée.

C. Antonymes. Trouvez le contraire des mots suivants.

1. le divorce
2. la jeunesse
3. la mort
4. une jeune fille
5. une personne qui continue à travailler
6. vieux

D. À des âges différents. Avec votre partenaire, imaginez les désirs, capacités (*abilities*) et responsabilités des personnes mentionnées ci-dessous, en utilisant les verbes suggérés. Faites chacun(e) une suggestion différente pour chaque personne. Suivez le modèle.

MODÈLE: un adolescent / (ne pas) vouloir...
É1: Un adolescent veut être indépendant.
É2: Il ne veut pas souvent parler avec ses parents de ses activités.

1. un adolescent / (ne pas) vouloir...
2. un bébé / (ne pas) pouvoir...
3. un garçon de 7 ans / (ne pas) aimer...
4. une retraitée / (ne pas) vouloir...
5. une jeune fille de 12 ans / (ne pas) pouvoir...
6. un adulte / (ne pas) devoir...
7. une personne du troisième âge / (ne pas) aimer...

Maintenant, parlez de votre enfance ou de votre adolescence avec votre partenaire. Y a-t-il des choses que vous avez voulu faire mais que vous n'avez pas pu faire? Qu'est-ce que vous avez pu faire?

E. Un portrait. Faites votre portrait à l'époque actuelle (*present time*). Vous êtes à quelle étape de votre vie? Quels sont vos espoirs (*hopes*)? vos déceptions (*disappointments*)? Quel est le moment idéal de la vie, selon vous?

Les médias

Le journal et ses rubriques (*f.*)

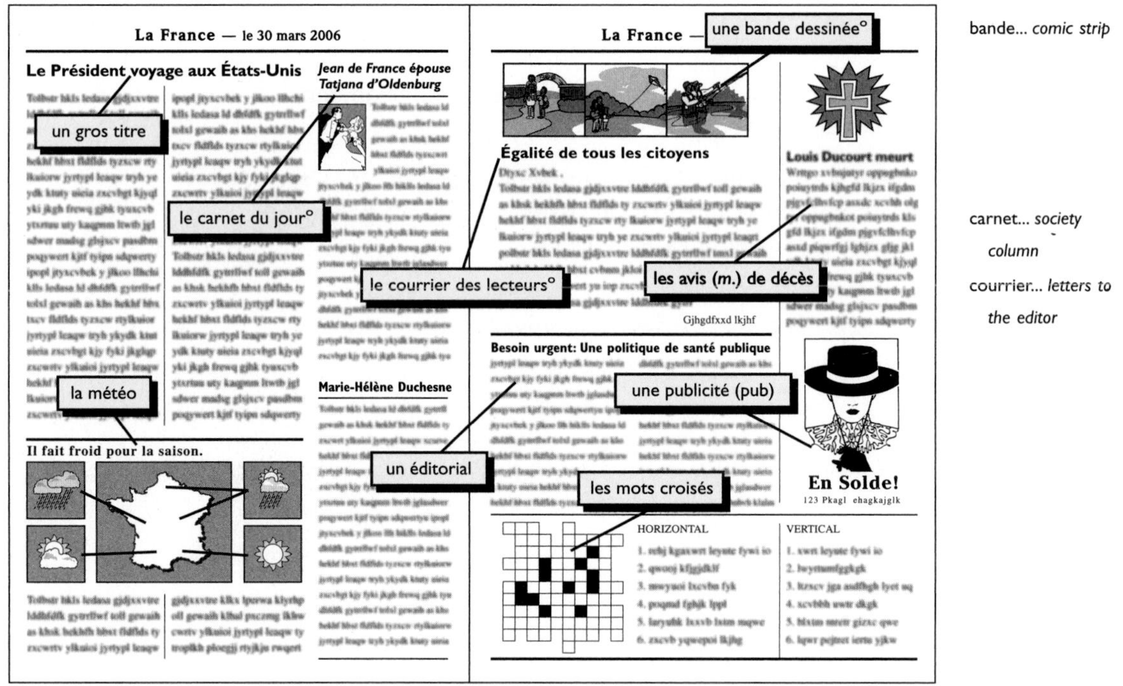

bande... *comic strip*

carnet... *society column*

courrier... *letters to the editor*

La télévision

TF1

6.05 Des filles dans le vent. Le secret.
6.30 TF1 info
6.40 TF1 jeunesse: Salut les toons
8.30 Téléshopping
9.05 La joyeuse tribu
10.05 Le siècle des intellectuels
11.15 Chicago Hope, la vie à tout prix Mort d'un brave chien.
12.05 Tac O Tac TV
12.10 Etre heureux comme
12.15 Le juste prix
12.50 A vrai dire
13.00 Journal
13.42 Bien Jardiner
Magazine.
13.50 Les feux de l'amour
Feuilleton. Etats-Unis. Inédit
Comme Paul sort de l'hôpital, Christine vient l'aider à faire sa valise. Sharon se défend d'avoir provoqué Matt qui la considère comme responsable.
14.45 Arabesque
Série.
15.40 Sydney Police
Série.

TF1

16.40 Sunset Beach
Série. Etats-Unis. Inédit
A peine rentrée à Sunset Beach, Olivia trouve Gregory au lit avec Annie. Betty découvre le corps d'Eddie. Cole fait la connaissance de son père.
17.35 Melrose Place
Série. Etats-Unis.
Retour de bâton.
Amanda et Billy poursuivent leur liaison. Alison démissionne. Peter et Michael partent en week-end pour participer à un concours de beauté.
18.25 Les amis
19.05 Le bigdil
19.57 Clic et net
Conquête spatiale.
20.00 Journal
20.35 Le journal de la Coupe du monde
20.50 Le juste prix
Jeu.

Autres mots utiles

à la une	on the front page
une chaîne	(*television*) station; network
une publicité	commercial, advertisement
une station (de radio)	(radio) station

Activités

A. Qu'est-ce que c'est? Donnez le mot qui correspond à la définition.

DANS LE JOURNAL

1. C'est la rubrique du journal où on annonce les naissances et les mariages.
2. C'est un jeu où il s'agit de trouver le mot correct.
3. C'est la partie du journal où on annonce les enterrements.
4. C'est un forum où les lecteurs du journal peuvent exprimer leurs opinions.
5. Ce sont des histoires amusantes en images que les enfants aiment beaucoup.

À LA TÉLÉVISION

6. Ce sont des mélodrames à la télé.
7. On regarde cette émission pour se tenir au courant (*to keep up to date*).
8. C'est une histoire en plusieurs épisodes.

B. C'est quoi? Complétez la phrase avec le mot juste (*right*).

DANS LE JOURNAL

1. On trouve un _____ au début d'un article.
2. Chaque journal exprime son opinion dans l'_____.
3. Si le président fait un voyage important, on le rapporte _____.

À LA TÉLÉVISION

4. Les petits enfants aiment beaucoup les _____ de Disney.
5. Il y a des _____ scientifiques sur la chaîne des sciences.
6. Aimez-vous les _____ comme *Scrubs* et *Arrested Development*?
7. Quel _____ était le plus amusant (*most fun*) à la télévision—*Qui veut être un millionnaire* ou *Tic-tac-toe de Hollywood*?
8. Chaque année, les chaînes américaines lancent de nouvelles _____.

C. Interview. Demandez à votre partenaire...

1. comment il/elle se tient au courant.
2. quels journaux ou magazines il/elle préfère.
3. quelle rubrique du journal il/elle préfère et pourquoi.
4. s'il / si elle aime faire les mots croisés dans le journal et pourquoi (pas).
5. quelle(s) émission(s) il/elle préfère regarder à la télévision.
6. quelle publicité récente à la télévision il/elle aime bien et pourquoi.
7. s'il / si elle aime les dessins animés et lequel (*which one*) il/elle préfère.
8. quelle station de radio il/elle aime et pourquoi.

Visionnement 1

Avant de visionner

Pour parler du passé. Vous avez déjà appris le **passé composé**. Mais en français, on utilise aussi un autre temps—l'**imparfait**—pour parler du passé. Vous allez apprendre l'imparfait dans ce chapitre. Mais maintenant, pour comprendre l'Épisode 12, lisez (*read*) les phrases suivantes et faites attention au sens (*meaning*).

Elle **était**[a] très calme...
Ses yeux **brillaient**,[b] comme les yeux d'un enfant à Noël...
Je **voulais**[c] discuter avec elle.

[a]*was* [b]*were shining* [c]*wanted*

Regardez encore une fois les verbes en caractères **gras**. Quels verbes décrivent (*describe*) des émotions? Quels verbes décrivent une action qui continue dans le passé?

Vocabulaire relatif à l'épisode

elle a souri	*she smiled*
un drôle de...	*a funny, strange...*
doucement	*gently*
qui a déchiré	*who tore up*
au moins	*at least*
une bourgade	*village*

Observez!

Dans l'Épisode 12, Camille apprend un autre détail important sur son grand-père. Pendant votre visionnement, essayez de trouver la réponse aux questions suivantes.

- Pourquoi Mado s'impatiente-t-elle contre Camille?
- Quelle est l'importance du titre de la chanson (*song*) préférée de Louise, *Mon Amant de Saint-Jean*?

Après le visionnement

A. Les détails. Qu'est-ce qu'on apprend dans cet épisode sur l'histoire de la famille Leclair? Répondez **vrai** si on trouve cette information dans l'épisode. Répondez **faux** si on ne la trouve pas.

Dans cet épisode, on apprend...

1. qui a déchiré les photos d'Antoine.
2. l'état d'esprit (*state of mind*) de Louise au moment de sa mort.
3. où Antoine est allé dans les Cévennes.
4. pourquoi on a déchiré les photos d'Antoine.
5. pourquoi *Mon Amant de Saint-Jean* était la chanson préférée de Louise.
6. où on a enterré (*buried*) Louise.

B. Réfléchissez. Selon vous, pourquoi Mado a-t-elle révélé le nom du village où Antoine est allé en 1943? Est-ce qu'elle se prépare à raconter l'histoire d'Antoine à Camille? Essaie-t-elle de calmer Camille, ou y a-t-il une autre explication?

L'imparfait (I)

Narrating in the past

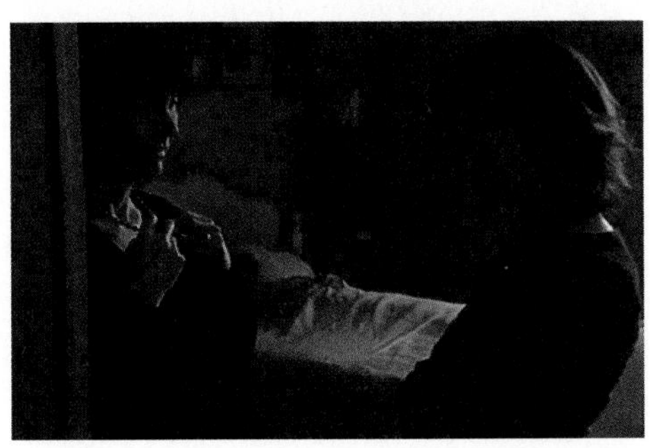

—Elle **était** très calme, tu sais.

The term *tense* means "time." There are several past tenses in French—that is to say, there are several ways of expressing past time. The **passé composé** is used to talk about past events that are completed before the time or at the time being discussed. The imperfect, **l'imparfait**, has a complementary function: It is used to describe conditions, emotions, states of mind, ongoing actions, and habitual actions in the past.

1. To form the **imparfait** of all verbs except **être**, drop the **-ons** ending from the **nous** form of the present tense and then add the endings **-ais**, **-ais**, **-ait**, **-ions**, **-iez**, **-aient** to the stem.

regarder (*nous regardons*)			
je	regard **ais**	nous	regard **ions**
tu	regard **ais**	vous	regard **iez**
il, elle, on	regard **ait**	ils, elles	regard **aient**

Camille **finissait** sa toilette quand Alex est arrivé.	*Camille was finishing getting dressed when Alex arrived.*
Je **voulais** discuter avec elle.	*I wanted to talk with her.*
Elle **avait** à peu près mon âge, à cette époque...	*She was about my age, at that time . . .*

For verbs like **commencer** and **manger**, the **ç** and **ge** of the present tense **nous** form are changed to **c** and **g** for **nous** and **vous** in the **imparfait** because the endings begin with **i**.

PRESENT TENSE		IMPARFAIT
nous commen**ç**ons	→	je commen**ç**ais, *but* nous commen**c**ions, vous commen**c**iez
nous man**ge**ons	→	je man**ge**ais, *but* nous man**g**ions, vous man**g**iez

2. The **imparfait** of **être** uses the stem **ét-** and the **imparfait** endings.

être (ét-)			
j'	ét **ais**	nous	ét **ions**
tu	ét **ais**	vous	ét **iez**
il, elle, on	ét **ait**	ils, elles	ét **aient**

C'**était** un petit village. *It was a small village.*

3. The **imparfait** is used to describe conditions, emotions, and states of mind in the past.

Louise **était** jeune en 1939. *Louise was young in 1939.*
Elle **était** très calme, tu sais. *You know, she was very calm.*
Je **voulais** discuter avec elle. *I wanted to talk with her.*

Activités

A. De bons souvenirs. (***Happy memories.***) Mettez les verbes entre parenthèses à l'imparfait pour comprendre les souvenirs de Louise.

Avant de mourir, Louise a beaucoup pensé au passé mais elle ____[1] (être) heureuse parce qu'il y _____[2] (avoir) beaucoup de bons souvenirs.

«Nous _____[3] (être) en 1939. Quand j'ai appris que je/j' ______[4] (attendre) (*was expecting*) un bébé, ça a été une grande joie. J'ai dit à Antoine: «C'est exactement ce que nous _____[5] (vouloir)—un enfant pour compléter notre vie de famille!» Et mes parents aussi _____[6] (adorer) l'idée d'avoir des petits-enfants. Ils nous ont dit: «Vous _____[7] (avoir envie) de commencer une famille, et voilà, ça commence!» Quand la guerre a éclaté (*broke out*), tout le monde _____[8] (s'inquiéter) beaucoup. Antoine et moi, nous _____[9] (être) conscients (*aware*) de la difficulté de notre situation, mais notre amour (*love*) pour notre petite Mado nous _____[10] (donner) des forces. Je _____[11] (réfléchir) à son avenir (*future*) et à ce que nous _____[12] (pouvoir) faire pour assurer sa sécurité. Je _____[13] (se demander) parfois pourquoi Antoine _____[14] (devoir) partir pour rejoindre les résistants (*to join the resistance fighters*) dans les Cévennes, mais je _____[15] (comprendre) aussi que je l'_____[16] (aimer) pour le courage qui l'_____[17] (obliger) à partir.»

B. Dans le journal d'hier. Décrivez ce que vous avez lu dans le journal d'hier et les réactions des lecteurs. Choisissez un des verbes de la liste pour compléter les phrases à l'imparfait. Les titres des rubriques vont vous aider.

Verbes: avoir, être, chercher, faire, parler, pleuvoir, pouvoir, se sentir, travailler, vendre

1. La météo: Hier, il _____ froid et il _____.
2. Une bande dessinée: C'_____ très drôle parce qu'il y _____ des petits personnages amusants.
3. Une publicité: Un grand magasin _____ des chaussures à moitié prix (*half price*).
4. Un éditorial: Deux jeunes femmes _____ des problèmes politiques dans la ville.
5. Les mots croisés: Je _____ un mot que je ne _____ pas trouver.
6. Les avis de décès: Vous _____ très triste parce que vous avez reconnu (*recognized*) le nom d'un ami de la famille.

C. Une interview. Posez à votre partenaire des questions sur son passé et le passé d'autres personnes. Utilisez les éléments donnés pour former vos questions. Suivez le modèle.

MODÈLE: tes amis / penser à / politique / il y a _____ ans
É1: Est-ce que tes amis pensaient à la politique il y a cinq ans?
É2: Non, ils ne pensaient pas à la politique. Ils pensaient aux matchs de base-ball.

1. tu / vouloir / faire des études universitaires / il y a _____ ans
2. tes parents / réfléchir à / vieillesse / il y a _____ ans
3. un(e) de tes ami(e)s / vouloir / travailler pour un journal / il y a _____ ans
4. tu / aimer / regarder les actualités à la télévision / il y a _____ ans
5. tes amis et toi / penser à / l'environnement / il y a _____ ans
6. tu / avoir / un chien (*dog*) ou un chat (*cat*) / il y a _____ ans
7. tes amis / avoir besoin de / étudier beaucoup / il y a _____ ans

Structure 37

L'imparfait (II)

Narrating in the past

—Ses yeux **brillaient**, comme les yeux d'un enfant à Noël...

1. The **imparfait** is also used to express ongoing actions in the past. This usage often can be thought of as meaning *was/were doing.*

Ses yeux **brillaient**, comme les yeux d'un enfant à Noël...	*Her eyes were shining, like a child's eyes at Christmas . . .*
Nous **pensions** à un voyage dans les Cévennes.	*We were thinking of (making) a trip to the Cévennes.*

2. Finally, the **imparfait** is used to express habitual past action, corresponding to the English *used to do.*

	Elle **demandait** toujours cette chanson à Alex.	*She always used to ask Alex for that song.*
	Camille **sortait** souvent avec Bruno.	*Camille used to go out often with Bruno.*
but	Hier, elle **a demandé** à Alex de jouer cette chanson.	*Yesterday, she asked Alex to play that song.*
	Camille **est sortie** avec Bruno hier.	*Camille went out with Bruno yesterday.*

Notez bien!

A number of expressions of time and frequency, some of which you already know, are very useful when talking about habitual past action. Many can, of course, also be used in the present tense.

autrefois	*formerly, in the past*
toujours	*always*
tous les jours	*every day*
d'habitude	*usually, normally*
souvent	*often*
quelquefois	*sometimes*
parfois	*sometimes*
de temps en temps	*from time to time*
rarement	*rarely*

Tous les jours, d'habitude, quelquefois, and **de temps en temps** can be placed at the beginning of a sentence. **Toujours, souvent, parfois,** and **rarement** usually follow the conjugated verb.

D'habitude, Alex jouait «Mon Amant de Saint-Jean» pour Louise. *Alex usually played "Mon Amant de Saint-Jean" for Louise.*

Camille arrive **toujours** à l'heure. Elle passe **souvent** quarante minutes au maquillage. *Camille always arrives on time. She often spends forty minutes in makeup.*

Activités

A. Une matinée difficile. Alex parle du jour où Louise est morte. Mettez les verbes entre parenthèses à l'imparfait.

Je ______[1] (s'installer) à ma place habituelle au marché Mouffetard quand le médecin est sorti de chez Louise. J'______[2] (avoir) mon accordéon avec moi, et je ______[3] (penser) jouer «Mon Amant de Saint-Jean» pour elle quand le médecin m'a demandé de monter dans son appartement. Je suis entré, et Louise ______[4] (être) là sur son lit. Mado la ______[5] (regarder) en silence. Elle ______[6] (ne pas pouvoir) parler.

Je lui ai dit: «C'______[7] (être) une femme extraordinaire, votre mère. Vous ______[8] (avoir) de la chance d'avoir une mère si gentille. Elle ______[9] (aimer) tous les gens du quartier, et nous l'______[10] (adorer) aussi.»

Je ______[11] (vouloir) vraiment faire quelque chose pour aider Mado. Nous ______[12] (parler) de sa mère quand Mado m'a pris les mains. Elle m'a demandé si je ______[13] (pouvoir) aller chez Camille pour lui dire (*tell*) la triste nouvelle en personne. Quand je suis arrivé chez Camille, elle ______[14] (faire) sa toilette. Elle ______[15] (se peigner) et elle ______[16] (porter) une vieille chemise. Elle a bien vu que j'______[17] (avoir) une mauvaise nouvelle.

Quand j'ai laissé Camille à la porte de l'immeuble de Louise, elle _____[18] (essayer) de se calmer, mais je _____[19] (comprendre) bien que la journée _____[20] (aller) être difficile, très difficile.

B. Quand j'avais ton âge. Un adolescent parle à ses grand-parents de sa vie. Imaginez ce que sa grand-mère ou son grand-père dirait (*would say*) qu'elle/il faisait dans les mêmes situations. Soyez logique.

MODÈLE: Je danse toute (*all*) la nuit. (avoir ton âge) →
Quand j'avais ton âge, je dansais aussi toute la nuit. (Quand j'avais ton âge, je ne dansais pas toute la nuit.)

1. Je parle avec mes amis. (être jeune)
2. Mes amis et moi, nous mangeons au restaurant. (avoir de l'argent)
3. Mes parents ne me comprennent pas. (faire des bêtises [*silly things*])
4. Tous mes amis regardent la télévision. (être jeunes)
5. Nous sortons dans des boîtes de nuit. (avoir 16 ans)
6. Je dois utiliser ma carte de crédit. (faire mes achats)
7. Mes amis font du roller tous les vendredis soirs. (être jeunes)
8. On boit beaucoup de coca. (avoir soif)
9. Ma grand-mère veut toujours me voir. (avoir 10 ans)
10. Ma petite amie étudie l'informatique. (avoir ton âge)
11. Nous réfléchissons à l'environnement. (être adolescents)

C. Interviews. Interviewez deux camarades de classe (ou votre professeur) pour savoir si, oui ou non, ils faisaient les mêmes activités que vous il y a cinq ans. D'abord, écrivez cinq questions à l'imparfait en utilisant les éléments des listes suivantes, puis faites vos interviews.

Expressions interrogatives: à quel(le)(s), à qui, avec qui, de quel(le)(s), où, quand, quel(le)(s), qu'est-ce que

Verbes: chanter (*to sing*), danser, dessiner (*to draw*), étudier, jouer à... , jouer de... , parler, prendre des photos, sortir le soir, travailler, ???

MODÈLE: É1: De quel instrument jouais-tu?
É2: Je jouais de la flûte.

Maintenant, comparez les réponses avec les réponses des autres étudiants de la classe. Y a-t-il des choses que tout le monde faisait? que peu de gens faisaient? que votre professeur faisait?

Regards sur la culture

Les étapes de la vie

Louise's death in this episode upsets Camille and seems to dash her hopes of finding out about what happened to her grandfather during World War II. It also modifies the relationship between Mado and Camille in subtle but important ways. In every culture, deaths, like births and marriages, are treated in special ways.

- French people don't give baby showers. A birth announcement is usually sent to family and friends, and many of these people visit the new baby, bringing gifts of the kind that North Americans give at a shower.
- Most French people see having a child as a major investment of time, energy, and affection. Children are looked after very closely all the way through childhood. As a result, many French families have only one child, and there is no particular sense that being an only child is a disadvantage. People who have many children are sometimes jokingly accused of being clumsy or of wanting to take advantage of the additional Social Security payments that they receive.
- French marriages take place in two parts. The civil ceremony is obligatory and is usually carried out complete with flowers and bridal gown. A religious ceremony is optional and in itself is not sufficient to legalize a marriage. This dual ceremony is the result of the separation of church and state that was mandated in early 20th-century France. The wedding reception usually consists of a huge dinner: As many as twelve or thirteen courses are presented over 5 hours or so, with dish after dish being commented on and appreciated. The meal is punctuated by individual speeches, toasts, and songs, and often is followed by dancing.

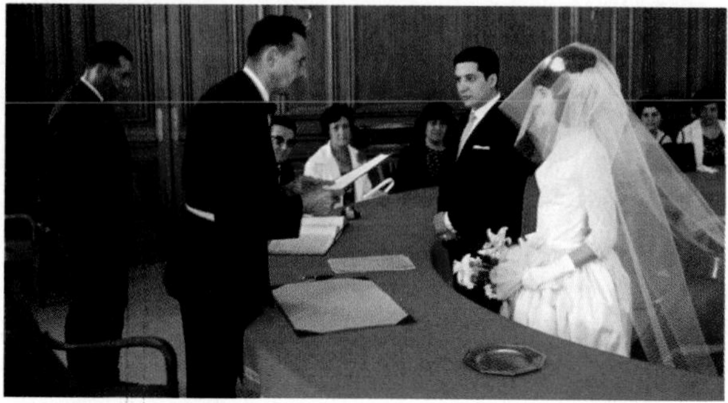
Un mariage civil à la mairie

- Career choice is often class-related. Since World War II, young people have often been discouraged by their families from entering agriculture, blue-collar jobs, and crafts. Another very important criterion in the choice is security. Finding a permanent, secure job (**une situation**) has traditionally been an obsession with French people. Most look for a job they can keep all their lives. This often means trying very hard to get a civil service job (anything from staff positions in government offices to teaching). Another criterion is location: Most people expect to find a job near home and family and to stay in it.
- **Ambition** is a word that has mainly negative connotations in France. It is impolite, at best, to be **ambitieux**. But for the French, ambition is not really necessary: French education and the system of competitive examinations are oriented toward finding people exactly the kind of job they should have.
- The average retirement age in France is 60. Most people receive 60 to 70% of their salary in retirement benefits. Many consider it selfish not to plan for an inheritance for one's children.
- Nearly every French person dreads the idea of dying in a hospital. People want to die at home, where friends and loved ones can watch over them and come to pay their last respects. Funerals and the clinical procedures surrounding death and burial are far simpler in France than they are in North America.

Considérez

Contrast French attitudes toward having children with those of your culture. What different values are involved? Why might this be? What might be the outward signs of these differences?

Les verbes dire, lire et écrire

Talking about everyday activities

—Maman? Que **dit** le médecin?

The verbs **dire**, **lire**, and **écrire** all have to do with communication. **Décrire** (*to describe*) is conjugated like **écrire**.

dire (*to say; to tell*)		**lire** (*to read*)		**écrire** (*to write*)	
je	**dis**	je	**lis**	j'	**écris**
tu	**dis**	tu	**lis**	tu	**écris**
il, elle, on	**dit**	il, elle, on	**lit**	il, elle, on	**écrit**
nous	**disons**	nous	**lisons**	nous	**écrivons**
vous	**dites**	vous	**lisez**	vous	**écrivez**
ils, elles	**disent**	ils, elles	**lisent**	ils, elles	**écrivent**
passé composé: j'**ai dit**		passé composé: j'**ai lu**		passé composé: j'**ai écrit**	

Yasmine **dit**: «C'est ma nouvelle école?»	*Yasmine says: "Is this my new school?"*
Elle **lit** sur l'écran de l'ordinateur.	*She reads on the computer screen.*
Les auteurs **écrivent** chaque jour.	*Authors write every day.*
Dites à David de venir tout de suite.	*Tell David to come right away.*
Il **a écrit** une lettre pour le quatrième anniversaire de sa fille.	*He wrote a letter for his daughter's fourth birthday.*
Des amis **ont lu** que la grand-mère de Camille était morte.	*Friends read that Camille's grandmother had died.*
Camille **décrit** la situation de ses grands-parents en 1939.	*Camille describes her grandparents' situation in 1939.*

Activités

A. Les médias. Faites des phrases avec les éléments donnés. N'oubliez pas d'utiliser **de** ou **que**, si nécessaire.

MODÈLE: nous / ne pas lire / le courrier des lecteurs tous les jours
Nous ne lisons pas le courrier des lecteurs tous les jours.

1. les journalistes / ne pas écrire / toujours clairement
2. la télévision / décrire / la misère humaine trop en détail
3. les jeunes / ne pas dire / les feuilletons sont intelligents
4. hier, je / lire / le président est à l'hôpital
5. tu / ne pas dire / toujours la vérité (*truth*)
6. le reporter / relire / son reportage très attentivement
7. quand vous / décrire / votre jeu télévisé préféré, qu'est-ce que vous / dire?
8. nous / dire / à nos enfants / jouer gentiment (*nicely*)

B. Ce n'est pas vrai! Un étudiant et sa petite amie sont fâchés l'un avec l'autre. L'un(e) dit ce qu'il/elle pense. Jouez le rôle de l'autre en répondant au passé composé avec **dire**, **lire**, **décrire** ou **écrire**.

MODÈLE: Je t'écris toujours des poèmes. (ne... jamais) →
Tu ne m'as jamais écrit de poèmes.

1. Je dis toujours la vérité. (ne... pas / hier)
2. Ton ancienne petite amie (*old girlfriend*) t'écrit souvent. (ne... pas)
3. Tu lis mon journal intime (*diary*). (ne... jamais)
4. Tes amis et toi, vous dites que je suis laide. (ne... jamais)
5. Tes amis lisent toutes mes lettres. (ne... pas)
6. Vous me décrivez comme si j'étais un idiot. (ne... jamais)

C. Quand ce journaliste était jeune… . Un étudiant en journalisme pose des questions à un vieux journaliste sur sa vie. Avec un(e) partenaire, jouez les deux rôles. Utilisez des éléments des trois colonnes pour former des questions à l'imparfait.

MODÈLE: ÉTUDIANT: Est-ce que votre femme était jalouse de votre travail?
JOURNALISTE: Non. Elle travaillait avec moi. (Oui, elle pensait que je travaillais trop.)

vous	lire	vos articles
votre rédacteur en chef	écrire	votre travail
vos collègues	aimer	une vie intéressante
votre femme	avoir	jaloux/ouse de votre travail
	être	content(e)(s) de vous

Visionnement 2

Observez!

Considérez les aspects culturels expliqués dans **Regards sur la culture**. Ensuite, regardez l'Épisode 12 encore une fois, et répondez aux questions suivantes.

- Louise meurt dans son lit, chez elle. Est-ce que cette scène reflète une situation typique en France ou non?
- Camille a-t-elle tort (*Is Camille wrong*) de vouloir parler de son grand-père juste après l'enterrement de Louise?

Après le visionnement

Faites l'activité pour le **Visionnement 2** dans le cahier.

Synthèse: Lecture

Mise en contexte

The **valse musette** is a blend of folk music from the Auvergne region and light Parisian music from the 19th century. It developed into its current form during the 1930s, under the influence of Italian immigrants. The **valse musette** is accompanied by an accordion; indeed, the term **musette** refers to a small, bagpipe-like instrument, played especially in the Auvergne. Louise's favorite song, *Mon Amant de Saint-Jean,* is a **valse musette** written during the Second World War and popularized by Lucienne Delyle. Louise probably associated the song's title with her longing to see her husband, who had gone to Saint-Jean de Causse.

Stratégie pour mieux lire

Understanding the structure of a song's lyrics

When you hear a song, you can readily perceive its musicality: You hear the changes in pitch, the rhythm, and the rhyme. But you may not be able to distinguish all the lyrics or the nuances of meaning in them, because they may be delivered rapidly or indistinctly.

The song *Mon Amant de Saint-Jean* tells a story that is narrated in the past. It is divided into three verses, each consisting of three stanzas, or groups of lines. Skim the verses and identify which stanza in each advances the story. Which stanzas are repeated from verse to verse? What is different about the last verse?

When you've identified the overall structure, read the lyrics more carefully. How would you summarize the story and the narrator's feelings at the end?

Mon Amant[1] de Saint-Jean

Je ne sais pourquoi j'allais danser
À Saint-Jean au musette
Mais il m'a suffi d'un seul baiser[2]
Pour que mon cœur soit[3] prisonnier.
Comment ne pas perdre la tête
Serrée[4] par des bras audacieux
Car l'on croit[5] toujours
Aux doux mots d'amour
Quand ils sont dits avec les yeux.
Moi qui l'aimais tant[6]
Je le trouvais le plus beau de Saint-Jean
Je restais grisée[7]
Sans volonté[8]
Sous ses baisers.

Sans plus réfléchir, je lui donnais
Le meilleur de mon être[9]
Beau parleur chaque fois qu'il mentait
Je le savais, mais je l'aimais.
Comment ne pas perdre la tête
Serrée par des bras audacieux
Car l'on croit toujours

[1]*Lover* [2]*il... one kiss was enough* [3]*Pour... To make my heart* [4]*Held tight* [5]*Car... For one believes* [6]*qui... who loved him so much* [7]*intoxicated* [8]*Sans... Without will* [9]*Le... The best of my being*

Aux doux mots d'amour
Quand ils sont dits avec les yeux.
Moi qui l'aimais tant
Je le trouvais le plus beau de Saint-Jean
Je restais grisée
Sans volonté
Sous ses baisers.

Mais hélas,[10] à Saint-Jean comme ailleurs[11]
Un serment n'est qu'un leurre[12]
J'étais folle de croire au bonheur
Et de vouloir garder[13] son cœur.
Comment ne pas perdre la tête
Serrée par des bras audacieux
Car l'on croit toujours
Aux doux mots d'amour
Quand ils sont dits avec les yeux.
Moi qui l'aimais tant
Mon bel amour, mon amant de Saint-Jean,
Il ne m'aime plus
C'est du passé
N'en parlons plus.

Musique: Émile Carrara
Paroles: Léon Agel
1945: Éditions Méridian

[10]*alas* [11]*elsewhere* [12]*Un... An oath is only a deception* [13]*to keep*

Après la lecture

A. Le bon résumé. Choisissez le bon résumé de la chanson parmi les possibilités suivantes.

a. Un homme essaie de séduire (*seduce*) une femme. Au début, elle résiste, parce qu'elle ne croit pas à ses doux mots d'amour. Enfin, elle tombe amoureuse de lui, mais il la trompe (*deceives her*) et la quitte.

b. Une femme tombe amoureuse d'un homme qu'elle connaît depuis longtemps. Mais il reste froid et distant. Elle est trop intoxiquée par son amour pour remarquer son indifférence. Finalement, elle se rend compte de sa folie.

c. Un homme séduit une femme par des baisers et des doux mots d'amour. Elle ne résiste pas, elle devient intoxiquée par son amour. Mais finalement, elle apprend qu'il mentait et qu'il ne l'aime pas.

B. Un portrait. Faites le portrait de la narratrice et de son amant. Au début, quel était l'état d'esprit de la narratrice? Était-elle optimiste, sincère, cynique, impuissante (*helpless*)? Pourquoi était-elle susceptible aux désirs de l'amant? Qui a trompé qui? Comment l'attitude de la narratrice a-t-elle changé à la fin?

C. La chanson. Lisez les paroles à haute voix (*aloud*). Comment imaginez-vous la chanson? La musique est-elle gaie? rythmée? triste? lugubre (*gloomy*)?

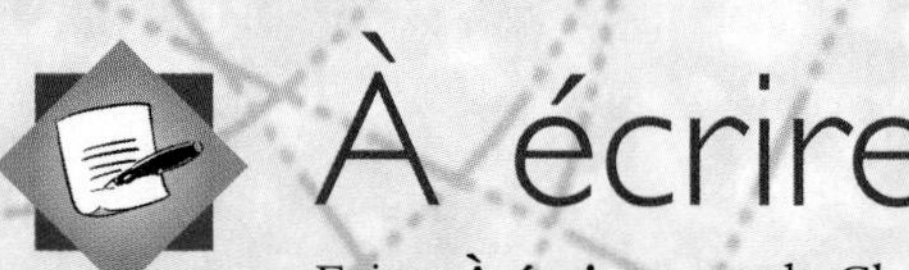

À écrire

Faites **À écrire** pour le Chapitre 12 dans le cahier.

Vocabulaire

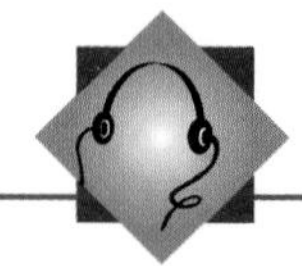

Les étapes de la vie

l'enfance (*f.*)	childhood
l'enterrement (*m.*)	burial
une étape	stage
un événement	event
un garçon	boy
une jeune fille	girl
la jeunesse	youth
la mort	death
la naissance	birth
un(e) retraité(e)	retiree, retired person
la vieillesse	old age

MOTS APPARENTÉS: **l'adolescence** (*f.*), **un(e) adolescent(e)** (*fam.* **un[e] ado**), **un(e) adulte, un bébé, le mariage**

À REVOIR: **la vie**

Les médias

les actualités (*f. pl.*)	news; news program
une bande dessinée	comic strip
le carnet du jour	society column
une chaîne	(*television*) station; network
le courrier des lecteurs	letters to the editor
un dessin animé	animated cartoon
un feuilleton	soap opera
un gros titre	headline
les informations (*f. pl.*)	news; news program
un journal (des journaux)	newspaper
les mots (*m.*) **croisés**	crossword puzzle
les avis (*m.*) **de décès**	obituary column; obituary
une publicité	commercial, advertisement
une rubrique	section, column

MOTS APPARENTÉS: **un documentaire, un éditorial (des éditoriaux), un magazine, les médias** (*m. pl.*), **une série, une sitcom, une station (de radio)**

À REVOIR: **un jeu (des jeux), la météo**

Adjectifs

joyeux/euse joyous, joyful

À REVOIR: **beau (bel, belle), jeune, nouveau (nouvel, nouvelle), vieux (vieil, vieille)**

Verbes

décrire	to describe
dire	to say; to tell
écrire	to write
lire	to read
prendre sa retraite	to retire

MOT APPARENTÉ: **divorcer**

Adverbes

autrefois	formerly, in the past
d'habitude	usually, normally
de temps en temps	from time to time
quelquefois	sometimes
tous les jours	every day

À REVOIR: **bien, mal, parfois, rarement, souvent, toujours**

Autres expressions utiles

à la une	on the front page
au/du troisième âge	elderly, in old age

Chapitre 13

Documents

Le Chemin du retour

Feuille de service du 22 janvier
7e jour de tournage
Horaires: 9h–19h

LIEU DE TOURNAGE: MARSEILLE—FRANCE 3—Bureau 108, 1er étage

Séquence	*Effets*	*Décors*	*Résumé*	*Rôles*
78E	INT.—JOUR	CANAL 7—Bureau Bruno-Rachid	Bruno rejoint Hélène. Ils recherchent° ensemble l'historien sur Internet.	BRUNO, HÉLÈNE

°*look for*

OBJECTIFS

In this episode, you will

- see how Bruno follows up on his offer to Camille
- find out more about Camille's grandfather, Antoine

In this chapter, you will

- talk about technology and methods of communication
- talk about university studies
- express the ideas of *nobody* and *nothing*
- discuss what and whom you know
- practice narration using the **passé composé** and the **imparfait** together
- learn about higher education in France
- read about SMS (Short Message Service) in France

Vocabulaire en contexte

Comment communiquer?

Les **gens**° (*m. pl.*) ne communiquent pas tous de la même façon.°

Les... *People* / *way*

Émilie écrit **une lettre**.

Benjamin **décroche** le combiné,° introduit sa carte, entend la tonalité et **compose**° le numéro. Il **laisse**° un message très long au répondeur, et enfin il **raccroche**.° Cet homme est **bavard**!°

décroche... *lifts the receiver*
dials
leaves
hangs up
talkative

Béatrice est **internaute**. Elle aime **naviguer (surfer) sur le Web**, et elle a **une page perso**.* Elle vient d'écrire un **mél**.† Maintenant, elle **clique** sur l'icone pour envoyer son message. Pour elle, **le courrier électronique semble** avoir **remplacé**° la poste.

semble... *seems to have replaced*

Autres expressions utiles

une boîte aux lettres électronique	electronic mailbox
une page d'accueil	home page
un signet	bookmark
un site Web	website
un(e) technophobe	person who is afraid of technology

*C'est une locution familière qui signifie **une page personnelle**.
†Le terme **mél** est utilisé en France. Les Canadiens disent **un courriel**.

Activités

A. Un dessin. Que font les personnes dans le dessin?

B. Qu'est-ce que c'est? Donnez le mot qui correspond à la définition.

1. C'est la première page d'un site Web.
2. C'est une personne qui navigue sur Internet.
3. Quand on est dans la rue, on peut téléphoner de cet endroit.
4. Pour ouvrir un document informatique, on fait cette action.
5. C'est un ordinateur qu'on peut utiliser quand on voyage.
6. C'est un message électronique qu'on envoie par Internet.
7. C'est l'endroit où on trouve son courrier électronique.
8. C'est une description d'une personne qui parle beaucoup.

C. Réflexions. Interviewez votre partenaire. Demandez-lui...

1. dans quelles circonstances il/elle écrit une lettre et ce dont (*what*) il/elle a besoin pour l'écrire.
2. les démarches (*steps*) qu'il/elle fait pour téléphoner à quelqu'un (*someone*).
3. s'il est recommandé d'utiliser un portable au restaurant ou en voiture.
4. s'il / si elle préfère le courrier électronique au téléphone. Demandez-lui d'expliquer (*to explain*).
5. s'il / si elle aime surfer sur le Web et quel est son site préféré.
6. pour quels sites il/elle a fait un signet, et pourquoi.
7. s'il / si elle a une page perso et, si oui, quelles informations il/elle met sur cette page. Demandez-lui si sa page est utile à son avis (*in his/her opinion*).
8. combien de fois par jour il/elle vérifie sa boîte aux lettres électronique.
9. pourquoi, à son avis, certaines personnes sont technophobes.
10. si Internet lui semble une invention utile, dangereuse, etc.

Les cours à l'université

Dans l'Épisode 13 du film, on cherche l'ami historien de Bruno. Il **enseigne** l'histoire contemporaine à l'université de Paris, mais en ce moment, il écrit sa **thèse de doctorat**. Un cousin d'Hélène donne des cours à l'université du Québec à Trois-Rivières. Voici **un plan** du campus de cette université canadienne.

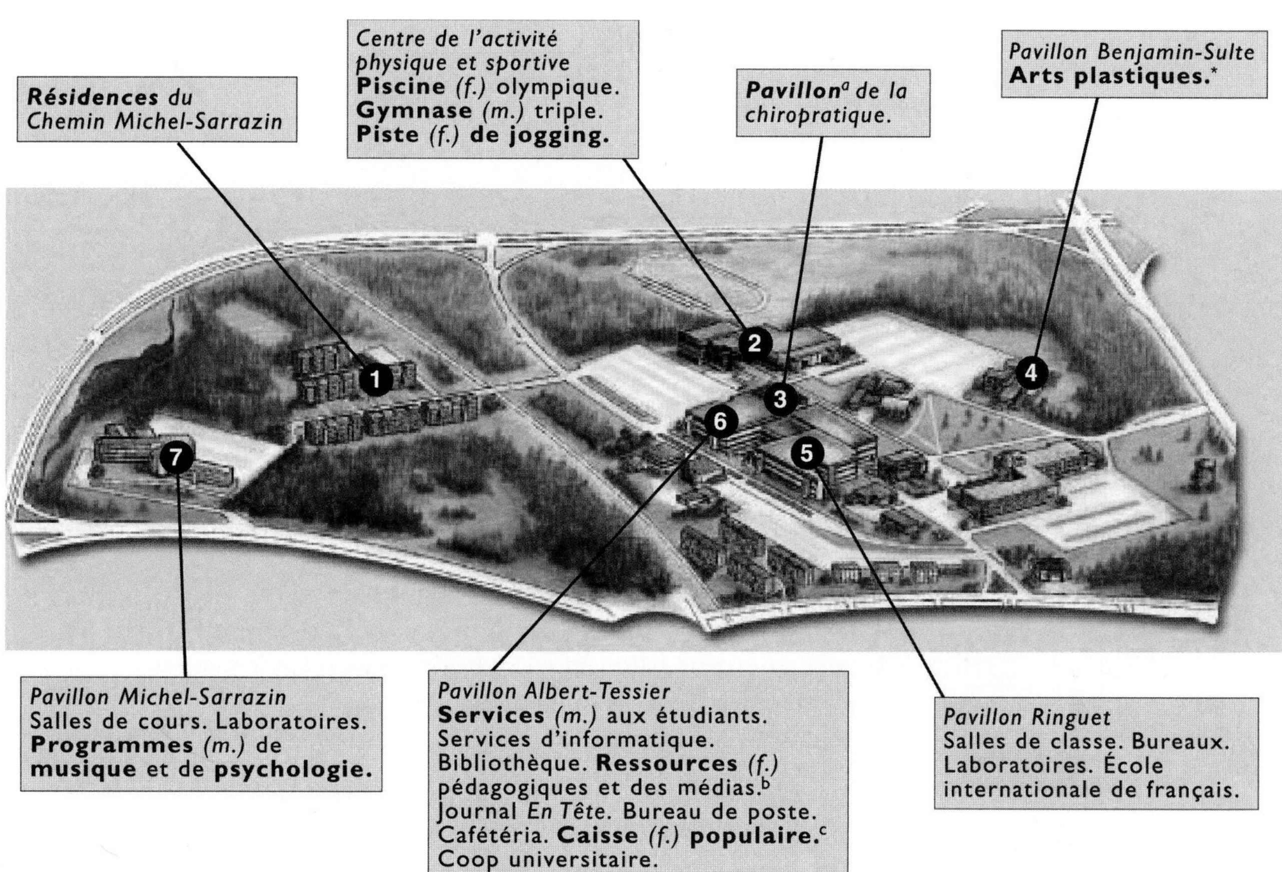

Résidences du *Chemin Michel-Sarrazin*

Centre de l'activité physique et sportive
Piscine *(f.)* olympique.
Gymnase *(m.)* triple.
Piste *(f.)* **de jogging.**

Pavillon[a] *de la chiropratique.*

Pavillon Benjamin-Sulte
Arts plastiques.*

Pavillon Michel-Sarrazin
Salles de cours. Laboratoires.
Programmes *(m.)* de **musique** et de **psychologie.**

Pavillon Albert-Tessier
Services *(m.)* aux étudiants.
Services d'informatique.
Bibliothèque. **Ressources** *(f.)* pédagogiques et des médias.[b]
Journal *En Tête*. Bureau de poste.
Cafétéria. **Caisse** *(f.)* **populaire.**[c]
Coop universitaire.

Pavillon Ringuet
Salles de classe. Bureaux. Laboratoires. École internationale de français.

[a]*Building* [b]Ressources... *Teaching and media resources* [c]Caisse... *Credit union*

Quelles autres **matières**° *(f.)* sont offertes° par cette université? On peut **faire des études** ou **se spécialiser** en

subjects / offered

- **administration** *(f.)* **des affaires**
- **arts** *(m.)* **dramatiques**
- **biochimie** *(f.)*
- **biologie** *(f.)*
- **chimie**° *(f.)*
- **économie** *(f.)* **de gestion**°

chemistry

économie... *business economics*

*Les arts plastiques sont les arts visuels comme la peinture (*painting*) et la sculpture.

- **enseignement**° (*m.*) **des langues**° (*f.*) **secondes*** — *teaching / languages*
- **enseignement secondaire**
- études françaises (études **littéraires** / études de **langue** et communication)
- **génie**° (*m.*) (chimique, électrique, industriel, mécanique) — *engineering*
- **philosophie** (*f.*)
- **physique**° (*f.*) — *physics*
- **traduction**° (*f.*) — *translation*

Autre terme utile

le droit law

Activités

A. Où? Où va-t-on sur votre campus ou dans votre ville pour faire les choses suivantes?

1. pour obtenir des renseignements sur les activités organisées pour les étudiants sur le campus
2. pour faire du jogging
3. pour étudier à fond (*in depth*) une question
4. pour faire une expérience (*experiment*)
5. pour réduire (*reduce*) le stress
6. pour voir des expositions d'arts plastiques
7. pour se coucher
8. pour trouver un bâtiment qu'on ne connaît pas sur le campus
9. pour faire de l'exercice ou pour nager (*swim*)
10. pour emprunter de l'argent

B. Trouvez la matière. Vous entendez des bribes (*bits*) de conversation dans le café. En quelle matière est-ce que chaque étudiant se spécialise?

MODÈLE: MARIE: ...la respiration des mammifères et des autres vertébrés... → Marie fait des études de biologie.

1. PIERRE: ...les cantates de Bach, «La Mer (*The Sea*)» de Debussy...
2. PHILIPPE: ...j'étudie le calcul des probabilités...
3. BENJAMIN: ...j'adore les romans (*novels*) de Marcel Proust...
4. NELLY: ...l'énergie électrostatique du condensateur...
5. LAURA: ...on fait des études sur les capacités cognitives...
6. NATHALIE: ...je lis les œuvres (*works*) de Sophocle et d'Euripide...
7. SYLVAIN: ...le code civil français n'a pas d'équivalent aux États-Unis...
8. DELPHINE: ...la combustion du carbone dans l'oxygène...
9. ANAÏS: ...l'inflation est causée par un excès de la demande...

*On peut aussi dire **des langues étrangères** (*foreign languages*).

C. Spécialisations. Quelle est l'opinion de la classe? Quelle spécialisation...

1. exige (*requires*) une thèse de doctorat? **2.** exige une personnalité extravertie? **3.** exige beaucoup de réflexion abstraite? **4.** exige des connaissances (*knowledge*) en statistique? **5.** exige des connaissances en langues étrangères?

D. En quoi te spécialises-tu? Demandez à six étudiants en quoi ils se spécialisent.

MODÈLE: En quoi est-ce que tu te spécialises? →
Je fais des études de biologie. (Je ne sais pas encore.)

Pour discuter° des études universitaires

discuss

Voici des questions utiles pour une conversation sur les études universitaires.

Tu fais tes études à quelle université?
En quelle année es-tu?
Quels cours est-ce que tu suis?°* — *are taking*
En quoi est-ce que tu te spécialises?
En général, est-ce que tu as de bonnes ou de mauvaises **notes**(*f.*)?° — *grades*
Est-ce que **tu as** déjà **échoué**° **à un examen**? — *failed*
Est-ce que **tu sèches**°† **tes cours** de temps en temps? — *skip, play hooky from*
Est-ce que **tu as préparé la leçon/l'examen** pour demain?
Est-ce que tu as fait tes devoirs?
Est-ce que **tu as passé un examen**° récemment? — passé... *taken an exam*
Quand vas-tu recevoir ton **diplôme**?

Activité

Une interview. Interviewez votre partenaire pour en savoir plus (*to learn more*) sur sa vie à l'université.

Demandez-lui...

1. quelle est sa spécialisation.
2. quels cours il/elle suit (*takes*) pour sa spécialisation.
3. s'il / si elle apprend des choses intéressantes et s'il / si elle a de bonnes notes.
4. s'il / si elle s'inquiète avant les examens et comment il/elle prépare généralement un examen.
5. s'il / si elle trouve les services réservés aux étudiants adéquats, et pourquoi (ou pourquoi pas).
6. de parler de l'équipement et des installations disponibles (*available*) dans les salles de cours, dans les laboratoires et au centre des sports, par exemple.
7. si, en général, il/elle a une bonne ou une mauvaise opinion de l'université.

*C'est le verbe **suivre**. Une réponse possible à cette question: **Je suis** un cours de (biologie).
†**Sécher** se conjugue comme **préférer**: je sèche, nous séchons.

Visionnement 1

Avant de visionner

Les actes de parole. Lisez les extraits suivants du scénario de l'Épisode 13. Ensuite, analysez les phrases en italique. Quelles sont leurs fonctions? Choisissez parmi les possibilités suivantes.

Vocabulaire relatif à l'épisode

type étrange	*strange guy*
vous avez découvert quelque chose	*you discovered something*
ont été détruites	*were destroyed*
partout	*throughout, everywhere*
aussi bien... que	*just as easily . . . as*
la preuve	*proof*
indice sérieux	*serious indication, clue*

demander une opinion	exprimer la reconnaissance (*gratitude*)
demander une précision	présenter ses condoléances
exprimer l'accord	faire un compliment
exprimer l'incrédulité	faire une demande

1. RACHID: Et je fais quoi, là-bas?
   CAMILLE: Interroge les gens sur la vie du village, pendant la guerre. Surtout les années 1942–43.
   RACHID: *D'accord.*
2. PRODUCTRICE: *Je suis désolée pour ta grand-mère.*
3. CAMILLE: L'autre jour, tu m'as parlé d'un ami historien, non?
   BRUNO: Je ne sais pas où il est, Camille. J'ai téléphoné, mais il a déménagé (*moved*).
   CAMILLE: *Dépêche-toi de le retrouver, s'il te plaît.*
4. HÉLÈNE: (après la mort de Louise) *Camille! Camille, je suis de tout cœur avec toi.*
5. CAMILLE: Au revoir. Merci, Bruno. Et toi aussi, Hélène. *Je suis contente de vous avoir comme amis.*
6. BRUNO: Alors? *Qu'est-ce que tu penses de... de David?* Un peu bizarre, non?
   HÉLÈNE: Non. *Non, il est plutôt* (rather) *bel homme... Hmmm?*
   BRUNO: *Bel homme? David?*

Observez!

Dans l'Épisode 13, Hélène et Bruno essaient de trouver l'historien qui peut aider Camille. Pendant le visionnement, essayez de trouver la réponse aux questions suivantes.

- Où est-ce que Camille demande à Rachid d'aller?
- Quelles méthodes de communication utilise-t-on pour trouver l'historien? Est-ce qu'on réussit?
- Qu'est-ce qui semble impliquer Antoine dans un acte de trahison (*treason*)?

Après le visionnement

A. Vrai ou faux? Vérifiez votre compréhension de l'épisode en indiquant si les phrases suivantes sont vraies ou fausses. Répondez **incertain** si l'épisode ne vous donne pas l'information nécessaire.

1. Rachid va à Alès pour parler aux gens du grand-père de Camille.
2. Bruno a du mal à trouver son ami historien.
3. Hélène trouve des renseignements sur Antoine Leclair aux Archives nationales.
4. Les Allemands et certains Français ont détruit beaucoup d'archives à la fin de la guerre.
5. Le laissez-passer (*pass*) que possédait (*possessed*) Antoine était contrefait (*counterfeit*).
6. Le laissez-passer a été signé par un officier allemand.
7. Il était normal de posséder un laissez-passer comme celui (*the one*) qu'avait Antoine.

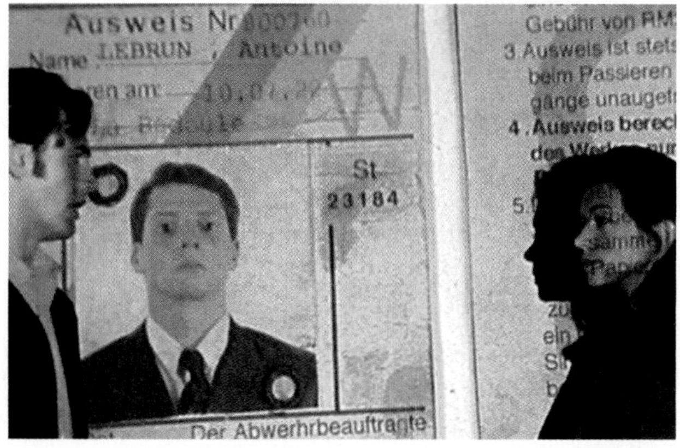

B. Réfléchissez. Selon l'historien, le laissez-passer n'est pas preuve de la culpabilité d'Antoine, mais c'est un indice sérieux. À votre avis, y a-t-il d'autres scénarios qui pourraient (*that could*) expliquer le laissez-passer? Voici quelques possibilités. Quelle explication est la plus convaincante?

1. Antoine a contrefait (*counterfeited*) le laissez-passer pour obtenir des renseignements sur les activités des Allemands.
2. Les Allemands ont fabriqué ce laissez-passer pour faire croire aux Français (*to make the French believe*) qu'Antoine était un collaborateur.
3. Tous les résistants avaient un laissez-passer contrefait pour les protéger (*to protect them*) au cas où ils seraient arrêtés (*in case they were arrested*) par la Gestapo.

Avez-vous une autre idée?

Structure 39

Ne... rien et ne... personne

Expressing the concepts of *nothing* and *nobody*

—Il **n'**y a **rien** aux Archives à propos d'Antoine Leclair. Et toi, tu as trouvé ton ami historien?

—Non. Non, je **n'**ai **rien** trouvé. Non. Il a déménagé et **personne ne** connaît sa nouvelle adresse.

You have been using several French negations since Chapter 1: **ne... pas** (*not*), **ne... pas du tout** (*not at all*), **ne... pas encore** (*not yet*), **ne... jamais** (*never*), and **ne... plus** (*no longer*). Two other negations are also very useful.

ne... rien	*nothing, not anything*
ne... personne	*nobody, no one, not anyone*

Ne... rien and **ne... personne** can act as the subject or object of a verb or as the object of a preposition. The position of the two parts of the expression depends on how they are being used.

1. When used as the subject of a sentence, **rien** and **personne** precede **ne** directly, just before the verb.

Rien ne peut le justifier.	*Nothing can justify that.*
Là-bas, **personne n'**envoie les Juifs en prison.	*Nobody sends Jews to prison there.*

2. When used as the object of a verb, the negations work just like **ne... pas**, that is, with **ne** before the verb and **rien** and **personne** after the verb.

Il **n'**y a **rien** aux Archives.	*There's nothing in the Archives.*
Bruno **ne** voit **personne** sur le plateau.	*Bruno doesn't see anyone on the set.*

When used as the object of a verb in the **passé composé**, **ne... rien** surrounds the auxiliary verb. **Ne... personne**, however, places **personne** after the past participle.

Je **n'**ai **rien** trouvé.	*I didn't find anything.*
Nous **n'**avons trouvé **personne**.	*We didn't find anyone.*

3. When a verb is followed by a preposition, **ne** is before the verb, and **rien** and **personne** follow the preposition.

Il **n'**a besoin de **rien**.	*He doesn't need anything.*
Elle **ne** parle à **personne**.	*She doesn't talk to anyone.*

4. **Rien** and **personne** can be used alone to answer a question.

—Qui va sortir avec toi?	*Who is going out with you?*
—**Personne.**	*Nobody.*
—Qu'est-ce que tu vas faire?	*What are you going to do?*
—**Rien.**	*Nothing.*

5. **Ne... rien** and **ne... personne** are related to the affirmative expressions **quelque chose** (*something*) and **quelqu'un** (*someone*).

—**Quelqu'un** a appelé?	*Did somebody call?*
—Non, **personne n'**a appelé.	*No, nobody called.*
—Tu as trouvé **quelque chose**?	*Did you find something?*
—Non, je **n'**ai **rien** trouvé.	*No, I didn't find anything.*

Pour en savoir plus...

Note that French routinely combines negatives within a sentence. When Bruno was blindfolded, he said

—Je **ne** vois **plus rien du tout**! *I no longer see anything at all!*

Activités

A. Problèmes de couple. Une femme n'est pas d'accord avec son mari et elle le contredit (*contradicts*). Utilisez les expressions négatives **ne... rien** et **ne... personne** pour donner les réponses négatives de la femme.

MODÈLE: Tout le monde nous croit le couple parfait. →
Personne ne nous croit le couple parfait.

1. Nous faisons quelque chose ce week-end.
2. Nous sortons avec nos amis, n'est-ce pas?
3. Tu aimes tout le monde dans ma famille. (Je...)
4. Tout (*Everything*) va bien chez nous.
5. Je parle de beaucoup de choses quand nous sommes ensemble. (Tu...)
6. Je te donne des cadeaux (*gifts*) et des fleurs (*flowers*). (Tu...)
7. Tout le monde nous invite à dîner.

B. À propos d'Antoine. Faites des phrases négatives pour parler d'Antoine. Utilisez les éléments donnés et mettez les phrases au passé composé.

1. Antoine / dire / rien / dans ses lettres au sujet de la guerre
2. personne / comprendre / la vérité
3. Mado / parler à / personne / de son père
4. rien / être / facile après la guerre pour Louise et Mado
5. Camille / apprendre / rien / sur son grand-père
6. personne / trouver / la vérité sur Antoine
7. certains Français / dire / rien / après la guerre au sujet des traîtres

C. Dans ma vie. Interviewez votre partenaire. S'il / Si elle veut répondre à la forme négative, il/elle peut employer une négation de la liste. Soyez prêt(e) à donner des détails sur la vie de votre partenaire à la classe pour comparer les réponses.

Vocabulaire utile: ne... jamais, ne... pas du tout, ne... pas encore, ne... personne, ne... plus, ne... rien

Demandez-lui...

1. s'il / si elle a déjà un diplôme universitaire.
2. s'il / si elle a fait la connaissance de quelqu'un juste avant le cours aujourd'hui.
3. s'il / si elle a acheté quelque chose sur Internet récemment (*recently*).
4. s'il / si elle habite toujours la ville de sa naissance.
5. s'il / si elle veut passer des examens cette semaine.
6. s'il / si elle trouve les émissions à la télévision à 3 h du matin intéressantes.
7. si quelqu'un va lui acheter une Ferrari.

Les verbes *savoir* et *connaître*

Talking about what and whom you know

—Il a déménagé et personne ne **connaît** sa nouvelle adresse.

—Il est professeur à l'université?

—Oui, oui. Seulement, actuellement, il ne donne pas de cours. Et puis **tu sais**, c'est un type étrange, un peu bizarre, très solitaire… **Je ne sais pas** quoi faire.

There are two verbs meaning *to know* in French: **savoir** and **connaître**. Each has its own special uses.

Savoir

1. The verb **savoir** means *to know* (*a fact*). You have already used it in **Je ne sais pas**.

savoir (*to know*)			
je	**sais**	nous	**savons**
tu	**sais**	vous	**savez**
il, elle, on	**sait**	ils, elles	**savent**
passé composé: **j'ai su** impératif: **sache, sachons, sachez**			

2. **Savoir** can take a direct object or it can be followed by a subordinate clause beginning with **que**, **comment**, **quand**, **pourquoi**, **combien de**, **où**, **qui**, etc.

Camille **sait son texte** par cœur.	*Camille knows her lines by heart.*
Je **sais que** Bruno et Camille sont deux bons professionnels.	*I know that Bruno and Camille are two good professionals.*
Camille veut **savoir comment et pourquoi** Antoine a disparu.	*Camille wants to know how and why Antoine disappeared.*

3. When followed by an infinitive, **savoir** means *to know how* (*to do something*).

Rachid **sait faire un reportage intéressant**.	*Rachid knows how to do an interesting report.*

Connaître

1. **Connaître** means *to know* in the sense of *to be acquainted with.*

connaître (*to know*)			
je	**connais**	nous	**connaissons**
tu	**connais**	vous	**connaissez**
il, elle, on	**connaît**	ils, elles	**connaissent**
passé composé: **j'ai connu**			

2. **Connaître** always takes a direct object: a person, a place, or something else that one might be familiar with, such as a song, a story, a road, and so on.

Je connais bien **le quartier**!	*I know the neighborhood well!*
Tu connais **quelqu'un** aux Archives nationales?	*Do you know anyone at the National Archives?*

3. Other verbs conjugated like **connaître** are **reconnaître** (*to recognize*), **paraître** (*to seem, appear*), **apparaître** (*to appear*), and **disparaître** (*to disappear*).

Vous le **reconnaissez**?	*Do you recognize him?*
Antoine **a disparu** pendant la guerre.	*Antoine disappeared during the war.*
Il **paraît** qu'Antoine était un traître.	*It seems that Antoine was a traitor.*

Activités

A. Que savent-ils faire? Parlez de ces personnes. Que savent-elles faire?

MODÈLE: une bonne boulangère →
Elle sait faire un bon pain.

1. une étudiante en littérature
2. un professeur d'informatique
3. un internaute
4. les journalistes à la télévision
5. vous, les professeurs de français
6. vos camarades de classe et vous

B. L'université du Québec à Trois-Rivières. Deux étudiantes américaines sont arrivées à Trois-Rivières au Québec pour faire des études. Elles ne connaissent pas encore le campus de l'université. Utilisez une forme du verbe **connaître** pour compléter leur conversation avec Isabelle, une autre étudiante.

KATHY: _____[1]-tu bien ce campus?

ISABELLE: Oui, je le _____[2] assez bien. Vous le _____[3] aussi, n'est-ce pas?

ANGELA: Non, nous _____[4] déjà un peu la ville de Trois-Rivières, et Kathy _____[5] un des professeurs, mais le campus, non.

KATHY: Au fait, je veux _____[6] l'adresse du bâtiment de psychologie.

ISABELLE: Je suis désolée! Je ne la _____[7] pas, mais j'ai deux amis qui étudient la psychologie. Ils _____[8] certainement l'adresse. Je peux leur téléphoner.

C. Le Café Internet. Regardez cette publicité. Dites ce que vous savez, ce que vous ne savez pas, ce que vous connaissez et ce que vous ne connaissez pas à propos de ce cybercafé à Paris.

MODÈLE: son numéro de fax →
Je sais son numéro de fax.
C'est le 33 (0) 1 40 25 73 51.

1. les horaires d'ouverture (*hours when it is open*)
2. où il se trouve
3. le nom du cybercafé
4. si on peut y (*there*) boire du café
5. l'adresse Internet
6. combien coûtent 15 minutes en ligne
7. la station R.E.R. la plus proche (*nearest*)
8. où on peut envoyer un mél
9. son propriétaire (*owner*)

Café Internet
93 boulevard Saint-Michel
75005 PARIS
RER B, station de Métro Luxembourg
BUS 85, 38, 89, 27, 21, 82
Email: Cybercafe@café-internet.net
http://www.café-internet.net
tél: +33 (0) 1 44 62 97 40
fax: +33 (0) 1 40 25 73 51
ouvert tous les jours
du lundi au samedi de 9 h à 23 h
le dimanche de 12 h à 22 h

D. L'épisode 13. Utilisez **apparaître**, **disparaître**, **paraître** et **reconnaître** pour compléter ce récit. Employez le passé composé (p.c.) si c'est indiqué.

Tout le monde à Canal 7 _____[1] que Camille est triste, et on veut l'aider. Bruno dit que l'historien est un type bizarre qui _____[2] de temps en temps, mais il essaie de le trouver. Selon Rachid, il _____[3] que les traces d'Antoine _____[4] (p.c.) de Saint-Jean de Causse. Enfin, l'historien _____[5] au bureau avec Bruno. Camille _____[6] contente. Malheureusement, des documents _____[7] souvent pendant les guerres, et David n'a trouvé que le laissez-passer incriminant.

E. Interview. Interviewez votre partenaire pour savoir ce qu'il/elle sait et ce qu'il/elle ne sait pas, ainsi que (*as well as*) les gens et les endroits (*places*) qu'il/elle connaît. Votre partenaire doit aussi parler d'autres personnes. Que savent-elles, qui connaissent-elles, etc.?

Vocabulaire utile: faire du ski, un(e) technophobe, un cybercafé, faire la cuisine, parler une autre langue, la statue de la Liberté, faire des recherches sur Internet, un site Internet intéressant, un(e) internaute passionné(e), ?

MODÈLE: É1: Est-ce que tu sais danser?
É2: Je ne sais pas danser, mais je sais jouer du piano.
É1: Connais-tu un endroit (*place*) où on danse dans cette ville?
É2: Oui, je connais des boîtes de nuit.
É1: Sais-tu quels jours les étudiants vont dans ces boîtes?, etc.

Maintenant, présentez à la classe un compte rendu (*report*) sur votre partenaire.

Regards sur la culture

L'enseignement supérieur°

L'enseignement... *Higher education*

In this episode, Bruno locates David, the college history professor. He is not teaching at the moment because he is writing his thesis. A North American would probably expect a college professor to have finished writing his thesis before getting a job in higher education. In fact, French higher education is different in many ways from the North American model.

- Almost everyone who receives a higher education in France attends public institutions, which are very inexpensive. The curricula are supervised by the Ministry of Education. Anyone who has earned the **baccalauréat*** may study at a public university.
- Since 1998, much work has been done to create diploma equivalencies among different European Union countries. In France, after earning **le bac**, students can go on to earn **la licence** after three more years, **le master** after five, and **le doctorat** after eight. A dissertation (**la thèse**), researched and written over several years, is required for **le doctorat**. Some university professors, like David in the film, teach before having completed their thesis.
- Students at the university are called **étudiant(e)s**. This is seen as a social, and almost a professional, category in France. College students have many advantages (reduced prices at the movies, for example) and generally enjoy a rich social life by taking advantage of the services of the city where their university is located.
- College courses revolve around the end-of-year examinations. Some (not all) students rarely go to class and work only in the late spring before exams.
- Relationships between students and professors at the university in France are usually impersonal and distant compared with those in North America.
- Some young people (around 10%) hope to enter one of France's **grandes écoles**, which is an entirely different educational track. Entry into one of these institutions requires two years of very stressful preparatory studies beyond the **baccalauréat**, followed by extremely difficult competitive examinations called **concours** that involve both written and oral tests. Only a small number of positions are available in the **grandes écoles**, and those with the best scores in the **concours** get them. Students on this track do very little but study. If they gain entry into a **grande école**, they are guaranteed a salary, great social prestige, and a very useful social network. Those who are not accepted start university studies from scratch.

Une cérémonie à l'École polytechnique

*The **baccalauréat** is a comprehensive examination of general knowledge and studies done in high school. It is taken in two parts: the first at the end of the next-to-last year of high school, the second at the end of the final year. The **bac** is essential for many jobs in France. About 77% of high school students pass it.

Considérez

Compare the system of higher education in France with that of your own country. What are some of the advantages of each? What do you think are some of each system's weaknesses?

Structure 41

Le passé composé et l'imparfait (I)

Narrating in the past

—Ce document **était** un laissez-passer spécial. Avec ça, on **pouvait** voyager partout en France. Aussi bien dans la zone occupée par les Allemands que dans la zone libre.

—Et beaucoup de gens **avaient** ce document?

—Non. Ce laissez-passer **a été** signé sur l'ordre d'un officier supérieur. Un officier allemand… Et ça, c'**était** assez rare.

—Alors, Antoine **a** peut-être **collaboré** ou **travaillé** avec les Allemands?

Both the **passé composé** and the **imparfait** are past tenses, although, as you have already seen, they are used to express different aspects of past time. These differences are summarized in the following chart.

Passé composé	**Answers the question…**
Past events or sequences of events	What happened?
Imparfait	**Answers the question…**
Descriptions in the past	What were the circumstances? What was someone's state of mind?
Ongoing past action	What was happening?
Habitual past action	What used to happen?

Notez bien!

You have already learned about some adverbs of sequence that are used to order events in a narration: **avant, d'abord, puis, ensuite, après, enfin.** You have also seen some adverbs and expressions that refer to the past, present, or future: **déjà, hier, bientôt, demain, tout de suite, plus tard.** Other expressions that are used to tell when something happened or will happen include

l'an, l'année, le mois, la semaine dernier/ière last year, month, week

l'an, l'année, le mois, la semaine prochain(e) next year, month, week

ce matin this morning

ce soir this evening

cet après-midi this afternoon

le lendemain the next day

Je pars au Canada **le mois prochain.** *I am going to Canada next month.*

J'ai étudié **ce matin.** *I studied this morning.*

Le lendemain, Rachid est allé dans les Cévennes. *The next day, Rachid went to the Cévennes.*

These adverbs and expressions can come at the beginning or end of a sentence.

1. When the two tenses are used in the same sentence, the **passé composé** expresses an event that interrupts the ongoing action expressed by the **imparfait**. In other words, the **imparfait** sets the scene for the event in the **passé composé**.

Camille **se brossait** les cheveux quand Alex **a frappé** à la porte.	*Camille was brushing her hair when Alex knocked at the door.*

2. Surrounding words, especially adverbs, sometimes give a good indication of the tense required. Words that indicate the precise time or number of repetitions of an action generally accompany the **passé composé**, and words that indicate habituality generally accompany the **imparfait**.

WORDS THAT SIGNAL THE *PASSÉ COMPOSÉ*	WORDS THAT SIGNAL THE *IMPARFAIT*
l'an dernier / l'année dernière	autrefois
le mois dernier	d'habitude
la semaine dernière	dans le temps (*in the past*)
lundi (dernier), etc.	de temps en temps
hier	le lundi, etc.
un jour	le week-end
un week-end	parfois
soudain (*suddenly*)	rarement
	souvent
	toujours
	tous les jours

D'habitude, Louise téléphonait à Mado **tous les jours.**	*Louise usually called Mado every day.*
La semaine dernière, Camille a préparé le dîner pour Louise.	*Last week, Camille prepared dinner for Louise.*

3. **Savoir** and **connaître** are normally used in the **imparfait** for past meanings. They have subtle differences in meaning when they are used in the **passé composé**.

IMPARFAIT	PASSÉ COMPOSÉ
Bruno **connaissait** l'historien.	Camille **a connu** l'historien.
*Bruno **knew** the historian.*	*Camille **met** the historian.*
Louise ne **savait** pas la vérité sur Antoine.	Louise **n'a pas su** la vérité sur Antoine.
*Louise didn't **know** the truth about Antoine.*	*Louise **didn't find out** the truth about Antoine.*

The verb **devoir** can mean *supposed to* in the **imparfait** and either *had to* or *probably* (*must have*) in the **passé composé**.

IMPARFAIT	PASSÉ COMPOSÉ
Ils **devaient** faire un voyage ensemble.	Ils ont **dû** faire un voyage ensemble.
*They **were supposed to** (**planned to**) take a trip together.*	*They **probably** took (**must have** taken) a trip together.*

Activités

A. L'histoire, c'est fantastique. Comment est-ce que David est devenu historien? Mettez les phrases au passé composé ou à l'imparfait selon le sens. Utilisez les mots clés et le contexte pour vous aider.

MODÈLE: Quand j'avais (avoir) 13 ans, je ne comprenais pas (ne pas comprendre) l'histoire.

1. Un jour, mon père ____ (trouver) un beau livre d'histoire à la bibliothèque.
2. Ce jour-là, nous ____ (regarder) toutes les images et nous ____ (parler) des hommes et des femmes importants.
3. Une semaine après, mon père ____ (retourner) à la bibliothèque et j'y ____ (aller) avec lui.
4. Ce jour-là, nous ____ (décider) d'étudier l'histoire ensemble.
5. Parfois, quand j'____ (avoir) des problèmes avec toutes les dates, mon père m'____ (aider) à les apprendre.
6. D'habitude, nous ____ (aller) à la bibliothèque le samedi matin, mais un jour nous ____ (visiter) le Musée de l'Homme.
7. Ce jour-là, au musée, je (j') ____ (comprendre) que l'histoire est le sujet le plus passionnant (*exciting*) et je (j') ____ (prendre) une décision importante. Je (J') ____ (choisir) ma profession!

À votre avis, est-il important d'étudier l'histoire? Quels cours d'histoire avez-vous suivis? Qu'est-ce que vous avez appris dans ces cours? Donnez des exemples.

B. La recherche continue... Utilisez les verbes au passé composé ou à l'imparfait pour expliquer où Camille en est dans ses recherches.

MODÈLE: Camille / donner / la photo d'Antoine à Louise →
Camille a donné la photo d'Antoine à Louise.

1. Louise / ne jamais vouloir / parler de son mari, mais elle / dire / certaines choses
2. «il / être / dans les Cévennes»
3. «il / me / envoyer / une lettre»
4. Camille et Louise / aller / partir ensemble quand Louise / mourir
5. un jour, Camille / expliquer / à sa mère qu'elle / avoir envie de / parler avec Louise
6. «on / devoir / faire un voyage dans les Cévennes»
7. «je / vouloir / discuter avec elle»
8. Mado / refuser toujours / d'en parler (*to talk about it*)
9. alors un soir Camille / demander / à Bruno de retrouver son ami historien
10. avec l'aide d'Hélène, Bruno / trouver David, qui / venir / parler avec Camille
11. Camille / être / très impatiente et elle / poser / tout de suite des questions
12. «alors, Antoine / collaborer / avec les Allemands?»
13. nous / comprendre / qu'Antoine / avoir / un laissez-passer
14. qu'est-ce que vous / apprendre / sur ce laissez-passer?

Maintenant, répondez à la question posée dans le numéro 14.

C. Hélène et Internet. La semaine dernière, Hélène a passé plusieurs heures devant son portable. Pour savoir ce qu'elle a fait, mettez les verbes à l'imparfait ou au passé composé, selon le cas (*depending on the case*).

1. Lundi, je/j' _____[1] (recevoir) un mél d'un ami québécois. Il _____[2] (ne pas savoir) que je/j' _____[3] (être) en France. Je lui _____[4] (expliquer) que je/j' _____[5] (lancer) un reportage sur la vie au Québec.
2. Mercredi, je/j' _____[6] (apprendre) la mort de la grand-mère de Camille. Quand je/j' _____[7] (voir) Camille, je lui _____[8] (dire) que je/j' _____[9] (être) désolée. Ce soir-là, je lui _____[10] (envoyer) un petit mél pour lui demander si elle _____[11] (avoir) besoin de quelque chose.
3. Jeudi, Bruno _____[12] (venir) me parler. Il _____[13] (chercher) toujours (*still*) son ami David, mais il _____[14] (ne pas savoir) comment le trouver. Nous _____[15] (faire) une recherche sur Internet et je/j' _____[16] (trouver) son adresse électronique. Je/J' _____[17] (dire) à Bruno: «Tu _____[18] (ne pas penser) à Internet.»
4. Avant Internet, des journalistes comme moi _____[19] (être) obligés de voyager pour faire des recherches. D'habitude, nous _____[20] (passer) beaucoup de temps en avion, alors nous _____[21] (ne jamais être) chez nous! Mais cette semaine, je/j' _____[22] (passer) dix heures devant mon ordinateur et je/j' _____[23] (ne pas voyager) du tout. Depuis Internet, ma vie _____[24] (changer beaucoup)!

D. Mon premier jour à la fac. (*My first day at university.*) Interviewez votre partenaire sur ce qui est arrivé pendant son premier jour à l'université. Utilisez les catégories suivantes pour vous guider dans vos questions.

Catégories:

une description (le temps, l'apparence du campus, l'ambiance sur le campus, etc.)

le matin	les étudiants	les professeurs	les cours
le déjeuner	l'après-midi	la fin de la journée	les classes

MODÈLE: É1: Fais-moi une description de ton premier jour à la fac.
É2: Mon premier jour était super. Il faisait beau et tous les étudiants étaient en short.
É1: As-tu bien trouvé tes classes?
É2: J'ai trouvé ma première classe sans problème...

Après votre conversation, faites un petit compte rendu sur le premier jour à la fac de votre partenaire.

MODÈLE: Michel m'a dit que son premier jour à la fac était super. Il faisait beau et tout le monde était en short. Michel a trouvé la classe pour son premier cours sans problème...

E. Une journée pas comme les autres. Décrivez à un(e) partenaire une journée importante de votre passé. Il/Elle vous pose des questions pour apprendre le plus de détails possible sur votre journée mémorable.

Visionnement 2

Observez!

Considérez les aspects culturels expliqués dans **Regards sur la culture**. Ensuite, regardez l'Épisode 13 encore une fois, et répondez aux questions suivantes.

- À votre avis, est-ce que David va finir sa thèse de doctorat bientôt? Pourquoi (pas)?
- Selon Hélène, pourquoi est-ce que Bruno est «un vrai Français»? Qu'est-ce qu'elle veut dire en ce qui concerne les Français et Internet?

Après le visionnement

Faites l'activité pour le **Visionnement 2** dans le cahier.

Synthèse: Culture

Les technologies de la communication

Dans le film, Hélène dit à Bruno qu'il est «un vrai Français» parce qu'il n'a pas pensé à utiliser Internet pour chercher l'historien, David. Même s'il est vrai que les Français utilisent moins Internet que les habitants de certains autres pays, ils sont très branchés[1] sur la technologie moderne pour communiquer.

On voit le téléphone portable, le mobile, partout en France; dans la rue, au café et même—malheureusement pour les professeurs—à l'école. 90% des jeunes entre 18 et 29 ans et presque 50% des adolescents possèdent un téléphone mobile. Évidemment, les adultes s'en servent[2] régulièrement, mais c'est chez les jeunes que l'utilisation n'est pas loin[3] de la «surconsommation». Comme les adolescents adorent parler avec leurs amis, le prix des communications devient vite trop élevé, alors pour éviter des notes[4] de téléphone astronomiques (et donc des problèmes

[1]*up-to-date; "into"* (fam.) [2]s'en... *use them* [3]*far* [4]*bills*

avec leurs parents), les jeunes ont trouvé autre chose. C'est par les SMS (Short Message Service) ou mini-messages (qui s'appellent aussi des «textos») tapés sur un téléphone portable que beaucoup de jeunes communiquent. Les compagnies de télécommunications ont rendu cette nouvelle forme de communication très économique; un message ne coûte que 15 centimes, et elles proposent des forfaits spéciaux[5] et des heures, le soir, où c'est encore moins cher. Selon une étude, les jeunes entre 11 et 18 ans disent qu'ils ont toujours leur portable avec eux et qu'ils le consultent plus de vingt fois par jour. C'est presque une obsession! Donc, si on veut prendre ou donner des nouvelles[6] ou confirmer un rendez-vous, il suffit de[7] taper un de ces petits messages.

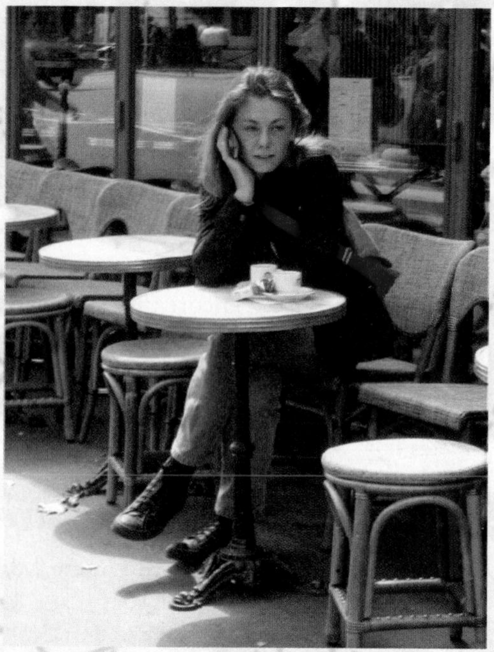
On aime son mobile.

Utilisez-vous votre téléphone mobile pour envoyer des SMS?
Champ: personnes disposant d'un téléphone mobile (en %)

	Juin 2003	
	18 ans et plus	**12–17 ans**
Oui	53	92
Non	44	7
Ne connaît pas les SMS	3	1
Ne sait pas	0	0
Total	**100**	**100**

[*Source:* CREDOC, enquête sur les «Conditions de vie et les Aspirations des Français», juin 2003.]

Catherine veut savoir ce que fait son ami. Alors elle tape: «KESTUFÉ?» (Qu'est-ce que tu fais?). Son ami répond: «Je V O 6né» (Je vais au ciné.). Après, pour savoir ce que son ami pense du film, Catherine tape «CKOMEN?» (C'est comment?). Ce nouveau langage pratique attire[8] beaucoup les jeunes, qui apprennent vite à taper leurs messages et à décoder ceux[9] de leurs amis. En plus, ils adorent faire partie

[5]*forfaits... special subscription rates* [6]*personal news* [7]*il... one simply has to* [8]*attracts* [9]*those*

d'une communauté qui a son propre[10] langage. Même si les adultes n'utilisent que rarement[11] les abréviations, ils sont tout aussi heureux de pouvoir laisser des messages (personnels et professionnels) et même d'envoyer leurs meilleurs vœux[12] pour la nouvelle année par SMS. Selon un reportage, le 1er janvier 2005 à 00 h 0, les Français ont envoyé 15 millions de «Bonne Année». C MANIFIK!

[10]*own* [11]n'utilisent... *rarely use* [12]meilleurs... *best wishes*

À vous

Un message SMS. Which SMS message would you send in the following circumstances? Several answers may be possible.

1. Votre professeur vient d'arriver pour commencer le cours.
2. Votre correspondant vient d'arriver dans le café où vous l'attendez.
3. C'est la fin du cours et vous pouvez recommencer à communiquer par SMS.
4. Votre ami vient d'envoyer un message très amusant.
5. Vous devez arrêter la communication, mais seulement (*only*) pour quelques minutes.
6. Vous voulez savoir si votre correspondant a compris ce que vous avez dit.

Petit lexique SMS

7 nui	cette nuit	J f1	j'ai faim.
A+	à plus tard	jtv	je te vois
A12C4	à un de ces quatre (On va se voir un de ces jours.)	Je deco	je me déconnecte
		mdr	mort de rire
ad taleur	à tout à l'heure	pdp	pas de problème
ama	à mon avis	plpp	pas libre pour parler
bjr	bonjour	rapv	rappeler vite
bsr	bonsoir	sdr	je suis de retour
Ki C?	c'est qui?	stvcqjvd	si tu vois ce que je veux dire

À écrire

Faites **À écrire** pour le Chapitre 13 dans le cahier.

Vocabulaire

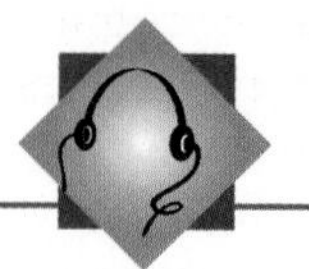

La communication

une boîte aux lettres électronique electronic mailbox
le courrier électronique e-mail
une feuille (de papier) leaf; sheet (of paper)
des gens (*m. pl.*) people
un(e) internaute Internet user
un mél e-mail message
une page d'accueil home page
un portable portable (cell) phone; laptop computer
un signet bookmark
un(e) technophobe person who is afraid of technology
un timbre stamp
la tonalité dial tone

MOTS APPARENTÉS: **une cabine téléphonique, une enveloppe, un icone, une lettre, une page perso, un site Web**

Pour parler de la communication

composer (un numéro) to dial (a number); to compose
décrocher to pick up (*the telephone receiver*)
raccrocher to hang up (*the telephone receiver*)

MOTS APPARENTÉS: **cliquer, naviguer (surfer) sur le Web**

À l'université

une caisse populaire credit union
un gymnase gymnasium
une note grade (on an exam, an assignment)
une piscine swimming pool
une piste (de jogging) (jogging) trail, track
un plan map (*subway, city, region*)
une ressource resource
une thèse thesis, dissertation

MOTS APPARENTÉS: **un diplôme, un doctorat, un programme, une résidence (universitaire), un service**

Les cours universitaires

l'administration (*f.*) **des affaires** business administration
les arts (*m. pl.*) **plastiques** visual arts (sculpture, painting, etc.)
la biochimie biochemistry
la chimie chemistry
le droit law
l'économie (*f.*) **de gestion** business economics
l'enseignement (*m.*) **(secondaire, des langues étrangères)** teaching (of secondary school, of foreign languages)
le génie (chimique, électrique, industriel, mécanique) (chemical, electrical, industrial, mechanical) engineering

une langue (étrangère)	(foreign) language
une matière	(*school*) subject
la physique	physics
la traduction	translation

MOTS APPARENTÉS: **les arts** (*m. pl.*) **dramatiques, la biologie, la musique, la philosophie, la psychologie**

Pour discuter des études universitaires

discuter de	to discuss
échouer (à un examen)	to fail (an exam)
enseigner	to teach
faire des études en	to major in, study (*a subject*)
passer un examen	to take an exam
préparer (une leçon, un examen)	to study for (a lesson, an exam)
sécher un cours	to skip, cut class
se spécialiser en	to major in

Autres verbes

apparaître	to appear
connaître	to know, be acquainted with
disparaître	to disappear
laisser	to leave; to allow
paraître	to seem, appear
reconnaître	to recognize
remplacer	to replace
savoir	to know (a fact)
sembler	to seem

Négations

ne... personne	nobody, no one
ne... rien	nothing

À REVOIR: **ne... jamais, ne... pas, ne... pas du tout, ne... pas encore, ne... plus**

Expressions de temps

ce matin	this morning
ce soir	this evening
cet après-midi	this afternoon
le lendemain	the next day

À REVOIR: **après, avant, bientôt, d'abord, déjà, demain, enfin, ensuite, hier, plus tard, puis, tout de suite**

Adjectifs

bavard(e)	talkative
dernier/ière	last
littéraire	literary
prochain(e)	next

Autres expressions utiles

quelque chose	something
quelqu'un	someone
Quels cours est-ce que tu suis?	What courses are you taking?

Chapitre 14

Une lettre

Le Chemin du retour

Feuille de service du 14 octobre
4e jour de tournage
Horaires: 9h–19h

LIEU DE TOURNAGE: PARIS—3, square Rapp, 7e

Séquence	*Effets*	*Décors*	*Résumé*	*Rôles*
87	INT.—JOUR	APPARTEMENT LOUISE—Séjour	Camille est dans l'appartement de Louise quand Mado arrive. Camille trouve des bijoux,° une lettre de son grand-père et des photos.	CAMILLE, MADO

° *jewelry*

OBJECTIFS

In this episode, you will

- watch as Camille finds a lead for her search
- learn what happened to all the photos of Antoine

In this chapter, you will

- talk about traveling by train, plane, and car
- learn about getting around in Paris
- talk about when things happened and for how long
- describe actions with adverbs
- talk about going *to* and *from* cities, countries, provinces, and states
- learn about various modes of transportation in France
- read correspondence from a sailor in World War II

Vocabulaire en contexte

Pour voyager

Pour aller de Paris dans les Cévennes, il y a **plusieurs**° possibilités. Choisissez votre **moyen** de transport préféré.

several

En train (*m.*)

De **la gare**° à Paris, prenez **le TGV.**°

station / Train à Grande Vitesse

Vous pouvez acheter **un billet**° au **guichet**,° par Minitel, sur Internet ou à un distributeur automatique. Il faut° préciser si vous désirez un **aller simple** ou un **aller-retour** et si vous voulez voyager en première classe ou en seconde. Attention: vous devez réserver **une place** à l'avance. Vous pouvez choisir **un wagon fumeurs**° ou **non-fumeurs**, **un siège couloir**° ou **fenêtre**.

ticket / *window*
Il... *It is necessary to*
wagon... *smoking car*
siège... *aisle seat*

Tous les **passagers**° (*m.*) doivent **composter** leur billet° avant de monter—les composteurs se trouvent à l'entrée des **quais**° (*m.*).

passengers
composter... *punch their ticket*
platforms

Descendez à Nîmes, où vous pouvez prendre un train en **correspondance**° (*f.*). Pour faire le voyage de Paris aux Cévennes, vous allez mettre entre 5 et 8 heures.

transfer

En avion° (*m.*)

airplane

De **l'aéroport** (*m.*) Orly-ouest, il y a plusieurs **vols**° (*m.*) par jour pour Nîmes. Par exemple, il y a un vol à 9 h qui arrive à Nîmes à 10 h 10. De Nîmes à Alès, vous pouvez prendre **un autocar**° ou **louer**° une voiture.

flights
intercity bus / *rent*

En avion, vous êtes limité à deux **valises** (*f.*) et un sac à main. Vous devez arriver à l'aéroport une heure et demie avant **le départ** de l'avion, pour **enregistrer**° vos valises, passer au poste de contrôle de sécurité et trouver **la porte d'embarquement.**°

check
porte... *gate*

En voiture

Prenez **l'autoroute** (*f.*) A7 jusqu'à Orange. **La limite de vitesse**° sur l'autoroute: 120 km/h.* Ensuite, suivez° la A9 jusqu'à **la sortie**° 19 direction Alès. Suivez **la route** D981 jusqu'à Alès.

limite... *speed limit*
follow / *exit*

Suggestion: évitez° **les heures de pointe**° et les grandes vacances° car° **la circulation**° est mauvaise et il y a des risques d'**embouteillages**° (*m.*).

Avoid / heures... *rush hour*
grandes... *summer vacation* / *since* / *traffic* / *traffic jams*

---

*km/h = kilomètres à l'heure

Comme Alès est en France, les Français n'ont pas besoin de **passer la douane**° et ils n'ont besoin ni° d'**un passeport**, ni° d'**un visa**.

customs / neither

nor

Autre mot utile

l'arrivée (*f.*) arrival

Activités

A. Quel moyen de transport? Quel moyen de transport—**le train**, **l'avion** ou **la voiture**—associez-vous aux mots suivants? Attention: parfois, il y a plusieurs possibilités.

MODÈLE: un vol → l'avion

1. une gare
2. enregistrer
3. un quai
4. un billet
5. composter
6. une correspondance
7. la limite de vitesse
8. un wagon non-fumeurs
9. une porte d'embarquement
10. un embouteillage
11. passer la douane

B. Avantages et inconvénients. Trouvez un avantage et un inconvénient des moyens de transport suivants.

AVANTAGES	INCONVÉNIENTS
a des sièges confortables	n'a pas de siège confortable
est bon(ne) pour la santé	est désagréable quand il pleut/neige
est économe	est cher (chère)
est non-polluant(e)	est polluant(e)
est pratique	n'est pas pratique
est rapide	est lent(e)
est toujours à l'heure	est souvent en retard
permet d'éviter (*avoid*) les embouteillages	est désagréable aux heures de pointe
laisse plus de liberté au voyageur	offre peu de flexibilité pour les heures de départ

MODÈLE: le vélo → Le vélo est bon pour la santé, mais il est lent.

1. la voiture
2. le train
3. l'avion
4. l'autocar
5. le taxi
6. le cheval (*horse*)

C. Un voyage. Dans quelle ville êtes-vous allé(e) récemment (*recently*)? Racontez votre voyage. Quel mode de transport avez-vous choisi? Pourquoi? Quels préparatifs avez-vous faits avant le départ? Le voyage s'est-il bien passé?

MODÈLE: Le week-end dernier, mes amis et moi, on est allés à San Francisco pour assister à un concert. On a pris la route de bonne heure (*early*) pour éviter les embouteillages. On a mis deux heures pour arriver au stade où avait lieu le concert (*where the concert took place*). Le voyage s'est bien passé.

Circuler° à Paris

To travel around

Il est très agréable de se promener à Paris. Mais si on est **pressé**,° il n'est pas toujours pratique d'aller d'**un endroit**° à l'autre **à pied**.° La solution? **Le métro**.

in a hurry

place / à… on foot

En métro

Le **réseau du métro**° dessert° toute la ville de Paris; on n'est jamais loin d'une station. Quel est le mode d'emploi du métro? Regardez le plan.

réseau… *subway system / serves*

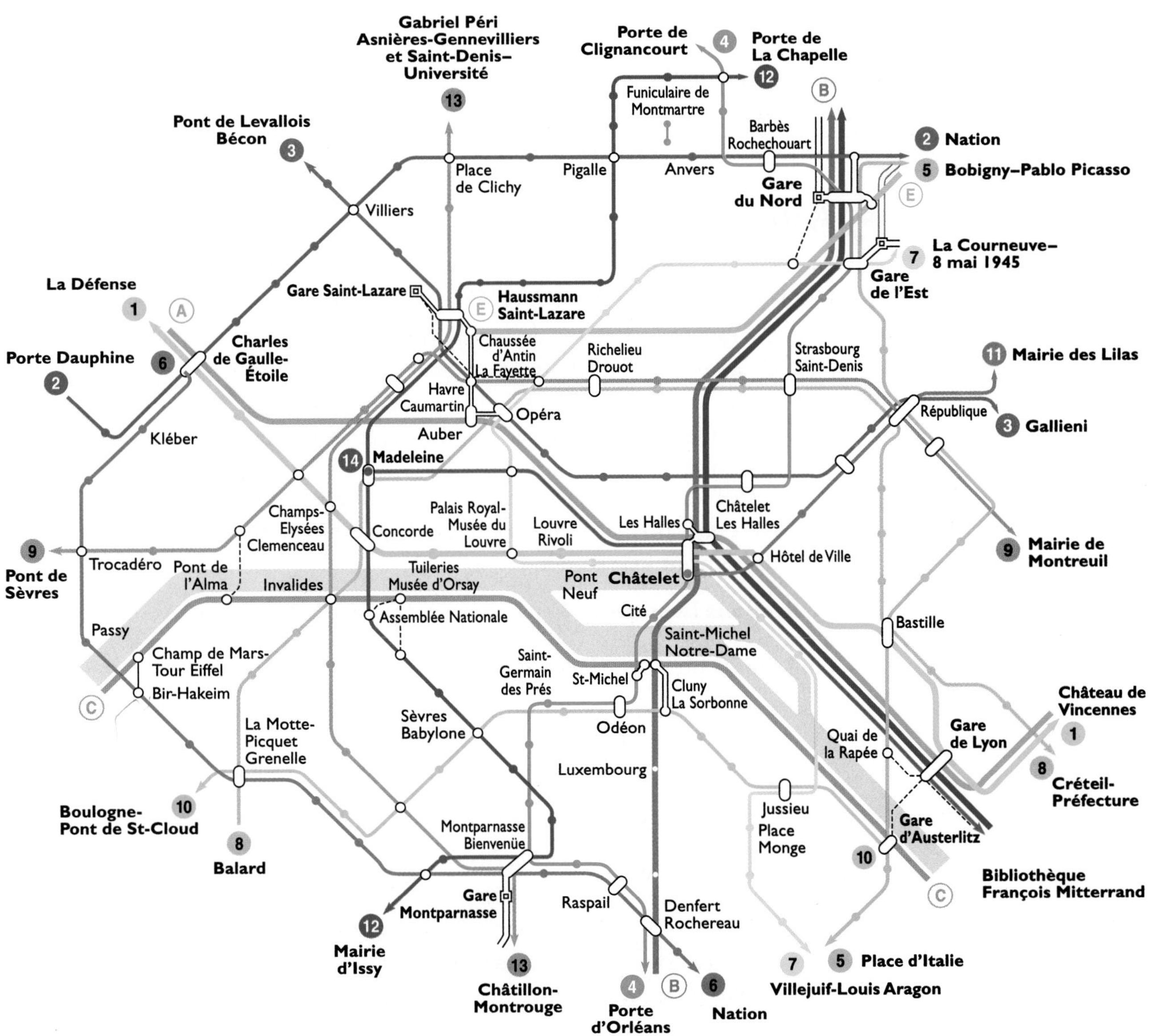

Quand Camille va de chez elle (métro Champ de Mars-Tour Eiffel) à l'appartement de Louise (métro Place Monge), elle achète **un ticket** et prend la ligne 6 **direction** (*f.*) Nation (c'est **le terminus** de la ligne). Elle descend à La Motte-Picquet Grenelle pour prendre sa correspondance sur la ligne 10, direction Gare d'Austerlitz. Elle descend à Jussieu et prend la correspondance sur la ligne 7, direction Villejuif-Louis Aragon. Elle descend à **l'arrêt**° suivant pour aller à pied chez Louise. *stop*

En bus

Pour mieux° connaître les quartiers de la ville, on peut prendre **le bus**. Comme ça, on peut même **rencontrer**° des gens qui y habitent, et on voit les monuments et les magasins. Paris est une belle ville! *better* / *meet*

En voiture

Il est déconseillé° de circuler en voiture. **Stationner**° dans la rue est souvent impossible, et les **parkings**° sont parfois **complets**.° *not advisable / Parking* / *parking lots / full*

Activités

A. C'est le... Précisez le moyen ou les moyens de transport décrit(s) dans les phrases suivantes. Est-ce **aller à pied**, **le métro**, **le bus** ou **la voiture**?

1. Ce n'est pas un moyen de transport très rapide.
2. C'est un moyen de transport souterrain (*underground*).
3. Les stations ne sont pas loin les unes des autres.
4. Il est difficile de stationner dans la rue, et les parkings sont souvent complets.
5. Il faut repérer (*locate*) le terminus pour choisir sa direction.
6. C'est un moyen de transport agréable, mais pas pratique quand on est pressé.
7. Ils circulent jour et nuit.

B. Prenons le métro! Vous faites du tourisme à Paris et vous voulez voir les monuments principaux. Vous choisissez de vous déplacer (*to get around*) en métro. Consultez le plan du métro parisien et dites comment vous allez...

MODÈLE: de votre hôtel (métro Odéon) à la tour Eiffel (métro Bir-Hakeim). Je prends la ligne 10, direction Boulogne-Pont de St-Cloud, et je descends à La Motte-Picquet Grenelle. Puis je prends la correspondance sur la ligne 6, direction Charles de Gaulle-Étoile. Je descends à la station Bir-Hakeim.

1. de la tour Eiffel (métro Bir-Hakeim) à l'Arc de Triomphe (métro Charles de Gaulle-Étoile).
2. de l'Arc de Triomphe au Sacré-Cœur (métro Anvers).
3. du Sacré-Cœur à la cathédrale Notre-Dame (métro Cité).
4. de Notre-Dame au Louvre (métro Palais Royal-Musée du Louvre).
5. du Louvre à votre hôtel (métro Odéon).

Visionnement 1

Avant de visionner

La répétition. Parfois, la même idée est répétée dans une phrase sous des formes différentes. Il s'agit de paraphrases ou d'explications du mot clé. Analysez les phrases suivantes. Les mots en *italique* ont le même sens ou renforcent le sens des mots en caractères **gras**. Que signifient les mots en italique?

1. CAMILLE: Regarde. Louise a gardé[a] cette photo **intacte**. Elle *ne l'a pas déchirée*, comme les autres.
2. CAMILLE: Elle aimait son mari. Elle l'a **toujours** aimé, *jusqu'à la fin de sa vie*.
3. MADO: J'avais 10 ou 11 ans. Un jour, à l'école, mes camarades *m'ont surnommée* la fille du traître. D'autres **disaient** la «fille du pourri»,[b] la «fille du collabo».

[a]a... *kept* [b]*rotten pig*

Notez bien!

The word **traître** means *traitor*. Camille didn't know the rumors about her grandfather and never understood the reason for her mother's shame until recently.

Observez!

Dans cet épisode, Camille et Mado apprennent des détails importants sur la vie d'Antoine pendant la guerre. Pendant votre visionnement de l'Épisode 14, essayez de trouver les réponses aux questions suivantes.

- Qu'est-ce que Rachid a appris pendant son voyage?
- Qu'est-ce que Mado et Camille ont trouvé dans le coffret (*little box*) de Louise?
- À quel sujet Mado a-t-elle changé d'avis (*changed her mind*)?
- Qui a découpé les photos de Louise avec son mari? Pourquoi?

Vocabulaire relatif à l'épisode

la serrure	*latch*
verrouillé(e)	*locked*
Il faut chercher la vérité.	*We must look for the truth.*
en courant	*running*
des ciseaux	*scissors*

Après le visionnement

A. Un résumé. Complétez le résumé de l'Épisode 14 en mettant dans chaque cas un des deux verbes proposés au passé composé ou à l'imparfait.

Rachid est revenu de son voyage dans les Cévennes. Il y _____[1] (rencontrer,[a] rentrer) des gens intéressants, mais il _____[2] (ne rien apprendre, ne rien comprendre) sur le grand-père de Camille.

Plus tard, chez Mado, Camille _____[3] (cacher,[b] trouver) un coffret qui _____[4] (rendre, appartenir) à sa grand-mère. Dans ce coffret, Mado a découvert[c] les bijoux[d] de sa mère. Le coffret _____[5] (contenir, vouloir) aussi

[a]*to meet, run into* [b]*to hide* [c]a... *discovered* [d]*jewelry*

Notez bien!

The verb **tenir** (*to hold*) is conjugated like **venir**.

je	**tiens**
tu	**tiens**
il, elle, on	**tient**
nous	**tenons**
vous	**tenez**
ils, elles	**tiennent**

Verbs like **tenir** are: **appartenir** (*to belong to*), **contenir** (*to contain*), and **obtenir** (*to obtain, get*). All of these verbs use the auxiliary **avoir** in the **passé composé**.

une lettre d'Antoine. Il avait écrit[e] cette lettre en 1943, quand il _____[6] (travailler, habiter) dans les Cévennes, chez Pierre et Jeanne Leblanc.

Le coffret _____[7] (tenir, contenir) également une photo de Louise avec Antoine. Louise _____[8] (garder, mentir) cette photo intacte; elle _____[9] (ne pas la montrer, ne pas la déchirer[f]).

De toute façon,[g] ce n'était pas Louise qui avait découpé[h] les photos; c'était Mado. Pourquoi? Parce qu'à l'école, tout le monde l'_____[10] (acheter, appeler) la «fille du collabo». Elle _____[11] (avoir honte, avoir froid). Alors,[i] elle _____[12] (décider, savoir) de «tuer» son père en découpant les photos avec des ciseaux.

[e]avait... *had written* [f]*to rip up* [g]De... *In any case* [h]avait... *had cut up* [i]*So*

B. Réfléchissez. Répondez aux questions suivantes.

1. Au début, Mado n'a pas voulu entendre parler de son père. Maintenant, elle encourage Camille à trouver la vérité à son sujet. Selon vous, pourquoi Mado a-t-elle changé d'avis (*changed her mind*)? Est-ce à cause de la mort de sa mère? du contenu du coffret? de l'insistance de Camille?
2. Mado a voulu «tuer» son père en découpant ses photos. Est-ce que cette action l'a aidée à surmonter sa honte? Expliquez.

Structure 42

Depuis et pendant

Talking about time

—Je sais, oui, je viens souvent ici **depuis** quelques mois.

—Et **pendant** la guerre, qu'est-ce qu'il a fait?

Depuis

1. To ask about the *duration* of an action that began in the past and is still continuing in the present, use **Depuis combien de temps** + present tense.

   Depuis combien de temps est-ce que Louise habite dans la rue Mouffetard? — ***How long** has Louise been living on the Rue Mouffetard?*

   To answer this type of question, use present tense + **depuis** + expression of time, for example **longtemps** (*a long time*), **hier**, **soixante ans**. Notice that French uses the present tense where English uses a past tense.

   Mado garde le secret de son père **depuis** longtemps. — *Mado has been keeping her father's secret **for** a long time.*

   In negatives, French uses the **passé composé** + **depuis** + unit of time.

   Antoine **n'a pas habité** dans la rue Mouffetard **depuis** soixante ans. — *Antoine has not lived on the Rue Mouffetard **for** sixty years.*

2. To ask about the *beginning time* of an action that began in the past and is still continuing in the present, use **Depuis quand** + present tense.

   Depuis quand est-ce que Louise habite dans la rue Mouffetard? — ***Since when** has Louise been living on the Rue Mouffetard?*

   To answer this type of question, use a present-tense verb + **depuis** + date (or a word designating an event).

   Louise habite dans la rue Mouffetard **depuis** 1938. — *Louise has been living on the Rue Mouffetard **since** 1938.*

   Camille cherche son médaillon **depuis** l'émission ce matin. — *Camille has been looking for her locket **since** the show this morning.*

Pendant

1. To ask about the *duration* of an action, you can also use **pendant combien de temps**. It can be followed by any tense, depending on the meaning of the question.

   Pendant combien de temps Bruno et Camille parlent-ils? — ***How long** do Bruno and Camille talk?*

   Pendant combien de temps Bruno et Camille ont-ils parlé? — ***How long** did Bruno and Camille talk?*

   To answer this type of question, use **pendant** + unit of time.

   Ils parlent (ont parlé) **pendant** trois heures. — *They talk (talked) **for** three hours.*

2. **Pendant** can mean *during* when followed by a noun.

   Pendant le repas, Bruno pose des questions à Camille. — ***During** the meal, Bruno asks Camille questions.*

   Pendant la guerre, Antoine a habité dans les Cévennes. — ***During** the war, Antoine lived in the Cévennes.*

Pour en savoir plus...

Pour means *for* when used to express time intended.

Je vais m'absenter **pour** deux semaines. *I'm going away for two weeks.*

However, it should not be used to express duration. For that meaning of *for*, use **pendant**.

J'ai été absent **pendant** deux semaines. *I was away for two weeks.*

Activités

A. Le journal intime de Martine. (*Martine's diary.*) Martine commence un journal intime aujourd'hui. Lisez ce paragraphe et répondez aux questions. Utilisez les expressions avec **pendant** et **depuis**.

MODÈLE: Depuis quand est-ce que Martine parle de sa vie dans un journal intime? →
Elle parle de sa vie intime dans son journal depuis aujourd'hui.

J'ai habité (*lived*) à Besançon entre 1959 et 1979, puis je suis venue dans la région parisienne pour étudier. J'ai commencé à travailler avec le groupe Canal 7 en 1996 et j'ai eu l'idée de l'émission en 1998. Du point de vue personnel, j'ai épousé (*married*) Philippe il y a vingt ans et notre fils, Patrick, est né il y a quinze ans. Nous avons aussi une fille, Christelle, qui est née quatre ans après Patrick. Nous avons déménagé (*moved*) il y a un mois et maintenant nous habitons au centre de Paris. Notre fils est entré dans son nouveau lycée il y a trois semaines. Comme je vais toujours au bureau vers 7 h, Philippe aide les enfants le matin avant de partir à son travail à 8 h 30. C'est vraiment une vie de rêve (*dream*).

1. Pendant combien de temps est-ce qu'elle a habité à Besançon?
2. Depuis quand est-ce qu'elle travaille avec le groupe Canal 7?
3. Depuis combien de temps est-ce qu'elle est mariée?
4. Pendant combien de temps est-ce qu'elle a été mariée mais sans enfant?
5. Pendant combien de temps est-ce que Patrick a été fils unique?
6. Depuis quand est-ce que Martine habite au centre de Paris?
7. Depuis combien de temps est-ce que Patrick est dans son nouveau lycée?
8. Pendant combien de temps Philippe aide-t-il les enfants chaque matin?

B. Pour faire connaissance. Interviewez trois camarades de classe pour découvrir (*discover*) certains détails de leur passé et de leur vie actuelle. Posez des questions en utilisant les expressions **depuis quand**, **depuis combien de temps** et **pendant combien de temps**.

MODÈLE: habiter la même maison →
É1: Pendant combien de temps as-tu habité la même maison?
É2: J'ai habité la même maison pendant dix ans.

1. étudier le français
2. habiter cette ville
3. aller à cette université
4. sortir avec les mêmes ami(e)s que maintenant
5. boire du café
6. aller au lycée
7. jouer avec des jouets d'enfant
8. croire au Père Noël

Maintenant, comparez la vie de vos camarades avec votre propre (*own*) vie.

shamon

La forme et la place des adverbes

Describing actions

—Tu le retrouves pour moi?
Rapidement?

Adverbs can modify verbs, adjectives, and other adverbs. In Chapter 6, you saw an overview of some common French adverbs and in Chapter 10, you practiced using adverbs of time. In this chapter, you learn about the formation and placement of many useful adverbs, especially adverbs of manner.

La forme des adverbes

1. Many adverbs are formed by adding **-ment** to the feminine form of an adjective. These adverbs often correspond to English adverbs ending in *-ly*. Here is a list of some useful adjectives and the adverbs formed from them. If you know the adjectives, you'll also know the adverb.

actuel(le)	*current, present*	**actuellement**	*currently*
discret/ète	*discreet; reserved*	**discrètement**	*discreetly; with reserve*
doux (douce)	*gentle*	**doucement**	*gently*
exact(e)	*exact, accurate*	**exactement**	*exactly, accurately*
franc(he)	*frank*	**franchement**	*frankly*
immédiat(e)	*immediate*	**immédiatement**	*immediately*
lent(e)	*slow*	**lentement**	*slowly*
rapide	*fast*	**rapidement**	*quickly*
seul(e)	*alone; sole*	**seulement**	*only*
sûr(e)	*sure*	**sûrement**	*surely*
tel(le)	*such; like*	**tellement**	*so (very), so much*

Je suis **tellement**... nerveuse, impatiente!	*I'm so . . . tense, impatient.*
Elle s'est endormie **doucement**.	*She fell asleep gently.*
Actuellement, il ne donne pas de cours.	*Currently, he's not teaching any classes.*

2. If the masculine form of an adjective ends with **i**, **é**, or **u**, the adverb is formed from the masculine adjective. The adjective **fou** (*crazy, mad*), however, builds the adverb from its feminine form, **folle**.

	vrai(e)	*true*	**vraiment**	*truly*
	absolu(e)	*absolute*	**absolument**	*absolutely*
but	**fou (folle)**	*crazy, mad*	**follement**	*madly, wildly*

Tu es **vraiment** un grand dragueur.	*You're really quite the pick-up artist.*
Camille veut **absolument** connaître la vérité.	*Camille absolutely wants to know the truth.*

3. To derive adverbs from adjectives ending in **-ant** or **-ent** in the masculine form, change these endings to **-amment** or **-emment**.

apparent(e)	*apparent*	**apparemment**	*apparently*
élégant(e)	*elegant*	**élégamment**	*elegantly*
évident(e)	*evident*	**évidemment**	*evidently, obviously*

Camille était habillée **élégamment**.	*Camille was dressed elegantly.*
Ben, **apparemment**, oui. Il faut croire!	*Well, apparently, yes. It looks like it!*
Oui, euh, à part la nôtre, **évidemment**.	*Yes, uh, except for ours, obviously.*

4. To form an adverb from **gentil**, drop the final **-l** of the masculine form and add **-ment**.

gentil → **gentiment** *nicely*

Rachid parle **gentiment** à sa fille.	*Rachid talks nicely to his daughter.*

5. Some adverbs, such as **bien** and **mal**, are not derived from adjectives at all. Another is **vite** (*fast, quickly*).

Pourquoi part-il aussi **vite**?	*Why is he leaving so fast?*

La place des adverbes

1. In the present tense or **imparfait**, adverbs of manner usually follow the verb they modify.

Camille **cherche nerveusement** dans son sac.	*Camille searches nervously in her purse.*
Pourquoi **part**-il aussi **vite**?	*Why is he leaving so fast?*
Mado **parlait furieusement** à Camille.	*Mado was speaking furiously to Camille.*

Notez bien!

Peut-être (*perhaps, maybe*) is not formed from an adjective. It usually follows the word it modifies. In the **passé composé**, it follows the auxiliary verb.

Il peut **peut-être** t'aider. *Maybe he can help you.*

Antoine est **peut-être** devenu un traître. *Maybe Antoine became a traitor.*

Peut-être may also begin a sentence, in which case it is followed either by **que** or by inversion of the subject and verb.

Peut-être qu'il peut t'aider. / **Peut-être** peut-il t'aider. } *Maybe he can help you.*

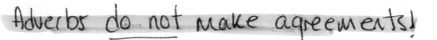

2. In the **passé composé**, adverbs of manner usually follow the past participle.

Mado a parlé **sévèrement** à sa fille.	*Mado spoke harshly to her daughter.*

Several common short adverbs, however, follow the auxiliary verb and precede the past participle.

Camille a **vite** répondu que ça ne la regardait pas.	*Camille quickly answered that it was none of her business.*
Elle a **bien** compris la situation.	*She understood the situation well.*
Mado a **trop** parlé.	*Mado spoke too much.*

Activités

A. Comment? Dites comment on fait les actions suivantes en ajoutant (*by adding*) l'adverbe qui correspond à l'adjectif entre parenthèses.

MODÈLE: Je parle de mes amis. (discret) →
Je parle discrètement de mes amis.

1. Je parle anglais avec les étrangers. (lent)
2. J'ai parlé à mon ami. (gentil)
3. J'ai parlé à mes parents. (méchant [*nasty*])
4. Je travaille. (rapide)
5. Je m'habille quand je sors avec mes amis. (mauvais)
6. J'ai préparé tous mes examens. (bon)
7. Je vais recevoir de bonnes notes. (sûr)
8. Je joue avec les enfants. (patient)
9. Je ne joue jamais avec les enfants. (violent)

Maintenant, pour chaque phrase, formulez une autre phrase qui exprime le contraire.

MODÈLE: Je parle de mes amis. (discret) →
Je parle indiscrètement de mes amis.

B. Une amie de Louise. Mettez les adverbes logiques à leur place pour compléter ce récit d'une amie de Louise.

Adverbes utiles: absolument, actuellement, apparemment, malheureusement, peut-être, sûrement, tellement

J'ai rencontré Louise quand j'avais 15 ans. _____[1], j'ai 81 ans et elle, elle avait le même âge. J'étais _____[2] triste d'apprendre sa mort la semaine dernière. _____[3], elle voulait partir en voyage avec sa petite-fille et pensait qu'elle avait _____[4] le temps de le faire avant de mourir. Elle voulait _____[5] parler avec la petite. _____[6], elle est morte trop tôt.

C. Conversation personnelle. Avec votre partenaire, parlez de vos activités en utilisant des adverbes. Ensuite, faites un résumé de vos résultats et comparez-les avec ceux (*those*) d'un autre petit groupe.

Vocabulaire utile: changer d'amis, danser, s'endormir, étudier, faire la cuisine, s'habiller, se lever, manger, parler à mes parents, parler français, partager mes possessions avec mes amis, travailler, voyager, etc.

MODÈLE: É1: Moi, je m'endors facilement pendant le cours de maths.
É2: Eh bien moi, je dors mal après trop de café. (*ou* Moi, je m'endors rapidement devant la télé.)

Regards sur la culture

Les transports et la société

When Rachid tells Camille how to get to Saint-Jean de Causse, he assumes that she will take the train, not drive there. Even in the area of transportation, French cultural attitudes differ greatly from those of North Americans.

- In France, nearly everyone uses the train. Although the network of rail lines has diminished since World War II, with many smaller and out-of-the-way places now linked to the rest of France by bus, people can get to most places quickly and easily by rail. The **Société nationale des chemins de fer français** (SNCF) is a public service known for its efficiency.

Le Train à Grande Vitesse (TGV)

- The **SNCF** is also known for its advanced technology. The **TGV** is a model of modern rail technology. In fact, Amtrak's high-speed train Acela, introduced in late 2000 on the East Coast, uses an electric propulsion system developed for the TGV. Designed by the French, the trains were built by a company in Quebec, Bombardier, which also invented the snowmobile.
- The **SNCF** is one of the leading employers in France. It also has one of the largest budgetary deficits of any French organization, but no government administration would dream of radically cutting rail services in order to balance the budget. Transportation is one of the services that the French expect from the government in return for their taxes.

- For many years, French experts downplayed the need for limited-access highways—**les autoroutes**. The Ministry of Transportation wanted to promote train travel and discourage long-distance car and truck use; this is one reason for the long delays in the development of the **autoroute** system in France as compared with Germany or Italy, for example. Although the attitude has changed in recent years, many large cities are still not linked to nearby urban areas by **autoroute**.
- The French sometimes find the North American atittude toward the automobile peculiar. They are surprised that people may prefer to live far from their place of work, take the car for the slightest errand, and often treat their cars with something akin to affection.
- In French cities, modes of transportation vary. There is a subway system—**le métro**—in cities such as Paris, Toulouse, Lyon, and Marseille. The Paris **métro**, opened in 1900, is famous for its completeness and ease of use. Its Art Nouveau entryways are considered artistic masterpieces.
- Most French cities did away with their tram lines in the 1950s, and bus transportation became the norm. Today, bus service is usually extensive and efficient in French cities. Like the trains, the buses often run at a deficit but are nonetheless considered an essential public service.
- In recent years, many French cities have reintroduced tram lines (**les tramways**), partly for ecological reasons, because trams do not pollute the way buses do. Lyon reintroduced the tram in 2000, and several other French cities, including Bordeaux, have similar projects underway.

Une entrée de métro à Paris

Considérez

In what ways do French cultural attitudes toward transportation differ from those in North America? Why did the automobile replace other forms of transportation in North America so much more than in Europe? How do you feel about government support for and control over transportation systems?

Structure 44

Les prépositions avec les noms géographiques

Locating places and people

—Ben, tu vas jusqu'à Alès. **À Alès,** tu loues une voiture et tu montes dans la montagne.

Le genre des noms géographiques

When used as the subject of a sentence or as the object of a verb such as **visiter** or **quitter**, place names need the correct definite article.* In order to determine the correct article to use, you must determine whether place names are masculine or feminine.

- Most continents are feminine: **l'Afrique**, **l'Europe**, **l'Asie**, **l'Australie**, **l'Amérique du Nord**, **l'Amérique du Sud**. *But* **l'Antarctique** (*m.*).
- Countries, states, and provinces that end in **-e** are feminine: **l'Algérie**, **l'Allemagne**, **l'Angleterre**, **la Caroline-du-Nord**, **la Chine**, **l'Espagne**, **la Floride**, **la France**, **la Louisiane**, **la Nouvelle-Écosse** (*Nova Scotia*), **Terre-Neuve** (*Newfoundland*), **la Virginie-Occidentale** (*West Virginia*), etc. One major exception is **le Mexique**.
- Countries, states, and provinces that end in other letters are masculine: **le Canada**, **les États-Unis**, **Israël**, **le Japon**, **le Québec**, **le Texas**, **le Viêtnam**, etc.

L'été prochain, je vais visiter **le Québec**.

La France a une longue histoire, mais **Israël** est un pays assez jeune.

L'Asie est un continent qui a aussi un passé riche.

*Two exceptions are **Israël** and **Terre-Neuve,** which have no article.

D'où venez-vous?

To express where a person comes *from* or is arriving *from,* use **de**.

1. For cities, for continents, and for countries, states, and provinces that are feminine or that start with a vowel sound, use **de** or **d'**.*

   Hélène arrive **de** Montréal et Ian arrive **de** Nouvelle-Écosse. Ils viennent **d'**Amérique du Nord.

   Camille et Bruno viennent **de** France, **de** Paris, plus exactement.

   Ce reporter vient **d'**Israël.

2. For masculine countries, states, or provinces, and for plural countries, **de** forms a contraction with the article.

   Le père de Rachid vient **du** Maroc. Mon père vient **des** États-Unis.

Où habitez-vous? Où êtes-vous? Où allez-vous?

To express the idea of *in, at,* or *to,* the preposition depends on the gender of the place name that follows it.

1. For cities, use **à**.

   Hélène habite **à** Montréal.†

   Camille habite **à** Paris.

2. For continents, and for countries, states, and provinces that are feminine or that start with a vowel sound, use **en**.

   Hélène arrive **en** Europe en avion. Elle fait un reportage **en** France.

   Le reporter qui vient de Jerusalem rentre **en** Israël.

3. For masculine countries, states, or provinces, and for plural countries, use **à** and form a contraction with the article.

   Hélène habite **au** Canada. Elle n'habite pas **aux** États-Unis.

	On vient... **On arrive...**	**On habite...** **On va...**
continent	de (d')	en
pays / état / province féminin	de (d')	en
pays / état / province masculin qui commence par une voyelle ou h muet	de (d')	en
pays / état / province masculin qui commence par une consonne	du	au
pays pluriel	des	aux
ville	de (d')	à

*Most city names do not have an article and are usually masculine: ***Paris* et *Lyon* sont grands.** Some, however, include an article: **Le Caire**, **Le Havre**, **La Nouvelle-Orléans**, **La Haye**. Always use the article with these names and form a contraction when necessary: **Elle vient *de La* Nouvelle-Orléans. Il vient *du* Havre.** The article is capitalized unless it forms a contraction.

†Again, city names that contain a definite article must include the capitalized article or a contraction: **Elle va *à La* Nouvelle-Orléans. Il va *au* Havre.**

Activités

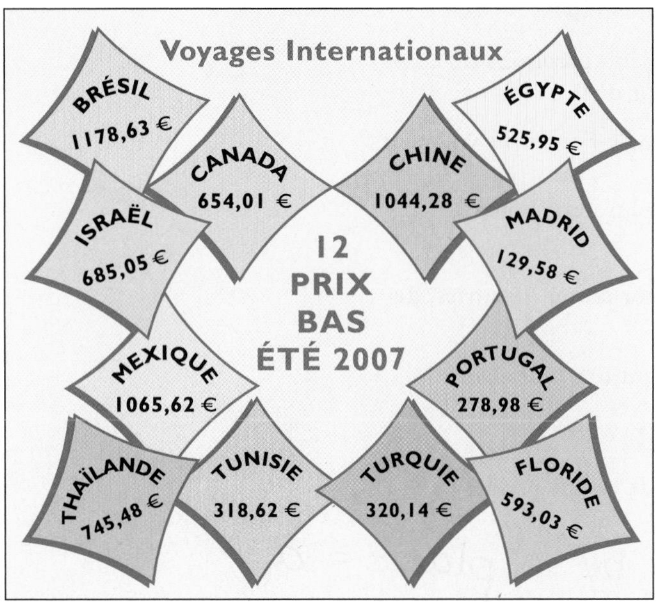

Voyages Internationaux
BRÉSIL
1178,63 €
CANADA
654,01 €
CHINE
1044,28 €
ÉGYPTE
525,95 €
ISRAËL
685,05 €
MADRID
129,58 €
12
PRIX
BAS
ÉTÉ 2007
MEXIQUE
1065,62 €
PORTUGAL
278,98 €
THAÏLANDE
745,48 €
TUNISIE
318,62 €
TURQUIE
320,14 €
FLORIDE
593,03 €

A. Destinations. Quel est le prix d'un voyage dans chaque pays mentionné dans cette brochure? Suivez le modèle en faisant bien attention à l'emploi de la préposition ou de l'article.

MODÈLE: On paie 525,95 euros pour aller en Égypte.

B. Villes, pays et continents. Dans quel pays et sur quel continent se trouvent les villes suivantes? Regardez les cartes dans votre livre pour les villes que vous ne connaissez pas.

Pays utiles: Algérie, Belgique, Côte-d'Ivoire, États-Unis, Guyane, Laos, Mali, Maroc, Sénégal, Suisse

MODÈLE: Tombouctou → Tombouctou se trouve au Mali. C'est en Afrique.

1. Abidjan
2. Alger
3. Berne
4. Bruxelles
5. Casablanca
6. Tunis
7. Dakar
8. La Nouvelle-Orléans

C. C'est logique. Faites une phrase avec les éléments donnés. Ensuite, utilisez un des verbes et un des pays donnés pour expliquer chaque situation. Attention aux temps des verbes!

Verbes utiles: aller, arriver, partir, venir, visiter

Pays et états utiles: Allemagne, Angleterre, Chine, Espagne, États-Unis, Japon, Maroc, Mexique, Texas

MODÈLE: Marta / danser / le flamenco. Elle...
Marta danse le flamenco. Elle vient d'Espagne.

1. l'avion de Paul / quitter / Denver International Airport. Paul...
2. la semaine dernière, Nadia / acheter / un beau livre en arabe. Elle...
3. dans 10 minutes, le train de Martin / rentrer / dans la gare de Berlin. Martin...
4. Yoko / naître / Tokyo en 1987. Elle...
5. Catherine / naître / Dallas en 1977. Elle...
6. le mois dernier, Abdul / monter / sur une pyramide maya. Il...
7. Karine / regarder / Big Ben la semaine prochaine. Elle...

D. Vos voyages. Avec votre partenaire, discutez des voyages que vous avez faits et de ceux (*those*) que vous voulez faire un jour. Parlez de ce que vous avez fait pendant vos voyages et de ce que vous voulez faire pendant votre voyage de rêve. Utilisez les éléments suivants pour vous inspirer.

VERBES	ENDROITS
aller	un continent
explorer	un état ou une province
partir	un monument
rester	un musée
visiter	un pays
voyager	un site touristique
	une ville

Visionnement 2

Avant de visionner

La gare de Lyon. In this episode, Rachid comes back to Paris with his report on Saint-Jean de Causse. Because he has been in the Cévennes, he comes into the **gare de Lyon**, where the trains from southeastern France arrive. The following map shows the area around this train station. Just across the Seine is the **gare d'Austerlitz**, named for a great victory in the Napoleonic wars. This is the station that serves southwestern France (Bordeaux, the Pyrenees, the Basque Country, etc.). You may recall from Chapter 1 that the **gare d'Austerlitz** is close to the **Jardin des Plantes** and Yasmine's school. Just to the north of the **gare de Lyon** is the **place de la Bastille**, former site of the infamous prison. Visitors to the square today see a monument to the July Revolution of 1830 and the new buildings of the **Opéra Bastille**. The outline of the now demolished Bastille is inscribed in the pavement of the square. South of the **gare de Lyon** is the **Ministère de l'Économie, des Finances et de l'Industrie**, one of the last great public building projects of the 20th century in Paris. In Chapter 2, you saw that Canal 7 is located not too far away, just down the right bank of the Seine, beyond the city limits.

Maintenant, regardez le plan à la page 322, et donnez le nom du bâtiment célèbre (*famous*) qui est en question dans les phrases suivantes.

1. Sylvie veut aller à Lourdes dans les Pyrénées. Vers quel bâtiment doit-elle aller?
2. Philippe veut voir *Carmen*. Vers quel bâtiment doit-il aller?
3. Bruno et Camille vont des Studios Canal 7 à la gare de Lyon. Quel bâtiment vont-ils voir en route?
4. Rachid va de la gare de Lyon à l'école de sa fille. Quel bâtiment va-t-il voir en route?
5. Hélène va de la gare de Lyon à la place de la Bastille. Quel bâtiment moderne va-t-elle voir en passant?

Les environs de la gare de Lyon

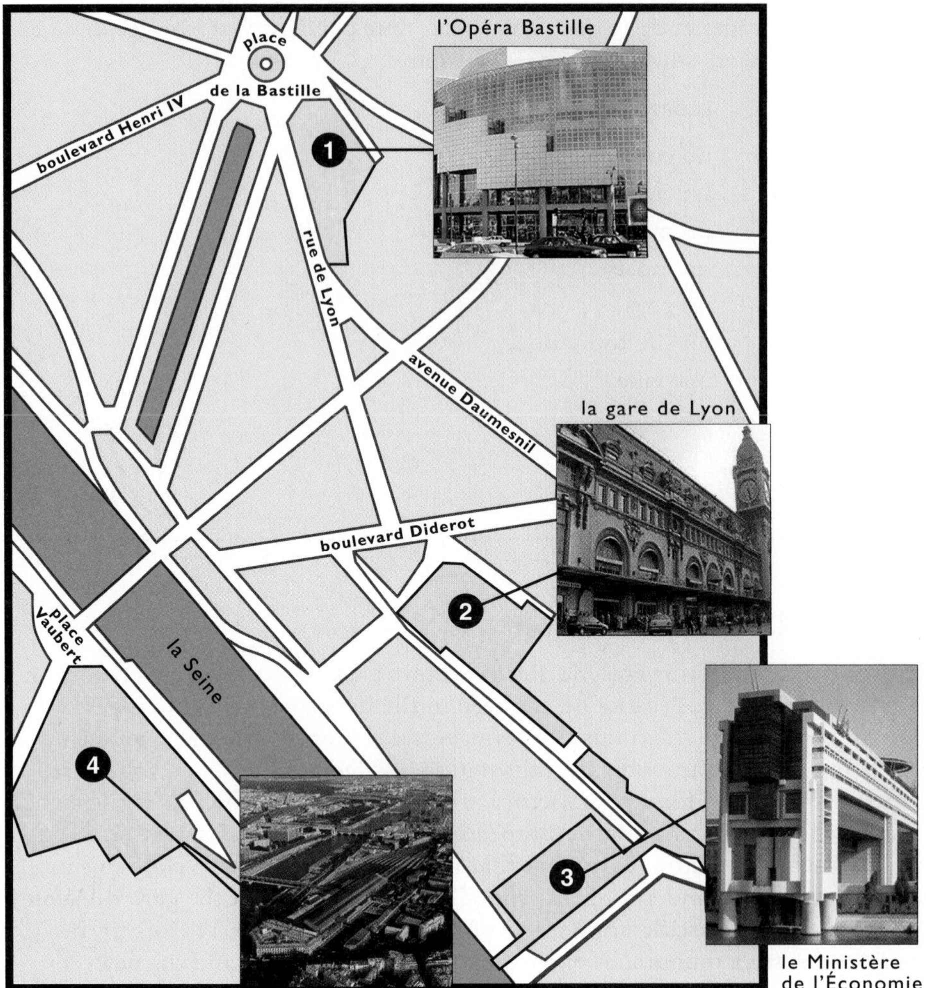

Observez!

Considérez les aspects culturels expliqués dans **Regards sur la culture**. Ensuite, regardez l'Épisode 14 encore une fois, et répondez aux questions suivantes.

- Quand Camille voit Rachid à la gare après son retour à Paris, il semble reposé et de bonne humeur. Que peut-on en conclure sur la qualité du service des trains en France?
- Enfant, Mado a été tourmentée par ses camarades à cause de son père. Que peut-on en conclure sur l'attitude des Français vis-à-vis des collaborateurs après la guerre?

Après le visionnement

Faites l'activité pour le **Visionnement 2** dans le cahier.

Synthèse: Lecture

Mise en contexte

During World War II, many soldiers sought penpals as a way of relieving the rigors of military life. These **correspondantes** provided comfort and support to men who were separated from their families and who risked their lives daily. As the penpals became acquainted, they began to address each other as **marraine** (*godmother*) and **filleul** (*godson*). These terms were simply signs of friendship and did not denote any family relationship.

In 1939, Yolande Pelletier, an 18-year-old Québécoise, began a correspondence with Carmen Pischella, a sailor from Corsica. After Yolande's death many years later, her daughter, Claudette Pelletier Deschênes, found Carmen's letters. You will be reading a few excerpts from them.

Mise en scène

Skim the following introduction to the letters. It is written by Yolande's daughter. What parallels do you see between her discovery of these letters and Camille's discovery of Antoine's letter in Episode 14? What parallels are there between Carmen and Antoine and their circumstances?

«Je savais depuis mon enfance que maman avait un correspondant pendant la guerre 39–45, j'ai toujours été curieuse de savoir les secrets que ces lettres contenaient. Maman gardait précieusement toutes les lettres de cet ami lointain[a] et elle nous refusait toujours la permission de les lire. Elle les gardait cachées et sous clé, pour une raison qu'elle ne nous a jamais dévoilée.[b] Nous pensions qu'elle considérait probablement ces lettres comme des lettres d'amour. … Quelques mois avant sa mort en 1983, elle a donné à ma nièce Julie un petit coffret de cèdre[c] contenant ses précieuses lettres avec l'instruction de les conserver en bon état.»

[a]*faraway* [b]ne… *never revealed to us* [c]coffret… *cedar box*

Stratégie pour mieux lire
Anticipating content

What kinds of information would you expect to find in the first letters from a penpal—name, address, age? What else? What other details? What might the person write about later? As you read, see if you accurately predicted the contents of Carmen's letters.

Marraine de Guerre

*Correspondance d'un matelot[1] corse à une jeune Canadienne pendant la Deuxième guerre mondiale**

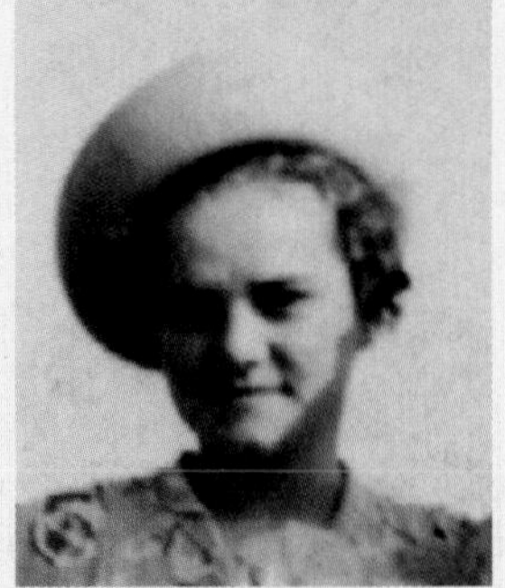

TOULON, le 18 mars 1939
Chère mademoiselle,

À présent je vais passer à ce qui vous préoccupe fort:[2] ma description. Je viens d'avoir, il y a douze jours, vingt ans et demi. Je ne suis pas originaire de Toulon, ville que vous ne connaissez pas, mais d'Ajaccio qui est plus petit mais dont vous devez certainement avoir entendu parler[3] comme ville où est né Napoléon Bonaparte.

J'ai eu ma première partie du Baccalauréat, je connais l'anglais assez passablement pour pouvoir l'écrire, avec quelques fautes, et me faire comprendre.[4] Je parle et j'écris parfaitement l'italien étant Corse et l'ayant étudié durant sept ans d'études secondaires.

J'ai encore deux ans et dix mois à faire dans la marine nationale, qui en France est la base de toute carrière civile.

J'oubliais de vous dire que je mesure en hauteur un mètre soixante et onze centimètres.

Je repars mardi prochain en Espagne où nous faisons le contrôle des armes[5] et d'où nous serons de retour[6] le vingt.

Amicalement,
Carmen

TOULON, le 7 mai 1939
Chère mademoiselle,

J'ai reçu votre gentille lettre le vingt-quatre avril, alors que j'étais bien loin de France où nous ne sommes rentrés que ce matin dimanche sept mai.

[1]*sailor* [2]*greatly* [3]dont… *of which you must have heard* [4]me… *make myself understood* [5]contrôle… *arms inspection* [6]serons… *will be back*

*Ces lettres représentent des extraits (*extracts*) de la correspondance entre Carmen et Yolande. Étant donné l'étendue (*given the length*) de la correspondance, on n'a pas pu reproduire le texte intégral.

Vous devez avoir appris par le journal que les événements étaient très graves en Europe, particulièrement entre la France et notre ennemie de toujours, l'Allemagne. Pour cette raison on nous envoie à Gibraltar qui est la porte de la Méditerranée, pour que, au cas où il se produirait quelque chose[7] nous soyons prêts à en interdire l'entrée ou la sortie.[8] C'est pour cela seul que je vous fais réponse treize jours en retard. ...

Je vous serre cordialement la main.
Carmen

AJACCIO, le 16 avril 1940
Chère Marraine,
Il fait un temps splendide, le soleil brille à longueur de journée, demain ou après demain j'irai[9] avec quelques amis à la pêche puis nous ferons[10] une bonne bouillabaisse sur les rochers. Sais-tu ce qu'est la bouillabaisse? C'est une soupe de poisson mais il faut[11] savoir la préparer et comme cuisine je ne sais faire que cela, je suis certain que si tu sais ce que c'est, l'eau t'en viendra à la bouche,[12] rien que d'y penser.[13] ...
en t'embrassant bien affectueusement. Carmen

[.....], le 12 novembre 1942
Très chère amie,

Ces quelques mots pour te dire que je suis encore vivant et en très excellente santé.

Où je suis? Sur le paquebot[14] «Ville d'Ajaccio» comme timonier signaleur,[15] depuis deux mois. Je pense que tu as entendu parler et que tu te seras même beaucoup intéressée[16] à la libération de la Corse, j'étais à Ajaccio à ce moment là et j'y ai participé.[17]

Et toi que deviens-tu? Peut-être es-tu mariée à l'heure actuelle, si oui je te souhaite[18] tout le bonheur que tu désires et tu le sais, c'est sincère. J'écris quand même à ton adresse de jeune fille[19] et j'espère que la lettre te parviendra.[20]

Je vais te quitter en espérant une prompte réponse et t'embrassant bien, bien fort. Ton petit. Carmen

[7]pour... *so that in case something happens* [8]à... *we are ready to block entrance or exit to it (the Mediterranean)* [9]*will go* [10]*will make* [11]*it's necessary* [12]l'eau... *your mouth will water* [13]rien... *just thinking about it* [14]*ocean liner* [15]timonier... *helmsman-signaler* [16]tu... *you will have even been very interested* [17]j'y... *I participated in it* [18]je... *I wish you* [19]de... *unmarried* [20]*will reach*

Après la lecture

A. Avez-vous bien anticipé? Quels éléments anticipés avez-vous trouvés dans les lettres du matelot? Quels autres thèmes avez-vous découverts? Donnez les renseignements (*information*) que vous avez trouvés.

1. son nom **2.** son adresse **3.** son âge **4.** autres thèmes que vous avez anticipés **5.** autres thèmes que vous n'avez pas anticipés. Nommez-en trois (*Name three of them*) si possible.

Maintenant, décrivez le matelot en résumant les renseignements qu'il a donnés à Yolande dans ses lettres.

B. L'éducation sentimentale. Quels détails dans ces lettres indiquent que les deux correspondants deviennent de plus en plus intimes?

C. L'histoire. Quels faits historiques sont mentionnés dans les lettres? Quel rôle Carmen a-t-il joué dans ces événements?

À écrire

Faites **À écrire** pour le Chapitre 14 dans le cahier.

Vocabulaire

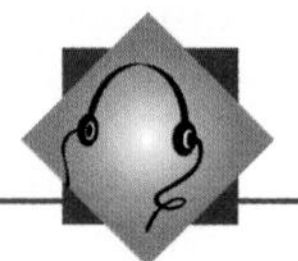

Pour voyager

un billet (aller simple, aller-retour) (one-way, round trip) ticket
un endroit place, location
un(e) passager/ère passenger
une place (*reserved*) seat
un siège (couloir, fenêtre) (aisle, window) seat
à pied on foot
circuler to get around
passer la douane to go through customs
prendre une correspondance to transfer

MOTS APPARENTÉS: **une arrivée, un départ, un passeport, une valise, un visa**
PRÉPOSITIONS À REVOIR: **à, de, en**

Pour voyager en train

une gare train station
un quai platform
un train à grande vitesse (*fam.* **un TGV**) high-speed train
un wagon (fumeurs, non-fumeurs) (smoking, nonsmoking) train car
composter to punch (*a ticket*)

MOT APPARENTÉ: **un train**

Pour voyager en avion

un avion airplane
une porte d'embarquement gate
un vol flight
enregistrer (une valise) to check (a suitcase)

MOT APPARENTÉ: **un aéroport**

Pour voyager en métro et en bus

un arrêt (*station*) stop
un autocar (*long distance, tour*) bus
un bus (*short distance, city*) bus
un guichet ticket window
le métro subway
un réseau (du métro) (subway) system, network
un ticket (de métro) (subway) ticket

MOTS APPARENTÉS: **la direction, un terminus**

Pour voyager en voiture

la circulation traffic
un embouteillage traffic jam
les heures (*f.*) **de pointe** rush hour
la limite de vitesse speed limit
une sortie exit
complet/ète full
louer to rent
stationner to park

MOTS APPARENTÉS: **une autoroute, une route**
À REVOIR: **un parking**

Substantifs

un moyen means; method; mode
un(e) traître / traîtresse traitor

Adjectifs

actuel(le) current, present
discret/ète discreet; reserved
doux (douce) gentle
exact(e) exact, accurate
fou (folle) crazy, mad
franc(he) frank
lent(e) slow
plusieurs several
pressé(e) in a hurry
seul(e) alone; sole
tel(le) such; like

MOTS APPARENTÉS: **absolu(e), apparent(e), élégant(e), évident(e), immédiat(e), rapide, sûr(e)**
À REVOIR: **gentil(le), vrai(e)**

Adverbes

peut-être perhaps
seulement only
tellement so (very), so much
vite fast, quickly

À REVOIR: **bien, mal**

Expressions de temps

depuis for; since
longtemps (for) a long time
pendant during; while

Verbes

appartenir to belong to
contenir to contain
obtenir to obtain
rencontrer to meet; to run into
tenir to hold

Continents

l'Afrique (*f.*), **l'Amérique** (*f.*) **du Nord, l'Amérique** (*f.*) **du Sud, l'Antarctique** (*m.*), **l'Asie** (*f.*), **l'Australie** (*f.*), **l'Europe** (*f.*)

Pays et régions

Israël (*m.*)

À REVOIR: **l'Algérie, l'Allemagne, l'Angleterre, le Canada, la Chine, l'Espagne, les États-Unis, la France, le Japon, le Mexique, le Québec, le Viêtnam**

Chapitre 15

Une piste!°

°Une... *A lead!*

Le Chemin du retour

Feuille de service du 12 octobre
2e jour de tournage
Horaires: 9h–19h

LIEU DE TOURNAGE: PARIS—18, rue des Rondeaux, 20e

Séquence	*Effets*	*Décors*	*Résumé*	*Rôles*
90B	INT.—NUIT	APPARTEMENT RACHID—Salle à manger	Camille mange un couscous chez Rachid.	CAMILLE, RACHID, YASMINE, SONIA

OBJECTIFS

In this episode, you will

- find out what Rachid learned in Saint-Jean de Causse
- learn more about Rachid's and Sonia's backgrounds

In this chapter, you will

- talk about popular foods in various parts of the world
- talk about countries and nationalities
- talk about everyday activities
- use the pronouns **y** and **en** to refer to places and things
- read about how immigration has affected French culture

Vocabulaire en contexte

La cuisine maghrébine*

Voici les ingrédients et **la recette**° pour **un** bon **couscous maghrébin.** — *recipe*

DES ÉPICES° (*f.*) ET DES CONDIMENTS — *spices*

la cannelle	cinnamon
la coriandre	coriander
le persil	parsley
le/la quatre-épices	*blend of pepper, nutmeg, ginger, cinnamon, or cloves used to flavor soups, stews, and vegetables*

Mettre le coucous dans le couscoussier° et **faire cuire à la vapeur**° pendant 15 minutes.
Dans l'évier,° **verser**° sur le couscous 1 litre d'eau.
Laisser égoutter° pendant 15 minutes.
Ensuite verser le coucous dans un très grand plat creux.°
Ajouter° une cuillère à café de sel et 2 cuillères à soupe d'huile et **mélanger.**°
Laisser reposer 20 minutes.

couscous cooker
faire... steam
kitchen sink / pour
drain
plat... deep dish
Add
mix

Pour lire une recette, les termes suivants sont aussi utiles.

une casserole	saucepan
couvrir	to cover
faire bouillir	to boil
faire cuire (quelque chose) **au four**	to bake
faire frire	to fry
(ré)chauffer	to (re)heat

*Le terme **le Maghreb** et l'adjectif **maghrébin(e)** se réfèrent aux pays de l'Afrique du Nord: principalement le Maroc, l'Algérie et la Tunisie.

Activités

A. Quels ingrédients? En utilisant le vocabulaire presenté, ainsi que (*as well as*) d'autres mots que vous connaissez, identifiez les ingrédients principaux dans les plats suivants.

MODÈLE: un ragoût (*stew*) de bœuf →
Dans un ragoût de bœuf, on met du bœuf, des pommes de terre, des carottes, des oignons...

1. une salade (du chef) **2.** une pizza **3.** une soupe aux légumes
4. une omelette **5.** des crudités (*raw vegetables*)

B. Méthodes de cuisson. (*Cooking methods.*) Identifiez la méthode de cuisson pour les plats suivants.

MODÈLE: des spaghettis → On fait bouillir les spaghettis.

1. des frites **2.** une tarte **3.** du riz **4.** un hamburger **5.** une pizza
6. des brocolis

C. Une recette. Formez des groupes de trois ou quatre personnes. Chaque membre du groupe donne le nom de son plat favori. Les autres étudiants posent alors des questions sur les ingrédients, la préparation, etc. Ensuite, chacun (*each one*) donne son opinion sur ce plat.

MODÈLE:
VOUS: Mon plat favori, c'est la soupe à l'oignon.
LE GROUPE: Quels sont les ingrédients principaux? Comment est-ce qu'on prépare cette soupe? Est-ce que tu manges ce plat au petit déjeuner, au déjeuner ou au dîner? Cela a l'air délicieux / trop piquant (*spicy*) / immangeable.

Spécialités du monde entier

Vallée du Kashmir
Visitez le Pakistan et l'Inde!
spécialités pakistanaises et indiennes
Tandoori au charbon de bois
Agneau,[a] poulet ou crevettes
dans une sauce curry
Riz basmati
Menu 9€ (midi seulement), 15€/25€.
Carte environ 12€/16€.
Ouvert 7/7. Service jusqu'à 23 h 30.
3, place de Vauban (7e)
01.45.85.86.73

Les Pakistanais et les Indiens aiment **le curry**, **le yaourt**, **les lentilles** (*f.*) et **la cardamome**.

La citronnelle[d] et la coriandre sont très populaires au Viêtnam. Les Chinois aiment **la sauce de soja**, **le gingembre**,[e] l'oignon vert et l'huile de sésame.

[a]*lamb* [b]Canard... *Peking duck* [c]*Prawns* [d]*lemon grass* [e]*ginger*

Douchka
Spécialités russes
Dîner aux chandelles[f]
avec ses musiciens
dans un décor vieille Russie
Menu 14€.
Carte environ 17€.
Ouvert tous les jours
jusqu'à minuit
79, rue Saint-Dominique (7e)
01.45.05.52.67

Mamma Léone
Ses spécialités italiennes vous transportent en Italie.
Pâtes fraîches maison
Carpaccio
Courgettes à la Piémontaise
Saladerie-Tarterie (le midi)
Menu 13€. Carte environ 16€.
Fermé dimanche et lundi midi.
54, rue de Bourgogne (7e)
01.45.82.57.58

La cuisine russe utilise **les betteraves**[g] (*f.*), les pommes de terre, **les champignons**[h] (*m.*) et la crème fraîche.

Les Italiens aiment **les pâtes**[i] (*f. pl.*) de toutes sortes, les courgettes, les tomates, le poisson et **l'ail**[j] (*m.*).

AUTRES CUISINES ET INGRÉDIENTS TYPIQUES

israélienne: les pois chiches, les salades, **le pain pita**
thaïlandaise: les **cacahouètes**[k] (*f.*), la **noix de coco**,[l] les pâtes

[f] *candles* [g] *beets* [h] *mushrooms* [i] *pasta* [j] *garlic* [k] *peanuts* [l] noix... *coconut*

Activités

A. Des ingrédients. Voici des ingrédients propres à (*characteristic of*) certaines cuisines nationales. Identifiez la nationalité et le pays.

MODÈLE: la coriandre →
C'est la cuisine maghrébine. Elle vient du Maroc ou d'Algérie.
(*ou* C'est la cuisine vietnamienne. Elle vient du Viêtnam.)

1. les lentilles **2.** la citronnelle **3.** le gingembre **4.** le curry **5.** les pâtes **6.** les pois chiches **7.** la sauce de soja **8.** le yaourt **9.** les betteraves

B. Présentez-vous! Décrivez-vous à la classe. Parlez de la nationalité de votre famille et de vos préférences alimentaires. Avez-vous des talents culinaires?

MODÈLE: Je m'appelle Thomas Trauth. Mes parents sont d'origine italienne et allemande,* mais je suis américain. J'aime la cuisine italienne parce que j'adore les pâtes et parce que l'ail est bon pour la santé.

C. Une interview. Interviewez votre partenaire pour déterminer ses goûts alimentaires. Demandez-lui...

1. quels ingrédients il/elle aime dans un plat, et quels ingrédients il/elle déteste.
2. s'il / si elle préfère la cuisine piquante ou les plats qui ne sont pas très épicés.
3. quel est son restaurant préféré et le plat qu'il/elle commande le plus fréquemment dans ce restaurant.
4. quels plats il/elle aime servir à l'occasion d'une fête.
5. la cuisine régionale (de son pays) qu'il/elle préfère.

---

*Le mot **origine** est un substantif féminin, alors il prend la forme féminine de l'adjectif.

Visionnement 1

Avant de visionner

Un dialogue incomplet. Voici l'extrait d'un dialogue entre Camille et Rachid, où on parle du voyage de Rachid dans les Cévennes. Complétez le passage en choisissant les mots logiques.

CAMILLE: _____[1] (Personne, Rien) ne t'a parlé de la guerre, apparemment?

RACHID: Les vieux sont discrets. Ils _____[2] (veulent, ne veulent pas) s'exprimer[a] devant une caméra. Et les jeunes n'ont pas _____[3] (connu, su) cette période.

CAMILLE: Comment faire pour _____[4] (retrouver, retourner) la trace de mon grand-père?

RACHID: 60 ans après la guerre, c'est _____[5] (utile, difficile).

CAMILLE: _____[6] (Pourquoi, Où) tu dis ça? On sait aujourd'hui comment vivait l'homme du Néandertal.[b] Et c'était _____[7] (quand, où)? Il y a 75.000 ans!

RACHID (*sourit*): Tu n'es jamais _____[8] (encouragée, découragée), hein?

[a]*to express themselves* [b]l'homme... *Neanderthal Man (ancient human ancestor)*

Vocabulaire relatif à l'épisode

y a séjourné	*stayed there*
une petite goutte	*a little drop*
as-tu rencontré	*did you meet*
C'est comme ça que ça s'écrit?	*Is that how it's spelled?*
c'est génial	*that's fantastic*
surtout pas	*definitely not*

Observez!

Dans l'Épisode 15, Camille pose des questions à Rachid sur son voyage dans les Cévennes. Pendant votre visionnement, essayez de trouver les réponses aux questions suivantes.

- À quels obstacles Rachid doit-il faire face dans ses recherches?
- De quelle piste est-ce que Camille parle?

Après le visionnement

A. Racontez l'épisode! Un étudiant donne une phrase qui commence le résumé. Un autre étudiant reprend le récit, jusqu'à ce que tout l'épisode soit (*is*) reconstitué.

B. Réfléchissez. Répondez aux questions suivantes.

1. Pourquoi les vieux de Saint-Jean de Causse sont-ils «discrets»? Pourquoi ne veulent-ils pas parler de la guerre? Est-ce qu'ils veulent oublier les événements tragiques? Est-ce qu'ils ont quelque chose à cacher (*to hide*)? Se méfient-ils des inconnus (*Do they mistrust strangers*)?
2. Pourquoi Camille ne veut-elle pas appeler les Leblanc tout de suite? A-t-elle peur d'apprendre la vérité? Veut-elle réfléchir avant d'agir (*before acting*)?

Les verbes comme *ouvrir*

Talking about everyday actions

—**J'ai découvert** les Cévennes. C'est somptueux.

The verb **ouvrir** (*to open*) is conjugated like a regular **-er** verb in the present tense, but the past participle is irregular.

ouvrir (*to open*)			
j'	ouvr**e**	nous	ouvr**ons**
tu	ouvr**es**	vous	ouvr**ez**
il, elle, on	ouvr**e**	ils, elles	ouvr**ent**
passé composé: j'ai **ouvert**			

1. Other verbs conjugated like **ouvrir** are

couvrir	*to cover*	**offrir**	*to offer; to give*
découvrir	*to discover*	**souffrir**	*to suffer*

Tu mets les ingrédients dans une casserole et puis **tu** la **couvres**. — *You put the ingredients in a saucepan and then you cover it.*

Mado **a** beaucoup **souffert** des injures de ses camarades. — *Mado suffered a great deal because of her classmates' insults.*

2. The opposite of **ouvrir** is **fermer** (*to close*). **Fermer** is a regular **-er** verb.

Tu **fermes** les fenêtres, petite? J'ai horreur des courants d'air. — *Will you close the windows, dear? I hate drafts.*

Activités

A. Découvertes culturelles. Complétez les paragraphes en utilisant correctement les verbes entre parenthèses. Utilisez le temps présent sauf (*except*) où vous devez mettre le passé composé (p.c. = passé composé).

1. Dans mon pays l'Algérie, on ____ (souffrir, p.c.) pendant la guerre entre 1954 et 1963. Nous ____ (découvrir, p.c.) que notre culture peut résister à tout, même si les gens ____ (souffrir) toujours des conflits internes violents.
2. Je ____ (découvrir) en ce moment beaucoup de choses sur l'Algérie. Mes parents m'____ (offrir, p.c.) un livre sur les cultures maghrébines pour mon anniversaire. Il ____ (couvrir) toute l'histoire de ces pays.
3. Les Français ____ (découvrir) la culture algérienne grâce à (*thanks to*) la cuisine. Récemment, mon frère ____ (ouvrir, p.c.) un restaurant algérien, et je travaille pour lui. Nous ____ (offrir) toutes sortes de couscous et de la chorba'dess, une soupe aux lentilles. Je ____ (découvrir) beaucoup de recettes similaires dans nos deux pays, et ça m'____ (ouvrir) vraiment les yeux.
4. Tu nous ____ (offrir) un repas au restaurant? Comme ça (*that way*), nous allons découvrir nous-mêmes (*ourselves*) cet aspect de ta culture!
5. Ah vous, les Français, vous ____ (découvrir) tout à travers (*through*) la gastronomie.

B. Alors... (*So*...) Dans chaque situation, il y a plusieurs actions possibles. Complétez les phrases de façon logique (*in a logical way*) en utilisant des termes des listes de vocabulaire utile.

Vocabulaire utile: les/des allergies, un bon plat aux courgettes et aux tomates, la/de la chaleur (*heat*), un chapitre du livre par jour, les/des fenêtres, les/des fleurs (*flowers*), un nouveau restaurant, le/du froid, un mal de tête, les pâtes et des sauces avec beaucoup d'ail

Verbes utiles: couvrir, découvrir, fermer, offrir, ouvrir, souffrir

MODÈLE: L'hiver arrive, alors la vieille dame... →
É1: L'hiver arrive, alors la vieille dame couvre les fleurs.
É2: L'hiver arrive, alors la vieille dame n'ouvre pas les fenêtres.

1. C'est le printemps, alors nous...
2. C'est l'été, alors vous...
3. C'est mon anniversaire, alors mon ami...
4. Je vais dans un restaurant végétarien, alors je...
5. Ce cours avance vite, alors le professeur...
6. Les étudiants voyagent en Italie, alors ils...
7. La cuisine indienne est très à la mode, alors M. Desai...

Structure 46

Les pronoms y et en

Avoiding repetition

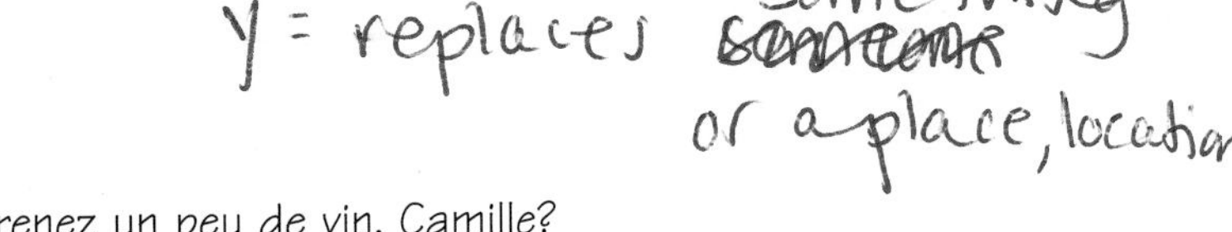

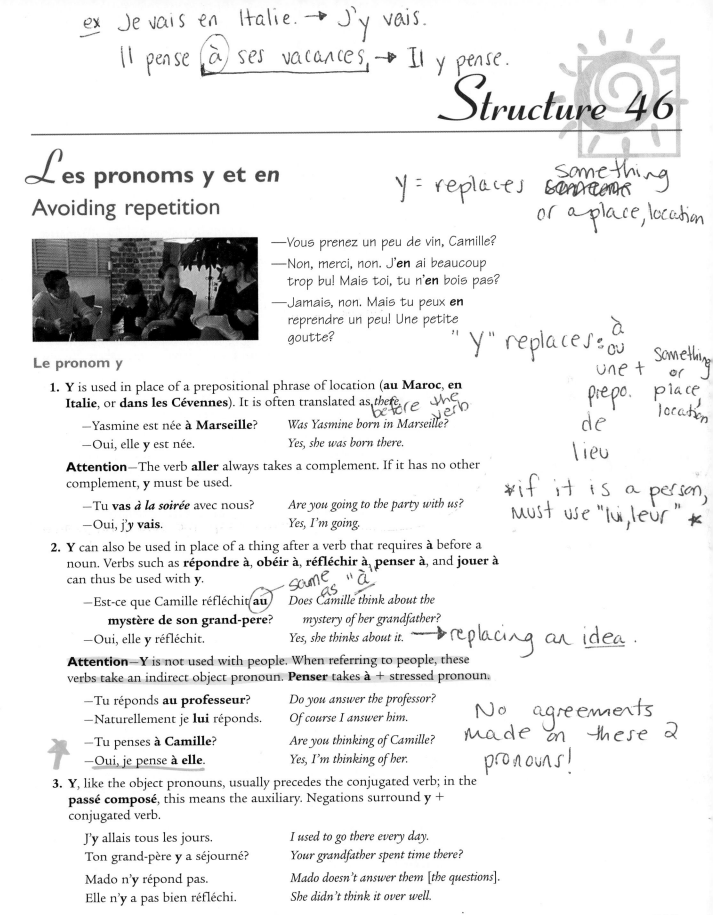

—Vous prenez un peu de vin, Camille?

—Non, merci, non. J'**en** ai beaucoup trop bu! Mais toi, tu n'**en** bois pas?

—Jamais, non. Mais tu peux **en** reprendre un peu! Une petite goutte?

Le pronom y

1. **Y** is used in place of a prepositional phrase of location (**au Maroc**, **en Italie**, or **dans les Cévennes**). It is often translated as *there*.

—Yasmine est née **à Marseille**?	*Was Yasmine born in Marseille?*
—Oui, elle **y** est née.	*Yes, she was born there.*

   Attention—The verb **aller** always takes a complement. If it has no other complement, **y** must be used.

—Tu **vas *à la soirée*** avec nous?	*Are you going to the party with us?*
—Oui, j'***y* vais**.	*Yes, I'm going.*

2. **Y** can also be used in place of a thing after a verb that requires **à** before a noun. Verbs such as **répondre à**, **obéir à**, **réfléchir à**, **penser à**, and **jouer à** can thus be used with **y**.

—Est-ce que Camille réfléchit **au mystère de son grand-pere**?	*Does Camille think about the mystery of her grandfather?*
—Oui, elle **y** réfléchit.	*Yes, she thinks about it.*

   Attention—**Y** is not used with people. When referring to people, these verbs take an indirect object pronoun. **Penser** takes **à** + stressed pronoun.

—Tu réponds **au professeur**?	*Do you answer the professor?*
—Naturellement je **lui** réponds.	*Of course I answer him.*
—Tu penses **à Camille**?	*Are you thinking of Camille?*
—Oui, je pense **à elle**.	*Yes, I'm thinking of her.*

3. **Y**, like the object pronouns, usually precedes the conjugated verb; in the **passé composé**, this means the auxiliary. Negations surround **y** + conjugated verb.

J'**y** allais tous les jours.	*I used to go there every day.*
Ton grand-père **y** a séjourné?	*Your grandfather spent time there?*
Mado n'**y** répond pas.	*Mado doesn't answer them [the questions].*
Elle n'**y** a pas bien réfléchi.	*She didn't think it over well.*

4. In verb + infinitive constructions, **y** is placed before the verb to which it is related (usually the infinitive).

Je vais **y** voyager un jour.	*I'm going to take a trip there some day.*

5. As with other pronouns, **y** follows the verb in the affirmative imperative but precedes it in the negative imperative.

Allez-**y**!	*Go ahead!*
N'**y** pense pas.	*Don't think about it.*

Attention—The **-s** in the **tu** form of **-er** verbs is restored in the affirmative imperative when **y** is used.

Reste**s**-y.	*Stay there.*

Le pronom en

1. **En** is used in place of a phrase containing an indefinite article, a partitive article, or an expression of quantity (**un bon couscous**, **des navets**, **du vin**, **quelques courges**, **un peu de quatre-épices**).

—Tu veux **des légumes**?	*Do you want any vegetables?*
—Oui, j'**en** veux.	*Yes, I'd like some.*

When a measurement (**un peu**, **une bouteille de**, **un kilo de**, etc.) or a number (**un**, **deux**, **trois**) would be indicated in a phrase using the noun, it must also be used with the pronoun **en**, following the conjugated verb.

—Tu veux encore **du vin**?	*Do you want some more wine?*
—Non, merci, j'**en** ai **trop** bu.	*I've drunk too much (of it).*
—Vous avez **trois sœurs**?	*Do you have three sisters?*
—C'est ça. J'**en** ai **trois**.	*That's right. I have three (of them).*

2. **En** can also be used with a verb that requires **de** before a noun. Verbs such as **avoir besoin/envie/honte/peur de**, **être content(e) de**, **parler de**, **penser de**, and **jouer de** can thus be used with **en**.

—Que penses-tu **de cette histoire**?	*What do you think of this story?*
—Qu'est-ce que tu **en** penses, toi?	*What do you think of it, yourself?*

Attention—**En** is not usually used to refer to people. When these verbs refer to people, they take **de** + stressed pronoun after the verb.

—Que penses-tu **de l'historien**?	*What do you think of the historian?*
—Qu'est-ce que tu penses **de lui**?	*What do you think of him?*

3. **En**, like **y** and the object pronouns, usually precedes the conjugated verb; in the **passé composé**, this means the auxiliary. Negations surround **en** + conjugated verb.

J'**en** *buvais* tous les jours.	*I used to drink some every day.*
Camille n'**en** *veut* pas.	*Camille doesn't want any.*
Elle n'**en** *a* pas souvent parlé.	*She didn't talk about it often.*

4. In verb + infinitive constructions, **en** is placed before the verb to which it is related (usually the infinitive).

Je vais **en** acheter deux.	*I'm going to buy two of them.*

5. Again, as with other pronouns, **en** follows the verb in the affirmative imperative but precedes it in the negative imperative. Note that, as with **y**, the **-s** in the **tu** form of **-er** verbs is restored in the affirmative imperative when **en** is used.

Achètes-**en**!	*Buy some!*
N'**en** parlons pas.	*Let's not talk about it.*

Activités

A. Chez Lorenzo. Regardez cette publicité pour un restaurant parisien et répondez aux questions suivantes. Utilisez **y** dans vos réponses.

MODÈLE: Pensez-vous qu'on mange bien ou mal dans ce restaurant? → Je pense qu'on y mange bien. (Je pense qu'on y mange mal.)

1. Quelle sorte de cuisine mange-t-on dans ce restaurant? **2.** Peut-on aller à l'Arc de Triomphe à pied? **3.** Est-ce que vous vous êtes déjà promené(e) dans ce quartier? **4.** Pensez-vous que le chef de cuisine habite à Marseille? **5.** Quels repas peut-on prendre dans ce restaurant—le petit déjeuner? le déjeuner? le dîner? **6.** À votre avis, est-ce que le chef de cuisine réfléchit à son menu chaque jour?

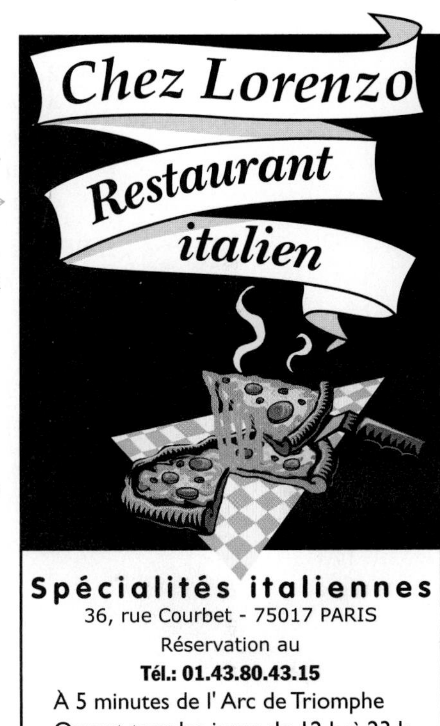

Chez Lorenzo
Restaurant
italien
Spécialités italiennes
36, rue Courbet - 75017 PARIS
Réservation au
Tél.: 01.43.80.43.15
À 5 minutes de l' Arc de Triomphe
Ouvert tous les jours de 12 h à 23 h

B. Un repas spécial. Deux camarades de chambre ont invité des amis pour un repas vietnamien ce soir, mais ils sont mal organisés. Le premier parle. Quelles sont les réponses du deuxième? Utilisez le pronom **en** dans chaque réponse.

MODÈLE: Tu as choisi des recettes pour ce soir, non? / Non, je... → Non, je n'en ai pas encore choisi.

1. Tu as acheté du vin? / Oui, j'...
2. Mais tu sais que Zaki et Irène ne boivent pas de vin. / C'est vrai, ils...
3. Alors, tu vas prendre une bouteille d'eau minérale? / D'accord, je...
4. Tu peux acheter des crevettes? / Oui, je...
5. Nous sommes quatre à manger, donc prends un kilo de crevettes. / OK, je...
6. Tu n'as pas peur de cette recette compliquée? / Non, je...
7. Est-ce que nos amis vont être contents de la soirée chez nous? / Bien sûr, ils...

C. Dans le film. Vous rappelez-vous ces événements importants dans le film? Répondez aux questions en utilisant **y** ou **en**, ou un pronom accentué (*stressed pronoun*). Justifiez votre réponse.

MODÈLE: Est-ce que Rachid habite toujours à Marseille? → Non, il n'y habite plus. Il habite à Paris.

1. Est-ce que Camille pense à la guerre? **2.** Est-ce qu'elle a envie de trouver des renseignements (*information*) sur son père? **3.** Est-ce que Rachid part en Allemagne? **4.** Est-ce que Camille a parlé de son grand-père avec Bruno?

5. Est-ce que Rachid est allé à Saint-Jean de Causse? **6.** Est-ce qu'Antoine a habité chez les Leblanc en 1943? **7.** Est-ce que les gens du village ont parlé d'Antoine? **8.** Est-ce que Louise et Camille sont allées dans les Cévennes? **9.** Est-ce que Camille est contente du dîner chez Rachid? **10.** Est-ce que Mado a peur de la vérité?

D. Pour faire une ratatouille. Richard veut faire une ratatouille et sa femme, Marie, est tout à fait d'accord avec tout ce qu'il dit! Que dit Marie? Faites une phrase à l'impératif en utilisant les pronoms **y** ou **en**.

MODÈLE: RICHARD: Je veux faire une ratatouille.
MARIE: Alors, fais-en une.

1. Je dois d'abord acheter des aubergines, des courgettes et des poivrons. **2.** Je ne dois pas acheter de vin. **3.** Je vais aller à l'épicerie pour les herbes. **4.** Je dois trouver ensuite quatre tomates. **5.** Je dois mettre l'huile d'olive dans la casserole. **6.** Je vais mettre beaucoup d'ail, aussi. **7.** Je ne veux pas ajouter beaucoup de persil. **8.** Je dois mettre la casserole sur la plaque électrique (*burner*).

E. Les restaurants. Posez des questions à deux camarades de classe. Ils/Elles vont vous répondre en utilisant **y** ou **en**. Prenez des notes pour pouvoir faire un compte rendu (*report*) à la classe. Demandez à chaque camarade...

1. s'il / si elle aime dîner au restaurant.
2. s'il / si elle est allé(e) dans ce restaurant récemment.
3. s'il / si elle essaie des plats qu'il/elle ne connaît pas. (par exemple?)
4. s'il / si elle va au restaurant seul(e). (sinon, avec qui?)
5. s'il / si elle boit du vin avec les repas. (pourquoi ou pourquoi pas?)
6. s'il / si elle pense aller dans un restaurant bientôt. (où et quand?)

Regards sur la culture

Transformations de la culture en France

Les éléments du couscous

In this episode, Rachid and Sonia have prepared **couscous**, a traditional North African dish, for Camille. In fact, **couscous** is one of a number of cultural elements from the Maghreb that are becoming assimilated into French culture. Immigration often changes the host society.

- People of North African origin are now the largest immigrant cultural group in France. Originating in Morocco, Tunisia, and especially Algeria, many of these people originally arrived in hopes of finding temporary work.
- At the time of Algeria's independence in 1962, nearly 1.5 million French citizens who had lived their entire lives in North Africa arrived en masse in France. These people included the **pieds-noirs**,

who were descendants of European settlers; Algerian Jews, whose ancestors had lived in North Africa for centuries; and North African Muslims.

- Among the customs brought by these people are a number of culinary specialities: **merguez** (a kind of spicy beef or lamb sausage), **méchoui** (a way of preparing a whole lamb on a spit over open coals), and **couscous**.
- Couscous is based on semolina wheat, which is steamed with the vapor from a stew of meat (usually lamb) and vegetables. At the table, one generally helps oneself to the couscous grain itself, the vegetables, the bouillon, and chickpeas out of separate serving dishes. One can then add **harissa**, a hot pepper sauce.
- Because of recent immigration patterns, Islam is now the second-largest religion in France after Roman Catholicism, with more adherents than Judaism or Protestantism. The children of North African immigrants, often called **beurs**, may or may not follow Islamic traditions.
- The wearing of the veil among certain Muslim groups has been a very touchy issue in France, because French public schools have traditionally forbidden the wearing of any outward religious symbol.
- The presence of **pieds-noirs** and, more recently, of **beurs** in French entertainment has brought a new accent to the culture. The most striking recent development has been the rising popularity among French young people of **raï**, the distinctive popular music of Algeria.

Considérez

What immigrant groups have succeeded in bringing changes to your own culture in recent times? What kinds of changes are these—food? games? music? something else?

Structure 47

Les verbes *vivre* et *suivre*

Talking about everyday actions

—On sait aujourd'hui comment **vivait** l'homme du Néandertal.

Two verbs, **vivre** (*to live*) and **suivre** (*to follow; to take* [*a course*]), are conjugated in the same way in the simple tenses, but their past participles differ.

vivre (*to live*)		**suivre** (*to follow; to take* [*a course*])	
je	**vis**	je	**suis**
tu	**vis**	tu	**suis**
il, elle, on	**vit**	il, elle, on	**suit**
nous	**vivons**	nous	**suivons**
vous	**vivez**	vous	**suivez**
ils, elles	**vivent**	ils, elles	**suivent**
passé composé: j'ai **vécu**		passé composé: j'ai **suivi**	

Le père de Camille **vit** à Londres. — *Camille's father lives in London.*

Actuellement, nous ne **suivons** pas de cours. Nous faisons des recherches. — *Currently, we aren't taking any courses. We're doing research.*

1. **Survivre** (*to survive*) is conjugated like **vivre**. **Poursuivre** (*to pursue*) is conjugated like **suivre**.

   Le grand-père de Camille **a**-t-il **survécu**? — *Did Camille's grandfather survive?*

   Camille **a poursuivi** sa quête. — *Camille pursued her quest.*

2. **Vivre** can be used in the same sense as **habiter** (*to inhabit, reside in, live in*), but it can also mean *to be alive, to live* in the sense of existing or having a certain lifestyle.

   J'**habite** dans la rue Mouffetard. — *I live on the rue Mouffetard.*

   Le père de Camille **vit** à Londres. — *Camille's father lives in London.*

   but Elle **vit** encore? — *Is she still alive?*

   Nous **vivons** bien en France. — *We live well in France.*

Activités

A. Qu'est-ce qu'on étudie dans chaque pays? Selon l'endroit où on vit, on suit parfois des cours différents. Mettez la forme correcte de **vivre** ou **suivre** pour parler de ces stéréotypes.

1. Je _____ en France, alors je _____ des cours de littérature française.
2. Nous _____ des cours d'histoire américaine parce que nous _____ aux États-Unis.
3. Les jeunes _____ des cours très difficiles s'ils _____ au Japon.
4. On _____ un cours de littérature portugaise si on _____ au Brésil.
5. Vous _____ en Italie, alors vous _____ un cours sur les poètes italiens.
6. Masha _____ en Russie, alors elle _____ un cours sur les arts dramatiques russes.

B. Deux histoires de la Résistance. Mettez les verbes suivants au passé composé ou à l'imparfait pour compléter les deux histoires.

Pendant la guerre, les résistants ______[1] (survivre) parce qu'ils ______[2] (vivre) en communauté. Jean Moulin, un célèbre résistant, ______[3] (vivre) entre 1899 et 1943. Il ______[4] (suivre) Charles de Gaulle en Angleterre en 1941. Quand il est retourné en France, les nazis le/l'______[5] (poursuivre). En 1943, la Gestapo ______[6] (suivre) un autre résistant à une réunion avec Jean Moulin. Ils ont arrêté Jean Moulin qui (*who*) ______[7] (survivre) à deux mois de torture sans rien révéler. Mais il est mort au cours de (*during*) son transfert en Allemagne.

Yves Salaun avait 16 ans en 1942. Il ______[8] (poursuivre) des études au lycée de St-Brieuc pendant l'Occupation. Tristes de voir leur pays occupé, deux de ses camarades et lui ______[9] (suivre) les résistants plus âgés. Ils ______[10] (vivre) ensemble pendant deux ans. Malheureusement, ils ______[11] (ne pas survivre) longtemps. Les nazis les ______[12] (poursuivre) et les ont attrapés. Ils ont été fusillés (*shot*) en 1944.

Que pensez-vous de ces deux histoires vraies?

C. La vie des gens. Utilisez des éléments de chaque colonne pour faire des phrases logiques. Conjuguez les verbes aux temps convenables (*appropriate*).

A	B	C
je	(ne... pas) habiter	dans la ville de ______
mes parents	(ne... pas) vivre	au XVIIe siècle (*century*)
Louis XIV		à Versailles
mon ami(e)		bien
mes grands-parents		encore
les étudiants		dans un appartement (dans une maison, à la cité universitaire [*dormitory*])

D. La moyenne. (*The average.*) Utilisez les éléments suivants pour poser des questions à quatre camarades de classe. Faites attention aux temps des verbes. Notez les noms et les réponses sur une feuille de papier et calculez les moyennes.

MODÈLE: depuis combien de temps / vivre / dans cette ville →
VOUS: Depuis combien de temps vis-tu dans cette ville?
PAUL: Depuis un an.
ANN: Depuis un an.
MARCOS: Depuis six mois.
ASTRID: Depuis un an et demi.
VOUS: La moyenne est un an.

1. depuis quand / vivre / ici **2.** combien de cours / suivre / maintenant **3.** pendant combien de temps / suivre / des cours au lycée **4.** combien de personnes / habiter / chez vous quand vous aviez 12 ans **5.** combien de personnes dans cette classe / suivre / un autre cours avec vous **6.** depuis combien de temps / vivre / dans ce pays

Visionnement 2

La ville de Paris

As you followed the lives of the characters through the first fifteen episodes of *Le Chemin du retour*, you examined six areas of Paris in some detail. Each of these is indicated by a chapter designation in a box on the map. As you can see, most of the action of the film has taken place near the center of Paris. Because the scene is about to shift to other parts of France, this is a good time to consolidate your knowledge about Paris.

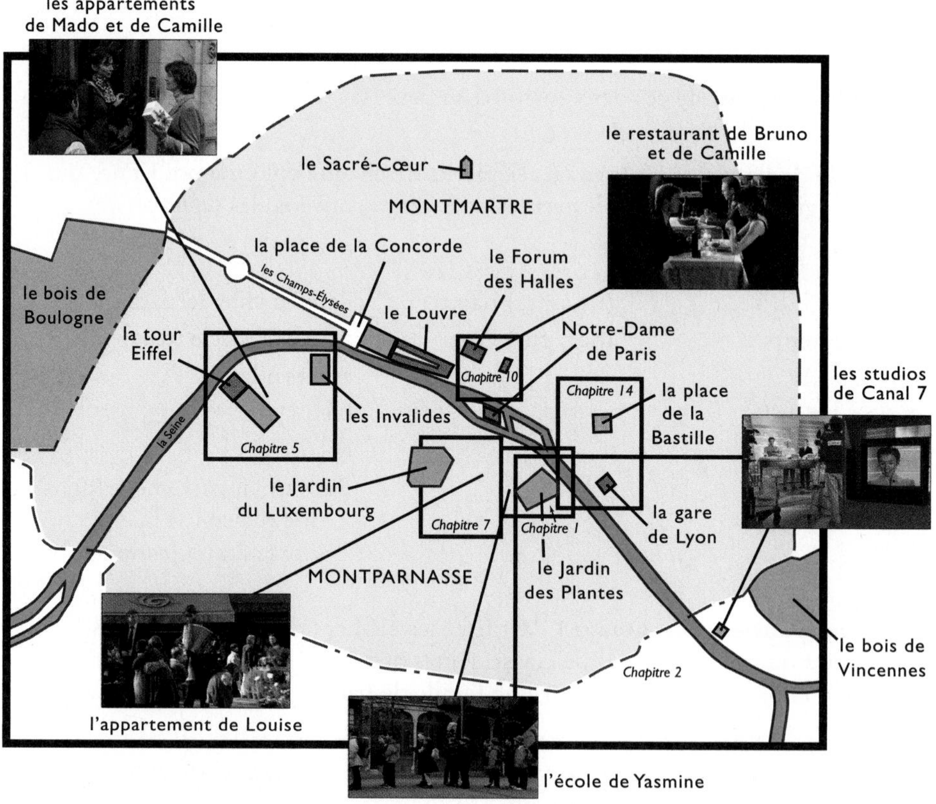

Vous souvenez-vous? Composez des phrases pour situer les endroits de la liste A par rapport (*with respect to*) aux endroits de la liste B.

Vocabulaire utile: près de, loin de, au nord de, au sud de, à l'est de, à l'ouest de

MODÈLES: Le Jardin des Plantes est près de l'école de Yasmine.
La place de la Concorde est loin des studios de Canal 7.
Montmartre est au nord du restaurant de Bruno et de Camille.

A	B
la Seine	l'appartement de Louise
la tour Eiffel	l'appartement de Mado
le Louvre	l'école de Yasmine
Montmartre	les studios de Canal 7
Notre-Dame de Paris	le restaurant de Bruno et de Camille
les Champs-Élysées	
Montparnasse	
la place de la Concorde	
le Jardin des Plantes	
la gare de Lyon	

Observez!

Considérez les aspects culturels expliqués dans **Regards sur la culture**. Ensuite, regardez l'Épisode 15 encore une fois, et répondez aux questions suivantes.

- Comment le couscous est-il présenté? Qu'est-ce qu'il y a dans un grand bol et qu'est-ce qu'il y a dans plusieurs petits bols?
- Quelle sorte de musique Rachid met-il à la radio? Pourquoi, à votre avis?

Après le visionnement

Faites l'activité pour le **Visionnement 2** dans le cahier.

Synthèse: Culture

Immigration et nationalité

Dans le film, Rachid et Sonia sont certainement de nationalité française, parce qu'ils sont nés à Marseille. Le père de Rachid et les parents de Sonia n'ont peut-être jamais pris la nationalité française, mais ils ont tous les avantages sociaux des Français.

Étrangers[1] en France

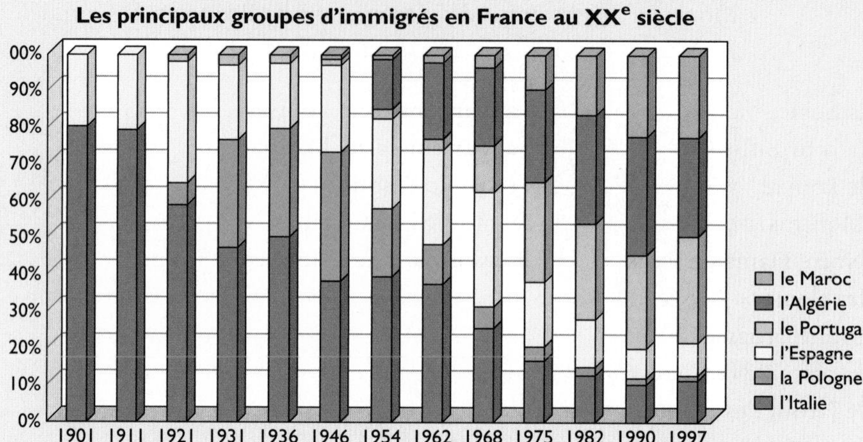

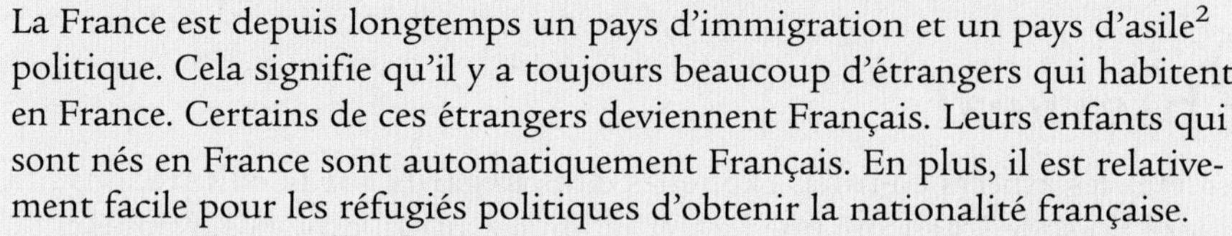

La France est depuis longtemps un pays d'immigration et un pays d'asile[2] politique. Cela signifie qu'il y a toujours beaucoup d'étrangers qui habitent en France. Certains de ces étrangers deviennent Français. Leurs enfants qui sont nés en France sont automatiquement Français. En plus, il est relativement facile pour les réfugiés politiques d'obtenir la nationalité française.

Dans certaines villes françaises, les étrangers qui y travaillent peuvent voter aux élections municipales. Et, depuis 1992, les citoyens[3] d'autres pays de l'Union européenne qui habitent en France peuvent voter lors des[4] élections municipales françaises.

La majorité des Français sont contents que la France reste un pays d'asile. Mais certains Français trouvent qu'il est trop facile d'obtenir la nationalité française. Ils pensent qu'on ne doit pas la donner aux enfants de personnes qui ne sont en France que pour le travail. Le Front national, un parti politique de droite,[5] pense qu'il faut renvoyer ces familles[6] dans leurs pays d'origine. Ces opinions s'intensifient en période de difficultés économiques. Mais le Front national ne représente qu'une petite minorité de la population. Les autres partis politiques veulent maintenir les droits[7] des immigrés.

Paris, 1999

[1]*Foreigners* [2]*asylum* [3]*citizens* [4]*lors… at the time of the* [5]*right (conservative)* [6]*il… these families should be forced to return (to their native country)* [7]*rights*

À vous

L'immigration. Choose one year from the graph. Imagine you are hiring a social worker in a French city in that year to deal with the foreign-born population. List the kinds of expertise you want in that person and the kinds of problems that person will have to help immigrants handle.

À écrire

Faites **À écrire** pour le Chapitre 15 dans le cahier.

Vocabulaire

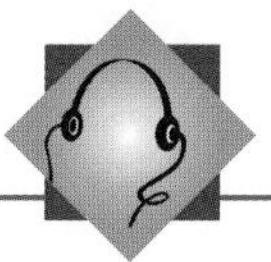

Aliments

l'ail (*m.*) garlic
une aubergine eggplant
une betterave beet
une cacahouète peanut
la cannelle cinnamon
un champignon mushroom
la citronnelle lemon grass
la coriandre coriander
une courge squash
une courgette zucchini
une épice spice
le gingembre ginger
l'huile (*f.*) **(d'olive, de sésame)** (olive, sesame) oil
un navet turnip
une noix de coco coconut
des pâtes (*f. pl.*) pasta
le persil parsley
des pois (*m.*) **chiches** chick-peas
le/la quatre-épices *blend of spices for soups, etc.*
des raisins (*m.*) **secs** raisins
le yaourt yogurt

MOTS APPARENTÉS: **la cardamome, le couscous, le curry, les grains** (*m.*) **de couscous, des lentilles** (*f.*), **le pain pita, la sauce de soja**

À REVOIR: **une carotte, des haricots** (*m.*) **verts, un oignon (vert), une pomme de terre, une tomate**

Pour faire la cuisine

une casserole saucepan
une recette recipe
chauffer to heat
faire bouillir to boil
faire cuire (à la vapeur, au four) to cook (to steam, to bake)
faire frire to fry
mélanger to mix
réchauffer to reheat
verser to pour

Pays et nationalités

l'Inde (*f.*) India
le Maghreb the Maghreb (Morocco, Algeria, Tunisia)
maghrébin(e) from the Maghreb
russe Russian

MOTS APPARENTÉS: **indien(ne), israélien(ne), l'Italie** (*f.*), **italien(ne), le Pakistan, pakistanais(e), la Russie, thaïlandais(e)**

À REVOIR: **la Chine, chinois(e), le Viêtnam, vietnamien(ne)**

Verbes

ajouter to add
couvrir to cover
découvrir to discover
fermer to close
offrir to offer; to give (*a gift*)
ouvrir to open
poursuivre to pursue
souffrir to suffer
suivre to follow
suivre un cours to take a class
survivre to survive
vivre to live, to be alive

À REVOIR: **aller, avoir besoin/envie/honte/peur (de), être content(e) (de), habiter, jouer à, jouer de, obéir à, parler de, penser à, penser de, réfléchir à, répondre à**

Pronoms

en some; any; of/from it/them/there
y there; it/them

Chapitre 16

Le départ

Le Chemin du retour

Feuille de service du 17 octobre
7e jour de tournage
Horaires: 9h–19h

LIEU DE TOURNAGE: PARIS—GARE DE LYON

Séquence	*Effets*	*Décors*	*Résumé*	*Rôles*
97	EXT.—JOUR	PARIS—GARE DE LYON	Bruno accompagne Camille à la gare de Lyon. Camille part dans les Cévennes.	CAMILLE, BRUNO

OBJECTIFS

In this episode, you will

- find out what Camille does about Rachid's discovery in Saint-Jean de Causse

In this chapter, you will

- talk about leisure activities in the Cévennes
- talk about vacation activities in Brittany
- compare and contrast actions and things
- ask questions using interrogative pronouns
- learn about the French concept of friendship
- read maxims about friendship and love written by famous French writers

Vocabulaire en contexte

Les loisirs° dans les Cévennes

Les... *Leisure activities*

Les **loisirs** (*m. pl.*) dans les Cévennes sont nombreux, **surtout**° les activités **en plein air**.°

especially / en... *outdoors*

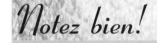

°*summertime*

Autres expressions utiles

un camping	campground
un casque	helmet
des patins (*m.*)	ice skates
une piste	trail; track; ski run
des vacances (*f. pl.*)	vacation
jouer au hockey	to play hockey
patiner, faire du patin à glace	to ice skate
prendre une photo	to take a photograph

*VTT = vélo tout terrain (*mountain bike*).

Notez bien!

Voilà quelques noms **d'animaux** (*m.*).

un cerf	deer, stag
un chat	cat
un cheval	horse
un chien	dog
un lapin	rabbit
un oiseau	bird
un ours	bear
un poisson	fish
une souris	mouse

Le terme **une souris** est aussi utilisé pour l'ordinateur.

Activités

A. Qu'est-qu'on fait? Indiquez quel(s) sport(s) ou quelle(s) activité(s) on associe avec les termes suivants.

MODÈLE: des patins → faire du patin à glace (patiner)

1. un cheval
2. des skis
3. des chaussures de marche
4. un beau lac
5. un ours
6. un sac à dos
7. une corde
8. un snowboard (une planche à neige)
9. un casque
10. un oiseau

B. Pour les amateurs de sport. Quelles activités peut-on faire aux endroits suivants? Faites des phrases complètes.

MODÈLE: en montagne →
On peut faire du vélo en montagne. (On peut faire du surf des neiges en montagne.)

1. sur une piste **2.** en l'air **3.** dans une forêt **4.** sur une pente (*slope*)

Pour en savoir plus...

Les salariés français ont un minimum de cinq semaines de congés (*time off*) payés. Certaines entreprises sont fermées pendant tout le mois d'août pour permettre à tout le monde de partir en vacances, car (*since*) pour la plupart des (*most*) Français, rester chez soi pour se reposer, ce n'est pas vraiment des vacances.

La fermeture annuelle

Les gloires° de la Bretagne

Les... *Glories*

Les gens qui vont **en vacances** en Bretagne peuvent y faire des activités bien variées.

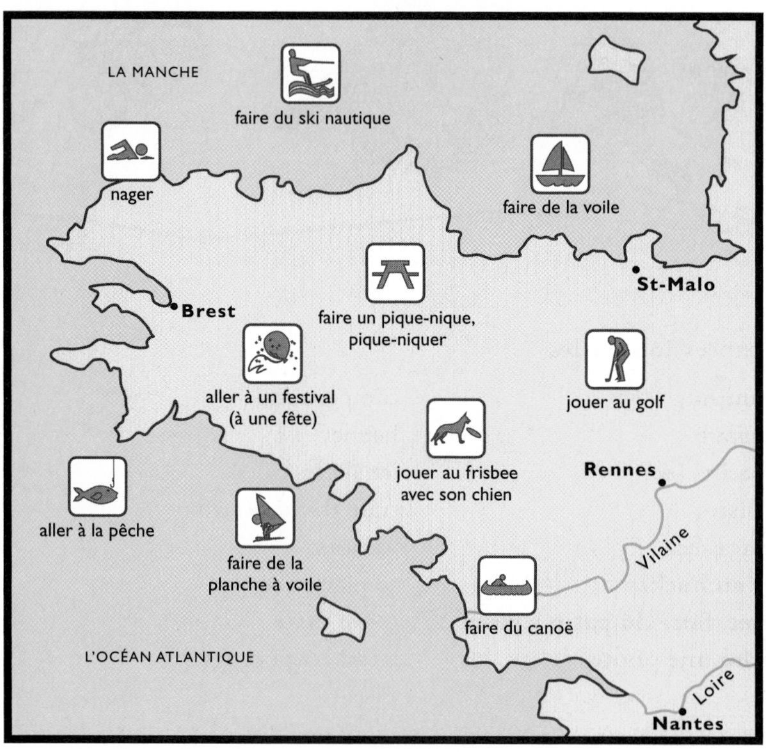

Autres mots utiles

une balle	ball (*not inflated with air*)
un ballon	ball (*inflated with air*)
un bateau (à voile)	(sail)boat
une équipe	team
un panier	basket
une plage	beach
jouer à la pétanque (aux boules)	to play lawn bowling

Activités

A. Soyez bien équipé(e)! Identifiez une activité qui correspond à l'équipement ou aux endroits suivants.

MODÈLES: un court de tennis → On joue au tennis sur un court de tennis.
une balle → On joue au golf avec une balle.

1. des boules **2.** un terrain de golf **3.** un ballon **4.** un bateau **5.** des patins **6.** une planche à voile **7.** une nappe et un panier de provisions

B. Les préférences sportives. Identifiez quelques activités que vous aimez faire dans les situations ou aux endroits indiqués.

MODÈLE: comme sport d'hiver →
Comme sport d'hiver, je préfère faire du ski de fond et du patin à glace.

1. à la plage **2.** au centre sportif **3.** dans un pays où il fait très froid **4.** à la mer (*sea*) **5.** sur un lac (*lake*) **6.** à la piscine **7.** en équipe **8.** seul(e) **9.** avec des amis

C. Interview. Demandez à votre partenaire...

1. s'il / si elle est plutôt sportif/ive ou sédentaire.
2. quels sports il/elle aime pratiquer.
3. combien de fois par semaine il/elle fait du sport.
4. quelle est la meilleure (*best*) équipe de l'université, selon lui/elle.
5. quels sports sont populaires dans sa région d'origine.

D. Racontez. Avec votre partenaire, parlez des vacances que vous avez passées en plein air (ou imaginez vos vacances idéales en plein air).

1. Où êtes-vous allé(e)?
2. Comment est-ce que vous avez voyagé?
3. Combien de temps votre voyage a-t-il duré?
4. Combien de temps avez-vous passé dans cette région?
5. Qu'est-ce que vous faisiez pendant la journée? la soirée?
6. Est-ce que vous vous êtes bien amusé(e)?
7. Dans quel état d'esprit (*frame of mind*) étiez-vous en partant?

Pour en savoir plus...

L'histoire de la Bretagne a commencé 6.000 ans avant l'ère chrétienne, mais ce n'est qu'après le départ des Romains au Ve siècle (*century*) que de nombreux Celtes de Grande-Bretagne ont immigré en Bretagne. La Bretagne est restée un état indépendant jusqu'en 1532. Un million de personnes parlent encore aujourd'hui l'ancienne langue bretonne.

La côte bretonne

Visionnement 1

Avant de visionner

Une discussion. Voici des lignes tirées de l'Épisode 16. C'est une conversation entre Camille et Martine, la productrice de «Bonjour!». Considérez l'histoire jusqu'ici et essayez de déterminer si c'est Camille ou la productrice qui parle.

1. Je pars en vacances aujourd'hui! **2.** Tu es folle? Tu penses à l'émission? **3.** Mais remplace-moi [...]! J'ai besoin de partir! **4.** Inutile (*It's pointless* [*to insist*]). J'ai pris ma décision... **5.** Tu es une professionnelle! Tu dois respecter ton contrat! **6.** Je suis mal en ce moment et j'ai besoin de repos (*rest*), tu peux comprendre ça? **7.** Incroyable (*Unbelievable*)! Cette fille a perdu la tête (*has lost her mind*).

Vocabulaire relatif à l'épisode

deux semaines de congé	*two weeks of vacation*
C'est si grave que ça?	*Is it as serious as that?*
le plus vite possible	*as soon as possible*
je tiens à toi	*I care about you*
elle a des soucis	*she has worries*
le moindre problème	*the slightest problem*

Observez!

Camille et la productrice se disputent dans l'Épisode 16. Essayez de répondre aux questions suivantes pendant votre visionnement de l'épisode.

- Qu'est-ce que Camille veut faire absolument?
- Quelle solution trouvent-elles pour régler (*resolve*) leur problème?

Après le visionnement

A. Une vive discussion. (*An intense discussion.*) Martine n'est pas contente de la décision de Camille de partir en vacances. Voici quelques-unes de ses objections. Comment est-ce que Camille y répond? Choisissez parmi les possibilités données.

1. MARTINE: Tu ne peux pas partir! C'est impossible...
CAMILLE: Pourquoi?
MARTINE: Tu es la vedette° de l'émission!
CAMILLE: a. Tu plaisantes!
b. Elle a des soucis!
c. Personne n'est irremplaçable.

°*star*

2. MARTINE: Camille, tu as des responsabilités.
CAMILLE: a. C'est le plus mauvais jour de ma vie.
b. Inutile. J'ai pris ma décision.
c. Tu es le meilleur.

3. MARTINE: Tu as signé un contrat avec moi! Tu es une professionnelle! Tu dois respecter ton contrat!
CAMILLE: a. Pourquoi?
b. Vraiment? C'est si grave que ça?
c. Peut-être, mais il est essentiel de vivre, aussi!

B. Les subtilités de l'amour. Quelle sorte de relation existe entre Camille et Bruno, selon vous? Est-ce un rapport d'amitié ou d'amour ou est-ce un mélange des deux? Considérez les scènes suivantes avant de répondre.

Structure 48

Le comparatif

Comparing and contrasting

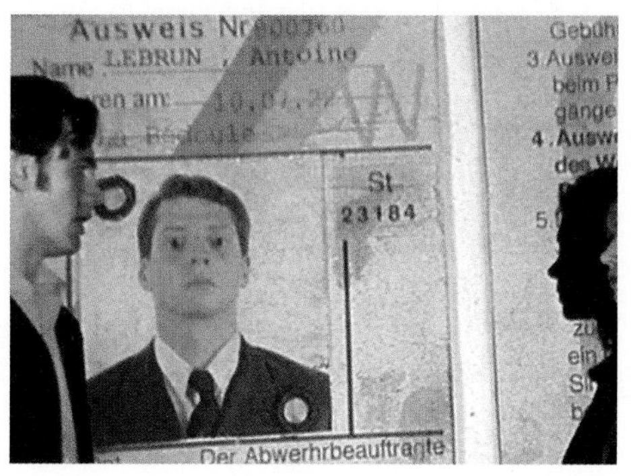

—*Ce document était un laissez-passer spécial. Avec ça, on pouvait voyager partout en France.* ***Aussi bien*** *dans la zone occupée par les Allemands* ***que*** *dans la zone libre.*

Comparisons in French are created using the comparison words **plus** (*more*) and **moins** (*less; fewer*). The words **aussi** (*as*) and **autant** (*as much; as many*) are used to express equality.

Comparatif des adjectifs and des adverbes

1. To use adjectives and adverbs in comparisons, use the following constructions.

plus **aussi** **moins**	+	adjective adverb	(+ **que**)

Notez bien!

Stressed pronouns: **les pronoms accentués**

je →	**moi**
tu →	**toi**
il →	**lui**
elle →	**elle**
on →	**soi**
nous →	**nous**
vous →	**vous**
ils →	**eux**
elles →	**elles**

Rachid est moins égocentrique que **lui** (Bruno). *Rachid is less egocentric than he* (*Bruno*) *is.*

In addition to their use in comparisons, stressed pronouns can be used after **c'est**, after prepositions, and to add emphasis.

C'est bien **lui**! *It's him!*

Tu vas travailler avec **eux**. *You'll be working with them.*

Eh ben, **moi**, je ne trouve pas ça amusant du tout! *Well, I don't find it funny at all!*

Vous êtes forts, Bruno et **vous**. *You're a strong team, you and Bruno.*

A phrase beginning with **que** is included if you need to clarify who or what is being compared. In place of the name of a person, a stressed pronoun can be used after **que**.

Mado pense que Camille agit **plus impulsivement qu'**elle.	*Mado thinks that Camille acts more impulsively than she does.*
Le bureau de Rachid est **aussi grand que** le bureau de Bruno.	*Rachid's desk is as big as Bruno's desk.*
Yasmine est **moins grande que** ses camarades de classe.	*Yasmine is not as tall as her classmates.*

2. **Bon** and **bien** have irregular comparatives: **meilleur(e)** (adjective) and **mieux** (adverb).

Camille dit que Bruno est un **meilleur** journaliste qu'elle.	*Camille says Bruno is a better journalist than she is.*
Ça va **mieux** aujourd'hui?	*Is it going better today?*

Comparatif des quantités

1. To compare quantities of nouns, use the following constructions.

plus de **autant de** **moins de**	+	noun	(+ **que**)

Camille a **autant d'**énergie que Bruno.	*Camille has as much energy as Bruno.*
Bruno a **moins de** patience que Martine.	*Bruno has less patience than Martine.*

2. To compare frequency of activity, use **plus**, **autant**, or **moins** after a verb.

Yasmine danse **plus** que ses parents.	*Yasmine dances more than her parents.*
Camille voyage **autant** qu'Hélène.	*Camille travels as much as Hélène.*

Activités

A. Comment les imaginez-vous? Comparez les personnages et les endroits du film en utilisant **plus**, **moins**, **aussi** ou **autant** et les éléments donnés. Faites tous les changements nécessaires.

MODÈLE: le boulanger / avoir un grand rôle / Bruno →
Le boulanger a un moins grand rôle que Bruno.

1. Martine / être malheureux / Camille
2. Camille / être joli / Martine
3. Bruno / être égoïste / Yasmine
4. Rachid / être un bon journaliste / Sonia
5. Saint-Jean de Causse / être important pour l'histoire d'Antoine / Paris

6. on / aller souvent à la pêche à Paris / dans les Cévennes
7. on / aller difficilement de Paris à Alès en autocar / en train
8. Camille / penser sérieusement à «Bonjour!» / Martine

B. Qu'est-ce qu'ils ont? Imaginez la vie des personnages du film et comparez les éléments suivants.

1. Hélène a _____ amies canadiennes _____ Camille.
2. Louise avait _____ souvenirs d'Antoine _____ Mado.
3. Sonia a _____ énergie _____ Hélène.
4. Rachid a _____ expérience professionnelle _____ Camille.
5. Camille a _____ responsabilités _____ Bruno pendant l'émission.
6. Rachid a _____ expérience _____ Bruno.
7. Quand Camille part, Martine a _____ soucis _____ Nicole, la scripte.
8. Rachid a _____ problèmes de famille _____ Camille.

C. Comparaisons. Répondez aux questions de votre camarade pour comparer la fréquence des activités des personnes suivantes. Pensez à combien de fois par mois chacune (*each one*) fait certaines choses. Employez **plus, autant** ou **moins** et des pronoms accentués.

MODÈLES: travailler plus / vous ou deux membres de votre famille →
É1: Qui travaille plus, toi ou ta mère et ton père?
É2: Moi ou eux? Euh... je travaille autant qu'eux.

1. chanter (*sing*) moins / deux membres de votre famille
2. danser plus / vous ou votre meilleur(e) ami(e)
3. sortir moins le soir / vous ou votre partenaire
4. aller plus au cinéma / deux de vos ami(e)s
5. manger plus au restaurant / vous ou votre partenaire et un(e) de ses ami(e)s
6. voyager moins / vous ou le président des États-Unis

D. Généralisations. Avec un(e) partenaire, comparez les personnes et les choses suivantes.

MODÈLE: les grandes villes / les petits villages (activités, cher, ?) →
É1: Les grandes villes ont plus d'activités pour les jeunes que les petits villages.
É2: D'accord. Mais les petits villages sont plus avantageux parce qu'on y trouve des maisons moins chères que dans les grandes villes. (*ou* Peut-être. Mais les petits villages ont autant d'avantages que les grandes villes, pour des raisons différentes.)

1. les étudiants / les professeurs (livres, danser, ?)
2. les films français / les films américains (violence, difficile à comprendre, ?)
3. les voitures d'aujourd'hui / les voitures des années 70 (rouler vite, bon, ?)
4. les skieurs / les joueurs de tennis (sportif, porter des vêtements chauds, ?)
5. les grands supermarchés / les petits magasins (les produits, ouvrir tôt, ?)
6. les hommes / les femmes (parler, bon, ?)

Maintenant, faites part de (*share*) vos opinions à la classe et discutez-en avec vos camarades qui ne sont pas d'accord avec vous.

Structure 49

Le superlatif

Comparing and contrasting

—Super! C'est **le plus mauvais** jour de ma vie!

Superlatives, like comparisons, use **plus** and **moins**, **meilleur** and **mieux**, but the definite article (**le**, **la**, **les**) is added.

Superlatif des adjectifs

1. To form the superlative of adjectives, use **le**, **la**, or **les** before the comparative.

   C'est **le plus mauvais** jour **de** ma vie. — *This is the worst day of my life.*

2. With adjectives, the superlative expression will precede or follow the noun, depending on the usual position of the adjective. If the superlative precedes the noun, the definite article appears only once, but if it follows the noun, the definite article is repeated. Note that the preposition **de** introduces the group, object, or concept to which the superlative item is being compared.

   Yasmine est **le** personnage **le moins âgé** de l'histoire. — *Yasmine is the youngest character in the story.*

   Camille est **la meilleure** amie de Bruno. — *Camille is Bruno's best friend.*

Superlatif des adverbes

Use **le plus** (*the most*) or **le moins** (*the least*) before the adverb to create a superlative. A superlative adverb follows the verb.

Rachid travaille **le plus sérieusement de** tous les reporters. — *Rachid works the most seriously of all the reporters.*

Dans sa famille, Rachid parle **le mieux** arabe. — *In his family, Rachid speaks Arabic the best.*

Superlatif des quantités

To express superlative quantities, use **le plus de** (*the most*) + noun for the largest quantity and **le moins de** (*the least/fewest*) + noun for the smallest quantity. For superlatives of verbs, put **le plus** or **le moins** after the verb.

Dans la famille, c'est Camille qui a **le plus de** responsabilités.	*In her family, Camille has the most responsibilities.*
C'est Camille qui travaille **le plus**.	*It's Camille who works the most.*

Activités

A. Réussir votre visite à Saint-Jean de Causse. Il y a plusieurs hôtels et restaurants près de Saint-Jean de Causse. Évaluez-les, puis faites deux phrases qui contiennent un superlatif. Suivez le modèle.

MODÈLE:
restaurant / grand →
Le plus grand restaurant est le Self Select. Le moins grand restaurant est Au Vieux Moulin.

1. hôtel / luxueux
2. restaurant / cher
3. logement / vieux
4. service / bon
5. hôtel / beau
6. cuisine / bon

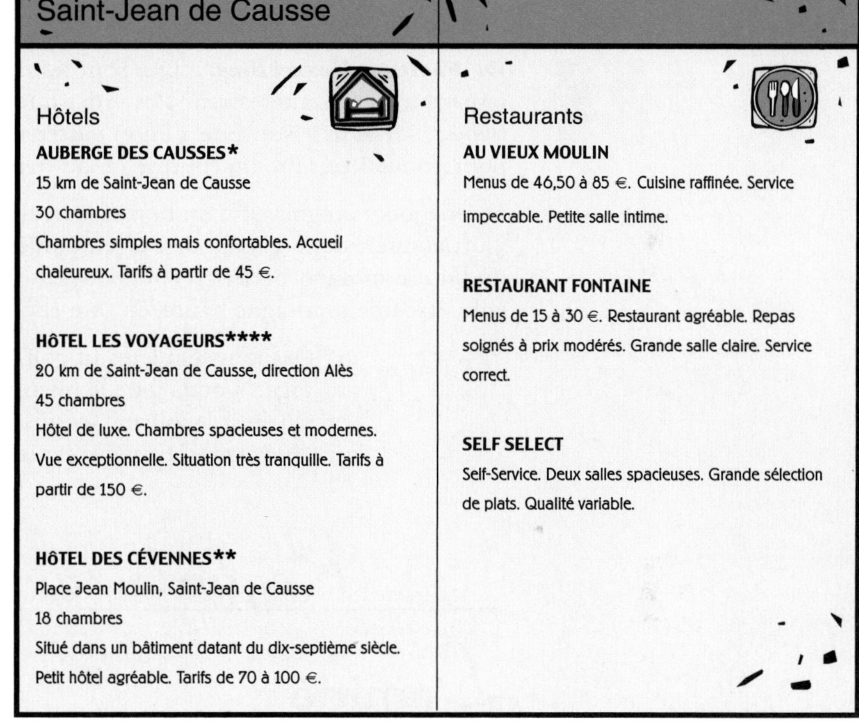
Saint-Jean de Causse

Hôtels

AUBERGE DES CAUSSES*
15 km de Saint-Jean de Causse
30 chambres
Chambres simples mais confortables. Accueil chaleureux. Tarifs à partir de 45 €.

HÔTEL LES VOYAGEURS****
20 km de Saint-Jean de Causse, direction Alès
45 chambres
Hôtel de luxe. Chambres spacieuses et modernes. Vue exceptionnelle. Situation très tranquille. Tarifs à partir de 150 €.

HÔTEL DES CÉVENNES**
Place Jean Moulin, Saint-Jean de Causse
18 chambres
Situé dans un bâtiment datant du dix-septième siècle. Petit hôtel agréable. Tarifs de 70 à 100 €.

Restaurants

AU VIEUX MOULIN
Menus de 46,50 à 85 €. Cuisine raffinée. Service impeccable. Petite salle intime.

RESTAURANT FONTAINE
Menus de 15 à 30 €. Restaurant agréable. Repas soignés à prix modérés. Grande salle claire. Service correct.

SELF SELECT
Self-Service. Deux salles spacieuses. Grande sélection de plats. Qualité variable.

B. Identifiez. Pour chacune des actions suivantes, indiquez qui, parmi (*among*) vos connaissances, représente chaque extrême. Suivez le modèle.

MODÈLE: travailler sérieusement →
Mon amie Lisa travaille le plus sérieusement. Mon frère John travaille le moins sérieusement.

1. faire régulièrement du sport
2. aller souvent en boîte
3. écouter patiemment vos problèmes
4. vous conseiller logiquement
5. s'habiller élégamment
6. parler vite
7. manger bien

C. Êtes-vous matérialiste? Posez des questions à trois membres de la classe. Ensuite, comparez les réponses. Pouvez-vous déterminer qui est l'étudiant le plus matérialiste de la classe?

MODÈLE: voitures →
VOUS: Combien de voitures avez-vous?
JOHN: J'en ai deux.
LISA: J'en ai deux aussi.
SETH: Moi, je n'en ai pas.
VOUS: John a autant de voitures que Lisa, mais Seth a le moins de voitures. Il n'a pas de voiture.

1. ordinateurs
2. CD
3. paires de chaussures
4. montres
5. appareils photo
6. téléphones portables

D. Parlons d'extrêmes. Qui sont les meilleurs acteurs du monde? Quel est le journal le moins intéressant? Posez des questions de ce genre sur cinq sujets (*subjects*) de la liste suivante à un(e) partenaire. Prenez des notes sur ses réponses pour pouvoir en faire un compte rendu (*report*).

Sujets: jouer au golf, être un bon acteur, être une ville agréable à vivre, être un journal intéressant, gagner de l'argent, jouer au football américain, chanter, être un bon restaurant, parler en cours de français, être une personne connue de votre ville, être une montagne haute, être un sport bien payé, être une bonne profession

MODÈLE: É1: Qui joue le mieux au golf?
É2: Tiger Woods joue le mieux au golf.
É2: Quel est le journal le moins intéressant?
É1: *The National Enquirer* est le journal le moins intéressant.

Regards sur la culture

L'amitié°

°Friendship

Meilleurs amis

In Episode 16, Bruno reminds Camille that she can always count on him, that he is ready to join her immediately in the Cévennes if she should encounter any problem at all. Camille recognizes that Bruno is her best friend.

- French people generally have only a few friends, because friendship to them is a deep relationship and one that makes serious demands on one's time and attention. They check up on a friend nearly every day, and they expect to go out of their way frequently to do good turns for a friend. In short, a friend in France would expect you to participate fairly intensely in his or her life.
- Friends are not expected to agree on everything. The pleasures of debate and argument are a normal part of friendship.
- Married people in France, both men and women, may maintain friendships that they do not share with their spouses.

- Neighbors in France, whether in single-family homes or in apartments, do not expect to be friends. Proximity does not inspire friendship; shared interests and personal trust do.
- In France, people do not usually invite acquaintances to their homes. They might go out to dinner with people they know casually, but only good friends are invited into the closed domain of the home. Many North Americans who live in France are frustrated at not being invited home by the people they know. In the South, however, people tend to meet with friends in less planned, more spontaneous ways than in the North.
- Even good friends would normally not consider that they have the right to go beyond a few areas of a friend's home. They would probably not go into the kitchen, for example, and might not ever see the bedrooms. French people are shocked at the freedom that visitors seem to have in North American homes. The idea of serving oneself something from the refrigerator is anathema to the French!
- Most French people who visit North America are thrilled to find that they make many friends so quickly. They comment favorably on the openness and kindness of Americans and Canadians. However, those who stay for more than a couple of weeks are often bitterly disappointed when they find out that what seemed like "friendships" to them in fact have none of the depth and intensity that they expect of such a relationship in France.

Considérez

What is your reaction to the French notion of friendship? Would you prefer to have just a few very intense friendships, or maintain a larger number of less committed relationships? Why? What are the advantages and disadvantages of each custom?

Structure 50

Les pronoms interrogatifs (*suite*)

Asking questions

—**Qu'est-ce qui** s'est passé dans les Cévennes?

In Chapter 6, you learned to recognize the forms and meanings of most interrogative pronouns.

Qui est parti dans les Cévennes?
À quoi s'intéresse-t-elle?
Qu'est-ce qu'elle cherche?
Avec qui veut-elle parler?
Que fait-elle pour trouver cette personne?
De quoi est-ce qu'elle a besoin?

Here is a complete chart of the interrogative pronouns. You already saw most of them in Chapter 6. The two new ones are the subject forms **qui est-ce qui** and **qu'est-ce qui**.

	PERSONNES	CHOSES
sujet	**qui**	—
	qui est-ce qui	**qu'est-ce qui**
objet	**qui**	**que**
objet d'une préposition	préposition + **qui**	préposition + **quoi**

Qui est-ce qui a parlé à Rachid? — *Who spoke to Rachid?*
Qu'est-ce qui inquiète Camille? — *What is worrying Camille?*

Remember—As objects, **qui**, **que**, and **quoi** can be followed by verb + subject (inversion) or by **est-ce que** + subject + verb.

De quoi Camille a-t-elle besoin?
De quoi est-ce que Camille a besoin?
} *What does Camille need?*

Activités

A. Rester chez moi? Jamais! On fait l'interview d'une vieille dame sportive. Indiquez à quelle question correspond chacune des réponses.

MODÈLE: Qu'est-ce que vous aimez faire le week-end? →
J'aime faire des randonnées.

1. Qu'est-ce que vous aimez faire le week-end?
2. De quoi avez vous besoin pour vos randonnées?
3. Qui est-ce que vous rencontrez (*meet*) pendant vos randonnées?
4. Qu'est-ce qui se passe (*happens*) quand vous vous rencontrez?
5. Qu'est-ce qu'ils vous demandent?
6. Que pensez-vous de leur question?
7. Qu'est-ce qui vous empêche (*prevents*) d'aller en randonnée?
8. À qui est-ce que vous dites où vous allez?

a. Je le dis à mon petit-fils. Sinon (*Otherwise*), il s'inquiète.
b. Je rencontre des jeunes (*young people*).
c. J'ai besoin de mes chaussures de marche.
d. Ils veulent savoir mon âge.
e. Nous nous parlons.
f. Je ne pars pas quand il fait trop froid.
g. J'aime faire des randonnées.
h. Je la trouve normale. J'ai 86 ans!

Maintenant, identifiez l'expression interrogative dans chaque question et la partie de la réponse qui y correspond.

B. Un voyage important. Imaginez une conversation entre Mado et Camille. Camille explique (*explains*) son voyage dans les Cévennes. Complétez chaque question avec la forme interrogative (**qui**, **qui est-ce qui**, **qu'est-ce qui**, **que**, **quoi**) qui correspond à la réponse. Utilisez une préposition si c'est nécessaire.

MODÈLE: MADO: Qu'est-ce qui t'a donné l'idée de partir?
CAMILLE: La lettre d'Antoine m'a donné l'idée de partir.

1. MADO: ____ t'a donné l'adresse de Mme Leblanc? Qui est-ce qui
   CAMILLE: Rachid m'a donné son adresse.
2. MADO: ____ a-t-il parlé quand il était à Saint-Jean? Avec qui
   CAMILLE: Il a parlé avec le petit-fils de Mme Leblanc.
3. MADO: ____ est-ce que tu penses quand tu penses au voyage? ~~Qu'est-ce que~~ À quoi
   CAMILLE: Je pense à ce village où mon grand-père a disparu.
4. MADO: ____ est-ce que tu penses de moi, avec cette histoire de photos découpées (*cut*)? Qu'est-ce que
   CAMILLE: Je pense que tu étais une petite fille malheureuse.
5. MADO: Que vas-tu faire en arrivant à Saint-Jean?
   CAMILLE: Je vais visiter le village.
6. MADO: Qui est-ce que tu vas voir après?
   CAMILLE: Je vais voir le petit-fils de Mme Leblanc.
7. MADO: Qui t'accompagne à la gare de Lyon?
   CAMILLE: Bruno m'accompagne à la gare.
8. CAMILLE: ____ t'inquiète, maman?
   MADO: J'ai peur d'apprendre que mon père était un traître.
9. MADO: ____ est-ce que tu as besoin pour le voyage?
   CAMILLE: J'ai simplement besoin de ton amour (*love*).

C. Les étudiants et les vacances. Imaginez que vous travaillez pour une agence de voyages qui se spécialise en vacances pour les étudiants. Posez cinq questions à deux étudiant(e)s. Ils/Elles doivent vous répondre en donnant leurs propres opinions.

MODÈLE: É1: Qu'est-ce qui intéresse les étudiants?
É2: Les sports en plein air intéressent les étudiants.

	aimer faire
À/Avec/De qui	avoir peur
À/Avec/De quoi	devoir penser avant le voyage
Qu'est-ce qui	inquiéter les parents
Qu'est-ce que	intéresser les étudiants
Qui est-ce qui	vouloir voyager
	?

Visionnement 2

Observez!

Considérez les aspects culturels expliqués dans **Regards sur la culture**. Ensuite, regardez l'Épisode 16 encore une fois, et répondez aux questions suivantes.

- Pourquoi Martine laisse-t-elle partir Camille? Est-ce une décision basée sur des critères professionnels ou sur une amitié personnelle?
- Comment Bruno montre-t-il son amitié pour Camille?

Après le visionnement

Faites l'activité pour le **Visionnement 2** dans le cahier.

Synthèse: Lecture

Mise en contexte

In the **Regards sur la culture** section of this chapter, you learned a few things about the French notion of friendship. This **Synthèse** section contains a few maxims—short, pithy observations about people and society—formulated by some well-known French writers over the centuries.* Although some were written over three hundred years ago, many people feel that they are still relevant today.

Stratégie pour mieux lire
Paraphrasing

Good maxims are finely crafted and concise. Still, restating the idea in a different language, or paraphrasing, may enable you to understand the nuances of their observations. For example, which paraphrase best explains this maxim?

> «Nous aimons toujours ceux qui (*those who*) nous admirent, et nous n'aimons pas toujours ceux que (*those whom*) nous admirons.»
>
> La Rochefoucauld (1613–1680)

*The French writers quoted are novelists (Balzac, Colette), playwrights (Molière, d'Harleville), and other men and women of letters (Chamfort, La Rochefoucauld, Mme de Staël).

a. We often mistake self-interest for friendship.

b. We like people who look up to us and not those whom we look up to.

As you read the following **maximes** about friendship and love, formulate a paraphrase in English that you think approximately expresses the meaning of each one. Also think about which one (if any) expresses your own observations about friendship or love.

L'amitié et l'amour

«Un ami est long à trouver et prompt à perdre.»
Anonyme

«Nous pardonnons aisément[1] à nos amis les défauts[2] qui ne nous regardent[3] pas.»
La Rochefoucauld (1613–1680)

«On est aisément dupé[4] par ce qu'on aime.»
Molière (1622–1673)

«Dans le monde, vous avez trois sortes d'amis: vos amis qui vous aiment, vos amis qui ne se soucient[5] pas de vous, et vos amis qui vous haïssent.[6]»
Chamfort (1741–1794)

«Il faut[7] aimer les gens, non pour soi, mais pour eux.»
Collin d'Harleville (1755–1806)

«L'amour est un égoïsme[8] à deux.»
Mme de Staël (1766–1817)

«On n'est point[9] l'ami d'une femme lorsqu'on[10] peut être son amant.[11]»
Honoré de Balzac (1799–1850)

«Quand on est aimé, on ne doute de rien. Quand on aime, on doute de tout.»
Colette (1873–1954)

[1]*easily* [2]*faults* [3]*concern* [4]*fooled* [5]se... *care* [6]*hate* [7]Il... *One must* [8]*selfishness* [9]*absolutely not* [10]*when one* [11]*lover*

Colette

Après la lecture

A. Avez-vous compris? Les phrases suivantes sont des paraphrases des maximes. Pour chacune, notez la maxime qui convient (*fits*).

1. Pourquoi rester ami si on peut devenir amant?
2. Il est facile de pardonner les actions d'un ami si ces actions ne vous blessent (*injure, hurt*) pas.
3. Ceux qui (*Those who*) se disent votre ami ne le sont pas tous.

4. L'amitié est une chose fragile.
5. On est aveuglé (*blinded*) par l'amitié.
6. Pour être l'ami de quelqu'un, il faut abandonner l'égoïsme.
7. Il est plus facile de se sentir (*feel*) sûr de soi quand on reçoit des preuves (*proof*) d'amour que quand on en donne.
8. L'amour entre deux personnes exclut les autres.

B. Réfléchissez. Répondez aux questions suivantes.

1. Choisissez une maxime qui exprime vos propres (*own*) idées sur le thème de l'amitié ou de l'amour. S'il n'y en a pas, créez (*create*) votre propre maxime.
2. Quelle maxime trouvez-vous la moins vraie?
3. Quelle maxime réflète le mieux une caractéristique de l'amitié qui existe entre Bruno et Camille? Est-ce que leur amitié contredit une des maximes? Laquelle (*Which one*)?

À écrire

Faites **À écrire** pour le Chapitre 16 dans le cahier.

Vocabulaire

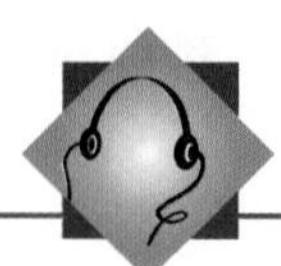

Les loisirs

aller à la pêche	to go fishing
faire de la planche à voile	to windsurf
faire de la voile	to sail
faire de l'escalade	to go rock climbing
faire du parapente	to hang glide
faire du patin à glace	to ice skate
faire du ski de fond	to cross-country ski
faire du ski nautique	to waterski
faire du surf des neiges	to snowboard
faire du vélo	to bike
faire du VTT	to mountain bike
faire une randonnée	to hike
jouer à la pétanque (aux boules)	to play lawn bowling
monter à cheval	to ride a horse
nager	to swim
patiner	to ice skate

MOTS APPARENTÉS: **faire de la photographie, faire du camping, faire du canoë, faire du ski, faire un pique-nique, jouer au golf, jouer au hockey, pique-niquer, prendre une photo, skier**

L'équipement et les lieux pour les loisirs

une balle	ball (*not inflated with air*)
un ballon	ball (*inflated with air*)
un bateau (à voile)	(sail)boat
un camping	campground
un casque	helmet
une équipe	team
des loisirs (*m. pl.*)	leisure activities
un panier	basket
des patins (*m.*)	ice skates
une piste	trail; track; ski run
une plage	beach
des vacances (*f. pl.*)	vacation

MOTS APPARENTÉS: **un festival (des festivals), un frisbee**

À REVOIR: **une fête**

Les animaux

un cerf	deer, stag
un chat	cat
un cheval	horse
un chien	dog
un lapin	rabbit
un oiseau	bird
un ours	bear
une souris	mouse; computer mouse

MOTS APPARENTÉS: **un animal (des animaux)**

À REVOIR: **un poisson**

Pronoms accentués

moi	me
toi	you
lui	him
elle	her
soi	oneself
nous	us
vous	you
eux	them (*m.*)
elles	them (*f.*)

Expressions interrogatives

qui est-ce qui	who (*subject of sentence*)
qu'est-ce qui	what (*subject of sentence*)

À REVOIR: **qui, que, quoi**

Pour faire des comparaisons

aussi... que	as . . . as
autant (de...) que	as much/many (. . . as)
meilleur(e)(s) (que)	better (than)
mieux (que)	better (than)
moins (de...)	less/fewer (. . .)
moins (que)	less/fewer (than)
plus (de...)	more (. . .)
plus (que)	more (than)
le/la/les meilleur(e)(s) (de)	the best (of)
le mieux (de)	the best (of)
le/la/les moins (de)	the least (of)
le/la/les plus (de)	the most (of)

Autres expressions utiles

en plein air	outdoors
en vacances	on vacation
surtout	especially

Chapitre 17

Je cherche la trace d'un homme.

Le Chemin du retour

Feuille de service du 17 janvier
2e jour de tournage
Horaires: 8h–17h30

LIEU DE TOURNAGE: POURRIÈRES—Rue en contrebas de° la Grand Place

en... *below*

Séquence	*Effets*	*Décors*	*Résumé*	*Rôles*
110	EXT.—JOUR	SAINT-JEAN, PLACE DU VILLAGE—Monument aux morts	Camille prend des photos du monument et découvre le nom de Pierre Leblanc.	CAMILLE

OBJECTIFS

In this episode, you will

- learn the possible consequences of Camille's "vacation" from the show
- meet a new character who helps Camille move forward in her quest

In this chapter, you will

- talk about geographical features
- ask and give directions
- talk about the future
- review the forms, uses, and placement of object pronouns
- use direct object and indirect object pronouns in the same sentence
- learn about the causes of population shifts in France and in Africa during the 20th century

Vocabulaire en contexte

Le relief° de la France

Le... *The topography*

Lexique géographique

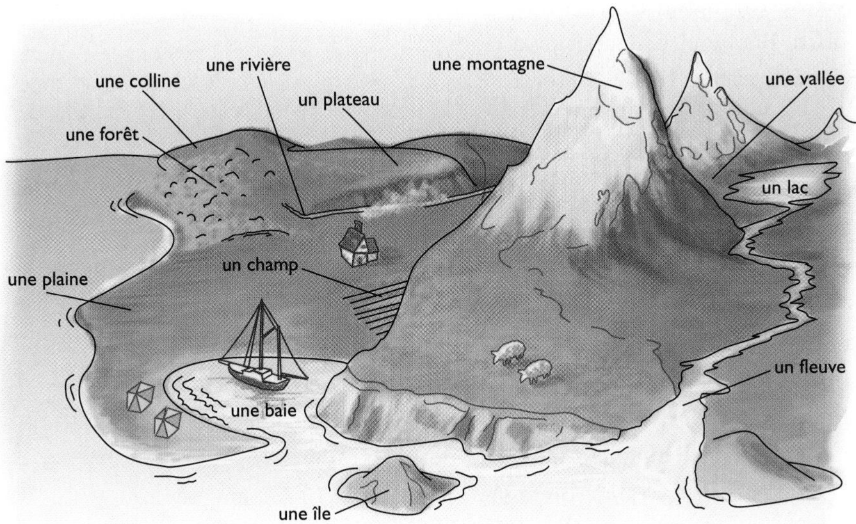

Autres expressions utiles

une côte	coast
au bord de	on the banks (shore, edge) of
à la campagne	in the country

La France a un relief varié. Au **nord** et à l'**ouest,** on trouve des **plaines,** des **collines** et des **vallées.** Au **sud** et à l'**est,** il y a des chaînes de **montagnes** très hautes. Au centre, le Massif central est fait de vieilles montagnes volcaniques.

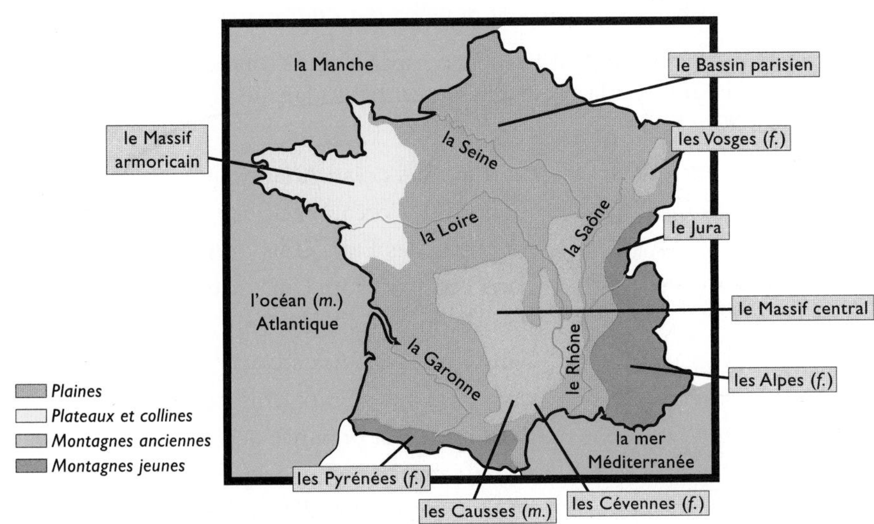

Activités

A. Le connaissez-vous? La liste suivante identifie des endroits très connus. Indiquez le terme géographique qui les décrit.

MODÈLE: Alpes, Rocheuses → Ce sont des montagnes.

1. Guam, Hawaii, Martinique, Porto Rico
2. Adriatique, Baltique, des Caraïbes, Méditerranée
3. Amazone, Mississippi, Saint-Laurent, Seine
4. Everest, Kilimandjaro, McKinley, Rainier
5. Baffin, Biscayne, Chesapeake, d'Hudson
6. Érié, Supérieur, Tahoe, Victoria

B. Repérez. Regardez la carte d'Europe au début de votre livre et situez les pays en suivant le modèle.

MODÈLE: la France / l'Allemagne / l'Espagne / la Grande-Bretagne →
La France se trouve à l'ouest de l'Allemagne, au nord de l'Espagne et au sud de la Grande-Bretagne.

1. la Suisse / la France / l'Allemagne / l'Italie
2. la Belgique / le Luxembourg / les Pays-Bas / la France
3. l'Espagne / la France / le Portugal / la mer Méditerranée
4. la Pologne / l'Allemagne / la Slovaquie / l'Ukraine
5. le Danemark / la Grande-Bretagne / la Norvège / l'Allemagne

C. Poursuite triviale géographique. Inventez des questions sur la géographie de votre pays et posez-les à votre partenaire. Vous pouvez utiliser les verbes **se trouver** et **se situer**, des adjectifs comme **grand**, **vaste** et **vieux** et les indications données. Vous pouvez aussi utiliser vos propres (*own*) idées.

MODÈLES: Quelle grande chaîne de montagnes se trouve dans l'ouest du Canada et des États-Unis? →
Les Rocheuses se trouvent dans l'ouest du Canada et des États-Unis.

Où est-ce qu'on peut être à la campagne dans l'état de New York? →
On peut être à la campagne au centre et dans le nord-est de l'état de New York.

une baie	au bord de l'océan Atlantique
des champs de blé (*wheat*)	au bord de l'océan Pacifique
des collines	au centre des États-Unis / du Canada
un fleuve / une rivière	dans l'est des États-Unis / du Canada
une forêt	dans le nord des États-Unis / du Canada
une île / des îles	dans l'ouest des États-Unis / du Canada
un lac / des lacs	dans le sud des États-Unis / du Canada
des montagnes	dans l'état / la province de...
un plateau	sur la côte est de l'Amérique du Nord
une vallée	sur la côte ouest de l'Amérique du Nord
à la campagne	?

Demander et donner le chemin°

Demander... *Asking and giving directions*

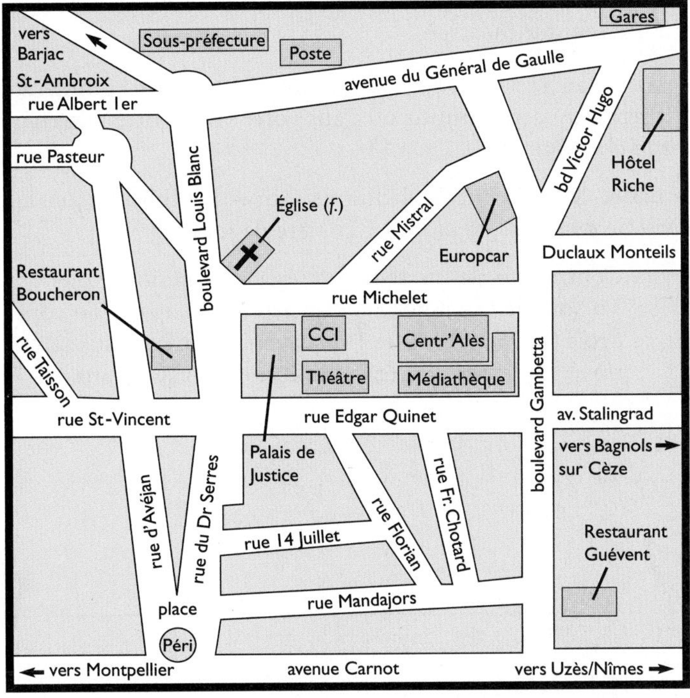

Un plan d'Alès

Camille arrive à la gare d'Alès et veut louer une voiture pour aller à Saint-Jean de Causse. Comment trouve-t-elle l'agence de location° Europcar?

agence... *rental agency*

CAMILLE: Pardon, monsieur, **est-ce que vous pourriez° m'indiquer le chemin pour aller à** une agence de location de voitures?

could

HOMME: Bien sûr, mademoiselle. **Descendez l'avenue** du Général de Gaulle, en allant **vers°** la poste. **Tournez à gauche°** à la deuxième rue, le boulevard Gambetta, et allez **tout droit.°** L'agence Europcar est au **coin°** de la rue Mistral.

toward / à... *to the left*
tout... *straight ahead*
corner

CAMILLE: Et pour aller à Saint-Jean de Causse, s'il vous plaît?

HOMME: **Remontez° l'avenue** du Général de Gaulle. Après **le** deuxième **feu,°** vous allez voir **un poteau indicateur°** pour la D904 direction Saint-Ambroix. Continuez jusqu'à la sortie pour la D906. Prenez la D906 direction Villefort.

Go back up / *traffic light*
poteau... *sign(post)*

Autres expressions utiles

à droite to/on the right **une carte** map **traverser** to cross

Activités

A. À Alès. Comment va-t-on...

1. du Palais de Justice à la poste?
2. de l'église au restaurant Guévent?

3. de la médiathèque à la place Péri?
4. du coin de l'avenue Carnot et du boulevard Gambetta au Centr'Alès?
5. du Centr'Alès à la sous-préfecture?
6. de la rue Pasteur au théâtre?

B. Chez vous. Demandez à votre partenaire de vous dire comment aller d'un endroit à un autre sur votre campus ou dans votre ville. Votre partenaire doit vous indiquer le chemin.

Vocabulaire utile: le bâtiment de l'administration, la bibliothèque, la cafétéria, le centre sportif, le gymnase, le parking, la piste de jogging

MODÈLE: É1: Comment va-t-on de la cafétéria à la bibliothèque?
É2: Tu sors de la cafétéria par l'entrée principale. Tu continues tout droit vers le gymnase. Tu vas voir le parking sur ta gauche. Tu traverses le parking et la bibliothèque est devant toi.

Visionnement 1

Avant de visionner

A. Le contexte. À la fin de l'Épisode 16, Camille est partie pour Saint-Jean de Causse. Martine n'était pas contente. Lisez cette conversation téléphonique qui introduit l'Épisode 17. Utilisez le contexte pour deviner (*guess*) la signification des mots en italique.

BRUNO: En fait,[a] tu sais, on a des problèmes ici, hein...
CAMILLE: Tu m'as choisi une remplaçante?[b] Comment est-elle?
BRUNO: Non, Camille. Je ne plaisante pas,[c] là! Je suis vraiment très *embêté*...
CAMILLE: Un problème d'argent. Combien te faut-il,[d] cette fois-ci?
BRUNO: Mais non, ce n'est pas ça! En fait, le problème, Camille, c'est toi, voilà! Ton absence est très mal acceptée par le président, et...
CAMILLE: Ah! Qu'est-ce qu'il a dit?
BRUNO: Ben,[e] officiellement, rien, mais, euh, il y a des rumeurs, hein! On parle d'un *licenciement* possible...
CAMILLE: Quoi, le président me met à la porte?!
BRUNO: *Méfie-toi*, il en est capable, tu sais!
CAMILLE: *Je m'en fiche!*
BRUNO: Quoi... ?
CAMILLE: Je m'en fiche, Bruno! Ce voyage est très important pour moi. Tu comprends, c'est pff![f]

[a]En... *In fact* [b]*replacement* [c]Je... *I'm not joking* [d]te... *do you need* [e]*Well* [f]c'est... *the rest is nothing!*

B. Quel ton? Regardez encore une fois le dialogue dans l'Activité A. De quel ton Bruno et Camille doivent-ils dire chacune (*each one*) des phrases dans cette scène?

d'un ton compatissant (*caringly*)	d'un ton indifférent
d'un ton fâché	d'un ton inquiet
d'un ton grave	d'un ton sérieux
d'un ton impatient	en plaisantant (*jokingly*)
d'un ton incrédule (*incredulously*)	

MODÈLE: En fait, tu sais, on a des problèmes ici, hein... →
Bruno dit ça d'un ton inquiet. (Bruno dit ça d'un ton sérieux.)

Observez!

Dans l'Épisode 17, Camille arrive à Saint-Jean de Causse. Regardez l'épisode, et trouvez les réponses aux questions suivantes.

- Qui est Éric? Qu'apprenez-vous sur sa famille et sur l'endroit où il habite?
- Est-ce que les attitudes de Louise et de Jeanne Leblanc envers (*toward*) la guerre se ressemblent?

Vocabulaire relatif à l'épisode

à peine	*hardly*
j'ai hérité de la ferme	*I inherited the farm*
il a disparu	*he disappeared*
ne vous le dira pas	*won't tell you*
son mari était un résistant	*her husband was a Resistance fighter*
l'ont tué	*killed him*

Après le visionnement

A. Pourquoi? Expliquez pourquoi les personnages du film font les actions suivantes dans l'Épisode 17.

1. Pourquoi Bruno téléphone-t-il à Camille?
2. Pourquoi Camille semble-t-elle indifférente à l'idée d'un licenciement éventuel?
3. Pourquoi Camille ne veut-elle pas téléphoner au président?
4. Pourquoi Camille cherche-t-elle à parler avec Éric?
5. Pourquoi y a-t-il peu de jeunes dans le village?
6. Pourquoi est-ce qu'Éric tient particulièrement à (*is fond of*) sa grand-mère?
7. Pourquoi Camille veut-elle parler avec la grand-mère d'Éric?
8. Pourquoi, selon Éric, est-ce que sa grand-mère ne va pas parler avec elle?

B. Réfléchissez. Répondez aux questions suivantes.

1. Comprenez-vous l'attitude du président envers Camille? A-t-il tort?
2. Bruno suggère à Camille de parler avec le président. Elle refuse, disant qu'elle ne le connaît pas. Prend-elle la bonne décision, ou non?

Notez bien!

To say that you miss someone or something, use the verb **manquer à**. In French, the person or thing missed is the subject of the sentence; an indirect object is used to identify the person who misses.

Tu **me manques**. *I miss you.*
Antoine **manque à** Louise. Il **lui manque**. *Louise misses Antoine. She misses him.*

Structure 51

Le futur

Narrating

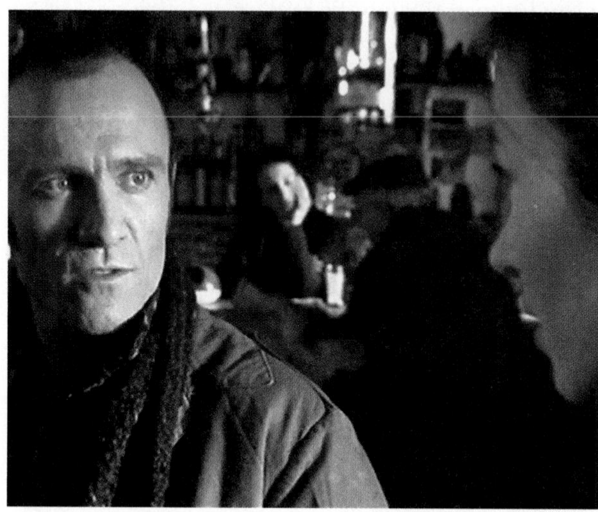

—En été, avec la nouvelle route, les touristes **pourront** monter plus facilement jusqu'au village.

Le temps futur

1. To form the future tense, add the endings **-ai**, **-as**, **-a**, **-ons**, **-ez**, **-ont** to the infinitive. In the case of **-re** verbs, the **e** of the infinitive ending is dropped before adding the ending.

	regarder	répondre	réussir
je	regarder**ai**	répondr**ai**	réussir**ai**
tu	regarder**as**	répondr**as**	réussir**as**
il, elle, on	regarder**a**	répondr**a**	réussir**a**
nous	regarder**ons**	répondr**ons**	réussir**ons**
vous	regarder**ez**	répondr**ez**	réussir**ez**
ils, elles	regarder**ont**	répondr**ont**	réussir**ont**

Mais ma grand-mère ne vous le **dira** pas. — *But my grandmother will not tell you.*

2. All verbs in the future tense have the same endings, but some verbs have irregular stems.

Irregular Verbs:

INFINITIF	RADICAL	FUTUR AVEC *JE*
aller	**ir-**	j'irai
avoir	**aur-**	j'aurai
devoir	**devr-**	je devrai
envoyer	**enverr-**	j'enverrai
être	**ser-**	je serai
faire	**fer-**	je ferai
pouvoir	**pourr-**	je pourrai
recevoir	**recevr-**	je recevrai
savoir	**saur-**	je saurai
venir	**viendr-**	je viendrai
voir	**verr-**	je verrai
vouloir	**voudr-**	je voudrai

Allez tout droit et vous **verrez** le monument aux morts devant vous. — *Go straight ahead and you will see the war memorial right in front of you.*

3. Some spelling-change verbs have an irregular stem in the future. Changement verbs·

VERBES COMME...	RADICAL	FUTUR AVEC *JE*
acheter	**achèter-**	j'achèterai
appeler	**appeller-**	j'appellerai
payer	**paier-**	je paierai

manger, commencer do not change

~~envoyer~~

Tu m'**achèteras** une bonne bouteille de champagne? — *Will you buy me a good bottle of champagne?*

However, verbs like **préférer** don't have a spelling change in the future.

Quel film est-ce que tu **préféreras** voir? — *Which movie will you prefer to see?*

Les phrases avec *si* et *quand*

1. To say that something will happen *if* another event occurs, use **si** + present tense for the possible event and the future tense for what will happen. The two clauses can appear in either order.

Si Camille **parle** à Mme Leblanc, est-ce qu'elle **apprendra** la vérité? — *If Camille talks to Mme Leblanc, will she learn the truth?*

Camille **apprendra** la vérité **si** elle **parle** à Mme Leblanc. — *Camille will learn the truth if she talks to Mme Leblanc.*

2. To say that something will happen *when* another event occurs, use **quand** + future tense for the upcoming event and another future-tense verb for what will happen when the first event occurs. The two clauses can appear in either order.

(*continued*)

Quand elle **arrivera** chez Mme Leblanc, Éric **sera** à la porte. — *When she arrives at Mme Leblanc's house, Éric will be at the door.*

Éric **sera** à la porte **quand** elle **arrivera** chez Mme Leblanc. — *Éric will be at the door when she arrives at Mme Leblanc's house.*

Activités

A. Qu'est-ce qui va se passer? Les personnages du film veulent faire certaines choses. Est-ce qu'ils réussiront? Transformez les phrases suivantes en utilisant le futur simple et mettez-les à l'affirmatif ou au négatif selon vos prédictions.

MODÈLE: Camille veut rencontrer Mme Leblanc. →
Camille rencontrera Mme Leblanc. (Camille ne rencontrera pas Mme Leblanc.)

1. Camille veut savoir la vérité.
2. Camille veut aller chez Jeanne Leblanc.
3. Camille veut voir Mme Leblanc.
4. Camille veut apprendre des détails sur son grand-père.
5. Bruno veut appeler Camille chaque jour.
6. Camille veut finir par trouver la trace de son grand-père.
7. Mado veut avoir l'amour de sa fille.

B. Une visite en France. Michel parle de ce qu'il fera avec ses amis quand ils viendront en France.

Mon ami Paul _____[1] (arriver) en juin avec sa nouvelle femme. Ils _____[2] (ne pas pouvoir) rester chez moi, parce qu'il y _____[3] (avoir) déjà un autre ami chez moi. Il _____[4] (venir) avec nous en voyage. Le premier soir, je _____[5] (préparer) un dîner où tout le monde _____[6] (pouvoir) faire connaissance.

Nous _____[7] (partir) pour Nice, où nous _____[8] (voir) la mer et la montagne. Ce _____[9] (être) super. On _____[10] (se lever) tard, on _____[11] (aller) à la plage, et on _____[12] (faire du roller). Je _____[13] (prendre) probablement un coup de soleil.° Paul et sa femme _____[14] (acheter) certainement des souvenirs et ils les _____[15] (payer) cher. Ensuite, dans la vallée du Rhône, nous _____[16] (boire) du bon vin et nous _____[17] (manger) des plats régionaux.

Nous _____[18] (devoir) retourner à Paris avant la fin du mois, mais je suis sûr que mes amis _____[19] (être) contents du voyage, et je pense que nous _____[20] (vouloir) passer d'autres vacances ensemble.

°coup... *sunburn*

C. Parler français. Faites des phrases au futur avec des éléments des quatre colonnes. Suivez le modèle, et faites attention au temps du verbe après **si** et **quand**.

MODÈLE: Vous parlerez français si vous allez en France. →
Vous parlerez français quand vous irez en France.

je	envoyer des cartes postales		aller en France
tu	lire un journal français		avoir de l'argent / le temps
un prof de français	parler (bien) français	si	choisir d'étudier à l'étranger
nous	habiter au Sénégal / à Montréal	quand	prendre des vacances au Québec
vous	regarder un film québécois		visiter Bruxelles
les étudiants	rendre visite à un(e) ami(e)		vivre à Paris

D. La vie des gens dans la classe. Terminez les phrases à votre façon (*in your own way*). Ensuite, comparez vos réponses avec celles de deux autres étudiant(e)s.

1. Si je suis fatigué(e) ce soir,...
2. Les étudiants iront au cinéma quand...
3. Si j'ai le temps ce week-end,...
4. J'aurai de bonnes notes en cours quand...

E. Âmes sœurs. (*Kindred spirits.*) Interviewez trois camarades de classe pour savoir où ils/elles seront dans cinq ans, quelle sera leur routine quotidienne, et ce qu'ils/elles feront pour s'amuser. Avec qui partagerez-vous les mêmes tendances?

Structure 52

Les pronoms compléments (révision)

Avoiding repetition

—Quoi, le président **me** met à la porte?!

—Méfie-toi, il **en** est capable, tu sais!

Pronouns are used to avoid repetition and enhance cohesion between sentences. They may replace a noun in the third person; in the first and second persons, they are used to refer to or to address someone. Study the following examples. Notice how the use of pronouns in the second paragraph results in a smoother and more concise style.

WITHOUT PRONOUNS: Bruno recherche David. Bruno trouve David à l'université. Bruno va à l'université et demande à David de donner des conseils à Camille. Camille a besoin de conseils parce que Camille a beaucoup de questions. David répond à toutes ses questions.

WITH PRONOUNS: Bruno recherche David. Il le trouve à l'université. Bruno y va et lui demande de donner des conseils à Camille. Elle en a besoin parce qu'elle a beaucoup de questions. David y répond.

1. Direct objects can refer to things or people. In the third person, you can identify a direct object *noun* because it is not preceded by any preposition (such as **à** or **de**). Direct object *pronouns* are **me**, **te**, **le**, **la**, **l'**, **nous**, **vous**, **les**.

   SIMPLE TENSE: Bruno trouve **David** à l'université. → Il **le** trouve à l'université.

   COMPOUND TENSE: Bruno a trouvé **David** à l'université. → Il **l'**a trouvé à l'université.

2. Indirect objects refer to people. In the third person, you can identify an indirect object *noun* because it is preceded by the preposition **à**. Indirect object *pronouns* are **me**, **te**, **lui**, **nous**, **vous**, **leur**.

   SIMPLE TENSE: Bruno demande **à David**... → Bruno **lui** demande...

   COMPOUND TENSE: Bruno a demandé **à David**... → Bruno **lui** a demandé...

3. The pronoun **y** is used to refer to a preposition of location (e.g, **sur**, **dans**, **à**) + place. It can also be used to replace **à** + thing.

   SIMPLE TENSE: Bruno va **à l'université**... → Bruno **y** va...

   COMPOUND TENSE: David a répondu **à toutes ses questions**. → David **y** a répondu.

4. The pronoun **en** is used to replace **de** + thing or **de** + noun after an expression of quantity. It can also replace a noun after a number.

   SIMPLE TENSE: Elle a besoin **de conseils**. → Elle **en** a besoin.

   COMPOUND TENSE: Elle a posé beaucoup **de questions**. → Elle **en** a posé beaucoup.

   or Elle a posé une question. → Elle **en** a posé une.

5. Placement:

   - As you probably noticed in the examples above, all object pronouns, including **y** and **en**, precede the verb of which they are the object. If that verb is in a compound tense, the pronoun precedes the auxiliary.

     SIMPLE TENSE: Bruno **le** trouve à l'université et **lui** demande de...

     COMPOUND TENSE: Bruno **l'**a trouvé à l'université et **lui** a demandé de...

- Negations surround the pronoun + verb sequence. The initial element **ne** precedes the pronoun and the second element (**pas**, **jamais**, etc.) follows the verb.

  SIMPLE TENSE: Bruno **ne** le trouve **pas** immédiatement.

  COMPOUND TENSE: Bruno **ne** l'a **pas** trouvé immédiatement.

Activités

A. Ils veulent visiter le Maroc. Complétez les phrases avec un pronom complément d'objet direct ou indirect, **y** ou **en**.

1. Daniel et Sophie font un voyage au Maroc. Ils vont ______ aller au printemps. Ils ______ sont très contents.
2. Ils ont choisi Royal Air Maroc, parce ce que cette compagnie ______ a proposé un prix (*price*) intéressant.
3. Ils ont cherché des hôtels sur Internet et ils ______ ont trouvé beaucoup. L'Hôtel Riad dar Zahr ______ a offert un tarif étudiant. La chambre coûte (*costs*) 46 euros, et ils ______ ont réservée avec une carte de crédit.
4. Ils vont partir pour Marrakech le 15 avril et ils vont ______ revenir le 2 mai.
5. Aujourd'hui, ils téléphonent à un ami qui ______ est déjà allé. Il ______ parle du palais (*palace*) de la Bahia. Ils veulent ______ visiter, alors ils achètent un guide touristique qui ______ parle.
6. Ce guide est super! Ils ______ trouvent beaucoup d'autres possibilités. Le Maroc a un relief très varié. Des montagnes? Il y ______ a beaucoup! Daniel veut absolument faire une randonnée dans le Haut-Atlas et visiter le village d'Ait Zitoun.
7. «Allons-______», ______ dit Sophie. «Mais écoute, on peut ______ visiter, ce village, mais est-ce qu'on peut ______ dormir?»
8. Daniel consulte le guide. Il ______ découvre que les habitants du village peuvent ______ loger, Sophie et lui. Et pendant deux semaines!
9. Daniel demande à Sophie d'appeler l'agent de voyages. Daniel dit: «Téléphone-______ pour ______ dire que la date du retour est bien trop tôt. Change-______. Nous allons rester au Maroc pendant un mois!»

B. Le voyage de Daniel et Sophie. Avec un(e) partenaire, posez des questions et répondez-y en utilisant les pronoms d'objet direct ou indirect, **y** ou **en**. Suivez le modèle en respectant le temps des verbes et en utilisant les informations de l'Activité A.

MODÈLE: Ils ont pensé *à un voyage au Sénégal?*
É1: Est-ce qu'ils y ont pensé?
É2: Non, ils n'y ont pas pensé. Ils ont pensé à un voyage au Maroc.

1. Ils ont acheté *des billets d'avion* chez Air France?
2. Ils vont aller *à Casablanca*?
3. Ils vont rendre visite *à leurs amis*?
4. Ils parlent *à un ami* qui a visité le Maroc?
5. Leur ami parle *à Daniel et à Sophie* d'un hôtel près de la plage?

6. Ils achètent *un guide*?
7. Ils trouvent *le guide* intéressant?
8. Ils vont visiter *le village d'Ait Zitoun*?
9. Ils vont revenir *du Maroc* après deux semaines?

Voudriez-vous faire ce voyage avec Daniel et Sophie? Pourquoi (pas)?

Regards sur la culture

Le déclin de la campagne

Camille notices that there are not many people around in Saint-Jean de Causse. Éric tells her, however, that a new road has been built to the village and that this will certainly bring in many tourists during the summer months. The situation of Saint-Jean de Causse is similar to that of many other villages in France.

- Paris has long been the undisputed center of France. In French, one is by definition either **Parisien** or **provincial**. Even those who live in large cities such as Lyon or Marseille are "provincials."
- At the same time, the villages of rural France are the backbone of many French people's vision of their country. Many urban dwellers speak of a rural region as their family's place of origin, even if they have lived their whole lives in the city.
- At the time of the Second World War, a very high percentage of France's population did work in agriculture as compared with other developed countries such as Britain and Germany. But today, fewer than 30% of the farms of that period are still active. This relatively rapid depopulation of rural France has been called **l'exode rural**.

Ancien village de Conques, Aveyron

- The economic shift away from agricultural work since the Second World War has also been a cultural shift, as young people moved to the cities. Young women were in the forefront of this movement, and, for the past forty years, young men who wanted to maintain the family farm were sometimes unable to find wives.
- Along with the decline of traditional agriculture, France is experiencing the decline and loss of many regional traditions that had their roots in rural populations, including the daily use of languages such as Breton, Basque, and Occitan.
- Villages such as Saint-Jean de Causse in the Cévennes that today might have fifty or sixty inhabitants could have had as many as five hundred in 1880. Two institutions seem to symbolize to local people the survival of a living village

community: the local grocery store and the elementary school. The closing of the school is always a particularly dramatic—and sad—event.

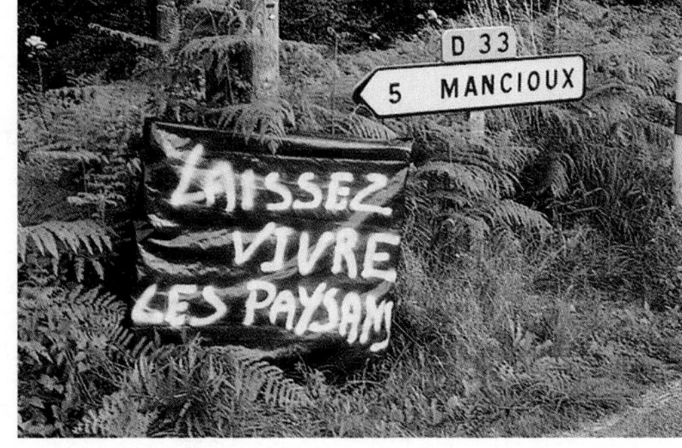

Dans les Pyrénées

- One result of the rural exodus is the existence of abandoned or nearly abandoned villages, particularly in areas that are difficult to reach. These places are often extraordinarily picturesque, and, in some cases, have been bought up by Europeans from other countries or by wealthy Parisians to serve as vacation sites.
- Despite this dramatic decline in rural populations and traditional farming, France is still a very important power in agriculture: It produces 21.4% of the agricultural output of the European Union, by far the largest percentage of any of the members (the next highest is Italy, with 16%).

Considérez

French attitudes toward farming as a career have been relatively negative for quite a long time. Today, a young person who decides to go into farming often feels a bit defensive. Why would this be? What perceptions and attitudes related to farming as an occupation are there in your culture?

Structure 53

Les pronoms compléments d'objet direct et indirect

Avoiding repetition

—Mais ma grand-mère ne **vous le** dira pas.

You have already learned how to place direct object pronouns and indirect object pronouns in a sentence. Now you will learn how to use them at the same time.

1. When there is more than one object pronoun in a declarative sentence, they are positioned in the following order.

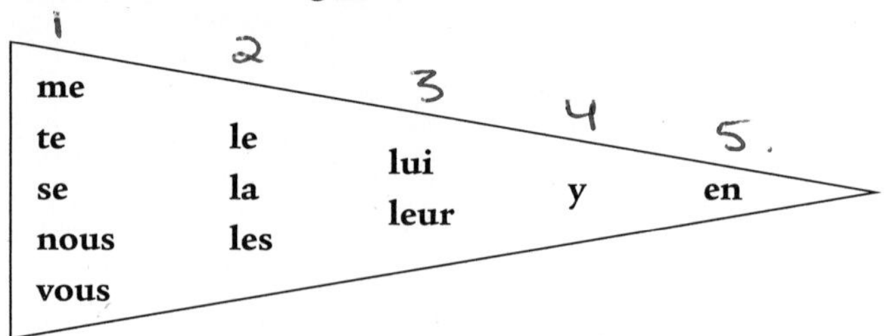

—Rachid donne-t-il l'adresse à Camille?	*Does Rachid give Camille the address?*
—Oui, il **la lui** donne.	*Yes, he gives it to her.*

In negative sentences, the pronouns follow **ne** and precede the verb.

—Tu ne conseilles pas cet hôtel?	*You don't recommend this hotel?*
—C'est ça. Je ne **te le** conseille pas.	*That's right. I don't recommend it to you.*

Remember—**Y** is never used to refer to people. To represent a phrase containing **à** + person, use an indirect object pronoun (**à Camille** → **lui**). **En** cannot be used to refer to **de** + person. In that case, use **de** + stressed pronoun after the verb (**de Camille** → **d'elle**). **En** can be used, however, to represent a person that is a direct object introduced by an indefinite article, partitive article, or expression of quantity (**Vous avez un enfant? Oui, j'en ai un.**)

2. The same rules for the placement of object pronouns apply for two pronouns as for one. In simple tenses (the present, the **imparfait**, and the future), object pronouns precede the verb. In compound tenses (the **passé composé**), object pronouns precede the auxiliary verb. In the **futur proche**, object pronouns precede the verb of which they are an object, usually the infinitive.

   Tu me choisis une remplaçante? → Tu **m'en** choisis une?
   Tu m'as choisi une remplaçante? → Tu **m'en** a choisi une?
   Tu vas me choisir une remplaçante? → Tu vas **m'en** choisir une?

Remember—In the **passé composé** with the auxiliary verb **avoir**, the past participle must agree with a preceding direct object pronoun.

La photo? Je **te l'**ai trouvé**e**.	*The photo? I found it for you.*

3. In the negative imperative, both object pronouns precede the verb.

Ne **lui en** parle pas!	*Don't talk to him about it!*

In the affirmative imperative, the object pronouns follow the verb and are joined to the verb by hyphens. **Me** and **te** become **moi** and **toi**, except when they come before **en**. The order of the pronouns with an affirmative imperative is as follows:

objet direct	objet indirect	**y**	**en**

Donne l'adresse à Camille! → Donne-**la-lui**. *Give it to her.*
Montrez-moi la photo! → Montrez-**la-moi**. *Show it to me.*
Conseille-moi un hôtel! → Conseille-**m'en** un. *Recommend one to me.*

Activités

A. Interactions. Répondez aux questions en remplaçant les mots soulignés par des compléments d'objet direct et indirect ou **y** ou **en**.

MODÈLE: Est-ce que Bruno donne des conseils à Camille? →
Oui, il lui en donne.

1. Bruno parle-t-il à Camille des problèmes?
2. Est-ce que Camille trouve des noms sur le monument aux morts?
3. Camille pose-t-elle des questions aux joueurs de pétanque?
4. Camille demande-t-elle des renseignements (*information*) à la patronne du bar?
5. Est-ce que la patronne du bar parle à Camille de la famille Leblanc?
6. Est-ce que la patronne montre Éric à Camille?
7. Camille parle-t-elle à Éric de son grand-père?
8. Est-ce qu'Éric donne l'adresse (*f.*) à Camille?

B. C'est déjà fait. Magali, Danielle et Carine organisent un week-end à la montagne. Magali suggère quelques préparatifs aux deux autres, mais elles ont déjà tout fait! Suivez le modèle.

MODÈLE: MAGALI: Empruntez (*Borrow*) les sacs à dos à vos frères.
DANIELLE ET CARINE: Nous les leur avons déjà empruntés.

1. Parlez de notre itinéraire (*m.*) à vos parents.
2. Donnez-moi l'argent pour la tente.
3. Mettez des chaussures de randonnée dans le sac.
4. Apportez-moi (*Bring me*) les provisions que vous avez achetées.
5. Cherchez une carte de la région dans le placard (*cupboard*).
6. Trouvez-moi mon appareil photo.
7. Expliquez notre itinéraire à mon frère.
8. Prenez de l'essence (*gasoline*) pour la voiture à la station-service.

C. Un adolescent mal élevé. Paul n'est pas gentil. Il refuse de faire ce que sa mère veut. Aidez sa mère à lui dire ce qu'il doit faire immédiatement. Suivez le modèle.

MODÈLE: PAUL: Je ne veux pas montrer mes livres à ma petite cousine!
SA MÈRE: Montre-les-lui maintenant!

1. Je refuse de donner le café à papa.
2. Je ne veux pas te parler de ma petite amie.
3. Je refuse de donner des cadeaux à mes grands-parents.
4. Je ne veux pas manger de la salade à la cantine.
5. Je ne veux pas écrire la lettre à tante Élisabeth.

6. Je n'ai pas envie de me regarder dans le miroir.
7. Je refuse de vous présenter mes amis de l'école.
8. Je ne veux pas parler de mes problèmes au psychiatre.

Maintenant, imaginez que la mère de Paul s'exaspère. Donnez les mêmes ordres au négatif en commençant par «Bon, très bien... »

MODÈLE: PAUL: Je ne veux pas montrer mes livres à ma petite cousine!
SA MÈRE: Bon, très bien, ne les lui montre pas!

D. Êtes-vous un bon ami / une bonne amie? Posez les questions suivantes à votre partenaire qui répondra en utilisant deux pronoms. Ensuite, analysez les réponses. Pensez-vous que votre partenaire a les traits d'un bon ami / d'une bonne amie?

MODÈLE: É1: Racontes-tu des mensonges (*lies*) à tes ami(e)s?
É2: Non, je ne leur en raconte pas. (Oui, je leur en raconte de temps en temps.)

Demandez à votre partenaire...

1. s'il / si elle parle de ses problèmes personnels à son meilleur ami / sa meilleure amie.
2. s'il / si elle offre parfois des cadeaux (*gifts*) à ses amis.
3. s'il / si elle cache (*hides*) ses émotions aux autres.
4. s'il / si elle oublie parfois d'envoyer une carte à son meilleur ami / sa meilleure amie pour son anniversaire.
5. s'il / si elle pardonne à ses amis leurs défauts (*faults*) de caractère.
6. s'il / si elle ne répète pas les secrets intimes de ses amis aux autres.

Visionnement 2

Les Cévennes. In order to get to Saint-Jean de Causse, Camille rode the train down the Rhône Valley and over to Nîmes. There, she changed to a local train that took her to Alès, a former center of silkworm breeding that lies in the plains near the edge of the Cévennes mountains. From Alès, Camille drove a rented car up to Saint-Jean de Causse. This is a region of rocky soils that has always been poor and isolated from the rest of France. It is one of the areas that has lost the largest percentage of its population over the past half century.

The Cévennes were a center of the Resistance in World War II, but the area's history of resistance goes much further back. In the early 1700s, it was a hotbed of Protestant revolt against royal authority. One tourist attraction in the Cévennes is the village of Le Mas Soubeyran (*The Upper Hamlet* or *Farm* in the Occitan language). It is the location of the house of the Protestant chief Rolland and a museum dedicated to the Protestant resistance.

Imaginez que vous allez passer une journée dans les Cévennes. Complétez les phrases suivantes à l'aide de la carte.

Demain, nous ferons une excursion dans le Massif central. Nous prendrons le train de nuit. Il passera à Avignon, mais il ne s'y arrêtera pas.[a] Nous descendrons à _____[1] pour prendre le train régional jusqu'à _____[2]. Là, nous louerons une voiture et nous monterons vers les _____[3]. Nous nous arrêterons pendant une heure au _____[4] parce que nous voulons comprendre l'histoire du protestantisme en France. Ensuite, nous monterons voir le village de _____[5], pour visiter la ferme de Jeanne Leblanc. Plus tard, nous irons faire du bateau dans les _____[6]. Et après, nous descendrons vers la Méditerranée pour passer la soirée[b] dans la ville de _____[7].

[a]ne... *will not stop there* [b]*evening*

Les Cévennes

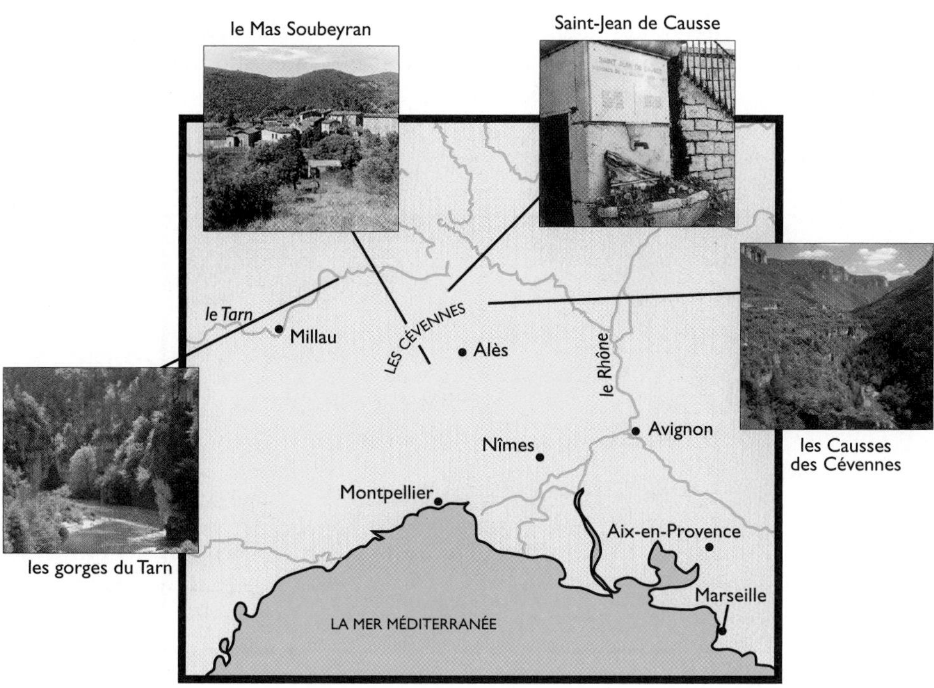

Observez!

Considérez les aspects culturels expliqués dans **Regards sur la culture**. Ensuite, regardez l'Épisode 17 encore une fois, et répondez aux questions suivantes.

- Est-ce qu'il y a beaucoup de jeunes au bar des Cévennes? Quel rôle le bar semble-t-il jouer dans ce petit village?
- Est-ce qu'il y a beaucoup de chômage dans cette région? Quel était le métier traditionnel dans cette région? Qu'est-ce qui va le remplacer?

Après le visionnement

Faites l'activité pour le **Visionnement 2** dans le cahier.

Synthèse: Culture

L'écologie et les mouvements de population

Au Québec, en France, au Sénégal, partout[1] dans le monde[2] francophone, on observe un mouvement des populations de la campagne vers les villes. Mais, pour des raisons écologiques, ce mouvement est plus dramatique dans certaines régions du monde. Par exemple, en Haïti et à Madagascar, la disparition[3] des forêts a provoqué une migration vers les villes.

Le Sahel, c'est une vaste région d'Afrique qui sépare le Sahara des zones tropicales. Dans le Sahel, il y a huit mois par an sans pluie.[4] On cultive le millet pendant la saison des pluies et on élève[5] des troupeaux[6] de bœufs, de moutons et de chameaux.[7]

Il y a eu[8] dans le passé des périodes de sécheresse[9] extrême dans le Sahel qui ont causé des famines et des maladies. Aujourd'hui, la sécheresse semble permanente. Certains pensent que le Sahara avance et que les terres[10] du Sahel ne seront plus jamais fertiles: c'est la désertification.

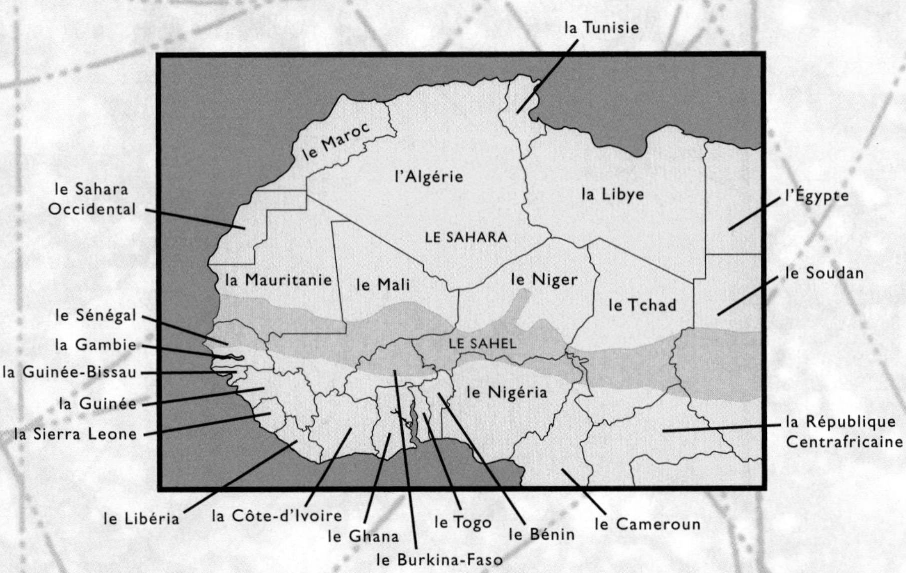

«Il y avait de la pluie et de l'eau partout. Nous cultivions et récoltions[11] et nous avions tout. Aujourd'hui, nous n'avons rien. Parfois, nous passons dix jours, vingt jours sans manger. Nos enfants meurent de faim.» (Citation d'une Malienne, victime de la désertification)

[1]*everywhere* [2]*world* [3]*disappearance* [4]*rain* [5]*raises* [6]*herds* [7]*camels* [8]*Il... There were* [9]*drought* [10]*soils* [11]*harvested*

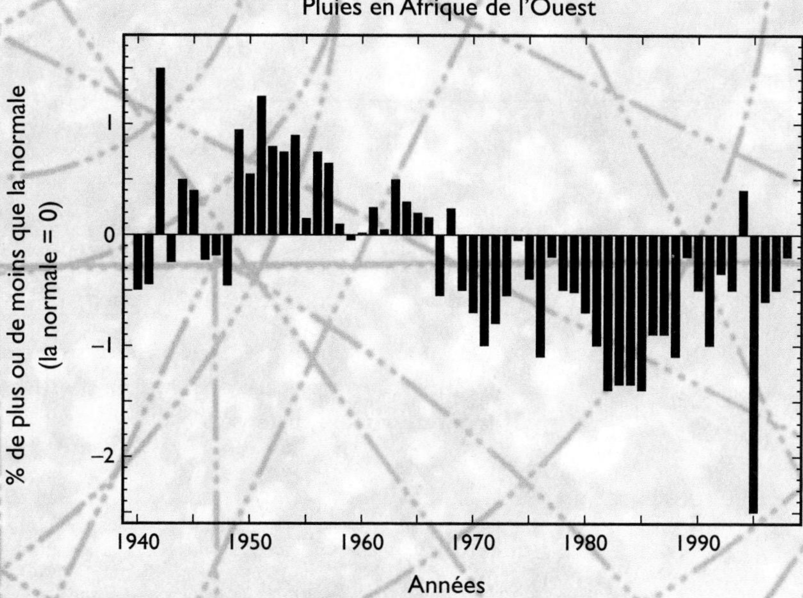

Les causes de la désertification sont souvent discutées: il y a sans doute des changements climatiques, mais il y a aussi des abus de ressources naturelles (la monoculture intensive de certaines plantes, par exemple) et l'augmentation excessive de la population.

La désertification provoque des migrations vers les villes ou vers des régions plus fertiles. Elle provoque aussi des antagonismes ethniques. Un exemple: la Mauritanie. En 1965, 70% des Mauritaniens étaient des nomades et vivaient comme leurs ancêtres depuis des siècles.[12] Aujourd'hui, avec la désertification du pays, il y a seulement 7% de nomades. Tous ces gens sont allés vers des villes: ce sont des «réfugiés écologiques». En général, ils restent très pauvres[13] et vivent dans des quartiers misérables parce que leurs connaissances ne sont pas adaptées à la vie urbaine.

[12] *centuries* [13] *poor*

À vous

Le problème de la désertification. Why do you think the Sahel desertification problem is of particular importance in the French-speaking world? Look at the map and list the French-speaking countries that lie in the Sahel region. What other countries are probably also affected?

À écrire

Faites **À écrire** pour le Chapitre 17 dans le cahier.

Vocabulaire

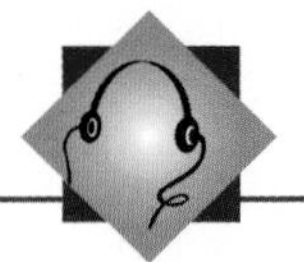

Le relief géographique

un champ	field
une colline	hill
une côte	coast
un fleuve	large river
une île	island
la Manche	English Channel
un massif	old, rounded mountain range
une mer	sea
un relief	topography, relief

MOTS APPARENTÉS: **une baie, un bassin, une forêt, un lac, une montagne, un océan, une plaine, un plateau, une rivière, une vallée**

Les points cardinaux

l'est (*m.*)	east
le nord	north
l'ouest (*m.*)	west
le sud	south

Demander et indiquer le chemin

une carte	map
le chemin	route, way
un coin	corner
une église	church
un feu	traffic light; fire
un poteau indicateur	sign(post)
Est-ce que vous pourriez m'indiquer le chemin pour aller à...	Could you show me the way to . . .
monter/descendre une rue	to go up/down a street
à droite	to/on the right
à gauche	to/on the left
tout droit	straight
vers	toward

MOTS APPARENTÉS: **indiquer, tourner**

Autres expressions utiles

à la campagne	in the country
au bord de	on the banks (shore, edge) of
manquer à	to be missed by (*someone*)
traverser	to cross

Chapitre 18

Histoires privées

Le Chemin du retour

Feuille de service du 15 janvier
1er jour de tournage
Horaires: 8h30–18h

LIEU DE TOURNAGE: SAINT-ANTONIN—DOMAINE BAYLE

Séquence	***Effets***	***Décors***	***Résumé***	***Rôles***
118	INT.—JOUR	MAISON JEANNE—Cuisine	Camille parle avec Jeanne et lui explique la raison de sa venue.°	CAMILLE, JEANNE LEBLANC

la... *why she came*

OBJECTIFS

In this episode, you will

- learn more about what Antoine did during the German occupation of France

In this chapter, you will

- talk about farm life
- discuss environmental issues
- describe people and things using relative clauses
- talk about everyday actions
- learn about how country life and city life relate to the geography of France
- read a folktale from the Cévennes

Vocabulaire en contexte

L'agriculture

Si les agriculteurs sont de moins en moins **nombreux**° en France, les techniques agricoles se sont cependant° transformées. Il en résulte une productivité considérablement augmentée.

numerous
nevertheless

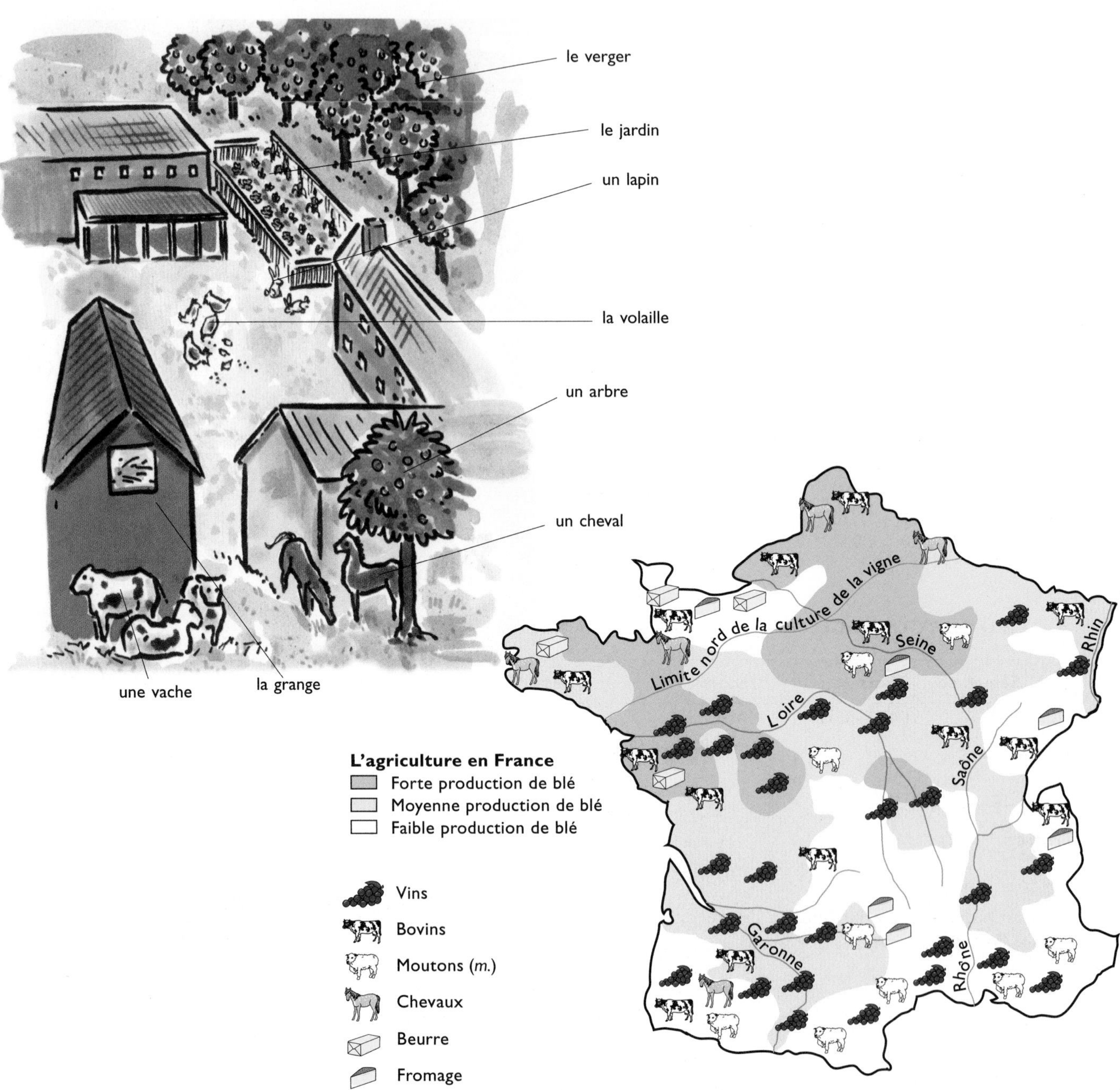

Les céréales° (*f.*)

Le blé° est **cultivé presque partout°** en France. L'agriculteur **plante** le blé au printemps et le **récolte** en automne. **Les fermes** (*f.*) françaises produisent aussi d'autres **céréales**: l'avoine,° l'orge,° le maïs et le riz.

Les... *Grains*

Wheat / presque... *almost everywhere*

oats / barley

La viticulture°

Les Français sont **fiers°** de leurs vins. **Les vignobles°** (*m.*) du Bordelais, de la Bourgogne et de la vallée du Rhône produisent des vins connus dans **le monde°** entier.

La... *Wine growing*

proud / vineyards

world

L'élevage°

Les vaches donnent leur lait, qui sert surtout à faire du fromage: tomme de Savoie, gruyère du Jura, cantal du Massif central. Le lait de **brebis°** (*f.*) des Causses donne un fromage célèbre, le roquefort. **Les fermiers** élèvent souvent aussi **des porcs** (*m.*), de la volaille et des lapins.

(*Animal*) *Breeding*

ewe

Autres mots utiles

une cheminée	fireplace; chimney
une marmite	*large iron cooking pot*
un(e) paysan(ne)	farmer
la récolte	harvest; crop
la terre	earth; soil
une vigne	vine
un village	village
pousser	to grow; to push
ramasser	to pick (up), gather (up)

Activités

A. Produits. De quel animal, quelle céréale ou quelle plante les produits suivants proviennent-ils?

MODÈLE: le pain → Le pain provient du blé.

1. le vin
2. le gruyère
3. le roquefort
4. des œufs
5. le cidre
6. le lait
7. le jambon

B. Une petite compétition. Mettez-vous en groupes de trois. Une personne posera les questions suivantes aux deux autres. La personne qui répondra le plus vite avec une réponse correcte obtiendra un point.

MODÈLE: Comment appelle-t-on la personne qui travaille la terre? → C'est un agriculteur. (C'est un fermier.) (C'est un paysan.)

1. Où est-ce qu'on cultive du raisin?
2. Quel produit est cultivé presque partout en France?

3. Quel est l'endroit où on garde (*keeps, stores*) le blé?
4. Quelles plantes poussent dans une forêt et donnent à la forêt son caractère?
5. Quelle tâche (*task*) l'agriculteur fait-il en automne?
6. Quels animaux les fermiers élèvent-ils souvent?
7. Où trouve-t-on beaucoup de fleurs?
8. Où les agriculteurs plantent-ils des graines (*seeds*)?

C. Chez nous. Quel est le rôle de l'agriculture dans votre pays? Répondez aux questions suivantes.

1. Quelles sont les activités agricoles principales de votre pays?
2. Dans quelle(s) région(s) de votre pays cultive-t-on les céréales?
3. Y a-t-il une région où la viticulture est importante? Quelle région? Avez-vous déjà bu des vins de cette région? Les aimez-vous?
4. Quelles régions sont connues pour leur production de fromage? Est-ce que ce fromage est fait à partir de lait de vache, de chèvre (*goat*) ou de brebis?
5. Dans quelles régions l'élevage est-il important? Quels animaux y sont élevés?

L'environnement

Les Français s'inquiètent de plus en plus pour **l'environnement** (*m.*) de la France et du monde. Le gouvernement fait de nombreux efforts pour réduire° **la pollution** de l'eau et de l'air. Il a lancé un système de **recyclage** (*m.*) et une politique de **conservation** (*f.*) pour faire baisser° **la consommation de l'essence**° (*f.*) et des ressources naturelles. Les Verts sont **un parti politique** qui joue un rôle important. Ils pensent beaucoup à **l'avenir**° (*m.*) et cherchent des moyens **efficaces**° pour réduire **l'effet** (*m.*) **de serre**,° et pour convaincre° le public de **consommer** moins et de **recycler** plus.

reduce

faire... *to lower* / *gasoline*

the future

efficient

l'effet... *the greenhouse effect* / *convince*

Activités

A. Conseils. Quels conseils peut-on donner aux personnes suivantes? Mettez vos phrases à l'impératif.

Verbes utiles: conserver, consommer, devenir, penser, recycler, réduire

MODÈLE: Jean-François pense que les partis politiques traditionnels négligent la question de l'environnement. →
Devenez vert. (Faites partie du parti des Verts. Adhérez aux Verts.)

1. Nathalie met tout dans la poubelle (*garbage can*).
2. Lise adore faire du shopping; elle achète beaucoup de choses inutiles.
3. Laurent laisse toutes les lumières allumées (*lit*) dans son appartement. Sa note d'électricité est très élevée; il s'en inquiète.
4. Le pot d'échappement (*exhaust pipe*) de la voiture de Michel ne marche pas du tout; il ne purifie absolument pas le gaz d'échappement.
5. Valérie utilise trop d'eau.

B. Et vous? Découvrez si votre partenaire s'inquiète de l'environnement. Demandez-lui...

1. s'il / si elle fait des efforts pour protéger l'environnement, s'il / si elle fait du recyclage et s'il / si elle essaie de consommer moins.
2. ce qu'il/elle peut faire pour réduire encore sa consommation d'essence. Est-ce que les transports en commun représentent une solution pratique pour lui/elle? le vélo? le covoiturage (voyager en voiture avec des camarades)?
3. quel est le sujet écologique le plus important en ce moment, selon lui/elle: l'effet de serre, le recyclage, la conservation des ressources naturelles ou autre chose? Demandez-lui d'expliquer.
4. s'il / si elle est optimiste ou pessimiste en ce qui concerne l'avenir de la planète et si, selon lui/elle, les habitants de son pays font le maximum pour protéger l'environnement.
5. si le mouvement écologiste est important dans sa région et s'il est efficace, selon lui/elle.
6. s'il / si elle est engagé(e) dans le mouvement écologiste et, si oui, quelles sont les activités principales de son groupe.

Visionnement 1

Avant de visionner

Vocabulaire relatif à l'épisode

Tenez!	*Take this!*
C'est une lettre qu'a écrite mon grand-père.	*It's a letter my grandfather wrote.*
la vérité	*truth*
cacher	*to hide*
Asseyez-vous	*Sit down*
l'aligot	*regional potato-and-cheese soup*
de la part d'un ami	*on the recommendation of a friend*
l'a accueilli	*welcomed him*
C'était de la folie!	*It was madness!*

La narration de Jeanne Leblanc. Dans cet épisode, Jeanne Leblanc raconte le séjour (*stay*) d'Antoine dans sa famille. Sa narration est au passé. Complétez le dialogue avec le passé composé ou l'imparfait. Justifiez votre choix en vous rappelant la fonction de chaque temps du verbe: le passé composé s'emploie pour raconter des événements achevés dans le passé; l'imparfait s'emploie pour des descriptions des circonstances et des situations, pour des actions habituelles et pour des actions en train de se dérouler (*unfolding*).

JEANNE: [Antoine] _____[1] (vouloir) faire de la Résistance. Pierre l'_____[2] (accueillir[a]) avec sympathie, et très vite ils _____[3] (devenir) copains[b]...

CAMILLE: Il _____[4] (habiter) dans cette maison?

JEANNE: Oui... Pierre lui _____[5] (faire) visiter la région. Puis il lui _____[6] (présenter) nos amis résistants. Antoine _____[7] (être) serviable,[c] sympathique.

CAMILLE: Il vous _____[8] (parler) souvent de sa femme?

JEANNE: Oui, et de sa fille aussi, qui _____[9] (être) encore toute petite. Antoine _____[10] (s'inquiéter) beaucoup pour elles. Il les _____[11] (savoir) seules à Paris. Elles n'_____[12] (avoir) pas d'argent...

CAMILLE: Mais alors, il _____[13] (lutter[d]) dans la Résistance avec votre mari?

JEANNE (*acquiesce*): Oui. Il y _____[14] (avoir) quatre copains avec eux. Ils détruisaient des ponts et des voies de chemin de fer.[e] Il _____[15] (être) essentiel de retarder les troupes allemandes... Mais Antoine _____[16] (être) impatient. Il _____[17] (dire) à mon mari: «Il faut frapper plus fort![f]».

CAMILLE: Plus fort?

JEANNE: Oui. Il _____[18] (vouloir) monter des opérations plus importantes! Et je vous le dis, Camille, notre malheur _____[19] (venir) de là!

[a]*to welcome* [b]*friends* [c]*willing to help* [d]*to fight* [e]détruisaient... *destroyed bridges and railroads* [f]Il... *We have to strike harder!*

Observez!

Dans l'Épisode 18, Camille essaie d'apprendre plus de détails sur Antoine. Écoutez la conversation entre Camille et Jeanne, en réfléchissant aux questions suivantes.

- Quel rapport s'établit (*is established*) entre Jeanne Leblanc et Camille?
- Pourquoi Antoine est-il allé dans les Cévennes? Comment a-t-il fait la connaissance de Pierre et Jeanne Leblanc?

Après le visionnement

A. Le carnet de Camille. (*Camille's notebook.*) Avant de rencontrer Jeanne, Camille a préparé une liste de questions qu'elle voulait lui poser. Voici les questions tirées de son carnet. Quelles réponses a-t-elle reçues?

1. Quand est-ce que mon grand-père Antoine est arrivé chez vous? **2.** Est-ce qu'il habitait dans votre maison? **3.** Est-ce qu'il vous parlait souvent de sa femme ou de sa fille? **4.** Quel était son état d'esprit quand il parlait de sa famille? Pourquoi? **5.** Est-ce qu'il a vraiment lutté dans la Résistance avec votre mari? **6.** Les opérations se sont-elles bien passées?

B. Réfléchissez. Répondez aux questions suivantes.

1. Quelle sorte de personne est Jeanne? Est-elle généreuse? contente? amère (*bitter*)? Expliquez, en donnant des exemples de l'épisode. **2.** Est-ce qu'elle mène (*leads*) une vie moderne ou plutôt (*rather*) traditionnelle? Justifiez votre réponse. **3.** Selon vous, pourquoi Jeanne décide-t-elle de raconter l'histoire d'Antoine à Camille?

Structure 54

Les pronoms relatifs

Combining related ideas

—Il vous parlait souvent de sa femme?

—Oui, et de sa fille aussi, **qui** était encore toute petite.

Relative pronouns join two related sentences or ideas into one longer sentence. When the two ideas are combined, one becomes dependent or "relative" to the other.

Three useful relative pronouns are **qui**, **que**, and **où**. The choice of which one to use depends on whether it will be the subject or object of the verb in the relative clause▲ or whether it refers back to a time or place mentioned in the independent clause.▲

Le pronom relatif *qui*

The relative pronoun **qui** can refer to either people or things. It serves as the *subject* of the verb in the relative clause and is followed by that verb. It makes no elision when it is followed by a word beginning with a vowel.

> Il parlait de **sa fille**. **Sa fille** était encore toute petite. →
> Il parlait de sa fille, **qui** était encore toute petite.
> *He spoke about his daughter,* ***who*** *was still very little.*

> Selon Jeanne, Antoine a monté **des opérations**. **Les opérations** ont causé la mort de Pierre. →
> Selon Jeanne, Antoine a monté des opérations **qui** ont causé la mort de Pierre.
> *According to Jeanne, Antoine organized operations* ***that*** *caused Pierre's death.*

> **Antoine** est arrivé en 1943. **Antoine** a vite rencontré des résistants. →
> Antoine, **qui** est arrivé en 1943, a vite rencontré des résistants.
> *Antoine,* ***who*** *arrived in 1943, soon met members of the Resistance.*

In these examples, **qui** is the *subject* of the verb in the relative clause.

Le pronom relatif *que*

The relative pronoun **que** can also refer to either people or things. It serves as the *object* of the verb in the relative clause and is followed by a noun or pronoun subject and the verb. **Que** makes elision if it is followed by a word beginning with a vowel.

> Camille rencontre **la femme**. Rachid a trouvé **la femme**. →
> Camille rencontre la femme **que** Rachid a trouvée.
> *Camille meets the woman* ***whom*** *Rachid located.*

> C'est un **pays**. On aime ce **pays**. →
> C'est un pays **qu'**on aime.
> *It's a country* ***that*** *people love.*

In these examples, **que** becomes the *direct object* of the verb in the relative clause.

Pour en savoir plus...

You learned in Chapter 10 that the past participle of a verb conjugated with **avoir** agrees in number and gender with a direct object that precedes it. Because **que** has the grammatical function of a direct object in the relative clause and precedes the verb of which it is the object, the past participle must agree.

> C'est **une lettre**. Mon grand-père a écrit **une lettre**. →
> C'est une lettre **que** mon grand-père a écrit**e** en 1943.*
> *It's a letter* ***that*** *my grandfather wrote in 1943.*

Le pronom relatif *où*

The relative pronoun **où** refers to places or times mentioned in the main clause. It is followed by a noun or pronoun subject and the verb of the relative clause.

PLACE: Camille s'approche du bar des Cévennes. Quelques hommes jouent à la pétanque **devant le bar des Cévennes**. →
Camille s'approche du bar des Cévennes **où** quelques hommes jouent à la pétanque.
Camille approaches the bar des Cévennes ***where*** *several men are playing pétanque.*

---

*In the film, Camille actually says, **C'est une lettre *qu'*a écrite mon grand-père en 1943.** This inversion of the subject and verb in the relative clause is a permissible stylistic variation. Notice that the past participle still agrees with its preceding direct object.

TIME: **À l'époque**, Antoine faisait de la Résistance dans les Cévennes. **À l'époque**, Louise et Mado vivaient à Paris. →

À l'époque **où** Antoine faisait de la Résistance dans les Cévennes, Louise et Mado vivaient à Paris.

*At the time **when** Antoine was a member of the Resistance in the Cévennes, Louise and Mado were living in Paris.*

The following chart summarizes the use of relative pronouns.

GRAMMATICAL FUNCTIONS OF NOUN	PRONOUN
subject	**qui**
object	**que**
place or time	**où**

Activités

A. Histoires privées. Employez le pronom relatif approprié pour compléter le commentaire sur l'Épisode 18.

Saint-Jean de Causse est le village _____[1] Antoine a passé les derniers jours de sa vie. C'est la vérité _____[2] intéresse Camille. La situation _____[3] Camille se trouve est délicate. Elle veut parler d'un sujet _____[4] Mme Leblanc n'aime pas. C'est un sujet _____[5] est très difficile pour tout le monde. La guerre est quelque chose _____[6] personne ne peut oublier[a] et _____[7] touche encore beaucoup de gens.

Pendant qu'elles parlent, Mme Leblanc prépare une recette _____[8] vient de sa grand-mère et _____[9] Camille trouve très bonne. Mme Leblanc sort une vieille boîte _____[10] contient des photos _____[11] quelqu'un a prises pendant la guerre. Ce sont des images _____[12] montrent Pierre Leblanc et Antoine. C'étaient des copains _____[13] s'aimaient beaucoup au moment _____[14] on a pris cette photo. Malheureusement, c'est une amitié[b] _____[15] a mal fini pour tout le monde.

[a]*forget* [b]*friendship*

B. Le monde rural. Liez les deux phrases à l'aide d'un pronom relatif.

1. Autrefois, la France était un pays essentiellement agricole. Ce pays était plus traditionnel qu'au XXI[e] siècle.
2. C'est une situation compliquée. Beaucoup de jeunes agriculteurs ne comprennent pas cette situation.
3. Les jeunes continuent à travailler dans les champs. Leurs grands-parents ont travaillé dans ces champs.
4. Des fermes industrielles remplacent les petites fermes. Ces petites fermes appartiennent à des familles.

5. Certaines familles vont vivre en ville. En ville, il y a plus de travail.
6. Le gouvernement essaie d'aider les fermes. Les familles veulent protéger (*protect*) ces fermes.
7. Il y a des lois européennes concernant l'agriculture. Ces lois n'aident pas tous les agriculteurs.

C. Vos études. Avec un(e) partenaire, parlez de votre situation à l'université. Complétez les descriptions suivantes en ajoutant une phrase qui commence avec **qui**, **que** ou **où** pour clarifier votre position.

MODÈLE: Dans notre université, il y a des gens qui/que... →
É1: Dans notre université, il y a des gens qui travaillent beaucoup. Ils sont très sérieux.
É2: Il y a aussi des gens que les professeurs admirent. Ce sont de bons étudiants.

1. ______ est une matière qui/que...
2. ______ est un lieu sur le campus qui/que/où...
3. ______ est un restaurant qui/que/où...
4. Mon dernier cours était un cours de ______. C'était un cours qui/que/où...
5. Dans mon cours de ______, il y avait une personne intéressante. C'était une personne qui/que...
6. La semaine dernière, j'ai étudié ______ (un endroit). C'est un endroit qui/que/où...
7. Dans notre université, il y a des professeurs qui/que...

Structure 55

Les verbes comme *conduire*

Talking about everyday actions

—Oui. Il y avait quatre copains avec eux. Ils **détruisaient** des ponts et des voies de chemin de fer.

The verb **conduire** (*to drive*) is irregular in the present tense, and it has an irregular past participle. The formation of the **futur** and the **imparfait** are regular.

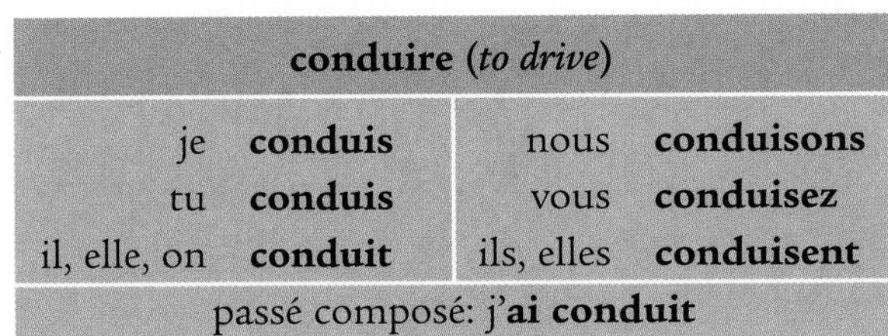

conduire (*to drive*)			
je	**conduis**	nous	**conduisons**
tu	**conduis**	vous	**conduisez**
il, elle, on	**conduit**	ils, elles	**conduisent**
passé composé: j'**ai conduit**			

Other verbs conjugated like **conduire** are

construire *to construct*
détruire *to destroy*
produire *to produce*
réduire *to reduce*
traduire *to translate*

L'historien **a traduit** le laissez-passer en français.	*The historian translated the pass into French.*
On **construit** une nouvelle autoroute.	*They're building a new highway.*
Sans Camille, il est difficile de **produire** «Bonjour!».	*Without Camille, it's difficult to produce "Bonjour!".*

Activités

A. Qui dit quoi? Complétez les phrases avec le présent d'un des verbes indiqués. Ensuite, imaginez qui est impliqué dans ces conversations—des amis, un étudiant, un traducteur, un agent de police, un journaliste, un homme d'affaires, un chauffeur de taxi, une victime de la guerre, ?

conduire, réduire, traduire

1. —Beaucoup de gens _____ trop souvent leur voiture. On ne _____ pas la pollution si on _____ tous les jours.
2. —Est-ce que tu _____ encore ton taxi tard le soir?
   —Non, je _____ mes heures de travail pour être avec ma famille.
3. —Vous _____ trop vite! Nous ne _____ pas à cette vitesse (*speed*) dans notre petit village! Comme ça, on _____ aussi le nombre d'accidents.
4. —Nous _____ des documents pour l'Organisation des Nations unies. Et toi? Qu'est-ce que tu _____?
   —Je _____ les lettres d'Albert Camus en anglais.

construire, détruire, produire

5. —Est-ce que les armées ennemies _____ vos villages?
   —Oui, et quand on _____ nos machines agricoles, les fermes _____ moins de nourriture.
6. —Vous et votre père, qu'est-ce que vous _____ dans votre usine (*factory*)?
   —Nous _____ du papier recyclé. Avec ses collègues, mon père _____ une nouvelle usine chaque année. Quand on recycle du papier, on _____ moins d'arbres.

B. Rêves et réalités. (***Dreams and realities.***) Complétez les phrases avec la forme correcte d'un des verbes de la liste. Attention aux temps des verbes.

Vocabulaire utile: conduire, construire, détruire, produire, réduire, traduire

Dans le passé, on ____[1] régulièrement les vieux bâtiments et les gens ____[2] des bâtiments plus modernes à la place. Dans votre ville, est-ce que les gens ____[3] beaucoup de nouveaux bâtiments récemment? Est-ce que votre famille ____[4] une nouvelle maison?

Dans le monde d'aujourd'hui, nous ne ____[5] pas la pollution de l'air parce que les gens ____[6] leurs voitures tous les jours. De plus, on ne ____[7] pas beaucoup de voitures électriques qui polluent moins. Et vos amis et vous, ____[8]-vous tous les jours?

Certains étudiants ne ____[9] pas du français en anglais dans leur tête. Est-ce que vous ____[10] du français en anglais quand vous lisez?

Dans le monde de demain, la vie sera parfaite.[a] Les régions agricoles ____[11] assez de céréales pour nourrir[b] le monde entier. Ainsi,[c] on ____[12] le nombre de gens qui ont faim. À votre avis, quel pays ____[13] le plus de nourriture dans ce monde idéal?

[a]*perfect* [b]*feed* [c]*In this way*

C. Interview. Formez des questions avec les éléments suivants. Interviewez trois camarades de classe pour obtenir des réponses à ces questions. Ensuite, comparez ces réponses avec celles de la classe.

MODÈLE: combien de fois par semaine / tes parents (tes enfants) / conduire / la voiture →
É1: Combien de fois par semaine est-ce que tes parents (tes enfants) conduisent la voiture?
É2: Ils conduisent la voiture au moins (*at least*) dix fois par semaine.

1. quand tu / lire / en français / traduire / tous les mots (*words*)
2. les agriculteurs de ton pays / produire / quelque chose de spécial
3. quel type de voiture / ton meilleur ami (ta meilleure amie) / conduire
4. quand / tu / ne... pas conduire
5. comment / tu / réduire / personnellement la pollution de l'air dans ta ville l'année dernière
6. quel type de bâtiment / ton université / construire / récemment

D. L'environnement, hier et aujourd'hui. Avec un(e) partenaire, jouez les rôles d'une jeune personne qui interviewe une personne âgée. La jeune personne veut savoir si on s'inquiétait autant de l'environnement autrefois qu'aujourd'hui.

MODÈLE: LE/LA JEUNE: Aujourd'hui, on réduit la pollution de l'air avec des voitures moins polluantes.
LA PERSONNE ÂGÉE: Autrefois, nous ne pensions pas à ce problème. Nous ne réduisions pas la pollution.

conduire
recycler (les journaux, le verre, le plastique, etc.)
conserver les ressources naturelles (les forêts, l'eau, etc.)
réduire la pollution de l'air (de l'eau, de la terre)
détruire de vieux bâtiments
réduire la consommation d'essence (d'électricité, de gaz naturel, d'énergie nucléaire)
produire (des voitures plus petites, des produits recyclables, etc.)

Regards sur la culture

La vie en ville et à la campagne

As you saw in this episode, Camille eventually finds the house in Saint-Jean de Causse where her grandfather spent part of the war. Jeanne and her grandson seem to have a fairly comfortable life.

Le village de Sainte-Engrâce dans les Pyrénées

- A farmhouse in the Cévennes would usually have the stable and barn on the ground floor. The family would live on the second floor, which would have an exterior stone staircase leading up to it. The roof would be covered with rough stone tiles. Jeanne's house is more elaborate and southern-looking. It has certainly been modified as the family became more prosperous. However, like most village homes in France, it is filled with a curious mix of traditional and modern elements.
- French people, both urban and rural, are very much attached to certain local traditions. For example, in the Central **Pyrénées**, everyone wants to be able to enjoy **la garbure** (a thick stew of cabbage, pork, rye bread, and preserved goose meat). And on special occasions, for example at a wedding dinner, everyone will sing the song "Aqueras montanhas" (*Those Mountains*) in Occitan, the traditional language of southern France.
- Until the 1970s or 1980s, the borders separating city from country were very distinct in most areas of France. Except for the special cases of a few very large cities, urban sprawl was absent. The past few decades, however, have seen the development of huge supermarkets and malls around even small towns.
- At the same time, the desire for North American–style suburban living is growing, not among the wealthiest people, who prefer urban environments, but in the middle class. Hosts of large **lotissements** (*developments*) are

appearing all over France. More and more people want to have their own **pavillon** (*small single-family home*), with garden and lawn.

Lyon la nuit

- Today, the major cities of France are developing very specific looks and personalities. Lille, in the north, aims to promote a modern image, with its Euralille district and high-tech public transportation. Montpellier, on the Mediterranean coast, has renovated its 18th-century center and has linked it to what is probably the most ambitious postmodern architectural development in France. Though they differ considerably one from the other, cities in France are in general very livable and intensely lived in. The North American city that is in large part emptied of its inhabitants at night is a shock to the French.

Considérez

The majority of French people would probably prefer to live in a city. Why do you think that this is true when so many North Americans would rather live in the suburbs or in the country?

Structure 56

La construction *verbe* + *préposition* + *infinitif*

Talking about everyday actions

—Tenez, s'il vous plaît. **Demandez**-lui simplement **de lire** ceci.

All verbs that follow a conjugated verb are in the infinitive form. You have been using these verb + infinitive constructions since Chapter 2.

Tu **vas travailler** avec eux. — *You're going to work with them.*

Je ne **sais** pas quoi **faire**. — *I don't know what to do.*

Je **veux** simplement **savoir** la vérité, pour moi. — *I only want to find out the truth, for me.*

Il **a voulu monter** des opérations plus importantes! — *He wanted to organize larger operations!*

1. Verbs that can take an infinitive directly after them include

adorer	désirer	espérer	savoir
aimer (mieux)	détester	pouvoir	vouloir
aller	devoir	préférer	

2. Some verbs use a preposition (usually **à** or **de**) before an infinitive. You've already learned some of these as well. These two categories of verbs include

VERBE + **à** + INFINITIF
apprendre à *to learn to (do)*
arriver à *to succeed in (doing)*
commencer à *to begin to (do)*
continuer à *to continue to (do)*
encourager (quelqu'un) à *to encourage (someone) to (do)*
hésiter à *to hesitate to (do)*
inviter (quelqu'un) à *to invite (someone) to (do)*
réfléchir à *to think about (doing)*
réussir à *to succeed in (doing)*

VERBE + **de** + INFINITIF
accepter de *to accept (doing)*
cesser de *to stop (doing)*
choisir de *to choose to (do)*
décider de *to decide to (do)*
demander (à quelqu'un) de *to ask (someone) to (do)*
se dépêcher de *to hurry to (do)*
dire (à quelqu'un) de *to tell (someone) to (do)*
essayer de *to try to (do)*
finir de *to finish (doing)*
permettre (à quelqu'un) de *to allow (someone) to (do)*
promettre (à quelqu'un) de *to promise (someone) to (do)*
refuser de *to refuse to (do)*
venir de *to have just (done)*

Je vous **invite à dîner**... — *I'm inviting you to dine . . .*

Écoute, n'**hésite** pas **à** m'**appeler**. — *Look, don't hesitate to call me.*

Dépêche-toi de le **retrouver**. — *Hurry and find him.*

...et **tu** lui **dis de venir** tout de suite! — *. . . and you tell him to come right away!*

Activités

A. Jeanne et Camille. Créez des phrases complètes avec les éléments suivants. N'oubliez pas la préposition si nécessaire.

1. Éric / dire / à Camille / partir
2. Camille / demander / à Éric / montrer / la lettre d'Antoine à Jeanne
3. Jeanne / accepter / parler à Camille
4. Camille / commencer / parler à Jeanne de sa quête
5. Jeanne / ne pas hésiter / montrer les photos à Camille

(*continued*)

6. Jeanne / décider / expliquer / comment Pierre et Antoine se sont connus
7. Camille / encourager / Jeanne / parler
8. Jeanne / essayer / raconter son histoire calmement
9. Camille / inviter / Jeanne / s'asseoir (*to sit down*)
10. Jeanne / permettre / Camille / l'aider

B. Au contraire. Vincent et Véronique sont des jumeaux (*twins*), mais ils ne se ressemblent pas. Complétez la première partie de la phrase avec une préposition et utilisez un verbe de la liste (avec une préposition, si nécessaire) pour terminer la phrase. Montrez que ces deux personnes n'agissent pas de la même façon.

Verbes utiles: arriver, choisir, commencer, continuer, hésiter, refuser

MODÈLE: Véronique cesse de fumer, mais Vincent commence à fumer.

1. Véronique accepte _____ parler aux gens, mais Vincent...
2. Véronique réussit _____ se faire des amis (*to make friends*), mais Vincent n'...
3. Véronique a fini _____ faire des bêtises (*silly things*) à l'âge de 12 ans, mais Vincent...
4. Véronique se dépêche _____ aider les gens, mais Vincent...
5. Véronique refuse _____ critiquer les gens, mais Vincent...

C. Actions et opinions. Terminez chaque phrase avec une construction qui utilise un verbe à l'infinitif. N'oubliez pas la préposition, si c'est nécessaire.

1. Je refuse...
2. Cette année, mon meilleur ami / ma meilleure amie va commencer...
3. Mes camarades de classe finissent...
4. J'adore parfois...
5. Les professeurs détestent...
6. Cette année, j'ai appris...
7. Mes amis me promettent...

Visionnement 2

Observez!

Considérez les aspects culturels expliqués dans **Regards sur la culture**. Ensuite, regardez l'Épisode 18 encore une fois, et répondez aux questions suivantes.

- De quelle région de France la famille de Jeanne vient-elle?
- Quelle est l'attitude de Jeanne envers son héritage régional? Que fait-elle dans cet épisode pour vous donner cette idée?

Faites l'activité pour le **Visionnement 2** dans le cahier.

Synthèse: Lecture

Mise en contexte

The reading selection in this chapter is a folktale that dates back to the Middle Ages.* Numerous versions have been found throughout France. It is also found in the Grimm† collection, which may explain its increased popularity in the late 19th and early 20th centuries. This version originated in the Cévennes region.

Stratégie pour mieux lire
Understanding oral tradition in written folktales

Folktales are transmitted orally and are addressed to a local audience. For this reason, they sometimes contain samples of regional dialect and exhibit characteristics of unplanned, spoken speech, such as repetition, incomplete sentences, exclamations, and a more flexible word order. Look at this example from the story that illustrates an oral style.

C'était un vilain,‡ un serf, quoi, et alors il voulait être riche.	*There was a villein, a serf, see, and, well, he wanted to be rich.*

Notice how the narrator refines his choice of vocabulary as he goes along and how he uses the expressions **quoi** and **alors** as interjections to give him time to think of what he will say next. Both of these are stylistically more like spoken narration than traditional written narration. Now look at another example.

Alors un jour, le diable, il y dit...	*So one day, the devil, he says to him . . .*

Here, the subject, **le diable**, is repeated in the pronoun **il**, and as an indication of dialect, **y** is used in place of **lui**. Again, these are indications of an oral presentation of the story.

---

*The Middle Ages refers to the period in European history often dated from 476 (fall of the Western Roman Empire) to 1453 (when Constantinople was conquered by the Turks).

†The German brothers Jakob Grimm (1785–1863) and Wilhelm Grimm (1786–1859) are known for their collection of folksongs and folktales. Between 1812 and 1822, they published these stories and songs in *Grimm's Fairy Tales* and other books.

‡Villein: a vile, brutish peasant; originally "feudal serf." A serf was a member of the lowest feudal class in medieval Europe, bound to the land and owned by a lord.

Now read the whole folktale. What is the moral of the story? What does it illustrate?

Le partage[1] de la récolte

C'était un vilain, un serf, quoi, et alors il voulait être riche. Alors il se plaignait[2] toujours:

—Oh! Moi si je savais! J'invoquerais[3] le diable! Même si… S'agit que j'aie des sous, quoi.[4]

Alors un jour, le diable, il y dit:

—Écoute, tu m'as invoqué. Je peux te venir en aide, seulement à une condition: nous allons partager la moitié[5] de tes récoltes. Alors, qu'est-ce que tu plantes cette année?

—Eh ben, je plante des pommes de terre…

—Ah! alors le diable y dit, ben écoute: tu plantes des pommes de terre, moi je me réserverai ce qui[6] sortira du champ.

—Bon, ça va. Moi je prendrai ce qui est dans la terre.

Alors quand la récolte arrive, pardi,[7] le diable se présente, et il est obligé de prendre la fane[8] des pommes de terre. Et lui, le paysan lui, il ramasse ce qu'il y avait dans la terre. Mais c'est tout des pommes de terre.

—Oooh! le diable dit, cette année tu m'as trompé! Mais l'année prochaine! Moi je veux prendre ce qui restera dans la terre!

Alors l'année d'après il sème[9] du blé, le bonhomme. Alors là, le diable arrive, quand c'est la fenaison,[10] là, et pardi bien sûr, le bonhomme, il ramasse la cime[11] du blé, quoi, ce qui est sorti de terre et le diable a été obligé de ramasser l'éteule,[12] les racines, ce qui restait, quoi. Ça, c'était le diablotin trompé par un vilain…

[1]*sharing* [2]*se… complained* [3]*I would invoke* [4]*S'agit… I need some money, see?* [5]*half* [6]*ce… that which* [7]*of course* [8]*useless part (the leaves)* [9]*sows* [10]*harvest time* [11]*top* [12]*stalks (straw)*

Après la lecture

A. Qui est-ce? Identifiez la personne dont on parle dans chacune des phrases suivantes. S'agit-il du paysan ou du diable?

1. Il a besoin d'argent.
2. Il est obligé de prendre la fane des pommes de terre.
3. Il ramasse des pommes de terre.
4. Il invoque le diable.
5. Il vient en aide.
6. Il plante du blé.
7. On l'a trompé.

B. La narration orale d'un conte. Voici quelques phrases tirées du texte. Comment ces phrases indiquent-elles que ce conte est une narration orale?

Possibilités:

répétition	expressions dialectales
exclamations	ordre flexible des éléments de la phrase
phrases incomplètes	expressions utilisées pour gagner du temps

1. Ah, alors, le diable y dit, ben, écoute.
2. Et lui, le paysan lui, il ramasse ce qu'il y avait dans la terre.
3. Alors là, le diable arrive, quand c'est la fenaison, là, et pardi, bien sûr, le bonhomme, il ramasse la cime du blé, quoi...

C. Réflexions. Réfléchissez aux questions suivantes.

1. D'habitude, quels traits associe-t-on avec un paysan? avec le diable? Est-ce que leurs portraits dans cette histoire correspondent à vos idées?
2. Quelles autres histoires ou fables connaissez-vous où une personne ou un animal redoutable (*fearsome*) est trompé par quelqu'un qui est moins puissant (*powerful*)?
3. Quelle est la morale du conte? Quelles caractéristiques de la nature humaine explore ce conte?

À écrire

Faites **À écrire** pour le Chapitre 18 dans le cahier.

Vocabulaire

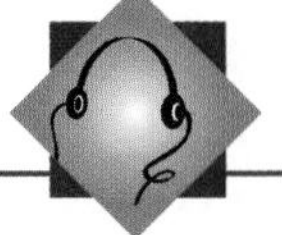

L'agriculture

un arbre	tree
le blé	wheat
une brebis	ewe
une céréale	grain
une cheminée	fireplace; chimney
l'élevage (*m.*)	(animal) breeding
une ferme	farm
un(e) fermier/ière	farmer
une grange	barn
un jardin	garden
une marmite	*large iron cooking pot*
un mouton	sheep
un(e) paysan(ne)	farmer
un porc	pig
la récolte	harvest; crop
la terre	earth; soil
une vache	cow
un verger	apple orchard
une vigne	vine
un vignoble	vineyard
la viticulture	wine growing
la volaille	poultry

pousser	to grow; to push
ramasser	to pick (up), gather (up)
récolter	to harvest

MOTS APPARENTÉS: **l'agriculture** (*f.*), **cultiver, planter, un village**

À REVOIR: **un(e) agriculteur/trice, le beurre, un cheval, le fromage, un lapin, le vin**

L'environnement

l'avenir (*m.*)	future	**consommer**	to consume
la consommation	consumption, usage		
l'effet (*m.*) **de serre**	greenhouse effect		
l'essence (*f.*)	gasoline		
le monde	world		

MOTS APPARENTÉS: **la conservation, l'environnement** (*m.*)**, un parti politique, la pollution, le recyclage, recycler**

Pronoms relatifs

que	whom, that, which	**où**	where, when
qui	who, that, which		

Autres verbes utiles

arriver (à)	to succeed in (doing)
cesser (de)	to stop (doing)
conduire	to drive
construire	to construct
détruire	to destroy
produire	to produce
réduire	to reduce
traduire	to translate

MOTS APPARENTÉS: **accepter (de), continuer (à), décider (de), hésiter (à), inviter (quelqu'un) à, refuser (de)**

À REVOIR: **adorer, aimer, aller, apprendre (à), choisir (de), commencer (à), demander (à quelqu'un) (de), se dépêcher (de), désirer, détester, devoir, dire (à quelqu'un) (de), encourager (quelqu'un) (à), espérer, essayer (de), finir (de), permettre (à quelqu'un) (de), pouvoir, préférer, promettre (à quelqu'un) (de), réfléchir (à), réussir (à), savoir, venir de, vouloir**

Adjectifs

efficace	efficient	**fort(e)**	strong; significant
faible	weak	**moyen(ne)**	moderate; average
fier (fière)	proud	**nombreux/euse**	numerous

Autres expressions utiles

partout	everywhere	**presque**	almost, nearly

Chapitre 19

Un certain Fergus

Le Chemin du retour

Feuille de service du 26 janvier
10e jour de tournage
Horaires: 13h–23h

LIEU DE TOURNAGE: FUVEAU—MUSÉE DES TRAINS

Séquence	*Effets*	*Décors*	*Résumé*	*Rôles*
122	EXT.—NUIT	COMBAT NOCTURNE FLASHBACK	Récit de Jeanne: la trahison° d'Antoine	ANTOINE 1940

treason

OBJECTIFS

In this episode, you will

- hear Jeanne tell what happened the night her husband was killed
- find out where Camille will go next on her quest

In this chapter, you will

- talk about wartime events
- discuss hypothetical situations and conditions
- use demonstrative pronouns to refer to specific things and people
- learn more about the Resistance movement in France during the Second World War
- read about Martinique and New Caledonia

Vocabulaire en contexte

Un reportage sur la Résistance

Le S

le 20 décembre 1943

MORT DE RÉSISTANTS

Alès—Les **résistants** continuent leur effort pour **retarder l'avance**° des **troupes** allemandes. Ils **frappent** plus **fort**,*° détruisant des **ponts**° et **des voies de chemin de fer**.°

La nuit du 17 décembre, sept résistants sont tombés dans **un piège**° tendu° par l'ennemi. Ils **ont attaqué** un train où les Allemands avaient entreposé° des **armes**—un train qu'ils croyaient **gardé** par seulement deux ou trois **soldats**. Les résistants sont passés un à un **silencieusement**° dans l'ombre° des wagons, mais **soudain**,†° la porte d'un wagon s'est ouverte et des soldats allemands **ont tiré sur**° les résistants. Ils ont été tous **tués**.°

Un résistant, grièvement blessé,° a pu **s'échapper**° et **se réfugier**° sous un wagon, mais il est mort le lendemain, le 18 décembre. Comme tous ses camarades, il est mort pour **la patrie**.°

En fait, les résistants attendaient **un camion**° pour transporter les armes. **Le conducteur**,° un certain Antoine Lebrun,‡ les avait poussés° à attaquer le train. Comme° ce camion n'est jamais arrivé, la Résistance **accuse** Antoine Lebrun de **trahison**° et le **recherche** activement. De son côté,° l'ennemi a commencé une campagne° de désinformation et a lancé des représailles:° plusieurs **otages**° ont déjà été **fusillés**.°

retarder... *to slow the advance*
frappent... *are striking harder* / *bridges*
voies... *railroad tracks*
trap / *set*
stored
silently
shadow / *suddenly*
ont... *fired on* / *killed*
grièvement... *seriously wounded* / *escape*
se... *take shelter*
la... *his country*
truck
driver
avait... *had pushed*
As
treason
De... *For its part*
campaign
reprisals / *hostages*
shot

Activités

A. Définitions. Voici des définitions de certains mots utilisés dans le reportage sur la Résistance. Donnez le mot convenable (*fitting*).

1. une sorte de prisonnier **2.** une personne qui participe au combat pendant une guerre **3.** le pays d'origine d'une personne **4.** les membres d'un groupe clandestin qui se battent contre (*fight against*) l'ennemi **5.** la personne qui conduit un véhicule **6.** un groupe de soldats **7.** la conséquence fatale d'une attaque

---

*Rappelez-vous que **fort(e)** est aussi un adjectif: **On devient fort quand on fait régulièrement de la musculation.**

†**Soudain(e)** est aussi un adjectif: **Il a eu une crise cardiaque soudaine.**

‡«Antoine Lebrun» est le nom pris par Antoine Leclair pour s'identifier sur son laissez-passer.

B. Événements d'une guerre. Complétez chaque phrase avec un des termes de la liste. Conjuguez les verbes au temps approprié et faites l'accord des substantifs et des adjectifs lorsque (*when*) c'est nécessaire.

Vocabulaire utile: accuser, attaquer, camion, fort, frapper, fusiller, piège, rechercher, retarder, silencieusement, soudain, voie de chemin de fer

1. L'ennemi a déjà envahi (*invaded*) plusieurs pays. Comment peut-on _____ son avance?
2. Ils _____ la ville et l'ont complètement détruite.
3. Personne n'attendait cette attaque. Ça a été un événement _____.
4. Les résistants ont perdu cette bataille (*battle*). L'ennemi était plus _____ qu'eux.
5. Les soldats _____ les résistants dans la forêt, mais ils ne les ont pas trouvés.
6. Pour tromper la Résistance, les troupes ont quitté la ville. Mais c'était un _____. Ils étaient cachés (*hidden*) près de la ville.
7. Les soldats ont avancé sans faire aucun bruit (*noise*). Ils ont avancé _____.
8. Les _____ roulaient sur les routes, chargés (*loaded*) d'armes et de bombes.
9. Les résistants ont voulu _____ plus fort contre l'ennemi.
10. Pour empêcher la livraison (*prevent the delivery*) des armes par train, les résistants ont détruit les _____.
11. On _____ un des résistants de trahison.

C. Qu'est-ce qu'ils font? Avec votre partenaire, inventez deux légendes pour chacun des dessins suivants. Une des légendes décrit le dessin, l'autre décrit ce qui se passera après. Mettez les substantifs au pluriel si nécessaire. Vous pouvez utiliser d'autres mots si vous voulez.

Substantifs utiles:
Allemands, armes, camion, otage, piège, pont, résistant, soldat, train, voie de chemin de fer, wagon

Verbes utiles: accuser, attaquer, détruire, s'échapper, frapper, garder, rechercher, se réfugier, retarder, tirer sur, tuer

1.

2.

3.

4.

Visionnement 1

Avant de visionner

Jeanne raconte son histoire. Dans le passage suivant, Jeanne raconte les événements de la nuit du 17 décembre 1943. À votre avis, qu'est-ce que les résistants allaient faire ce soir là? Qu'est-ce qui ne s'est pas passé comme prévu (*as planned*)?

Mon mari est arrivé le premier, avec les autres résistants. Antoine était en retard. Il devait le rejoindre[a] avec un camion, pour transporter les armes. Pierre était nerveux. Il savait qu'il risquait sa vie et celle[b] de ses camarades. Mais mon mari avait confiance:[c] Il croyait qu'Antoine était son ami. Et Antoine leur avait assuré[d] qu'il y aurait[e] très peu de soldats ce soir-là.

[a]*meet* [b]*that* [c]avait … *trusted him* [d]leur… *had assured them* [e]il… *there would be*

Vocabulaire relatif à l'épisode

il faut les empêcher de combattre	*we have to keep them from fighting*
un type	*guy*
Nous saisirons ces armes!	*We'll seize these arms!*
tout s'est précipité	*everything began happening quickly*
se traîner	*to move slowly, with difficulty; to crawl*
il a disparu	*he disappeared*
le chagrin	*pain, sorrow*

Observez!

Regardez l'épisode pour répondre aux questions suivantes.

- Qui était Fergus? Quelle «preuve» (*proof*) a-t-on de sa trahison?
- Qui a accusé Antoine de trahison? Pourquoi?

Après le visionnement

A. Ordre chronologique. Classez les événements suivants par ordre chronologique de 1 à 10.

__4__ **a.** Pierre est arrivé le premier au rendez-vous, avec les autres résistants.
__1__ **b.** Antoine a voulu frapper plus fort.
__10__ **c.** Éric donne une photo de Fergus à Camille.
__5__ **d.** Pierre a été grièvement blessé.
__3__ **e.** Fergus a demandé à Pierre de réunir (*gather together*) tous ses amis résistants.
__7__ **f.** Pierre s'est traîné jusque chez lui.
__2__ **g.** Fergus est arrivé de Paris.
__8__ **h.** Jeanne a soigné (*took care of*) Pierre.
__9__ **i.** Pierre a accusé Antoine de trahison.
__6__ **j.** Pierre a pu s'échapper.

B. Réfléchissez. Répondez aux questions suivantes.

1. À la fin de l'épisode, Jeanne demande à Camille de partir. Selon vous, regrette-t-elle sa décision d'accueillir Camille? Est-ce que le récit des événements de la nuit du 17 décembre 1943 a été trop pénible (*painful; difficult*) pour elle? Jeanne ressent-elle de la haine (*does she feel hatred*) envers Camille, la petite-fille d'Antoine?
2. Jeanne demande à Éric de donner la photo de Fergus à Camille. Est-ce que les remarques de Camille l'ont incitée à revoir sa façon de penser en ce qui concerne l'histoire d'Antoine? Veut-elle savoir elle-même la vérité?

Le conditionnel

Being polite and talking about possibilities

—Où **serait** la France sans l'effort des résistants, des héros de la guerre?

You have already studied the use of verbs in two verbal moods▲: the *indicative* (present, **passé composé**, **imparfait**, and future) and the *imperative*.

The *conditional* is another mood. It is used to make polite requests, to offer advice politely, and to talk about things that might happen.

1. To form the conditional, use the same stem as in the future tense but add the endings of the **imparfait**.

regarder		répondre	réussir
je	regarder**ais**	répondr**ais**	réussir**ais**
tu	regarder**ais**	répondr**ais**	réussir**ais**
il, elle, on	regarder**ait**	répondr**ait**	réussir**ait**
nous	regarder**ions**	répondr**ions**	réussir**ions**
vous	regarder**iez**	répondr**iez**	réussir**iez**
ils, elles	regarder**aient**	répondr**aient**	réussir**aient**

Camille explique qu'elle **aimerait** rencontrer la grand-mère d'Éric. — *Camille explains that she would like to meet Éric's grandmother.*

Verbs with irregular future stems have the same stems in the conditional. The endings are always regular.

Je **serais** contente de voir votre grand-mère. — *I would be happy to see your grandmother.*

Auriez-vous une photo des résistants? — *Would you have a photo of the resistance fighters?*

2. You have already seen examples of the conditional of *politeness*, a form used to soften a request or a piece of advice.

- Requests made with the present tense are not considered as polite as those made using the conditional.

  David, est-ce que vous **pourriez** m'aider dans mes recherches? — *David, could you help me with my research?*

- Advice can be given using the conditional of **devoir** + infinitive or by beginning with the expression **À ta (votre) place.**

  Tu **devrais** appeler le président, Camille. — *You should call the president, Camille.*

  À ta place, Camille, j'**abandonnerais** cette idée. — *If I were you, Camille, I would give up that idea.*

3. The conditional expresses a hypothetical occurrence. It can stand alone in sentences about hypothetical situations such as a description of a perfect world.

   Dans un monde parfait, il n'y **aurait** plus jamais de guerre. — *In a perfect world, there would be no more war.*

Activités

A. Une université parfaite. Complétez les phrases avec un verbe au conditionnel pour indiquer comment les choses seraient dans une université parfaite.

MODÈLE: Les professeurs ____ (ne pas donner) d'examens. →
Les professeurs ne donneraient pas d'examens.

1. On ____ (avoir) du bon café dans toutes les salles de classe.
2. La librairie ____ (vendre) les livres pour un dollar.
3. Vous ____ (réussir) à tous vos examens sans les préparer.
4. Je ____ (pouvoir) me lever tard le matin.
5. Les professeurs ____ (faire) les devoirs pour les étudiants (et pas le contraire).

6. Tu _____ (venir) sur le campus une fois par semaine.
7. Je _____ (ne pas travailler) à la bibliothèque tous les soirs.
8. Vous _____ (finir) tous vos cours à midi.
9. Nous _____ (recevoir) nos diplômes après un an d'études.

B. À votre place... / Vous devriez... Antoine Leclair donne des conseils à Pierre Leblanc et leur ami résistant David Berg. Quels sont les conseils? Commencez les phrases avec **À votre place, je...**

MODÈLE: contacter tous les résistants de la région →
À votre place, je contacterais tous les résistants de la région.

1. essayer de tout faire pour prendre les armes des Allemands
2. aller à la voie de chemin de fer
3. prendre les armes qui sont dans le train
4. ne rien dire à vos femmes
5. faire très attention

Pierre donne des conseils à Antoine aussi. Commencez les phrases avec **À ta place, je...**

6. être très prudent (*careful*)
7. ne pas parler tout de suite de ce projet
8. attendre encore un peu

Maintenant, donnez les mêmes conseils en utilisant **vous** ou **tu** avec le verbe **devoir** au conditionnel. Suivez le modèle.

MODÈLE: contacter tous les résistants de la région →
Vous devriez contacter tous les résistants de la région.

C. Dans un monde de rêve. Avec un(e) partenaire, parlez d'un monde où tout serait parfait parce que les gens feraient ou ne feraient pas certaines choses. Suivez le modèle, mais faites preuve d'imagination.

MODÈLE: mes parents →
Dans un monde de rêve, mes parents me donneraient beaucoup d'argent. (Dans un monde de rêve, mes parents ne se disputeraient pas.)

1. mes parents / mes enfants
2. mon meilleur ami / ma meilleure amie
3. je
4. mon professeur de _____ (*subject*)
5. les étudiants de cette classe
6. les jeunes en général
7. le président du pays
8. les célébrités

Structure 58

Les phrases avec *si*

Expressing hypothetical situations and conditions

—**Si** Camille ne **cherchait** pas la vérité, elle ne la **saurait** jamais.

You have already learned that in order to say something *will* happen *if* another event occurs, you should use **si** + present + future. You also know that the two clauses can appear in either order.

Si Camille ne **retourne** pas immédiatement à Canal 7, **sera**-t-elle licenciée?	*If Camille does not return to Channel 7 immediately, will she be fired?*
Est-ce que Camille **abandonnera** sa quête **si** elle ne **trouve** pas Fergus?	*Will Camille abandon her quest if she doesn't find Fergus?*

If "si" is at the beginning of the sentence, the first verb must be imparfait.

1. To say that something *would probably* happen *if* another event occurred, the construction **si** + **imparfait** + conditional is used. The two clauses can appear in either order.

Si Louise **était** encore vivante, elle **ferait** le voyage avec Camille.	*If Louise were still living, she would make the trip with Camille.*
Est-ce que le président **accepterait** l'absence de Camille **si** Martine **était** moins convaincante?	*Would the president accept Camille's absence if Martine were less convincing?*

Sometimes the **si** clause is understood but not expressed.

Tu **ferais** ça pour moi?	*You would do that for me?*

2. **Si j'étais toi (vous)** + conditional can be used to give advice. Used this way, it plays the same role as **À ta (votre) place.**

Si j'**étais** toi, Camille, j'**abandonnerais** cette idée.	*If I were you, Camille, I would give up that idea.*

Pour en savoir plus...

The structure **si** + **imparfait** can be used alone to make suggestions or invitations.

Si on **allait** au restaurant ce soir? *How about going out to eat tonight?*

Si nous **prenions** un pot ensemble? *What about having a drink together?*

Activités

A. Le Vercors. Le Vercors, une région pas loin des Alpes, était, comme les Cévennes, un lieu important pour la Résistance. On y trouve aujourd'hui le *Site national historique de la Résistance en Vercors*. Faites des phrases avec les éléments donnés en utilisant l'imparfait et le conditionnel pour faire des hypothèses.

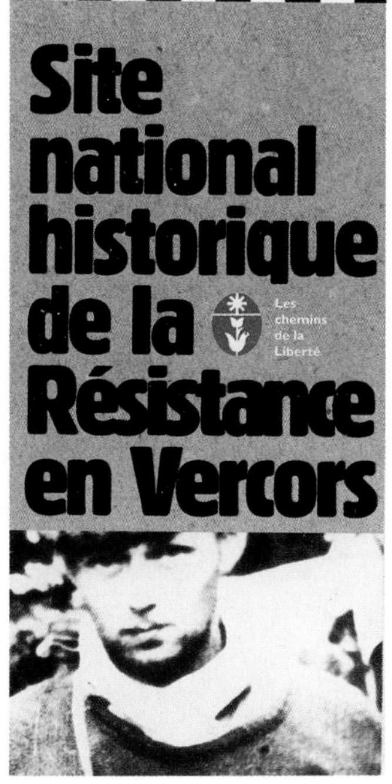

1. si nous / aller à cet endroit, / nous / visiter / un site national
2. je / trouver / facilement le Mémorial / si je / passer / par le village de Vassieux-en-Vercors
3. nous / ne pas avoir / le temps de visiter le Mémorial / si nous / arriver après 17 h
4. si les gens / venir / un dimanche en mai, / ils / pouvoir / visiter le Mémorial
5. si vous / voir / cet endroit, / vous / être sans doute touché(e) par l'héroïsme des résistants
6. si les Français / ne pas comprendre / l'importance de l'histoire, / ils / ne pas construire / des sites comme cela

Maintenant, parlez d'un autre endroit à visiter. Utilisez les phrases ci-dessus (*above*) comme modèle.

B. Situations normales et situations absurdes. Terminez les phrases suivantes avec une proposition contenant un verbe au présent, au futur, à l'imparfait ou au conditionnel, selon le sens de la phrase.

1. Si j'ai le temps ce soir, ...
2. Si j'avais un crocodile, ...
3. Mes amis et moi, nous mangerions au restaurant si...
4. Si mon ami(e) ne trouve pas de travail après les études, ...
5. Si mes parents étaient des extra-terrestres, ...
6. Si mes amis oublient mon anniversaire, ...
7. Je serais triste si...
8. Si mon professeur nous donnait des examens faciles, ...
9. Si les étudiants avaient moins de travail, ...
10. Les étudiants parleraient bien français si...
11. Si j'avais trois pieds, ...
12. Si je trouvais cent dollars dans la rue, ...

C. Que ferait-on? Interviewez trois camarades de classe pour savoir ce qu'ils/elles feraient seul(e)s et ce qu'ils/elles feraient ensemble dans votre région par les temps indiqués. Faites attention aux temps et aux modes des verbes.

MODÈLES: automne / il pleut →
É1: Que ferais-tu en automne s'il pleuvait?
É2: S'il pleuvait, je visiterais le musée d'art.
É1: Que feriez-vous ensemble en automne s'il pleuvait?
É1, 2, 3: S'il pleuvait, nous danserions dans la rue.

1. hiver / il fait du soleil
2. été / il fait très chaud
3. printemps / il fait mauvais et il pleut
4. automne / il fait frais mais beau
5. hiver / il neige

Regards sur la culture

La Résistance

Antoine avec ses camarades de la Résistance

During the years immediately following the Second World War, those who had served in the Resistance were seen as heros and saviors of France.

- In 1940, shortly after the French defeat, General Charles de Gaulle made a radio broadcast from London, encouraging the French nation not to cooperate with the German victors or their French allies but rather to fight to free France. By this act, he became the leader of the Free French forces.
- The Resistance movement that emerged little by little in occupied France engaged in secret military action (sabotage, assassinations, etc.), intelligence missions, medical service, and political contact. It had its own underground newspapers and periodicals. With the Resistance fighting both the German occupiers and the French Vichy government, World War II became a French civil war.
- After Germany turned against Russia in 1941, many well-organized French Communist groups became active members of the Resistance. The participation of these people made the movement far more effective.
- Much of the Resistance operated out of remote areas in the French countryside. Many groups were centered in rural southern France, where they came to be known as **maquisards** after the region's scrubby vegetation, **le maquis**.
- By the time of the Allied landings in Normandy in 1944, many who had originally supported Vichy started considering themselves members of the Resistance. By the end of the war, the number of **résistants** had multiplied considerably.
- A number of well-known French writers joined the Resistance through the underground **Comité national des écrivains**. Among these were Camus, Aragon, Éluard, and Malraux. One of the most important outcomes of this period was the tendency for intellectuals to become **engagés**, in other words, to be political activists. Many joined the French Communist Party. For nearly 25 years after the war, famous literary figures, like Jean-Paul Sartre, were significant political opinion makers.

Considérez

In 1940, France was defeated and partly occupied, but there was a French government operating from Vichy, with a popular man (le Maréchal Pétain) at its head. Why might some people have joined the Resistance when it seemed like a doubtful cause and when it made them traitors to the existing government?

Structure 59

Les pronoms démonstratifs

Avoiding repetition

—Il savait qu'il risquait sa vie et **celle** de ses camarades.

Demonstrative pronouns▲ are used to mean *this/that* (*one*) or *these/those* (*ones*).

1. The four demonstrative pronouns correspond in gender and number to the noun they represent.

	SINGULIER	PLURIEL
masculin	celui	ceux
féminin	celle	celles

2. Demonstrative pronouns must be followed by one of the following constructions.

   - **-ci** (to indicate proximity) or **-là** (to indicate distance)

     —Dans **quel train** les Allemands ont-ils entreposé des armes? — *In which train did the Germans store weapons?*

     —Ils en ont entreposé dans **celui-ci**. — *They stored some in this one.*

     —**Quels hommes** ont fait partie de la Résistance? — *Which men were in the Resistance?*

     —**Ceux-là!** — *Those!*

   - **de** + noun (to express possession)

     —Savait-il qu'il risquait **la vie de** ses camarades? — *Did he know he was risking his buddies' lives?*

     —Oui. Il savait qu'il risquait sa vie et **celle de** ses camarades. — *Yes. He knew he was risking his life and those of his buddies.*

- a relative clause introduced by **qui**, **que**, or **où** (to give more information)

—**Quel camion** attendaient-ils?	*Which truck were they waiting for?*
—Ils attendaient **celui qu**'Antoine conduisait.	*They were waiting for the one that Antoine was driving.*

Activités

A. Vous rappelez-vous les personnages? Utilisez un pronom démonstratif pour lier (*join*) logiquement les éléments de la colonne de gauche avec ceux de la colonne de droite.

MODÈLE: Hélène est celle qui vient du Québec

1. Hélène est	**a.** qui aide Camille à comprendre le laissez-passer
2. David est	**b.** que Pierre a vu avec un uniforme nazi
3. Roger et Nicole sont	**c.** qui ont organisé l'attaque contre le train
4. Pierre et Antoine sont	**d.** qui travaillent avec Martine à la régie
5. Roland Fergus est	**e.** qui aiment Camille de tout cœur
6. Mado et Louise sont	**f.** qui vient du Québec

B. Comparaisons. Mettez-vous par groupes de trois ou quatre. Comparez-vous à un ou plusieurs membre(s) de votre groupe. Vos camarades vont vous dire s'ils / si elles sont d'accord avec vous. Utilisez les catégories suivantes.

MODÈLE: cheveux →
É1: Mes cheveux sont plus courts que ceux de Suzanne.
É2: Je ne suis pas d'accord. Tes cheveux sont plus longs que ceux de Suzanne. (*ou* D'accord. Ceux de Suzanne sont plus longs.)

1. voiture	**3.** famille	**5.** études	**7.** yeux
2. travail	**4.** cours	**6.** vêtements	**8.** sac à dos

Visionnement 2

Observez!

Considérez les aspects culturels expliqués dans **Regards sur la culture**. Ensuite, regardez l'Épisode 19 encore une fois, et répondez aux questions suivantes.

- Comment la Résistance a-t-elle essayé d'infiltrer les Allemands?
- Dans quel quartier de Marseille Fergus habitait-il avant la guerre?

Après le visionnement

Faites l'activité pour le **Visionnement 2** dans le cahier.

Synthèse: Culture

Deux îles françaises loin de la France

En 1939, l'empire français était vingt-deux fois plus grand que la France métropolitaine, c'est-à-dire que la France elle-même. Il y avait des colonies aux Caraïbes,[1] en Afrique, dans l'océan Indien, en Indochine et dans le Pacifique. La Deuxième Guerre mondiale et la période 1945–1960 ont transformé la situation. Beaucoup de colonies sont devenues indépendantes; d'autres sont restées françaises.

La Martinique

La population:

- Traditionnellement ouvriers et paysans, **les Noirs** sont aujourd'hui souvent de la classe moyenne aussi.
- Les blancs des grandes familles traditionnelles (l'élite de la population) sont **les Békés**.
- Les personnes de race mixte, **les Mulâtres** sont en général de la classe moyenne.
- **Les Blancs créoles**, nés dans l'île, sont souvent des artisans et des commerçants.
- Les Français de France (professeurs, policiers, administrateurs) sont surnommés **les Métros**.

Un marché à Fort-de-France en Martinique

En 1940, la Martinique, aux Antilles, était dominée par douze grandes familles, «les Békés», c'est-à-dire les blancs qui possédaient les grandes plantations. Au moment de la Deuxième Guerre mondiale, ces familles sont restées fidèles[2] au gouvernement de Vichy. Mais beaucoup de Noirs sont partis à la Dominique, l'île située au nord, pour rejoindre l'armée de Charles de Gaulle.

En 1945, les Martiniquais ont voté pour l'union politique avec la France. Aujourd'hui, l'île est un «département d'outre-mer» (DOM)[3] de la France et les Martiniquais sont donc des citoyens[4] français. La situation économique de la Martinique est difficile. La ressource traditionnelle était la canne à sucre, mais l'agriculture ne prospère plus aujourd'hui. Plus de 50% des salaires dans l'île sont payés par le gouvernement. Cependant,[5] avec l'assistance de la France, la Martinique est plus prospère que les autres pays de la région.

[1]*Caribbean* [2]*loyal* [3]*overseas department (state)* [4]*citizens* [5]*Nevertheless*

La Nouvelle-Calédonie

Un village kanak en Nouvelle-Calédonie

La population:

- Les Mélanésiens, **les Kanaks**, étaient les premiers habitants de l'île. Ouvriers et paysans, ils habitent en général à la campagne.
- Les blancs qui sont nés sur l'île, **les Caldoches**, vivent sur leurs terres ou dans les villes.
- Les Français de France (professeurs, policiers, administrateurs, ingénieurs) sont surnommés **les Zozos** (ou **Zoreilles**).
- Il y a aussi les autres, les enfants d'immigrés asiatiques (Polynésiens, Vietnamiens, par exemple). Ce sont en général des ouvriers, des artisans et des commerçants.

En 1940, le gouvernement de Vichy n'a pas pu contrôler toutes les colonies: la Nouvelle-Calédonie a déclaré son soutien[6] pour de Gaulle et les Forces françaises libres. Les partisans de Vichy sont partis à Saïgon, au Viêtnam. Après l'attaque contre Pearl Harbor, la Nouvelle-Calédonie est devenue une base importante pour les troupes américaines. Les militaires sont arrivés avec beaucoup d'argent. Ils ont construit des aéroports, des hôpitaux et des routes. Beaucoup de Kanaks ont vu pour la première fois des bulldozers et des jeeps. Ils ont vu aussi que certains des soldats américains étaient noirs. Cette présence américaine a transformé les mentalités.

Après la guerre, la Nouvelle-Calédonie est devenue un «territoire d'outre-mer» (TOM)* de la France et ses habitants sont devenus citoyens français. La prospérité est arrivée après 1960 avec l'exploitation du minerai nickel. L'île a 40% des ressources du monde en nickel. Mais les Kanaks n'ont pas autant profité des avantages de cette expansion économique et les années 80 ont vu une montée du mouvement indépendantiste kanak. Entre 1984 et 1988 il y a eu une période de violence anti-française. Aujourd'hui, la situation est plus calme, mais les Kanaks sont toujours beaucoup plus pauvres que les Caldoches. Et maintenant, ils sont minoritaires dans l'île.

[6]*support*

À vous

Un reportage. En petits groupes, préparez une présentation orale où vous comparerez la Martinique et la Nouvelle-Calédonie. Utilisez les suggestions suivantes.

1. ...une colonie française...
2. ...la société est dominée par...
3. ...les plus pauvres sont...
4. ...on appelle les gens qui représentent la France...
5. ...pendant la guerre de 39–45...
6. ...les ressources naturelles...
7. ...est près de pays pauvres/riches...
8. ...il y a eu de la violence...

*Les DOM sont plus intégrés au système politique français que les TOM. Les habitants des DOM ont les mêmes droits (*rights*) et les mêmes devoirs que les citoyens français en France. Les TOM diffèrent entre eux par leurs lois (*laws*) et par leurs relations avec la France.

À écrire

Faites **À écrire** pour le Chapitre 19 dans le cahier.

Vocabulaire

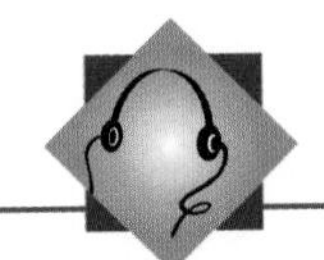

La guerre

une arme (*f.*)	weapon, arm	**un pont**	bridge
un camion	truck	**un soldat**	soldier
un(e) conducteur/trice	driver	**la trahison**	treason
un otage	hostage	**une voie de chemin de fer**	railroad tracks
la patrie	homeland		
un piège	trap		

MOTS APPARENTÉS: **un résistant, des troupes** (*f.*)

Verbes

s'échapper	to escape	**se réfugier**	to hide, take refuge
frapper	to strike, hit	**retarder l'avance**	to slow the advance
fusiller	to execute (*somebody*) by shooting	**tirer sur**	to fire on, shoot at
garder	to guard; to keep	**tuer**	to kill
rechercher	to search for; to research		

MOTS APPARENTÉS: **accuser, attaquer**

Les pronoms démonstratifs

celui, celle; ceux, celles	this/that; these/those

Adjectifs et adverbes

fort (*adj.*)	with strength; with effort	**soudain(e)** (*adj.*)	sudden
silencieusement	silently		
soudain (*adv.*)	suddenly		

À REVOIR: **fort(e)** (*adv.*)

Autres expressions utiles

à ta (votre) place	in your place, if I were you

À REVOIR: **-ci, -là, si**

Chapitre 20

Risques

Le Chemin du retour

Feuille de service du 21 janvier
6e jour de tournage
Horaires : 9h–19h

LIEU DE TOURNAGE : MARSEILLE—FRANCE 3—Grand plateau au rez-de-chaussée

Séquence	*Effets*	*Décors*	*Résumé*	*Rôles*
130	INT.—JOUR	CANAL 7—Plateau de l'émission «BONJOUR!»	Le président veut renvoyer° Camille. La productrice menace° alors de démissionner° avec toute l'équipe. Le président accorde une extension d'une semaine.	PRODUCTRICE, PRÉSIDENT

fire
threatens
quit

OBJECTIFS

In this episode, you will

- find out what Martine says to the station president about Camille
- watch as Camille looks for Roland Fergus

In this chapter, you will

- talk about the city of Marseille
- discuss the world of work and money
- express judgments, necessity, and obligation using infinitives
- express obligation and will, using the subjunctive
- learn about workplace customs in France
- read an excerpt of a story by Jules Verne

Vocabulaire en contexte

La ville de Marseille

Marseille: 795.600 **habitants** (*m.*), deuxième ville de France.

La situation géographique de Marseille, premier **port** en France, a favorisé **au cours des siècles**° (*m.*) l'implantation sur son sol° de différentes nationalités avec une forte proportion d'**immigrés** (*m.*) des pays d'Afrique du Nord, mais aussi des Italiens, des Turcs, des Espagnols et des Portugais.

au... *through the centuries* / *soil*

L'accent marseillais, rendu si populaire dans les films de Marcel Pagnol, est **célèbre** dans le monde entier. Les Marseillais sont **réputés** pour **la chaleur**° de leur **accueil** (*m.*) et leur **joie** (*f.*) **de vivre**.°

warmth

joie... *joyful attitude (toward life)*

Marseille est divisé en seize **arrondissements**° (*m.*) dont° plusieurs quartiers et **sites** (*m.*) **touristiques** comme:

districts / *including*

- *Le Vieux-Port:* port de plaisance,° hôtels, restaurants, cafés, boutiques
- *Le Panier:* quartier aux **ruelles**° **étroites**° anciennement **délabrées**° mais maintenant en pleine **rénovation**, boutiques, **galeries** (*f.*)
- *Notre-Dame de la Garde:* basilique° du XIXe siècle, perchée sur une colline qui **donne sur**° le port
- *Le cours Julien:* **rue piétonne**,° **antiquaires**° (*m., f.*), librairies, cafés, restaurants

port... *marina*

alleyways / *narrow* / *dilapidated*

basilica (large Roman Catholic church)

donne... *overlooks*

rue... *pedestrian street* / *antique dealers*

Pour en savoir plus...

L'écrivain et cinéaste Marcel Pagnol (1895–1974) est très connu pour sa description du paysage et des habitants de la Provence, y compris (*including*) la célèbre trilogie marseillaise *Marius*, *Fanny* et *César*. Il décrit sa jeunesse dans la région dans ses deux films *La Gloire de mon père* (1957) et *Le Château de ma mère* (1958), qui ont été refaits par le cinéaste Yves Robert en 1991.

Activités

A. Définitions. Donnez le mot qui correspond aux définitions suivantes. Attention: Faites des phrases complètes!

MODÈLE: un commerçant qui vend des objets devenus plus précieux au cours des années →
Un antiquaire est un commerçant qui vend des objets devenus plus précieux au cours des années.

1. un étranger qui s'installe dans un nouveau pays **2.** une division administrative d'une ville **3.** une zone où la circulation automobile est interdite (*prohibited*) **4.** une période de cent ans **5.** un endroit où les bateaux arrivent **6.** un adjectif qui décrit un bâtiment qui a besoin d'être rénové

Pour en savoir plus...

Voici quelques mots du dialecte marseillais. Leur origine est la langue occitane (le provençal). Leur équivalent dans le langage «standard» est indiqué.

bazarette = une personne qui parle beaucoup, un(e) bavard(e)

fada = fou ou passionné de quelqu'un ou de quelque chose

pitchoun ou **pitchon** = petit enfant

Qu'es aco? = Qu'est-ce que c'est?

testard = têtu (*stubborn*)

B. Chez vous. Identifiez une ville...

1. où il y a une cathédrale célèbre. De quel siècle date cette cathédrale?
2. où il y a un port. C'est un port de plaisance ou un port maritime (*shipping*)?
3. qui est réputée pour la chaleur de son accueil. Comment sont ses habitants?
4. qui est célèbre dans le monde entier. Quels sites touristiques y trouve-t-on? Quelles galeries? Quelles boutiques?
5. où il y a un accent particulier. Cet accent est-il lent? rythmé? prestigieux?
6. qui accueille beaucoup d'immigrés. Quel(s) groupe(s) d'immigrés y trouve-t-on?

C. Une annonce publicitaire. Avec un(e) partenaire, créez une annonce publicitaire pour votre ville ou région. Suivez le modèle donné dans la présentation sur Marseille, et décrivez, par exemple, des rues piétonnes ou des ruelles pittoresques, des bâtiments ou de grandes maisons qui donnent sur des jardins, des ports de plaisance, des sites touristiques célèbres, la joie de vivre des habitants, etc.

Le monde du travail et de l'argent

Quand Martine, la productrice à Canal 7, **a engagé**° Camille, les deux ont signé **un contrat**. Avec son **équipe**, Martine **a formé**° Camille, qui est bientôt devenue **la vedette**° de l'émission «Bonjour!». Maintenant Camille reçoit **un** très bon **salaire**. Chaque mois, elle **dépose**° un chèque d'un **montant** important° sur son **compte**° à **la banque**.

Camille décide de prendre **un congé**° de deux semaines sans en parler à Martine. Le président de Canal 7 n'en est pas du tout content. Il va peut-être **licencier**° Camille. Bruno a peur qu'il le fasse° et que Camille se retrouve **au chômage**.°

a... *hired*
a... *trained*
star
deposits
montant... *large amount* / *account*
time off
to fire
le... *might do it*
au... *unemployed*

Autres expressions utiles

un carnet de chèques	checkbook
faire un chèque	to write a check
toucher un chèque	to cash a check

Langage fonctionnel

Pour trouver un emploi

Expressions pour parler de la recherche d'un emploi

rédiger/soumettre son curriculum vitæ (C.V.)	*to write/submit one's CV (resumé)*
poser sa candidature	*to apply, submit one's candidacy*
avoir un entretien d'embauche	*to have a job interview*
être payé(e) [10 dollars] de l'heure	*to be paid [10 dollars] per hour*
un(e) chômeur/euse	*unemployed person*

Questions souvent posées à un entretien d'embauche

Pourquoi avez-vous répondu à notre annonce?	*Why did you respond to our ad?*
Pourquoi avez-vous quitté votre dernier emploi?	*Why did you leave your last job?*
Quelles sont vos qualifications?	*What are your qualifications?*
Que savez-vous de notre société?	*What do you know about our company?*

Quand je cherche un nouvel emploi, je **rédige mon curriculum vitæ** et je **pose ma candidature** dans plusieurs entreprises. Quand j'obtiens **un entretien d'embauche**, on me demande parfois de parler de **mes qualifications**.

Activités

A. Le monde du travail. Complétez les phrases suivantes par le mot ou l'expression qui convient. S'il s'agit d'un verbe, conjuguez-le au temps convenable. Si c'est un substantif, mettez l'article si nécessaire.

1. Camille est l'animatrice la plus connue et la plus aimée de Canal 7. C'est _____ (congé, vedette) de «Bonjour!»
2. Quand Martine l'a engagée, Camille avait très peu d'expérience. Martine la (l') _____ (former, licencier) et maintenant, c'est la meilleure journaliste.
3. Camille reçoit un bon _____ (argent, salaire). Chaque mois, elle _____ (déposer un chèque, être au chômage) d'un montant important.
4. Pour des raisons personnelles, Camille a pris _____ (congé, contrat) et sera absente pour deux semaines.
5. Le président n'est pas content de l'absence de Camille. Après tout, elle a signé _____ (chèque, contrat).
6. Si le président ne se calme pas, il va sûrement _____ (former, licencier) Camille. Elle n'aura plus d'emploi à Canal 7.

B. Questions personnelles. Posez les questions suivantes à votre partenaire. Demandez-lui...

1. s'il / si elle préfère travailler en équipe ou seul(e). Quels sont les avantages et les inconvénients de chaque situation?
2. s'il / si elle préférerait gagner un bon salaire en faisant un travail qu'il/elle n'aime pas ou un salaire médiocre en faisant un travail qui l'intéresse.
3. ce qu'il/elle ferait s'il / si elle pouvait interrompre (*interrupt*) ses études ou son travail et prendre des congés.
4. ce qu'une personne qui est au chômage devrait faire pour trouver un emploi.
5. s'il / si elle pense que Camille va être licenciée. Pourquoi ou pourquoi pas?

C. Comment trouver un emploi. Expliquez quelles démarches (*steps*) vous devez faire pour trouver un emploi. Utilisez les adverbes **d'abord**, **ensuite**, **puis** et **enfin**.

MODÈLE: D'abord, je rédige mon curriculum vitæ. Ensuite,...

Visionnement 1

Avant de visionner

Vocabulaire relatif à l'épisode

elle était censée être...	*she was supposed to be . . .*
elle a changé d'avis	*she changed her mind*
démissionner	*to quit, resign*
rédactrice	*editor*
faites-lui confiance	*trust her*
Vous êtes de passage à...	*Are you traveling through . . .*

Confrontation professionnelle. Dans l'Épisode 20, la productrice, Martine, doit parler avec le président de Canal 7. Il est furieux à cause de l'absence de Camille. Voilà quelques paroles du président. À votre avis, qu'est-ce que Martine pourrait répondre?

1. Martine, vous me connaissez depuis longtemps. Je n'accepte pas les caprices. L'attitude de Camille est intolérable!
2. Personne n'a le droit (*right*) de déserter son poste. Rien ne peut le justifier.
3. C'est nous qui l'avons découverte, formée et rendue célèbre. Elle nous doit quelque chose, n'est-ce pas?
4. Je lui accorde (*I'll give her*) deux jours. Pas un jour de plus!

Observez!

Dans cet épisode, Martine est convoquée (*summoned*) chez le président. Ils discutent les actions de Camille. Maintenant, regardez l'Épisode 20 et répondez aux questions suivantes.

- Quel effet a l'absence de Camille sur les indices d'audience (*ratings*) de Canal 7?
- À quelle solution de compromis est-ce que Martine et le président arrivent à la fin de leur discussion?
- Que fait Camille pour essayer de trouver Roland Fergus?

Après le visionnement

A. Reconstituez. Mettez les répliques du dialogue dans l'ordre logique.

DIALOGUE A: MARTINE ET BRUNO

3 MARTINE: À Marseille. Qu'est-ce qu'elle va faire à Marseille?
5 MARTINE: Elle a changé d'avis. Et pourquoi?
1 MARTINE: Est-ce que quelqu'un a des nouvelles de Camille?
2 BRUNO: Oui. Elle a appelé. Elle est à Marseille.
4 BRUNO: Elle a peut-être changé d'avis!

DIALOGUE B: LE PATRON DU BAR ET CAMILLE

_____ PATRON: Alors, vous êtes de passage à Marseille?
_____ PATRON: Fergus... ? Fergus... ? Je connais tout le monde dans cette ville.
_____ PATRON: Oui. Je vous trouve son adresse pour demain matin.
_____ CAMILLE: C'est vrai?
_____ CAMILLE: Je cherche cet homme. Il s'appelle Roland Fergus... . Autrefois, son père avait un garage sur le Vieux-Port.

B. Réfléchissez. À votre avis, est-ce que le président est trop sévère envers Camille ou a-t-il raison? Justifiez votre réponse.

Structure 60

Les expressions impersonnelles + infinitif

Expressing judgments, necessity, and obligation

—La vérité... Savez-vous qu'**il n'est pas** toujours **bon de** la **connaître**?

—Peut-être. Mais **il n'est jamais bon de** la **cacher**, surtout à un enfant.

Impersonal expressions are those that have no specific person as the subject. In English, they are usually expressed as *It is important to . . . , One needs to . . . ,* and so on.

Pour en savoir plus...

The impersonal expression **il vaut mieux** (*it is better*) can also be used before an infinitive to express a judgment.

Il vaut mieux savoir la vérité. *It is better to know the truth.*

It may also be used in the future and the conditional.

Il vaudra mieux... *It will be better . . .*

Il vaudrait mieux... *It would be better . . .*

1. The construction **Il est** + adjective + **de** + infinitive can be used to express judgments about situations and circumstances. Adjectives such as **bon**, **essentiel**, **important**, **impossible**, **inutile**, **juste** (*right*), **préférable**, **triste**, and **utile** can be used in this way. The verb **être** can be in almost any tense.

Il sera essentiel de retarder les troupes allemandes...	*It will be essential to slow the German troops . . .*
Il était triste de penser aux événements de la guerre.	*It was sad to think about the events of the war.*
Il est juste de chercher la vérité.	*It is right to look for the truth.*

2. Impersonal expressions can also be used before an infinitive to talk about obligation or necessity. Three common expressions are

il faut	+ infinitive	*it is necessary to; one must*
il est nécessaire de	+ infinitive	*it is necessary to*
il suffit de	+ infinitive	*it is enough to, all that is necessary is to*

In English, these impersonal expressions are sometimes expressed with personal pronoun subjects.

Il est nécessaire de chercher la vérité sur mon père.	***We** need to look for the truth about my father.*
Il faut frapper plus fort.	***We** need to strike harder.*
Il suffit de tromper l'ennemi.	*All **you** need to do is to trick the enemy.*

Attention—**Il ne faut pas** means (*someone*) *should not.* Use **il n'est pas nécessaire de** to mean *it is not necessary to.*

Il ne faut pas mentir à un enfant.	*You shouldn't lie to a child.*
Il n'est pas nécessaire de mentir à un enfant.	*It's not necessary to lie to a child.*

Pour en savoir plus...

It is useful to learn to recognize **il faut** and **il suffit** in other tenses.

PASSÉ COMPOSÉ: **il a fallu, il a suffi**

IMPARFAIT: **il fallait, il suffisait**

FUTUR: **il faudra, il suffira**

CONDITIONNEL: **il faudrait, il suffirait**

3. You have already learned a few other constructions that can also be used with an infinitive to express judgment and necessity. In such cases, the infinitive has the same subject as the conjugated verb.

JUDGMENT: Camille **est heureuse d'avoir** Bruno comme ami.
Es-tu **content de voir** ces indices d'audience?

NECESSITY: Camille **a besoin d'aller** à Marseille.
Martine **doit parler** au président de Canal 7.

Activités

A. Marseille, une ville au service de ses habitants. Imaginez que les personnes suivantes se trouvent à Marseille. Pour chaque personne, indiquez quels services publics sont importants, essentiels, inutiles, etc., en utilisant une expression impersonnelle.

Vocabulaire utile: bon, essentiel, important, impossible, indispensable, inutile, préférable, triste, utile

MODÈLE: Pour un jeune de 16 ans sans voiture, il est essentiel d'avoir un plan du métro. Il est inutile de connaître le parking du Vieux-Port.

PERSONNES	SERVICES PUBLICS
1. un jeune de 16 ans sans voiture	**a.** avoir un plan du métro
2. un touriste qui ne connaît pas la ville	**b.** visiter le centre pédagogique de la mer
3. une employée qui téléphone aux restaurants pour réserver	**c.** utiliser les pages jaunes
4. un homme d'affaires qui conduit une voiture mais qui n'a pas d'enfants	**d.** demander un permis de construire
5. un instituteur qui veut enseigner l'importance de la protection des eaux	**e.** trouver l'Office du Tourisme et des Congrès
6. une dame avec des enfants qui veulent nager	**f.** pouvoir consulter le site Internet «Marseille et ses plages»
7. un père célibataire avec une petite fille	**g.** connaître le parking du Vieux-Port
8. un couple qui veut ajouter un garage à la maison	**h.** contacter les services de la Direction de la Petite Enfance

Maintenant, avec un(e) camarade de classe, décidez lesquels de ces services (ne) vous seraient (pas) utiles lors d'une visite à Marseille. Expliquez pourquoi.

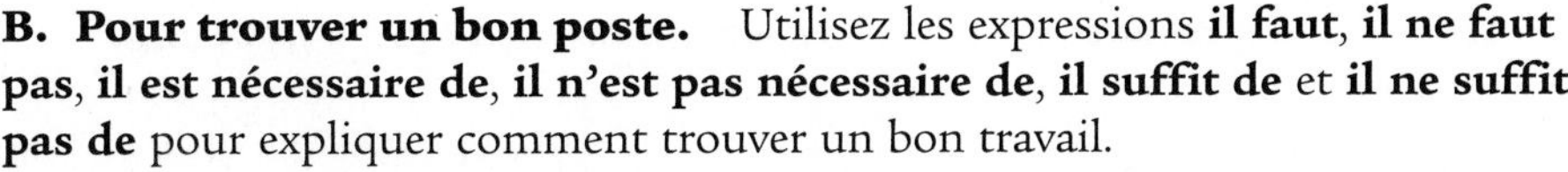

B. Pour trouver un bon poste. Utilisez les expressions **il faut**, **il ne faut pas**, **il est nécessaire de**, **il n'est pas nécessaire de**, **il suffit de** et **il ne suffit pas de** pour expliquer comment trouver un bon travail.

MODÈLE: savoir négocier un bon salaire →
Il faut savoir négocier un bon salaire.

1. répondre à l'annonce
2. connaître le patron
3. donner des cadeaux au patron
4. poser sa candidature
5. envoyer son dossier
6. rédiger son curriculum vitæ
7. faire une demande d'emploi par téléphone
8. s'habiller en short pour l'entretien d'embauche
9. parler de ses qualifications
10. engager un avocat

Maintenant, parlez avec un(e) camarade de classe de ce que vous (n')avez (pas) fait quand vous avez cherché du travail.

Structure 61

Le subjonctif

Expressing obligation and necessity

—**Il faut que Camille attende** jusqu'au lendemain pour obtenir l'adresse de Roland Fergus.

Up until now, the tenses you have learned are in verbal moods▲ called the *indicative*, the *imperative*, and the *conditional.* The subjunctive is another verbal mood that is used in very predictable and specific instances.

In this section, you will learn the formation of the present tense of the subjunctive and a set of expressions that trigger its use.

1. To form the subjunctive of all regular verbs, use the stem of the **ils/elles** form of the present indicative as the stem of the subjunctive and add the endings **-e**, **-es**, **-e**, **-ions**, **-iez**, **-ent**.

	travailler	attendre	finir
que je (j')	travaill**e**	attend**e**	finiss**e**
que tu	travaill**es**	attend**es**	finiss**es**
qu'il, qu'elle, qu'on	travaill**e**	attend**e**	finiss**e**
que nous	travaill**ions**	attend**ions**	finiss**ions**
que vous	travaill**iez**	attend**iez**	finiss**iez**
qu'ils, qu'elles	travaill**ent**	attend**ent**	finiss**ent**

Il faut que Camille finisse sa quête. *Camille has to finish her quest.*

The following verbs also form the subjunctive this way: **connaître**, **dire**, **écrire**, **lire**, **mettre**, and all verbs conjugated like **conduire**, **ouvrir**, **sortir**, and **vivre**.

Il est important que Mme Leblanc **lise** la lettre d'Antoine. *It is important that Mme Leblanc read the letter from Antoine.*

2. The verb + infinitive construction that you have already seen is used when a generalization is being made or when the subject of the infinitive is understood. But the infinitive has to be turned into a clause with the subjunctive when the following two things are *both* true:

- an expression that triggers the subjunctive (such as **il faut**) is used
- there are different subjects for the two verbs

ONE SUBJECT	Il faut **frapper** plus fort.
TWO SUBJECTS	Il faut **que vous frappiez** plus fort.
ONE SUBJECT	Il suffit de **lire** la lettre.
TWO SUBJECTS	Il suffit **qu'elle lise** la lettre.

Activités

A. Pour changer sa vie. Quand on veut changer sa vie, il faut prendre beaucoup de décisions. Transformez les phrases pour les rendre plus personnelles en utilisant le subjonctif et en faisant les autres changements nécessaires.

MODÈLE: Il faut penser à ses problèmes (nous) →
Il faut que nous pensions à nos problèmes.

1. Il ne faut pas oublier ses amis. (vous)
2. Il est essentiel de poser beaucoup de questions. (je)
3. Il n'est pas nécessaire de changer radicalement. (tu)
4. Il suffit de choisir un nouveau style de vie. (on)
5. Il est important de regarder le monde avec beaucoup d'attention. (les gens)
6. Il est très important de mettre fin aux activités nuisibles (*harmful*). (vous)
7. Il faut réfléchir longuement. (nous)
8. Il est nécessaire d'attendre le bon moment pour changer sa vie. (je)

Maintenant, parlez avec un(e) camarade de classe pour choisir les trois activités essentielles pour changer sa vie.

B. Une audition ratée. (*A failed audition.*) Votre ami est allé passer une audition à Canal 7. Malheureusement, il l'a complètement ratée. Il vous raconte les critiques de la productrice. Conseillez-le en vous inspirant des idées suivantes et en utilisant des expressions d'obligation + le subjonctif.

se calmer	se laver les cheveux	porter un nouveau costume
lire des notes	réfléchir avant de parler	choisir des sujets intéressants
parler moins vite	bien connaître les sujets	dire au caméraman de faire attention

MODÈLE: Elle n'aime pas mes vêtements. →
Il faut que tu portes un nouveau costume.

1. Elle dit que je suis difficile à comprendre quand je parle. **2.** Elle trouve que mes cheveux ne sont pas beaux. **3.** Elle dit que les spectateurs n'aimeront pas les sujets de l'émission. **4.** J'ai oublié le nom de mon invité. **5.** Elle pense probablement que je ne suis pas très intelligent. **6.** Elle dit que j'ai l'air nerveux. **7.** Elle dit que les spectateurs ne peuvent pas me voir clairement.

Regards sur la culture

Le monde du travail

You have probably noticed that the working relationships between Camille, Bruno, Rachid, and Martine are quite informal. In this segment, however, you see that the president of Canal 7 maintains a somewhat different connection with those who work there.

Martine parle avec le président de Canal 7

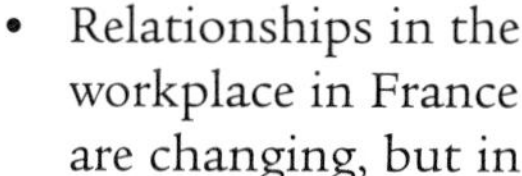

- Relationships in the workplace in France are changing, but in most cases they are more formal than in North America. The fact that Martine addresses her boss as **Monsieur le président**, even in an industry like broadcasting where informal relationships are more common, would not surprise French people. Coworkers rarely call each other by their first names, unless they have become friends outside of work. Familiarity in the world of work is not equated with friendship.
- Adhering to schedules is not as important in the French workplace as it is in North America, probably because people expect to be taking care of several things at once and know that new obligations may easily take precedence over old ones.* There is also a sense that relationships need to be maintained even at the expense of deadlines and promptness for appointments.
- It is usually considered rude in a meeting to "get down to business" right away. The French expect a certain amount of time to be spent on general conversation, making the personal relationships work, before real work can get done.
- The French are raised to be individualists. They do not join clubs and organizations nearly as much as North Americans do and sometimes consider that those who do are unacceptably conformist. As a result, French people in the workplace often resist teamwork, preferring to do their jobs separately.
- At the same time, however, the French have a long tradition of joining together for the defense of their professions and jobs. The power and appeal of labor unions in France is much greater than it is in North America, partly because

---

*Edward Hall, an anthropologist particularly interested in nonverbal communication, has called this approach "polychronic." He contrasts French attitudes with respect to time to the "monochronic" approach of North Americans, for whom fixed deadlines are a fairly serious matter.

social class is perceived to be a more important factor in one's identity in France.

- Just as authority is centralized in the French political system (although that is changing slowly), control tends to be vested in a few individuals in the workplace. Decisions made by the central power source seem more natural to French workers than attempts at creating consensus, which are often felt to be a waste of time.
- Mealtimes are usually considered more important than any normal work obligations. Traditionally, French businesses and offices were closed for two hours between 12:00 and 2:00 P.M., so that employees could go home for lunch and relaxation. This is still considered the norm, although the situation is slowly changing. The expression **la journée continue** describes business situations where this lunch break is not taken.
- July and August are vacation time in France, and, because everyone has at least five weeks of paid vacation, many businesses simply shut down for several weeks during this period.

Considérez

Few people in France would admit to being workaholics. What differences in priorities regarding work do you see when you compare the French situation with that in your culture?

Structure 62

Les formes subjonctives irrégulières et le subjonctif de volonté

Expressing wishes and desires

—Bonjour, petite! **Vous voulez que je vous serve** quelque chose?

Les formes subjonctives irrégulières

Irregular verbs in the subjunctive can be classified according to the number of stems used in their conjugation. All of them use the standard endings, except **avoir** and **être**.

1. Verbs with one subjunctive stem: **faire**, **pouvoir**, **savoir**

	faire	pouvoir	savoir
	fass-	*puiss-*	*sach-*
que je	**fasse**	**puisse**	**sache**
que tu	**fasses**	**puisses**	**saches**
qu'il, qu'elle, qu'on	**fasse**	**puisse**	**sache**
que nous	**fassions**	**puissions**	**sachions**
que vous	**fassiez**	**puissiez**	**sachiez**
qu'ils, qu'elles	**fassent**	**puissent**	**sachent**

2. Verbs with two subjunctive stems (one irregular, one derived from the present indicative **nous** form): **aller**, **vouloir**

	aller	vouloir
	aill-; all-	*veuill-; voul-*
que je (j')	**aille**	**veuille**
que tu	**ailles**	**veuilles**
qu'il, qu'elle, qu'on	**aille**	**veuille**
que nous	**allions**	**voulions**
que vous	**alliez**	**vouliez**
qu'ils, qu'elles	**aillent**	**veuillent**

3. Verbs with two subjunctive stems (one derived from the present indicative **ils/elles** form, one derived from the present indicative **nous** form): **boire**, **croire**, **devoir**, **prendre**, **recevoir**, **venir**

	boire	croire	devoir	prendre	recevoir	venir
	boiv-; buv-	*croi-; croy-*	*doiv-; dev-*	*prenn-; pren-*	*reçoiv-; recev-*	*vienn-; ven-*
que je	**boive**	**croie**	**doive**	**prenne**	**reçoive**	**vienne**
que tu	**boives**	**croies**	**doives**	**prennes**	**reçoives**	**viennes**
qu'il, qu'elle, qu'on	**boive**	**croie**	**doive**	**prenne**	**reçoive**	**vienne**
que nous	**buvions**	**croyions**	**devions**	**prenions**	**recevions**	**venions**
que vous	**buviez**	**croyiez**	**deviez**	**preniez**	**receviez**	**veniez**
qu'ils, qu'elles	**boivent**	**croient**	**doivent**	**prennent**	**reçoivent**	**viennent**

4. Only two verbs have both irregular stems and irregular endings: **avoir**, **être**.

	avoir	être
	ai-; ay-	*soi-; soy-*
que je (j')	**aie**	**sois**
que tu	**aies**	**sois**
qu'il, qu'elle, qu'on	**ait**	**soit**
que nous	**ayons**	**soyons**
que vous	**ayez**	**soyez**
qu'ils, qu'elles	**aient**	**soient**

Le subjonctif de volonté

Besides being used after verbs that express judgment and necessity, the subjunctive is used after verbs that express desire or will, for example **désirer**, **exiger** (*to demand; to require*), and **vouloir**. Once again, if there is no change of subject, an infinitive can follow the expression of will. But if there is a change of subject, the second verb will be in the subjunctive in a dependent clause introduced by **que**. Compare the following examples.

ONE SUBJECT	Je voudrais **savoir** la vérité.
TWO SUBJECTS	Je voudrais **que tu saches** la vérité.
ONE SUBJECT	Camille ne désire pas **revenir** à Paris.
TWO SUBJECTS	Le président désire que Camille **revienne** tout de suite à Paris.

Activités

A. Une visite de Marseille. Dominique, une jeune Marseillaise, explique à deux touristes, Thérèse et Paul, ce qu'il faut faire pour profiter de sa ville. Choisissez un verbe qui convient, et mettez-le au subjonctif pour compléter les phrases. Plus d'un verbe est parfois logique.

Vocabulaire utile: aller, avoir, boire, comprendre, croire, être, faire, pouvoir, prendre, savoir

1. Il faut que vous _____ attention quand vous buvez du pastis.* C'est de l'alcool.
2. Je veux que Paul _____ visiter le Château d'If. Il peut y aller demain s'il fait beau.
3. Je voudrais que nous _____ au musée d'Archéologie méditerranéenne ensemble.
4. Thérèse, il faut que tu _____ le temps d'acheter du tissu provençal dans une des boutiques «Les Olivades».

*__Le pastis__ est une boisson alcoolisée à l'anis, qui sent le réglisse (*licorice*). On prononce le **s** final de **pastis** et d'**anis**.

5. Paul, je veux que tu _____ comment aller au Vieux-Port. Il faut prendre le métro ligne 1 à la gare.
6. Il ne faut pas que vous _____ peur de vous promener le soir dans les rues piétonnes.
7. Il n'est pas nécessaire que vous _____ la langue provençale. Mais il faut comprendre l'accent marseillais.
8. Je voudrais que l'Opéra de Marseille _____ ouvert pendant votre visite.
9. Thérèse, il faut que tu _____ du vin de pays pendant ta visite.

B. Les problèmes de Camille. Faites des phrases complètes avec les éléments donnés pour imaginer des bribes (*snatches*) de conversation entre Camille et Bruno quand elle lui téléphone de Marseille.

MODÈLES: BRUNO: le président/ exiger / tu / être / au travail demain →
Le président exige que tu sois au travail demain.
CAMILLE: Je / ne pas vouloir / être / au travail demain. →
Je ne veux pas être au travail demain.

1. BRUNO: Martine / vouloir / je / te parler / sérieusement
   CAMILLE: d'accord / je / accepter de / te parler / sérieusement
2. CAMILLE: je / ne pas vouloir / revenir / tout de suite
   BRUNO: nous / désirer vraiment / tu / revenir
3. BRUNO: je / vouloir / tu / savoir / le numéro de mon portable
   CAMILLE: je / vouloir / aussi / savoir / le numéro de ton portable
4. BRUNO: Martine / aller / voir le président
   CAMILLE: je / ne pas vouloir / Martine / aller / voir le président
5. BRUNO: le président / vouloir / recevoir / tes excuses pour ce «caprice»
   CAMILLE: je / vouloir simplement / il / comprendre / que cette absence est importante pour moi
6. CAMILLE: je / vouloir / tu / faire / une chose pour moi
   BRUNO: je / désirer vraiment / faire / quelque chose pour toi
7. CAMILLE: à mon retour, je / vouloir / nous / prendre / un verre ensemble
   BRUNO: je / vouloir / te revoir / le plus vite possible
8. BRUNO: je / vouloir / tu / avoir confiance en moi
   CAMILLE: je sais: je / pouvoir / avoir confiance en toi

Maintenant, expliquez à un(e) camarade de classe ce que certaines personnes dans votre vie veulent que vous fassiez.

MODÈLE: Mes grands-parents veulent que je leur rende visite plus souvent.

C. Pour réussir. Avec un(e) partenaire, jouez les rôles d'un conseiller universitaire et d'un étudiant / d'une étudiante qui a des difficultés. Utilisez des éléments des deux colonnes et changez de rôle après avoir donné cinq conseils.

MODÈLE: ÉTUDIANT: Qu'est-ce qu'il faut que je fasse pour réussir aux examens?
CONSEILLER: Je veux que vous veniez me voir plus souvent.

ÉTUDIANT(E)	CONSEILLER
1. pour réussir aux examens	vouloir bien participer
2. pour avoir de bonnes notes	finir tous les cours
3. pour finir mes études cette année	venir me voir plus souvent
4. pour comprendre le livre	aller à la bibliothèque
5. pour mieux étudier	faire tous les devoirs
6. pour parler en classe	écrire les réponses dans le cahier
	arrêter (*stop*) de regarder la télé
	lire attentivement

Visionnement 2

Observez!

Considérez les aspects culturels expliqués dans **Regards sur la culture**. Ensuite, regardez l'Épisode 20 encore une fois, et répondez aux questions suivantes.

- Écoutez le français du patron du bar. En quoi son accent est-il différent du français que vous avez entendu jusqu'ici?
- D'après ce que dit le patron du bar, qu'est-ce qui indiquerait que Marseille a certaines caractéristiques d'une petite ville?

Après le visionnement

Faites l'activité pour le **Visionnement 2** dans le cahier.

Synthèse: Lecture

Mise en contexte

Jules Verne (1828–1905) is often considered the father of science fiction. He wrote sixty-eight novels—including ***Le Tour du monde en 80 jours*** (*Around the World in 80 Days*), ***Vingt mille lieues sous les mers*** (*20,000 Leagues Under the Sea*), and ***Voyage au centre de la terre*** (*Journey to the Center of the Earth*)—short stories, a geography of

France, theatrical works, and an essay on Edgar Allan Poe. The United States fascinated Verne, and twenty-three of his novels took place there. This story was published in 1910, after his death, in a collection of previously unpublished works.

In this excerpt, Jules Verne imagines a day in the life of Francis Bennett, director of the newspaper *The Earth Herald* in the year 2890. Bennett, **roi des journalistes** (*king of journalists*), is the latest in the line of newspaper magnates descended from Gordon Bennett, who, twenty-five generations earlier, founded the *New York Herald*. Since that time, the American capital has been transferred from Washington, D.C., to Universal City, capital of the United Americas. Although this is a fictional account of a workplace very distant in time and set in America, can you find any parallels with the French workplace described in **Regards sur la culture**?

Stratégie pour mieux lire
Understanding the passé simple

In this passage, Verne uses a tense called the **passé simple** to narrate the events. The **passé simple** is used primarily in literary and historical contexts but is otherwise equivalent to the **passé composé**; both are used to talk about completed past actions.

You do not need to learn to use the forms of the **passé simple** to understand this passage; you need to recognize and understand only the **il/elle** form. The **il/elle** form is usually made up of the infinitive stem and an ending. For **-er** verbs, the ending is **-a**, and for **-re** and **-ir** verbs, the ending is **-it**.

gagner	il gagna la salle de rédaction	*he entered the editing room*
répondre	il répondit	*he answered*
finir	il finit	*he finished*

Some verbs are irregular in the **passé simple**. In this excerpt, you will see only one example.

voir	il vit	*he saw*

Stratégie pour mieux lire
Discerning the author's point of view

As Verne imagines the future, he also expresses his social vision and attitudes toward change. For example, read the following sentence, in which he begins to describe a new invention used in the offices of *The Earth Herald*. Try to identify which elements in the sentence represent the author's point of view on the new invention.

> Grâce à[a] un ingénieux système, d'ailleurs,[b] une partie de cette publicité se propage[c] sous une forme absolument nouvelle....
>
> [a]Grâce... *Thanks to* [b]*moreover* [c]se... *spreads*

Phrases such as **Grâce à**, **ingénieux**, and **absolument nouvelle** express Verne's admiration, even awe, for this mechanical advance.

As you read, look for other phrases that reflect Verne's attitude toward life in the 29th century. Does he think that society is always just? How do people and nature interact?

Au XXIXe siècle ou La journée d'un journaliste américain en 2890

Francis Bennett poursuit son inspection et pénètre dans la salle de reportage. Ses quinze cents reporters, placés alors devant un égal[1] nombre de téléphones, communiquaient aux abonnés[2] les nouvelles reçues pendant la nuit des quatre coins du monde. L'organisation de cet incomparable service a été souvent décrite. Outre[3] son téléphone, chaque reporter a devant lui une série de commutateurs,[4] permettant d'établir la communication avec telle ou telle[5] ligne téléphotique.[6] Les abonnés ont donc non seulement le récit,[7] mais la vue des événements, obtenue par la photographie intensive.

Francis Bennett interpelle[8] un des dix reporters astronomiques, attachés à ce service, qui accroîtra[9] avec les nouvelles découvertes opérées dans le monde stellaire.

—Et bien, Cash, qu'avez-vous reçu?...

—Des phototélégrammes de Mercure, de Vénus et de Mars, monsieur.

—Intéressant, ce dernier?...

—Oui! une révolution dans le Central Empire, au profit des démocrates libéraux contre les républicains conservateurs.

—Comme chez nous, alors. Et de Jupiter?

—Rien encore! Nous n'arrivons pas à comprendre les signaux des Joviens.[10] Peut-être les nôtres[11] ne leur parviennent[12]-ils pas?

—Cela vous regarde,[13] et je vous en rends responsable, Monsieur Cash! répondit Francis Bennett, qui, fort mécontent, gagna la salle de rédaction scientifique.

«Cela vous regarde, et je vous en rends responsable, Monsieur Cash!»

La salle adjacente, vaste galerie longue d'un demi-kilomètre, était consacrée[14] à la publicité, et l'on[15] imagine aisément[16] ce que doit être la publicité d'un journal tel que le *Earth Herald*. Elle rapporte en moyenne[17] trois millions de dollars par jour. Grâce à un ingénieux système, d'ailleurs, une partie de cette publicité se propage sous une forme absolument nouvelle, due à un brevet[18] acheté au prix de trois dollars à un pauvre diable qui est mort de faim. Ce sont d'immenses affiches, réfléchies par les nuages, et dont la dimension est telle que l'on peut les apercevoir[19] d'une contrée toute entière.

De cette galerie, mille projecteurs étaient sans cesse occupés à envoyer aux nues,[20] qui les reproduisaient en couleur, ces annonces démesurées.[21]

[1]*equal* [2]*subscribers* [3]*In addition to* [4]*switches* [5]telle... *any* [6]ligne... *an invention imagined by Verne that reproduces the image at the other end of the line* [7]*words* [8]*calls out to* [9]*will grow* [10]*inhabitants of Jupiter* [11]*ours* [12]*reach* [13]Cela... *It's your business* [14]*devoted* [15]= on [16]*easily* [17]rapporte... *brings in on average* [18]*patent* [19]*see* [20]*clouds* [21]*excessive, oversized*

Mais, ce jour-là, lorsque[22] Francis Bennett entra dans la salle de publicité, il vit que les mécaniciens se croisaient les bras auprès de[23] leurs projecteurs inactifs. Il s'informe... Pour toute réponse, on lui montre le ciel d'un bleu pur.

—Oui!... du beau temps, murmure-t-il, et pas de publicité aérienne possible! Que faire? S'il ne s'agissait que de pluie,[24] on pourrait la produire! Mais ce n'est pas de la pluie, ce sont des nuages qu'il nous faudrait!...

—Oui... de beaux nuages bien blancs, répondit le mécanicien-chef.

—Eh bien! Monsieur Samuel Mark, vous vous adresserez à la rédaction scientifique, service météorologique. Vous lui direz de ma part qu'elle s'occupe activement de la question des nuages artificiels. On ne peut vraiment pas rester ainsi[25] à la merci du beau temps.

Jules Verne
Illustration de Georges Roux

[22]*when* [23]auprès... *near* [24]S'il... *If it were only rain* [25]*like this*

Après la lecture

A. Avez-vous compris? Répondez aux questions suivantes.

1. Comment M. Bennett passe-t-il sa journée?
2. Quelles sont les deux inventions décrites? Est-ce qu'elles marchent bien?
3. Quelle est l'attitude de M. Bennett devant un problème? Est-il défaitiste (*defeatist*)? réfléchi (*thoughtful*)? prêt à agir (*act*)?

B. Le point de vue de l'auteur. Avec un(e) partenaire, analysez le texte pour trouver...

1. une remarque de l'auteur qui indique que les riches exploitent les pauvres.
2. des expressions qui expriment l'attitude de l'auteur envers la nouvelle technologie.
3. un exemple où l'auteur envisage que l'homme peut dompter (*overcome*) la nature.

C. Le lieu de travail. Comment est le lieu de travail décrit par Verne? Est-ce qu'on travaille en équipe ou seul? Y a-t-il une hiérarchie dans cette entreprise? Comment est le rapport patron-travailleur?

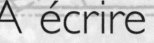

À écrire

Faites **À écrire** pour le Chapitre 20 dans le cahier.

Vocabulaire

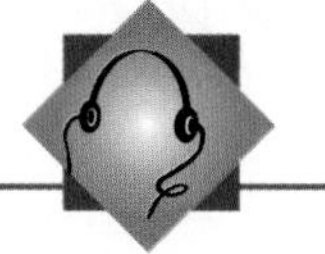

La ville de Marseille

l'accueil (*m.*)	welcome; greeting
un(e) antiquaire	antique dealer
un arrondissement	district
un(e) habitant(e)	inhabitant
une ruelle	alleyway
une rue piétonne	pedestrian street

MOTS APPARENTÉS: **une galerie, un(e) immigré(e), la joie de vivre, un port, la rénovation, un site touristique**

Le monde du travail

un congé	holiday, time off
une vedette	star (*of a show, movie*)
engager	to hire
former	to train; to form
licencier	to fire
au chômage	unemployed

MOTS APPARENTÉS: **un contrat, un salaire**

Le monde de l'argent

une banque	bank
un carnet de chèques	checkbook
un compte (en banque)	(bank) account
un montant	amount (*of a check or sale*)
déposer un chèque	to deposit a check
faire un chèque	to write a check
toucher un chèque	to cash a check

Expressions d'opinion, de nécessité, d'obligation et de volonté

il est bon	it is good
il est juste (injuste)	it is right (not right)
il est triste	it is sad
il est utile (inutile)	it is useful (useless, no use)
il faut	it is necessary; (one) must, should
il ne faut pas	(one) must not, should not
il suffit	it is enough, all it takes is

MOTS APPARENTÉS: **il est essentiel (important, impossible, nécessaire, préférable), il n'est pas nécessaire**

Substantifs

la chaleur	warmth; heat
un siècle	century

Verbes

donner sur (le port)	to overlook, have a view of (the port)
exiger	to demand; to require

À REVOIR: **désirer, vouloir**

Adjectifs

célèbre	famous
délabré(e)	dilapidated
étroit(e)	narrow
réputé(e)	well known

Autres expressions utiles

au cours de	throughout (*time*)

Chapitre 21

D'où vient cette photo?

Le Chemin du retour

Feuille de service du 19 janvier
4e jour de tournage
Horaires : 8h–18h

LIEU DE TOURNAGE : MARSEILLE—MÉMORIAL DES CAMPS DE LA MORT—Salle 1er étage

Séquence	*Effets*	*Décors*	*Résumé*	*Rôles*
148	EXT.—JOUR	MUSÉE MÉMORIAL—Salles d'exposition	Camille discute avec la conservatrice° du musée et lui montre la photo de Fergus.	CAMILLE, CONSERVATRICE DU MUSÉE

° curator

OBJECTIFS

In this episode, you will

- see Camille pursue leads in Marseille
- meet a band of musicians who play raï music

In this chapter, you will

- talk about art, music, and other cultural opportunities in Marseille
- use the subjunctive to talk about emotions
- use the subjunctive to talk about doubt and uncertainty
- use the subjunctive in other contexts
- learn about museums as institutions in French society
- read about cultural policy in Quebec

Vocabulaire en contexte

*S*pectacles et manifestations culturelles° à Marseille

Spectacles… *Entertainment and cultural events*

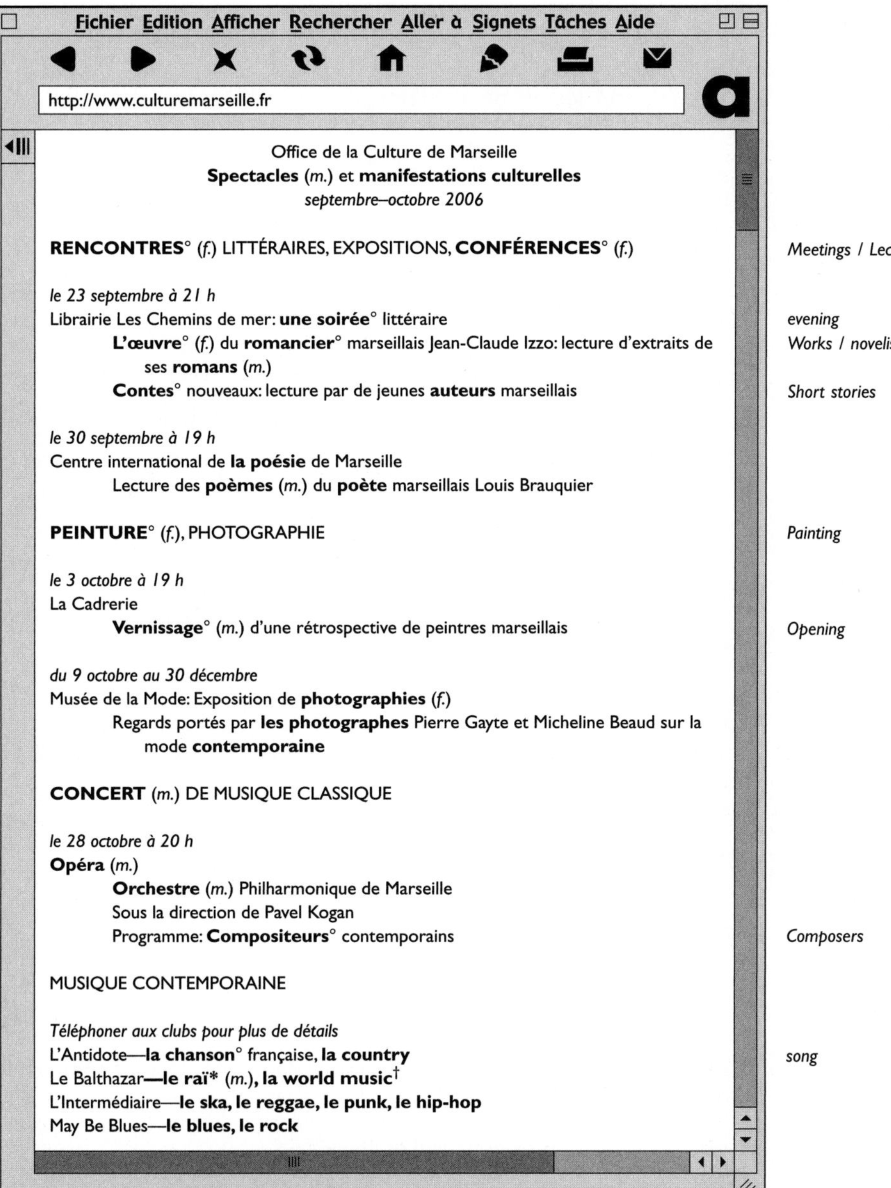

Office de la Culture de Marseille
Spectacles (*m.*) et **manifestations culturelles**
septembre–octobre 2006

RENCONTRES° (*f.*) LITTÉRAIRES, EXPOSITIONS, **CONFÉRENCES**° (*f.*)

le 23 septembre à 21 h
Librairie Les Chemins de mer: **une soirée**° littéraire
L'œuvre° (*f.*) du **romancier**° marseillais Jean-Claude Izzo: lecture d'extraits de ses **romans** (*m.*)
Contes° nouveaux: lecture par de jeunes **auteurs** marseillais

le 30 septembre à 19 h
Centre international de **la poésie** de Marseille
Lecture des **poèmes** (*m.*) du **poète** marseillais Louis Brauquier

PEINTURE° (*f.*), PHOTOGRAPHIE

le 3 octobre à 19 h
La Cadrerie
Vernissage° (*m.*) d'une rétrospective de peintres marseillais

du 9 octobre au 30 décembre
Musée de la Mode: Exposition de **photographies** (*f.*)
Regards portés par **les photographes** Pierre Gayte et Micheline Beaud sur la mode **contemporaine**

CONCERT (*m.*) DE MUSIQUE CLASSIQUE

le 28 octobre à 20 h
Opéra (*m.*)
Orchestre (*m.*) Philharmonique de Marseille
Sous la direction de Pavel Kogan
Programme: **Compositeurs**° contemporains

MUSIQUE CONTEMPORAINE

Téléphoner aux clubs pour plus de détails
L'Antidote—**la chanson**° française, **la country**
Le Balthazar—**le raï*** (*m.*), **la world music**†
L'Intermédiaire—**le ska, le reggae, le punk, le hip-hop**
May Be Blues—**le blues, le rock**

Meetings / Lectures
evening
Works / novelist
Short stories
Painting
Opening
Composers
song

Notez bien!

Many nouns designating artists have clear masculine and feminine forms; for example,

un(e) chanteur/euse singer
un(e) compositeur/trice composer
un(e) musicien(ne) musician
un(e) photographe photographer
un(e) romancier/ière novelist

Female painters, poets, and authors can be called either by the masculine forms **un peintre, un poète, un auteur** or by the feminine forms **une femme peintre, une femme poète, une femme auteur.**

***Le raï** est une sorte de musique qui est populaire dans les pays maghrébins.
†Le terme **world music** désigne les différentes musiques du Tiers-Monde (*Third World*) et des groupes minoritaires dans les pays développés. Il s'agit en général de styles qui combinent la tradition de ces régions avec des éléments du rock occidental (*western*).

Pour en savoir plus...

La ville de Marseille a beaucoup d'espaces (*venues*) consacrés aux événements musicaux. Les spectacles d'opéra et de musique symphonique ont lieu à l'Opéra municipal. De grands concerts de musique contemporaine ont lieu au Théâtre National de Marseille, la Criée. Il existe aussi d'autres endroits, plus petits, où on peut écouter de la musique populaire, tels que *L'Antidote*, *L'Intermédiaire* et *Le Balthazar*. Le programme culturel du *Balthazar*, qui se déclare «Ouvert à toutes les musiques et à toutes les rencontres artistiques», reflète la diversité de la ville de Marseille.

Autres expressions utiles

une pièce (de théâtre)	play
un tableau	painting (*picture*)
avoir lieu	to take place

Langage fonctionnel

Pour parler des spectacles

Pour parler de votre réaction à une chanson, un film, une pièce de théâtre, une exposition d'art, etc., utilisez les éléments suivants.

J'ai adoré...		*I loved . . .*	
Je n'ai pas du tout aimé...		*I didn't like . . . at all.*	
J'ai détesté...		*I hated . . .*	
C'est nul.		*It's awful.*	
Je le/la trouve	bien (mal) interprété(e).	*I find it*	*well (badly) performed.*
	bien (mal) joué(e).		*well (badly) acted.*
Il/Elle est	génial(e).	*It is*	*brilliant, inspired.*
	médiocre.		*mediocre, dull.*
	passionnant(e).		*fascinating, gripping.*
	sans intérêt.		*uninteresting.*
	très réussi(e).		*very well done.*
C'est	un succès.		*a success.*

—**J'adore** les films de Polanski. Et toi? — *I love Polanski's films. Do you?*

—J'en ai vu un récemment et **je l'ai trouvé** tout à fait **médiocre**! — *I saw one recently and thought it was really dull!*

—Mais non! Il faut que tu voies un de ses chefs-d'œuvre: Polanski est vraiment **génial**! — *Not at all! You must see one of his masterpieces: Polanski is really brilliant.*

Activités

A. L'artiste et son œuvre. Quelle est la spécialité de chaque artiste? Suivez le modèle, et faites des phrases complètes.

MODÈLE: Un poète... → Un poète écrit de la poésie.

1. Un peintre...
2. Une photographe...
3. Une romancière...
4. Une musicienne...
5. Un chanteur...
6. Une compositrice...

B. Une visite à Marseille. Vous passez quelques semaines à Marseille. Divisez en trois groupes les activités culturelles présentées dans le vocabulaire à la page 441.

- «les musts»: celles auxquelles (*at which*) il faut assister à tout prix
- les activités que vous ferez si vous avez le temps
- les activités qui ne vous intéressent pas du tout

Organisez votre itinéraire et présentez-le à la classe. Expliquez votre classement.

MODÈLE: Il faut absolument que j'aille au Balthazar, parce que j'adore le raï.

C. Une interview. Posez les questions suivantes à votre partenaire pour déterminer plus précisément ses intérêts culturels. Demandez-lui...

1. quelles sorties culturelles il/elle a faites récemment.
2. quelle activité culturelle il/elle aime le mieux.
3. quelle activité culturelle il/elle trouve la plus ennuyeuse et pourquoi.
4. quel genre de musique il/elle préfère et quel est son musicien préféré.
5. si ses goûts culturels sont les mêmes ou différents de ceux de ses parents et de ses amis.
6. ses opinions sur un film (un roman, une pièce) récent(e).

Visionnement 1

Avant de visionner

Vrai ou faux? Lisez le dialogue. Ensuite, lisez les phrases qui suivent et dites si elles sont vraies ou fausses. Si elles sont fausses, corrigez-les (*correct them*).

—Cet homme, Roland Fergus, qui est-il exactement? Vous savez quelque chose sur lui?

—Je sais qu'il est marseillais et qu'il a quitté la ville au début de la guerre pour se rendre dans les Cévennes.

—Ici, nous conservons les photos qui sont de provenance[a] incertaine ou douteuse.

—C'est-à-dire?[b]

—Nous avons reçu beaucoup de photos. Impossible de tout exposer![c] Alors, nous avons écarté[d] les photos des gens que nous ne pouvions pas identifier.

—Ceux qui ont collaboré avec les Allemands?

—Pas seulement... Marseille a beaucoup souffert de la guerre. Des familles entières sont mortes. Des milliers de personnes.

[a]*origin* [b]c'est... *Which means?* [c]*exhibit* [d]*set aside*

1. Cette scène se passe probablement dans un bar.
2. Il y a des photos dont (*of which*) personne ne sait l'origine.
3. On a exposé toutes les photos.
4. On a exposé des photos de ceux qui ont collaboré avec les Allemands.
5. Beaucoup de Marseillais ont souffert pendant la guerre.

Vocabulaire relatif à l'épisode

vous longez les quais	*you walk along the docks*
déçu(e)	*disappointed*
40 ter	*40c (in a street address)*
vous squattez ce local?	*are you squatters here?*
l'accord de la mairie	*approval of the mayor's office*
ce mec	*this guy*
une piste	*lead, clue*

Observez!

Dans cet épisode, Camille trouve l'adresse du garage de Fergus et de son père. Maintenant, regardez l'Épisode 21, et cherchez les réponses aux questions suivantes.

- Comment Camille trouve-t-elle le garage de Fergus?
- Où va-t-elle ensuite pour s'informer?
- Qu'est-ce que Camille apprend de plus sur Fergus?
- Est-ce qu'on établit l'identité de Fergus comme collaborateur?

Après le visionnement

A. De qui s'agit-il et quelle est la réponse? Lisez les extraits du dialogue et déterminez qui parle avec qui: Camille, le patron du bar, un musicien, la conservatrice du musée. Choisissez ensuite la réplique correcte.

1. ______: Vous voyez? Mon bar est ici. Vous prenez à gauche... Vous longez les quais. Vous tournez à droite... jusqu'au boulevard de la Corderie, et c'est là.

______: **a.** J'ai peur que vous soyez déçue, vous savez.
b. Où est-ce?
c. Je peux garder cette carte?

2. ______: Vous squattez ce local?

______: **a.** Il a travaillé dans la Résistance.
b. Non, non. On a l'accord de la mairie...
c. Le propriétaire? Personne ne l'a jamais vu.

3. ______: Alors, nous avons écarté les photos des gens que nous ne pouvions pas identifier.

______: **a.** Des familles entières sont mortes. Des milliers de personnes.
b. Du Maroc. Il y a bien ce nom, Fergus.
c. Ceux qui ont collaboré avec les Allemands?

4. ______: Mais c'est lui! C'est lui! C'est Roland Fergus. D'où vient cette photo?

______: **a.** Regardez ceci...
b. Du Maroc. Il y a bien ce nom, Fergus. Et il y a une adresse à Casablanca.
c. Nous avons reçu beaucoup de photos.

B. Réfléchissez. Les musiciens expliquent à Camille qu'ils squattent le garage avec la permission de la mairie. À votre avis, pourquoi veulent-ils utiliser le garage pour leurs répétitions?

Structure 63

Le subjonctif d'émotion et d'opinion

Expressing emotion and opinion

—**J'ai peur que vous soyez** déçue, vous savez.

In Chapter 20, you saw that the subjunctive is used after verbs of obligation, necessity, and will, when the subject of the verb in the subordinate clause is different from the subject of the independent clause.

1. The subjunctive is also used after expressions of emotion as long as a *second* subject is used in the subordinate clause. Expressions of emotion include the following:

    avoir peur que
    être content (**heureux, ravi** [*thrilled*]) **que**
    être fâché (**furieux**) **que**
    être surpris (**étonné** [*astonished*]) **que**
    être triste (**désolé** [*sorry*]) **que**
    il est bon (**bizarre**, **dommage** [*too bad*], **incroyable** [*incredible*], **formidable**, **ridicule**) **que**
    préférer que
    regretter que
    souhaiter (*to wish, hope*) **que**

Le patron du bar **souhaite que** Camille **ait** de la chance.	*The bartender hopes that Camille will have good luck.*
Camille **est ravie que** les musiciens lui **donnent** une piste.	*Camille is delighted that the musicians give her a lead.*
Mado **est contente que** Camille **fasse** ce voyage.	*Mado is happy that Camille is making this trip.*
Il est dommage que Camille ne **puisse** pas trouver Fergus.	*It's a shame that Camille can't find Fergus.*

Remember—When only one subject is involved in the action, use **de** + infinitive after these expressions. In the case of **préférer** and **souhaiter**, the infinitive follows the conjugated verb directly.

Camille **a peur de perdre** la trace de Fergus.	*Camille is afraid of losing track of Fergus.*
Les musiciens **souhaitent jouer** au *Balthazar.*	*The musicians hope to play at the Balthazar.*

2. One verb of emotion, **espérer**, is followed by the indicative (present, future, etc.), not the subjunctive.

Le patron du bar **espère que** Camille **aura** de la chance.	*The bartender hopes that Camille will have good luck.*

However, with only one subject, **espérer** is followed by the infinitive.

Elle **espère apprendre** la vérité sur son grand-père.	*She hopes to find out the truth about her grandfather.*

Activités

A. Au Conservatoire National de Région de Marseille. Le Conservatoire National de Région de Marseille donne matière à réflexion. Exprimez ces pensées à l'aide du subjonctif, de l'indicatif ou de l'infinitif des verbes entre parenthèses.

MODÈLE: Il est incroyable que cette école _____ (pouvoir) enseigner la musique à 16.000 jeunes. →
Il est incroyable que cette école *puisse* enseigner la musique à 16.000 jeunes.

1. Alexandre regrette qu'il y _____ (avoir) si peu de cours d'improvisation.
2. Annie a peur de _____ (faire) son récital en public.
3. Il est triste que le Premier Prix du Conservatoire _____ (être) si difficile à obtenir.
4. Benjamin préfère que les cours de jazz _____ (finir) avant 6 h.
5. M. Goya sera ravi de _____ (découvrir) un jeune guitariste avec du talent.
6. Certains parents espèrent que la musique _____ (ne pas devenir) trop importante pour leurs enfants.
7. Beaucoup d'enfants souhaitent _____ (aller) au Conservatoire.
8. Il est dommage que ce jeune homme ne _____ (réussir) pas à tous ses cours.
9. Les jeunes musiciens sont étonnés que les études _____ (pouvoir) prendre près de quinze ans.
10. Beaucoup de jeunes musiciens espèrent _____ (jouer) dans une des nouvelles salles de concerts au conservatoire.
11. Il est bon que le Conservatoire _____ (offrir) beaucoup de cours intéressants aux jeunes musiciens.

Maintenant, inspirez-vous des éléments de cette description pour parler avec un(e) camarade de classe de votre propre université.

MODÈLE: Il est fantastique que notre université puisse proposer sept cours de langues différentes.

B. Le Festival d'Avignon. Parlez du festival qui se passe chaque été en Avignon en complétant chaque phrase avec les choix suggérés entre parenthèses. Faites l'élision avec **qu'** si nécessaire.

MODÈLE: Les commerçants de la ville sont contents que les gens achètent beaucoup de souvenirs.

1. Les commerçants de la ville sont contents que... (a, f)
2. Les metteurs en scène sont ravis que... (e, h)
3. Le jeune spectateur est triste que... (b, c)
4. Il est dommage que... (b, c, i)
5. Le directeur du Centre Acanthes pour la création musicale est surpris que... (d, j)
6. Une actrice est furieuse que... (c, g, i)
7. Il est ridicule que... (b, c, i)
8. Il est formidable que... (a, d, f, h, j)

a. il / y avoir / beaucoup de touristes pendant le festival
b. les places au théâtre / être / si chères
c. les auteurs / ne pas pouvoir / toujours venir aux lectures de leurs pièces
d. beaucoup de jeunes / vouloir / étudier la musique contemporaine
e. tant de spectateurs / aller / à leurs pièces
f. les gens / acheter / beaucoup de souvenirs
g. son rôle / être / trop limité
h. une femme auteur / faire / une lecture publique de sa pièce
i. un journaliste / dire / de mauvaises choses sur la pièce
j. les danseurs allemands / venir / en Avignon pour présenter leur création

C. Camille continue ses recherches. Voilà quelques commentaires sur le film. En vous basant sur le modèle, créez de nouvelles phrases pour dire que la deuxième personne partage les sentiments de la première. Utilisez les pronoms compléments d'objet direct et indirect si possible.

MODÈLE: Le patron du bar est content de savoir l'ancienne adresse de Fergus. (Camille) → Et Camille est contente qu'il la sache.

1. Camille a peur de ne pas pouvoir trouver le garage. (le patron du bar)
2. Camille est surprise de reconnaître le visage de Fergus sur l'une des photos. (la conservatrice)
3. Le patron du bar est heureux de donner la carte à Camille. (Camille)
4. Camille est contente d'entendre la chanson de raï. (les musiciens)
5. La conservatrice est ravie de trouver l'adresse au dos de la photo. (Camille)
6. Un musicien est heureux d'avoir une piste. (Camille)
7. La conservatrice regrette de ne pas avoir plus d'informations. (Camille)

D. Vous, vos amis et vos vies. Terminez chaque phrase. Utilisez un verbe au subjonctif ou à l'indicatif selon le cas.

MODÈLES: Dans cinq ans, j'espère que mon meilleur ami... →
Dans cinq ans, j'espère que mon meilleur ami aura un bon travail.

Mes amis souhaitent que... →
Mes amis souhaitent que je vienne chez eux pendant les vacances.

1. Je regrette que mes amis...
2. Mes amis ont peur que leurs cours...
3. Nous, les étudiants, sommes désolés que les professeurs...
4. Mon meilleur ami espère que je...
5. Les professeurs sont toujours contents que les étudiants...
6. Ma meilleure amie préfère que son travail...
7. Les jeunes souhaitent...
8. Il est bizarre que les professeurs...

Structure 64

Le subjonctif de doute, d'incertitude et de possibilité

Expressing doubt, uncertainty, and possibility

Camille **n'est pas certaine que** la conservatrice du musée **puisse** l'aider.

1. The subjunctive is also used after expressions of doubt, uncertainty, or possibility as long as a second subject occurs in the subordinate clause. Expressions of doubt and uncertainty include the following:

douter (*to doubt*) **que**	**il est incertain que**
être incertain que	**il est peu probable** (*unlikely*) **que**
il est douteux (*doubtful*) **que**	**il est possible que**
il est impossible que	**il se peut** (*it could be*) **que**

Le patron du bar doute que Fergus soit toujours à Marseille.	*The bartender doubts that Fergus is still in Marseille.*
Mais **il se peut que les musiciens aient** une piste.	*But it could be that the musicians have a lead.*

2. Some expressions are followed by the subjunctive only when they are in the negative.

ne pas être certain (sûr) que
ne pas croire que
ne pas penser que

Je ne crois pas qu'il soit un collaborateur.	*I don't believe he is a collaborator.*

3. Used in questions, **croire que**, **penser que**, and **être certain (sûr) que** are followed by the subjunctive when the issue is questionable, vague, or uncertain or when the questioner considers it as such.

Croyez-vous que ce soit une photo de Roland Fergus?	*Do you think that this is a photo of Roland Fergus?*

4. The indicative is used in affirmative statements after **croire que**, **penser que**, **être certain (sûr) que**, and **il est probable (clair, évident, vrai, certain, sûr) que** because the element of doubt is not present in these expressions. Instead, they imply probability or certainty. This is also true of **ne pas douter que**.

Il est clair que Camille essaiera de trouver Fergus à tout prix.	*It's clear that Camille will try to find Fergus at any cost.*
Rachid **ne doute pas que Camille réussira.**	*Rachid doesn't doubt that Camille will succeed.*

Remember—When there is only one subject involved in the action, use **de** + infinitive after these expressions. In the case of **ne pas croire** and **ne pas penser**, the infinitive follows the conjugated verb directly.

Je **ne crois pas** savoir l'adresse.	*I don't believe I know the address.*
Il **ne pense pas** avoir envie d'y aller.	*He doesn't think he feels like going.*
Il est impossible de tout exposer.	*It is impossible to exhibit everything.*

Activités

A. Malik Musique. Un site Internet propose toutes sortes de musique arabe à écouter et à acheter. Mettez les verbes au mode indiqué.

INDICATIF PRÉSENT OU CONDITIONNEL, SELON LE CAS

1. Je pense qu'on ____ (pouvoir) y trouver le CD «Sahara» de Naima Ababsa.
2. Il est certain qu'on ____ (entendre) beaucoup de raï sur ce site.
3. Je n'y trouve pas le CD «La Musique judéo-arabe» de Leïla Sfez. Mais je crois qu'il ____ (être) facile à trouver sur d'autres sites.
4. Je suis sûr(e) que cela ____ (prendre) des heures si on voulait écouter toutes les chansons sur le site!

SUBJONCTIF

5. Il est impossible que nous ____ (écouter) toutes les chansons sur ce site.
6. Nous doutons que le site ____ (vendre) des CD de Madonna.
7. Il est peu probable que nous ____ (trouver) le CD «Alger, Alger» de Lili Boniche dans la catégorie «musique tunisienne».
8. Pensez-vous que ce site ____ (vouloir) annoncer des concerts de musique sénégalaise? Ou croyez-vous qu'il ____ (faire) de la publicité pour des chants berbères?
9. Je ne crois pas que le webmestre ____ (mettre) beaucoup de musique techno sur son site. Mais est-il possible qu'il ____ (dire) aux clients où ils peuvent trouver d'autres sites sur la musique?

B. Conseils à un entrepreneur. Jacques décide de lancer une «start-up». C'est une bonne idée? Faites des phrases avec les éléments donnés pour découvrir les conseils de ses amis, Philippe et Nicole. Mettez les verbes à l'indicatif (présent ou futur), à l'infinitif ou au subjonctif, selon le cas.

MODÈLE: NICOLE: «Écoute, Jacques, je / ne pas être sûre que / cette start-up / être / une bonne idée.» →
Écoute, Jacques, je ne suis pas sûre que cette start-up soit une bonne idée.

1. JACQUES: «Je / être sûr de / trouver / un grand public, mais j'aurai besoin d'une équipe.»
2. NICOLE ET PHILIPPE: «Nous / ne pas penser que / les amis / vouloir / y participer.»
3. NICOLE: «Il / être douteux que / les internautes / choisir / d'acheter en ligne.»
4. PHILIPPE: «Il / se pouvoir que / tu / avoir / quelques clients...
5. ... mais il / être probable que / ce projet / finir / mal.»
6. JACQUES: «Je / ne pas croire que / vous / bien comprendre / l'e-commerce.»
7. NICOLE ET PHILIPPE: «Au contraire, il est clair que / les gens / préférer / les entreprises brique et mortier (*brick and mortar*).»
8. JACQUES: «Alors, vous / croire que / la netéconomie / être en train de / perdre son attrait?»

Êtes-vous plutôt d'accord avec Jacques ou avec Nicole et Philippe? Expliquez pourquoi, à un(e) camarade de classe.

C. Devant un nouveau musée d'art. Mettez-vous à trois et jouez les rôles suivants: un(e) journaliste, quelqu'un qui pense que l'art est très important dans la vie et une autre personne qui pense que l'art n'est pas important du tout. Le/La journaliste doit poser cinq questions et les deux autres se contredisent, en suivant le modèle.

MODÈLE: vous pensez / ce musée / être / important pour la ville →
É1: Pensez-vous que ce musée soit important pour la ville?
É2: Oui, je pense qu'il est très important.
É3: Moi, je ne pense pas qu'il soit important.

1. il est vrai / les enfants / venir souvent au musée
2. il est évident / ces tableaux / avoir / beaucoup de valeur
3. vous pensez / les statuettes africaines / être / intéressantes
4. il est possible / l'aquarelle berbère / devoir / être protégée (*protected*) du soleil
5. il est incertain / la boutique du musée / vendre / des CD-ROM sur l'art

Regards sur la culture

La notion du musée

Camille's search leads her to the **Musée de la Résistance**, a historical museum of the type that one could find anywhere in Europe or North America.

- The modern concept of the museum developed out of the Enlightenment and came into its own in the 19th century, when the notion of educating the masses for participation in democracy began to dominate the thinking of Euro-American intellectuals. The Louvre itself, originally made up of the confiscated collections of the monarchy, opened in 1793, in the middle of the French Revolution. It stood for the new order of things, where works of beauty could be admired not just by the wealthy, but by the common people as well.

Le musée d'Orsay à Paris

- The typical museum has thus aimed to provide examples of beauty and moments of instruction. In Marseille, there are museums that display works of art, archeological finds, and other historically significant objects. Larger museums, such as the Louvre, often display a combination of all three, with objects ranging from the Code of Hammurabi (18th c. B.C.E.) to **la Joconde** (*Mona Lisa*) by Leonardo da Vinci (16th c.) and the Crown Jewels of France.
- Over the two centuries since the founding of the Louvre, the notion of the museum has developed and expanded in many ways. Museums of technology and of natural history were developed very early on and continue to be popular. As time has gone by, more and more kinds of phenomena have found their way into specific sorts of museums, often for educational rather than

aesthetic goals. Paris, for example, has a **Musée de la Contrefaçon** (*counterfeiting*).

- For tourists, the many churches, palaces, and other historic buildings of France are museums in a sense, too. The Palace of Versailles is one of the most heavily visited buildings in Europe, and most people move through it and view it just as they would an art museum.
- There are even whole villages, towns, and cities in France that are thought of as **villes-musées**. For example, the walled city of Carcassonne, the ruins of Roman cities such as Vaison-la-Romaine, and the parts of Avignon that lie inside the medieval ramparts are felt to be museum-like and are treated so by visitors.
- European museums usually have an aesthetic and instructional goal, but American and Canadian museums have been particularly concerned about combining instruction and entertainment. Science museums in particular are usually more didactic in France than they are in North America. The point of view that the museum can be a place of entertainment is not particularly common in France.

La fontaine Stravinsky à côté du Centre Pompidou à Paris

Considérez

Most museums in France are publicly funded, whereas the majority of North American museums are private. How might this difference relate to the higher entertainment value found in North American museums? What are the advantages and disadvantages of the two systems?

Structure 65

Autres usages du subjonctif

Un musicien donne une piste à Camille **pour qu'elle puisse** trouver Roland Fergus.

1. Certain conjunctions▲ must be followed by the subjunctive when the two clauses in the sentence have different subjects.

afin que	*in order that, so that*
avant que	*before*
bien que	*although*
jusqu'à ce que	*until*
pour que	*in order that, so that*
sans que	*unless; without*

Camille fait ce voyage **pour que son grand-père soit** innocenté.	*Camille is making this trip so that her grandfather will be vindicated.*
Le président ne sera pas content **jusqu'à ce que Camille revienne**.	*The president won't be happy until Camille returns.*

2. When only one subject is involved in both actions, the conjunctions **bien que** and **jusqu'à ce que** still take the subjunctive, but the other conjunctions are replaced by the following prepositions + infinitive.

afin de
avant de
pour
sans } + infinitive

Bien que Camille ait l'adresse, elle ne connaît pas le chemin.	*Although Camille has the address, she doesn't know how to get there.*
Camille continuera **jusqu'à ce qu'elle sache** la vérité.	*Camille will continue until she knows the truth.*
Que faisait Camille **avant de travailler** pour nous?	*What did Camille do before working for us?*
Il a quitté la ville **pour se rendre** dans les Cévennes.	*He left the city to go to the Cévennes.*
Martine plaisante **sans sourire**.	*Martine jokes without smiling.*

3. When only one subject is involved in both actions, you can use **après** and the *past infinitive*. The past infinitive consists of the infinitive form of **avoir** or **être** followed by a past participle.

Fergus s'est installé à Casablanca **après avoir quitté** Marseille.	*Fergus moved to Casablanca after leaving Marseille.*
Après s'être renseignée auprès des musiciens, Camille est allée au musée.	*After having gotten some information from the musicians, Camille went to the museum.*

Pour en savoir plus...

The subjunctive can also be used in a clause beginning with **que** to express a wish. Louise used it this way in Episode 11, when she said good-bye to Samuel Lévy.

—Que Dieu te **protège**.	*May God protect you.*

Activités

A. Avec la conservatrice du musée. Choisissez la bonne conjonction ou préposition de la liste pour faire des phrases complètes. Il y a parfois deux possibilités.

Conjonctions: afin que, avant que, bien que, jusqu'à ce que, pour que, sans que
Prépositions: afin de, après, avant de, pour, sans

1. _____ rencontrer la conservatrice, Camille commence à perdre l'espoir (*hope*).
2. La conservatrice vient vers Camille _____ l'aider.
3. Camille parle à la conservatrice _____ elle comprenne la situation.
4. La conservatrice s'excuse _____ aller chercher une boîte de photos _____ savoir s'il y a une photo de Fergus.
5. _____ il y ait beaucoup de photos, elles trouvent celles qu'elles cherchent.
6. _____ partir, Camille comprend qu'il faut aller au Maroc.
7. _____ Camille puisse trouver Fergus, la conservatrice lui donne l'adresse à Casablanca.
8. Camille ne va pas parler à ses collègues à Paris. Elle va partir au Maroc _____ le président de Canal 7 le sache.
9. Camille cherchera Fergus _____ elle le trouve.
10. _____ avoir quitté le musée, Camille a plus d'espoir.

B. Quelques conseils. Complétez chaque conseil en utilisant une des constructions suivantes: **après** + substantif, **après** + infinitif passé, **avant** + substantif, **avant de** + infinitif, **avant que** + subjonctif.

MODÈLE: avant / se mettre au lit / ne regardez pas la télévision. →
Avant de vous mettre au lit, ne regardez pas la télévision.

Pour une bonne nuit de sommeil

1. Ne buvez pas de caféine / après / le dîner.
2. Gardez du temps pour vous détendre / avant / aller au lit.
3. Il est important de prendre un léger goûter / avant / vous / se coucher.
4. Apprenez à pratiquer les techniques de relaxation avant / manger / et avant / l'heure où vous vous couchez d'habitude.
5. Pour vous détendre, prenez un bain chaud une heure / avant / se mettre au lit.
6. Après / se reposer, vous vous sentirez bien.

Pour éviter le décalage horaire

7. Quelques semaines / avant / le départ, / essayez d'établir un horaire fixe.
8. Les médecins conseillent de cesser de boire du café trois jours / avant / vous / partir.
9. Après / votre arrivée, / ne faites pas de sieste.
10. Après / arriver, / sortez le plus possible au soleil.

Avec un(e) camarade de classe, parlez des conseils pour une bonne nuit de sommeil. Lesquels (n')avez-vous (pas) respectés? Pourquoi?

C. Les musées d'histoire. Quel est le rôle d'un musée d'histoire? Avec un(e) partenaire, parlez de ce rôle en utilisant les phrases suivantes comme point de départ. Suivez le modèle.

MODÈLE: Les gens gardent des objets du passé afin de / afin que... →
É1: Les gens gardent des objets du passé afin de se souvenir des événements.
É2: Et ils les gardent aussi afin que les jeunes puissent mieux comprendre l'histoire.

1. Ces musées doivent exister pour que... / pour...
2. Les gens ne peuvent pas les visiter sans... / sans que...
3. On montre des images horrifiantes afin que... / afin de...
4. Les jeunes ne comprennent pas l'histoire avant... / avant que...
5. Nous devons tous étudier l'histoire jusqu'à ce que... / bien que...

Visionnement 2

La ville de Marseille. Marseille est la ville la plus ancienne de France. Fondée par les Grecs vers 600 avant J.-C.,* elle était célèbre pour son port magnifique. Aujourd'hui, on trouve des cafés et des restaurants autour du Vieux-Port. Il y a aussi un marché aux poissons tous les matins.

La ville de Marseille est très différente de Paris: c'est une ville méditerranéenne qui ressemble un peu à Naples ou à Alger. Dans le quartier du Panier, on voit de petites rues étroites qui montent et qui descendent comme en Italie. La Canebière est la grande rue où les Marseillais aiment se promener. L'église Notre-Dame de la Garde domine la ville et semble la protéger.

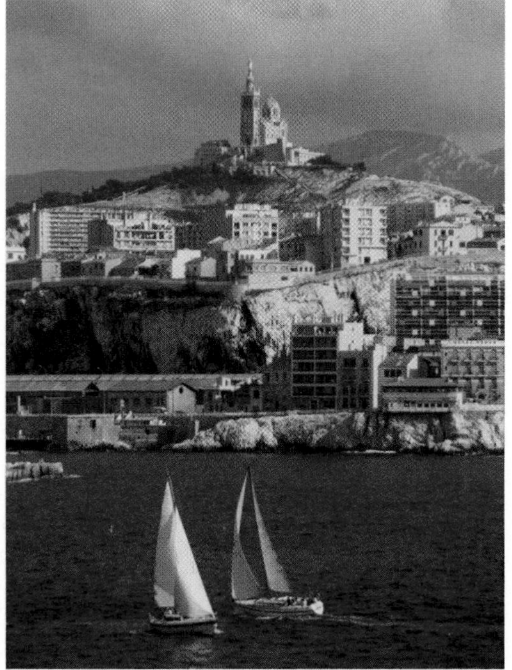

La ville de Marseille

*avant J.-C. = avant Jésus-Christ. En anglais, on écrit B.C. ou B.C.E. (*before the common era*). *600* B.C.

La ville de Marseille

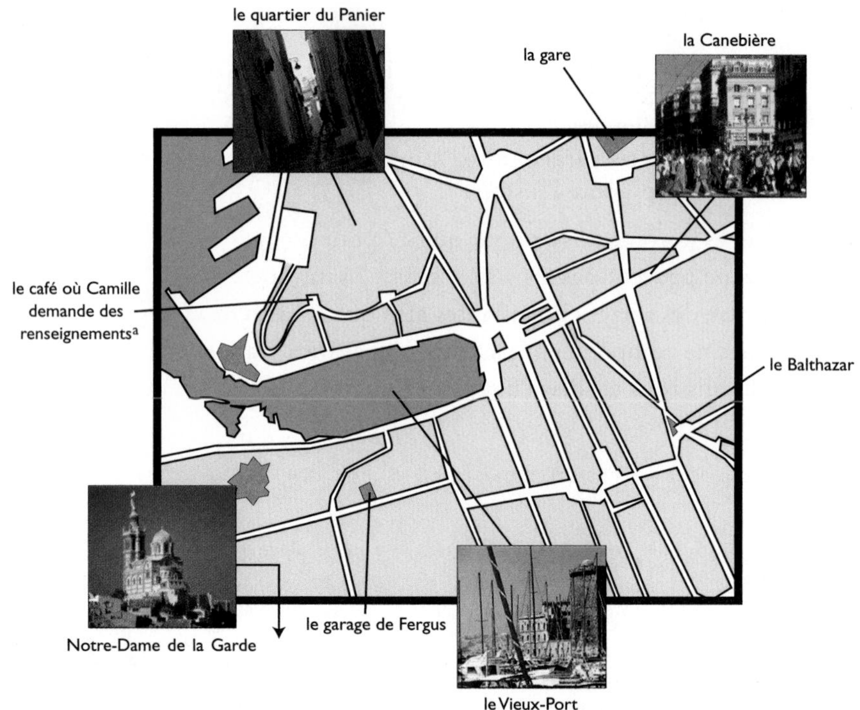

Complétez le paragraphe à l'aide de la carte et de la lecture à la page 455.

Camille a pris le train à Nîmes, et elle est arrivée dans la ville de Marseille à ____[1]. Elle est allée à pied jusqu'au grand boulevard qui s'appelle ____[2] et où tout le monde se promène. Elle a continué dans cette rue, et elle est arrivée au ____[3], où elle a vu le marché aux poissons. Mais elle était pressée. Dans le quartier du ____[4], elle est entrée dans un petit ____[5] pour demander des renseignements. Le patron du bar lui a dit de revenir le lendemain matin. Le soir, elle a rendu visite aux parents de Rachid.

Le lendemain, elle est retournée au ____[6] et le patron du bar lui a dit qu'il fallait chercher le boulevard de la Corderie de l'autre côté du ____[7]. Elle y est allée, mais le ____[8] avait disparu:[b] le bâtiment était vide.[c] Elle y a trouvé des musiciens qui jouaient de la musique raï. Est-elle montée sur la colline pour voir ____[9], qui domine la ville? Non, elle s'est dépêchée d'aller au musée de la Résistance.

[a]des... *information* [b]avait... *had disappeared* [c]*empty*

Observez!

Considérez les aspects culturels expliqués dans **Regards sur la culture**. Ensuite, regardez l'Épisode 21 encore une fois, et répondez aux questions suivantes.

- Quelles expressions le patron du bar utilise-t-il pour expliquer à Camille comment aller au garage de Fergus? Quelles expressions utilisez-vous quand vous indiquez le chemin dans votre ville? Trouvez-vous des différences entre l'usage français et l'usage nord-américain?
- Dans le film, qu'est-ce qui montre le mélange de cultures qui caractérise la ville de Marseille?

Après le visionnement

Faites l'activité pour le **Visionnement 2** dans le cahier.

Synthèse: Culture

La politique culturelle au Québec

Dans le monde francophone, la culture est un sujet politique important, et les problèmes linguistiques dominent souvent dans les débats politiques. Par exemple, pendant longtemps, la France, comme les États-Unis, n'avait pas de langue officielle. Mais en 1992, après des débats très difficiles, la constitution a été modifiée et le français est devenu la langue officielle de la République. C'était une réaction, en partie, contre la domination de l'anglais dans les sciences et dans la politique internationale.

Au Québec, les problèmes linguistiques ont beaucoup d'importance. Les francophones sont une minorité au Canada, et l'environnement nord-américain est dominé par l'anglais, qui est en expansion.

Les drapeaux canadien et québécois

Année	Population du Canada	% de Francophones
1951	14.010.000	29%
est. 2005	32.078.819	22.9%

La situation en 1971

En 1971, beaucoup de Québécois parlaient français et anglais. Mais le bilinguisme mène[1] à l'assimilation, et presque toutes les communautés francophones de l'ouest du Canada et de la Nouvelle-Angleterre sont devenues progressivement anglophones.

L'anglais était la langue des affaires et de l'industrie au Québec. Les anglophones étaient souvent à la tête des entreprises. Les immigrés préféraient envoyer leurs enfants dans les écoles anglophones. En 1971, 79% des enfants des immigrés étaient dans une école anglophone. Depuis la Conquête,* le français canadien adoptait beaucoup de mots anglais. Dans les régions anglophones, on avait peu de respect pour le français nord-américain. À Toronto, à Vancouver, même dans les écoles anglophones du Québec, on apprenait généralement le français de Paris.

1977: La charte de la langue française

La «charte de la langue française» était un acte de politique culturelle unique au monde. Son but[2] était d'assurer à la langue française le premier rôle dans la société québécoise et de permettre au français de survivre en Amérique du Nord.

PROVISIONS DE LA CHARTE

1. Le français est obligatoire dans l'administration de la province (dans les bureaux, pour les contrats, sur les routes, etc.).
2. Le français est la langue ordinaire des entreprises qui ont une importance publique (le téléphone, les transports, l'électricité, etc.). Les documents peuvent contenir aussi une traduction en anglais.
3. Le français est la langue officielle des relations du travail. La communication officielle dans les entreprises doit être en français.
4. Les affiches, les inscriptions sur les produits doivent être en français. Une traduction en anglais est possible, mais le texte français doit dominer.
5. L'accès aux écoles anglophones est limité. Les enfants des immigrés doivent aller à l'école française.

Aujourd'hui

Après 1977, certaines grandes entreprises ont quitté Montréal pour Toronto pour protester contre ces mesures. Mais aujourd'hui, le Québec est transformé, surtout à Montréal. Plus de 70% des enfants d'immigrés sont à l'école française. La plupart[3] des anglophones sont devenus bilingues, et le français domine partout.

Malheureusement, bien que le français se stabilise au Québec, la langue continue à décliner dans le reste du Canada.

[1]*leads* [2]*goal* [3]La... *Most*

*La Conquête se réfère à la victoire de l'Angleterre au moment de la bataille des plaines d'Abraham à Québec en 1759.

À vous

Une petite ville francophone en Louisiane. Mettez-vous par groupes de quatre. Imaginez que vous êtes le conseil municipal d'une petite ville cajun dans le sud-ouest de la Louisiane. On vous a suggéré d'adopter une politique linguistique pour protéger le français dans votre ville. Décidez quelle sera votre politique linguistique. Considérez les domaines suivants: l'administration de la ville, les contrats locaux, la signalisation routière (*road signs*), les affiches, l'école. Présentez votre «charte» à la classe.

Expressions utiles: on peut; on doit; il faut que

À écrire

Faites **À écrire** pour le Chapitre 21 dans le cahier.

Vocabulaire

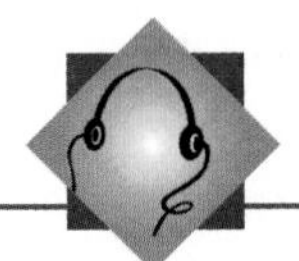

Les beaux-arts

la peinture	painting (*action, art*)
un(e) photographe	photographer
une photographie (*fam.* **une photo**)	photograph
un tableau	painting (*picture*)
un vernissage	opening, preview

À REVOIR: **un(e) conservateur/trice, un(e) peintre / femme peintre**

La musique

une chanson	song
un(e) chanteur/euse	singer
un(e) compositeur/trice	composer

MOTS APPARENTÉS: **le blues, un concert, la country, le hip-hop, un opéra, un orchestre, le punk, le raï, le reggae, le rock, le ska, la world music**

À REVOIR: **un(e) musicien(ne)**

La littérature et le théâtre

un(e) auteur / femme auteur	author
un conte	short story
une pièce (de théâtre)	play
la poésie	poetry
un roman	novel
un(e) romancier/ière	novelist

MOTS APPARENTÉS: **un poème, un(e) poète / femme poète**

Substantifs

une conférence	lecture	**une rencontre**	meeting, encounter
une manifestation (culturelle)	(cultural) event; (*public, political*) demonstration	**une soirée**	evening
une œuvre	literary or art work, musical composition	**un spectacle**	entertainment, show

Adjectif

contemporain(e)	contemporary

Expressions d'émotion et d'opinion

être désolé(e) que	to be sorry that
être étonné(e) que	to be astonished that
être ravi(e) que	to be thrilled that
il est dommage que	it is too bad that
il est incroyable que	it is incredible that
souhaiter que	to wish, hope that

MOTS APPARENTÉS: **être furieux/euse (surpris[e]) que, il est bizarre que, regretter que**

À REVOIR: **avoir peur que, espérer que, être content(e) (fâché[e], heureux/euse, triste) que, il est bon (formidable, ridicule) que, préférer que**

Expressions de doute et d'incertitude

douter que	to doubt that
il est douteux que	it is doubtful that
il est peu probable que	it is unlikely that
il se peut que	it could be that, it is possible that

MOTS APPARENTÉS: **être incertain(e) que, il est incertain que, ne pas être certain(e) que**

À REVOIR: **il est impossible (possible) que, ne pas croire que, ne pas être sûr(e) que, ne pas penser que**

Expressions de probabilité et de certitude

il est clair que	it is clear that
ne pas douter que	not to doubt that

MOTS APPARENTÉS: **être certain(e) que, il est certain (probable) que**

À REVOIR: **croire que, être sûr(e) que, il est évident (sûr, vrai) que, penser que**

Conjonctions

afin que	so that, in order that	**pour que**	so that, in order that
avant que	before	**sans que**	unless; without
bien que	although		
jusqu'à ce que	until		

Prépositions

afin de	in order to
avant de	before

À REVOIR: **après, pour, sans**

Autre expression utile

avoir lieu	to take place

Chapitre 22

Secrets dévoilés

Le Chemin du retour

Feuille de service du 20 janvier
11e jour de tournage
Horaires : 9 h–19 h

LIEU DE TOURNAGE : CASABLANCA—À DÉFINIR° — *°to be determined*

Séquence	***Effets***	***Décors***	***Résumé***	***Rôles***
160	INT.—FIN DU JOUR	VILLA FERGUS— Salon Fergus	Camille est reçue par les Fergus. Roland raconte sa version des faits. Il est très faible et son fils, Thomas, continue le récit et donne une boîte de documents à Camille.	CAMILLE, THOMAS FERGUS, ROLAND FERGUS

OBJECTIFS

In this episode, you will

- meet the person who reveals the truth to Camille

In this chapter, you will

- talk about traveling to other countries
- review narrating with the **passé composé** and the **imparfait**
- narrate stories that include events at various points in the past
- learn to understand indirect discourse in narration
- learn about the culture of Casablanca
- read about a boy of Algerian descent who learns something about his heritage

Vocabulaire en contexte

En voyage à Casablanca

Aperçu° de la ville

Métropole cosmopolite, Casablanca est une ville de contrastes: un côté oriental—**arabe** et **berbère**°*—et un côté occidental, les habitants **riches** et leurs **voisins° pauvres,** la vie traditionnelle et les développements modernes. On voit des voitures de luxe et des chariots,° des femmes **en décolleté°** et robe **courte°** et des femmes musulmanes qui s'habillent **dignement°** en djellabas† (*f.*) ou qui portent des foulards sur la tête.

Comme **la plupart des** villes marocaines, Casablanca comporte° deux parties distinctes. **La médina°** offre un spectacle **étonnant**;° un labyrinthe de ruelles **sombres°** et d'impasses étroites, où on découvre des **mosquées** (*f.*), des hammams° et des marchés. **À l'écart** (*m.*) **de°** la médina, le vingtième siècle a donné naissance à un nouveau type de ville: le long de **larges°** avenues, les bâtiments officiels alternent avec des commerces. À l'arrière, ce sont des villas° qu'on trouve **au milieu des°** jardins.

Overview, Quick look
Berber
neighbors
carts / en... *in low-cut clothing*
short
with dignity
includes
old city
amazing
dark
baths / À... *Away from*
wide
(detached) houses / au... *in the middle of*

Activités

A. Familles de mots. Identifiez le mot ou la phrase du vocabulaire qui est de la même famille que l'expression donnée. Puis, dites si la réponse est un substantif, un adjectif, un adverbe ou une phrase prépositionnelle.

MODÈLE: écarté (*separated*) → à l'écart de (phrase prépositionnelle)

1. un Berbère
2. le décolleté
3. la dignité
4. un Arabe
5. l'étonnement (*m.*) (*astonishment*)
6. le voisinage (*neighborhood*)
7. le milieu
8. la pauvreté
9. la richesse

*Les Berbères sont un groupe ethnique nord-africain (distincts des Arabes).
†Une djellaba est un vêtement (une robe) long à manches (*sleeves*) et à capuchon (*hood*), porté par les hommes et les femmes, en Afrique du Nord.

B. Associations. Avec quel côté de la ville de Casablanca associez-vous les expressions suivantes—le côté moderne et occidental ou le côté traditionnel et oriental?

MODÈLE: une mosquée →
J'associe une mosquée avec le côté traditionnel et oriental de Casablanca.

1. des bâtiments officiels
2. des femmes en robes courtes
3. des hommes en djellabas
4. les ruelles sombres de la médina
5. des villas et de larges avenues
6. des femmes habillées dignement

C. Pour découvrir une ville. Interviewez votre partenaire pour découvrir ses souvenirs d'une ville à l'étranger (*abroad*). Il/Elle peut imaginer un voyage à Marseille ou à Casablanca s'il / si elle n'est jamais allé(e) à l'étranger.

Demandez à votre partenaire...

1. quelle ville il/elle a visitée et pourquoi il/elle a décidé d'y aller.
2. si cette ville ressemblait à la plupart des villes qu'il/elle connaissait déjà. Demandez-lui d'expliquer pourquoi ou pourquoi pas.
3. s'il / si elle a pu distinguer des quartiers différents dans la ville et en quoi ils étaient distincts. Demandez-lui de décrire les quartiers résidentiels.
4. ce qu'il/elle a vu d'intéressant (d'étonnant, de fabuleux).
5. ce qu'il/elle a aimé le plus dans cette ville.
6. s'il / si elle voudrait retourner dans cette ville pour une visite plus longue ou pour y habiter. Demandez-lui d'expliquer sa réponse.

Visionnement 1

Avant de visionner

Étude de vocabulaire. Parfois, on peut deviner (*guess*) la nouvelle signification d'un mot en analysant son emploi dans des contextes familiers. D'abord, lisez les phrases que vous avez déjà rencontrées dans le film. Ensuite, lisez la phrase où le nouvel emploi apparaît, et essayez de préciser le sens du nouvel usage.

1. **Famille *prendre***
   Il rentre à Paris, il retrouve sa femme, *reprend* son travail...
   Mais tu peux en *reprendre* un peu! Une petite goutte (just a drop)?
   NOUVEL EMPLOI: Les Allemands ***ont repris*** cette rumeur à leur compte (*to their advantage*)!
2. **Famille *lancer***
   Je *lance* une série de reportages sur la vie au Québec.
   NOUVEAUX EMPLOIS: C'est lui qui ***a lancé*** la rumeur...
   C'était un bon prétexte pour ***lancer*** des représailles.

Vocabulaire relatif à l'épisode

Puis-je vous être utile?	*Can I help you?*
Il a demandé qu'on ne le dérange pas.	*He asked not to be disturbed.*
Inutile d'insister.	*There's no use insisting.*
C'est ce que tout le monde était censé croire.	*That's what everyone was supposed to believe.*
On ne peut pas abandonner les copains!	*We can't abandon our friends!*
crever	*to die (slang)*
les avait aperçus	*had caught sight of / seen them*

3. **Famille *rendre***

   Dans quelle ville *s'est-il rendu*?

   Donc, c'est nous qui l'avons découverte, formée et *rendue* célèbre.

   Je sais qu'il est Marseillais et qu'il a quitté la ville au début de la guerre pour *se rendre* dans les Cévennes.

   NOUVEAUX EMPLOIS: La Résistance avait ***rendez-vous*** avec Antoine et moi.
   Mais aujourd'hui, croyez-vous qu'il est possible de ***rendre justice*** à... ?

4. **Famille *mettre***

   Quoi, le président me *met* à la porte?!

   On y *met* de la tomme fraîche du Cantal.

   Elle aussi, elle est désolée de vous *avoir mise* à la porte.

   NOUVEAUX EMPLOIS: J'***avais mis*** un uniforme...
   La Résistance ***a mis*** des mois à ***s'en remettre***.

Observez!

Dans l'Épisode 22, Camille rencontre Fergus, l'homme mystérieux qu'elle cherche depuis sa visite avec Jeanne Leblanc. Regardez l'épisode, et essayez de trouver les réponses aux questions suivantes.

- Comment l'histoire racontée par Fergus diffère-t-elle de celle racontée par Jeanne Leblanc? Quels détails ajoute-t-il?
- Pourquoi Fergus a-t-il quitté la France pour vivre à Casablanca?

Après le visionnement

A. Le récit de Fergus. Dans cet épisode, Roland Fergus et son fils Thomas racontent les événements du 17 décembre 1943 du point de vue de Fergus père. Classez les actions dans l'ordre chronologique de 1 à 5.

_____ ROLAND FERGUS: Les Allemands ont repris cette rumeur à leur compte! Ils ont dit que nous travaillions pour eux et que c'est la Résistance qui avait tué[a] Antoine.

_____ ROLAND FERGUS: Antoine a vu que ses amis étaient tombés[b] dans un piège. Les Allemands les tuaient un à un, comme des lapins!

_____ THOMAS FERGUS (FILS): Un résistant, un certain Pierre Leblanc, les avait aperçus. Il avait vu votre grand-père, Antoine, avec mon père qui portait un insigne nazi. C'est lui qui a lancé la rumeur...

_____ ROLAND FERGUS: Antoine voulait rejoindre les résistants. Mais j'ai vu que ce combat était perdu.

_____ ROLAND FERGUS: C'était un bon prétexte pour lancer des représailles et pour commencer une campagne de désinformation! Ils ont pris vingt-cinq hommes au hasard,[c] dans la région, et ils les ont fusillés![d] La Résistance a mis des mois à s'en remettre.

[a]avait... *had killed* [b]étaient... *had fallen* [c]au... *at random* [d]les... *shot them*

B. De graves malentendus. Qu'est-ce que Pierre Leblanc a vu et qu'est-ce qui l'a mené (*led*) à la conclusion que Fergus et Antoine étaient des traîtres? En quoi s'était-il trompé (*had he been mistaken*)?

Structure 66

Le passé composé et l'imparfait (II)

—C'est ce que tout le monde **était** censé croire. Ma venue de Paris **était** un secret bien gardé. Nous sommes... nous **sommes arrivés** à la gare... mais les Allemands **étaient** déjà là.

The French system of past tenses does not present a one-to-one correspondence with the English system, and therefore requires special attention. The goal of this section is to review and expand your knowledge of the **passé composé** and the **imparfait**, and to provide further opportunities for practice.

Le passé composé

Formation

1. As you already know, the **passé composé** always consists of an auxiliary verb conjugated in the present tense and followed by a past participle. For most verbs, the auxiliary is **avoir**.

David **a réussi** à trouver des documents sur Antoine Leclair.	*David succeeded in finding documents pertaining to Antoine Leclair.*
Jeanne Leblanc n'**a** pas **voulu** parler de la guerre.	*Jeanne Leblanc didn't want to talk about the war.*

Past participles of regular verbs are formed by dropping the infinitive ending and adding **-é** (for **-er** verbs), **-u** (for **-re** verbs), and **-i** (for **-ir** verbs, both the **finir** type and the **sortir** type). Irregular past participles are listed on page 225 and in Appendix B.

habiter	**habité**
descendre	**descendu**
finir	**fini**
sortir	**sorti**

A direct object can precede the verb if it is an object pronoun or if it is the relative pronoun **que** referring to an antecedent noun. When the direct object precedes the verb this way, the past participle agrees with it in gender and number.

Jeanne Leblanc? Camille **l'**a rencontrée à Saint-Jean de Causse. — *Jeanne Leblanc? Camille met her in Saint-Jean de Causse.*

La femme **que** Camille a rencontrée s'appellait Jeanne Leblanc. — *The woman whom Camille met was named Jeanne Leblanc.*

2. A small group of verbs that indicate a change of state form the **passé composé** with the auxiliary **être**. All are intransitive; that is, they are not followed by a direct object. When these verbs are used, the past participle agrees with the subject of the sentence.

Pour aller à Saint-Jean de Causse, Rachid **est descendu** du train à Alès. — *To go to Saint-Jean de Causse, Rachid got off the train in Alès.*

Mado **est née** en 1942. — *Mado was born in 1942.*

Attention: Not all intransitive verbs that indicate a change in state belong to this group. Many, for example, **courir** (*to run*), use the auxiliary **avoir**. See page 248 for a list of the verbs that take **être**.

3. The verbs **descendre**, **monter**, **passer**, and **sortir** can sometimes be followed by a direct object. In that case, they are conjugated with **avoir** and the past participle does *not* agree with the subject.

Camille **a sorti** une photo d'Antoine de son sac. — *Camille took a photo of Antoine out of her purse.*

Mado et le médecin **ont descendu** l'escalier. — *Mado and the doctor descended the stairs.*

4. Pronominal verbs are conjugated with the auxiliary **être** in the **passé composé**.

Bruno **s'est rasé** avant d'aller au restaurant avec Camille. — *Bruno shaved before going to the restaurant with Camille.*

Camille et Bruno **se sont dépêchés** pour arriver à l'heure. — *Camille and Bruno hurried in order to arrive on time.*

Pronouns in pronominal verbs can serve as direct or indirect objects. For pronominal verbs in the **passé composé**, the past participle agrees with the pronoun if it is a preceding *direct* object.

Camille **s'est couchée** tôt la veille de son départ. — *Camille went to bed early the night before her departure.*

Mado et Camille **se sont disputées**. — *Mado and Camille argued.*

Camille et Rachid **se sont** téléphoné avant d'aller à la gare. — *Camille and Rachid called each other before going to the station.*

Function

The **passé composé** is used to express completed events in past time. It is used to narrate what happened.

Camille **a trouvé** des pistes à Marseille.	*Camille found clues in Marseille.*
Les Allemands **ont envahi** la France en 1939.	*The Germans invaded France in 1939.*

L'imparfait

Formation

The **imparfait** (of all verbs except **être)** is formed by dropping the **-ons** ending of the present-tense **nous** form of the verb and adding the endings **-ais**, **-ais**, **-ait**, **-ions**, **-iez**, **-aient**.

Louise **aimait** la chanson «Mon Amant de Saint-Jean».	*Louise loved the song "Mon Amant de Saint-Jean."*
Tous les jours, Louise **descendait** dans la rue pour parler à Alex.	*Every day, Louise went down to the street to talk to Alex.*
Les habitants de Saint-Jean de Causse **agissaient** avec une prudence extrême pendant la guerre.	*The people of Saint-Jean de Causse acted with extreme care during the war.*

The **imparfait** of **être** is formed with the same endings added to the stem **ét-**.

Jeanne et Pierre Leblanc **étaient** très hospitaliers envers Antoine.	*Jeanne and Pierre Leblanc were very hospitable to Antoine.*

Functions

1. The **imparfait** is used for describing in past time. In this function, it is used to describe states of mind or a state of affairs.

Bruno **était** ravi de revoir Hélène.	*Bruno was happy to see Hélène again.*
Tout le monde **pensait** qu'Antoine **était** un collaborateur; on **avait** peur d'apprendre la vérité.	*Everybody thought that Antoine was a collaborator; they were afraid to learn the truth.*
Il **faisait** froid la nuit de la mort de Pierre Leblanc.	*It was cold the night of Pierre Leblanc's death.*

2. The **imparfait** also expresses ongoing past action (*what was happening*).

Hélène **cherchait** l'adresse de David sur Internet quand Bruno est entré.	*Hélène was looking for David's address on the Internet when Bruno came in.*
Alex **jouait** de l'accordéon pendant que Mado **parlait** au docteur.	*Alex was playing the accordion while Mado was talking to the doctor.*

3. Finally, the **imparfait** is used to express repeated and habitual past actions (*what used to happen*).

Bruno **déjeunait** avec ses collègues tous les jours à la cafétéria.	*Bruno used to eat lunch with his colleagues every day in the cafeteria.*
Autrefois, les Français **consommaient** plus de pain.	*In the past, the French ate more bread.*

Activité

Une année difficile. Chantal parle de son école préparatoire et du concours. Mettez les verbes à l'imparfait ou au passé composé, selon le cas (*depending on the case*).

Le premier jour, je _____[1] (ne pas descendre) du bus là où je _____[2] (devoir) et je _____[3] (se perdre). Je _____[4] (ne pas pouvoir) trouver mon école. Quand je _____[5] (aller) au bureau principal, il y _____[6] (avoir) trente élèves qui _____[7] (attendre) l'arrivée de la secrétaire. Je _____[8] (ne connaître personne). Nous _____[9] (commencer) à nous impatienter quand elle _____[10] (arriver enfin), mais elle nous _____[11] (faire) attendre encore un quart d'heure. Nous _____[12] (être) furieux. En plus, quand c'était mon tour, elle _____[13] (me dire): «Vous _____[14] (arriver) trop tard. Revenez demain.» Encore plus furieuse, je _____[15] (retourner) au bureau le lendemain. Enfin, je _____[16] (s'inscrire) à l'école préparatoire.

Pendant l'année, nous _____[17] (travailler) tous les jours comme des fous. Nous _____[18] (avoir) trois heures de maths par jour et à côté de ça, les deux heures de philo _____[19] (sembler) faciles. Enfin, je _____[20] (ne que faire) étudier pendant toute l'année. Je _____[21] (savoir) que le concours _____[22] (aller) être difficile.

Enfin le jour du concours _____[23] (arriver)! Les cinquante candidats _____[24] (se trouver) dans une salle et nous _____[25] (avoir) tous peur. Mais quand le pion (*assistant*) _____[26] (nous donner) le sujet pour l'écrit, nous _____[27] (comprendre) que nous _____[28] (être) bien préparés. Merci, les professeurs!

Structure 67

Le plus-que-parfait

Narrating

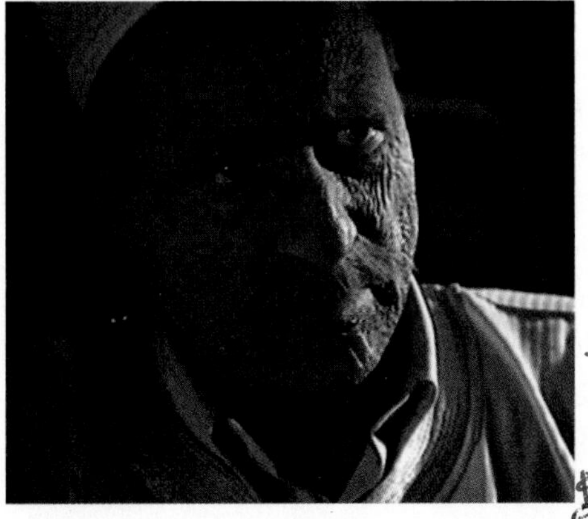

—Oui. Mais je ne travaillais pas pour les nazis! J'**avais mis** un uniforme pour tromper l'ennemi [...] Antoine a vu que ses amis **étaient tombés** dans un piège.

You have already learned to use the **passé composé** and the **imparfait**. In this section, you will learn another past tense, the **plus-que-parfait**, which is useful in narrating a series of past events.

1. The **plus-que-parfait** is formed by conjugating the auxiliary—**avoir** or **être**—in the **imparfait** and adding the past participle.

répondre			
j'	**avais répondu**	nous	**avions répondu**
tu	**avais répondu**	vous	**aviez répondu**
il, elle, on	**avait répondu**	ils, elles	**avaient répondu**

aller			
j'	**étais allé(e)**	nous	**étions allé(e)s**
tu	**étais allé(e)**	vous	**étiez allé(e)(s)**
il, elle, on	**était allé(e)**	ils, elles	**étaient allé(e)s**

2. The **plus-que-parfait** is used to talk about an action that occurred before another past action. It occurs frequently in longer narrations in past time, where multiple events are recounted in sequence.

Nous n'avons jamais su qui nous **avait trahis**.	*We never found out who (had) betrayed us.*
Antoine **avait donné** rendez-vous aux résistants.	*Antoine had set up a meeting with the resistance fighters.*

Activités

A. Pour connaître le Maroc. À la fin (*end*) de leur cours sur la culture marocaine, les étudiants se sont rendus compte de toutes les activités auxquelles (*in which*) ils avaient participé au courant du semestre. Formez des phrases selon le modèle. Attention aux auxiliaires.

MODÈLE: le professeur / inviter / la classe à étudier le Maroc →
Le professeur avait invité la classe à étudier le Maroc.

1. un ami marocain du professeur / venir / pour nous parler de son enfance
2. les étudiants / apprendre / certaines expressions en arabe
3. Anne / décrire / ses vacances à Marrakech de l'année précédente
4. nous / regarder / des photos de Fès et de Marrakech
5. nous / chercher / des sites Internet sur le Maroc
6. tu / lire / un livre de Tahar Ben Jelloun*
7. je / recevoir / une carte postale d'un étudiant à Casablanca
8. les étudiants / apporter / des CD de raï en classe
9. vous / découvrir / la musique berbère
10. vous / rester / après le cours pour écouter plus de musique
11. nous / préparer / des loukoums† en classe
12. les étudiants / aller / dans un restaurant marocain
13. je / manger / un couscous délicieux
14. tu / boire / du thé à la menthe (*mint*)

B. Imaginez. Que s'était-il passé avant? Avec votre partenaire, considérez les actions et les situations des personnes suivantes et imaginez des actions ou des situations qui les avaient précédées.

MODÈLE: Marta a bu un grand verre d'eau. →
É1: Avant, elle avait couru un marathon.
É2: Avant, elle était restée au soleil pendant trois heures.

1. Jean-Philippe a préparé un grand repas pour ses amis.
2. Vous avez passé un examen difficile.
3. J'ai acheté une nouvelle voiture.
4. Le patron a fermé le bar.
5. Magalie était très fatiguée le matin.
6. Nous avons choisi un concert.
7. L'étudiant avait mal à la tête le matin.
8. Nous avons réussi à nos examens.
9. J'ai rendu une rédaction (*composition*) en cours d'anglais.

---

*Tahar Ben Jelloun est un écrivain marocain de langue française, né à Fès en 1944.

†**Le loukoum** est une sorte de bonbon du Moyen-Orient qui est populaire au Maroc.

Regards sur la culture

La culture à Casablanca

When Camille decides to go to Casablanca, she does not seem bothered by the intercultural difficulties that such a trip will involve. It is true that the city has one of the largest populations of French citizens of any outside Europe. Still, Morocco is very different from Europe, despite its many historical connections with Spain and France.

La tradition et la modernité à Casablanca

- Morocco is only 8 miles (13 kilometers) from Europe and has had close historical links with both Spain and France. The country became a French protectorate in 1912. Although theoretically France was responsible only for maintaining order, it also directed foreign and economic policy. As Morocco became something very much like a French colony, it also underwent a process of modernization and Europeanization. During World War II, the sultan supported the Allies but met secretly with Churchill and Roosevelt in an attempt to build support for independence. Morocco finally did become independent in 1956. The French presence had an enormous impact, however, and is still a source of conflict and disagreement among Moroccans.
- The city of Dar el-Beida (*White House*)—best known abroad by its Spanish name, Casablanca—is the largest city in the entire Maghreb region (Morocco, Algeria, Tunisia) and the fourth largest city in Africa. The harbor of Casablanca, which was developed by the French in the early 20th century, has made the city the economic center of the country.
- Casa, as it is sometimes called in French, is considered a loud, aggressive, and cosmopolitan city. Parts of it look very modern and European, with restaurants, cafés, banks, and luxury stores. Other parts, like the Old Medina, resemble the traditional Muslim cities that have dominated the landscape of North Africa for centuries. On the outskirts are shantytowns, where country people, attracted by the economic dynamism of the city, often locate after moving to the city. Outsiders feel about Casablanca much as they do about Marseille or New York.
- Although it is situated on the Atlantic, Casablanca has a kind of Mediterranean climate. The weather is generally mild. Average temperatures range from 12 degrees Celsius (54 Fahrenheit) in January to 23 degrees C (73 F) in August.

- The official language in Morocco today is Arabic. But many Moroccan families have relatives living and working in France, and the constant communication back and forth maintains some knowledge of French at all levels of society.
- There has been a strong Jewish presence in the Maghreb since Roman times. In 1950, the Jewish population of Morocco was estimated at 300,000, but in recent years, many of the old Jewish communities have dwindled and disappeared, as their inhabitants moved to Israel or France. Today, there are only about 8,000 Moroccan Jews, and most of them live in Casablanca.
- Among the most important sights of Casablanca is the largest mosque and Islamic cultural center outside Saudi Arabia. The Hassan II Mosque, named for the late King of Morocco, was completed in 1988. It was built with contributions from Moroccans all over the world.

Considérez

If you were planning to go to Casablanca on business, what kinds of information and training would you want to have before going? Think about questions of language, religion, social customs, relations between the sexes, etiquette, work habits, food and drink, and so on.

Structure 68

Le discours indirect

Telling what others said

—Les Allemands ont repris cette rumeur à leur compte! Ils ont dit **que nous travaillions pour eux** et **que c'est la Résistance qui avait tué Antoine.**

Important—The information in this section is meant to help you understand when people tell what someone else said. You do not need to learn to create sentences like this, but you should learn to understand them when others use them.

Le discours direct

Direct discourse quotes a speaker's exact words. Sometimes, the quote is accompanied by a verb of communication such as **dire** and **demander**.

Jeanne Leblanc m'a dit: «Il n'était pas supposé être à ce rendez-vous.»	*Jeanne Leblanc told me, "He wasn't supposed to be at that meeting."*
Camille demande à l'employé: «Est-ce que M. Fergus est là?»	*Camille asks the employee, "Is Mr. Fergus here?"*

Le discours indirect

Indirect discourse tells what somebody said without using a direct quotation.

1. A speaker's statement is reported in a subordinate clause beginning with **que**. Just as in indirect discourse in English, pronouns change as necessary. Jeanne Leblanc used the pronoun **il** to refer to Fergus in the previous example of direct discourse. Hence, Camille uses **vous** when reporting the comment to Fergus himself in this example:

Jeanne Leblanc m'a dit **que vous** n'**étiez** pas supposé être là.	*Jeanne Leblanc told me you weren't supposed to be there.*

   Yes/no questions are reported indirectly in a subordinate clause beginning with **si**. Questions are phrased as statements, so question marks are not used.

Camille demande à l'employé **si** M. Fergus est là.	*Camille asks the employee if Mr. Fergus is there.*

2. When the verb of communication (**dire**, **demander**, etc.) in indirect discourse is in the *present* tense, the tense of the verb in the subordinate clause is the same as in direct discourse.

DIRECT DISCOURSE	Bruno demande à Camille: «Est-ce que tu **vas** au bureau aujourd'hui?»
INDIRECT DISCOURSE	Bruno demande à Camille si elle **va** au bureau aujourd'hui.

3. When the verb of communication in indirect discourse is in a *past* tense, the tense in the subordinate clause changes, according to certain rules.

DIRECT DISCOURSE VERB		INDIRECT DISCOURSE SUBORDINATE CLAUSE VERB
present	→	imparfait
imparfait	→	imparfait (*no change*)
passé composé	→	plus-que-parfait

DIRECT DISCOURSE	La conservatrice a dit: «Fergus **est** à Casablanca.»
INDIRECT DISCOURSE	La conservatrice a dit que Fergus **était** à Casablanca.
DIRECT DISCOURSE	Fergus a dit: «J'avais peur mais j'ai **ai mis** l'uniforme nazi pour tromper l'ennemi.»
INDIRECT DISCOURSE	Fergus a dit qu'il avait peur mais qu'il **avait mis** l'uniforme nazi pour tromper l'ennemi.

Pour en savoir plus...

You already know several verbs that are often used to introduce indirect discourse: **ajouter**, **demander**, **dire**, **écrire**, **indiquer**, and **répondre**. A few others that you may have seen or heard are

annoncer	*to announce*
déclarer	*to declare*
expliquer	*to explain*
préciser	*to specify*
rapporter	*to report*

Activités

A. Qui dit... ? Choisissez le personnage qui dit chaque chose. Ensuite, transformez chaque phrase indirecte en phrase directe, en faisant tous les changements nécessaires. Suivez le modèle.

Personnages: l'employé, Thomas Fergus (fils), Roland Fergus, Camille

MODÈLE: L'employé dit que M. Fergus est absent. «Monsieur Fergus est absent.»

1. _____ explique que M. Fergus est malade.
2. _____ répond qu'elle est la petite fille d'Antoine Leclair.
3. _____ annonce que M. Fergus veut bien la recevoir chez lui.
4. _____ demande à la femme si elle a dit à M. Fergus qu'elle était arrivée.
5. _____ explique que Fergus est son ancien nom.
6. _____ dit que les autres membres de la Résistance avaient rendez-vous avec Antoine et lui.
7. _____ explique qu'à la Libération son père a voulu rétablir la vérité.

B. Qu'est-ce qu'ils ont dit? Plusieurs étudiants qui ont vu *Le Chemin du retour* ont parlé du film. Transformez les phrases indirectes en phrases directes en faisant tous les changements nécessaires.

MODÈLES: Le professeur a demandé si les étudiants avaient aimé le film. → «Est-ce que vous avez aimé le film?»

Chris a dit qu'il aimait tous les films français. → «J'aime tous les films français.»

1. Esmeralda a demandé si tout le monde avait compris le film.
2. Lori a expliqué que le film était un peu difficile mais très intéressant.
3. Tamara a ajouté que parfois les acteurs parlaient un peu vite.
4. Corey a demandé si les autres avaient aimé le jeu des acteurs.
5. Chris et Mark ont dit que les acteurs étaient très bons.
6. Corey a dit qu'il n'avait jamais vu les Cévennes avant.
7. Courtney a annoncé qu'elle avait reconnu le quartier Mouffetard.
8. Tamara a déclaré qu'elle préférait la scène à Casablanca.
9. Mark a demandé si la classe pouvait voir tout le film à la fin du semestre.
10. Le professeur a dit que c'était une excellente idée.
11. Brandon a ajouté qu'il préférait regarder le film au lieu de passer un examen de fin de semestre!

Maintenant, donnez votre propre opinion en ce qui concerne les questions et les commentaires que vous venez de lire.

MODÈLES: Le professeur a demandé si les étudiants avaient aimé le film. → Oui, j'ai aimé le film. (Non, je n'ai pas aimé le film.)

Chris a dit qu'il aimait tous les films français. → Moi aussi, j'aime tous les films français. Ils sont tellement différents des films américains. (Moi, non. Je n'aime pas la plupart des films français. Ils sont ennuyeux.)

Visionnement 2

Le Maroc. Camille arrive à l'aéroport international Mohammed V de **Casablanca**, qui est la ville où vivent la majorité des juifs marocains et la plupart des Français. Mais le Maroc est très varié. Chacune (*Each one*) de ses villes a une réputation différente. **Rabat**, la capitale, est une ville élégante et calme. On y trouve des quartiers historiques, mais aussi des ambassades, le Palais Royal et l'université. **Marrakech**, la ville la plus importante du sud, a conservé un caractère traditionnel. C'est le point de rencontre des populations de la montagne de l'Atlas et du désert. **Fès** est le centre religieux et intellectuel traditionnel du Maroc, où des gens de toutes origines se rencontrent. La ville a la réputation d'être la plus raffinée du Maroc.

Le Maroc

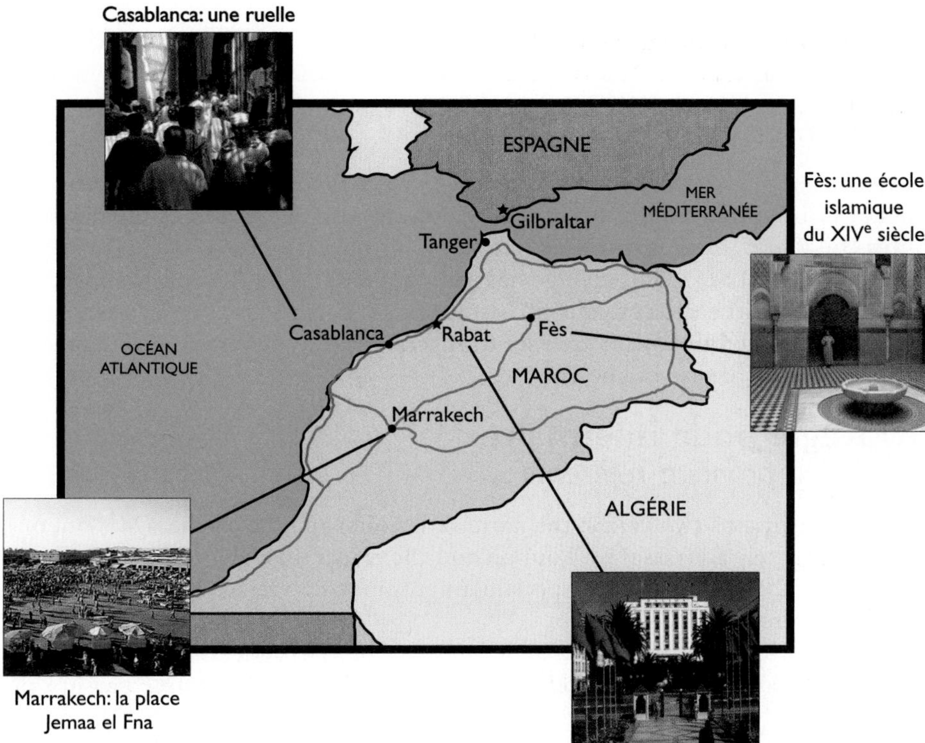

Casablanca: une ruelle

Fès: une école islamique du XIVe siècle

Marrakech: la place Jemaa el Fna

Rabat: quartier des ambassades

Indiquez la ville que vous choisiriez pour faire les choses suivantes.

MODÈLE: voir la capitale → Si je voulais voir la capitale, j'irais à Rabat.

1. regarder l'océan **2.** faire une promenade dans la montagne de l'Atlas **3.** voir une école islamique médiévale **4.** visiter une synagogue **5.** aller à l'ambassade américaine **6.** voir un grand port **7.** connaître les traditions intellectuelles marocaines **8.** voir le palais du roi (*king's palace*)

Pour en savoir plus...

Le thé, symbole d'hospitalité

Le thé au sucre et à la menthe fait partie intégrale de la vie marocaine: il est caractéristique de tous les milieux, à toute heure, dans toutes les circonstances. Sa préparation comporte de nombreux gestes (*movements*) traditionnels. À la fin, il est versé en tenant la théière (*teapot*) de plus en plus haut: on le boit avec les doigts écartés parce que le verre est très chaud.

Observez!

Considérez les aspects culturels expliqués dans **Regards sur la culture**. Ensuite, regardez l'Épisode 22 encore une fois, et répondez aux questions suivantes.

- Comment conseille-t-on à Camille de s'habiller pour aller voir Fergus?
- Comment est-ce qu'on accueille Camille quand elle arrive chez Fergus?

Après le visionnement

Faites l'activité pour le **Visionnement 2** dans le cahier.

Synthèse: Lecture

Mise en contexte

Azouz Begag, a first-generation French citizen of Algerian descent, was born outside of Lyon in 1957. In this autobiographical work, he describes the poverty of his childhood. After many years in a slum, his family moves to state-subsidized housing (**une HLM***). This change has profound effects on the cultural identity of his family. In the excerpt you will be reading, his high school French teacher, M. Loubon, a **pied-noir** who grew up in Algeria, tries to raise Azouz's awareness of an Algeria he has never known.

Stratégie pour mieux lire

Identifying pronoun referents

This scene contains two voices: the narrator (Azouz) and his teacher (M. Loubon). Azouz alternately addresses M. Loubon and the reader. In order to follow the direction of the narrative, it is especially important to understand the various pronoun references.

The following sentences are taken from the text. Try to identify the person to whom each italicized pronoun refers. Is it Azouz, M. Loubon, Azouz's parents, or the reader?

1. —Azouz! *Vous* savez comment on dit «le Maroc» en arabe?, *me* demande tout à coup M. Loubon...
2. Depuis maintenant de longs mois, le prof a pris l'habitude de *me* faire parler en classe, de moi, de ma famille...
3. Savez-*vous* comment on dit les allumettes (*matches*) chez *nous*, par exemple? Li zalimite.

***HLM** = Habitation à loyer (*rent*) modéré

4. —Ah non, m'sieur. Mon père et ma mère, *ils* disent jamais ce mot. Pour appeler un Marocain, *ils* disent Marrocci.
5. Puis *il* reprit son cours pendant quelques minutes avant de s'adresser à nouveau à *moi*...
6. *Il* me dit: —*Vous* ne savez pas qu'en arabe on appelle le Maroc le «pays du soleil couchant»?

Now read the entire text, paying close attention to the identity of the speaker and to whom the pronouns refer. Think, too, about M. Loubon's motivation in calling on Azouz.

M. Loubon

—Azouz! Vous savez comment on dit «le Maroc» en arabe?, me demande tout à coup[1] M. Loubon alors qu'il était en train d'écrire au tableau quelques phrases de style conjuguées au subjonctif.

La question ne me surprend pas. Depuis maintenant de longs mois, le prof a pris l'habitude de me faire parler en classe, de moi, de ma famille, de cette Algérie que je ne connais pas mais que je découvre de jour en jour avec lui.

À la maison, l'arabe que nous parlons ferait certainement rougir de colère un habitant de La Mecque.[2]* Savez-vous comment on dit les allumettes chez nous, par exemple? Li zalimite. C'est simple et tout le monde comprend. Et une automobile? La taumobile. Et un chiffon?[3] Le chiffoun. Vous voyez, c'est un dialecte particulier qu'on peut assimiler aisément lorsque[4] l'oreille est suffisamment entraînée.[5] Le Maroc? Mes parents ont toujours dit el-Marroc, en accentuant le *o*. Alors je réponds à M. Loubon:

—Le Maroc, m'sieur, ça se dit el-Marroc!

D'abord, il paraît un peu stupéfait, puis il poursuit:

—On ne dit pas el-Maghreb?

—Ah non, m'sieur. Mon père et ma mère, ils disent jamais ce mot. Pour appeler un Marocain, ils disent Marrocci.

M. Loubon reprend, amusé:

—En arabe littéraire,[6] on dit el-Maghreb et ça s'écrit comme ça.

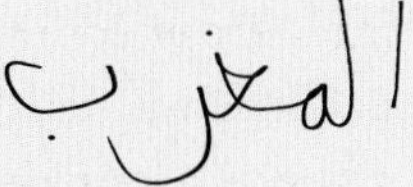

Il dessine quelques lettres arabes au tableau sous les regards ébahis[7] des élèves. Je précise pendant qu'il écrit:

—J'ai déjà entendu mes parents prononcer ce mot.

Il me dit:

—Vous ne savez pas qu'en arabe on appelle le Maroc le «pays du soleil couchant»?

[1]tout... *suddenly* [2]ferait... *would certainly cause an inhabitant of Mecca to grow red with anger* [3]*rag* [4]*when* [5]*trained* [6]arabe... *classical Arabic* [7]*dumbfounded*

*La Mecque est une ville sainte en Arabie Saoudite, où se rendent tous les ans des musulmans pratiquants pour accomplir le pèlerinage (*pilgrimage*) nommé «le hajj», qui est une des obligations de l'Islam.

—Non, m'sieur.»

Puis il reprit[8] son cours pendant quelques minutes avant de s'adresser à nouveau à moi:

—Vous savez ce que cela veut dire? me relance-t-il en dessinant des hiéroglyphes.

J'ai dit non. Que je ne savais pas lire ni écrire l'arabe.

—Ça c'est alif, un *a*. Ça c'est un *l* et ça c'est un autre *a*, explique-t-il. Alors, qu'est-ce que ça veut dire?

J'hésite un instant avant de réagir:

—Ala! dis-je mais sans saisir la signification de ce mot.

—Pas Ala, dit M. Loubon. Allah! Vous savez qui c'est Allah?...

Je souris[9] légèrement de son accent berbère:

—Oui, m'sieur. Bien sûr. Allah, c'est le Dieu des musulmans!

Azouz Begag (*Le Gone du Chaâba*, 1986)

[8]*continued* [9]*smile*

Après la lecture

A. Analyse des pronoms. Relisez le passage en réfléchissant aux questions suivantes.

1. À qui se réfèrent les pronoms de la première personne (**je, me, nous**)?
2. Qui est le **il** du récit?
3. Entre quelles personnes s'emploie le pronom **vous**? Pourquoi?

B. Réfléchissez. Réfléchissez à l'histoire pour répondre aux questions suivantes.

1. Qui connaît mieux l'arabe littéraire et écrit? Est-il fier de cette connaissance?
2. Qui connaît mieux l'arabe parlé? Est-il fier de son dialecte?
3. Azouz sait-il lire et écrire l'arabe? Et ses parents?
4. Azouz a-t-il une formation (*education, upbringing*) religieuse?
5. Avec qui Azouz se sent-il confortable—avec ses parents? M. Loubon? le lecteur? Comment ce sentiment se montre-t-il sur le plan linguistique?
6. Pourquoi M. Loubon pose-t-il ces questions à Azouz? Pourquoi montre-t-il comment écrire ces deux mots en arabe?

À écrire

Faites **À écrire** pour le Chapitre 22 dans le cahier.

Vocabulaire

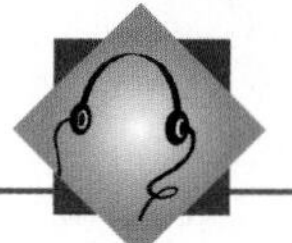

Au Maroc

une médina *old portion of an Arab city*

MOTS APPARENTÉS: **arabe, berbère, une mosquée**

Substantif

un(e) voisin(e) neighbor

Adjectifs

court(e) short
étonnant(e) surprising, amazing, shocking
large wide
pauvre poor
sombre dark

MOT APPARENTÉ: **riche**

Adverbe

dignement with dignity

Autres expressions utiles

à l'écart de away from
au milieu de in the middle of
en décolleté in low-cut clothing
la plupart de most (of)

Épilogue

Le Chemin du retour

Le Chemin du retour

Feuille de service du 13 octobre
3e jour de tournage
Horaires : 8 h 30–18 h 30

LIEU DE TOURNAGE : PARIS—Champs de Mars

Séquence	*Effets*	*Décors*	*Résumé*	*Rôles*
183B	EXT.—FIN DU JOUR	CHAMPS DE MARS	Conclusion et retrouvailles° entre Camille et sa mère, Mado.	CAMILLE, MADO

°reunion

OBJECTIFS

In this episode, you will

- get hints about the direction Camille's life may take now that she has learned the truth

In this chapter, you will

- talk about the characters in the film and predict their future
- learn about the history and characteristics of French filmmaking

Visionnement 1

Avant de visionner

A. Analyse. En visionnant *Le Chemin du retour* jusqu'ici, vous avez eu l'occasion d'analyser les actions et le caractère des personnages. En groupes de trois, discutez des questions suivantes.

1. Quel est le caractère de Camille? de Bruno? de Mado?
2. Quel est le rapport entre Camille et Bruno? entre Camille et Mado?

B. Changements. Maintenant, lisez les échanges suivants, extraits de l'Épilogue du film. D'après (*Based on*) ces dialogues, est-ce que le caractère de ces personnages a changé depuis qu'on les a rencontrés au début du film? Leurs rapports les uns avec les autres ont-ils changé?

1. Considérez d'abord Bruno.

BRUNO: Euh, excusez-moi. Quelqu'un sait où est Camille? (*vers la régie*) Euh, la régie? Quelqu'un peut me dire où se trouve Camille?

PRODUCTRICE: (*off*) Ne t'affole pas,[a] Bruno! Elle arrive!

BRUNO: Je suis sûr qu'elle est encore au maquillage!... C'est dingue,[b] ça! Non, mais qu'est-ce qu'on lui fait, un lifting[c] peut-être?

Et encore...

BRUNO: Excuse-moi, Camille. Excuse-moi. J'ai été ridicule, comme d'habitude. Au fond, je suis un type[d] banal, tu sais, un journaliste sans talent, sans avenir. Je comprends que tu ne veuilles pas de moi!

[a]*Ne... Don't get upset* [b]*crazy* [c]*facelift* [d]*guy*

Est-ce le même Bruno dont (*of whom*) on a fait la connaissance au début du film ou est-ce un Bruno transformé par les événements de l'histoire?

2. Maintenant, lisez les réflexions de Mado.

MADO: J'ai été tellement stupide pendant toutes ces années, tellement lâche.° Maintenant, c'est fini, c'est trop tard... Je ne veux pas te perdre!

°*cowardly*

Le caractère de Mado a-t-il changé?

3. Finalement, lisez l'échange suivant.

MADO: Je n'ai pas le souvenir d'un seul jour où tu n'aies été impatiente avec moi, nerveuse.

CAMILLE: (*réfléchit une seconde*) C'est vrai. Mais maintenant, c'est fini. Ça va changer!

MADO: Vraiment? Tu ne pousseras plus de soupirs[a] à chaque fois que je parle?

[a]*Tu... You won't sigh any more*

CAMILLE: Non!

MADO: Tu ne lèveras plus les yeux au ciel?

CAMILLE: Jamais plus!

MADO: (*pour elle*[b]) Oh, c'est sûrement un rêve,[c] mais c'est tellement bon à entendre!

[b]*pour... to herself* [c]*dream*

Le rapport entre Mado et Camille a-t-il changé? Expliquez.

Vocabulaire relatif à l'épisode

libérée d'un poids	*freed from a burden*
sa femme l'a pleuré	*his wife mourned him*
ils se réuniront	*they will be meeting*
décerné(e)	*awarded*
Ça, je vous fais confiance	*I trust you on that*
déranger	*to disturb*
me gronder	*scold me*
s'il y a bien une chose dont on n'a pas à avoir peur	*if there's anything one doesn't need to fear*

Observez!

Camille a découvert la vérité sur son grand-père, Antoine. Qu'est-ce qui va se passer maintenant? Pendant votre visionnement de l'Épilogue, essayez de trouver la réponse aux questions suivantes.

- Quel moment de l'épisode est le plus difficile pour Camille? le plus satisfaisant?
- À la fin de l'épisode, peut-on dire que Camille est une «nouvelle» femme? Justifiez votre réponse.

Après le visionnement

A. Avez-vous compris? Dites si les phrases suivantes sont vraies ou fausses et corrigez celles qui sont fausses.

1. En rentrant de son voyage, Camille téléphone immédiatement à Mado pour lui raconter les nouvelles.
2. Au retour de Camille, Camille et Bruno se disputent.
3. Bruno s'impatiente parce que Camille arrive en retard pour l'émission «Bonjour!».
4. David explique à Camille qu'un comité a refusé de revoir le cas d'Antoine.
5. Camille est très mécontente des nouvelles que David lui donne.
6. À la fin, Camille et Mado s'entendent bien.

B. Le passé... et l'avenir. Répondez aux questions suivantes.

1. Quelle est la réaction de Bruno quand il entend les nouvelles de Camille à propos d'Antoine? Comment Camille répond-elle aux remarques de Bruno?
2. Pourquoi David apporte-t-il des fleurs à Camille? A-t-il peut-être une autre motivation que celle qu'il annonce?
3. Selon vous, quel sera l'avenir de Camille et David? de Camille et Bruno? de Camille et Mado? de Camille et ses supérieurs? Est-ce que leurs rapports vont changer?

C. Hypothèses. Selon vous, pourquoi Camille a-t-elle persisté dans ses efforts pour trouver la vérité? Qu'est-ce qui l'a encouragée pendant les moments difficiles?

Regards sur la culture

Le cinéma français

Vous voilà arrivés maintenant à la fin du *Chemin du retour,* et c'est le moment de réfléchir au cinéma en général et à sa relation avec la culture française. Le cinéaste[1] de ce film est américain, mais le scénariste[2] et les acteurs sont français. Le film a donc[3] un caractère interculturel.

- Le cinéma, tel que[4] nous le connaissons aujourd'hui, est l'invention de deux Français: les frères Louis et Auguste Lumière. Ils ont organisé la première présentation publique du cinéma en 1895 au Grand Café de Paris. L'originalité de leur conception (par rapport à celle de Thomas Edison, par exemple) se trouve dans l'idée d'une projection publique sur grand écran. C'est ce qui a déterminé le caractère social du cinéma, une caractéristique qui existe encore aujourd'hui, plus de cent ans plus tard.
- Le cinéma s'est développé rapidement en France. Le premier film de fiction a été créé[5] par Georges Méliès en 1897. C'est Méliès aussi qui a créé *Le Voyage dans la lune*[6] (1902), un film bien connu des amateurs du cinéma aujourd'hui. En réalité, la France a dominé le monde du cinéma jusqu'à la Première guerre mondiale. Plus tard, c'est l'industrie américaine qui a pris la première place.

Une scène du *Voyage dans la lune* de Méliès

- En ce qui concerne le nombre de films produits par an, la France est en cinquième position (après l'Inde, les États-Unis, le Japon et la Chine). Mais l'influence du cinéma français est primordial.[7] Le Festival du film de Cannes symbolise le rôle important joué par la France dans cette industrie.
- Beaucoup de Français prennent le cinéma très au sérieux. Les jeunes assistent souvent à des séances[8] de ciné-club, où l'on[9] visionne et discute de films exceptionnels ou expérimentaux. De nombreux jeunes Français connaissent suffisament l'histoire du cinéma pour pouvoir comparer et évaluer les œuvres des grands cinéastes français et américains.
- La politique culturelle française prend le cinéma au sérieux aussi. L'État finance en grande partie la Cinémathèque, qui conserve et restaure les films anciens et organise la projection de toutes sortes de films. L'État finance aussi la formation[10] des professionnels du cinéma et essaie de favoriser la promotion et la diffusion du cinéma français dans le monde.
- L'influence internationale du cinéma français a été particulièrement importante à la fin des années 50, quand la Nouvelle Vague (*New Wave*) est née. Ce mouvement, qui représentait une nouvelle spontanéité dans la création cinématographique, a accordé une grande importance au cinéaste en tant qu'«auteur»[11] de son film. Le caractère innovateur et expérimental des œuvres de la Nouvelle Vague—les films de François Truffaut et de Jean-Luc Godard, par exemple—a influencé des cinéastes dans le monde entier.

Le cinéaste François Truffaut au travail

- Puisque[12] les spectateurs nord-américains n'aiment pas beaucoup les films doublés[13] ou sous-titrés, il n'est pas rare qu'un film français soit refait en version américaine. Ces films, qu'on appelle «*remakes*» en anglais, ont souvent

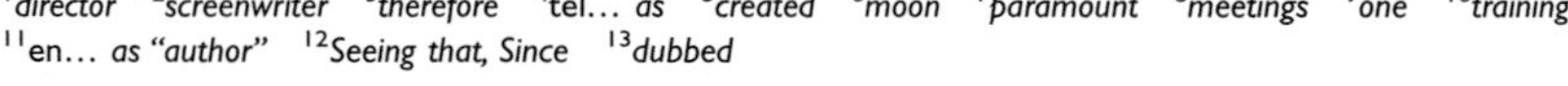

[1]*director* [2]*screenwriter* [3]*therefore* [4]*tel... as* [5]*created* [6]*moon* [7]*paramount* [8]*meetings* [9]*one* [10]*training* [11]*en... as "author"* [12]*Seeing that, Since* [13]*dubbed*

eu beaucoup de succès en Amérique du Nord, et quelquefois en France aussi, où le public peut donc voir la même histoire sous deux formes différentes. Mais les spécialistes du cinéma considèrent souvent que ces films américains n'ont pas la qualité artistique des versions d'origine. Quelques exemples de films français et de leurs versions américaines:

Boudu sauvé des eaux (Renoir, 1932)	*Down and Out in Beverly Hills* (Mazursky, 1986)
Diabolique (Clouzot, 1955)	*Diabolique* (Chechik, 1996)
À bout de souffle (Godard, 1959)	*Breathless* (McBride, 1983)
La Femme infidèle (Chabrol, 1969)	*Unfaithful* (Lyne, 2002)
Trois Hommes et un couffin (Serreau, 1985)	*Three Men and a Baby* (Nimoy, 1987)
Les Visiteurs (Poiré, 1993)	*Just Visiting* (Gaubert, 2001)
Taxi (Pirès, 1998)	*Taxi* (Story, 2004)

La Cage aux folles de Molinaro (1978)

The Birdcage de Nichols (1996)

Considérez

Réfléchissez aux différences culturelles entre la France et l'Amérique du Nord que vous avez eu l'occasion d'observer dans ce cours. Ensuite, choisissez un de vos films nord-américains préférés et essayez de déterminer ce qu'on changerait pour en faire une version française. Considérez les éléments suivants:

- l'environnement (urbain ou rural, bâtiments, etc.)
- les relations familiales qui sont illustrées dans le film
- la conception de l'amitié dans le film
- le rôle de la nourriture, des voitures et d'autres objets
- les valeurs morales des personnages
- le ton ou le contenu moral du film
- la fin du film

Visionnement 2

À présent, regardez le film encore une fois, sans interruption. Vous allez voir que vous comprenez maintenant toute l'histoire et une grande partie du dialogue. Et après le visionnement, n'oubliez pas de vous offrir une petite récompense pour tous vos efforts. Bravo!

Appendice A

Glossary of Grammatical Terms

ADJECTIVE (ADJECTIF, *m.*) A word that describes a noun or a pronoun. It agrees in number and gender with the word it modifies.	
demonstrative adjective (adjectif démonstratif) An adjective that points out a particular noun.	**ce** garçon, **ces** livres ***this** boy, **these** books*
interrogative adjective (adjectif interrogatif) An adjective used to form questions.	**Quelles** affiches cherchez-vous? ***Which** posters are you looking for?*
possessive adjective (adjectif possessif) An adjective that indicates possession or a special relationship.	**leur** voiture, **ma** sœur ***their** car, **my** sister*
ADVERB (ADVERBE, *m.*) A word that describes an adjective, a verb, or another adverb.	Il écrit **très bien**. *He writes **very well**.* Elle est **plus** efficace. *She is **more** efficient.*
AGREEMENT (ACCORD, *m.*) Nouns in French are marked for gender and number: any word that modifies a noun must reflect that noun's gender and number. This principle is known as agreement. Adjectives, articles, and past participles of verbs conjugated with **être** show agreement, for example.	C'est **une femme indépendante**. *She is an independent woman.* **Elles sont arrivées** à temps. *They arrived in time.*
ARTICLE (ARTICLE, *m.*) A word that signals an upcoming noun.	
definite article (article défini) An article that indicates a specific noun or a noun used in a generic or abstract sense.	**le** pays, **la** chaise, **les** femmes ***the** country, **the** chair, **the** women*
indefinite article (article indéfini) An article that indicates an unspecified noun or an unspecified quantity of a count noun.	**un** garçon, **une** ville, **des** carottes ***a** boy, **a** city, (**some**) carrots*
partitive article (article partitif) In French, an article that indicates an unspecified quantity of a mass (noncount) noun.	**du** chocolat, **de la** tarte, **de l'**eau (***some***) *chocolate,* (***some***) *pie,* (***some***) *water*

CLAUSE (PROPOSITION, *f.*) A construction that contains a subject and a verb.	
independent (main) clause (proposition principale) A clause that stands on its own and expresses a complete idea.	**Je cherche la femme** qui joue au tennis. ***I'm looking for the woman*** *who plays tennis.*
relative clause (proposition relative) A subordinate clause that refers back to a person, thing, place, or time mentioned in the main clause.	Je cherche la femme **qui joue au tennis**. *I'm looking for the woman* ***who plays tennis****.*
subordinate clause (proposition subordonnée) A clause that cannot stand on its own because it does not express a complete idea.	Je la cherche **parce que j'ai besoin d'elle**. *I'm looking for her* ***because I need her****.*
COMPARATIVE (COMPARATIF, *m.*) An expression used to compare two adjectives, adverbs, nouns, or actions.	Léa est **moins** bavarde **que** Julien. *Léa is* ***less*** *talkative* ***than*** *Julien.* Elle court **plus** vite **que** lui. *She runs* ***faster than*** *he does.*
CONDITIONAL (CONDITIONNEL, *m.*)	See **Mood**.
CONJUGATION (CONJUGAISON, *f.*) The different forms of a verb for a particular tense or mood. A present indicative conjugation:	je parle — *I speak* tu parles — *you speak* il, elle, on parle — *he, she, it, one speaks* nous parlons — *we speak* vous parlez — *you speak* ils, elles parlent — *they speak*
CONJUNCTION (CONJONCTION, *f.*) An expression that connects words, phrases, or clauses.	Christophe **et** Diane sont sérieux **mais** sympas. *Christophe* ***and*** *Diane are serious* ***but*** *nice.*
GENDER (GENRE, *m.*) A grammatical category of words. In French, there are two genders: feminine and masculine. Gender applies to nouns, articles, adjectives, and pronouns.	*m.* / *f.* articles and nouns: **le** disque / **la** cassette adjectives: **lent, beau** / **lente, belle** pronouns: **il, celui** / **elle, celle**
IMPERATIVE (IMPÉRATIF, *m.*)	See **Mood**.
IMPERFECT (IMPARFAIT, *m.*) A verb tense that expresses habitual past actions, past descriptions, past states of mind, or ongoing actions in the past.	Nous **nagions** souvent. *We* ***used to swim*** *often.*
INDIRECT DISCOURSE (DISCOURS INDIRECT, *m.*) The reporting of what someone said using a subordinate clause.	Elle a dit **que la chanson était super**. *She said* ***that the song was terrific****.*

INFINITIVE (INFINITIF, *m.*)	See **Mood**.
MOOD (MODE, *m.*) A set of categories for verbs that indicates the speaker's attitude toward what he/she is saying.	
conditional mood (mode conditionnel) A verb form conveying possibility.	J'**irais** si j'avais le temps. *I **would go** if I had time.*
imperative mood (mode impératif) A verb form expressing a command.	**Allez**-y! ***Go** ahead!*
indicative mood (mode indicatif) A verb form denoting actions or states that are considered facts.	Je **vais** à la bibliothèque. *I **am going** to the library.*
infinitive mood (mode infinitif) A verb form introduced in English by *to*.	**jouer, vendre, venir** ***to play, to sell, to come***
subjunctive mood (mode subjonctif) A verb form, uncommon in English, used primarily in subordinate clauses after expressions of obligation, desire, doubt, or emotion. French constructions with the subjunctive have many possible English equivalents.	Je veux que vous y **alliez**. *I want you to go there.*
NOUN (NOM, *m.* ou SUBSTANTIF, *m.*) A word that denotes a person, place, thing, or idea. Proper nouns are capitalized names.	**avocat, ville, journal, Louise** ***lawyer, city, newspaper, Louise***
NUMBER (NOMBRE, *m.*) A grammatical category of words. It indicates whether a noun, article, adjective, or pronoun is singular or plural.	singulier Le fromage est bon. pluriel Les fromages sont bons.
OBJECT (OBJET, *m.*) A noun that follows a verb or a preposition, or a pronoun that takes the place of or refers to this noun.	
direct object (objet direct) A noun that follows the verb directly, i.e., without an intervening preposition, and that receives the action of that verb. It could also be a pronoun that refers to this noun. It answers the question *What?* or *Whom?*	J'ai vu **le film**. Tu **l'**as vu aussi. *I saw **the film**. You saw **it** too.* Est-ce que tu connais **cette femme**? *Do you know **that woman**?*
indirect object (objet indirect) A noun, designating a person, that follows the verb and is introduced by the preposition **à**, or a pronoun that refers to this noun.	Tu téléphones souvent à **tes amis**? *Do you call your friends often?* Oui, je **leur** parle tous les jours. *Yes, I talk to them every day.*
PASSÉ COMPOSÉ (*m.*) In French, a verb tense that expresses a past action with a definite ending. It consists of the present indicative of the auxiliary verb (**avoir** or **être**) and the past participle of the conjugated verb.	**j'ai mangé** *I **ate**, I **did eat**, I **have eaten*** elle **est tombée** *she **fell**, she **did fall**, she **has fallen***

PAST PARTICIPLE (PARTICIPE PASSÉ, *m.*) The form of a verb used in a compound tense (like the **passé composé**) with forms of *to have* in English, and with **avoir** and **être** in French.	**mangé, fini, perdu** ***eaten, finished, lost***
PLUS-QUE-PARFAIT (*m.*) A tense that denotes an action that took place before another past action.	Quand je suis arrivé, mes parents **étaient** déjà **partis**. *When I arrived, my parents **had** already **left**.*
PREPOSITION (PRÉPOSITION, *f.*) A word or phrase that specifies the relationship of one word (usually a noun or a pronoun) to another. The relationship is usually spatial or temporal.	**près de** l'aéroport, **avec** lui, **avant** 11 h ***near** the airport, **with** him, **before** 11:00*
PRESENT PARTICIPLE (PARTICIPE PRÉSENT, *m.*) A verb form used to express near simultaneity and/or how an action is performed. French constructions with the present participle have many possible English equivalents.	En **entrant**, il a remarqué le changement du décor. *As he entered, he noticed the change in décor.* Elle travaille en **écoutant** la radio. *She works while listening to the radio.*
PRONOUN (PRONOM, *m.*) A word used in place of one or more nouns.	
demonstrative pronoun (pronom démonstratif) A pronoun that singles out a particular person or thing.	Voici trois livres: **celui-ci** est intéressant, mais **ceux-là** sont ennuyeux. *Here are three books: **this one** is interesting, but **those** are boring.*
interrogative pronoun (pronom interrogatif) A pronoun used to ask a question.	**Qui** parle? ***Who** is speaking?* **Qu'est-ce que** vous voulez? ***What** do you want?*
object pronoun (pronom complément d'objet) A pronoun that replaces a direct object noun or an indirect object noun.	direct: Je vois Alain. Je **le** vois. *I see Alain. I see **him**.* indirect: Je donne le livre à Daniel. Je **lui** donne le livre. *I give the book to Daniel. I give **him** the book.*
possessive pronoun (pronom possessif) A pronoun that represents an object belonging to someone.	Quel stylo est **le mien**? *Which pen is **mine**?*
reflexive pronoun (pronom réfléchi) A pronoun that represents the subject of the verb.	Je **me** regarde dans le miroir. *I am looking at **myself** in the mirror.*
relative pronoun (pronom relatif) A pronoun that introduces a subordinate clause and denotes a noun already mentioned.	On parle à la femme **qui** habite ici. *We're talking to the woman who lives here.* C'est le stylo **que** vous cherchez? *Is this the pen (**that**) you are looking for?*
stressed pronoun (pronom accentué ou pronom disjoint) In French, a pronoun used for emphasis, after **C'est**, or as the object of a preposition.	**Toi**, tu es incroyable! *You are unbelievable!* C'est **moi**! *It's me! (It's I!)* Je travaille avec **lui**. *I work with **him**.*

subject pronoun (pronom sujet) A pronoun representing the person or thing performing the action of the verb.	**Ils** travaillent bien ensemble. ***They** work well together.*
SUBJECT (SUJET, *m.*) The word(s) denoting the person, place, or thing performing an action or existing in a state.	**Mon ordinateur** est là-bas. ***My computer** is over there.* **Marc** arrive demain. ***Marc** arrives tomorrow.*
SUBJUNCTIVE (SUBJONCTIF, *m.*)	See **Mood**.
SUPERLATIVE (SUPERLATIF, *m.*) An expression used to compare more than two adjectives, adverbs, nouns, or actions.	Elle a choisi la robe **la plus chère**. *She chose **the most expensive** dress.* Béatrice court **le plus vite**. *Béatrice runs **the fastest**.*
VERB (VERBE, *m.*) A word that reports an action or state.	Elle **est arrivée** hier. *She **arrived** yesterday.* Elle **était** fatiguée. *She **was** tired.*
auxiliary verb (verbe auxiliaire) A verb used in conjunction with an infinitive or a participle to convey distinctions of tense and mood. In French, the main auxiliaries are **avoir** and **être**.	J'**ai** fait mes devoirs. *I did my homework.* Nous **sommes** allés au cinéma. *We went to the movies.*
impersonal verb (verbe impersonnel) A verbal expression introduced by the impersonal pronoun **il**.	**Il fait** beau aujourd'hui. ***It is** nice today.* **Il faut** travailler fort. ***One has** to work hard.*
irregular verb (verbe irrégulier) A verb whose conjugation cannot be determined by the form of the infinitive.	**être: je suis, tu es, il/elle/on est, nous sommes, vous êtes, ils/elles sont** *to be: I am, you are, he/she/one is, we are, you are, they are*
pronominal verb (verbe pronominal) A verb conjugated with a pronoun (**me**, **te**, **se**, **nous**, **vous**) that corresponds to the subject pronoun. A pronominal verb may express reflexive or reciprocal action, or it may be idiomatic in usage.	**Il se coupe** quand **il se rase**. ***He cuts himself** when **he shaves** (**himself**).* **Ils se téléphonent.** *They call **each other**.* **se souvenir, je me souviens** *to remember, I remember*
regular verb (verbe régulier) A verb whose conjugation can be determined by the form of the infinitive. In French, there are three groups of regular verbs: those whose infinitives end in **-er, -ir,** and **-re.**	**regarder:** je regarde, tu regard**es**, il/elle/on regard**e**, nous regard**ons**, vous regard**ez**, ils/elles regard**ent** ***to look at:** I look at, you look at, he/she/one looks at, we look at, you look at, they look at* **finir:** je fin**is**, tu fin**is**, il/elle/on fin**it**, nous fin**issons**, vous fin**issez**, ils/elles fin**issent** ***to finish:** I finish, you finish, he/she/one finishes, we finish, you finish, they finish* **répondre:** je répond**s**, tu répond**s**, il/elle/on répond, nous répond**ons**, vous répond**ez**, ils/elles répond**ent** ***to answer:** I answer, you answer, he/she/one answers, we answer, you answer, they answer*

Appendice B

Verbes

Verbes réguliers

INFINITIF ET PARTICIPE PRÉSENT	PRÉSENT	PASSÉ COMPOSÉ	IMPARFAIT	FUTUR	CONDITIONNEL	SUBJONCTIF	IMPÉRATIF
1. **chercher** cherchant	je cherche tu cherches il/elle/on cherche nous cherchons vous cherchez ils/elles cherchent	j' ai cherché tu as cherché il/elle/on a cherché nous avons cherché vous avez cherché ils/elles ont cherché	je cherchais tu cherchais il/elle/on cherchait nous cherchions vous cherchiez ils/elles cherchaient	je chercherai tu chercheras il/elle/on cherchera nous chercherons vous chercherez ils/elles chercheront	je chercherais tu chercherais il/elle/on chercherait nous chercherions vous chercheriez ils/elles chercheraient	que je cherche que tu cherches qu' il/elle/on cherche que nous cherchions que vous cherchiez qu' ils/elles cherchent	cherche cherchons cherchez
2. **répondre** répondant	je réponds tu réponds il/elle/on répond nous répondons vous répondez ils/elles répondent	j' ai répondu tu as répondu il/elle/on a répondu nous avons répondu vous avez répondu ils/elles ont répondu	je répondais tu répondais il/elle/on répondait nous répondions vous répondiez ils/elles répondaient	je répondrai tu répondras il/elle/on répondra nous répondrons vous répondrez ils/elles répondront	je répondrais tu répondrais il/elle/on répondrait nous répondrions vous répondriez ils/elles répondraient	que je réponde que tu répondes qu' il/elle/on réponde que nous répondions que vous répondiez qu' ils/elles répondent	réponds répondons répondez
3. **finir** finissant	je finis tu finis il/elle/on finit nous finissons vous finissez ils/elles finissent	j' ai fini tu as fini il/elle/on a fini nous avons fini vous avez fini ils/elles ont fini	je finissais tu finissais il/elle/on finissait nous finissions vous finissiez ils/elles finissaient	je finirai tu finiras il/elle/on finira nous finirons vous finirez ils/elles finiront	je finirais tu finirais il/elle/on finirait nous finirions vous finiriez ils/elles finiraient	que je finisse que tu finisses qu' il/elle/on finisse que nous finissions que vous finissiez qu' ils/elles finissent	finis finissons finissez
4. **se laver**[*] (se) lavant	je me lave tu te laves il/on se lave elle se lave nous nous lavons vous vous lavez ils se lavent elles se lavent	je me suis lavé(e) tu t'es lavé(e) il/on s'est lavé elle s'est lavée nous nous sommes lavé(e)s vous vous êtes lavé(e)(s) ils se sont lavés elles se sont lavées	je me lavais tu te lavais il/on se lavait elle se lavait nous nous lavions vous vous laviez ils se lavaient elles se lavaient	je me laverai tu te laveras il/on se lavera elle se lavera nous nous laverons vous vous laverez ils se laveront elles se laveront	je me laverais tu te laverais il/on se laverait elle se laverait nous nous laverions vous vous laveriez ils se laveraient elles se laveraient	que je me lave que tu te laves qu' il/on se lave qu' elle se lave que nous nous lavions que vous vous laviez qu' ils se lavent qu' elles se lavent	lave-toi lavons-nous lavez-vous

Verbes réguliers avec changements orthographiques

INFINITIF ET PARTICIPE PRÉSENT	PRÉSENT		PASSÉ COMPOSÉ	IMPARFAIT	FUTUR	CONDITIONNEL	SUBJONCTIF	IMPÉRATIF	*AUTRES VERBES*
1. **commencer** commençant	je commence tu commences il/elle/on commence	nous commen**ç**ons vous commencez ils/elles commencent	j'ai commencé	je commen**ç**ais nous commencions	je commencerai	je commencerais	que je commence que nous commencions	commence commen**ç**ons commencez	divorcer, lancer, remplacer
2. **manger** mangeant	je mange tu manges il/elle/on mange	nous mang**e**ons vous mangez ils/elles mangent	j'ai mangé	je mang**e**ais nous mangions	je mangerai	je mangerais	que je mange que nous mangions	mange mang**e**ons mangez	changer, encourager, engager, exiger, mélanger, nager, partager, voyager
3. **préférer** préférant	je préf**è**re tu préf**è**res il/elle/on préf**è**re	nous préférons vous préférez ils/elles préf**è**rent	j'ai préféré	je préférais	je préférerai	je préférerais	que je préf**è**re que nous préférions	préf**è**re préférons préférez	espérer, répéter, s'inquiéter, sécher
4. **payer** payant	je pa**i**e tu pa**i**es il/elle/on pa**i**e	nous payons vous payez ils/elles pa**i**ent	j'ai payé	je payais	je pa**i**erai	je pa**i**erais	que je pa**i**e que nous payions	pa**i**e payons payez	employer, envoyer, essayer
5. **appeler** appelant	j' appe**ll**e tu appe**ll**es il/elle/on appe**ll**e	nous appelons vous appelez ils/elles appe**ll**ent	j'ai appelé	j'appelais	j'appe**ll**erai	j'appe**ll**erais	que j'appe**ll**e que nous appelions	appe**ll**e appelons appelez	s'appeler, se rappeler
6. **acheter** achetant	j' ach**è**te tu ach**è**tes il/elle/on ach**è**te	nous achetons vous achetez ils/elles ach**è**tent	j'ai acheté	j'achetais	j'ach**è**terai	j'ach**è**terais	que j'ach**è**te que nous achetions	ach**è**te achetons achetez	se lever, se promener

Verbes irréguliers

INFINITIF ET PARTICIPE PRÉSENT	PRÉSENT		PASSÉ COMPOSÉ	IMPARFAIT	FUTUR	CONDITIONNEL	SUBJONCTIF	IMPÉRATIF	*AUTRES VERBES*
1. **aller**[*] allant	je vais tu vas il/elle/on va	nous allons vous allez ils/elles vont	je suis allé(e)	j'allais	j'irai	j'irais	que j'aille que nous allions	va allons allez	
2. **avoir** ayant	j' ai tu as il/elle/on a	nous avons vous avez ils/elles ont	j'ai eu	j'avais	j'aurai	j'aurais	que j'aie que nous ayons	aie ayons ayez	
3. **boire** buvant	je bois tu bois il/elle/on boit	nous buvons vous buvez ils/elles boivent	j'ai bu	je buvais	je boirai	je boirais	que je boive que nous buvions	bois buvons buvez	
4. **conduire** conduisant	je conduis tu conduis il/elle/on conduit	nous conduisons vous conduisez ils/elles conduisent	j'ai conduit	je conduisais	je conduirai	je conduirais	que je conduise que nous conduisions	conduis conduisons conduisez	construire, détruire, produire, réduire, traduire
5. **connaître** connaissant	je connais tu connais il/elle/on connaît	nous connaissons vous connaissez ils/elles connaissent	j'ai connu	je connaissais	je connaîtrai	je connaîtrais	que je connaisse que nous connaissions	connais connaissons connaissez	apparaître, disparaître, paraître, reconnaître
6. **croire** croyant	je crois tu crois il/elle/on croit	nous croyons vous croyez ils/elles croient	j'ai cru	je croyais	je croirai	je croirais	que je croie que nous croyions	crois croyons croyez	
7. **cueillir** cueillant	je cueille tu cueilles il/elle/on cueille	nous cueillons vous cueillez ils/elles cueillent	j'ai cueilli	je cueillais	je cueillerai	je cueillerais	que je cueille que nous cueillions	cueille cueillons cueillez	accueillir, recueillir
8. **devoir** devant	je dois tu dois il/elle/on doit	nous devons vous devez ils/elles doivent	j'ai dû	je devais	je devrai	je devrais	que je doive que nous devions	dois devons devez	
9. **dire** disant	je dis tu dis il/elle/on dit	nous disons vous dites ils/elles disent	j'ai dit	je disais	je dirai	je dirais	que je dise que nous disions	dis disons dites	
10. **écrire** écrivant	j' écris tu écris il/elle/on écrit	nous écrivons vous écrivez ils/elles écrivent	j'ai écrit	j'écrivais	j'écrirai	j'écrirais	que j'écrive que nous écrivions	écris écrivons écrivez	décrire

[*]Verbs followed by an asterisk[*] are conjugated with **être** in the compound tenses.

Verbes irréguliers (*suite*)

INFINITIF ET PARTICIPE PRÉSENT	PRÉSENT		PASSÉ COMPOSÉ	IMPARFAIT	FUTUR	CONDITIONNEL	SUBJONCTIF	IMPÉRATIF	*AUTRES VERBES*
11. **être** étant	je suis tu es il/elle/on est	nous sommes vous êtes ils/elles sont	j'ai été	j'étais	je serai	je serais	que je sois que nous soyons	sois soyons soyez	
12. **faire** faisant	je fais tu fais il/elle/on fait	nous faisons vous faites ils/elles font	j'ai fait	je faisais	je ferai	je ferais	que je fasse que nous fassions	fais faisons faites	
13. **falloir**	il faut		il a fallu	il fallait	il faudra	il faudrait	qu'il faille	—	
14. **lire** lisant	je lis tu lis il/elle/on lit	nous lisons vous lisez ils/elles lisent	j'ai lu	je lisais	je lirai	je lirais	que je lise que nous lisions	lis lisons lisez	
15. **mettre** mettant	je mets tu mets il/elle/on met	nous mettons vous mettez ils/elles mettent	j'ai mis	je mettais	je mettrai	je mettrais	que je mette que nous mettions	mets mettons mettez	permettre, promettre
16. **mourir*** mourant	je meurs tu meurs il/elle/on meurt	nous mourons vous mourez ils/elles meurent	je suis mort(e)	je mourais	je mourrai	je mourrais	que je meure que nous mourions	meurs mourons mourez	
17. **naître*** naissant	je nais tu nais il/elle/on naît	nous naissons vous naissez ils/elles naissent	je suis né(e)	je naissais	je naîtrai	je naîtrais	que je naisse que nous naissions	nais naissons naissez	
18. **ouvrir** ouvrant	j' ouvre tu ouvres il/elle/on ouvre	nous ouvrons vous ouvrez ils/elles ouvrent	j'ai ouvert	j'ouvrais	j'ouvrirai	j'ouvrirais	que j'ouvre que nous ouvrions	ouvre ouvrons ouvrez	couvrir, découvrir, offrir, souffrir
19. **partir*** partant	je pars tu pars il/elle/on part	nous partons vous partez ils/elles partent	je suis parti(e)	je partais	je partirai	je partirais	que je parte que nous partions	pars partons partez	dormir, mentir, s'endormir,* sentir, servir, sortir*

*Verbs followed by an asterisk * are conjugated with **être** in the compound tenses.

Verbes irréguliers (*suite*)

INFINITIF ET PARTICIPE PRÉSENT	PRÉSENT		PASSÉ COMPOSÉ	IMPARFAIT	FUTUR	CONDITIONNEL	SUBJONCTIF	IMPÉRATIF	*AUTRES VERBES*
21. **pouvoir** pouvant	je peux** tu peux il/elle/on peut	nous pouvons vous pouvez ils/elles peuvent	j'ai pu	je pouvais	je pourrai	je pourrais	que je puisse que nous puissions	—	
22. **prendre** prenant	je prends tu prends il/elle/on prend	nous prenons vous prenez ils/elles prennent	j'ai pris	je prenais	je prendrai	je prendrais	que je prenne que nous prenions	prends prenons prenez	apprendre, comprendre
23. **recevoir** recevant	je reçois tu reçois il/elle/on reçoit	nous recevons vous recevez ils/elles reçoivent	j'ai reçu	je recevais	je recevrai	je recevrais	que je reçoive que nous recevions	reçois recevons recevez	
24. **savoir** sachant	je sais tu sais il/elle/on sait	nous savons vous savez ils/elles savent	j'ai su	je savais	je saurai	je saurais	que je sache que nous sachions	sache sachons sachez	
25. **suivre** suivant	je suis tu suis il/elle/on suit	nous suivons vous suivez ils/elles suivent	j'ai suivi	je suivais	je suivrai	je suivrais	que je suive que nous suivions	suis suivons suivez	poursuivre
26. **venir*** venant	je viens tu viens il/elle/on vient	nous venons vous venez ils/elles viennent	je suis venu(e)	je venais	je viendrai	je viendrais	que je vienne que nous venions	viens venons venez	appartenir, contenir, devenir,* obtenir, revenir,* tenir
27. **vivre** vivant	je vis tu vis il/elle/on vit	nous vivons vous vivez ils/elles vivent	j'ai vécu	je vivais	je vivrai	je vivrais	que je vive que nous vivions	vis vivons vivez	survivre
28. **voir** voyant	je vois tu vois il/elle/on voit	nous voyons vous voyez ils/elles voient	j'ai vu	je voyais	je verrai	je verrais	que je voie que nous voyions	vois voyons voyez	revoir
29. **vouloir** voulant	je veux tu veux il/elle/on veut	nous voulons vous voulez ils/elles veulent	j'ai voulu	je voulais	je voudrai	je voudrais	que je veuille que nous voulions	veuille veuillons veuillez	

If **je peux is inverted to form a question, it becomes **puis-je... ?**

*Verbs followed by an asterisk * are conjugated with **être** in the compound tenses.

Lexique français-anglais

This end vocabulary provides contextual meanings of French words used in this text. It does not include proper nouns (unless presented as active vocabulary or unless the French equivalent is quite different in spelling from English), most abbreviations, adjectives that are exact cognates, past participles used as adjectives if the infinitive is listed, or regular adverbs formed from adjectives listed. Adjectives are listed in the masculine singular form; feminine endings or forms are included. An asterisk (*) indicates words beginning with an aspirate *h*. Active vocabulary is indicated by the number of the chapter in which it is activated.

Abbreviations

ab.	abbreviation	*indef.*	indefinite	*p.p.*	past participle
adj.	adjective	*inf.*	infinitive	*prep.*	preposition
adv.	adverb	*interj.*	interjection	*pron.*	pronoun
art.	article	*interr.*	interrogative	*Q.*	Quebec usage
colloq.	colloquial	*inv.*	invariable	*rel.*	relative
conj.	conjunction	*irreg.*	irregular	*s.*	singular
fam.	familiar or colloquial	*m.*	masculine noun	*s.o.*	someone
f.	feminine noun	*n.*	noun	*s.th.*	something
Gram.	grammatical term	*pl.*	plural	*v.*	verb

à *prep.* to; at (1); in; **à bientôt** see you soon (P); **à coté de** next to, beside (3); **à demain** see you tomorrow (P); **à droite (gauche)** to/on the right (left) (17); **à haute voix** aloud; **à la campagne** in the country (17); **à la garçonne** boyish; **à la une** on the front page (12); **à l'heure** on time (5); **à mi-temps** part-time (11); **à nouveau** again; **à Paris** in Paris; **à pied** on foot (14); **à table** at the table; **à temps partiel** part-time; **à votre (ta) place** if I were you (19)
abandonner to abandon, desert
abolition *f.* abolition
abonné(e) *m., f.* user, subscriber
abord: d'abord *adv.* first, first of all, at first (10)
absence (de) *f.* absence (from)
absent(e) *adj.* absent
absolu(e) *adj.* absolute (14)
abstrait(e) *adj.* abstract
absurde *adj.* absurd; silly
abus *m.* abuse, misuse
Académie Française *f.* French Academy (*official body that rules on language questions*)
accent *m.* accent; emphasis; accent mark; **accent aigu (grave, circonflexe)** acute (grave, circumflex) accent
accentuer to emphasize; **s'accentuer** to grow stronger
accepter (de) to accept (*to do s.th.*) (18)
accès *m.* access
accessoire *m.* accessory
accident *m.* accident
accompagner to accompany, go along (with)
accord *m.* approval; agreement; **d'accord (je suis d'accord)** okay; agreed (I agree) (2)
accorder to give
accordéon *m.* accordion
accordéoniste *m., f.* accordionist
accroître (*p.p.* **accru**) *irreg.* to grow, increase
accueil *m.* welcome, greeting (20); **famille (*f.*) d'accueil** host family; **page (*f.*) d'accueil** home page (13)
accueillir *irreg.* to welcome
accuser (de) to accuse (*of s.th.*); to blame (19)
achat *m.* purchase; **faire des achats** to make purchases
acheter (j'achète) to buy (6); **acheter à quelqu'un** to buy for someone
acide *adj.* sour; tart
acrylique *adj.* acrylic
acte *f.* act; action
acteur/trice *m., f.* actor/actress (P)
actif/ive *adj.* active (2)
action *f.* action, deed
activité *f.* activity
actualités *f. pl.* news; news program (12)
actuel(le) *adj.* current, present (14)
acuponcture *f.* acupuncture
adapté(e) *adj.* adapted
addition *f.* check, bill (*in a restaurant*)
adéquat(e) *adj.* adequate
adhérer (j'adhère) to join (*a political party*)
adjacent(e) *adj.* adjacent
adjectif *m., Gram.* adjective
administrateur/trice *m., f.* administrator; manager
administratif/ive *adj.* administrative
administration *f.* administration; management; **administration des affaires** business administration (13)
admirer to admire
adolescence *f.* adolescence (12)
adolescent(e) (*fam.* **ado**) *m., f.* adolescent, teenager (12)
adopter to adopt; to take up
adorer to love, adore (2)
adresse *f.* address
adresser: s'adresser à to address, speak to
adulte *m., f.* adult (12)
adverbe *m., Gram.* adverb
adversité *f.* adversity
aérien(ne) *adj.* aerial
aéroport *m.* airport (14)
affaire *f.* affair; subject; **affaires** (*f. pl.*) business (11); **homme (femme)** (*m., f.*) **d'affaires** businessman (woman)
affichage: tableau (*m.*) **d'affichage** bulletin board (11)

affiche *f.* poster (5)
affirmatif/ive *adj.* affirmative
affoler to panic; **ne t'affole pas** don't get upset
afin de *prep.* in order to (21)
afin que *prep.* in order that, so that (21)
africain(e) *adj.* African; **Africain(e)** *m., f.* African (*person*)
âge *m.* age; **au troisième âge** in old age (12); **quel âge avez-vous (as-tu) (a-t-il,** *etc.***)?** how old are you (is he, etc.)?
âgé(e) *adj.* old; elderly
agence *f.* agency; **agence de location** car rental agency; **agence de voyages** travel agency
agent(e) *m., f.* agent; **agent(e) de police** police officer; **agent(e) de sécurité** security guard (11)
agir to act; **il s'agit de** it's a question of, it's about
agneau *m.* lamb
agrandir to enlarge
agréable *adj.* pleasant, nice
agression *f.* aggression
agricole *adj.* agricultural
agriculteur/trice *m., f.* farmer (11)
agriculture *f.* agriculture, farming (18)
ah bien *interj.* well then
aide *f.* help, assistance; **à l'aide de** with the help of
aider to help
aigu: accent (*m.*) **aigu** acute accent (**é**)
ail *m.* garlic (15)
ailleurs *adv.* elsewhere; **d'ailleurs** moreover, besides
aimable *adv.* lovable
aimer to like; to love (2); **aimer bien** to like; **aimer mieux** to prefer (2); **j'aimerais** I would like; **s'aimer** to love each other
ainsi *conj.* thus, in this way, like this; **ainsi que** as well as
air *m.* air; tune; **avoir l'air** to look, seem (4); **courant** (*m.*) **d'air** breeze, draft; **en plein air** outdoors (16)
aisément *adv.* easily
ajouter to add (15)
album-photo *m.* photo album
alcool *m.* alcohol
alcoolisé(e) *adj.* alcoholic (*beverage*)
Algérie *f.* Algeria (3)
algérien(ne) *adj.* Algerian (3); **Algérien(ne)** *m., f.* Algerian (*person*)
algue *f.* seaweed
aligot *m. regional potato-and-cheese soup*
aliment *m.* food (7)
alimentaire *adj.* alimentary, pertaining to food
Allemagne *f.* Germany (3)
allemand(e) *adj.* German (3); **Allemand(e)** *m., f.* German (*person*) (3)
aller *irreg.* to go (3); **aller** + *inf.* to be going (*to do s.th.*) (3); **aller à la pêche** to go fishing (16); **billet** (*m.*) **aller-retour** roundtrip ticket (14); **billet** (*m.*) **aller simple** one-way ticket (14); **allez-y!** go ahead!; **ça va?** how's it going? (P); **ça va bien** I'm fine (P); **comment allez-vous (vas-tu)?** how are you? (P); **je vais bien** I'm fine (P)
allergie *f.* allergy
allergique *adj.* allergic
alliance *f.* alliance, union
alliés *m. pl.* allies
allumer to light
allumette *f.* match
allusion *f.*: **faire allusion à** to make reference to
alors *adv.* so; then, in that case (i)
alphabet *m.* alphabet
alsacien(ne) *adj.* Alsatian; **Alsacien(ne)** *m., f.* Alsatian (*person*)
amant(e) *m., f.* lover
amateur de *m.* fan of, enthusiast of
ambassade *f.* embassy
ambiance *f.* atmosphere, ambiance
ambitieux/euse *adj.* ambitious
ambition *f.* ambition
âme *f.* soul; **âme sœur** kindred spirit; **âmes perdues** lost souls
amère *adj.* bitter
américain(e) *adj.* American (3); **Américain(e)** *m., f.* American (*person*); **football** (*m.*) **américain** football (10)
Amérique (*f.*) **du Nord** North America (14)
Amérique (*f.*) **du Sud** South America (14)
ami(e) *m., f.* friend (P); **faux ami** false cognate; **petit(e) ami(e)** *m., f.* boyfriend (girlfriend); **se faire des amis** to make friends
amicalement *adv.* amicably
amitié *f.* friendship
amour *m.* love; **lettre** (*f.*) **d'amour** love letter
amoureux/euse *adj.* in love; **tomber amoureux/euse** to fall in love
amphithéâtre (*fam.* **amphi**) *m.* amphitheater, lecture hall
ampleur *f.* fullness
amusant(e) *adj.* amusing, funny (2)
amuser: s'amuser (à) to have a good time (9)
an *m.* year (4); **j'ai (il a,** *etc.***) (vingt) ans** I am (he is, *etc.*) (twenty) years old (4); **nouvel an** New Year's Day (11)
analyse *f.* analysis
analyser to analyze
ancêtre *m., f.* ancestor
ancien(ne) *adj.* ancient; old; former
anglais(e) *adj.* English (3); **anglais** *m.* English (*language*) (1); **Anglais(e)** *m., f.* English person (3)
Angleterre *f.* England (3)
anglophone *adj.* English-speaking
animal *m.* animal (16)
animateur/trice *m., f.* television anchor
animé(e) *adj.* animated; **dessin** (*m.*) **animé** animated cartoon (12)
anis *m.* anise
année *f.* year (4); **année prochaine (dernière)** next (last) year; **les années cinquante** the fifties; **années de l'avant-guerre** prewar years
anniversaire *m.* birthday (4); **anniversaire de mariage** wedding anniversary (11)
annonce *f.* advertisement; **petites annonces** classified ads (11)
annoncer (nous annonçons) to announce; to state
annuaire *m.* telephone book
anonyme *adj.* anonymous
antagonisme *m.* antagonism
Antarctique *m.* Antarctica (14)
anthropologie *f.* anthropology
antibiotique *m.* antibiotic
anticiper to anticipate, expect
antidote *m.* antidote
antillais(e) *adj.* West Indian; **Antillais(e)** *m., f.* West Indian (*person*)
antiquaire *m., f.* antique dealer (20)
août *m.* August (4)
apaiser to appease
apercevoir (*like* **recevoir**) *irreg.* to see; to notice
apéritif *m.* cocktail
apostrophe *m.* apostrophe
apparaître (*like* **connaître**) *irreg.* to appear (13)
appareil photo *m.* camera (5)
apparent(e) *adj.* apparent (14)
apparenté(e) *adj.* related, similar; **mots** (*m. pl.*) **apparentés** cognates
apparition *f.* appearance
appartement *m.* apartment, flat (5)
appartenir (*like* **tenir**) (*irreg.*) **à** to belong to (14)
appel *m.* call
appeler (j'appelle) to call (6); **il (elle) s'appelle** his (her) name is (4); **je m'appelle** my name is (P); **s'appeler** to be named (9); **comment t'appelles-tu?** what's your name? (*fam. s.*) (P); **comment vous appelez-vous?** what's your name? (*fam. pl.*; *formal s. and pl.*) (P)
appétit *m.* appetite; **bon appétit** enjoy your meal
applaudir to applaud (11)
apporter to bring
appréciation *f.* appreciation

apprécier to appreciate
apprendre (*like* **prendre**) *irreg.* to learn (7)
approcher to approach, draw near; **s'approcher (de)** to approach (*s.th.*)
approprié(e) *adj.* appropriate, fitting
après *prep.* after (8); **après que** after (21); **d'après** based on, according to
après-demain *adv.* day after tomorrow
après-guerre *m.* postwar period
après-midi *m. or f.* afternoon (5); **cet après-midi** this afternoon (13); **de l'après-midi** in the afternoon (5)
aquarelle *f.* watercolor
aquatique *adj.* aquatic
arabe *adj.* Arab (22); **Arabe** *m., f.* Arab (*person*); **arabe** (*m.*) **littéraire** classical Arabic
arborer: arborant sporting; wearing
arbre *m.* tree (18)
arc *m.* arch
archéologie *f.* archeology
architectural(e) *adj.* architectural
archives *f. pl.* archives
arène *f.* arena
argent *m.* money (6)
arithméthique *f.* arithmetic
armée *f.* army
arme *f.* arm, weapon (19)
armistice *m.* armistice
armoire *f.* armoire, wardrobe (*furniture*) (5)
arrestation *f.* arrest
arrêt *m.* (station) stop (14)
arrêter (de) to stop, cease; to arrest; **des opinions** (*f. pl.*) **arrêtées** definite opinions; **s'arrêter** to stop (*oneself*)
arrière *adv.* (in the) back; **arrière-grand-parent** *m.* great-grandparent; **arrière plan** *m.* background
arrivée *f.* arrival (14)
arriver (à) to arrive (11); to happen; to succeed in (doing) (18); **qu'est-ce qui lui arrive?** what's going on with him?
arrondissement *m.* district (20)
art *m.* art (10); **arts dramatiques** dramatic arts (13); **arts plastiques** visual arts (*sculpture, painting, etc.*) (13); **beaux-arts** fine arts
arteriel(le) *adj.* arterial
article *m., Gram.* article
artifice: feux (*m. pl.*) **d'artifice** fireworks
artisan(e) *m., f.* craftsman, artisan (11)
artisanal(e) *adj.* hand-crafted; **pain** (*m.*) **artisanal** hand-crafted bread
artiste *m., f.* artist
artistique *adj.* artistic
ascenseur *m.* elevator
asiatique *adj.* Asian; **Asiatique** *m., f.* Asian (*person*)
Asie *f.* Asia (14)
asile *m.* asylum; **asile politique** political asylum
aspect *m.* aspect, feature
aspiré(e) *adj.* spoken, aspirated; **h aspiré** letter *h* not allowing liaison or elision
aspirine *f.* aspirin (9)
asseoir (*p.p.* **assis**) *irreg.* to seat; **asseyez-vous (assieds-toi)** sit down; **s'asseoir** to sit down
assez *adv.* rather, somewhat, quite; **assez de** *adv.* enough (7); **assez jeune** quite young
assiette *f.* plate (8)
assimiler to assimilate
assistance *f.* assistance, help
assistant(e) *m., f.* assistant
assister à to attend (*an event*) (10)
associer to associate
assorti(e) *adj.* matching; **bien assorti(e)** well-matched
assumer to take on
assurer to ensure
astronomique *adj.* astronomical
atelier *m.* workshop
athlète *m., f.* athlete
atmosphère *f.* atmosphere
attacher to attach; **s'attacher à** to become attached to (*s.th.*)
attaque *f.* attack
attaquer to attack (19)
attendre to wait (for) (8)
attention *f.* attention; **attention!** *interj.* watch out!; **faire attention (à)** to pay attention (to) (5)
attentivement *adv.* attentively
attirer to attract
attitude *f.* attitude
attraper to trap
aubergine *f.* eggplant (15)
au revoir *m.* good-bye (P)
audacieux/euse *adj.* daring, bold
audience *f.* audience; **indices** (*m. pl.*) **d'audience** ratings
augmentation *f.* increase; rise
augmenter to increase
aujourd'hui *adv.* today (3); nowadays; **nous sommes le combien aujourd'hui?** What date is it?
auprès de *prep.* near, close to
aussi *adv.* also (P); as; so; **aussi... que** as . . . as (16); **aussi bien que** just as easily as
Australie *f.* Australia (14)
autant; autant de + *noun* + **que** *adv.* as much/many + *noun* + as (16); **autant que** as much as (16)
auteur (femme auteur) *m., f.* author (21); **en tant qu'auteur** as author
autocar *m.* (tour) bus (14)
autographe *m.* autograph
automatique *adj.* automatic
automne *m.* autumn, fall (10); **en automne** in the fall (10)
automobile (*fam.* **auto**) *f.* automobile
autoritaire *adj.* authoritarian
autoroute *f.* highway (14)
autour de *prep.* around
autre *adj., pron.* other, another (2); **autre chose?** something else?; **l'autre / les autres** the other(s)
autrefois *adv.* formerly, in the past (12)
auxiliaire *m., Gram.* auxiliary (*verb*)
avance *f.* advance; **en avance** early (5); **retarder l'avance** to slow the advance (19)
avancer (nous avançons) to advance
avant *adv.* before (in time) (8); *prep.* before, in advance of; **avant de** before (21); **avant-guerre** *n. m.* prewar period; **avant que** *conj.* before (21)
avantage *m.* advantage, benefit
avantageux/euse *adj.* advantageous; profitable
avare *m., f.* miser
avec *prep.* with (1)
avenir *m.* future (18)
avenue *f.* avenue; **monter l'avenue** to go up the avenue (17)
aveugle *adv.* blind
avion *m.* airplane (14); **billet** (*m.*) **d'avion** airplane ticket; **en avion** by airplane
avis *m.* opinion; notice; **avis de décès** *s.* obituary, *pl.* obituary section (*of newspaper*) (12); **à votre (ton) avis** in your opinion; **changer d'avis** to change one's mind
avocat(e) *m., f.* lawyer (11)
avoine *f.* oats
avoir (*p.p.* **eu**) *irreg.* to have (4); **avoir (vingt) ans** to be (twenty) years old; **avoir besoin (de)** to need (4); **avoir chaud** to feel hot (4); **avoir confiance en** to have confidence in; **avoir du mal (à)** to have a hard time (*doing s.th.*); **avoir envie de** to be in the mood for (4); **avoir faim** to be hungry (4); **avoir froid** to be cold (4); **avoir honte (de)** to be ashamed (of) (4); **avoir horreur de** to hate, detest; **avoir l'air** to look, seem (4); **avoir les cheveux châtain** to have brown hair (4); **avoir les yeux marron** to have brown eyes (4); **avoir lieu** to take place (21); **avoir l'occasion** to have the chance; **avoir mal à** to have pain, an ache in; to have a sore . . . (9); **avoir mal au cœur** to feel nauseated (9); **avoir peur (de)** to be afraid (of) (4); **avoir raison** to be right; **avoir soif** to be thirsty (4); **avoir sommeil** to be sleepy; **avoir tort** to be wrong, to be mistaken
avril *m.* April (4)

baby-boom *m.* baby boom
baby-sitter *m., f.* babysitter (11)
baccalauréat *m.* (*fam.* **bac**) *high school diploma*
baguette *f.* French bread, baguette
baie *f.* bay (17)
baignoire *f.* bathtub
bain *m.* bath; **bain thermal** spa bath (*spring water*); **maillot** (*m.*) **de bain** swimsuit (6); **salle** (*f.*) **de bains** bathroom (5)
baiser *m.* kiss
baisser to lower
balle *f.* ball (*not inflated with air*) (16)
ballon *m.* ball (*inflated with air*) (16)
banal(e) *adj.* trite, superficial, banal
bande (*f.*) **dessinée** comic strip (12)
bandé(e) *adj.*: **yeux** (*m. pl.*) **bandés** blindfolded
banlieue *f.* suburb (3)
bancaire: carte (*f.*) **bancaire** bank (*debit*) card (6)
banque *f.* bank (20); **banque de données** database
baptisé(e) *adj.* baptized, christened
bar *m.* bar, pub
base *f.* basis; base (*military*); **à base de** based on, from
base-ball *m.* baseball (10)
baser to base; **baser sur** to base on
basique *adj.* basic
bassin *m.* basin (17)
bataille *f.* battle
bateau *m.* boat; **bateau à voile** sailboat (16); **en bateau** by boat; **faire du bateau** to go sailing
bâtiment *m.* building (3)
bavard(e) *adj.* talkative (13)
bavarder to gossip; to talk a lot
beau (bel, belle [*pl.* **beaux, belles**]) *adj.* handsome; beautiful (2); **beau temps** nice weather; **il fait beau** it's nice (weather) out (10)
beaucoup (de) *adv.* much, many, a lot (of) (7); **beaucoup plus** much more, many more
beau-frère *m.* stepbrother; brother-in-law (4)
beau-père *m.* stepfather; father-in-law (4)
beauté *f.* beauty; **institut** (*m.*) **de beauté** beauty parlor
bébé *m.* baby (12)
belle-mère *f.* stepmother; mother-in-law (4)
belle-sœur *f.* stepsister; sister-in-law (4)
ben *interj. fam.* well
berbère *adj.* Berber (22)
béret *m.* beret
besoin *m.* need; **avoir besoin de** to need (4)
bêtise *f.* foolishness; **faire des bêtises** to make mistakes; to do silly things
betterave *f.* beet (15)
beurre *m.* butter (7)
bibliothèque *f.* library (3)
bien *adv.* well, good (P); **bien payé** well paid; **bien que** although (21); **bien sûr que non** of course not (2); **bien sûr (que oui)** (yes), of course; (2); **ça va bien** I'm fine, I'm well (P); **je vais bien** I'm fine (P); **s'entendre bien (avec)** to get along well (with) (9); **très bien** very well (P); **vouloir bien** to be glad, willing (*to do s.th.*) (6)
bientôt *adv.* soon (3); **à bientôt** *interj.* see you soon (P)
bière *f.* beer
bijoux *m. pl.* jewelry
bilingue *adj.* bilingual
bilinguisme *m.* bilingualism
billard *m.* billiards (10)
billet *m.* ticket (14); **billet aller-retour** roundtrip ticket (14); **billet aller simple** one-way ticket (14); **billet d'avion** airplane ticket
biochimie *f.* biochemistry (13)
biographique *adj.* bibliographical
biologie *f.* biology (13)
bisou *m. fam.* kiss (*child's language*)
bizarre *adj.* weird, strange (21)
blanc *m.* blank; space; **remplir les blancs** to fill in the blanks
blanc(he) *adj.* white (4, 6)
blé *m.* wheat (18)
bled *m. fam.* small village
blesser to wound, injure
bleu(e) *adj.* blue (4, 6); **carte** (*f.*) **bleue** bank card
bloc-notes *m.* pad of paper (P)
blond(e) *adj.* blond (4)
blues *m. s. inv.* blues music (21)
bœuf *m.* beef (7); **les bœufs** oxen
boire (*p.p.* **bu**) *irreg.* to drink (7)
bois *m.* woods, wooded area
boisson *f.* beverage, drink (8)
boîte *f.* box, can (7); **boîte aux lettres électronique** electronic mailbox (13); **boîte de nuit** nightclub (10)
bol *m.* bowl
bombe *f.* bomb
bon(ne) *adj.* good (2); **bon appétit** enjoy your meal; **bon ben** *interj.* all right then; **bonne chance** good luck (1); **bonne humeur** good mood; **bonne journée** have a good day; **en bonne forme** in good shape (9)
bonbon *m.* piece of candy
bonjour *interj.* hello, good day (P)
bord *m.* edge; bank; **au bord de** on the banks (shore, edge) of (17)
bordelais(e) *adj.* from Bordeaux (*region*)
botte *f.* boot (6)
bouche *f.* mouth (9)
boucher/ère *m., f.* butcher (7)
boucherie *f.* butcher shop (7)
bouddhisme *m.* Buddhism
bouddhiste *adj.* Buddhist
boue *f.* mud
bougie *f.* candle
bouillabaisse *f. fish soup*
bouillir (*p.p.* **bouilli**) *irreg.* to boil; **faire bouillir** to boil (*food*) (15)
boulanger/ère *m., f.* (bread) baker (7)
boulangerie *f.* (bread) bakery (7)
boule *f.* bowling ball; **jouer aux boules** to play lawn bowling
boulevard *m.* boulevard
bouleversement *m.* upheaval, disruption
bourgade *f.* village
bourgeois(e) *adj.* bourgeois, middle-class
bourguignon(ne) *adj.* from Burgundy (*region*)
bout *m.* end; **à bout de souffle** out of breath, breathless
bouteille *f.* bottle 7
boutique *f.* small shop, boutique
bowling *m.* bowling (10)
boxe *f.* boxing; **match** (*m.*) **de boxe** boxing match (10)
branché(e) *adj.* up-to-date, hip (*fam.*)
bras *m.* arm (9); **se croiser les bras** to cross one's arms
brebis *f.* ewe (18)
breton(ne) *adj.* from Brittany (*region*)
brevet *m.* patent
bribes *f. pl.* snatches; bits
brie *m.* Brie cheese
briller to shine
brocoli *m.* broccoli
bronchite *f.* bronchitis; bad cough
brosser to brush; **se brosser (les cheveux, les dents)** to brush (one's hair, teeth) (9)
bruit *m.* noise; **le bruit court** rumor has it
brûler to burn
brun(e) *adj.* brown (6)
buffet *m.* buffet; sideboard (5)
bureau *m.* desk (1); office (3); **bureau de poste** post office building
bus *m.* (city) bus (14)
but *m.* goal

ça *pron.* this, that, it; **ça marche** that works for me; **ça me va?** does it suit me?; **ça va?** how's it going? (P); **ça va bien** I'm fine, I'm well (P); **c'est ça?** is that right? (3); **qu'est-ce que c'est que ça?** what is that? (P)
cabine *f.* cabin; booth; **cabine téléphonique** telephone booth (13)
cacahouète *f.* peanut (15)
cacher to hide
cachemire *m.* cashmere
cadeau *m.* gift
cadre *m., f.* executive (11)

café *m.* coffee (8); café; **café au lait** coffee with milk (8)
cafétéria *f.* cafeteria
cage *f.* animal cage
cahier *m.* notebook, workbook (P)
caillé: lait (*m.*) **caillé** curdled milk (*similar to sour cream*)
caisse *f.* checkout (6); **caisse populaire** credit union (13)
calcul *m.* calculus
calculatrice *f.* calculator (P)
calendrier *m.* calendar
calme *adj.* calm
calmer to calm; **se calmer** to calm down
calorie *f.* calorie
camarade *m., f.* friend; **camarade de classe** classmate (P)
camembert *m.* Camembert cheese
caméra *f.* movie camera
cameraman (*pl.* **cameramen**) *m.* cameraman
camion *m.* truck (19)
camp *m.* camp
campagne *f.* country(side); campaign (*publicity, military*); **à la campagne** in the country (17); **pain** (*m.*) **de campagne** country-style wheat bread
camping *m.* campground (16); **faire du camping** to go camping (16)
campus *m.* campus
Canada *m.* Canada (3)
canadien(ne) *adj.* Canadian (3); **Canadien(ne)** *m., f.* Canadian (*person*)
canal *m.* channel
canapé *m.* sofa (5)
canard *m.* duck; **canard laqué** Peking duck
candidat(e) *m., f.* candidate
candidature *f.* candidacy; **poser sa candidature** to submit one's application
canne (*f.*) **à sucre** sugarcane
cannelle *f.* cinnamon (15)
canoë *m.* canoe; **faire du canoë** to go canoeing (16)
cantate *f.* cantata
cantine *f.* cafeteria
capable *adj.* capable; **il en est capable** he can do it
capacité *f.* skill
capitale *f.* capital (city)
caprice *m.* caprice, whim
capuchon *m.* hood
car *conj.* for, because, since
caractère *m.* character (*personal quality*); **caractères gras** boldface type
caractériser to characterize; **se caractériser (par)** to be characterized (by)
caractéristique *f.* caracteristic
carbone *m.* carbon
carbonnade (*f.*) **flamande** regional meat stew
cardamome *f.* cardamom (15)
cardiaque *adj.* cardiac; **crise** (*f.*) **cardiaque** heart attack
cardinal(e) (*pl.* **cardinaux**) *adj.* essential, cardinal
carême *m.* Lent
carnet *m.* notebook; **carnet de chèques** checkbook (20); **carnet du jour** society column (12)
carotte *f.* carrot (7)
carrière *f.* career
carte *f.* map (17); (greeting) card; menu; **carte bancaire** bank (*debit*) card (6); **carte bleue** bank card; **carte de crédit** credit card (6); **carte météorologique** weather map; **carte postale** postcard; **par carte de crédit** by credit card
cas *m.* case; **au cas où** in case, in the event that; **selon le cas** as the case may be
casque *m.* helmet (16)
casser to break; **se casser** to break (*a limb*) (9)
casserole *f.* saucepan (15)
catégorie *f.* category
cathédrale *f.* cathedral
catholicisme *m.* Catholicism
catholique *adj.* Catholic
cause *f.* cause; **à cause de** because of
causer to cause
CD *m.* compact disc (CD)
ce (cet, cette, *pl.* **ces)** *adj.* this, that, these, those (5); **ce (c')** *pron.* it, this, that; **ce matin** this morning (13); **ce soir** this evening (13); **c'est** this/that/it is (P); **cet après-midi** this afternoon (13); **n'est-ce pas?** isn't that right? (3)
ceci *pron.* this
céder (je cède) to give in
cédille *f.* cedilla (**ç**)
cèdre *m.* cedar
ceinture *f.* belt (6)
cela (ça) *pron.* that; **à part cela (ça)** besides that; **c'est pour cela seul** it's only for that reason; **cela (ne) vous regarde (pas)** that is (not) your problem
célèbre *adj.* famous (20)
célébrer (je célèbre) to celebrate
célébrité *f.* fame; celebrity
célibataire *adj.* unmarried, single (4)
celle *pron. f. s.* the/this/that one (19)
celles *pron. f. pl.* these/those (ones) (19)
cellule *f.* nucleus
celte *adj.* Celtic; **Celte** *m., f.* Celtic (*person*)
celui *pron. m. s.* this/that one (19)
censé(e) *adj.*: **être censé(e) faire** to be supposed to do (*s.th.*)
cent *adj.* hundred (4); **pour cent** percent
centimètre *m.* centimeter
central(e) *adj.* central; primary
centralisé(e) *adj.* centralized
centre *m.* center; **centre commercial** shopping center; **centre sportif** sports center (3); **centre-ville** (*m.*) downtown
cependant *adv.* nevertheless
céréale *f.* grain (18)
cerf *m.* deer, stag (16)
cerise *f.* cherry (7)
certain(e) *adj.* certain; sure (21)
certitude *m.* certainty
cerveau *m.* brain (9)
cesser (de) to stop (*doing*) (18)
c'est-à-dire *conj.* that is to say, I mean
ceux *pron. m. pl.* these/those ones (19)
chacun(e) *pron.* each (one), every one
chagrin *m.* sorrow
chaîne *f.* (television, radio) station; network (12); **chaîne privée payante** private subscription channel
chaîne stéréo *f.* stereo system (5)
chaise *f.* chair (1)
chaleur *f.* warmth (20); heat
chambre *f.* bedroom (5); **camarade** (*m., f.*) **de chambre** roommate
chameau *m.* camel
champ *m.* field (17)
champagne *m.* champagne (7)
champignon *m.* mushroom (15)
champion *m.* champion
chance *f.* luck; **avoir de la chance** to be lucky; **bonne chance** good luck (1)
chancelier *m.* chancellor
chandelle *f.* candle
changer (nous changeons) to change (6); **changer d'avis** to change one's mind
changement *m.* change
chanson *f.* song (21)
chant *m.* chant, song
chanter to sing
chanteur/euse *m., f.* singer (21)
chapeau *m.* hat (6)
chaque *adj.* each, every (7)
charcuterie *f.* pork butcher shop (7); delicatessen (7); pork products (8)
charcutier/ière *m., f.* butcher
chargé(e) *adj.* loaded (*weapon*)
charmant(e) *adj.* charming
charte *f.* charter; chart
chat *m.* cat (16)
châtain *adj. inv.* brown (*hair color*) (4)
château (*pl.* **châteaux**) *m.* castle; **châteaux en Espagne** castles in the air
chaud(e) *adj.* warm, hot; **avoir chaud** to feel hot (4); **il fait chaud** it's hot (weather) out (5)
chauffer to heat (15); **réchauffer** to reheat (15)
chauffeur *m.* driver
chaussée *f.* pavement; **rez-de-chaussée** (*m.*) ground floor

chaussette *f.* sock (6)
chaussure *f.* shoe (6); **chaussures de marche** walking shoes
chef *m.* chief; chef
chef-d'œuvre (*pl.* **chefs-d'œuvre**) *m.* masterpiece
chemin *m.* route, way (17); **chemin de fer** railroad; **est-ce que vous pourriez m'indiquer le chemin pour aller à... ?** could you show me the way to . . . ? (17); **voie** (*f.*) **de chemin de fer** railroad tracks (19)
cheminée *f.* fireplace; chimney (18)
chemise *f.* shirt (6)
chemisier *m.* blouse (6)
chèque *m.* check (6); **carnet** (*m.*) **de chèques** checkbook (20); **déposer un chèque** to deposit a check (20); **faire un chèque** to write a check (20); **par chèque** by check; **toucher un chèque** to cash a check (20)
cher (chère) *adj.* dear; expensive (2)
chercher to look for (2)
chéri(e) *m., f.* dear, darling, honey
cheval (*pl.* **chevaux**) *m.* horse (16); **monter à cheval** to go horseback riding (16)
cheveux *m. pl.* hair (9); **avoir les cheveux blonds (châtain, noirs, roux, blancs)** to have blond (brown, black, red, white) hair (4); **se brosser les cheveux** to brush one's hair (9)
chèvre *m.* goat; goat cheese
chez *prep.* at the home (business) of (3); **chez moi** at my place; **chez les jeunes** among young people
chiches: pois (*m.*) **chiches** chickpeas
chien *m.* dog (16); **nom** (*m.*) **d'un chien!** *interj.* darn it!
chiffon *m.* rag
chiffre *m.* number
chimie *f.* chemistry (13)
chimique *adj.* chemical; **génie** (*m.*) **chimique** chemical engineering (13)
Chine *f.* China (3)
chinois(e) *adj.* Chinese (3); **Chinois(e)** *m., f.* Chinese person
chiropratique *f. Q.* chiropractic
chocolat *m.* chocolate (8); **mousse** (*f.*) **au chocolat** chocolate mousse (8)
choisir to choose (11)
choix *m.* choice; **à vous le choix** your choice; **de premier choix** top quality
cholestérol *m.* cholesterol
chômage *m.* unemployment; **au chômage** *adj.* unemployed (20)
chômeur/euse *m., f.* unemployed person
chose *f.* thing (8); **autre chose** something else; **quelque chose** something (13)
choux (*m. pl.*) **de bruxelles** Brussels sprouts
chrétien(ne) *adj.* Christian
christianisme *m.* Christianity
chronologie *f.* chronology
chronologique *adj.* chronological
cidre *m.* cider
ciel *m.* sky (10); **le ciel est couvert (clair)** the sky is cloudy (clear) (10)
cimetière *m.* cemetery
cinéaste *m., f.* filmmaker
ciné-club *m.* film club
cinéma *m.* movie business; movie theater (P)
cinémathèque *f.* film store, film library
cinématographe *m., f.* cinematographer
cinéphile *m., f.* movie lover
cinq *adj.* five (P)
cinquante *adj.* fifty (P)
cinquième *adj.* fifth (11)
circonflexe: accent (*m.*) **circonflexe** *Gram.* circumflex accent (**â**)
circonstances *f. pl.* circumstances
circulation *f.* traffic (14)
circulatoire *adj.* circulatory
circuler to travel around (14)
cirque *m.* circus (10)
ciseaux *m. pl.* scissors
cité *m.* area in a city; **cité universitaire** dormitory
citoyen(ne) *m., f.* citizen
citron *m.* lemon (7); **citron vert** lime
citronnelle *f.* lemongrass (15)
civil *m.* general public; civilian; **civil(e)** *adj.* public; **code civil** civil code, common law; **état** (*m.*) **civil** civil status
clair(e) *adj.* clear (10, 21); **le ciel est clair** the sky is clear (10)
clandestin(e) *adj.* clandestine
clarifier to clarify
classe *f.* class (P); **camarade** (*m., f.*) **de classe** classmate (P); **classe moyenne** middle class; **salle** (*f.*) **de classe** classroom (P)
classement *m.* classification
classer to classify
classique *adj.* classic; classical
clé *f.* key; **moments** (*m. pl.*) **clés** key moments; **mot clé** *m.* key word; **sous clé** under lock and key
client(e) *m., f.* client (6)
clientèle *f.* clientele
climat *m.* climate
climatique *adj.* pertaining to climate
cliquer (sur) to click (on) (13)
clochard(e) *m., f.* hobo, tramp
clown *m.* clown
club *m.* club (*social*); **ciné-club** *m.* film club
coca *m.* Coca Cola (8)
cochon *m.* pig; pork
coco: noix (*f.*) **de coco** coconut (15)
code *m.* numerical code; **code civil** civil code, common law
cœur *m.* heart (9); **avoir mal au cœur** to feel nauseous (9); **savoir par cœur** to know by heart; **de tout cœur** with all one's heart; **greffe** (*f.*) **du cœur** heart transplant
coexistence *f.* coexistence
coexister to coexist
coffret *m.* little box
cognitif/ive *adj.* cognitive
cohabitation *f.* cohabitation
cohabiter to live together
coin *m.* corner (17); **les quatres coins du monde** the four corners (far reaches) of the world
coïncidence *f.* coincidence
colère *f.* anger
collaborateur/trice (*fam.* **collabo**) *m., f.* collaborator
collaborer to collaborate
collection *f.* collection
collègue *m., f.* colleague
colline *f.* hill (17)
colonne *f.* column
coloris *m.* coloring
combat *m.* combat, fighting
combattre (*like* **battre**) *irreg.* to fight (*against*)
combien (de) *adv.* how much? how many? (4); **depuis combien de temps?** how long?; **nous sommes le combien aujourd'hui?** what date is it today?
combiné *m.* (telephone) receiver
combustion *f.* combustion
comédie *f.* comedy
comique *adj.* comic
comité *m.* committee
commander to give orders; to order (*in a restaurant*)
comme *adv.* as, like (8); since, seeing that; **comme ça** this way; **comme d'habitude** as usual; **comme prévu** as expected
commémorer to commemorate
commencer (nous commençons) to begin (6)
comment *adv.* how (4); **comment allez-vous (vas-tu)?** how are you? (P); **comment est/sont... ?** what is/are . . . like? (2); **comment t'appelles-tu?** what's your name? (*fam. s.*) (P); **comment vous appelez-vous?** what's your name? (*fam. pl.; formal s. and pl.*) (P)
commentaire *m.* commentary
commerçant(e) *m., f.* tradesperson
commerce *m.* commerce (11); **commerce international** international commerce (11)
commercial(e) *adj.* commercial; **centre** (*m.*) **commercial** shopping center
commode *f.* dresser
commun(e) *adj.* common
communauté *m.* community
communication *f.* communication

communiquer to communicate
communiste *m., f.; adj.* communist
commutateur *m.* switch
compagnie *f.* company, business
comparaison *f.* comparison
comparatif/ive *adj.* comparative
comparer to compare
compatissant(e) *adj.* caring
compétition *f.* competition
complément *m.* complement; **pronom complément d'objet direct (indirect)** *Gram.* direct (indirect) object pronoun
complet/ète *adj.* full (14)
compléter (je complète) to complete
compliment *m.* compliment
compliqué(e) *adj.* complicated
comportement *m.* behavior
comporter to involve, include
composé(e) *adj.* composed; **passé** (*m.*) **composé** compound past tense
composer to compose (13); **composer un numéro** to dial a (telephone) number (13)
compositeur/trice *m., f.* composer (21)
composter to punch (*a ticket*) (14)
composteur *m.* dating stamp; ticket puncher
compréhension *f.* understanding
comprendre (*like* **prendre**) *irreg.* to understand (7); to include
comprimé *m.* tablet (9)
compris(e) *adj.* included
compromis *m.* compromise
comptable *m., f.* accountant (11)
compte *m.* account; **à leur compte** to their advantage; **compte en banque** bank account (20); **compte rendu** report; **se rendre compte (de)** to realize (9)
conception *f.* conception
concerner to concern; **en ce qui concerne** concerning (*s.o. or s.th.*)
concert *m.* concert (21)
conclure (*p.p.* **conclu**) *irreg.* to conclude
conclusion *f.* conclusion
concours *m.* competitive examination
conçu(e) *adj.* conceived, designed
condensateur *m.* condenser
condiments *m. pl.* condiments
condition *f.* condition
conditionnel *m., Gram.* conditional (*verb tense*)
condoléances *f. pl.* condolences
conducteur/trice *m., f.* driver (19)
conduire (*p.p.* **conduit**) *irreg.* to drive (18)
conférence *f.* lecture (21)
conférer (je confère) to confer, give
confiance *f.* confidence; **avoir confiance en** to have confidence in; **faire confiance (à)** to trust (*s.o.*)
configuration *f.* configuration
confirmation *f.* confirmation
confiture *f.* jam (7)
conflit *m.* conflict; dispute
confortable *adj.* comfortable
confrontation *f.* confrontation
congé *m.* holiday, time off (20); **prendre du congé** to take time off
congrès *m.* congress
conjonction *f., Gram.* conjunction
conjugaison *f., Gram.* conjugation
conjuguer to conjugate
connaissance *f.* knowledge; acquaintance; **faire la connaissance de** to meet (*a new person*) (5)
connaître (*p.p.* **connu**) *irreg.* to know, be acquainted with (13)
conquérir (*p.p.* **conquis**) *irreg.* to conquer
conquête *f.* conquest
consacré(e) *adj.* devoted
conscient(e) *adj.* aware
conseil *m.* advice; **donner des conseils** to give advice
conseiller to advise; **conseiller/ère** *m., f.* counselor
conséquence *f.* consequence
conservateur/trice *m., f.* curator (11); *adj.* (politically) conservative
conservation *f.* conservation (18)
conservatoire *m.* conservatory
conserver to conserve
considérable *adj.* considerable
considérer (je considère) to consider; **se considérer** to believe oneself to be
console *f.* console
consommation *f.* consumption (18)
consommer to consume, use (18)
consonne *f.* consonant
constitution *f.* constitution
constructeur *m.* manufacturer
construction *f.* construction
construire (*like* **conduire**) *irreg.* to construct (18)
consultation *f.* consultation
consulter to consult
contacter to contact
conte *m.* short story (21)
contemporain(e) *adj.* contemporary (21)
contenir (*like* **tenir**) *irreg.* to contain (14)
content(e) *adj.* happy
contenu *m.* content
contexte *m.* context
continent *m.* continent
continuer to continue (18)
contraceptive *adj.*: **pilule** (*f.*) **contraceptive** contraceptive pill
contraire *m.* opposite; **au contraire** on the contrary
contrat *m.* contract (20)
contre *prep.* against; **le pour et le contre** pros and cons
contredire (*like* **dire**, *but* **vous contredisez**) *irreg.* to contradict
contrée *f.* homeland; region
contrefaçon *f.* counterfeiting
contrefait(e) *adj.* counterfeit
contribuer to contribute
contrôler to control
contrôleur/euse *m., f.* ticket collector; conductor
convaincre (*p.p.* **convaincu**) *irreg.* to convince
convaincant(e) *adj.* convincing
convenable *adj.* fitting, appropriate
convenir (*like* **venir**) *irreg.* to suit, be suitable for
conversation *f.* conversation
convoqué(e) *adj.* summoned
copain (copine) *m., f. fam.* friend, pal
corde *f.* rope
cordialement *adv.* cordially
cordialité *f.* cordiality
coriandre *f.* coriander (15)
corps *m.* body (9); **Corps de la paix** Peace Corps; **extrémité** (*m.*) **du corps** limb; **partie** (*f.*) **du corps** part of the body
correct(e) *adj.* correct
correspondance *f.* correspondence; transfer, change (*of trains*); **faire/prendre une correspondance** to transfer (14)
correspondant(e) *m., f.* correspondent
correspondre to correspond
corse *adj.* Corsican; **Corse** *m., f.* Corsican (*person*)
costume *m.* man's suit (6)
costumier/ière *m., f.* wardrobe-keeper
côte *f.* coast (17)
côté *m.* side; **à côté de** beside (3); **d'un côté** on the one hand
coton *m.* cotton
coucher to put to bed; **se coucher** to go to bed (9)
couler to flow; **avoir le nez qui coule** to have a runny nose (9)
couleur *f.* color
couloir *m.* hallway; **siège** (*m.*) **couloir** aisle seat (14)
country *f.* country music (21)
coup *m.* blow; **coup de soleil** sunburn; **coup de téléphone** telephone call; **tout à coup** suddenly
couper to cut
couple *m.* couple
cour *f.* courtyard
courant *m.* current; **courant d'air** breeze, draft; **tenir au courant** to keep up to date
courge *f.* squash (15)
courgette *f.* zucchini (15)
courir (*p.p.* **couru**) *irreg.* to run; **le bruit court** rumor has it

courrier *m.* mail; **courrier des lecteurs** letters to the editor (12); **courrier électronique** e-mail (13)
cours *m.* class; course (1); **au cours de** throughout (*time*) (20); **au cours des siècles** through the centuries; **échouer à un cours** to fail a course (13); **quels cours est-ce que vous suivez (tu suis)?** what courses are you taking? (13); **sécher un cours** to cut a class (13)
course *f.* errand; **course à pied** running race (10); **faire les courses** to do errands (5)
court(e) *adj.* short (22)
couscous *m.* couscous (15); **grains** (*m. pl.*) **de couscous** grains of couscous (15)
cousin(e) *m., f.* cousin (4)
coûter to cost; **combien est-ce que ça coûte?** how much does it cost?
couteau *m.* knife (8)
couture *f.* sewing; **haute couture** high fashion
couturier *m.* fashion designer
couvert(e) *adj.* covered; **le ciel est couvert** the sky is cloudy
couvrir (*like* **ouvrir**) *irreg.* to cover (15)
craie *f.* chalk (1)
cravate *f.* tie (6)
crayon *m.* pencil (P)
créateur *m.* creator, designer
création *f.* creation
crédit *m.* credit; **carte** (*f.*) **de crédit** credit card (6)
créer to create
crème *f.* cream (7)
crémerie *f.* dairy store (7)
crémier/ière *m., f.* dairyman, dairywoman
créole *adj.* creole
crêpe *f.* crepe
crever (je crève) *fam.* to die
crevettes *f. pl.* shrimp (7)
criée *f.* auction
crier to shout, yell; **crier au scandale** to call it a scandal
crise *f.* attack; crisis; **crise cardiaque** heart attack; **crise de foie** queasy feeling
critère *m.* criteria
critique *m., f.* critic; *f.* criticism
critiquer to criticize
crocodile *m.* crocodile
croire (*p.p.* **cru**) *irreg.* to believe (10); **croire à** to believe in (*s.th.*); **il faut croire** it looks as if, it seems like it
croiser to cross; **mots** (*m. pl.*) **croisés** crossword puzzle (12); **se croiser les bras** to cross one's arms
croissant *m.* croissant, crescent roll (8)
croustillant(e) *adj.* crusty
crudités *f. pl.* raw vegetables
cruel(le) *adj.* cruel
cueillir *irreg.* to pick, collect (*flowers*)
cuillère *f.* spoon (8)
cuir *m.* leather
cuire to cook; **faire cuire à la vapeur** to steam (15); **faire cuire au four** to bake (15)
cuisine *f.* food; kitchen (5); **faire la cuisine** to cook (5)
cuisiner to cook
cuisinier/ière *m., f.* cook (11)
cuisinière *f.* stove (5)
cuisson *f.* cooking; **méthodes** (*f. pl.*) **de cuisson** cooking methods
culinaire *adj.* culinary
culpabilité *f.* guilt
cultiver to cultivate, grow, raise (18)
culture *f.* culture
culturel(le) *adj.* cultural; **manifestation** (*f.*) **culturelle** cultural event (21)
curieux/euse *adj.* curious
curriculum vitæ *m.* résumé, CV
curry *m.* curry (15)
cybercafé *m.* cybercafe
cycliste *m., f.* cyclist
cynique *adj.* cynical

d'abord *adv.* first, first of all, at first (10)
d'accord *interj.* okay, agreed (2); **d'accord?** okay? (3); **je suis d'accord** I agree (2)
d'ailleurs *adv.* moreover, besides
dame *f.* lady
dangereux/euse *adj.* dangerous
dans *prep.* in (P); within; **dans cinq ans** in five years; **dans la rue...** on . . . Street (3)
danser to dance
danseur/euse *m., f.* dancer
date *f.* date (*time*)
dater de to date from
daube *f.*: **daube de veau** veal stew
de *prep.* of; from (P); **de... à** from . . . to (5); **de l'après-midi** in the afternoon (5); **de nouveau** again; **de plus en plus** more and more; **de temps en temps** from time to time (12)
débarquement *m.* landing
débarquer to land
débat *m.* debate
début *m.* beginning; **au début (de)** in/at the beginning (of)
décembre *m.* December (4)
déception *f.* disappointment
décerner to award
décevoir (*p.p.* **déçu**) *irreg.* to disappoint
déchirer to tear up
décider (de) to decide (to) (18)
décision *f.* decision; **prendre une décision** to make a decision (7)
déclaration *f.* declaration
déclarer to declare
déclin *m.* decline
décliner to decline
décolleté: en décolleté in low-cut clothing (22)
décolonisation *f.* decolonization
déconseiller to advise against
décontracté(e) *adj.* relaxed; casual
décor *m.* decor; (stage) set
découper to cut (up)
découragé(e) *adj.* discouraged
découvrir (*like* **ouvrir**) *irreg.* to discover (15)
décrire (*like* **écrire**) *irreg.* to describe (12)
décrocher to pick up (*the telephone receiver*) (13)
décroissant(e) *adj.* descending
dedans *adv.* inside (it)
défaite *f.* defeat
défaitiste *adj.* defeatist
défaut *m.* fault (*character*)
défendre to defend
défilé *m.* parade
défiler to walk in procession, march
défini: article (*m.*) **défini** *Gram.* definite article
définition *f.* definition
déformation *f.* distortion, corruption
degré *m.* degree
déjà *adv.* already; ever (10); yet
déjeuner to have lunch (8); *m.* lunch (8); **petit déjeuner** *m.* breakfast (8)
délabré(e) *adj.* dilapidated (20)
délicat(e) *adj.* delicate
délicieux/euse *adj.* delicious; **cela a l'air délicieux** that looks delicious
demain *adv.* tomorrow (3); **à demain** see you tomorrow (P)
demande *f.* demand
demander (si) to ask (if, whether) (7)
démarche *f.* step
déménagement *m.* move (*to a new residence*)
déménager (nous déménageons) to move (*to a new residence*)
démesuré(e) *adj.* excessive
demi(e) *adj.* half; **et demi(e)** half-past (*the hour*) (5); **un an et demi** a year and a half
demi-kilo *m.* half-kilogram (7)
démissionner to quit, resign
démocrate *adj.* democrat
démonstratif/ive *adj.* demonstrative; **pronom (adjectif)** (*m.*) **démonstratif** *Gram.* demonstrative pronoun (adjective)
dent *f.* tooth (9); **se brosser les dents** to brush one's teeth (9)
dentelle *f.* lace
départ *m.* departure (14); **point** (*m.*) **de départ** starting point
département *m.* department; **département d'outre-mer (DOM)** overseas department

dépêcher: se dépêcher (de) to hurry up (*to do s.th.*) (9)
déplacer: se déplacer (nous nous déplaçons) to move around; to travel
déplaire (*like* **plaire**) *irreg.* to displease
dépliant *m.* brochure
déportation *f.* deportation
déposer to deposit; **déposer un chèque** to deposit a check (20)
dépression *f.* depression, low area
depuis *prep.* for; since (14); **depuis combien de temps?** how long?; **depuis quand?** since when?; **depuis six ans** for the past six years
déranger (nous dérangeons) to disturb, bother
dérangement: Le Grand Dérangement The Great Disturbance
dernier/ière *m., f.; adj.* last (13); latter; **ces deux derniers** the latter two; **la semaine dernière** last week
dérouler: se dérouler to unfold, happen
derrière *adv.* in back of, behind (3)
dès *prep.* from, since, beginning in
désaccord *m.* disagreement
désagréable *adj.* unpleasant
descendre (de) to descend; to get down (*from s.th.*); to get off (8); **descendre une rue** to go down a street (17)
description *f.* description
désert *m.* desert
déserter to desert
désertification *f.* desertification
désigner to designate
désinformation *f.* misinformation
désir *m.* wish, desire
désirer to want, desire (2)
désolé(e) *adj.* sorry (21)
désordre *m.* disorder; **en désordre** disorderly
dessert *m.* dessert (8)
desservir (*like* **dormir**) *irreg.* to serve
dessin *m.* drawing; **dessin animé** animated cartoon (12)
dessiné(e): bande (*f.*) **dessinée** comic strip (12)
dessiner to draw
dessous: au-dessous (de), en dessous (de) *prep.* below (3)
dessus: au-dessus (de), en dessus (de) *prep.* above, over (3)
déstabilisation *f.* destabilization
destination *f.* destination
destruction *f.* destruction
détail *m.* detail
déterminer to determine; to figure out
détester to detest, hate (2)
détruire (*like* **conduire**) *irreg.* to destroy (18)
deux *adj.* two (P)
deuxième *adj.* second (11)
deux-pièces *m.s.* one-bedroom apartment
devant *prep.* in front of (3)
développement *m.* development
développer: se développer to develop, expand
devenir (*like* **venir**) *irreg.* to become (3)
deviner to guess
devise *f.* motto
dévoiler to reveal
devoir (*p.p.* **dû**) *irreg.* to have to, must; to owe (9); *m.* homework; duty; **faire les devoirs** to do homework (5)
dévoué(e) *adj.* devoted
d'habitude *adv.* usually, normally (12); **comme d'habitude** as usual
diable *m.* devil
dialectal(e) *adj.* dialectal
dialecte *m.* dialect
dialogue *m.* dialogue
dictature *f.* dictatorship
dictionnaire *m.* dictionary (P)
dieu *m.* god
différence *f.* difference
différent(e) *adj.* different
différer (je diffère) (de) to differ (from)
difficile *adj.* difficult (2)
difficulté *f.* difficulty
diffusé(e) *adj.* broadcast
diffusion *f.* broadcasting
digestif/ive *adj.* digestive
dignement *adv.* with dignity (22)
diligemment *adv.* diligently
dimanche *m.* Sunday (4)
dimension *f.* dimension, size
diminuer to diminish
dîner to dine, eat dinner (2); *m.* dinner (8)
dingue *adj., fam.* crazy
dinosaure *m.* dinosaur
diplôme *m.* diploma (13)
dire (*p.p.* **dit**) *irreg.* to tell; to say (12); **c'est-à-dire** that is to say; **dire à quelqu'un** to tell someone; **vouloir dire** to mean (6)
direct(e) *adj.* direct; **pronom** (*m.*) **complément d'object direct** *Gram.* direct object pronoun
directeur/trice *m., f.* director, manager
direction *f.* direction (14)
discothèque *f.* discotheque
discours *m.* discourse, speech; **discours direct (indirect)** *Gram.* direct (indirect) speech
discret/ète *adj.* discreet; reserved (14)
discussion *f.* discussion
discuter to discuss (13)
disparaître (*like* **connaître**) *irreg.* to disappear (13)
disparition *f.* disappearance
disponible *adj.* available
dispute *f.* dispute
disputer: se disputer to argue (9)
disque *m.* record; **disques compacts** compact discs
distant(e) *adj.* distant
distinct(e) *adj.* distinct; separate
distinguer to distinguish, tell apart
distractions *f. pl.* leisure activities (10); entertainment, amusement
distribuer to distribute
distributeur (*m.*) **automatique** (ticket) vending machine
divers(e) *adj.* various; diverse
diversité *f.* diversity
diviser to divide; **se diviser (en)** to divide / be divided (into)
division *f.* division
divorce *m.* divorce
divorcé(e) *adj.* divorced (4)
divorcer (nous divorçons) to get a divorce (12)
dix *adj.* ten (P); **dix-huit** eighteen (P); **dix-neuf** nineteen (P); **dix-sept** seventeen (P)
dixième *adj.* tenth (11)
doctorat *m.* doctorate (13); **thèse** (*m.*) **de doctorat** doctoral dissertation
document *m.* document
documentaire *m.* documentary (12)
domaine *m.* domain, field
dôme *m.* dome
domicile *m.* domicile, residence; **sans domicile fixe** homeless
domination *f.* domination
dominer to dominate
dommage *m.*: **il est dommage que** it's too bad that (21)
dompter to overcome
donc *conj.* therefore; thus; so
donner to give (2); **donner des conseils** to give advice; **donner sur (le port)** to have a view of, overlook (the port) (20)
dont *pron.* whose, of which; including
dormir (je dors) *irreg.* to sleep (8)
dos *m.* back (9); **sac** (*m.*) **à dos** backpack (P)
dossier *m.* résumé; papers
douane *f.* customs; **passer la douane** to go through customs (14)
douanier/ière *m., f.* customs officer
doublé(e) *adj.* dubbed; **film** (*m.*) **doublé** dubbed film
douche *f.* shower; **douche au jet** high-pressure shower
doué(e) *adj.* talented, gifted
douleur *f.* ache, pain (9)
doute *m.* doubt; **sans doute** probably, no doubt; **sans aucun doute** without a doubt

douter que to doubt that (21)
douteux/euse *adj.* doubtful (21)
doux (douce) *adj.* gentle (14); soft; sweet; **doux mots** (*m. pl.*) **d'amour** sweet nothings; **il fait doux** it's mild (weather) out (10); **médecine** (*f.*) **douce** alternative medicine
douzaine (de) *f.* dozen (of) (7)
douze *adj.* twelve (P)
dragueur *m.* flirt
dramatique *adj.* dramatic; **arts** (*m. pl.*) **dramatiques** performing arts
drame *m.* drama; **psycho-drame** psychological drama
dresser: se dresser to stand (*as a statue*)
droit *m.* law (13); (*legal*) right
droit(e) *adj.* right; straight; **tout droit** *adv.* straight ahead (17)
droite *f.* right (side), right-hand side; **à droite** to/on the right (17)
drôle *adj.* odd; comical, funny; **drôle d'idée** *f.* odd idea
du (de la) *art. Gram.* some (7); **du matin** in the morning (5); **du soir** in the evening (5)
dû (due) à owing to
duo *m.* duet
dupé(e) *adj.* duped
dur(e) *adj.* hard; **œuf** (*m.*) **dur mayonnaise** hard-boiled egg with mayonnaise (8)
durant *prep.* during
durer to last
dynamique *adj.* dynamic (2)

eau *f.* water (7); **eau de source** spring water; **eau minérale gazeuse (plate)** carbonated (noncarbonated, flat) mineral water (7); **l'eau t'en viendra à la bouche** your mouth will water
eaux *f. pl.* bodies of water
ébahi(e) *adj.* dumbfounded
ébéniste *m., f.* cabinet maker
écart *m.*: **à l'écart de** away from (22)
écarter to set aside
échange *m.* exchange
échappement *m.* exhaust; **gaz** (*m.*) **d'échappement** exhaust fumes; **pot** (*m.*) **d'échappement** muffler
échapper: s'échapper to escape (19)
écharpe *f.* scarf (6)
échouer to fail (13); **échouer à un examen** to fail an exam (13)
éclair *m.* eclair (*pastry*)
éclairagiste *m., f.* lighting engineer
éclaircir to shed light on
école *f.* (elementary) school (1); **école maternelle** preschool, nursery school; **école primaire** elementary school
écologie *f.* ecology
écologique *adj.* ecological
écologiste *m., f.* ecologist; *adj.* ecological
économe *adj.* thrifty, economical
économie *f.* economy; **économie de gestion** business economics (13)
économique *adj.* economic
écouter to listen (to); **écouter la radio** to listen to the radio (2)
écran *m.* screen (*film, computer*) (2); **petit écran** television
écrire (*p.p.* **écrit**) *irreg.* to write (12); **comment s'écrit... ?** how do you spell . . . ?
écrit *m.* written examination
écriture *f.* penmanship (1)
écrivain (femme écrivain) *m., f.* writer (11)
édicter to enact
édifice *m.* building
éditeur/trice *m., f.* publisher
édition *f.* edition
éditorial *m.* editorial (12)
éducatif/ive *adj.* educational
éducation *f.* training
effet *m.* effect; **effet de serre** greenhouse effect (18)
efficace *adj.* effective; efficient (18)
effort *m.* effort; **faire un effort** to try, make an effort
égal(e) *adj.* equal
égalité *f.* equality
église *f.* church (17)
égocentrique *adj.* self-centered
égoïsme *m.* selfishness
égoïste *adj.* selfish; egotistical
élection *f.* election
électricité *f.* electricity; **panne** (*f.*) **d'électricité** power outage
électrique *adj.* electric; **génie** (*m.*) **électrique** electrical engineering (13); **plaque** (*f.*) **électrique** burner (*on a stove*)
électronique *adj.* electronic; **boîte** (*f.*) **aux lettres électronique** electronic mailbox (13); **courrier** (*m.*) **électronique** e-mail (13); **message** (*m.*) **électronique** e-mail message
électrostatique *adj.* electrostatic
élégant(e) *adv.* elegant (14)
élément *m.* element
élémentaire *adj.* elementary
éléphant *m.* elephant
élevage *m.* animal breeding (18)
élève *m., f.* pupil (1)
élevé(e) *adj.* high
élision *f., Gram.* elision
élite *f.* elite
éloigner: s'éloigner to walk off, move away
elle *pron.* she, it; her (1, 16); **elle-même** herself
elles *pron.* they; them (1, 16)
émanciper: s'émanciper to become independent
embarquement *m.*: **porte** (*f.*) **d'embarquement** (*airport*) gate (14)
embauche: entretien (*m.*) **d'embauche** job interview
embaucher to hire
embellissant(e) *adj.* flattering
embêté(e) *adj.* upset
embouteillage *m.* traffic jam (14)
embrasser: s'embrasser to kiss (each other) (9)
émission *f.* program (*television*) (2)
émotion *f.* emotion
empêcher to hinder, prevent
empereur *m.* emperor
empire *m.* empire
emploi *m.* work; employment; job (11); **emploi à mi-temps** part-time job; **mode** (*f.*) **d'emploi** directions for use
employé(e) *m., f.* employee; *adj.* employed; **employé(e) de fast-food** fast-food worker (11)
employer to employ; to use (6); **s'employer** to be used
emprunter to borrow
en *prep.* in; by; while; *pron.* of/from it/them/there; some; any (15); **en avance** early (5); **en bonne (pleine) forme** in good (great) shape; feeling good (9); **en décolleté** in low-cut clothing (22); **en espèces** in cash (6); **en face de** opposite, facing (3); **en plein air** outdoors (16); **en plus** in addition; **en réalité** in fact, actually; **en retard** late (5); **en solde** on sale; **en train** by train; **être en train de** to be in the process of; **en vacances** on vacation (16)
enchaîner: s'enchaîner to be linked
enchanté(e) *adj.* delighted; it's nice to meet you (P)
encore *adv.* again; still (3); more; **encore une fois** once again; **ne... pas encore** not yet (1)
encourager (nous encourageons) to encourage (6)
endormir: s'endormir (*like* **dormir**) *irreg.* to fall asleep (9)
endroit *m.* place, location (14)
énergie *f.* energy
enfance *f.* childhood (12)
enfant *m., f.* child (1)
enfin *adv.* at last, finally (10); *interj.* well; in short (10)
engager (nous engageons) to hire (20)
ennemi(e) *m., f.* enemy
ennuyeux/euse *adj.* boring (2); annoying, tiresome
enquête *f.* investigation; survey

enregistrer to register, check (in) (14); **enregister une valise** to check a suitcase (14)
enseignement *m.* teaching, education (13); **enseignement des langues étrangères** foreign language teaching (13); **enseignement secondaire** secondary school teaching (13); **enseignement supérieur** higher education
enseigner to teach
ensemble *adv.* together (7); *m.* collection, group
ensuite *adv.* next, then (10)
entendre to hear (8); **s'entendre (bien, mal) (avec)** to get along (well, badly) (with) (9)
enterrement *m.* burial (12)
enterrer to bury
enthousiasme *m.* enthusiasm
enthousiaste *adj.* enthusiastic
entier/ière *adj.* entire, whole
entraîner: s'entraîner to train, be in training
entre *prep.* between (3); among
entrée *f.* first course (*meal*) (8); entrance (*to a building*)
entreposer to warehouse, store
entreprise *f.* business
entrer to enter (11)
entretien *m.*: **entretien d'embauche** job interview
envahir to invade
enveloppe *f.* envelope (13)
envers *prep.* toward
envie *f.*: **avoir envie de** to feel like, want (4)
environ *adj.* about
environnement *m.* environment (18)
environs *m., f.* surroundings
envisager (nous envisageons) to envisage, imagine
envoyer (j'envoie) to send (6)
épais(e) *adj.* thick
épaule *f.* shoulder (9)
épice *f.* spice (15); **quatre-épices** *m., f. s.* blend of spices for soups, etc. (15)
épicé(e) *adj.* spicy
épicerie *f.* grocery store (7)
épicier/ière *m., f.* grocer (7)
épilogue *m.* epilogue
épisode *m.* episode
éponge *f.* sponge; blackboard eraser (1)
époque *f.* period; era; **à l'époque** at that time
épouser to marry
époux (épouse) *m., f.* husband (wife); **ex-époux (ex-épouse)** ex-husband (ex-wife)
équilibre *m.* balance
équipe *f.* team (16)
équipement *m.* equipment
équiper to equip
équivalent(e) *m.* equivalent
escalade *f.*: **faire de l'escalade** to go rock climbing (16)
escalier *m.* flight of stairs
escargot *m.* snail
esclavage *m.* slavery
esclave *m., f.* slave
espace *m.* space; venue
Espagne *f.* Spain (3); **châteaux** (*m. pl.*) **en Espagne** castles in the air
espagnol(e) *adj.* Spanish (3); **Espagnol(e)** *m., f.* Spaniard
espèce *f.*: **en espèces** in cash (6)
espérer (j'espère) to hope (6)
espoir *m.* hope
esprit *m.* spirit; mind; **état** (*m.*) **d'esprit** state of mind; **ouvert(e) d'esprit** open-minded
essai *m.* essay, composition
essayer (j'essaie) to try; to try on (6)
essence *f.* gasoline (18)
essentiel(le) *adj.* essential (20)
est *m.* east
esthéthique *adj.* esthetic
estival(e) *adj.* summertime
estomac *m.* stomach (9)
et *conj.* and (P); **et demi(e)** half-past (*the hour*) (5); **et quart** quarter past (*the hour*) (5); **et toi?** (*fam. s.*) and you? (P); **et vous?** (*fam. pl.; formal s. and pl.*) and you? (P)
établir to establish; **s'établir** to be established, evolve
étage *m.* floor (*of building*) (5); **premier étage** first floor (*above ground floor*)
étagère *f.* shelf
étape *f.* stage (12)
état *m.* state; **état civil** civil status; **état d'esprit** state of mind
États-Unis *m. pl.* United States (3)
été *m.* summer (10); **en été** in summer (10)
éternel(le) *adj.* eternal
étonné(e) *adj.* astonished, surprised (21)
étonnant(e) *adj.* amazing, surprising, shocking (22)
étrange *adj.* strange; odd
étranger/ère *adj.* foreign; unfamiliar *m., f.* foreigner; stranger; **à l'étranger** abroad; **langue** (*f.*) **étrangère** foreign language (13)
être (*p.p.* **été**) *irreg.* to be; **ce ne sont pas** these/those/they are not (P); **ce n'est pas** this/that/it is not (P); **c'est...** this/that/it is . . . (4); **c'est ça?** is that right? (3); **comment est/sont... ?** what is/are . . . like? (2); **est-ce... ?** is this/that . . . ? (4); **est-ce que... ?** is it so (*true*) that . . . ? (1); **il est (cinq) heures** it is (five) o'clock (5); **être de passage** to be passing through; **être de retour** to be back
étroit(e) *adj.* narrow (20)
études *f. pl.* studies (1); **faire des études en** to major in (13)
étudiant(e) *adj.* (male/female) university student (P)
étudier to study (2)
euh... *interj.* uh . . .
euro *m.* euro
Europe *f.* Europe (14)
européen(ne) *adj.* European
eux *pron., m. pl.* them (16); **eux-mêmes** themselves
évaluer to evaluate
événement *m.* event (12)
éventuel(e) *adj.* possible
évidemment *adv.* evidently, obviously
évident(e) *adj.* evident (14)
évier *m.* (kitchen) sink
éviter to avoid
évoluer to evolve
évoquer to recall
exact(e) *adj.* exact, accurate (14)
exagérer (j'exagère) to exaggerate
examen (*fam.* **exam**) examination, test; **échouer à un examen** to fail an exam (13); **passer un examen** to take an exam (13); **réussir à un examen** to pass a test (11)
examiner to examine
excellent(e) *adj.* excellent
exceptionnel(le) *adj.* exceptional
excès *m.* excess
exclusion *f.* exclusion; **mesure** (*f.*) **d'exclusion** segregation policy
excursion *f.* excursion, trip
excuser: s'excuser to excuse oneself; to apologize; **excusez-moi** excuse me
exemple *m.* example; **par exemple** for example
ex-époux (ex-épouse) *m., f.* ex-husband (ex-wife)
exercer (nous exerçons) to practice (*a profession*)
exiger (nous exigeons) to demand, require (20)
exister to exist
exode *m.* exodus
exotique *adj.* exotic
expansion *f.* expansion
expérience *f.* experience; experiment
expérimental(e) *adj.* experimental
expert(e) *adj.* expert
explication *f.* explanation
expliquer to explain
exploiter to exploit
explorer to explore
exposer to exhibit
exposition (*f.*) **d'art** art exhibit (10)
express *adj. inv.* express; **transport** (*m.*) **express régional** regional express train

expression *f.* expression
exprimer to express; **s'exprimer** to express oneself
expulser to expel
extermination *f.*: **camp** (*m.*) **d'extermination** concentration camp
exterminer to exterminate
extrait *m.* extract
extraordinaire *adj.* extraordinary
extraterrestre *m., f.* extraterrestrial
extraverti(e) *adj.* extroverted
extrême *adj.* extreme
extrémité *f.* extremity; **extrémité du corps** limb

fable *f.* fable
fabriquer to build
fabuleux/euse *adj.* fabulous; amazing
façade *f.* façade; side
face *f.* side; **en face de** opposite, facing (3); **face à** in the face of, facing; **faire face à** to face, confront
fâché(e) *adj.* angry (2)
fâcher: se fâcher (contre) to become angry (with) (9)
facile *adj.* easy (2)
façon *f.* manner, way; **à sa façon** in his (her) own way; **de façon sérieuse** in a serious way; **de toute façon** in any case
facteur *m.* letter carrier
faculté (*fam.* **fac**) *f.* faculty (*university department for a specific field of study*)
faible *adj.* weak (18); low
faim *m.* hunger; **avoir faim** to be hungry (4)
faire (*p.p.* **fait**) *irreg.* to make; to do (5); **faire allusion** to make reference to; **faire attention (à)** to pay attention (to) (5); **faire beau (il fait beau)** to be nice out (10); **faire bouillir** to boil (15); **faire chaud (il fait chaud)** to be hot out (10); **faire confiance à** to trust (*s.o.*); **faire cuire à la vapeur** to steam (15); **faire cuire au four** to bake (15); **faire de la photographie** to take photographs (16); **faire de la planche à voile** to windsurf (16); **faire de la voile** to go sailing (16); **faire de l'escalade** to go rock climbing (16); **faire des achats** to make purchases; **faire des bêtises** to make mistakes, do silly things; **faire des études (en)** to major (in) (13); **faire des recherches** to do research; **faire doux (il fait doux)** to be mild out (10); **faire du bateau** to go sailing; **faire du camping** to go camping (16); **faire du canoë** to go canoeing (16); **faire du jogging** to go jogging; **faire du parapente** to hang glide (16); **faire du patin à glace** to go ice skating (16); **faire du roller** to roller-skate; **faire du shopping** to go shopping (5); **faire du ski** to go skiing (16); **faire du ski de fond** to cross-country ski (16); **faire du ski nautique** to waterski (16); **faire du soleil (il fait du soleil)** it's sunny out (10); **faire du sport** to play sports; **faire du surf des neiges** to snowboard (16); **faire du tourisme** to go sightseeing; **faire du tricot** to knit; **faire du vélo (du VTT)** to bike (mountain bike) (16); **faire du vent (il fait du vent)** to be windy (10); **faire face à** to face, confront; **faire frais (il fait frais)** to be chilly (10); **faire frire** to fry (15); **faire froid (il fait froid)** to be cold out (10); **faire la connaissance (de)** to meet (*a new person*) (5); **faire la cuisine** to cook (5); **faire la fête** to have a party (5); **faire la lessive** to do the laundry (5); **faire la queue** to stand in line (5); **faire la vaisselle** to do the dishes (5); **faire le lit** to make the bed (5); **faire le ménage** to do housework (5); **faire les courses** to run errands (5); **faire les devoirs** to do homework (5); **faire mauvais (il fait mauvais)** to be bad weather (10); **faire partie de** to be a part of; to belong to; **faire peur (à)** to frighten; **faire sa toilette** to wash up; **faire un chèque** to write a check (20); **faire une correspondance** to transfer (14); **faire un effort** to try, make an effort; **faire une promenade** to take a walk (5); **faire une randonnée** to hike, go hiking (16); **faire un pique-nique** to have a picnic (16); **faire un reportage** to prepare/give a report (*TV*); **faire un stage** to do an internship; **faire un voyage** to take a trip (5); **je ne sais pas quoi faire** I don't know what to do; **se faire des amis** to make friends; **se faire mal (à)** to hurt (a part of one's body) (9)
fait *m.* fact, **tout à fait** completely
falloir (*p.p.* **fallu**) *irreg.* to be necessary; **il fallait** it was necessary to; **il faut** it is necessary (to); one must, one should (20); **il ne faut pas** one must (should) not (20)
familial(e) *adj.* relating to the family
familier/ière *adj.* familiar
famille *f.* family
famine *f.* famine
fanatique: fanatique (*m., f.*) **de sport** sports fan (10)
fantaisie *f.* fantasy
fantaisiste *adj.* fanciful
fantastique *adj.* fantastic; **c'est fantastique** it's fantastic; **film** (*m.*) **fantastique** fantasy film
fascinant(e) *adj.* fascinating
fasciné(e) *adj.* fascinated
fast-food *m.* fast food (8)
fatal(e) (*pl.* **fatal(e)s**) *adj.* fatal
fatigué(e) *adj.* tired (2)
faut: il faut it is necessary (to); one must, one should (20)
faute *f.* fault; mistake
fauteuil *m.* armchair (5)
faux (fausse) *adj.* false (2); **c'est faux** that's wrong (2); **faux ami** *m.* false cognate; **vrai ou faux?** true or false?
favori(te) *adj.* favorite
favoriser to favor
félicitations *f. pl.* congratulations
féliciter to congratulate
féminin(e) *adj.* feminine
femme *f.* woman (P); wife (4); **femme écrivain** (woman) writer (11); **femme ingénieur** (woman) engineer (11); **femme médecin** (woman) doctor (9); **femme peintre** (woman) painter (11); **femme poète** (woman) poet (21); **femme sculpteur** woman sculptor
fenêtre *f.* window (1); **siège** (*m.*) **fenêtre** window seat (14)
fer *m.* iron; **chemin** (*m.*) **de fer** railroad; **voie** (*f.*) **de chemin de fer** railroad tracks (19)
férié(e) *adj.*: **jour** (*m.*) **férié** legal holiday (11)
ferme *f.* farm (18)
fermer to close (15)
fermeture *f.* closure
fermier/ière *m., f.* farmer (18)
festival (*pl.* **festivals**) *m.* festival (16)
fête *f.* celebration; festival; Saint's day; party (11); **fête des Mères** Mother's Day; **fête du Travail** Labor Day (11); **faire la fête** to have a party (5); **fête nationale** national holiday (11)
feu *m.* traffic light; fire (17); **feux d'artifice** fireworks
feuille *f.* leaf; **feuille (de papier)** sheet (of paper) (13); **feuille de service** call sheet
feuilleton *m.* soap opera (12)
février *m.* February (4)
fiançailles *f. pl.* engagement
fiancer: se fiancer (nous nous fiançons) to get engaged
ficher: je m'en fiche *fam.* I don't care
fiction *f.* fiction
fier (fière) *adj.* proud (18)
fièvre *f.* fever (9); **avoir de la fièvre** to have a fever (9)
figurer (dans) to figure (in)
fille *f.* girl; daughter (4); **jeune fille** girl (12); unmarried woman; **petite fille** granddaughter (4)
filleul *m.* godson
film *m.* film (P)
filmer to film

fils *m.* son (4); **fils unique** only son; **petit-fils** *m.* grandson (4)
fixe *adj.*: **sans domicile fixe** homeless
fin *f.* end; **en fin de journée** at the end of the day; **mettre fin à** to put an end to
finalement *adv.* finally
financer (nous finançons) to finance
financier/ière *adj.* financial
finir to finish (11)
flamand(e) *adj.* Flemish; **Flamand(e)** *m., f.* Flemish person; **carbonnade** (*f.*) **flamande** Flemish regional stew
flamenco *m.* flamenco
fleur *f.* flower (1)
fleuve *m.* large river (17)
flexible *adj.* flexible
flipper *m.*: **jouer au flipper** to play pinball
flirter to flirt
flou(e) *adj.* blurry
flûte *f.* flute
foie *m.* liver; **crise** (*f.*) **de foie** queasy feeling
fois *f.* time (*occasion*) (5); **encore une fois** once again
folie *f.* madness
follement *adv.* madly, wildly
fonction *f.* function
fonctionnaire *m., f.* civil servant, government worker (11)
fonctionnel(le) *adj.* functional, useful
fonctionner to function
fond *m.* bottom; back; background; **à fond** in depth; **au fond** basically; **faire du ski de fond** to cross-country ski (16)
fonder to found
fontaine *f.* fountain
football (*fam.* **foot**) *m.* soccer (10); **football américain** football (10); **match** (*m.*) **de foot** soccer match (10)
footing *m.* jogging, running (10)
forces *f. pl.* (armed) forces
forêt *f.* forest (17)
forfait *m.* fixed price
formation *f.* education, training; upbringing
forme *f.* form; **en bonne (pleine) forme** in good (great) shape; feeling good (9)
former to train; to form (20)
formidable *adj.* terrific, wonderful (2)
formule *f.* formula
formuler to formulate
fort(e) *adj.* strong; significant (18); *adv.* with strength, with effort (19); **frapper plus fort** to strike harder
forum *m.* forum
fou (folle) *adj.* crazy, mad (14)
foulard *m.* lightweight scarf (6)
four *m.* oven (5); **faire cuire au four** to bake (15); **four à micro-ondes** microwave oven (5)
fourchette *f.* fork (8)
frais (fraîche) *adj.* cool; fresh; **il fait frais** it's chilly out (10)
franc (franche) *adj.* frank (14)
français(e) *adj.* French (1); *m.* French (*language*) (1); **Français(e)** *m., f.* French person (3)
France *f.* France (3)
francophone *adj.* French-speaking (3); **monde** (*m.*) **francophone** French-speaking world
frapper to strike, hit (19); **frapper plus fort** to strike harder
fraternité *f.* brotherhood
fréquence *f.* frequency
fréquent(e) *adj.* frequent
fréquenter to frequent
frère *m.* brother (4); **beau-frère** stepbrother, brother-in-law (4)
frigo *m., fam.* fridge, refrigerator (5)
frire: faire frire to fry (15)
Frisbee *m.* Frisbee (16)
frites *f. pl.* French fries (8); **poulet-frites** *m.* chicken with French fries (8); **steak-frites** *m.* steak with French fries
froid *m.* cold; **avoir froid** to feel cold (4); **il fait froid** it's cold out (10)
fromage *m.* cheese (7)
Front national *m.* National Front (*political party*)
frontière *f.* border
fruit *m.* fruit (7); **fruits de mer** seafood (7)
fume-cigarette *m.* cigarette holder
fumer to smoke
fumeurs: wagon (*m.*) **fumeurs** smoking train car (14)
furieux/euse *adj.* furious (21)
fusil *m.* gun
fusiller to execute (*s.o.*) by shooting (19)
futur(e) *adj.* future; **futur** *m., Gram.* future tense; **futur proche** *Gram.* near future

gagner to earn; to win
gai(e) *adj.* cheerful, happy
galerie *f.* (art) gallery (2)
garage *m.* garage
garagiste *m., f.* garage owner
garçon *m.* boy (12)
garde-malade *m., f.* nurse's aide (11)
garder to guard; to keep (19)
gardien(ne) *m., f.* attendant; **gardien(ne) d'immeuble** building superintendent (11)
gare *f.* train station (14)
garer to park
gastronomie *f.* gastronomy
gastronomique *adj.* gastronomical
gauche *adj.* left; *f.* left (side), left-hand side; **à gauche** to/on the left (17)
gaz *m.* gas; **gaz d'échappement** exhaust fumes
gazeux/euse *adj.* carbonated; **eau** (*f.*) **minérale gazeuse** carbonated mineral water (7)
gendre *m.* son-in-law (4)
général(e) *adj.* general; **en général** in general
générale *f.* dress rehearsal
généralisation *f.* generalization
généraliser to generalize
génération *f.* generation
généreux/euse *adj.* generous
générique *adj.* generic
génial(e) *adj.* brilliant, inspired; fantastic
génie *m.* engineering (13); **génie chimique (électrique, industriel, mécanique)** chemical (electrical, industrial, mechanical) engineering (13)
genou *m.* knee (9)
genre *m.* type
gens *m. pl.* people (13)
gentil(le) *adj.* nice, kind; well-behaved (2)
gentilhomme *m.* gentleman
gentillesse *f.* kindness
géographie *f.* geography (1)
géographique *adj.* geographical
germanique *adj.* Germanic
gestapo *f.* Gestapo
gestion *f.* management (11); **économie** (*f.*) **de gestion** business economics (13)
gifle *m.* slap
gingembre *m.* ginger (15)
glace *f.* ice cream (8); ice; **faire du patin à glace** to ice skate (16)
gloire *f.* glory
golf *m.* golf (16); **mini-golf** *m.* miniature golf
gorge *f.* throat (9); **avoir mal à la gorge** to have a sore throat (9)
goût *m.* taste
goûter to taste
goutte *f.* little drop
gouvernement *m.* government
grâce à *prep.* thanks to
grain *m.* grain; **grains de couscous** couscous grains (15)
graine *f.* seed
gramme *m.* gram
grand(e) *adj.* large, big; tall (2); **Le Grand Dérangement** The Great Disturbance; **grandes vacances** *f. pl.* summer vacation; **grand magasin** *m.* department store; **grand-mère** *f.* grandmother (4); **grand-père** *m.* grandfather (4); **grands-parents** *m. pl.* grandparents; **train** (*m.*) **à grande vitesse (TGV)** French high-speed train (14)

grange *f.* granary, barn (18)
gras(se) *adj.* fatty; thick; **en caractères** (*m. pl.*) **gras** in boldface type; **matières** (*f. pl.*) **grasses** (*meat*) fat
gratuitement *adv.* for free
grave *adj.* serious, grave; **accent** (*m.*) **grave** *Gram.* grave accent (**è**)
graveur *m.* engraver
gravité *f.* gravity
greffe *f.* graft; **greffe du cœur** heart transplant
grièvement *adv.* gravely
grippe *f.* flu, influenza (9)
gris(e) *adj.* grey (6)
grisé(e) *adj.* intoxicated
grommeler (je grommelle) to grumble
gronder to scold
gros(se) *adj.* large, big; fat; **gros titre** *m.* headline (12)
grotte *f.* cave
groupe *m.* group
gruyère *m.* Gruyere (Swiss) cheese
guérir to cure; to heal
guerre *f.* war (8); **Deuxième Guerre mondiale** Second World War; **Première Guerre mondiale** First World War
guichet *m.* ticket window (14)
guide *m.* guidebook
guider to guide
guitare *f.* guitar (5)
guitariste *m., f.* guitar player
gymnase *m.* gymnasium (13)
gymnastique *adj.* gymnastic

habillé(e) *adj.* dressed; **mal (bien) habillé(e)** badly (well) dressed
habiller: s'habiller (en) to get dressed (in) (9)
habit *m.* clothing, dress
habitant(e) *m., f.* inhabitant (20)
habitation *f.* dwelling, residence; **habitation à loyer modéré (HLM)** low-income housing
habiter to live (in a place), reside (2)
habitude *f.* habit; **comme d'habitude** as usual; **d'habitude** usually, normally (10)
***haine** *f.* hatred
***haïr (je hais)** to hate
***halle** *f.* covered market
***hamburger** *m.* hamburger
***handicap** *m.* handicap
***Hanukkah** *m.* Hanukkah (11)
***haricot** *m.* bean; **haricots verts** green beans (7)
***hasard** *m.* chance; **au hasard** by chance, accidentally
***haut(e)** *adj.* high; **à haute voix** aloud **haute couture** *f.* high fashion; **haute technologie** *f.* high tech
***hauteur** *f.* elevation, height
***hein?** *interj. fam.* eh?; all right?
***hélas** *interj.* alas
herbe *f.* grass; herb
héritage *m.* inheritance; heritage
hériter (de) to inherit (*s.th.*)
***héroïsme** *m.* heroism
hésiter (à) to hesitate (*to do s.th.*) (18)
heure *f.* hour; time (*on a clock*) (5); **à... heure(s)** at . . . o'clock (5); **à l'heure** on time (5); **à quelle heure?** at what time? (5); **à toute heure** at any time; **de bonne heure** early; **heures de pointe** rush hour (14); **il est... heure(s)** it is . . . o'clock (5); **kilomètres** (*m. pl.*) **à l'heure** kilometers per hour; **quelle heure est-il?** what time is it? (5)
heureux/euse *adj.* happy (2)
hier *adv.* yesterday (10)
***hiérarchie** *f.* hierarchy
***hiéroglyphe** *m.* hieroglyphic
***hip-hop** *m.* hip-hop music (21)
histoire *f.* story (P); history (1); **histoire naturelle** natural history
historien(ne) *m., f.* historian
historique *adj.* historical
hiver *m.* winter (10); **en hiver** in winter (10) **sports** (*m.*) **d'hiver** winter sports
hivernage *m.* rainy season
***hockey** *m.* hockey (16)
homéopathie *f.* homeopathy
homme *m.* man (P); **homme d'affaires** businessman
honnête *adj.* honest
honneur *m.* honor
***honte** *f.* shame; **avoir honte (de)** to be ashamed (of) (4)
hôpital *m.* hospital (9)
horaire *m.* schedule, timetable; **horaires d'ouverture** hours when open
horloge *f.* clock (1)
horreur *f.* horror; **avoir horreur de** to hate, detest; **j'ai horreur de** I can't stand
***hors (de)** *adj.* outside (of)
hospitalité *f.* hospitality
hostile *adj.* hostile
hôtel *m.* hotel
hôtesse *f.* hostess
huile *f.* oil (15); **huile d'olive (de sésame)** olive (sesame) oil (15)
***huit** eight (P)
***huitième** *adj.* eighth (11)
humain(e) *adj.* human
humeur *f.* mood; **de bonne (mauvaise) humeur** in a good (bad) mood
humide *adj.* humid
hymne *m.* hymn
hypertension (*f.*) **artérielle** high blood pressure
hypothèse *f.* hypothesis
ici *adv.* here (3)
icone *m.* computer icon (13)
idéal(e) *adj.* ideal
idéaliste *adj.* idealistic
idée *f.* idea; **drôle d'idée** odd idea
identification *f.* identification
identifier to identify
identité *f.* identity
idiot(e) *adj.* idiot
il *pron.* he, it (1); **il y a** there is / there are (*for counting*) (P); **il y a (dix ans)** (ten years) ago (10)
île *f.* island (17)
illustration *f.* illustration
illustrer to illustrate; to exemplify
ils *pron.* they (1)
image *f.* picture; image
imaginaire *adj.* imaginary
imagination *f.* imagination
imaginer to imagine
immangeable *adj.* uneatable, inedible
immédiat(e) *adj.* immediate (14)
immeuble *m.* apartment building (5); **gardien(ne)** (*m., f.*) **d'immeuble** building superintendant (11)
immigration *f.* immigration
immigré(e) *m., f.* immigrant (20)
immigrer to immigrate
imparfait *m., Gram.* imperfect (*verb tense*)
impatience *f.* impatience
impatient(e) *adj.* impatient
impatienter: s'impatienter to become impatient
impératif/ive *adj.* imperative; **impératif** *m., Gram.* imperative; command
impersonnel(le) *adj.* impersonal
implantation *f.* planting
impliquer to implicate
impoli(e) *adj.* impolite
importance *f.* importance
important(e) *adj.* important; big (20)
impossible *adj.* impossible (20)
impressionné(e) *adj.* impressed
impressionnisme *m.* impressionism
impressionniste *m., f.* impressionist
imprimé(e) *adj.* printed
improvisation *f.* improvisation
improviste: à l'improviste *adv.* unexpectedly
impuissant(e) *adj.* helpless
impulsif/ive *adj.* impulsive
inactif/ive *adj.* inactive
incertain(e) *adj.* uncertain (21)
incertitude *f.* indecision
inciter to prompt
inclure (*p.p.* **inclu**) *irreg.* to include
incomparable *adj.* incomparable
incomplet/ète *adj.* incomplete
inconnu(e) *adj.* unknown

inconscient(e) (de) *adj.* unaware (of)
inconvénient *m.* inconvenience
incorporer to include
incrédule *adj.* incredulous; **d'un ton incrédule** incredulously
incrédulité *f.* disbelief
incroyable *adj.* unbelievable (21)
incrusté(e) *adj.* inlaid
Inde *f.* India (15)
indécis(e) *adj.* indecisive
indéfini(e) *adj.* indefinite; **article** (*m.*) **indéfini** *Gram.* indefinite article
indépendance *f.* independence
indépendant(e) *adj.* independent
indépendantiste *adj.* separatist
indicateur/trice *adj.*: **poteau** (*m.*) **indicateur** signpost
indicatif *m., Gram.* indicative (*verb tense*)
indice *m.* indication; **indices d'audience** ratings
indien(ne) *adj.* Indian (15); **Indien(e)** *m., f.* Indian (*person*)
indifférence *f.* indifference
indifférent(e) *adj.* indifferent
indiquer to show, indicate (17); **est-ce que vous pourriez m'indiquer le chemin pour aller à... ?** could you show me the way to . . . ? (17)
indirect(e) *adj.* indirect; **discours** (*m.*) **indirect** *Gram.* indirect speech; **pronom** (*m.*) **complément d'objet indirect** *Gram.* indirect object pronoun
indiscret/ète *adj.* indiscreet
indispensable *adj.* indispensable
industrie *f.* industry
industriel(le) *adj.* commercial; **génie** (*m.*) **industriel** industrial engineering (13)
inférieur(e) *adj.* inferior
infiltrer to infiltrate
infinitif *m., Gram.* infinitive
infirmier/ière *m., f.* nurse (9)
inflation *f.* inflation
inflexible *adj.* inflexible
influence *f.* influence
influencer (nous influençons) to influence
information *f.* information; data
informations *f. pl.* news; news program (12)
informatique *f.* computer science (1); **réseau** (*m.*) **informatique** computer network
informer: s'informer to find out, become informed
ingénieur (femme ingénieur) *m., f.* engineer (11)
ingénieux/euse *adj.* ingenious
ingrédient *m.* ingredient
injuste *adj.* unjust, not right (20)
innocence *f.* innocence
innocent(e) *adj.* innocent
innovateur/trice *adj.* innovative

inquiet (inquiète) *adj.* anxious, worried (2)
inquiéter: s'inquiéter (de, pour) (je m'inquiète) to worry (about) (9)
inquiétude *f.* worry, anxiety
inscription *f.* inscription; writing
inscrire: s'inscrire (*like* **écrire**) *irreg.* to register
insigne *m.* badge, insignia
insistance *f.* insistence, tenacity
insister to insist
inspirer to inspire
installer: s'installer to settle, set up (*house*)
instant *m.* instant, moment
institut *m.* institute; **institut de beauté** beauty parlor
instituteur/trice *m., f.* elementary school teacher (1)
instruction *f.* instruction, education
instrument *m.* (musical) instrument; **jouer d'un instrument** to play a musical instrument
intacte *adj.* intact
intégrant(e) *adj.* essential; **partie** (*f.*) **intégrante** essential/integral part
intégration *f.* integration
intellectuel(le) *adj.* intellectual (2)
intelligent(e) *adj.* intelligent
intensif/ive *adj.* intensive
intensifier: s'intensifier to intensify
interculturel(le) *adj.* intercultural
interdire (*like* **dire,** *but* **vous interdisez**) *irreg.* to forbid
interdit(e) *adj.* prohibited
intéressant(e) *adj.* interesting (2)
intéresser to interest; **s'intéresser à** to be interested in (9)
intérêt *m.* interest; concern; **sans intérêt** of no interest
intérieur(e) *adj.* interior; **intérieur** *m.* interior; **à l'intérieur des terres** in the center of the country
interjection *f., Gram.* interjection
intermédiaire *m.* intermediary
international(e) *adj.* international
internaute *m., f.* Internet user (13)
interne *adj.* internal
Internet: sur Internet on the Internet (11)
interpeller to call out to
interprétation *f.* interpretation
interprète *m., f.* interpreter (11)
interrogatif/ive *adj., Gram.* interrogative
interroger (nous interrogeons) to question
interrompre (*like* **rompre**) *irreg.* to interrupt
interruption *f.* interruption
interview *f.* interview
interviewer to interview

intime *adj.* intimate; personal; **journal** (*m.*) **intime** diary
intolérable *adj.* intolerable
intonation *f.* intonation
intoxiqué(e) *adj.* intoxicated
introduction *f.* introduction
introduire (*like* **conduire**) *irreg.* to introduce
intrus(e) *m., f.* intruder
inutile *adj.* useless, no use (20)
invasion *f.* invasion
inventer to invent
invention *f.* invention
inversion *f.* reversal
invitation *f.* invitation
inviter (à) to invite (*s.o.*) (to) (18)
invoquer to invoke, call upon
ironique *adj.* ironic
irrégulier/ière *adj., Gram.* irregular
irremplaçable *adj.* irreplaceable
irrité(e) *adj.* irritated
islamique *adj.* Islamic
isoler to isolate
Israël *m.* Israel (15)
israélien(ne) *adj.* Israeli (15); **Israélien(ne)** *m., f.* Israeli (*person*)
Italie *f.* Italy (15)
italien(ne) *adj.* Italian (15); **Italien(ne)** *m., f.* Italian (*person*)
italique *m.*: **en italique** in italic type
itinéraire *m.* itinerary

jamais *adv.* never; **jamais plus** never again; **ne... jamais** never, not ever (1)
jambe *f.* leg (9)
jambon *m.* ham (7)
janvier *m.* January (4)
Japon *m.* Japan (3)
japonais(e) *adj.* Japanese (3); **Japonais(e)** *m., f.* Japanese (*person*)
jardin *m.* garden (18); **jardin des plantes** botanical garden
jarret (*m.*) **de porc** ham hocks
jaune *adj.* yellow (6); **pages** (*f. pl.*) **jaunes** yellow pages
jazz *m.* jazz
je *pron.* I (1); **j'ai (vingt) ans** I'm (twenty) years old (4); **je m'appelle...** my name is . . . (P); **je ne sais pas** I don't know (P); **je (ne) suis (pas) d'accord** I (don't) agree (2); **je suppose** I suppose (3); **je vais bien** I'm fine (P); **je voudrais** I would like (6)
jean *m. s.* jeans (6)
jeep *m.* jeep
jet *m.*: **douche** (*f.*) **au jet** high-pressure shower
jeter (je jette) to throw
jeu (*pl.* **jeux**) *m.* game (10); **jeu de rôle** role play

jeudi *m.* Thursday (4)
jeune *adj.* young (2); **jeune fille** *f.* girl (12); unmarried woman
jeûner to fast
jeunesse *f.* youth (12)
job *m.* job
Joconde: la Joconde *f.* Mona Lisa (*painting*)
jogging *m.* jogging (10); **faire du jogging** to go jogging; **piste** (*f.*) **de jogging** jogging trail (13)
joie *f.* joy; **joie de vivre** joy in living (20)
joindre (je joins, nous joignons) (*p.p.* joint) *irreg.* to join
joli(e) *adj.* pretty (2)
jouer to play (10); to act; **jouer à un sport/un jeu** to play a sport/game (10); **jouer d'un instrument** to play a musical instrument (10)
jouet *m.* toy
joueur/euse *m., f.* player
jour *m.* day (1); **carnet du jour** society column; **jour férié** legal holiday (11); **par jour** per day; **plat** (*m.*) **du jour** today's special; **quel jour sommes-nous?** what day is it today?; **tous les jours** every day (10)
journal (*pl.* **journaux**) *m.* newspaper (12); **journal intime** diary; **journal universitaire** college newspaper
journalisme *m.* journalism
journaliste *m., f.* journalist (2)
journée *f.* (*whole*) day; **bonne journée** have a good day; **en fin** (*f.*) **de journée** at the end of the day; **toute la journée** all day
jovien(ne) *m., f.* inhabitant of Jupiter
joyeux/euse *adj.* joyous, joyful (12)
judaïsme *m.* Judaism
judas *m.* peephole
judéo-arabe *adj.* Judeo-Arab
juge *m.* judge
jugement *m.* judgment
juif (juive) *adj.* Jewish
juillet *m.* July (4)
juin *m.* June (4)
jumeau (jumelle) *m., f.* twin
jupe *f.* skirt (6)
jus *m.* juice; **jus d'orange** orange juice (8)
jusque (jusqu'à, jusqu'en) *prep.* up to; as far as; until; **jusqu'à** until (3); **jusqu'à ce que** until (21)
juste *adj.* just; fair (20)
justice *f.* justice; **rendre justice à** to do justice to
justifier to justify

kilo *m.* kilogram (7); **demi-kilo** half kilogram (7)
kilomètre (km) *m.* kilometer; **kilomètres à l'heure** kilometers per hour
kiosque *m.* kiosk

la (l') *art., f. s.* the (P); *pron., f. s.* her, it (9)
là *adv.* there (P); **là-bas** over there
laboratoire *m.* laboratory (P)
lac *m.* lake (17); **au bord d'un lac** on a lake shore
lâche *adj.* cowardly
laid(e) *adj.* ugly (2)
laine *f.* wool
laisser to leave (13); to allow (13)
laissez-passer *m.* security pass
lait *m.* milk (8); **café** (*m.*) **au lait** coffee with milk; **lait caillé** curdled milk (*similar to sour cream*)
laitier/ière *adj.* dairy; **produits** (*m. pl.*) **laitiers** dairy products
lampe *f.* lamp
lancer (nous lançons) to launch (6)
langage *m.* language, speech
langue *f.* language; **langue étrangère** foreign language (13); **langue seconde** second/foreign language
lapin *m.* rabbit (16)
large *adj.* wide (22)
larme *f.* tear; **au bord des larmes** on the verge of tears
latin(e) *adj.* Latin; **Quartier** (*m.*) **latin** Latin quarter (Paris)
lavabo *m.* bathroom sink (5)
lave-linge *m.* washing machine
laver: se laver to get washed, wash up (9); **se laver les cheveux (les mains)** to wash one's hair (hands)
lave-vaisselle *f.* dishwasher
le (l') *art., m. s.* the (P); *pron., m. s.* him, it (9)
leçon *f.* lesson (1)
lecteur *m.* reader; **courrier** (*m.*) **des lecteurs** letters to the editor (12); **lecteur de CD/DVD** CD/DVD player (5)
lecture *f.* reading (1)
légende *f.* caption
léger/ère *adj.* light (*weight*) (8)
légion (*f.*) **d'honneur** legion of honor
légume *m.* vegetable (7)
lendemain *m.* next day (10)
lent(e) *adj.* slow (14)
lentilles *f. pl.* lentils (15)
lequel (laquelle, lesquels, lesquelles) *pron.* who; whom; which
les *art., m., f., pl.* the (P); *pron., m., f., pl.* them (9)
lessive *f.* laundry; **faire la lessive** to do the laundry (5)
lettre *f.* letter (13); **boîte** (*f.*) **aux lettres electronique** electronic mailbox; **lettre d'amour** love letter
leur (*pl.* **leurs**) *adj.* their (4); **leur** *pron. m., f., pl.* to/for them (7); **le/la/les leur(s)** *pron.* theirs
leurre *m.* deception

levain *m.* yeast
lever: se lever (je me lève) to get up (*out of bed*); to stand up (9)
lexique *m.* glossary
liaison *f., Gram.* liaison
libéral(e) *adj.* liberal
libération *f.* liberation
libéré(e) *adj.* liberated
liberté *f.* liberty
librairie *f.* bookstore (3)
libre *adj.* free; **ils vivent en union libre** they are living together (without marriage) (4); **zone** (*f.*) **libre** free zone
licenciement *m.* dismissal, firing (*from a job*)
licencier to fire (*from a job*) (20)
lifting *m.* facelift
lier to link, join
lieu (*pl.* **lieux**) *m.* place, location (3); **au lieu de** instead of; **avoir lieu** to take place (21); **lieu de naissance** birthplace; **lieu de tournage** film location
lieue *f.* league (*unit of measure*)
ligne *f.* line; **ligne téléphonique** telephone line
limite *f.* limit; **limite de vitesse** speed limit (14)
limiter to limit, restrict
linge *m.* laundry; **lave-linge** *m.* washing machine
linguistique *adj.* linguistic
lire (*p.p.* **lu**) *irreg.* to read (12)
lit *m.* bed (5); **faire le lit** to make the bed (5)
lithium *m.* lithium
littéraire *adj.* literary (13); **arabe littéraire** classical Arabic
littérature *f.* literature
livraison *f.* delivery
livre *m.* book (P)
livre *f.* pound (*approx. half kilo*) (7)
local(e) *adj* local
local (*pl.* **locaux**) *m.* premises; business; facility
location *f.* rental; **agence** (*f.*) **de location** car rental agency
logement *m.* lodging; place of residence
logique *f.* logic; *adj.* logical
loi *f.* law
loin *adv.* far; **loin de** *prep.* far from (3)
lointain *adj.* faraway, distant
loisirs *m. pl.* leisure activities (16)
long(ue) *adj.* long
longer (nous longeons) to walk along
longtemps *adv.* (for) a long time (14)
longueur *f.* length
lors de *prep.* at the time of
lorsque *conj.* when
lôtissement *m.* (housing) development
louer to rent (14)
loyer *m.* rent; **habitation** (*f.*) **à loyer modéré (HLM)** low-income housing

lugubre *adj.* gloomy
lui *pron., m., f.* him; to/for him/her (7, 16)
lumière *f.* light; **mettre la lumière** turn on the light (7)
lundi *m.* Monday (4)
lune *f.* moon
lunettes *f. pl.* glasses; **lunettes de soleil** sunglasses (6)
lutter to fight
luxueux/euse *adj.* luxurious
lycée *m.* secondary school (1)
lyceén(ne) *m., f.* high school student (1)

ma *adj.* my
machine (*f.*) **à laver** washing machine
madame (*ab.* **Mme**) (*pl.* **mesdames**) *f.* madam; ma'am (*ab.* Mrs.) (P)
mademoiselle (*ab.* **Mlle**) (*pl.* **mesdemoiselles**) *f.* miss (*ab.* Miss) (P)
magasin *m.* store; **grand magasin** department store (6)
magazine *m.* magazine (12)
Maghreb *m.* Maghreb (Morocco, Algeria, Tunisia) (15)
maghrébin(e) *adj.* from the Maghreb (15)
magie *f.* magic
magnétoscope *m.* videocassette recorder (VCR) (5)
magnifique *adj.* magnificent, great (2)
mai *m.* May (4)
maillot (*m.*) **de bain** swimsuit (6)
main *f.* hand (9); **sac** (*m.*) **à main** handbag
main-d'œuvre *f.* manpower, workforce
maintenant *adv.* now (3)
mairie *f.* mayor's office
mais *conj.* but (2)
maïs *m.* corn (7)
maison *f.* house (5); **maison particulière** private home; **rentrer à la maison** to go home
maître (maîtresse) *m., f.* elementary school teacher (1)
majeur(e) *adj.* major
majorité *f.* majority
majuscule *adj., Gram.* uppercase (*alphabet letter*)
mal *adv.* badly (9); **au plus mal** very ill; **avoir du mal (à)** to have a hard time (*doing s.th.*); **avoir mal (à)** to have pain / an ache (in); to have a sore... (9); **avoir mal au cœur** to feel nauseated (9); **avoir mal au ventre** to have a stomachache (9); **se faire mal (à)** to hurt (a part of one's body) (9)
malade *adj.* sick (9); *m., f.* sick person; patient; **garde-malade** *m., f.* nurse's aide (11); **tomber malade** to fall ill (9)
maladie *f.* illness
malaise *m.* weakness, fainting spell
malentendu *m.* misunderstanding
malheur *m.* unhappiness, misery
malheureux/euse *adj.* unhappy, miserable (2)
malhonnête *adj.* dishonest
malien(ne) *adj.* from Mali; **Malien(ne)** *m., f.* person from Mali
maman *f., fam.* mommy
mammifère *m.* mammal
manche *f.* sleeve; **la Manche** English Channel (17)
mandarin(e) *adj.* Mandarin
manger (nous mangeons) to eat (6); **salle** (*f.*) **à manger** dining room (5)
manifestation *f.* (*public, political*) demonstration; outward sign; **manifestation culturelle** cultural event (21)
manquer à to be missed by (*s.o.*); **tu me manques** I miss you
manteau *m.* overcoat (6)
mantille *f.* mantilla
manuscrit *m.* manuscript
maquillage *m.* makeup; makeup room
maquiller: se maquiller to put on makeup (9)
maquis *m.* scrub, bush; French Resistance
maquisard(e) *m., f.* French Resistance fighter
marathon *m.* marathon race
marchand(e) *m., f.* merchant (7)
marché *m.* market (7); **bon marché** cheap; **supermarché** *m.* supermarket (3)
marcher to walk; to work (properly); **ça marche** that works for me
mardi *m.* Tuesday (4)
maréchal *m.* marshal, field marshal
mari *m.* husband (4)
mariage *m.* marriage (12); **anniversaire** (*m.*) **de mariage** wedding anniversary (11)
marié(e) *adj.* married (4)
marier: se marier to get married
marine (*f.*) **nationale** Marines
marketing *m.* marketing (11)
marmite *f. large, iron cooking pot* (18)
Maroc *m.* Morroco (3)
marocain(e) *adj.* Moroccan (3); **Marocain(e)** *m., f.* Moroccan (*person*) (3)
marque *f.* brand
marquer to mark
marraine *f.* godmother
marron *adj., inv.* chestnut brown (4, 6)
mars *m.* March (4)
marseillais(e) *adj.* from Marseille; **Marseillais(e)** *m., f.* person from Marseille
martiniquais(e) *adj.* from Martinique; **Martiniquais(e)** *m., f.* person from Martinique
martyr *m.* martyr
masculin(e) *adj.* masculine
massacre *m.* massacre
massage *m.* massage
massif *m. old, rounded mountain range* (17)
match *m.* **(de foot, de boxe)** (soccer, boxing) match (10)
matelot *m.* sailor
matérialiste *adj.* materialistic
maternel(e) *adj.* maternal; **école** (*f.*) **maternelle** nursery school, preschool
mathématiques (*fam.* **maths**) *f. pl.* mathematics (1)
matière *f.* (school) subject (13); substance; **matières grasses** (*meat*) fat
matin *m.* morning (5); **ce matin** this morning (13); **du matin** in the morning (5)
matinée *f.* morning (*duration*)
mauritanien(ne) *adj.* Mauritanian; **Mauritanien(ne)** *m., f.* Mauritanian (*person*)
mauvais(e) *adj.* bad (2); **de mauvaise humeur** in a bad mood; **il fait mauvais** it's bad weather (10)
maxichaud(e) *adj., fam.* extremely warm
maxima *f.* maximum
maximal(e) *adj.* highest
maxime *f.* maxim, saying
mayonnaise *f.* mayonnaise; **œuf** (*m.*) **dur mayonnaise** hard-boiled egg with mayonnaise (8)
me (m') *pron.* me; to/for me (7, 9)
mec *m., fam.* guy
mécanicien(ne) *m.* mechanic
mécanique *adj.* mechanical; **génie** (*m.*) **mécanique** mechanical engineering (13)
méchant(e) *adj.* mean, nasty
méchoui *m. whole lamb roasted on a spit over open coals*
mécontent(e) *adj.* displeased
mecque: La Mecque Mecca
médaillon *m.* locket
médecin (femme médecin) *m., f.* doctor (9)
médecine *f.* medicine (*profession*); **médecine douce** alternative medicine
médias *m. pl.* media (12)
médiathèque *f.* media library
médical(e) (*pl.* **médicaux, médicales**) *adj.* medical; **soins** (*m. pl.*) **médicaux** health care
médicament *m.* medicine, drug (9)
médiéval(e) *adj.* medieval
médina *f. old portion of an Arab city* (22)
médiocre *adj.* mediocre; dull
méditation *f.* meditation
méditerranéen(ne) *adj.* Mediterranean
méfiant(e) *adj.* suspicious
méfier: se méfier to distrust
meilleur(e) *adj.* **(que)** better (than) (16); **le/la/les meilleur(e)(s)** the best

mél *m.* e-mail message (13)
mélanésien(ne) *adj.* Melanesian; **Mélanésien(ne)** *m., f.* Melanesian (*person*)
mélange *m.* mixture
mélanger (nous mélangeons) to mix (15)
mélodrame *m.* melodrama
membre *m.* member
même *adj.* same (5); **elle-même** herself; **même chose** *f.* same thing; **nous-mêmes** ourselves
mémoires *m. pl.* memoires
mémorial (*pl.* **mémoriaux**) *m.* memorial
ménage *m.* housekeeping; **faire le ménage** to do housework (5)
mener (je mène) (à) to lead (to)
mensonge *m.* lie
mentalité *f.* mindset, attitude
menteur/euse *m., f.* liar
menthe *f.* mint; **thé** (*m.*) **à la menthe** mint tea
mentionné(e) *adj.* mentioned
mentir (*like* **sortir**) *irreg.* to lie (8)
mer *f.* sea (17); **département** (*m.*) **d'outre-mer (DOM)** overseas department; **fruits** (*m. pl.*) **de mer** seafood (7); **territoire** (*m.*) **d'outre-mer (TOM)** overseas territory
merci *interj.* thank you (P)
mercredi *m.* Wednesday (4)
mercure *m.* Mercury
mère *f.* mother (4); **belle-mère** *f.* stepmother; mother-in-law (4); **fête** (*f.*) **des Mères** Mother's Day; **grand-mère** *f.* grandmother (4)
mériter to deserve
mes *adj.* my
message *m.* message; **message électronique** e-mail message
messe *f.* mass
mesure *f.* measure; **mesure d'exclusion** segregation policy
mesurer to measure
métabolique *adj.* metabolical
métamorphoser to change
météo *f., fam.* weather report, forecast (10)
météorologique *adj.* meteorological; **carte** (*f.*) **météorologique** weather map
méthode *f.* method; **méthodes de cuisson** cooking methods
métier *m.* skilled trade (11)
métro *m.* subway (14); **plan** (*m.*) **du métro** subway map; **réseau** (*m.*) **du métro** subway system (14)
métropolitain(e) *adj.* metropolitan
metteur (*m.*) **en scène** director (*theatrical*)
mettre (*p.p.* **mis**) *irreg.* to put (on); to turn on (7); **mettre du temps à** to spend time on (7); **mettre en ordre** to put in order; **mettre fin à** to put an end to; **mettre la radio/télé/lumière** to turn on the radio/TV/light (7); **mettre la table** to set the table (7); **mettre un vêtement** to put on a piece of clothing (7)
meuble *m.* piece of furniture (5)
meurette: en meurette in wine sauce
mexicain(e) *adj.* Mexican (3); **Mexicain(e)** *m., f.* Mexican (*person*)
Mexique *m.* Mexico (3)
micro-ondes: four (*m.*) **à micro-ondes** microwave oven (5)
micro-ordinateur *m.* personal computer
microphone *m.* microphone
microscope *m.* microscope
midi *m.* noon (5); **cet après-midi** this afternoon (13); **de l'après-midi** in the afternoon (5); **il est midi** it is noon
mien: le/la/les mien(ne)(s) *pron.* mine
mieux *adv.* **(que)** better (than) (16); **aimer mieux** to prefer (2); **ça va mieux?** are you feeling better?
migraine *f.* migraine (headache)
migration *f.* migration
mil *m.* millet
milice *f.* militia
milieu *m.* environment; middle; **au milieu de** in the middle of (22)
militaire *adj.* military; *m. pl.* the military
mille *adj.* thousand (4)
millénaire *m.* millennium
milliard *m.* one billion (4)
millier *m.* (around) a thousand
millimètre *m.* millimeter
million *m.* one million (4)
millionaire *m.* millionaire
mime *m., f.* mime
mince *adj.* thin
minérai *m.* ore; **exploitation** (*f.*) **du minérai** mining of the ore
minéral(e) *adj.* mineral; **eau** (*f.*) **minérale gazeuse (plate)** carbonated (noncarbonated, flat) mineral water (7)
minéralogie *f.* mineralogy
minéraux *m. pl.* minerals
mini-golf *m.* miniature golf
minima *f.* minimum
minimal(e) *adj.* minimal
minimum *m.* minimum
ministère *m.* ministry
ministre *m.* minister; **premier ministre** prime minister
Minitel *m.* Minitel (*French personal communication system*)
minoritaire *adj.* minority
minorité *f.* minority
minuit *m.* midnight (5)
minuscule *adj., Gram.* lowercase (*alphabet letter*)
minute *f.* minute
miroir *m.* mirror (5)
misanthrope *m.* misanthrope
mise *f.* putting; placing; **mise en contexte** putting into context; **mise en scène** (theatrical) production
misérable *adj.* miserable
mi-temps *f. inv.*: **à mi-temps** part-time (11)
mixte *adj.* mixed
mobile *adj.* mobile; *n. m.* cell phone
moche *adj., fam.* awful; ugly
mode *f.* fashion
mode *m.* method; *Gram.* mood; **mode d'emploi** directions for use
modèle *m.* model
modéré(e) *adj.* moderate; **habitation** (*f.*) **à loyer modéré (HLM)** low-income housing
moderne *adj.* modern
moelleux/euse *adj.* smooth, velvety
moi *pron., s.* me; I (*emphatic*) (16); **à moi** mine; **chez moi** at my place; **excusez-moi** excuse me
moindre *adj.*: **le moindre problème** the slightest problem
moins *adv.* less; minus; before (the hour) (5); fewer (16); **au moins** at least; **de moins en moins** less and less; **le moins** + *adv.* the least + *adv.* (16); **le/la/les moins** + *adj.* the least + *adj.* (16); **le/la/les moins de** + *n.* the least/fewest + *n.* (16); **moins** + *adj./adv.* + **que** less + *adj./adv.* + than (16); **moins de** + *n.* + **que** less/fewer + *n.* + than (16); **moins le quart** quarter to (the hour) (5); *v.* + **le moins** *v.* + the least (16); *v.* + **moins que** *v.* + less than (16)
mois *m.* month (4)
moitié *f.* half
moment *m.* moment; **moments clés** key moments
mon *adj.* my
monde *m.* world (18); **les quatre coins du monde** the far reaches of the world, the four corners of the world; **monde du travail** work world; **monde francophone** French-speaking world; **le Nouveau Monde** the New World; **tout le monde** everyone (1)
mondial(e) *adj.* worldwide; **Deuxième Guerre** (*f.*) **mondiale** Second World War
monoculture *f.* monoculture
monoparental(e) *adj.* single-parent
monotone *adj.* monotonous
monsieur (*ab.* **M.**) (*pl.* **messieurs**) *m.* sir; mister (*ab.* Mr.) (P)
mont *m.* mount; mountain
montagne *f.* mountain (17)
montant *m.* amount (*of a check or sale*) (20)

montée *f.* climb; ascendancy
monter to go up; to climb (11); **monter à cheval** to go horseback riding (16); **monter une rue** to go up a street (17)
montréalais(e) *adj.* from Montreal; **Montréalais(e)** *m., f.* person from Montreal
montrer to show (7)
monument *m.* monument
moral(e) *adj.* moral
morale *f.* moral (*philosophy*)
morceau *m.* piece (7)
mort *f.* death (12)
mosquée *f.* mosque (22)
mot *m.* word; **doux mots d'amour** sweet nothings; **le mot juste** the right word; **mot clé** *m.* key word; **mot apparenté** cognate; **mots croisés** crossword puzzle (12)
motivation *f.* motivation
moto *f., fam.* motorcycle
mouchoir *m.* handkerchief; **mouchoir en papier** facial tissue (9)
moules *f. pl.* mussels
moulin *m.* mill
mourir (*p.p.* **mort**) *irreg.* to die (11)
mousse *f.* mousse; **mousse au chocolat** chocolate mousse
mousseline (*f.*) **de soie** chiffon
mouton *m.* sheep; mutton (8)
mouvement *m.* movement
mouvementé(e) *adj.* lively
moyen *m.* means, method, mode (14); **moyen de transport** means of transportation
moyen(ne) *adj.* moderate, average (18); **classe** (*f.*) **moyenne** middle class; **en moyenne** on average
mulâtre *adj.* mulatto, of mixed race
multiplication *f.* multiplication
multiplicité *f.* multiplicity
municipal(e) (*pl.* **municipaux**) *adj.* municipal
mur *m.* wall (1)
muscle *m.* muscle (9)
musculaire *adj.* muscular
musculation *f.* weight training (10)
musée *m.* museum (10); **conservateur/trice** (*m., f.*) **de musée** museum curator; **musée d'art (de sciences naturelles)** art (natural science) museum (10)
musical(e) (*pl.* **musicaux**) *adj.* musical
musicien(ne) *m., f.* musician (11)
musique *f.* music (13)
musts *m. pl.* things one must do or have
musulman(e) *adj.* Muslim
mystère *m.* mystery
mystérieux/euse *adj.* mysterious

mythe *m.* myth
mythique *adj.* mythical

nager (nous nageons) to swim (16)
naissance *f.* birth (12); **anniversaire** (*m.*) **de naissance** birthday; **date** (*f.*) **de naissance** birth date; **lieu** (*m.*) **de naissance** birthplace
naître (*p.p.* **né**) *irreg.* to be born (11)
nappe *f.* tablecloth (8)
narrateur/trice *m., f.* narrator
narration *f.* narrative, account
natal(e) *adj.* native; **ville** (*f.*) **natale** birthplace
nation *f.* nation
national(e) (*pl.* **nationaux**) *adj.* national; **fête** (*f.*) **nationale** national holiday (11)
nationalisme *m.* nationalism
nationalité *f.* nationality
nature *f.* nature
naturel(le) *adj.* natural; **histoire** (*f.*) **naturelle** natural history; **sciences** (*f. pl.*) **naturelles** natural science (1)
nautique *adj.* nautical; **faire du ski nautique** to waterski (16)
navet *m.* turnip (15); **c'est un navet** it's awful, terrible, a flop
naviguer to navigate; **naviguer le Web** to surf the Web (13)
nazi(e) *adj.* Nazi
ne (n') *adv.* no; not; **ce n'est pas** this/that/it is not (P); **ce ne sont pas** these/those/they are not (P); **il n'est pas nécessaire** it is not necessary (20); **ne... aucun(e)** not any; **ne... jamais** not ever, never (1); **ne... ni... ni...** neither . . . nor; **ne... pas** not (1); **ne... pas du tout** not at all, absolutely not (1); **ne... pas encore** not yet (1); **ne... personne** no one, nobody (13); **ne... plus** not anymore, no longer (10); **ne... point** absolutely not; **ne... que** only; **ne... rien** nothing (13); **n'est-ce pas?** isn't that right? (3)
néandertal *m.*: **homme** (*m.*) **du Néandertal** Neanderthal man
néanmoins *adv.* nevertheless
nécessaire *adj.* necessary (20); **si nécessaire** if necessary
nécessité *f.* necessity
négatif/ive *adj.* negative
négation *f., Gram.* negative
négliger (nous négligeons) to neglect
négocier to negotiate
neige *f.* snow; **faire du surf des neiges** to snowboard (16); **planche** (*f.*) **à neige** snowboard
neiger to snow; **il neige** it's snowing (10)
nerveux/euse *adj.* nervous, high-strung
neuf *adj.* nine (P); **dix-neuf** nineteen (P)

neuf (neuve) *adj.* new
neuvième *adj.* ninth (11)
neveu *m.* nephew (4)
nez *m.* nose (9); **nez qui coule** runny nose (9)
ni *conj.* neither, nor; **ne... ni... ni...** neither . . . nor
nièce *f.* niece (4)
noces *f. pl.* wedding; **voyage** (*m.*) **de noces** honeymoon
Noël *m.* Christmas (11); **père** (*m.*) **Noël** Santa Claus
noir(e) *adj.* black (4, 6); **pieds-noirs** *m. pl.* *French people born in North Africa*
noisette *adj. inv.* hazel (*eyecolor*) (4)
noix *f.* nut; **noix de coco** coconut (15)
nom *m.* name; **nom d'un chien!** *interj.* darn it!
nomade *m., f.* nomad
nombre *m.* number; **nombres ordinaux** ordinal numbers
nombreux/euse *adj.* numerous (18)
nommer to name
non *interj.* no (P), not; **bien sûr que non!** of course not! (2); **non?** isn't that right? (3); **non plus** neither, not either
non-fumeurs: wagon (*m.*) **non-fumeurs** nonsmoking train car (14)
non-polluant(e) *adj.* nonpolluting
nord *m.* north (17)
normal(e) *adj.* normal; **il est normal** it's to be expected
nos *adj.* our (4)
note *f.* grade (*on a school paper*) (13); note; **bloc-notes** (*pl.* **blocs-notes**) *m.* pad of paper (P); **note de téléphone** telephone bill; **prendre des notes** to take notes
noter to take note (of); to notice; to grade (*papers*); **notez bien** take note
notre *adj.* our (4)
nôtre: le/la/les nôtre(s) *pron.* ours
nourrir to feed
nourriture *f.* food
nous *pron.* we; us; to/for us (1, 7, 9, 16); **nous-mêmes** ourselves
nouveau (nouvel, nouvelle [*pl.* **nouveaux, nouvelles**]) *adj.* new (2); **à/de nouveau** again; **le nouvel an** New Year's Day (11); **le Nouveau Monde** the New World
nouveauté *f.* novelty; change
nouvelle *f.* piece of news
Nouvelle-Écosse *f.* Nova Scotia
novembre *m.* November (4)
nuage *m.* cloud
nuageux/euse *adj.* cloudy (10)
nucléaire *adj.* nuclear
nue *f.* cloud
nuisible *adj.* harmful

nuit *f.* night (10); **boîte** (*f.*) **de nuit** nightclub (10); **bonne nuit** good night
numéro *m.* number; **composer un numéro** dial a (phone) number (13)

obéir (à) to obey (11)
obésité *f.* obesity
objectif *m.* objective
objectif/ive *adj.* objective
objection *f.* objection
objet *m.* object; **pronom** (*m.*) **complément d'objet direct (indirect)** *Gram.* direct (indirect) object pronoun
obligation *f.* obligation
obligatoire *adj.* obligatory
obligé(e) *adj.* obligated
observateur/trice *m., f.* observer
observation *f.* observation
observer to observe
obstacle *m.* obstacle
obtenir (*like* **tenir**) *irreg.* to obtain (14)
occasion *f.* opportunity; occasion; **à l'occasion de** at the time of; **avoir l'occasion** to have the chance
occidental(e) (*pl.* **occidentaux**) *adj.* western
occitan(e) *adj.* of the Provençal language
occupation *f.* occupation
occuper to occupy; **s'occuper de** to take care of
océan *m.* ocean (17)
octobre *m.* October (4)
ode *f.* ode
odeur *f.* odor, smell
œil (*pl.* **yeux**) *m.* eye (9)
œuf *m.* egg; **œuf dur mayonnaise** hard-boiled egg with mayonnaise (8); **œufs en meurette** eggs in wine sauce
œuvre *f.* work (of art, literature, music); body of work (21); **chef-d'œuvre** (*pl.* **chefs-d'œuvre**) *m.* masterpiece; **main-d'œuvre** *f.* manpower, workforce
office *m.* office
officiel(le) *adj.* official
officier *m.* officer
offrir (*like* **ouvrir**) *irreg.* to offer; to give (15)
oignon *m.* onion (7); **oignon vert** green onion; **soupe** (*f.*) **à l'oignon** French onion soup
oiseau *m.* bird (16)
O.K.? *interj.* okay? (3)
olive *f.* olive; **huile** (*f.*) **d'olive** olive oil (15)
olympique *adj.* olympic
omelette *f.* omelet (8)
on *pron.* one; we, they, people, you (1)
oncle *m.* uncle (4)
onde *f.* wave; **four** (*m.*) **à micro-ondes** microwave oven (5)
ondulé(e) *adj.* wavy
onze *adj.* eleven (P)
opéra *m.* opera (21)
opération *f.* operation; tactic
opéré(e) *adj.* operated
opinion *f.* opinion
optimiste *adj.* optimistic
option *f.* option
orage *m.* thunderstorm (10)
oral(e) *adj.* oral
orange *adj., inv.* orange (6); *m.* orange (*color*); *f.* orange (*fruit*); **jus** (*m.*) **d'orange** orange juice (8)
orchestre *m.* orchestra (21); band
ordinaire *adj.* ordinary; regular
ordinal(e) *adj.* ordinal; **nombres** (*m. pl.*) **ordinaux** ordinal numbers
ordinateur *m.* computer (1)
ordonnance *f.* prescription (9)
ordre *m.* order; **mettre en ordre** to put in order
oreille *f.* ear (9)
organe *m.* organ (*body part*)
organisation *f.* organization
organiser to organize; **s'organiser** to organize oneself
orge *f.* barley
oriental(e) (*pl.* **orientaux**) *adj.* oriental, eastern
originaire (*adj.*) **de** originating from
originalité *f.* originality
origine *f.* origin
orthographe *f.* spelling
otage *m., f.* hostage (19)
ou *conj.* or (P)
où *adv., pron.* where (4); when: in/on which (18); **où se trouve...** ? where is . . . ? (3)
oublier to forget (6)
ouest *m.* west (17); **sud-ouest** *m.* southwest
oui *interj.* yes (P); **bien sûr que oui!** yes, of course! (2)
ours *m.* bear (16)
outre *prep.* besides, over and above; **département** (*m.*) **d'outre-mer (DOM)** overseas department; **outre-mer** *adv.* overseas; **territoire** (*m.*) **d'outre-mer (TOM)** overseas territory
ouvert(e) *adj.* open; **ouvert(e) d'esprit** open-minded
ouverture *f.* opening; **horaires** (*m. pl.*) **d'ouverture** hours when open
ouvrier/ière *m., f.* manual laborer (11)
ouvrir (*p.p.* **ouvert**) *irreg.* to open (15)
oxygène *m.* oxygen

page *f.* page; **page d'accueil** home page (13); **page perso** personal home page (13); **pages jaunes** yellow pages
pain *m.* bread (7); **pain artisanal** hand-crafted bread; **pain de campagne** country-style wheat bread; **petit pain** bread roll (8)
paire *f.* pair
paix *f.* peace; **Corps** (*m.*) **de la paix** Peace Corps
Pakistan *m.* Pakistan (15)
pakistanais(e) *adj.* Pakistani (15); **Pakistanais(e)** *m., f.* Pakistani (*person*)
palais *m.* palace; **palais du roi** king's palace
pâle *adj.* pale
panier *m.* basket (16)
panne *f.* breakdown (*mechanical*); **panne d'électricité** power outage
pantalon *m. s.* pants, trousers (6)
papa *m., fam.* papa, daddy
papeterie *f.* stationery store
papier *m.* paper; **feuille** (*f.*) **de papier** sheet of paper (13); **mouchoir** (*m.*) **en papier** facial tissue (9)
papy *m., fam.* grandpa
Pâque *f.* Passover (11)
paquebot *m.* ocean liner
Pâques *f. pl.* Easter (11)
par *prep.* by; per (6); **par chèque (carte de crédit)** by check (credit card); **par cœur** by heart; **par exemple** for example; **par jour (semaine,** *etc.*) per day (week, *etc.*); **par rapport à** with respect to; **par train (avion,** *etc.*) by train (plane, *etc.*); **passer par** to pass by (13)
paragraphe *m.* paragraph
paraître (*like* **connaître**) *irreg.* to seem, appear (13)
parallèlement *adv.* in parallel, at the same time
parapente *m.*: **faire du parapente** to hang glide (16)
paraphrase *f.* paraphrase
parc *m.* park
parcourir (*like* **courir**) *irreg.* to scan
pardon *interj.* pardon me
pardonner to excuse
parenté *f.* kinship, relationship; **quelle parenté?** what's the relationship?
parenthèse *f.* parenthesis; **entre parenthèses** in parentheses
parents *m. pl.* relatives; parents (4); **arrière-grands-parents** great-grandparents; **grands-parents** grandparents
parfait(e) *adj.* perfect
parfois *adv.* sometimes (2)
parfum *m.* perfume
parisien(ne) *adj.* Parisian; **Parisien(ne)** *m., f.* Parisian (*person*)
parking *m.* parking lot, parking garage (3)
parler to talk; to speak (2); **se parler** to talk to oneself
parmi *prep.* among
parole *f.* word
part *f.*: **à part cela** besides that; **de ma part** on my behalf; as for me, in my opinion; **quelque part** *adv.* somewhere

partage *m.* sharing
partager (nous partageons) to share (6)
partenaire *m., f.* partner
parti *m.*: **parti politique** political party (18)
participe *m., Gram.* participle
participer to participate
particularité *f.* particularity
particulier/ière *adj.* particular; **en particulier** in particular; **maison** (*f.*) **particulière** private home
partie *f.* part (9); **faire partie de** to be a part of, belong to; **partie du corps** part of the body; **partie intégrante** essential/integral part
partiel(le) *adj.* partial; **à temps partiel** part-time
partir (*like* **dormir**) *irreg.* to leave (*a place*) (8); **à partir de** beginning, starting from; **partir en voyage (vacances)** to go on a trip (vacation)
partisan(e) *m., f.* partisan, follower
partitif/ive *adj., Gram.* partitive
partout *adv.* everywhere (18); **presque partout** almost everywhere
parvenir (*like* **venir**) *irreg.* to reach
pas: ne... pas *adv.* not (1); **ce n'est pas** this/that it is not (P); **ne... pas du tout** not at all, absolutely not (1); **ne... pas encore** not yet (1); (21); **pas de problème** no problem; **pourquoi pas?** why not?
passablement *adv.* fairly well
passage *m.* passage; **être de passage** to be passing through
passager/ère *m., f.* passenger (14)
passé *m.* past; **passé composé** *Gram.* compound past tense
passeport *m.* passport (14)
passer to pass; to spend; to be showing (*a film*); **en passant** in passing; **laissez-passer** *m.* security pass; **passer la douane** to go through customs (14); **passer le week-end** to spend the weekend; **passer par** to pass by (11); **passer un examen** to take an exam (13); **qu'est-ce qui se passe?** what's going on?; **se passer** to take place, to happen (9)
passionnant(e) *adj.* fascinating, gripping, exciting
passionné(e) *adj.* crazy/mad about
pastelliste *m., f.* artist who works in pastels
pastille *f.* lozenge, cough drop (9)
pastis *m. aperitif made with anise*
pâté *m.* liver paste; pâté
paternel(le) *adj.* paternal
pâtes *f. pl.* pasta (15)
patience *f.* patience; **perdre patience** to lose patience (8)
patient(e) *adj.* patient
patin *m.* ice skate; **faire du patin à glace** to ice skate (16)
patiner to ice skate (16)
patisserie *f.* pastry bakery (7); pastry (7)
patissier/ière *m., f.* pastry chef (7)
patrie *f.* one's country, homeland (19)
patriotique *adj.* patriotic
patron(ne) *m., f.* owner; boss (11)
pauvre *adj.* poor (22); *m., f.* poor person
pavillon *m.* large building; private house
payant(e) *adj.* for which one must pay, not free; **chaîne** (*f.*) **privée payante** private subscription channel
payer (je paie) to pay (6)
pays *m.* country (3)
paysage *m.* landscape; scenery
paysan(ne) *m., f.* peasant, farmer (18)
pêche *f.* fishing; **aller à la pêche** to go fishing (16)
pêcher to fish
pédagogique *adj.* pedagogical
peigner: se peigner to comb one's hair (9)
peine *f.* punishment; **à peine** hardly
peintre (femme peintre) *m., f.* painter (11)
peinture *f.* painting (21)
pèlerinage *m.* pilgrimage
pendant *prep.* during; while (14); **pendant (cinq) heures** for (five) hours; **pendant combien de temps... ?** for how long . . . ?; **pendant les vacances** during vacation
pénétrer (je pénètre) to enter, penetrate
pénible *adj.* painful; difficult
penicilline *f.* penicillin
penser to think (2); **penser à** to think about; **penser de** to think of, to have an opinion about; **penser que** to think that
pente *f.* slope
perception *f.* perception
perché(e) *adj.* perched
perdre to lose (8); **perdre la tête** to lose one's mind (8); **perdre patience** to lose patience (8); **se perdre** to get lost
perdu(e) *adj.* lost; **âmes** (*f. pl.*) **perdues** lost souls
père *m.* father (4); **beau-père** *m.* father-in-law, stepfather (4); **grand-père** *m.* grandfather (4); **père Noël** Santa Claus
période *f.* period (*of time*); **en période de** during times of
périphérique *adj.* peripheral
permanent(e) *adj.* permanent
permettre (*like* **mettre**) *irreg.* to permit, allow (7)
permis *m.* permit
persil *m.* parsley (15)
persistent(e) *adj.* persistent
persister to persist, perservere
perso: page (*f.*) **perso** personal home page (13)
personnage *m.* character (P)
personnalité *f.* personality
personne *f.* person (P); **ne... personne** *pron. indef.* nobody, no one (13)
personnel(le) *adj.* personal
pessimiste *adj.* pessimistic
pétanque: jouer à la pétanque to play lawn bowling (16)
pétillant(e) *adj.* sparkling; fizzy; **vin** (*m.*) **pétillant** sparkling wine
petit(e) *adj.* small (2); **petit(e) ami(e)** *m., f.* boyfriend (girlfriend); **petit déjeuner** *m.* breakfast (8); **petit écran** *m.* small screen (TV); **petite-fille** *f.* granddaughter (4); **petites annonces** *f. pl.* classified ads (11); **petit-fils** *m.* grandson (4); **petit pain** *m.* bread roll (8); **petits pois** *m. pl.* peas (7); **tout(e) petit(e)** very little; at a young age
peu *adv.* little; few (7); hardly; **à peu près** about, nearly; **il est peu probable que** it is unlikely that (21); **un peu (de)** a little (of), (7)
peur *f.* fear; **avoir peur (de)** to be afraid (of) (4); **faire peur à** to frighten
peut-être *adv.* perhaps (14)
pharmacien(ne) *m., f.* pharmacist
phénomène *m.* phenomenon
philosophie (*fam.* **philo**) *f.* philosophy (13)
photographie (*fam.* **photo**) *f.* photograph (21); **album-photo** *m.* photo album; **appareil photo** *m.* camera (5); **faire de la photographie** to take photographs (16); **prendre une photo** to take a photograph (16)
photographe *m., f.* photographer (21)
phrase *f.* sentence
physique *f.* physics (13); *adj.* physical
piano *m.* piano (5)
pièce *f.* room (5); **deux-pièces** *m. s.* one-bedroom apartment **pièce de théâtre** play (21)
pied *m.* foot (9); **à pied** on foot (14); **course** (*f.*) **à pied** running race (10); **pieds-noirs** *pl. French people born in North Africa*
piège *m.* trap (19)
piéton(ne) *m., f.* pedestrian; **rue** (*f.*) **piétonne** pedestrian street (20)
pilule (*f.*) **contraceptive** contraceptive pill
piment *m.* pimento, hot pepper

pion *m.* assistant (*in a school*)
piquant(e) *adj.* spicy
pique-nique *m.* picnic; **faire un pique-nique** to have a picnic (16)
pique-niquer to have a picnic (16)
piscine *f.* swimming pool (13)
piste *f.* trail, track (13); ski run (16); lead; **piste de jogging** jogging trail (13)
pita *m.* pita (bread) (15)
pittoresque *adj.* picturesque
pizza *f.* pizza (8); **pizza surgelée** frozen pizza
placard *m.* cupboard
place *f.* place; (reserved) seat (14); public square; **à votre (ta) place** if I were you (19)
plage *f.* beach (16)
plaindre: se plaindre (*p.p.* **plaint**) *irreg.* to complain
plaine *f.* plain (17)
plainte *f.* complaint
plaire (*p.p.* **plu**) *irreg.* to please; **s'il vous (te) plaît** *interj.* please
plaisance *f.*: **port** (*m.*) **de plaisance** marina
plaisanter to joke/kid around
plaisanterie *f.* joke
plaisir *m.* pleasure; **avec plaisir** with pleasure, gladly
plan *m.* map (*subway, city, region*) (13); plane; **arrière plan** background; **plan du métro** subway map; **sur le plan linguistique** linguistically
planche *f.* board; **faire de la planche à voile** to windsurf (16); **planche à neige** snowboard
planète *f.* planet
planifier to plan
plantation *f.* planting
plante *f.* plant; **jardin** (*m.*) **des plantes** botanical garden
planter to plant (18)
plaque *f.*: **plaque électrique** burner (*on a stove*)
plastique *m., adj.* plastic; **arts** (*m. pl.*) **plastiques** visual arts (*sculpture, painting, etc.*) (13)
plat *m.* dish (8); **plat (chaud, principal)** (hot, main) dish (8); **plat du jour** today's special
plat(e) *adj.* flat; **eau** (*f.*) **minérale plate** noncarbonated (flat) mineral water (7)
plateau (*pl.* **plateaux**) *m.* plateau (17); set, stage (*cinema, television*) (2)
plein(e) *adj.* full; **à plein temps** full-time (11); **en plein air** outdoors (16); **en pleine forme** in great shape (9)
pleut: il pleut it's raining (10)
pleurer to cry
pleuvoir (*p.p.* **plu**) *irreg.* to rain; **il pleut** it's raining (10)
plier to fold
pluie *f.* rain
plupart *f.*: **la plupart (de)** most (of), the majority (of) (22)
pluriel *m., Gram.* plural
plus *adv.* more (16); **au plus mal** very ill; **beaucoup plus** much more; **de plus en plus** more and more; **de plus en plus tôt** earlier and earlier; **en plus** in addition; **le plus** + *adv.* the most + *adv.* (16); **le/la/les plus** + *adj.* the most + *adj.* (16); **le/la/les plus de** + *n.* the most + *n.* (16); **ne... plus** not any more, no longer (10); **non plus** neither; **plus** + *adj./adv.* + **que** more + *adj./adv.* + than (16); **plus de** + *n.* + **que** more + *n.* + than (16); **plus rien** nothing more; **plus tard** later (10); *v.* + **le plus** *v.* + the most (16); *v.* + **plus que** *v.* + more than (16)
plusieurs *adj., indef. pron.* several (14)
plûtot *adv.* rather; instead
poche *f.* pocket
poème *m.* poem (21)
poésie *f.* poetry (21)
poète (femme poète) *m., f.* poet (21)
poids *m.* weight
point *m.* point; **ne... point** *adv.* absolutely not; **point de départ** starting point; **point de repère** landmark; **point de vue** point of view
pointe: heures (*f. pl.*) **de pointe** rush hour (14)
pois *m. pl.* peas; **petits pois** green peas (7); **pois chiches** chickpeas (15)
poisson *m.* fish (7); **soupe** (*f.*) **de poisson** fish soup
poissonnerie *f.* fish store (7)
poissonnier/ière *m., f.* fishmonger
poitrine *f.* chest (9)
poivre *m.* pepper (8)
poivron *m.* bell pepper
poli(e) *adj.* polite
police *f.* police; **agent(e)** (*m., f.*) **de police** police officer
policier/ière *m., f.* police officer
politesse *f.* courtesy, good manners
politique *f.* politics; policy; *adj.* political; **parti** (*m.*) **politique** political party (18)
polluant(e) *adj.* polluting
polluer to pollute
pollution *f.* pollution (18)
pomme *f.* apple (7); **pomme de terre** potato (7); **tarte** (*f.*) **aux pommes** apple pie
ponctuation *f.* punctuation
pont *m.* bridge (19)
populaire *adj.* popular; **caisse** (*f.*) **populaire** credit union (13)
population *f.* population
porc *m.* pork (7); pig (18); **jarret** (*m.*) **de porc** ham hocks
porcelaine *f.* porcelain
port *m.* port (20); **port de plaisance** marina; **port maritime** shipping port
portable *m.* laptop computer (5); cell phone (5)
porte *f.* door (1); **porte d'embarquement** (*airport*) gate (14)
porter to wear (2); to carry; **prêt-à-porter** off-the-rack/ready-to-wear clothing
portrait *m.* portrait
portugais(e) *adj.* Portuguese; **Portugais(e)** *m., f.* Portuguese (*person*)
poser: poser sa candidature to submit one's application; **poser une question** to ask a question
position *f.* position; place
posséder (je possède) to possess
possessif/ive *adj.* possessive
possibilité *f.* possibility
possible *adj.* possible; **autant que possible** as much as possible (16); **il est possible (que)** it is possible (that); **le plus vite possible** as soon as possible
postal(e) *adj.* postal; **carte** (*f.*) **postale** postcard
poste *f.* mail (3); post office; **bureau** (*m.*) **de poste** post office building
poste *m.* position, job (11)
pot *m.*: **prendre un pot** to have a drink; **pot d'échappement** muffler
poteau (*m.*) **indicateur** signpost (17)
poubelle *f.* garbage can
poulet *m.* chicken (*meat*) (7); **poulet-frites** *m.* chicken with French fries (8)
poumon *m.* lung (9)
poupée *f.* doll
pour *prep.* for (1); **c'est pour cela** it's for that reason; **le pour et le contre** the pros and cons; **pour cent** percent; **pour que** so that, in order that (21); **s'inquiéter pour** to worry about
pourcentage *m.* percentage
pourquoi *adv., conj.* why (4); **pourquoi pas?** why not?
pourri(e) *m., f.* rotten person
poursuivre (*like* **suivre**) *irreg.* to pursue (15)
pousser to grow; to push (18); **pousser des soupirs** to sigh
pouvoir (*p.p.* **pu**) *irreg.* to be able, can; to be allowed (6); **est-ce que vous pourriez m'indiquer le chemin pour aller à... ?** could you show me the way to . . . ? (17); **il se peut que** it is possible that (21)
pratiquant(e) *adj.* practicing
pratique *f.* practice; *adj.* practical

pratiquer to practice
précédent(e) *adj.* preceding
précieux/euse *adj.* precious
précipiter: se précipiter to happen quickly
précisement *adv.* precisely, to be precise
préciser to specify
précision *f.* clarification
prédiction *f.* prediction
préfecture *f.* prefecture
préférable *adj.* preferable (20)
préférer (je préfère) to prefer (6)
préférence *f.* preference
premier/ière *adj.* first (11); **le premier** the first of the month (4); **premier choix** *m.* top quality; **premier étage** *m.* first floor (*above ground level*)
prendre (*p.p.* **pris**) *irreg.* to take (7); to have (*s.th. to eat/drink*) (7); **prendre des notes** to take notes; **prendre du temps** to take a long time (7); **prendre sa retraite** to retire (12); **prendre un congé** to take time off; **prendre une correspondance** to transfer; **prendre une décision** to make a decision (7); **prendre une photo** to take a photograph; **prendre un verre (un pot)** to have a drink (7); **prenez soin de vous** take care of yourself
prénom *m.* first name
préoccuper to preoccupy
préparatif *m.* preparation
préparation *f.* preparation
préparatoire *adj.* preparatory
préparer to prepare; **préparer (une leçon, un examen)** to study for (a lesson; a test) (13); **se préparer** to get ready
préposition *f., Gram.* preposition
près (de) *adv.* near (3); **à peu près** about, nearly
présence *f.* presence
présent *m.* present (*time*); **à présent** now, currently
présentation *f.* presentation
présent(e) *adj.* present
présenter to present; to introduce; **se présenter** to introduce oneself
président(e) *m., f.* president
presque *adv.* almost, nearly (18); **presque partout** almost everywhere
presse *f.* news media; press
pressé(e) *adj.* in a hurry (14)
prestigieux/euse *adj.* prestigious
prêt(e) *adj.* ready (2); **prêt-à-porter** *m.* off-the-rack/ready-to-wear clothing
prêter to lend; **prêter serment à** to swear allegiance to
prétexte *m.* pretext
preuve *f.* proof
prévision *f.* forecast
prévoir (*like* **voir**) *irreg.* to foresee, anticipate; **comme prévu** as expected
primaire *adj.* primary; **école** (*f.*) **primaire** elementary school
primordial(e) *adj.* paramount
prince *m.* prince
principal(e) *adj.* principal, main; **plat** (*m.*) **principal** main course (8)
principe *m.* principle
printemps *m.* spring (10); **au printemps** in spring (10)
prison *f.* prison
prisonnier/ière *m., f.* prisoner
privé(e) *adj.* private; **chaîne** (*f.*) **privée payante** private subscription channel; **vie** (*f.*) **privée** private life
prix *m.* price; prize; **à tout prix** at all costs
probabilité *f.* probability
probable *adj.* probable (21)
problème *m.* problem; **le moindre problème** the slightest problem; **pas de problème** no problem
prochain(e) *adj.* next (13); **la semaine (l'année,** *etc.***) prochaine** next week (year, etc.)
proche (de) *adj., adv.* near, close; **futur** (*m.*) **proche** *Gram.* near future
proclamer to proclaim
producteur/trice *m., f.* producer (2)
production *f.* production
productivité *f.* productivity
produire (*like* **conduire**) *irreg.* to produce (18)
produit *m.* product; **produits laitiers** dairy products
professeur *m.* professor (P); **professeure** *f. Q.* female professor (2); **prof** *m., f. fam.* professor (2)
profession *f.* profession (11)
professionnel(le) *adj., m., f.* professional
profit *m.* profit; **au profit de** at the expense of
profiter to take advantage of; to profit from
programme *m.* program (13)
progressivement *adv.* progressively
projecteur *m.* projector
projection *f.* projection
projet *m.* project
promenade *f.* walk; **faire une promenade** to take a walk (5)
promener: se promener (je me promène) to take a walk (9)
promettre (*like* **mettre**) *irreg.* to promise (7)
promotion *f.* promotion
prompt(e) *adj.* prompt
pronom *m., Gram.* pronoun; **pronom complément d'objet direct (indirect)** direct (indirect) object pronoun; **pronom (démonstratif, possessif, relatif)** (demonstrative, possessive, relative) pronoun
pronominal *adj., Gram.* pronominal; **verbe** (*m.*) **pronominal** *Gram.* pronominal (reflexive) verb
prononcer (nous prononçons) to pronounce
propager: se propager (nous nous propageons) to be disseminated, spread
propos *m.*: **à propos de** about, concerning
proposer to propose, suggest
propre *adj.* own; **propre à** characteristic of; **sa propre opinion** *f.* his (her) own opinion
propriétaire *m., f.* owner
prospère *adj.* prosperous
prospérer (je prospère) to prosper
prospérité *f.* prosperity
protéger (je protège, nous protégeons) to protect
protestant(e) *adj.* Protestant; **Protestant(e)** *m., f.* Protestant (*person*)
protestantisme *m.* Protestantism
protester to protest
provenance *f.*: **de provenance** originating in/from
provençal(e) *adj.* from Provence (*region*)
provenir (*like* **venir**) *irreg.* to come from, to originate in
province *f.* province
provincial(e) *adj.* provincial
provision *f.* provision; *pl.* food (*supplies*)
provoquer to provoke
prudent(e) *adj.* careful
psychiatre *m., f.* psychiatrist
psychiatrique *adj.* psychiatric
psycho-drame *m.* psychological drama
psychologie *f.* psychology (13)
public *m.* public; **en public** in public
public (publique) *adj.* public
publicitaire *adj.* advertising
publicité *f.* commercial, advertisement (12)
publier to publish
puce *f.* flea; **ma puce** *fam.* sweetheart
puis *adv.* then (10)
puisque *conj.* since, seeing that
puissant(e) *adj.* powerful
pull-over (*fam.* **pull**) *m.* pullover (*sweater*) (6)
punk *m.* punk music (21)
pur(e) *adj.* pure
purifier to purify
pyjama *m.* pyjamas
pyramide *f.* pyramid

quai *m.* platform (14); dock
qualification *f.* qualification
qualifier to characterize

qualité *f.* quality
quand *adv., conj.* when (4); **depuis quand?** since when?
quantité *f.* quantity
quarante *adj.* forty (P)
quart *m.* quarter, fourth; quarter of an hour; **et quart** quarter past (*the hour*) (5); **moins le quart** quarter to (*the hour*) (5)
quartier *m.* neighborhood, area of town (3); **Quartier latin** Latin Quarter (Paris)
quatorze *adj.* fourteen (P)
quatre *adj.* four (P); **quatre-vingt-dix** ninety (4); **quatre-vingts** eighty (4)
quatre-épices *m., f. blend of spices for soups, etc.* (15)
quatrième *adj.* fourth (11)
que (qu') *conj.* that; than; as; *interr. pron.* what (6); *rel. pron.* whom, that, which (18); **ne... que** only (10); **pour que** in order to (21); **qu'est-ce que** what (*object*) (6); **qu'est-ce que c'est?** what is it/this/that? (P); **qu'est-ce qui** what (*subject*) (16)
Québec *m.* Quebec (3)
québécois(e) *adj.* from Quebec (3); **Québécois(e)** *m., f.* person from Quebec
quel(le)(s) *interr. adj.* what?, which? (5); **quel âge avez-vous (as-tu) (a-t-il,** *etc.***)?** how old are you (is he, etc.)? (4); **quel jour sommes-nous?** what day is it today?; **quel temps fait-it?** what's the weather like? (10); **quelle heure est-il?** what time is it? (5); **quels cours est-ce que vous suivez (tu suis)?** what courses are you taking? (13)
quelque(s) *indef. adj.* several, some; a few (8); **quelque chose** *indef. pron.* something (13); **quelque part** *adv.* somewhere
quelquefois *adv.* sometimes (12)
quelques-uns/unes *indef. pron., pl.* some, a few
quelqu'un *indef. pron.* someone (13)
question *f.* question; **poser une question** to ask a question
quête *f.* quest
queue *f.* queue, line; **faire la queue** to stand in line (5)
qui *interr. pron.* who, whom (6); *rel. pron.* who, that, which (18); **qui est-ce?** who is it? (P); **qui est-ce que** whom (*object*); **qui est-ce qui** who (*subject*) (16)
quinze *adj.* fifteen (P)
quitter to leave (*s.o. or someplace*) (8)
quoi *pron.* what (6); **à quoi tu joues?** are you playing games?; **de quoi parlez-vous (parles-tu)?** what are you talking about? **je ne sais pas quoi faire** I don't know what to do
quotidien(ne) *adj.* daily
raccrocher to hang up (*the telephone receiver*) (13)
race *f.* race (*ethnicity*)
racine *f.* root
racisme *m.* racism
raconter to tell (about) (8)
radicalement *adv.* radically
radieux/euse *adj.* glorious, radiant
radio *f.* radio (5); **écouter la radio** to listen to the radio; **mettre la radio** to turn on the radio (7); **station** (*f.*) **de radio** radio station (12)
radioactif/ive *adj.* radioactive
raffiné(e) *adj.* refined
ragoût *m.* stew
raï *m.* raï music (21)
raisin *m.*: **du raisin** (or **des raisins**) grapes (7); **raisin sec** raisin (15)
raison *f.* reason; **avoir raison** to be right
raisonnable *adj.* reasonable
ralentir to slow down
ramadan *m.* Ramadan (11)
ramasser to pick (up), gather (up); to dig up (18)
randonnée *f.* hike; **faire une randonnée** to hike (16)
rap *m.* rap music
rapide *adj.* fast, rapid (14)
rapidité *f.* speed
rappeler: se rappeler (je me rappelle) to remember (9)
rappeur *m.* rap musician
rapport *m.* relation; **par rapport à** with respect to
rapporter to report; to bring in; to bring back
rarement *adv.* rarely (2)
raser: se raser to shave (9)
rassurer to reassure, comfort
ratatouille *f.* ratatouille
ravi(e) *adj.* thrilled (21)
ravissant(e) *adj.* beautiful, delightful
rayon *m.* department (*in a store*) (6)
réaction *f.* reaction
réagir to react
réalisateur/trice *m., f.* director
réalisme *adj.* realism
réaliste *adj.* realistic
réalité *f.* reality; **en réalité** in fact, actually
rébellion *f.* rebellion
récent(e) *adj.* recent
recette *f.* recipe (15)
recevoir (*p.p.* **reçu**) *irreg.* to receive (10)
réchauffer to reheat (15)
recherche *f.* research; **à la recherche de** in search of; **faire des recherches** to do research
rechercher to search for; to research (19)
récit *m.* narrative, story
récolte *f.* harvest, crop (18)
récolter to harvest (18)
recommander to recommend
récompense *f.* reward
réconforter to comfort
reconnaissance *f.* gratitude
reconnaître (*like* **connaître**) *irreg.* to recognize (13)
reconstituer to restore
recoucher: se recoucher to go back to bed
recueillir (*like* **cueillir**) *irreg.* to collect (16)
recyclable *adj.* recyclable
recyclage *m.* recycling (18)
recycler to recycle (18)
rédacteur/trice *m., f.* editor
rédaction *f.* composition; **salle** (*f.*) **de rédaction** editing room
rédiger (nous rédigeons) to write, compose
redoutable *adj.* fearsome
redresser to rebuild
réduire (*like* **conduire**) *irreg.* to reduce (18)
refait(e) *adj.* remade (*movie*)
référer: se référer (je me réfère) to refer (back) to
refermer to close again
réfléchi(e) *adj.* thoughtful
réfléchir à to reflect (on), think (about) (11)
refléter (je reflète) to reflect, mirror
réflexion *f.* reflection; thought
réfrigérateur (*fam.* **frigo**) *m.* refrigerator (fridge) (5)
réfugié(e) *m., f.* refugee
réfugier: se réfugier to take refuge (19)
refuser (de) to refuse (*to do s.th.*) (18)
regard *m.* look, glance
regarder to watch, look at (2); **cela (ne) vous regarde (pas)** that is (not) your problem; **regarder la télé** to watch TV
reggae *m.* reggae music (21)
régie *f.* control room (2)
régime *m.* regime; diet
région *f.* region
régional(e) *adj.* regional
régler (je règle) to resolve, settle
réglisse *m.* licorice
regret *m.* regret, remorse
regretter to regret, be sorry; **regretter que** to be sorry that (21)
régulier/ière *adj.* regular
rejoindre (*p.p.* **rejoint**) *irreg.* to join; to meet
relatif/ive *adj.* relative; **pronom** (*m.*) **relatif** *Gram.* relative pronoun
relation *f.* relationship
relativement *adv.* relatively
relief *m.* topography, relief (17)
religieux/euse *adj.* religious
religion *f.* religion
relire (*like* **lire**) *irreg.* to reread

remarquable *adj.* remarkable
remarque *f.* remark, comment
remarquer to notice
rembrunir: se rembrunir to become somber/disgruntled/darker; to cloud over
remède *m.* remedy, treatment, fix
remercier to thank
remettre: se remettre (*like* **mettre**) *irreg.* to recover
remonter to go back (up)
remplaçant(e) *m., f.* replacement
remplacer (nous remplaçons) to replace (13)
remplir to fill out (*a form*); **remplir les blancs** to fill in the blanks
renaissance: la Renaissance *f.* the Renaissance
rencontre *f.* meeting, encounter (21)
rencontrer to meet; to run into, encounter (14)
rendez-vous *m.* meeting; appointment
rendre to return (*s.th.*); to render, make (8); **rendre justice** (*f.*) **à** to do justice to; **rendre visite à** to visit (*s.o.*) (8); **se rendre à** to go to; **se rendre compte (de)** to realize (9)
renforcer (nous renforçons) to reinforce
rénovation *f.* renovation (20)
renseignements *m. pl.* information
rentrée *f.* back-to-school day
rentrer to come/go back (home) (11); **rentrer à la maison** to go home
renvoyer (je renvoie) to send back, return
répandre: se répandre to spread
repartir (*like* **partir**) *irreg.* to leave again
repas *m.* meal (8); **commander un repas** to order a meal
repère: point (*m.*) **de repère** landmark
repérer (je repère) to locate
répéter (je répète) to repeat (6)
répétition *f.* rehearsal
réplique *f.* response
répondeur *m.* answering machine
répondre to answer, respond (8)
réponse *f.* response
reportage *m.* report; **faire un reportage** to prepare/give a report (*TV*)
reporter *m.* reporter (2)
repos *m.* rest
reposé(e) *adj.* rested
reposer: se reposer to rest
reprendre (*like* **prendre**) *irreg.* to take up again, continue; to take more (*food*)
représailles *f. pl.* reprisals
représenter to represent
reproduire (*like* **conduire**) *irreg.* to reproduce
républicain(e) *m., f.* Republican
république *f.* republic
réputation *f.* reputation
réputé(e) *adj.* well known (20)
réseau *m.* network (14); system; **réseau du métro** subway system (14); **réseau informatique** computer network
réserver to reserve
résidence *f.* residence (13); **résidence universitaire** dormitory building (13)
résidentiel(le) *adj.* residential
résistance *f.* resistance
résistant(e) *m., f.* French Resistance fighter (19)
résister to resist
résoudre (*p.p.* **résolu**) *irreg.* to resolve
respecter to respect
respectif/ive *adj.* respective
respectueux/euse *adj.* respectful
respiration *f.* breathing
responsabilité *f.* responsibility
responsable *adj.* responsible
ressemblance *f.* resemblance
ressentir (*like* **dormir**) *irreg.* to feel
resservir (*like* **dormir**) *irreg.* to serve again (*food*)
ressource *f.* resource (13); **ressources naturelles** natural resources
restaurant (*fam.* **restau**) *m.* restaurant (3)
rester to stay (11)
résultat *m.* result
résulter (en) to result in
résumé *m.* summary
résumer to summarize
rétablir to reestablish
retard *m.* delay; **en retard** late (5)
retarder to slow; **retarder l'avance** to slow the advance (19)
retenir (*like* **tenir**) *irreg.* to keep
retour *m.* return; **être de retour** to be back
retourner to return; to turn around (11)
retraite *f.* retirement (12); **prendre sa retraite** to retire (12)
retraité(e) *m., f.* retiree (12)
rétroprojecteur *m.* overhead projector
retrouver to find (again); **se retrouver** to find oneself; to meet by prior arrangement
réunion *f.* meeting
réunir to gather together; **se réunir** to get together
réussir (à) to succeed (11); to pass (*a course or an exam*) (11)
rêve *m.* dream
réveiller to wake (*s.o.*); **se réveiller** to wake up (9)
réveillon *m.* Christmas Eve; New Year's Eve
révéler (je révèle) to reveal
revenir (*like* **venir**) *irreg.* to come back, return (3)
révision *f.* review
revoir (*like* **voir**) *irreg.* to see again (10); **au revoir** good-bye (P)
révolte *f.* revolt
révolution *f.* revolution
rez-de-chaussée *m.* ground floor (5)
rhubarbe *f.* rhubarb
rhume *m.* common cold (9)
riche *adj.* rich (22)
richesse *f.* wealth
ridicule *adj.* ridiculous (2)
ridiculiser to make fun of, mock
rien: ne... rien *indef. pron.* nothing (13); **plus rien** nothing more
ringard(e) *adj.* out-of-date
risque *m.* risk
risquer to risk
rivière *f.* small river (17)
riz *m.* rice (8)
robe *f.* dress (6)
rocher *m.* rock
rocheux/euse *adj.* rocky
rock *m.* rock music (21)
roi *m.* king; **palais** (*m.*) **du roi** king's palace
rôle *m.* role; **jeu** (*m.*) **de rôle** role play
roller *m.* roller skating (10); **faire du roller** to roller-skate
romain(e) *adj.* Roman
roman *m.* novel (21)
romancier/ière *m., f.* novelist (21)
romantique *adj.* romantic
rompre (*p.p.* **rompu**) *irreg.* to break
roquefort *m.* Roquefort cheese
rose *adj.* pink (6)
rosé(e) *adj.* rosy; **vin** (*m.*) **rosé** rosé wine
rôti *m.* roast; **rôti(e)** *adj.* roasted
rouge *adj.* red (6)
rougir to blush
rouler to travel (*in a car*); to roll (along)
route *f.* road, highway (14); **en route** on the way
routier/ière *adj.* pertaining to the road; **signalisation** (*f.*) **routière** road signs
routine *f.* routine
roux (rousse) *adj.* red (*hair color*) (4)
royal(e) *adj.* royal
rubrique *f.* section, column (*in a newspaper*) (12)
rue *f.* street; **dans la rue...** on . . . Street (3); **descendre une rue** to go down a street (17); **monter une rue** to go up a street (17); **rue piétonne** pedestrian street (20)
ruelle *f.* alleyway (20)
ruine *f.* ruin
rumeur *f.* rumor
rural(e) *adj.* rural
russe *adj.* Russian (15); **Russe** *m., f.* Russian (*person*)
Russie *f.* Russia (15)
rythme *m.* rhythm
rythmé(e) *adj.* rhythmic

sa *adj.* his, her, its, one's (4)
sac *m.* bag; **sac à dos** backpack (P); **sac à main** handbag
sacré(e) *adj.* sacred
sacrifice *m.* sacrifice
sage *adj.* well-behaved
saint(e) *m., f.* saint
saisir to seize; to grasp
saison *f.* season (10)
salade *f.* lettuce; salad (8); **salade verte** green salad
salaire *m.* salary (20)
salarié(e) *m., f.* full-time employee
sale *adj.* dirty
salle *f.* room; **salle à manger** dining room (5); **salle de bains** bathroom (5); **salle de classe** classroom (P); **salle de rédaction** editing room; **salle de séjour** living room (5)
saluer to greet
salut *interj.* hi; bye (P)
salutations *f.* greetings
samedi *m.* Saturday (4)
sandwich *m.* sandwich (8)
sans *prep.* without (2); **sans aucun doute** without a doubt; **sans domicile fixe** homeless; **sans doute** probably, no doubt (2); **sans intérêt** of no interest; **sans que** unless; without (21)
santé *f.* health (9)
satisfaisant(e) *adj.* satisfying
sauce *f.* sauce (8); **sauce de soja** soy sauce (15)
saucisse *f.* sausage link (7)
saucisson *m.* sausage
sauf *prep.* except
saumon *m.* salmon (7)
sauna *m.* sauna
sauter to jump
sauver to save
savoir (*p.p.* **su**) *irreg.* to know (*a fact*) (13); **je ne sais pas** I don't know (P); **je ne sais pas quoi faire** I don't know what to do
scandale *m.* scandal; **crier au scandale** to call it a scandal
scanner *m.* scanner
scénario *m.* script; scenario
scénariste *m., f.* screenwriter
scène *f.* scene (P); **metteur** (*m.*) **en scène** director (*theatrical*); **mise** (*f.*) **en scène** (*theatrical*) production
science *f.* science; **sciences naturelles** natural science (1)
scientifique *adj.* scientific
scoop *m.* scoop (*news*)
script *m.* script
scripte *f.* script coordinator
sculpteur (femme sculpteur) *m., f.* sculptor
sculpture *f.* sculpture
se (s') *pron.* oneself; himself; herself, itself, themselves; to oneself, etc.; each other
séance *f.* meeting; showing (*of a film*)
sec (sèche) *adj.* dry; **raisin** (*m.*) **sec** raisin (15)
sécher (je sèche) to dry; **sécher un cours** to cut a class (13)
sécheresse *f.* drought
séchoir *m.* dryer
secondaire *adj.* secondary; **enseignement** (*m.*) **secondaire** secondary school teaching (13)
seconde *f.* second (*sixtieth of a minute*); **second(e)** *adj.* second; **langue** (*f.*) **seconde** second/foreign language
secret *m.* secret
secrétaire *m., f.* secretary (11)
secrètement *adv.* secretly
sécurité *f.* security; **agent (e)** (*m., f.*) **de sécurité** security guard (11)
sédentaire *adj.* sedentary
séduire (*like* **conduire**) *irreg.* to seduce, charm
seize *adj.* sixteen (P)
séjour *m.* stay; trip; **salle** (*f.*) **de séjour** living room (5)
séjourner to stay (*in a place*)
sel *m.* salt (8)
self-sélect *m.* self-service restaurant
selon *prep.* according to (2); **selon le cas** depending on the case; **selon vous** in your opinion
semaine *f.* week (4); **par semaine** per week; **la semaine dernière (prochaine)** last (next) week
sembler to seem (13)
semer (je sème) to sow
semestre *m.* semester
sénégalais(e) *adj.* Senegalese; **Sénégalais(e)** *m., f.* Senegalese (*person*)
sens *m.* meaning
sentiment *m.* sentiment, emotion
sentimental(e) *adj.* sentimental
sentir (*like* **dormir**) *irreg.* to smell, to feel (8); **se sentir** to feel (*an emotion*)
séparer to separate
sept *adj.* seven (P)
septembre *m.* September (14)
septième *adj.* seventh (11)
série *f.* series (12)
sérieux/euse *adj.* serious
serre *f.* greenhouse; **effet** (*m.*) **de serre** greenhouse effect (18)
serré(e) *adj.* tight
serrure *f.* latch
serveur/euse *m., f.* waiter/waitress
serviable *adj.* willing (*to do s.th.*)
service *m.* service (13); department; **station** (*f.*) **service** service station
serviette *f.* napkin (8)
servir (*like* **dormir**) *irreg.* to serve (8); **s'en servir** to make use of it/them
ses *adj.* his, her, its, one's
sésame *m.* sesame; **huile** (*f.*) **de sésame** sesame oil (15)
seul(e) *adj.* alone; sole (14); **c'est pour cela seul** it's only for that reason
seulement *adv.* only (14)
sévère *adj.* severe
sexe *m.* sex
shopping *m.* shopping; **faire du shopping** to go shopping (5)
short *m.* shorts (6)
si *adv.* so (very); so much; yes (*response to negative question*); **si (s')** *conj.* if, whether (7); **s'il vous (te) plaît** *interj.* please
SIDA *m.* AIDS
siècle *m.* century (20); **au cours des siècles** through the centuries
siège *m.* seat (14); **siège couloir (fenêtre)** aisle (window) seat (14)
sien: le/la/les sien(ne)(s) *pron.* his, hers
signaleur *m.* signalman; **timonier** (*m.*) **signaleur** helmsman-signalman
signalisation *f.* signage; **signalisation routière** road signs
signe *m.* sign
signer to sign
signet *m.* bookmark (13)
signification *f.* significance
signifier to mean, signify
silence *f.* silence
silencieux/euse *adj.* silent
silencieusement *adv.* silently (19)
similaire *adj.* similar
similarité *f.* similarity
sincère *adj.* sincere
sincérité *f.* sincerity
singulier/ière *adj.* singular; *m., Gram.* singular (*form*)
sinon *prep.* if not, otherwise
sitcom *f.* situation comedy (12)
site *m.* site; **site touristique** tourist site (20); **site web** website (13)
situation *f.* situation; placement
situer to situate; **se situer** to be located
six *adj.* six (P)
sixième *adj.* sixth (11)
ska *m.* ska music (21)
skate *m.* skateboarding (10)
ski *m.* skiing; ski; **faire du ski** to go skiing (16); **faire du ski de fond (ski nautique)** to cross-country ski (waterski) (16)
skier to ski (16)
SMS *m.* Short Message Service, text messaging
snob *m.* snob
sociable *adj.* friendly
social(e) *adj.* social

socialiste *adj.* socialist
société *f.* company (11); society, organization
socio-économique *adj.* socioeconomic
sœur *f.* sister (4); **âme** (*f.*) **sœur** kindred spirit; **belle-sœur** *f.* sister-in-law, stepsister (4)
soi (soi-même) *pron.* oneself, herself, himself, itself (16); **sûr de soi** self-confident
soie *f.* silk
soif *f.* thirst; **avoir soif** to be thirsty (4)
soigner to take care of, nurse
soin *m.* care, treatment; **prenez soin de vous** take care of yourself; **soins médicaux** health care
soir *m.* evening (5); **ce soir** this evening (13); **du soir** in the evening (5)
soirée *f.* evening (21); party
soixante *adj.* sixty (4)
soixante-dix *adj.* seventy (4)
soja *m.* soy; **sauce** (*f.*) **de soja** soy sauce (15)
sol *m.* ground; **sous-sol** *m.* basement
soldat *m.* soldier (19)
solde *f.* sale; **en solde** on sale
soleil *m.* sun; **coup** (*m.*) **de soleil** sunburn; **il fait du soleil** it's sunny out (10); **lunettes** (*f. pl.*) **de soleil** sunglasses (6)
solitaire *adj.* solitary
solitude *f.* solitude
sombre *adj.* dark (22)
sommeil *m.* sleep; **avoir sommeil** to be sleepy
somptueux/euse *adj.* sumptuous
son *adj.* his, her, its, one's (4)
sondage *m.* survey
sonner to ring (*telephone, bell*)
sorte *f.* sort, type
sortie *f.* exit (14)
sortir (*like* **dormir**) *irreg.* to go out (8); **sortir avec** to go out with (*s.o.*)
soucier: se soucier de to care about
souci *m.* worry, concern
soudain *adv.* suddenly (19); **soudain(e)** *adj.* sudden (19)
souffle *m.* breath; **à bout de souffle** out of breath, breathless
souffrance *f.* suffering
souffrir (*like* **ouvrir**) *irreg.* to suffer (15)
souhaiter (que) to wish, hope (that) (21)
soumettre (*like* **mettre**) *irreg.* to hand in; to submit
soupe *f.* soup (8); **soupe à l'oignon** French onion soup; **soupe de poisson** fish soup
soupir *m.* sigh; **pousser des soupirs** to sigh
source *f.* source; **eau** (*f.*) **de source** spring water
sourd(e) *adj.* deaf; *m., f.* deaf person
sourire (*p.p.* **souri**) *irreg.* to smile
souris *f.* mouse; computer mouse (16)
sous *prep.* under (3); **sous clé** under lock and key; **sous-préfecture** *f.* subprefecture; **sous-sol** *m.* basement; **sous-titre** *m.* subtitle
souterrain(e) *adj.* underground
soutenir (*like* **tenir**) *irreg.* to support
soutien *m.* support
souvenir *m.* memory
souvenir: se souvenir (*like* **venir**) *irreg.* **de** to remember (9)
souvent *adv.* often (2)
spaghettis *m. pl.* spaghetti
spécial(e) *adj.* special
spécialisation *f.* (*educational*) major
spécialiser: se spécialiser en to major in
spécialiste *m., f.* specialist, expert
spécialité *f.* specialty
spectacle *m.* entertainment; show (21)
spectateur/trice *m., f.* spectator
splendide *adj.* splendid, wonderful
spontanéité *f.* spontaneity
sport *m.* sports; **faire du sport** to play sports; **fanatique** (*m., f.*) **de sport** sports fan (10); **sports d'hiver** winter sports; **voiture** (*f.*) **de sport** sportscar
sportif/ive *adj.* athletic (2); **centre** (*m.*) **sportif** sports center (3)
squatter to squat (*claim a residence*)
stabiliser: se stabiliser to become stable
stade *m.* stadium
stage *m.* internship (11); **faire un stage** to do an internship
standard *m.* standard
star *f.* star (*celebrity*)
station *f.* station; **station de radio** radio station (12); **station service** service station; **station thermale** spa, health resort
stationner to park (14)
statistique *f.* statistics
statuette *f.* statuette
statut *m.* status; statute
steak-frites *m.* steak with French fries
stéréo *adj.* stereo; **chaîne** (*f.*) **stéréo** stereo system (5)
stéréotype *m.* stereotype
stratégie *f.* strategy
stress *m.* stress
stressé(e) *adj.* stressed
structure *f.* structure
studio *m.* studio (P); studio apartment
stupéfait(e) *adj.* stupefied, dumbfounded
stupide *adj.* stupid
style *m.* style
stylo *m.* pen (P)
subjonctif *m., Gram.* subjunctive (*mood*)
substantif *m., Gram.* noun
subtilité *f.* subtlety
succès *m.* success
sucre *m.* sugar (7); **canne** (*f.*) **à sucre** sugarcane
sucré(e) *adj.* sweet (8)
sucrerie *f.* sweets
sud *m.* south (17); **sud-ouest** southwest
suffisamment *adv.* sufficiently
suffire (*p.p.* **suffi**) *irreg.* to suffice; **ça suffit** that's enough; **il suffit** it's enough (20)
suggérer (je suggère) to suggest
suicider: se suicider to commit suicide
suite *f.* outcome; **tout de suite** right away (10)
suivant(e) *adj.* following
suivre (*p.p.* **suivi**) *irreg.* to follow; to take (*a class*) (15)
sujet *m.* subject; **au sujet de** concerning
super *adj.* super, great (2)
supérieur(e) *adj.* superior; **enseignement** (*m.*) **supérieur** higher education
superlatif *m., Gram.* superlative
supermarché *m.* supermarket (3)
supplémentaire *adj.* supplementary, extra
supposer to suppose; **je suppose?** I suppose? (3)
supprimer to eliminate, abolish
sur *prep.* on, on top of (3); **donner sur** to overlook, have a view of (20); **sur Internet** on the Internet (11); **tirer sur** to fire on, shoot at (19)
sûr(e) *adj.* sure, certain (14); **bien sûr, bien sûr que oui (non)!** of course (not)! (2); **sûr de soi** self-confident
surconsommation *f.* overconsumption
surf (*m.*) **des neiges** snowboarding; **faire du surf des neiges** to snowboard (16)
surfer (le Web) to surf (the Web) (13)
surgelé(e) *adj.* frozen; **pizza** (*f.*) **surgelée** frozen pizza
surmonter to overcome
surnommer to name, call; to nickname
surprendre (*like* **prendre**) *irreg.* to surprise
surpris(e) *adj.* surprised (21)
surprise *f.* surprise
surtout *adv.* especially (16); above all; **surtout pas** definitely not
surveillé(e) *adj.* managed
survivre (*like* **vivre**) *irreg.* to survive (15)
sweatshirt (*fam.* **sweat**) *m.* sweatshirt (6)
symbole *m.* symbol
symboliser to symbolize
sympathie *f.* friendliness, liking
sympathique (*fam.* **sympa**) *adj.* nice (1)
symphonie *f.* symphony
symptôme *m.* symptom
synagogue *f.* synagogue
syndicat *m.* union

syntaxe *f.* syntax
synthèse *f.* synthesis
système *m.* system

ta *adj.* your (4)
table *f.* table (P); **à table** at the table; **mettre la table** to set the table (7)
tableau (*pl.* **tableaux**) *m.* blackboard (1); painting (*picture*) (21); **tableau d'affichage** bulletin board (11)
tâche *f.* task
tailleur *m.* woman's suit (6)
talent *m.* talent
talons (*m. pl.*) **aiguilles** stiletto heels
tant *adj.* so much; so many; **en tant qu'auteur** as author; **tant de spectateurs** so many spectators
tante *f.* aunt (4)
taper to type
tapis *m.* rug (5)
taquiner to tease
tard *adv.* late (3); **plus tard** later (10)
tarte *f.* pie (7); **tarte aux pommes** apple pie
tartine *f. bread with butter and jam* (8)
tasse *f.* cup (8)
taxi *m.* taxi
te (t') *pron., s., fam.* you; to/for you (7, 9); **combien te faut-il?** how much do you need?; **s'il te plaît** please
technicien(ne) *m., f.* technician
technique *adj.* technical
technologie *f.* technology; **haute technologie** high tech
technophobe *m., f.* technophobe (13)
tee-shirt *m.* T-shirt (6)
tel(le) *adj.* such; like (14); **tel(le) ou tel(le)** this or that; **tel que** like, such as
télé *fam.* TV (2)
téléphone *m.* telephone (5); **coup** (*m.*) **de téléphone** phone call; **téléphone portable** mobile (cell) phone (13)
téléphoner (à) to phone (*s.o.*) (7)
téléphonique *adj.* telephone; **annuaire** (*f.*) **téléphonique** phone book; **cabine** (*f.*) **téléphonique** phone booth (13); **ligne** (*f.*) **téléphonique** telephone line
télévisé(e) *adj.* televised
télévision (*fam.* **télé**) *f.* television set (5); (TV) (2); **mettre la télé** to turn on the TV (7); **regarder la télé** to watch TV
tellement *adv.* so (very), so much (14)
température *f.* temperature (10)
temps *m.* time (5); weather (10); *Gram.* tense; **à mi-temps** part-time (11); **à temps partiel** part-time; **beau temps** nice weather; **dans le temps** in the past; **de temps en temps** from time to time (12); **depuis combien de temps?** how long?; **il fait un temps splendide** it's a gorgeous day; **mettre du temps à** to spend time on (7); **prendre du temps** to take a long time (7); **quel temps fait-il?** what's the weather like? (10)
tenir (*p.p.* **tenu**) *irreg.* to hold (14); to keep; **je tiens à toi** I care about you; **tenir au courant** to stay up to date
tennis *m.* tennis (10)
tension *f.* tension
tente *f.* tent
tenue *f.* outfit
terme *m.* term
terminal(e) *adj.* terminal, final
terminer to finish; **c'est terminé?** are you finished?
terminus *m.* terminus, last stop (14)
terrain *m.* ground; **terrain de golf** golf course; **vélo** (*m.*) **tout terrain** (*fam.* **VTT**) mountain bike (16)
terre *f.* earth; soil; land (18); **à l'intérieur des terres** in the center of the country; **pomme** (*f.*) **de terre** potato (7); **par terre** to/on the ground
terrestre *adj.* earthly; **extraterrestre** *m., f.* extraterrestrial
terrible *adj.* terrible, awful
territoire *m.* territory; **territoire d'outre-mer (TOM)** overseas territory
tes *adj.* your
test *m.* test
tête *f.* head (9); **avoir mal à la tête** to have a headache; **perdre la tête** to lose one's mind (8)
têtu(e) *adj.* stubborn
texte *m.* text
texto *m. fam.* text message
TGV (train à grande vitesse) *m.* French high-speed train (14)
thaïlandais(e) *adj.* Thai; **Thaïlandais(e)** *m., f.* Thai (*person*)
thé *m.* tea (8); **thé à la menthe** mint tea
théâtre *m.* theater (10); **pièce** (*f.*) **de théâtre** play (21)
théière *f.* teapot
thème *m.* theme, subject
thérapeutique *adj.* therapeutic
thermal(e) *adj.* thermal; **bain** (*m.*) **thermal** spa bath (*hot spring water*); **station** (*f.*) **thermale** spa, health resort
thermalisme *m.* science of therapeutic baths
thèse *f.* thesis, dissertation (13); **thèse de doctorat** doctoral dissertation
thon *m.* tuna (7)
ticket (de métro) *m.* (subway) ticket (14)
tien: le/la/les tien(ne)(s) *pron.* yours
tiers *m.* third; **deux-tiers** two-thirds
tigre *m.* tiger
timbre *m.* stamp (13)
timonier-signaleur *m.* helmsman-signalman
tiré(e) *adj.* **de** taken from, excerpted from
tirer sur to fire on, shoot at (19)
tissu *m.* fabric
titre *m.* title; **gros titre** headline (12); **sous-titre** *m.* subtitle
tofu *m.* tofu
toi *pron., s., fam.* you (16); **et toi?** and you? (P)
toilette *f.*: **faire sa toilette** to wash up, get ready to go out; *pl.* restroom
tomate *f.* tomato (7)
tomber to fall (11); **ça tombe un mardi** that falls on a Tuesday; **tomber amoureux/euse** to fall in love; **tomber malade** to fall ill (9)
tomme *f. type of regional cheese*
ton *adj.* your (4)
ton *m.* tone
tonalité *f.* dial tone (13)
torse *m.* torso
tort *m.* wrong; **avoir tort** to be wrong, to be mistaken
torture *f.* torture
tôt *adv.* early (3); **de plus en plus tôt** earlier and earlier
totalitaire *adj.* totalitarian
touché(e) *adj.* touched; moved
toucher to touch; **toucher un chèque** to cash a check (20)
toujours *adv.* always (2, 3); still (10); **est-ce qu'il vit toujours?** is he still living?
tour *f.* tower; *m.* walk; turn; **c'était mon tour** it was my turn
tourisme *m.* tourism; **faire du tourisme** to go sightseeing
touriste *m., f.* tourist
touristique *adj.* tourist; **site** (*m.*) **touristique** tourist site (20)
tourmenté(e) *adj.* tormented
tournage *m.* filming
tourner to turn (17); to film (*a movie*); **tournez (tourne) à droite** turn right
Toussaint *f.* All Saints' Day (11)
tousser to cough (9)
tout(e) (*pl.* **tous, toutes**) *adj., indef. pron.* all, every (one), the whole (4); very; **à toute heure** at any time; **à tout prix** at all costs; **ne... pas du tout** not at all, absolutely not (1); **tous les jours** every day (12); **tous les lundis** every (each) Monday (4); **tout à coup** suddenly; **tout à fait** completely; **tout de suite** right away (3); **tout droit** straight ahead (17); **tout heureux/euse** very happy; **toute la**

journée all day; **toute une semaine** a whole week (4) **tout le monde** everyone (1); **tout le printemps** all spring (4)
trace *f.* trace
traditionnel(le) *adj.* traditional
traduction *f.* translation (13)
traduire (*like* **conduire**) *irreg.* to translate (18)
tragédie *f.* tragedy
tragique *adj.* tragic
trahir to betray
trahison *f.* treason (19)
train *m.* train (14); **en train** by train; **être en train de** to be in the process of; **par train** by train; **train à grande vitesse** (*fam.* **TGV**) French high-speed train (14)
traîner: se traîner to move slowly, with difficulty; to crawl
trait *m.* trait, feature; **trait d'union** hyphen
traitement *m.* treatment
traiter to treat, behave toward
traître/tresse *m., f.* traitor (14)
trajet *m.* journey (14)
tramway *m.* tramway, trolley car
tranquille *adj.* calm, peaceful
tranquillité *f.* calm, tranquillity
transformer to change, transform
transport *m.* transportation; **moyen** (*m.*) **de transport** means of transportation; **transport express régional** regional express train
travail *m.* work; job (2); **au travail** at work; **fête** (*f.*) **du Travail** Labor Day (11); **monde** (*m.*) **du travail** work world
travailler to work (2)
travailleur/euse *adj.* hardworking
travers: à travers *prep.* through
traverser to cross (17)
treize *adj.* thirteen (P)
tréma *m.* umlaut (ë)
trente *adj.* thirty (P)
très *adv.* very (P); **très bien** very well (P)
tricot *m.* knitting; **faire du tricot** to knit
tricoter to knit
trilogie *f.* trilogy
trimestre *m.* trimester
triomphe *f.* triumph
triste *adj.* sad (2)
trivial(e) *adj.* commonplace
trois *adj.* three (P)
troisième *adj.* third (11); **au/du troisième âge** elderly, in old age (12)
tromper to deceive, trick; **se tromper** to make a mistake, be mistaken (9)
trop (de) *adv.* too much (of), too many (of) (7); **trop tard** too late
tropical(e) *adj.* tropical
troublant(e) *adj.* troubling
troupe *f.* group; troop (19)
troupeau *m.* herd; flock
trouver to find; to consider (2); **où se trouve... ?** where is . . . ? (3); **se trouver** to be located (situated; found)
tu *pron.* you (1)
tuer to kill (19)
tunisien(ne) *adj.* Tunisian; **Tunisien(ne)** *m., f.* Tunisian (*person*)
turc (turque) *adj.* Turkish; **Turc (Turque)** *m., f.* Turk (*person*)
type *m.* type, kind; *fam.* guy
typique *adj.* typical

un(e) (*pl.* **des**) *indef. art.* a, an (P); *inv. adj.* one (P); *pron.* one; **à la une** on the front page (12); **les uns avec les autres** with each other; **un peu (de)** a little (of) (7)
uni(e) *adj.* united
unième: vingt et unième *adj.* twenty-first
uniforme *m.* uniform
union *f.* union; **ils vivent en union libre** they're living together (without marriage) (4); **trait** (*m.*) **d'union** hyphen
unique *adj.* sole, only; **fils** (*m.*) **unique** only son
unir to unite
univers *m.* universe
universitaire *adj.* (*of or belonging to the*) university; **cité** (*f.*) **universitaire** dormitory; **journal** (*m.*) **universitaire** college newspaper; **résidence** (*f.*) **universitaire** dormitory building (13)
université *f.* university (P)
urbain(e) *adj.* urban; **vie** (*f.*) **urbaine** city life (10)
urinaire *adj.* urinary
usage *m.* use; *Gram.* usage
utile *adj.* useful (20)
utilisation *f.* use
utiliser to use

vacances *f. pl.* vacation (16); **grandes vacances** summer vacation; **partir en vacances** to go on vacation (16); **pendant les vacances** during vacation; **vacances de Noël** Christmas vacation
vache *f.* cow (18)
vachement *adv., fam.* very, tremendously
vague *f.* wave; **Nouvelle Vague** New Wave (*films*)
vaisselle *f.* dishes; **faire la vaisselle** to do the dishes (5); **lave-vaisselle** *f.* dishwasher
valeur *f.* value
valise *f.* suitcase (14); **enregistrer une valise** to check a suitcase (14)
vallée *f.* valley (17)
valse *f.* waltz
vapeur *f.* steam; **faire cuire à la vapeur** to steam (*food*) (15)
varié(e) *adj.* varied, diverse
varier to vary
variété *f.* variety show
vaste *adj.* vast
veau *m.* veal (8); calf; **daube** (*f.*) **de veau** veal stew
vedette *f.* star (*of a show, movie*) (20)
végétarien(ne) *adj.* vegetarian
véhicule *m.* vehicle
vélo *m.* bicycle (5); **faire du vélo (du VTT)** to bike (mountain bike) (16); **vélo tout terrain (VTT)** mountain bike (16)
vendeur/euse *m., f.* sales clerk (6)
vendre to sell (8)
vendredi *m.* Friday (4)
venir (*p.p.* **venu**) *irreg.* to come (3); **venir de** + *inf.* to have just (*done s.th.*) (4)
vent *m.* wind; **il fait du vent** it's windy (10)
ventre *m.* belly (9); stomach; **avoir mal au ventre** to have a stomachache
verbe *m.* verb; **verbe pronominal** *Gram.* pronominal (reflexive) verb
verger *m.* orchard (18)
vérifier to check; to verify
vérité *f.* truth
vernissage *m.* opening; preview (21)
verre *m.* glass (8); **prendre un verre** to have a drink (7); **verre d'eau** glass of water
verrouillé(e) *adj.* locked
vers *prep.* toward; to (17)
verser to pour (15)
version *f.* version; **version originale** original-language version, not dubbed (*film*); **version française** French-language version (*film*)
vert(e) *adj.* green (6); **citron** (*m.*) **vert** lime; ***haricots** (*m. pl.*) **verts** green beans (7); **oignon** (*m.*) **vert** green onion; **salade** (*f.*) **verte** green salad
vertébré *m.* vertebrate
veste *f.* sports coat (6)
vêtement *m.* piece of clothing (6); *pl.* clothes; **mettre un vêtement** to put on a piece of clothing (7)
veuf (veuve) *adj.* widowed (4)
viande *f.* meat (7)
vice-versa *adv.* vice versa
victime *f.* victim (*male or female*)
victoire *f.* victory
vide *adj.* empty
vidéo *f.* videotape; *adj.* video
vidéotex *adj.* on-screen text
vie *f.* life (10); **étape** (*f.*) **de la vie** stage of life; **vie privée** private life; **vie urbaine** city life (10)
vieillesse *f.* old age (12)

Viêtnam *m.* Vietnam (3)
vietnamien(ne) *adj.* Vietnamese (3); **Vietnamien(ne)** *m., f.* Vietnamese (*person*)
vieux (vieil, vieille [*pl.* **vieux, vieilles**]) *adj.* old (2); *m., f.* old man, old woman; *m. pl.* the elderly
vif (vive) *adj.* lively; spirited; intense
vigne *f.* vine (18)
vignoble *m.* vineyard (18)
vilain *m.* brutish peasant
villa *f.* single-family house; villa
village *m.* village (18)
ville *f.* city (10); **centre-ville** *m.* downtown; **en ville** in the city; **ville natale** birthplace
vin *m.* wine (7); **vin pétillant** sparkling wine; **vin rouge (blanc, rosé)** red (white, rosé) wine (7)
vingt *adj.* twenty (P); **vingt et un (vingt-deux,** etc.) twenty-one (twenty-two, etc.); **vingt et unième** twenty-first (11)
vingtième *adj.* twentieth (11)
violence *f.* violence
violent(e) *adj.* violent
violet(te) *adj.* purple (6)
violoniste *m., f.* violinist
virgule *m.* comma
vis-à-vis *prep.* with respect to
visa *m.* visa (14)
visage *m.* face (9)
visionnement *m.* viewing
visionner to watch, view
visite *f.* visit; **rendre visite à** to visit (*s.o.*) (8)
visiter to visit (*a place*) (8)
visiteur/euse *m., f.* visitor
vite *adv.* fast, quickly (14)
vitesse *f.* speed; **limite** (*f.*) **de vitesse** speed limit; **train** (*m.*) **à grande vitesse (TGV)** French high-speed train
viticulture *f.* wine growing (18)
vitre *f.* pane of glass; windowpane
vivant(e) *adj.* alive, living
vivre (*p.p.* **vécu**) *irreg.* to live, be alive (15); **est-ce qu'il vit toujours?** is he still living?; **joie** (*f.*) **de vivre** joy in living (20); **ils vivent en union libre** they're living together (without marriage) (4)
vocabulaire *m.* vocabulary
vœu (*pl.* **vœux**) m. wish; **meilleurs vœux** best wishes
voici *prep.* here is/are (1)
voie *f.* road, lane; **voie de chemin de fer** railroad tracks (19)
voilà *prep.* there is/are, here is/are (*for pointing out*) (1)
voile *f.* sail; **bateau** (*m.*) **à voile** sailboat (16); **faire de la planche à voile** to windsurf (16); **faire de la voile** to sail (16)
voir (*p.p.* **vu**) *irreg.* to see (10)
voisin(e) *m., f.* neighbor (22)
voiture *f.* car (5); **voiture de sport** sportscar
voix *f.* voice; **à haute voix** aloud
vol *m.* flight (14)
volaille *f.* poultry; group of chickens (18)
volcanique *adj.* volcanic
volley-ball *m.* volleyball (10)
volonté *f.* will
volontiers *adv.* willingly, gladly
vos *adj.* your
vote *m.* vote
voter to vote
votre *adj.* your (4)
vôtre: le/la/les vôtre(s) *pron.* yours
vouloir (*p.p.* **voulu**) *irreg.* to want (6); **je voudrais** I would like (6); **vouloir bien** to be glad, to be willing (*to do s.th.*) (6); **vouloir dire** to mean (6)
vous *pron.* you; to/for you (1, 7, 9, 16); **comment allez-vous?** how are you? (P); **et vous?** and you? (P); **quel âge avez-vous?** how old are you? (4)
voyage *m.* trip; **agence** (*f.*) **de voyages** travel agency; **faire un voyage** to take a trip (5); **partir en voyage** to go on a trip; **voyage de noces** honeymoon
voyager (nous voyageons) to take a trip, travel (6)
voyageur/euse *m., f.* traveler
voyelle *f.* vowel
vrai(e) *adj.* true (2); **c'est vrai** that's true (2); **vrai ou faux?** true or false?
vraiment *adv.* truly
VTT (vélo tout terrain) *m.* mountain bike (16)
vue *f.* view; panorama; **point** (*m.*) **de vue** point of view

wagon *m.* (train) car (14); **wagon fumeurs (non-fumeurs)** smoking (nonsmoking) train car (14)
Web *m.* World Wide Web; **site** (*m.*) **Web** website (13); **sur le Web** on the Web; **surfer le Web** to surf the Web (13); **webmestre** *m.* webmaster
week-end *m.* weekend (4); **passer le week-end** to spend the weekend
world music *f.* world music (21)

y *pron.* there, to/about it/them (15); **il y a** there is / there are (*for counting*) (P); **il y a (dix ans)** (ten years) ago (10)
yaourt *m.* yogurt (15)
yeux (*pl. of* **œil**) *m. pl.* eyes (9); **avoir les yeux marron (noisette, bleus)** to have brown (hazel, blue) eyes (4); **les yeux bandés** blindfolded
yoga *m.* yoga

zéro *m.* zero (P)
zone *f.* zone; **zone libre** free zone
zoo *m.* zoo
zut! *interj.* rats!

Lexique anglais-français

This English-French end vocabulary contains the words in the active vocabulary lists of all chapters. See the introduction to the *Lexique français-anglais* for a list of abbreviations used.

abdomen ventre *m.* (9)
able: to be able pouvoir *irreg.* (6)
above au-dessus de (3)
absolute absolu(e) (14)
absolutely: absolutely not ne... pas du tout (1)
accept accepter (de) (18)
according to selon (2)
account: bank account compte *m.* en banque (20)
accountant comptable *m., f.* (11)
accurate exact(e) (14)
accuse accuser (19)
ache: douleur *f.* (9); **to have an ache in** avoir (*irreg.*) mal à (9)
acquaintance: to make the acquaintance of faire (*irreg.*) la connaissance de (5)
active actif/ive (2)
actor acteur/trice *m., f.* (P)
ad: classified ad petite annonce *f.* (11)
add ajouter (15)
adolescence adolescence *f.* (12)
adolescent adolescent(e) (*fam.* ado) *m., f.* (12)
adore adorer (2)
adult adulte *m., f.* (12)
advertisement publicité *f.* (12)
afraid: to be afraid of avoir (*irreg.*) peur de (4)
Africa Afrique *f.* (14)
after après (8); après que (21)
afternoon après-midi *m., f.* (5); **in the afternoon** de l'après-midi (5); **this afternoon** cet après-midi (13)
again encore (3)
age âge (*m.*); **in old age** au/du troisième âge (12); **old age** vieillesse *f.* (12)
ago: ten years ago il y a dix ans (10)
agree: I (don't) agree je (ne) suis (pas) d'accord (2)
agriculture agriculture *f.* (18)
airplane avion *m.* (14)
airport aéroport *m.* (14)
aisle seat siège (*m.*) couloir (14)
Algeria Algérie *f.* (3)
Algerian *adj.* algérien(ne) (3)
alive: to be alive vivre (15)
all tout, toute, tous, toutes (4); **all it takes is** il suffit de (20); **All Saints' Day** Toussaint *f.* (11); **all spring** tout le printemps (4)
alleyway ruelle *f.* (20)
allow permettre *irreg.* (7); laisser (13); **to be allowed** pouvoir (6)
almost presque (18)
alone seul(e) (14)
already déjà (10)
also aussi (P)
although bien que (21)
always toujours (2, 3)
amazing étonnant(e) (22)
American *adj.* américain(e) (3); **American football** football (*m.*) américain (10)
amount (*of check or sale*) montant *m.* (20)
amusing amusant(e) (2)
and et (P); **and you?** et vous (toi)? (P)
angry fâché(e) (2); **to get angry** se fâcher (9)
animal animal *m.* (*pl.* animaux) (16); **animal breeding** élevage *m.* (18)
animated cartoon dessin (*m.*) animé (12)
anniversary (*wedding*) anniversaire (*m.*) de mariage (11)
answer *v.* répondre (8)
Antarctica Antarctique *m.* (14)
antique dealer antiquaire *m., f.* (20)
anxious inquiet (inquiète) (2)
any *pron.* en (15); **there is/are not any** il n'y en a pas (de) (4)
apartment appartement *m.* (5); **apartment building** immeuble *m.* (5)
apparent apparent(e) (14)
appear apparaître *irreg.* (13); paraître *irreg.* (13)
applaud applaudir (11)
apple pomme *f.* (7)
April avril *m.* (4)
Arab *adj.* arabe (22); **old portion of an Arab city** médina *f.* (22)
argue se disputer (9)
arm bras *m.* (9); (*weapon*) arme *f.* (19)
armchair fauteuil *m.* (5)
armoire armoire *f.* (5)
arrival arrivée *f.* (14)
arrive arriver (11)
artisan artisan(e) *m., f.* (11)
as comme (8); **as . . . as** aussi... que (16); **as many/much (. . .) as** autant (de...) que (16)
ashamed: to be ashamed (of) avoir (*irreg.*) honte (de) (4)
Asia Asie *f.* (14)
ask demander (7)
asleep: to fall asleep s'endormir *irreg.* (9)
aspirin aspirine *f.* (9)
astonished: to be astonished that être (*irreg.*) étonné(e) que (21)
at à (1); **at . . . o'clock** à... heure(s) (5); **at first** d'abord (10); **at last** enfin (10); **at the home (business) of** chez (3); **at what time?** à quelle heure? (5)
athletic sportif/ive (2)
attack *v.* attaquer (19)
attend (*an event*) assister à (10)
attention: to pay attention faire (*irreg.*) attention (5)
August août *m.* (4)
aunt tante *f.* (4)
Australia Australie *f.* (14)
author auteur / femme auteur *m., f.* (21)
automobile voiture *f.* (5)
autoroute autoroute *f.* (14)
autumn automne *m.* (10); **in autumn** en automne (10)
average *adj.* moyen(ne) (18)
away from à l'écart de (22)

baby bébé *m.* (12)
babysitter baby-sitter *m., f.* (11)
back dos *m.* (9); **to go back home** rentrer (11); **in back of** derrière (3)
backpack sac à dos *m.* (P)
bad mauvais(e) (2); **it's bad weather** il fait mauvais (10); **it is too bad that** il est dommage que (21)
badly mal (9)
bake faire (*irreg.*) cuire au four (15)
baker (*of bread*) boulanger/ère *m., f.* (7); **pastry** chef patissier/ière *m., f.* (7)
bakery (*for bread*) boulangerie *f.* (7)
ball (*inflated with air*) ballon *m.* (16); (*not inflated with air*) balle *f.* (16)

bank banque *f.* (20); **bank account** compte (*m.*) en banque (20); **bank (debit) card** carte (*f.*) bancaire (6)
banks: on the banks of au bord de (17)
bar bar *m.* (11)
barn grange *f.* (18)
baseball base-ball *m.* (10)
basin bassin *m.* (17); **bathroom basin** lavabo *m.* (5)
basket panier *m.* (16)
bathing suit maillot (*m.*) de bain (6)
bathroom salle (*f.*) de bains (5); **bathroom basin** lavabo *m.* (5)
bay baie *f.* (17)
be être *irreg.* (1); **there is/are** (*counting*) il y a (P); **there is/are, here is/are** (*pointing out*) voilà (1); **these/those/they are (not)** ce (ne) sont (pas) (P); **to be alive** (*to live*) vivre (15); **to be mistaken (about)** se tromper (de) (9); **to be named** s'appeler (9); **to be (twenty) years old** avoir (vingt) ans (4)
beach plage *f.* (16)
beans: green beans haricots (*m. pl.*) verts (7)
bear ours *m.* (16)
beautiful beau (bel, belle, beaux, belles) (2)
because parce que (4)
become devenir *irreg.* (3); **to become angry (with)** se fâcher (contre) (9); **to become sick** tomber malade (9)
bed lit *m.* (5); **to go to bed** se coucher (9); **to make the bed** faire (*irreg.*) le lit (5)
bedroom chambre *f.* (5)
beef bœuf *m.* (7)
beet betterave *f.* (15)
before avant (8); avant de (21); avant que (21); **before** (*the hour*) moins (5)
begin commencer (6)
behaved: well-behaved gentil(le) (2)
behind derrière (3)
believe croire *irreg.* (10)
belly ventre *m.* (9)
belong to appartenir (*irreg.*) à (14)
below au-dessous de (3)
belt ceinture *f.* (6)
Berber berbère (22)
beside à côté de (3)
best: the best *adj.* le/la/les meilleur(e)(s) (16); *adv.* le mieux (16)
better *adj.* meilleur(e) (16); *adv.* mieux (16)
between entre (3)
bicycle vélo *m.* (5); **to go bicycling (to bike)** faire (*irreg.*) du vélo (16); **to mountain bike** faire (*irreg.*) du VTT (16)
big grand(e) (2)
billiards billard *m.* (10)
billion milliard *m.* (4)
biochemistry biochimie *f.* (13)
biology biologie *f.* (13)
bird oiseau *m.* (16)
birth naissance *f.* (12)
birthday anniversaire *m.* (4)
black noir(e) (4, 6)
blackboard tableau *m.* (*pl.* tableaux) (1); **blackboard eraser** éponge *f.* (1)
blond blond(e) (4)
blouse chemisier *m.* (6)
blue bleu(e) (4, 6); **blues** (*music*) blues *m.* (21)
board: blackboard tableau *m.* (*pl.* tableaux) (1); **bulletin board** tableau d'affichage (11)
boat bateau *m.* (16); **sailboat** bateau à voile (16)
body corps *m.* (9); **body of work** œuvre *f.* (21)
boil faire (*irreg.*) bouillir (15)
book livre *m.* (P)
bookmark signet *m.* (13)
bookstore librairie *f.* (3)
boot botte *f.* (6)
booth: telephone booth cabine (*f.*) téléphonique (13)
boring ennuyeux/euse (2)
born: to be born naître *irreg.* (11)
boss patron(ne) *m., f.* (11)
bottle bouteille *f.* (7)
bowling bowling *m.* (10)
box boîte *f.* (7)
boy garçon *m.* (12)
brain cerveau *m.* (9)
bread pain *m.* (7); **bread roll** petit pain *m.* (8); **bread with butter and jam** tartine *f.* (8)
break (*a limb*) se casser (9)
breakfast petit déjeuner *m.* (8)
breeding: animal breeding (*farming*) l'élevage *m.* (18)
bridge pont *m.* (19)
brother frère *m.* (4); **brother-in-law, stepbrother** beau-frère *m.* (*pl.* beaux-frères) (4)
brown brun(e) (6); (*hair color*) châtain *inv.* (4); **chestnut brown** marron *inv.* (4, 6)
brush (one's teeth, hair) se brosser (les dents, les cheveux) (9)
buffet buffet *m.* (5)
building bâtiment *m.* (3); **apartment building** immeuble *m.* (5) **building superintendent** gardien(ne) (*m., f.*) d'immeuble (11)
bulletin board tableau (*m.*) d'affichage (11)
burial enterrement *m.* (12)
bus: short distance, city bus bus *m.* (14); **long distance, tour bus** autocar *m.* (14)
business affaires *f. pl.* (11); **at the business of** chez (3); **business administration** administration (*f.*) des affaires (13); **business economics** économie (*f.*) de gestion (13)
but mais (2)
butcher boucher/ère *m., f.* (7); **butcher shop** boucherie *f.* (7)
butter beurre *m.* (7)
buy *v.* acheter (6)
by par (6)
'bye salut (P)

café café *m.* (3)
calculator calculatrice *f.* (P)
call *v.* appeler (6)
camera appareil photo *m.* (5)
campground camping *m.* (16)
camping: to go camping faire (*irreg.*) du camping (16)
can (to be able) pouvoir *irreg.* (6)
can (*container*) boîte *f.* (7)
Canada Canada *m.* (3)
Canadian *adj.* canadien(ne) (3)
canoeing: to go canoeing faire (*irreg.*) du canoë (16)
car voiture *f.* (5); **train car** wagon *m.* (14)
carbonated *adj.* gazeux/euse (7)
card carte *f.* (6); **credit card** carte de crédit (6); **bank (debit) card** carte bancaire (6)
cardamom cardamome *m.* (15)
carrot carotte *f.* (7)
cartoon: animated cartoon dessin (*m.*) animé (12)
case: in that case alors (1)
cash: in cash en espèces (6); **to cash a check** toucher un chèque (20)
cat chat *m.* (16)
CD player lecteur (*m.*) de CD (5)
celebration fête *f.* (11)
cell phone mobile *m.*; portable *m.* (5)
century siècle *m.* (20)
certain certain(e) (21); sûr(e) (14)
chair chaise *f.* (1)
chalk craie *f.* (1)
champagne champagne *m.* (7)
change *v.* changer (6)
character (*in a story*) personnage *m.* (P)
check chèque *m.* (6); **to cash a check** toucher un chèque (20); **to check a suitcase** enregistrer une valise (14); **to deposit a check** déposer un chèque (20); **to write a check** faire (*irreg.*) un chèque (20)
checkbook carnet (*m.*) de chèques (20)
checkout caisse *f.* (6)
cheese fromage *m.* (7)
chemistry chimie *f.* (13)
cherry cerise *f.* (7)
chest poitrine *f.* (9)
chestnut brown marron *inv.* (4, 6)
chicken poulet *m.* (7); **chicken with French fries** poulet-frites *m.* (8); **group of chickens** volaille *f.* (18)
chick peas pois (*m. pl.*) chiches (15)

child enfant *m., f.* (1)
childhood enfance *f.* (12)
chimney cheminée *f.* (18)
China Chine *f.* (3)
Chinese chinois(e) *adj.* (3)
chocolate chocolat *m.* (8); **chocolate mousse** mousse (*f.*) au chocolat (8)
choose choisir (11)
Christmas Noël *m.* (11)
church église *f.* (17)
cinnamon cannelle *f.* (15)
circus cirque *m.* (10)
city ville *f.* (10); **city life** vie (*f.*) urbaine (10); **old portion of an Arab city** médina *f.* (22)
civil servant fonctionnaire *m., f.* (11)
class classe *f.* (P); **to cut a class** sécher un cours (13)
classified ad petite annonce *f.* (11)
classmate camarade (*m., f.*) de classe (P)
classroom salle (*f.*) de classe (P)
clear clair(e) (10); **the sky is clear** le ciel est clair (10)
click (on) cliquer (sur) (13)
client client(e) *m., f.* (6)
climb *v.* monter (11)
clock horloge *f.* (1)
close *v.* fermer (15)
clothing (*article*) vêtement *m.* (6); **to put on a piece of clothing** mettre (*irreg.*) un vêtement (7)
cloudy nuageux/euse (10); **the sky is cloudy** le ciel est couvert (10)
coast côte *f.* (17)
coat: overcoat manteau (*m.*) (6); **sport coat** veste *f.* (6)
Coca Cola coca *m.* (8)
coconut noix (*f.*) de coco (15)
coffee café *m.* (8); **coffee with an equal amount of milk** café au lait (8)
cold: to be cold avoir (*irreg.*) froid (4); **it's cold out** il fait froid (10); **common cold** rhume *m.* (9)
column (*newspaper*) rubrique *f.* (12); **society column** carnet (*m.*) du jour (12)
comb (one's hair) se peigner (les cheveux) (9)
come venir *irreg.* (3); **to come back** revenir *irreg.* (3), rentrer (11); **to come home** rentrer (11)
comic strip bande (*f.*) dessinée (12)
commerce commerce *m.* (11)
commercial publicité *f.* (12)
company société *f.* (11)
compose composer (13)
composer compositeur/trice *m., f.* (21)
composition (*literary, artwork, musical*) œuvre *m.* (21)
computer ordinateur *m.* (1); **computer mouse** souris *f.* (16); **computer science** informatique *f.* (1); **laptop computer** portable *m.* (5)
concert concert *m.* (21)
conservation conservation *f.* (18)
consider (*s.o., s.th.*) **to be** trouver (2)
construct *v.* construire *irreg.* (18)
consume consommer (18)
consumption consommation *f.* (18)
contain contenir *irreg.* (14)
contemporary contemporain(e) (21)
continue continuer (18)
contract contrat *m.* (20)
control room régie *f.* (2)
cook cuisinier/ière *m., f.* (11); **to cook** (*s.th.*) faire (*irreg.*) cuire (15) **to cook (make) a meal** faire (*irreg.*) la cuisine (5)
cooking pot (*large, iron*) marmite *f.* (18)
cool: it's cool out il fait frais (10)
coriander coriandre *f.* (15)
corn maïs *m.* (7)
corner coin *m.* (17)
cough *v.* tousser (9); **cough drop** pastille *f.* (9)
could you show me the way to . . . ? est-ce que vous pourriez m'indiquer le chemin pour aller à... ? (17)
country pays *m.* (3); **country music** country *f.* (21); **in the country** à la campagne (17)
course cours *m.* (1); **first course** (*meal*) entrée *f.* (8); **of course** bien sûr (que oui) (2); **of course not** bien sûr que non (2); **to fail a course** échouer à un cours (13); **to pass a course** réussir à un cours (11); **to take a course** suivre un cours (15); **What courses are you taking?** Quels cours est-ce que tu suis? (13)
couscous couscous *m.* (15); **couscous grains** grains (*m. pl.*) de couscous (15)
cousin cousin(e) *m., f.* (4)
cover *v.* couvrir *irreg.* (15)
cow vache *f.* (18)
craftsperson artisan(e) *m., f.* (11)
crazy fou (folle) (14)
cream crème *f.* (7)
credit: credit card carte (*f.*) de crédit (6); **credit union** caisse (*f.*) populaire (13)
croissant croissant *m.* (8)
crop récolte *f.* (18)
cross *v.* traverser (17)
cross-country: to cross-country ski faire (*irreg.*) du ski de fond (16)
crossword puzzle mots (*m. pl.*) croisés (12)
cultivate cultiver (18)
cup tasse *f.* (8)
curator (of a museum) conservateur/trice *m., f.* (de musée) (11)
current *adj.* actuel(le) (14)
curry curry *m.* (15)
customs douane *f.* (14); **to go through customs** passer la douane (14)

dairy product store crémerie *f.* (7); **dairyman (woman)** crémier/ière *m., f.* (7)
dark *adj.* sombre (22)
daughter fille *f.* (4)
day jour *m.* (1)
dear cher (chère) (2)
death mort *f.* (12)
December décembre *m.* (4)
decide (to do) décider (de) (18)
decision: to make a decision prendre (*irreg.*) une décision (7)
deer cerf *m.* (16)
delicatessen charcuterie *f.* (7)
demand *v.* exiger (20)
demonstration (*public, political*) manifestation *f.* (21)
department (*in a store*) rayon *m.* (6); **department store** grand magasin *m.* (6)
departure départ *m.* (14)
deposit *v.*: **deposit a check** déposer un chèque (20)
descend descendre (8)
describe décrire *irreg.* (12)
desire *v.* désirer (2)
desk bureau *m.* (*pl.* bureaux) (1)
dessert dessert *m.* (8)
destroy détruire *irreg.* (18)
detest détester (2)
dial (a phone number) composer un numéro (13); **dial tone** tonalité *f.* (13)
dictionary dictionnaire *m.* (P)
die *v.* mourir *irreg.* (11)
difficult difficile (2)
dignity: with dignity dignement (22)
dilapidated délabré(e) (20)
dine dîner (2)
dining room salle (*f.*) à manger (5)
dinner dîner *m.* (8); **to eat dinner** dîner (2)
diploma diplôme *m.* (13)
direction direction *f.* (14)
disappear disparaître *irreg.* (13)
discover découvrir *irreg.* (15)
discreet discret/ète (14)
discuss discuter (13)
dish: hot dish plat (*m.*) chaud; **main dish** plat (*m.*) principal (8); **to do the dishes** faire (*irreg.*) la vaisselle (5)
dissertation thèse *m.* (13)
district arrondissement *m.* (20)
divorce *v.* **(to get divorced)** divorcer (12); **divorced** divorcé(e) (4)
do faire *irreg.* (5); **to do errands** faire les courses (5); **to do homework** faire les devoirs (5); **to do housework** faire le ménage (5); **to do the dishes** faire la vaisselle (5); **to do the laundry** faire la lessive (5)

doctor médecin / femme médecin *m., f.* (9)
doctorate doctorat *m.* (13)
documentary documentaire *m.* (12)
dog chien *m.* (16)
door porte *f.* (1)
doubt *v.* douter (21); **it is doubtful that** il est douteux que (21); **no doubt** sans doute (2)
down: to get/go down descendre (8); **to go down a street** descendre une rue (17)
dozen douzaine *f.* (7)
dramatic arts arts (*m. pl.*) dramatiques (13)
dress robe *f.* (6); **to get dressed (in)** s'habiller (en) (9)
dresser commode *m.*
drink boisson *f.* (8); **to drink** boire *irreg.* (7); **to have a drink** prendre (*irreg.*) un verre (7)
drive conduire *irreg.* (18)
driver conducteur/trice *m., f.* (19)
drug (medicine) médicament *m.* (9)
during pendant (14)
DVD player lecteur (*m.*) de DVD (5)
dynamic dynamique (2)

each chaque (7)
ear oreille *f.* (9)
early en avance (5); tôt (3)
earth terre *f.* (18)
east est *m.* (17)
Easter Pâques *f. pl.* (11)
easy facile (2)
eat manger (6); **to eat dinner** dîner (2)
economics: business economics économie (*f.*) de gestion (13)
edge: on the edge of au bord de (17)
editor: letters to the editor courrier (*m.*) des lecteurs (12)
editorial éditorial *m.* (*pl.* éditoriaux) (12)
efficient efficace (18)
effort: with effort fort (19)
egg œuf *m.;* **hard-boiled egg with mayonnaise** œuf dur mayonnaise (8)
eggplant aubergine *f.* (15)
eight huit (P)
eighteen dix-huit (P)
eighth huitième (11)
eighty quatre-vingts (4)
elderly au/du troisième âge (12)
electronic mailbox boîte (*f.*) aux lettres électronique (13)
elegant élégant(e) (14)
eleven onze (P)
e-mail courrier (*m.*) électronique (13); **e-mail message** mél *m.* (13)
employ *v.* employer (6)
encounter rencontre *f.* (21)
encourage encourager (6)
engineer ingénieur / femme ingénieur *m., f.* (11)
engineering génie *m.* (13); **chemical (electrical, industrial, mechanical) engineering** génie chimique (électrique, industriel, mécanique) (13)
England Angleterre *f.* (3)
English *adj.* anglais(e) (3); (*language*) anglais *m.* (1)
English Channel Manche *f.* (17)
enough assez (de) (7); **it is enough** il suffit (20)
enter entrer (11)
entertainment (*show*) spectacle *m.* (21)
envelope enveloppe *f.* (13)
environment environnement *m.* (18)
eraser gomme *f.*; **blackboard eraser** éponge *f.* (1)
errands: to do errands faire (*irreg.*) les courses (5)
escape *v.* s'échapper (19)
especially surtout (16)
essential: it is essential il est essentiel (20)
Europe Europe *f.* (14)
evening soir *m.* (5); soirée *f.* (21); **in the evening** du soir (5); **this evening** ce soir (13)
event événement *m.* (12); **cultural event** manifestation (*f.*) culturelle (21); **in the event that** au cas où (19); **special event** spectacle *m.* (21)
ever déjà (10)
every tout, toute, tous, toutes (4); **every day** tous les jours (10)
everyone tout le monde (1)
everywhere partout (18)
evident évident(e) (14)
ewe brebis *f.* (18)
exact exact(e) (14)
exam examen *m.* (13); **to fail an exam** échouer à un examen (13); **to pass an exam** réussir à un examen; **to study for an exam** préparer un examen (13); **to take an exam** passer un examen (13)
execute (*s.o.*) **by shooting** fusiller (19)
executive cadre *m., f.* (11)
exhibit: art exhibit exposition (*f.*) d'art (10)
exit sortie *f.* (14)
expensive cher (chère) (2)
eye œil *m.* (*pl.* yeux) (9); **to have brown (hazel, blue) eyes** avoir les yeux marron (noisette, bleus) (4)

face visage *m.* (9)
facial tissue mouchoir (*m.*) en papier (9)
facing en face de (3)
fail échouer (13); **to fail an exam** échouer à un examen (13)
fall *v.* tomber (11); (*season*) automne *m.* (10); **in the fall** en automne (10); **to fall asleep** s'endormir *irreg.* (9)
false faux (fausse) (2); **that's (it's) false (wrong)** c'est faux (2)
famous célèbre (20)
far (from) loin (de) (3)
farm ferme *f.* (18)
farmer agriculteur/trice *m., f.* (11); fermier/ière *m., f.* (18); paysan(ne) *m., f.* (18)
fast *adj.* rapide (14); *adv.* vite (14); **fast food** fast-food *m.* (8); **fast-food worker** employé(e) (*m., f.*) de fast-food (11)
father père *m.* (4); **father-in-law, stepfather** beau-père *m.* (*pl.* beaux-pères) (4)
February février *m.* (4)
feel: to feel like (*doing*) avoir (*irreg.*) envie de (4); **to feel nauseated** avoir mal au cœur (9)
festival festival *m.* (*pl.* festivals) (16); fête *f.* (11)
fever fièvre *f.* (9)
few peu (de) (7); **a few** quelques (8)
fewer (. . .) than moins (de...) que (16)
fewest: the fewest le moins (de) (16)
field champ *m.* (17)
fifteen quinze (P)
fifth cinquième (11)
fifty cinquante (P)
film film *m.* (P)
finally enfin (10)
find *v.* trouver (2)
fine: I'm fine ça va bien (P), je vais bien (P)
finish *v.* finir (11)
fire feu *m.* (17); **to fire** licencier (20); **to fire on** tirer sur (19)
fireplace cheminée *f.* (18)
first *adj.* premier/ière (11); **at first, first (of all)** *adv.* d'abord (10); **first course** (*meal*) entrée *f.* (8); **first of the month** premier *m.* (4)
fish poisson *m.* (7); **fish store** poissonnerie *f.* (7); **fishmonger** poissonnier/ière *m., f.* (7); **to go fishing** aller (*irreg.*) à la pêche (16)
five cinq (P)
flight vol *m.* (14)
floor (*of building*) étage (5)
flower fleur *f.* (1)
flu grippe *f.* (9)
follow suivre *irreg.* (15)
food aliment *m.* (7)
foot pied *m.* (9); **on foot** à pied (14)
football (American) football (*m.*) américain (10)
for pour (1); (*time*) depuis (14)
forest forêt *f.* (17)
foreign *adj.* étranger/ère (13); **foreign language** langue (*f.*) étrangère (13)

forget oublier (6)
fork fourchette *f.* (8)
form *v.* former (20)
formerly autrefois (12)
forty quarante (P)
four quatre (P)
fourteen quatorze (P)
fourth quatrième (11)
France France *f.* (3)
frank franc(he) (14)
French français(e) (3); (*language*) français *m.* (1); **French fries** frites *f. pl.* (8); **French-speaking** francophone (3)
Friday vendredi *m.* (4)
friend ami(e) *m., f.* (P)
Frisbee Frisbee *m.* (16)
from de (P); **from . . . to . . .** de... à... (5); **from time to time** de temps en temps (12)
front: in front of devant (3); **on the front page** (*newspaper*) à la une (12)
fruit fruit *m.* (7)
fry faire (*irreg.*) frire (15)
full complet/ète (14); **full-time** à plein temps (11)
funny amusant(e) (2)
furious furieux/euse (21)
furniture (piece of) meuble *m.* (5)
future avenir *m.* (18)

gallery galerie *f.* (20)
game jeu *m.* (*pl.* jeux) (10)
garden jardin *m.* (18)
garlic ail *m.* (15)
gasoline essence *f.* (18)
gate (*airport*) porte (*f.*) d'embarquement (14)
gather (*flowers*) cueillir *irreg.* (16); **to gather up** (*toys, etc.*) ramasser (18)
gentle doux (douce) (14)
geography géographie *f.* (1)
German *adj.* allemand(e) (3)
Germany Allemagne *f.* (3)
get: to get along well (poorly) (with) s'entendre bien (mal) (avec) (9); **to get around** circuler (14); **to get down** (off) descendre (de) (8); **to get dressed (in, as)** s'habiller (en) (7); **to get up** se lever (9)
ginger gingembre *m.* (15)
girl jeune fille *f.* (12)
give *v.* donner (2); **to give a gift** offrir (*irreg.*) un cadeau (15)
glad: to be glad to vouloir (*irreg.*) bien (6)
glass verre *m.* (8)
go aller *irreg.* (3); **to go back (home)** rentrer (11); **to go camping** faire (*irreg.*) du camping (16); **to go canoeing** faire (*irreg.*) du canoë (16); **to go down** descendre (8); **to go down (up) a street** descendre (monter) une rue (17); **to go fishing** aller à la pêche (16); **to go horseback riding** monter à cheval (16); **to go out** sortir *irreg.* (8); **to go rock climbing** faire de l'escalade (16); **to go shopping** faire (*irreg.*) du shopping (5); **to go through customs** passer la douane (14); **to go to bed** se coucher (9) **to go up** monter (11)
golf: to play golf jouer au golf (16)
good bon(ne) (2); **good-bye** au revoir (P); **good-looking** beau (bel, belle, beaux, belles) (12); **good luck** bonne chance; **to have a good time** s'amuser (9)
grade (*on a paper*) note *f.* (13)
grain céréale *f.* (18)
granddaughter petite-fille *f.* (*pl.* petites-filles)(4)
grandfather grand-père *m.* (*pl.* grands-pères) (4)
grandmother grand-mère *f.* (*pl.* grands-mères) (4)
grandparents grands-parents *m. pl.* (4)
grandson petit-fils *m.* (*pl.* petits-fils) (4)
grape raisin *m.* (7)
great super (2); magnifique (2)
green vert(e) (6); **green beans** haricots (*m. pl.*) verts (7)
greenhouse effect effet (*m.*) de serre (18)
greeting accueil *m.* (20)
gray gris(e) (6)
grocer épicier/ière *m., f.* (7); **grocery store** épicerie *f.* (7)
ground floor rez-de-chaussée *m.* (5)
grow pousser (18)
guard *v.* garder (19); **security guard** agent(e) *m., f.* de sécurité (11)
guitar guitare *f.* (5)
gymnasium gymnase *m.* (13)

hair cheveux *m. pl.* (9); **to have blond (brown, black, red, white) hair** avoir les cheveux blonds (châtain, noirs, roux, blancs) (4)
half: half-kilogram demi-kilo *m.*, (7); **half-past** (*the hour*) et demi(e) (5); **half-time** à mi-temps (11)
ham jambon *m.* (7)
hamburger hamburger *m.* (8)
hand main *f.* (9)
handkerchief: paper handkerchief mouchoir (*m.*) en papier (9)
handsome beau (bel, belle, beaux, belles) (2)
hang glide faire (*irreg.*) du parapente (16)
hang up (*the telephone receiver*) *v.* raccrocher (13)
Hanukkah Hanukkah (11)
happen se passer (9)
happy heureux/euse (2)
harvest récolte *f.* (18); **to harvest** récolter (18)
hat chapeau *m.* (6)
hate *v.* détester (2)
have avoir *irreg.* (4); **to have** (*s.th. to eat*) prendre *irreg.* (7); **to have a drink** prendre un verre (7); **to have a good time** s'amuser (9); **to have a party** faire (*irreg.*) la fête (5); **to have a picnic** faire un pique-nique, pique-niquer (16); **to have a stomachache** avoir mal au ventre (9); **to have a view of (the port)** donner sur (le port) (20); **to have blond (brown, black, red, white) hair** avoir les cheveux blonds (châtain, noirs, roux, blancs) (4); **to have lunch** déjeuner (8); **to have pain, an ache in, to have a sore . . .** avoir mal à (9); **to have to** (*must*) devoir *irreg.* (9)
hazel (*eye color*) noisette *adj. inv.* (4)
he il (1)
head tête *f.* (9)
headline gros titre *m.* (12)
health santé *f.* (9)
hear entendre (8)
heart cœur *m.* (9)
heat *v.* chauffer (15); *n.* chaleur *f.* (20)
hello bonjour (P)
helmet casque *m.* (16)
here ici (3); là (1); **here is (here are)** voici (1)
hesitate (*to do*) hésiter (à) (18)
hi salut (P)
hide se réfugier (19)
high school lycée *m.* (1); **high school student** lycéen(ne) *m., f.* (1)
high-speed train train (*m.*) à grande vitesse (*fam.* TGV) (14)
highway autoroute *f.* (14)
hike *v.* faire *irreg.* une randonnée (16)
hill colline *f.* (17)
hip-hop music hip-hop *m.* (21)
hire engager (20)
history histoire *f.* (1)
hit *v.* frapper (19)
hockey: to play hockey jouer au hockey (16)
hold *v.* tenir *irreg.* (14)
holiday congé *m.* (20); fête *f.* (11); **legal holiday** jour (*m.*) férié (11)
home: at the home of chez (3); **home page** page (*f.*) d'accueil (13); **personal home page** page (*f.*) perso (13); **to come home** rentrer (11)
homeland patrie *f.* (19)
homework devoir *m.* (5); **to do homework** faire (*irreg.*) les devoirs (5)
hope *v.* espérer (6); souhaiter (21)
horse cheval *m.* (16); **to go horseback riding** monter à cheval (16)
hospital hôpital *m.* (9)
hostage otage *m.* (19)
hot: to feel hot avoir (*irreg.*) chaud (4); **it's hot out** il fait chaud (10)

hotel hôtel *m.* (3)
hour heure *f.* (5); **rush hour** heures (*f. pl.*) de pointe (14)
house maison *f.* (5)
housework: to do the housework faire (*irreg.*) le ménage (5)
how comment (4); **how are you?** comment allez-vous? (vas-tu?) (P); **how many, how much** combien de (4); **how old are you (is he,** *etc.***)?** quel âge avez-vous (a-t-il, *etc.*)? (4); **how's it going?** ça va? (P)
hundred cent (4)
hungry: to be hungry avoir (*irreg.*) faim (4)
hurry *v.* se dépêcher (9); **in a hurry** pressé(e) (14)
husband mari *m.* (4)

I je (1)
ice cream glace *f.* (8)
ice skate *n.* patin *m.* (16); *v.* patiner (16); faire (*irreg.*) du patin à glace (16)
icon (computer) icone *m.* (13)
if si (7); **if I were you** à ta (votre) place (19)
immediate immédiat(e) (14)
immigrant immigré(e) *m., f.* (20)
important important(e) (20)
impossible impossible (20)
in dans (P); **in a hurry** pressé(e) (14); **in back of** derrière (3); **in cash** en espèces (6); **in front of** devant (3); **in good (great) shape** en bonne (pleine) forme (9); **in old age** au troisième âge (12); **in order to/that** afin de/que (21), pour que (21); **in short** *interj.* enfin (10); **in that case** alors (1); **in the afternoon** de l'après-midi (5); **in the country** à la campagne (17); **in the evening** du soir (5); **in the middle of** au milieu de (22); **in the morning** du matin (5); **in the past** autrefois (12); **in your place** à ta (votre) place (19)
incredible incroyable (21)
India Inde *f.* (15)
Indian *adj.* indien(ne) (15)
indicate indiquer (17)
inhabitant habitant(e) *m., f.* (20)
intellectual intellectuel(le) (2)
interesting intéressant(e) (2); **to be interested in** s'intéresser à (9)
Internet: Internet user internaute *m., f.* (13); **on the Internet** sur Internet (11)
internship stage *m.* (11)
interpreter interprète *m., f.* (11)
invite inviter (18)
is: to be être (1); **is it so** (*true*) **that . . .** Est-ce que... (1); **isn't that right?** n'est-ce pas? (3); non? (3); **is that right?** c'est ça? (P); **is this (that, it) . . . ?** est-ce... ? (4); **it could be that, it is possible that** il se peut que (21)
island île *f.* (17)

Israel Israél *m.* (14)
Israeli *adj.* israélien(ne) (15)
it il/elle *m., f.* (1); **it could be that** il se peut que (21); **it is . . .** c'est... (P); **it is not . . .** ce n'est pas... (P); **it's (ten) o'clock** il est (dix) heures (5); **it's a pleasure** (*to meet you*) enchanté(e) (P)
Italian italien(ne) *adj.* (15)
Italy Italie *f.* (15)

jam confiture *f.* (7)
January janvier *m.* (4)
Japan Japon *m.* (3)
Japanese *adj.* japonais(e) (3)
jeans jean *m., s.* (6)
job emploi *m.* (11); poste *m.* (11); travail *m.* (2)
jogging jogging *m.* (10); **jogging trail** piste (*f.*) de jogging (13)
journalist journaliste *m., f.* (2)
joyful, joyous joyeux/euse (12); **joyful attitude** (*toward life*) joie (*f.*) de vivre (20)
juice (orange) jus *m.* (d'orange) (8)
July juillet *m.* (4)
June juin *m.* (4)
just: to have just (*done s.th.*) venir (*irreg.*) de + *inf.* (4)

keep garder (19)
kill *v.* tuer (19)
kilogram kilo *m.* (7); **half kilogram** demi-kilo *m.* (7)
kind *adj.* gentil(le) (2)
kiss (each other) *v.* s'embrasser (9)
kitchen cuisine *f.* (5)
knee genou *m.* (9)
knife couteau *m.* (8)
know: to be acquainted with connaître *irreg.* (13); **I don't know** je ne sais pas (P); **to know** (*a fact*) savoir *irreg.* (13)

Labor Day fête (*f.*) du Travail (11)
laboratory laboratoire *m.* (P)
laborer: manual laborer ouvrier/ière *m., f.* (11)
lake lac *m.* (17)
language langue *f.* (13); **foreign language** langue étrangère (13); **foreign language teaching** enseignement (*m.*) des langues étrangères (13)
laptop computer portable *m.* (5)
last *adj.* dernier/ière (13); **at last** enfin (10); **last stop** terminus *m.* (14)
late en retard (5); tard (3)
later plus tard (10)
launch *v.* lancer (6)
laundry: to do the laundry faire (*irreg.*) la lessive (5)
law droit *m.* (13)
lawn bowling: to play lawn bowling jouer à la pétanque (aux boules) (16)

lawyer avocat(e) *m., f.* (11)
leaf feuille *f.* (13)
learn apprendre *irreg.* (7)
least: the least le/la/les moins (16)
leave partir *irreg.* (8); **to leave** (*s.o., a place*) quitter (8); **to leave** (*s.th. somewhere*) laisser (13)
lecture conférence *f.* (21)
left: to/on the left à gauche (17)
leg jambe *f.* (9)
legal holiday jour (*m.*) férié (11)
leisure activities distractions *f. pl.* (10); loisirs *m. pl.* (16)
lemon citron *m.* (7)
lemongrass citronnelle *f.* (15)
lentil lentille *f.* (15)
less moins (5); **less (. . .)** moins (de...) (16); **less (than)** moins (que) (16)
lesson leçon *f.* (1); **to study for a lesson** préparer une leçon (13)
let laisser (13)
letter lettre *f.* (13); **letters to the editor** courrier (*m.*) des lecteurs (12)
lettuce salade *f.* (8)
library bibliothèque *f.* (3)
lie *v.* mentir *irreg.* (8)
life vie *f.* (10); **city life** vie urbaine (10)
light: to turn on the light mettre (*irreg.*) la lumière (7); **traffic light** feu *m.* (17)
light (*weight*) léger (légère) (8)
like *prep.* comme (8); *adj.* tel(le) (14)
like: *v.* aimer (2); **I would like** je voudrais (6)
likely: it is (un)likely that il est (peu) probable que (21)
line: to stand in line faire (*irreg.*) la queue (5)
listen (to) écouter (2)
literary littéraire (13)
little peu (de) (7); **a little** un peu (de) (7)
live *v.* (*reside*) habiter (2); (*to be alive*) vivre *irreg.* (15); **they are living together (without marriage)** ils vivent en union libre (4)
living: joy in living joie (*f.*) de vivre (20); **living room** salle (*f.*) de séjour (5)
location endroit *m.* (14); lieu *m.* (*pl.* lieux) (3)
long time: for a long time longtemps (14)
look (at) regarder (2); **to look for** chercher (2); **to look (like)** avoir (*irreg.*) l'air (4)
lose perdre (8); **to lose one's mind** perdre la tête (8); **to lose patience** perdre patience (8)
lot: a lot (of) beaucoup (de) (7)
love *v.* aimer (2)
low-cut: in low-cut clothing en décolleté (22)
lozenge (*cough drop*) pastille *f.* (9)

lunch déjeuner *m.* (8); **to have lunch** déjeuner *v.* (8)
lung poumon *m.* (9)

madam (Mrs.) madame (Mme) (P)
magazine magazine *m.* (12)
Maghreb Maghreb *m.* (15); **from the Maghreb** maghrébin(e) (15)
magnificent magnifique (2)
mail *n.* poste *f.* (3); (*letters, etc.*) courrier *m.* (12)
major in se spécialiser en (13); faire (*irreg.*) des études en (13)
make faire *irreg.* (5), rendre (8); **to make a decision** prendre (*irreg.*) une décision (7); **to make a meal** faire (*irreg.*) la cuisine (5); **to make a mistake (about)** se tromper (de) (9); **to make the acquaintance of** faire (*irreg.*) la connaissance de (5); **to make the bed** faire (*irreg.*) le lit (5)
makeup: to put on makeup se maquiller (9)
man homme *m.* (P)
management gestion *f.* (11)
manual laborer ouvrier/ière *m., f.* (11)
many beaucoup (de) (7); **how many** combien de (4); **too many** trop (de) (7)
map carte *f.* (17); (*subway, city, region*) plan *m.* (13)
March mars *m.* (4)
market marché *m.* (7)
marketing marketing *m.* (11)
marriage mariage *m.* (12)
married marié(e) (4)
match (soccer, boxing) match *m.* (de foot, de boxe) (10)
mathematics (math) mathématiques (maths) *f. pl.* (1)
May mai *m.* (4)
meal repas *m.* (8); **to cook a meal** faire (*irreg.*) la cuisine (5)
mean *v.* vouloir (*irreg.*) dire (6)
means moyen *m.* (14)
meat viande *f.* (7)
medicine médicament *m.* (9)
media médias *m. pl.* (12)
meet *v.* rencontrer (14) **nice to meet you** enchanté(e) (P)
meeting rencontre *f.* (21); (*business*) réunion *f.*
merchant marchand(e) *m., f.* (7)
method moyen *m.* (14)
Mexican mexicain(e) (3)
Mexico Mexique *m.* (3)
microwave oven four (*m.*) à micro-ondes (5)
middle: in the middle of au milieu de (22)
midnight minuit *m.* (5)
mild: it's mild out il fait doux (10)
milk lait *m.* (8)
million million *m.* (4)
mind: to lose one's mind perdre la tête (8)
mineral water eau (*f.*) minérale (7)
minus moins (5)
mirror miroir *m.* (5)
miserable malheureux/euse (2)
Miss mademoiselle (Mlle) (P)
miss: to be missed by (*s.o.*) manquer à (17); **I miss you** tu me manques
mistake: to make a mistake, be mistaken (about) se tromper (de) (9)
mix *v.* mélanger (15)
mode moyen *m.* (14)
moderate moyen(ne) (18)
Monday lundi *m.* (4)
money argent *m.* (6)
month mois *m.* (4)
more: more (. . .) plus (de) (16); **more (than)** plus (que) (16)
morning matin *m.* (5); **in the morning** du matin (5); **this morning** ce matin (13)
Moroccan *adj.* marocain(e) (3)
Morocco Maroc *m.* (3)
mosque mosquée *f.* (22)
most (of) la plupart (de) (22); **the most (of)** le/la/les plus (de) (16)
mother mère *f.* (4); **mother-in-law, stepmother** belle-mère *f.* (*pl.* belles-mères) (4)
mountain montagne *f.* (17); **mountain bike** vélo *m.* tout terrain (VTT) (16); **old, rounded mountain range** massif *m.* (17)
mouse souris *f.* (16); **computer mouse** souris *f.* (16)
mousse: chocolate mousse mousse (*f.*) au chocolat (8)
mouth bouche *f.* (9)
movie theater cinéma *m.* (P)
much beaucoup (de) (7); **how much** combien de (4); **so much** tellement (12); **too much** trop (de) (7)
muscle muscle *m.* (9)
museum musée *m.* (10); **art (natural science) museum** musée d'art (de sciences naturelles) (10); **museum curator** conservateur/trice (*m., f.*) de musée (11)
mushroom champignon *m.* (15)
music musique *f.* (13)
musician musicien(ne) *m., f.* (11)
must: one must (not) il (ne) faut (pas) (20); **must (to have to)** devoir *irreg.* (9)
mutton mouton *m.* (8)
my name is je m'appelle (P)
name: to be named s'appeler (9); **his (her) name is** il (elle) s'appelle (4); **my name is** je m'appelle (P); **what's your name?** comment vous appelez-vous? (P); comment t'appelles-tu? (P)
napkin serviette *f.* (8)
narrow étroit(e) (20)
national holiday fête (*f.*) nationale (11)
nauseated: to feel nauseated avoir (*irreg.*) mal au cœur (9)
near près (de) (3)
nearly presque (18)
necessary: it is necessary il est nécessaire (20), il faut (20); **it is not necessary** il n'est pas nécessaire (20)
need: to need avoir (*irreg.*) besoin de (4)
neighbor voisin(e) *m., f.* (22)
neighborhood quartier *m.* (3)
nephew neveu *m.* (4)
network (*system*) réseau *m.* (14); **television network** chaîne *f.* (12)
never ne... jamais (1)
new nouveau (nouvel, nouvelle, nouveaux, nouvelles) (2); **New Year's Day** nouvel an *m.* (11)
news actualités *f. pl.* (12), informations *f. pl.* (12); **news program** actualités *f. pl.* (12), informations *f. pl.* (12)
newspaper journal *m.* (*pl.* journaux) (12); **newspaper section, column** rubrique *f.* (12)
next *adj.* prochain(e) (13); *adv.* ensuite (10); puis (10); **the next day** le lendemain (10)
nice (*person*) gentil(le) (2); sympathique (*fam.* sympa) (1); (*weather*) beau (10); **it's nice out** il fait beau (10); **nice to meet you** enchanté(e) (P)
niece nièce *f.* (4)
night nuit *f.* (10); **nightclub** boîte (*f.*) de nuit (10)
nine neuf (P)
nineteen dix-neuf (P)
ninety quatre-vingt-dix (4)
ninth neuvième (11)
no non (P); **no doubt** sans doute (2); **no one** ne... personne (13)
nobody ne... personne (13)
noncarbonated *adj.* plat(e) (7)
nonsmoking (train) car wagon (*m.*) non-fumeurs (14)
noon midi *m.* (5)
normally d'habitude (12)
north nord *m.* (17)
North America Amérique (*f.*) du Nord (14)
nose nez *m.* (9); **runny nose** le nez qui coule (9)

not ne... pas (1); **not anymore** ne... plus (1); **not at all, absolutely not** ne... pas du tout (1); **not ever** ne... jamais (1); **not yet** ne... pas encore (1)
notebook cahier *m.* (P)
nothing ne... rien (13)
novel roman *m.* (21)
novelist romancier/ière *m., f.* (21)
November novembre *m.* (4)
now maintenant (3)
numerous nombreux/euse (18)
nurse infirmier/ière *m., f.* (9); **nurse's aide** garde-malade *m., f.* (11)

obey obéir (à) (11)
obituary avis (*m.*) de décès (12); **obituary column** les avis de décès (12)
obtain obtenir *irreg.* (14)
ocean océan *m.* (17)
o'clock: it's (five) o'clock il est (cinq) heures (5); **at (five) o'clock** à (cinq) heures (5)
October octobre *m.* (4)
of de (P); **of course** bien sûr (que oui) (2); **of course not** bien sûr que non (2); **of it/them/there** en (15)
offer *v.* offrir *irreg.* (15)
office bureau *m.* (*pl.* bureaux) (3)
often souvent (2)
oil (olive, sesame) huile *f.* (d'olive, de sésame) (15)
okay d'accord (2); **I'm okay** ça va; **okay?** d'accord? (3); OK? (3)
old vieux (vieil, vieille, vieux, vieilles) (2); **elderly, in old age** au/du troisième âge (12); **old age** vieillesse *f.* (12); **old portion of an Arab city** médina *f.* (22)
omelet omelette *f.* (8)
on sur (3); **on foot** à pied (14); **on the street** dans la rue (3); **on the banks (shore, edge) of** au bord de (17); **on the front page** à la une (12); **on the Internet** sur Internet (11); **on the left/right** à gauche/droite (17); **on time** à l'heure (5); **on vacation** en vacances (16)
one (*numeral*) un; (*number, amount*) un(e) (P); (*people in general*) on (1)
onion oignon *m.* (7)
only ne... que (10); seulement (14)
open *v.* ouvrir *irreg.* (15)
opening (*of an art exhibit*) vernissage *m.* (21)
opera opéra *m.* (21)
or ou (P)
orange *adj.* orange *inv.* (6)
orchard verger *m.* (18)
orchestra orchestre *m.* (21)
order: in order that afin que (21); pour que (21); **in order to** afin de (21)
other autre (2)
out: to go out sortir *irreg.* (8)
outdoors en plein air (16)
oven four *m.* (5); **microwave oven** four à micro-ondes (5)
over au-dessus de (3)
overcoat manteau *m.* (6)
overlook (the port) donner sur (le port) (20)
owe devoir *irreg.* (9)
owner (*of a bar, restaurant*) patron(ne) *m., f.* (11)

pad of paper bloc-notes *m.* (P)
page page *f.* (13); **home page** page d'accueil (13); **on the front page** à la une (12); **personal home page** page perso (13)
pain douleur *f.* (9); **to have pain in** avoir (*irreg.*) mal à (9)
painter peintre / femme peintre *m., f.* (11)
painting (*action, art*) peinture *f.* (21); (*picture*) tableau *m.* (21)
Pakistan Pakistan *m.* (15)
Pakistani *adj.* pakistanais(e) (15)
pants pantalon *m. s.* (6)
paper: pad of paper bloc-notes *m.* (P); **paper handkerchief** mouchoir (*m.*) en papier (9); **sheet of paper** feuille (*f.*) de papier
parents parents *m., pl.* (4)
park *n.* parc *m.*; *v.* stationner (14)
parking lot, parking garage parking *m.* (3)
parsley persil *m.* (15)
part partie *f.* (9)
party fête *f.* (11); **to have a party** faire (*irreg.*) la fête (5); **political party** parti (*m.*) politique (18)
pass (by) passer (par) (11); **to pass a course (exam)** réussir à un cours (à un examen) (11)
passenger passager/ère *m., f.* (14)
Passover Pâque *f.* (11)
passport passeport *m.* (14)
past: in the past autrefois (12)
pasta pâtes *f. pl.* (15)
pastry pâtisserie *f.* (7); **pastry chef** pâtissier/ière *m., f.* (7); **pastry shop** pâtisserie *f.* (7)
patience: to lose patience perdre patience (8)
pay payer (6); **to pay attention** faire (*irreg.*) attention (5)
peanut cacahouète *f.* (*alt. spelling* cacahuète) (15)
peas petits pois *m. pl.* (7); **chick-peas** pois (*m. pl.*) chiches (15)
peasant paysan(ne) *m., f.* (18)
pedestrian street rue (*f.*) piétonne (20)
pen stylo *m.* (P)
pencil crayon *m.* (P)
penmanship écriture *f.* (1)
people on (1); gens *m. pl.* (13)
pepper poivre *m.* (8)
per par (6)
permit *v.* permettre *irreg.* (7)
perhaps peut-être (14)
person personne *f.* (P); **person who is afraid of technology** technophobe *m., f.* (13)
philosophy philosophie *f.* (13)
phone: *See* **telephone.**
photograph: photographie (*fam.* photo) *f.* (21); **to take photographs** faire (*irreg.*) de la photographie (16); **to take a photograph** prendre (*irreg.*) une photo (16)
photographer photographe *m., f.* (21)
physics physique *f.* (13)
piano piano *m.* (5)
pick: to pick up (*toys, etc.*) ramasser (18); **to pick up** (*the telephone receiver*) décrocher (13)
picnic: to have a picnic faire (*irreg.*) un pique-nique (16), pique-niquer (16)
pie tarte *f.* (7)
piece (of) morceau *m.* (de) (7)
pig porc *m.* (18)
pink rose (6)
pita (bread) (pain) pita *m.* (15)
pizza pizza *f.* (8)
place (*location*) endroit *m.* (14); lieu *m.* (*pl.* lieux) (3); **in your place** à ta (votre) place (19); **to take place** avoir (*irreg.*) lieu (21)
plain *n.* plaine *f.* (17)
plant *v.* planter (18)
plate assiette *f.* (8)
plateau plateau *m.* (17)
platform quai *m.* (14)
play *v.* jouer (10); *n.* pièce *f.* (de théâtre) (21); **to play** (*a sport*) jouer à (10); faire du sport (5); **to play** (*a musical instrument*) jouer de (10)
pleasure: it's a pleasure (*to meet you*) enchanté(e) (P)
poem poème *m.* (21)
poet poète / femme poète *m., f.* (21)
poetry poésie *f.* (21)
political party parti (*m.*) politique (18)
pollution pollution *f.* (18)
pool (*swimming*) piscine *f.* (13)
poor pauvre (22)
pork porc *m.* (7); **pork butcher shop (delicatessen)** charcuterie *f.* (7); **pork products** charcuterie *f.* (8)
port port *m.* (20)
position (*job*) poste *m.* (11)
possible: it is possible that il est possible que (21); il se peut que (21)
poster affiche *f.* (5)
pot: large, iron cooking pot marmite *f.* (18)

potato pomme (*f.*) de terre (7)
poultry volaille *f.* (18)
pound (*approx. half kilo*) livre *f.* (7)
pour *v.* verser (15)
prefer aimer mieux (2); préférer (6); **it is preferable** il est préférable (20)
prescription ordonnance *f.* (9)
pretty joli(e) (2)
preview (*of an art exhibit*) vernissage *m.* (21)
probable probable (21)
probably sans doute (2)
produce *v.* produire *irreg.* (18)
producer producteur/trice *m., f.* (2)
profession profession *f.* (11)
professor professeur *m.* (P)
program émission *f.* (2); programme *m.* (13)
promise *v.* promettre *irreg.* (7)
proud fier (fière) (18)
psychology psychologie *f.* (13)
pullover pull-over (*fam.* pull) *m.* (6)
punch (*a ticket*) composter (14)
punk music punk *m.* (21)
pupil élève *m., f.* (1)
purple violet(te) (6)
pursue poursuivre *irreg.* (15)
push *v.* pousser (18)
put mettre *irreg.* (7); **to put on a piece of clothing** mettre (*irreg.*) un vêtement (7); **to put on makeup** se maquiller (9)

quarter: quarter past (*the hour*) et quart (5); **quarter to** (*the hour*) moins le quart (5)
Quebec Québec *m.* (3); **from Quebec** québécois(e) (3)
quickly vite (14)

rabbit lapin *m.* (16)
race: running race course (*f.*) à pied (10)
radio radio *f.* (5); **to put/turn on the radio** mettre (*irreg.*) la radio (7); **radio station** station (*f.*) de radio (12)
raï music raï *m.* (21)
railroad tracks voie (*f.*) de chemin de fer (19)
rain: it's raining il pleut (10)
raisin raisin (*m.*) sec (15)
Ramadan ramadan *m.* (11)
rapid rapide (14); **rapidly** rapidement (12); vite (12)
rarely rarement (2)
read lire *irreg.* (12)
reading lecture *f.* (1)
ready prêt(e) (2)
realize se rendre compte (9)
receive recevoir *irreg.* (10)
recipe recette *f.* (15)
recognize reconnaître *irreg.* (13)
recycle recycler (18); **recycling** recyclage *m.* (18)
red rouge (6); (*hair color*) roux (rousse) (4)
reduce réduire *irreg.* (18)
reflect (on) réfléchir (à) (11)
refrigerator réfrigérateur (*fam.* frigo) *m.* (5)
refuge: to take refuge se réfugier (19)
refuse (to do) refuser (de) (18)
reggae music reggae *m.* (21)
register (check in) *v.* enregistrer (14)
regret *v.* regretter (21)
reheat réchauffer (15)
relatives parents *m., pl.* (4)
relief (*topography*) relief *m.* (17)
remember se rappeler (9); se souvenir *irreg.* (de) (9)
render (*make*) rendre (8)
renovation rénovation *f.* (20)
rent *v.* louer (14)
repeat répéter (6)
replace remplacer (13)
reporter reporter *m.* (2)
require exiger (20)
research *v.* rechercher (19)
reserved (*person*) discret/ète (14)
reside habiter (2)
residence résidence *f.* (13); **university dormitory** résidence universitaire (13)
Resistance fighter résistant(e) *m., f.* (19)
resource ressource *f.* (13)
rest *v.* se reposer (9)
restaurant restaurant *m.* (3)
retire prendre (*irreg.*) sa retraite (12)
retiree retraité(e) *m., f.* (12)
return (*something*) rendre (8); **to return** retourner (11)
rice riz *m.* (8)
rich riche (22)
ride: ride a horse monter à cheval (16)
ridiculous ridicule (2)
right: to/on the right à droite (17); **it is right (not right)** il est juste (injuste) (20); **is that right**? c'est ça? (3); **isn't that right?** n'est-ce pas? (3), non? (3); c'est ca? (3); **right away** tout de suite (10)
river: rivière *f.* (17); **large river** fleuve *m.* (17)
rock: to go rock climbing faire (*irreg.*) de l'escalade (16)
rock music rock *m.* (21)
roll (*bread*) petit pain *m.* (8)
roller skating roller *m.* (10); **to roller skate** faire (*irreg.*) du roller
room (*in a home*) pièce *f.* (5); **bathroom** salle (*f.*) de bains (5); **bedroom** chambre *f.* (5); **classroom** salle (*f.*) de classe (P); **dining room** salle (*f.*) à manger (5); **living room** salle (*f.*) de séjour (5)
route chemin *m.* (17); route *f.* (14)
rug tapis *m.* (5)
run: to run into (*meet*) rencontrer (14)
running (*jogging*) footing *m.* (10) jogging *m.* (10); **running race** course (*f.*) à pied (10)
runny nose le nez qui coule (9)
rush hour heures (*f. pl.*) de pointe (14)
Russia Russie *f.* (15)
Russian *adj.* russe (15)

sad triste (2); **it is sad** il est triste (20)
sail *v.* faire (*irreg.*) de la voile (16)
sailboat bateau (*m.*) à voile (16)
saint's day fête *f.* (11)
salad salade *f.* (8)
salary salaire *m.* (20)
salesclerk vendeur/euse *m., f.* (6)
salmon saumon *m.* (7)
salt sel *m.* (8)
same même (5)
sandwich sandwich *f.* (8)
Saturday samedi *m.* (4)
sauce sauce *f.* (8)
saucepan casserole *f.* (15)
sausage saucisson *m.* (8); **link sausage** saucisse *f.* (7)
say dire *irreg.* (12)
scarf écharpe (6); (*lightweight*) foulard (6)
scene scène *f.* (P)
school: elementary school école *f.* (1); **secondary school** lycée *m.* (1)
science: natural science sciences (*f. pl.*) naturelles (1)
screen écran *m.* (2)
sea mer *f.* (17)
seafood fruits (*m. pl.*) de mer (7)
search for rechercher (19)
season saison *f.* (10)
seat siège *m.* (14); **aisle (window) seat** siège (*m.*) couloir (fenêtre) (14); **(reserved) seat** place *f.* (14)
second deuxième (11)
secretary secrétaire *m., f.* (11)
section (*newspaper*) rubrique *f.* (12)
security guard agent(e) (*m., f.*) de sécurité (11)
see voir *irreg.* (10); **see you soon** à bientôt (P); **see you tomorrow** à demain (P); **to see again** revoir *irreg.* (10)
seem avoir (*irreg.*) l'air (4); sembler (13); paraître *irreg.* (13)
sell vendre (8)
send envoyer (6)
September septembre *m.* (4)
series série *f.* (12)
serve servir *irreg.* (8)
service service *m.* (13)
set (*TV, theater, cinema*) plateau *m.* (2); **to set the table** mettre (*irreg.*) la table (7)
seven sept (P)
seventeen dix-sept (P)
seventh septième (11)

seventy soixante-dix (4)
several plusieurs (14); quelques (8)
shape: in good (great) shape en bonne (pleine) forme (9)
share *v.* partager (6)
shave *v.* se raser (9)
she elle (1)
sheep mouton *m.* (18)
sheet (of paper) feuille *f.* (de papier) (13)
shirt chemise *f.* (6)
shocking étonnant(e) (22)
shoe chaussure *f.* (6)
shoot at tirer sur (19)
shopping: to go shopping faire (*irreg.*) du shopping (5)
shore: on the shore of au bord de (17)
short court(e) (22); **in short** *interj.* enfin (10)
short story conte *m.* (21)
shorts short *m. s.* (6)
should: one should (you should, etc.) (not) il (ne) faut (pas) (20)
shoulder épaule *f.* (9)
show *v.* montrer (7); indiquer (17); *n.* spectacle *m.* (21); **could you show me the way to** est-ce que vous pourriez m'indiquer le chemin pour aller à (17)
shrimp crevettes *f. pl.* (7)
sick malade (9); **to become sick** tomber malade (9)
sideboard buffet *m.* (5)
significant fort(e) (18)
signpost poteau (*m.*) indicateur (17)
silently silencieusement (19)
since (*time*) depuis (14)
singer chanteur/euse *m., f.* (21)
single (*unmarried*) célibataire (4)
sir (Mr.) monsieur (M.) (P)
sister sœur *f.* (4); **sister-in-law, stepsister** belle-sœur *f.* (*pl.* belles-sœurs) (4)
site site *m.* (13); **tourist site** site touristique (20); **website** site Web (13)
situation comedy (sitcom) sitcom *f.* (12)
six six (P)
sixteen seize (P)
sixth sixième (11)
sixty soixante (4)
ska music ska *m.* (21)
skateboarding skate *m.* (10)
ski *v.* skier, faire (*irreg.*) du ski (16); **ski run** piste *f.* (16); **to cross-country ski** faire (*irreg.*) du ski de fond (16)
skip: to skip class sécher un cours (13)
skirt jupe *f.* (6)
sky ciel *m.* (10); **the sky is cloudy (clear)** le ciel est couvert (clair) (10)
sleep dormir *irreg.* (8)
slow lent(e) (14); **to slow the advance** retarder l'avance (19)
small petit(e) (2)
smell *v.* sentir *irreg.* (8)
smoking (nonsmoking) train car wagon (*m.*) fumeurs (non-fumeurs) (14)
snow: it's snowing il neige (10)
snowboard *v.* faire (*irreg.*) du surf des neiges (16)
so *conj.* alors (1); **so** (*very*) tellement (14); **so that** afin que (21); pour que (21)
soap opera feuilleton *m.* (12)
soccer football (*fam.* foot) *m.* (10)
society column carnet (*m.*) du jour (12)
sock chaussette *f.* (6)
sofa canapé *m.* (5)
soil terre *f.* (18)
soldier soldat *m.* (19)
sole seul(e) (14)
some des (P); quelques (8); *pron.* en (15)
someone quelqu'un (13)
something quelque chose (13)
sometimes parfois (2); quelquefois (12)
son fils *m.* (4)
son-in-law gendre *m.* (4)
song chanson *f.* (21)
soon bientôt (3); **see you soon** à bientôt (P)
sore: to have a sore . . . avoir (*irreg.*) mal à (9)
sorry: to be sorry (that) être (*irreg.*) désolé(e) (que) (21)
soup soupe *f.* (8)
south sud *m.* (17)
South America Amérique (*f.*) du Sud (14)
soy sauce sauce (*f.*) de soja (15)
Spain Espagne *f.* (3)
Spanish *adj.* espagnol(e) (3)
speak parler (2)
special event spectacle *m.* (21)
speed limit limite (*f.*) de vitesse (14)
spend: to spend time on mettre (*irreg.*) du temps à (7)
spice épice *f.* (15); **blend of spices** (*for soups, etc.*) quatre-épices *m., f.* (15)
sponge éponge *f.* (1)
spoon cuillère *f.* (8)
sport: play/do sports faire (*irreg.*) du sport (5)
sports center centre (*m.*) sportif (3)
sport coat veste *f.* (6)
sports fan fanatique (*m., f.*) du sport (10)
spring printemps *m.* (10); **in spring** au printemps (10)
squash courge *f.* (15)
stage (*in a process*) étape *f.* (12); (*theater*) scène *f.*
stamp timbre *m.* (13)
stand: to stand up se lever (9); **to stand in line** faire (*irreg.*) la queue (5)
star (*of a show, movie*) vedette *f.* (20)
station: (*bus, métro*) **station stop** arrêt *m.* (14); **radio station** station (*f.*) de radio (12); **television station** chaîne *f.* (12); **train station** gare *f.* (14)
stay *v.* rester (11)
steam *v.* faire (*irreg.*) cuire à la vapeur (15)
step: stepbrother beau-frère *m.* (4); **stepfather** beau-père *m.* (4); **stepmother** belle-mère *f.* (4); **stepsister** belle-sœur *f.* (4)
stereo chaîne (*f.*) stéréo (5)
still encore (3); toujours (10)
stomach estomac *m.* (9); **to have a stomachache** avoir (*irreg.*) mal au ventre (9)
stop *v.* cesser (de) (18); **stop** (*bus métro*) arrêt *m.* (14); **last stop** terminus *m.* (14)
store magasin *m.* (6); **bread store** boulangerie *f.* (7); **butcher shop** boucherie *f.* (7); **dairy products store** crémerie *f.* (7); **department store** grand magasin *m.* (6); **fish store** poissonnerie *f.* (7); **grocery store** épicerie *f.* (7), supermarché *m.* (3); **pastry shop** pâtisserie *f.* (7); **pork butcher shop** charcuterie *f.* (7)
storm (*thunder and lightning*) orage *m.* (10)
story histoire *f.* (P); **short story** conte *m.* (21)
stove cuisinière *f.* (5)
straight (ahead) tout droit (17)
street: on (Mouffetard) Street dans la rue (Mouffetard) (3); **on the street** dans la rue (3); **pedestrian street** rue (*f.*) piétonne (20)
strength: with strength fort (19)
strike *v.* frapper (19)
strong fort(e) (18)
student (*university*) étudiant(e) *m., f.* (P)
studies études *f. pl.* (1)
studio studio *m.* (P)
study *v.* étudier (2); **to study** (*a subject*) faire (*irreg.*) des études en (13); **to study for (a lesson, an exam)** préparer (une leçon, un examen) (13)
subject (*school*) matière *f.* (13)
suburb banlieue *f.* (3)
subway métro *m.* (14); **subway system** réseau (*m.*) du métro (14); **subway ticket** ticket (*m.*) de métro (14)
succeed réussir (à) (11); **to succeed in (doing)** arriver à (18)
such tel(le) (14); **such a** un(e) tel(le) (14)
sudden soudain(e) (19)
suddenly soudain (19)
suffer souffrir *irreg.* (15)
sugar sucre *m.* (7)
suit (*man's*) costume *m.* (6); (*woman's*) tailleur *m.* (6)
suitcase valise *f.* (14)
summer été *m.* (10); **in summer** en été (10)
Sunday dimanche *m.* (4)
sunglasses lunettes (*f. pl.*) de soleil (6)
sunny: it's sunny out il fait du soleil (10)

superintendent: building superintendent gardien(ne) (*m., f.*) d'immeuble (11)
supermarket supermarché *m.* (3)
suppose: I suppose je suppose (3)
sure sûr(e) (14); certain(e) (21)
surf: to surf the Web naviguer (surfer) le Web (13)
surprised surpris(e) (21)
surprising étonnant(e) (22)
survive survivre *irreg.* (15)
sweatshirt sweatshirt (*fam.* sweat) *m.* (6)
sweet sucré(e) (8)
swim *v.* nager (16)
swimming pool piscine *f.* (13)
system (*network*) réseau *m.* (14); **subway system** reseau du métro (14)

table table *f.* (P); **to set the table** mettre (*irreg.*) la table (7)
tablecloth nappe *f.* (8)
tablet (*medicinal*) comprimé *m.* (9)
take prendre *irreg.* (7); **all it takes is** il suffit de (20); **I take it** je suppose (3); **to take a course** suivre (*irreg.*) un cours (15); **to take (a long) time** prendre du temps (7); **to take a trip** faire (*irreg.*) un voyage (5), voyager (6); **to take a walk** faire (*irreg.*) une promenade (5), se promener (9); **to take an exam** passer un examen (13); **to take a photograph** prendre (*irreg.*) une photo (16); **to take photographs** faire (*irreg.*) de la photographie (16); **to take place** avoir (*irreg.*) lieu (21); **to take refuge** se réfugier (19)
talk *v.* parler (2)
talkative bavard(e) (13)
tall grand(e) (2)
tea thé *m.* (8)
teach enseigner
teacher (*elementary school*) instituteur/trice *m., f.* (1), maître (maîtresse) *m., f.* (1)
teaching enseignement *m.* (13); **foreign language teaching** enseignement des langues étrangères (13); **secondary school teaching** enseignement secondaire (13)
team équipe *f.* (16)
telephone téléphone *m.* (5); **cell phone** portable *m.* (13); **telephone booth** cabine (*f.*) téléphonique (13); **to telephone** téléphoner (à) (7)
television télévision (*fam.* télé) *f.* (2); **television station** chaîne *f.* (12); **to put/turn on the television** mettre (*irreg.*) la télévision (7)
tell dire *irreg.* (12); **to tell about** raconter (8)
temperature température *f.* (10)
ten dix (P)
tennis tennis *m.* (10)
tenth dixième (11)
terminus terminus *m.* (14)
terrific formidable (2)
thank you merci (P)
that *adj.* ce, cet, cette (5); *rel. pron.* que (18); *rel. pron.* qui (18); **that is** c'est (P); **that is not** ce n'est pas (P); **that (one)** celle, celui (19)
theater théâtre *m.* (10)
then ensuite (10); puis (10); alors (1)
there *adv.* là (P); *pron.* y (15); **there is/are** (*pointing out*) voilà (1); (*counting*) il y a (P); **there is/are not** il n'y a pas de (4)
therefore alors (1)
these *adj.* ces (5); *pron.* celles, ceux (19); **these are (not)** ce (ne) sont (pas) (P)
thesis thèse *m.* (13)
they ils/elles/on (1); **they are (not)** ce (ne) sont (pas) (P)
thing chose *f.* (8)
think penser (2); **to think (about)** réfléchir (à) (11)
third troisième (11)
thirsty: to be thirsty avoir (*irreg.*) soif (4)
thirteen treize (P)
thirty trente (P)
this *adj.* ce, cet, cette (5); **this is** c'est (P); **this is not** ce n'est pas (P); **this (one)** celle, celui (19)
those *adj.* ces (5); *pron.* celles, ceux (19); **those are (not)** ce (ne) sont pas (P)
thousand mille (4)
three trois (P)
thrilled ravi(e) (21)
throat gorge *f.* (9)
throughout (*time*) au cours de (20)
thunder and lightening storm orage *m.* (10)
Thursday jeudi *m.* (4)
ticket billet *m.* (14); (subway) ticket (de métro) *m.* (14); **one-way (round trip) ticket** billet aller simple (aller-retour) (14) **ticket window** guichet *m.* (14)
tie cravate *f.* (6)
time fois *f.* (5); temps *m.* (5); heure *f.* (5); **at what time . . . ?** à quelle heure... ? (5); **from time to time** de temps en temps (12); **for a long time** longtemps (14); **full-time** à plein temps (11); **half-time** à mi-temps (11); **on time** à l'heure (5); **time off** congé *m.* (20); **to have a good time** s'amuser (9); **to spend time on** mettre (*irreg.*) du temps à (7); **to take (a long) time** prendre (*irreg.*) du temps (7); **what time is it?** quelle heure est-il? (5)
tired fatigué(e) (2)
tissue (*facial*) mouchoir (*m.*) en papier (9)
to à (1); en (14)
today aujourd'hui (3)
together ensemble (7)
tomato tomate *f.* (7)
tomorrow demain (3); **see you tomorrow** à demain (P)
too: too much, too many trop (de) (7); **that's too bad** c'est dommage; **it is too bad that** il est dommage que (21)
tooth dent *f.* (9)
topography relief *m.* (17)
tourist site site (*m.*) touristique (20)
toward vers (17)
track piste *f.* (16); **railroad tracks** voie (*f.*) de chemin de fer (19)
trade (*craft*) métier *m.* (11)
traffic circulation *f.* (14); **traffic jam** embouteillage *m.* (14); **traffic light** feu *m.* (17)
trail piste *f.* (16)
train train *m.* (14); **high-speed train** train à grande vitesse (*fam.* TGV) (14); **train car** wagon *m.* (14); **train station** gare *f.* (14); **to train** (*teach*) former (20)
traitor traître/tresse *m., f.* (14)
transfer *v.* faire/prendre (*irreg.*) une correspondance (14)
translate traduire *irreg.* (18)
translation traduction *f.* (13)
trap piège *m.* (19)
treason trahison *m.* (19)
tree arbre *f.* (18)
trip voyage *m.* (5); **to take a trip** faire (*irreg.*) un voyage (5), voyager (6)
troops troupes *f. pl.* (19)
trousers pantalon *m. s.* (6)
truck camion *m.* (19)
true vrai(e) (2); **is it true that . . . ?** est-ce vrai que... ? (1); **that is (it's) true** c'est vrai (2)
try (on) essayer (6)
T-shirt tee-shirt *m.* (6)
Tuesday mardi *m.* (4)
tuna thon *m.* (7)
turn *v.* tourner (17); **turn around** retourner (11); **turn on the radio (TV, light)** mettre (*irreg.*) la radio (télé, lumière) (7)
turnip navet *m.* (15)
twelve douze (P)
twentieth vingtième (11)
twenty vingt (P)
twenty-first vingt et unième (11)
two deux (P)

ugly laid(e) (2)
uncertain incertain(e) (21)
uncle oncle *m.* (4)
under sous (3)
understand comprendre *irreg.* (7)
unemployed au chômage (20)
unhappy malheureux/euse (2)
United States États-Unis *m. pl.* (3)

university université *f.* (P); **university residence** (*dormitory*) résidence (*f.*) universitaire (13); **university student** étudiant(e) *m., f.* (P)
unless sans que (21)
unlikely: it is unlikely (that) il est peu probable (que) (21)
until jusqu'à (3); jusqu'à ce que (21)
up: to get up, stand up se lever (9); **to go up** monter (11)
use *v.* employer (6)
useful utile (20)
useless (*no use*) inutile (20)
usually d'habitude (12)

vacation vacances *f. pl.* (16); **on vacation** en vacances (16)
valley vallée *f.* (17)
veal veau *m.* (8)
vegetable légume *m.* (7)
very très (P); **very well** très bien (P)
videocassette recorder (VCR) magnétoscope *m.* (5)
Vietnam Viêtnam *m.* (3)
Vietnamese *adj.* vietnamien(ne) (3)
view: to have a view of (the port) donner sur (le port) (20)
village village *m.* (18)
vine vigne *f.* (18)
vineyard vignoble *m.* (18)
visa visa *m.* (14)
visit: to visit (*a person*) rendre visite à (8); **to visit** (*a place*) visiter (8)
visual arts arts (*m. pl.*) plastiques (13)
volleyball volley-ball *m.* (10)

wait (for) attendre (8)
wake up se réveiller (9)
walk: to take a walk faire (*irreg.*) une promenade (5), se promener (9)
wall mur *m.* (1)
want avoir (*irreg.*) envie de (4); vouloir *irreg.* (6)
war guerre *f.* (8)
wardrobe (*furniture*) armoire *f.* (5)
warmth chaleur *f.* (20)
wash: to get washed, wash up se laver (9)
watch *v.* regarder (2)
water eau (*f.*) (7); **(carbonated, noncarbonated) mineral water** eau minérale (gazeuse, plate) (7)
waterski *v.* faire (*irreg.*) du ski nautique (16)
way route *f.* (14); chemin *m.* (17); **could you show me the way to** est-ce que vous pourriez m'indiquer le chemin pour aller à (17)
we nous/on (1)
weak faible (18)
weapon arme (*f.*) (19)
wear porter (2)
weather temps *m.* (10); **weather report** météo *f.* (10); **what's the weather?** quel temps fait-il? (10)
website site (*m.*) Web (13)
wedding anniversary anniversaire (*m.*) de mariage (11)
Wednesday mercredi *m.* (4)
week semaine *f.* (4)
weekend week-end *m.* (4)
weight training musculation *f.* (10)
weird bizarre (21)
welcome accueil *m.* (20); **to welcome** accueillir *irreg.*
well *adv.* bien (P); **I'm well** ça va bien (P); **very well** très bien (P); **well** *interj.* enfin (10); **well behaved** gentil(le) (2); **well known** réputé(e) (20)
west ouest *m.* (17)
what *interr. pron.* que (6); qu'est-ce que (6); qu'est-ce qui (16); quoi (6); **at what time?** à quelle heure? (5); **what courses are you taking?** quels cours est-ce que tu suis (vous suivez)? (13); **what is it/this/that?** qu'est-ce que c'est? (P); **what is/are . . . like?** comment est/sont... ? (2); **what's the weather?** quel temps fait-il? (10); **what's your name?** comment vous appelez-vous? (P), comment t'appelles-tu? (P); **what time is it?** quelle heure est-il? (5)
wheat blé *m.* (18)
when quand (4); *rel. pron.* où (18)
where *adv.* où (4); *rel. pron.* où (18); **where is . . . ?** où se trouve... ? (3)
whether si (7)
which *interr. adj.* quel (quelle, quels, quelles) (5); *rel. pron.* que (18); qui (18)
while pendant (14)
white blanc(he) (4, 6)
who *interr. pron.* qui (6); qui est-ce qui (16); *rel. pron.* qui (18) **who is it/this/that?** qui est-ce? (P)
whole: the whole . . . tout le / toute la... (4); **a whole week** toute une semaine (4)
whom *interr. pron.* qui (6); *rel. pron.* que (18)
why pourquoi (4)
wide large (22)
widowed veuf (veuve) (4)
wife femme *f.* (4)
willing: to be willing vouloir (*irreg.*) bien (6)
window fenêtre *f.* (1); **ticket window** guichet *m.* (14); **window seat** siège (*m.*) fenêtre (14)
windsurf faire (*irreg.*) de la planche à voile (16)
windy: it's windy out il fait du vent (10)
wine vin *m.* (7); **red (white, rosé) wine** vin rouge (blanc, rosé) (7); **wine growing** viticulture *f.* (18)
winter hiver *m.* (10); **in winter** en hiver (10)
wish *v.* souhaiter (21)
with avec (1); **with dignity** dignement (22); **with strength, with effort** fort (19)
without sans (2); sans que (21)
woman femme *f.* (P)
wonderful formidable (2)
work travail *m.* (2); **to work** travailler (2); **work (of art, literature, music); body of work** œuvre *f.* (21)
workbook cahier *m.* (P)
world monde *m.* (18)
world music world music *f.* (21)
worried inquiet/inquiète (2)
worry (about) *v.* s'inquiéter (de, pour) (9)
write écrire *irreg.* (12); **to write a check** faire (*irreg.*) un chèque (20)
writer écrivain/femme écrivain) *m., f.* (11)
wrong faux/fausse (2)

year an *m.* (4); année *f.* (4); **to be (twenty) years old** avoir (vingt) ans (4)
yellow jaune (6)
yes oui (P); **yes, of course!** bien sûr que oui! (2)
yesterday hier (10)
yogurt yaourt *m.* (15)
you tu/vous (1); **and you?** et vous (toi)? (P)
young jeune (2)
youth jeunesse *f.* (12)

zero zéro (P)
zucchini courgette *f.* (15)

Index

This index has four sections: Grammar, Culture, Vocabulary, and Reading Strategies. Topics treated within the Grammar index are cross-referenced. The Culture, Vocabulary, and Reading Strategies indexes are short; their contents are, for the most part, not cross-referenced. Page references followed by "n" refer specifically to footnotes or marginal notes.

Note: No references are given to the appendices. Appendice A (pp. A1–A5) provides definitions of grammatical terms, with examples. Appendice B (pp. A6–A10) is a table of verb forms and conjugations for active verbs in this text.

Grammar

Culture

Vocabulary

Reading Strategies

Credits

Photos

Page 34 (*top left*) Beryl Goldberg, (*top right*) Franz-Marc Freil/Corbis, (*bottom right*) © Ann Williams; *36* (*top*) Robert Fried/Stock Boston, (*bottom*) Philippe Girand/Corbis Sygma; *50* Becky Luigart-Stayner/Corbis; *58* (*clockwise from top left*) © Ann Williams, Toutain Dorbec Pierre/Corbis Sygma, Hekimian/Corbis Sygma, Ann Williams; *97* (*clockwise from top left*) Walter Rapho/The Liaison Agency, Michael A. Dwyer/Stock Boston, Nik Wheeler/Corbis, Catherine Ursillo/Photo Researchers Inc., Lee Snider/The Image Works, James Andanson/Corbis Sygma; *104* David Simson/Stock Boston; *121* R. Lucas/The Image Works; *124* (*clockwise from top left*) © Corbis, Corbis, Ann Williams, Bill Ross/Corbis; *126* © Thomas T. Field; *142* (*top and bottom*) Lee Snider/The Image Works; *146* (*left*) Rue des Archives/The Granger Collection, New York, (*right*) © Condé Nast Archive/Corbis; *147* (*bottom left*) © Condé Nast Archive/Corbis, (*middle*) © Bettmann/Corbis, (*top right*) © Pierre Vauthey/Corbis Sygma, (*bottom right*) © Petre Buzoianu/Avantis/Avantis/Time Life Pictures/Getty Images; *164* (*top*) Owen Franken/Stock Boston, (*bottom*) R. Lucas/The Image Works; 169 (*top left*) © Ann Williams, (*top right*) Yann Arthus-Bertrand/Corbis, (*bottom right*) © Ann Williams; *170* OPT, M. Schneider; *171* Owen Franken/Stock Boston; *213* Michael Nicholson/Corbis; *221* © William A. Allard/National Geographic/Getty Images, © Chad Ehlers/Stone/Getty Images; *258* © James Leynse/Corbis; *272* Dean Conger/Corbis; *294* Chip Hires/The Liaison Agency; *316* © Corbis; *317* Robert Holmes/Corbis; *322* (*top*) © Ann Williams, (*middle right*) © Ann Williams, (*bottom right*) Art on File/Corbis, (*bottom left*) Yann Arthus-Bertrand/Corbis; *324* Used by permission of Claudette Pelletier Deschênes; *344* © Ann Williams; *348* © Ann Williams; *349* © Ann Williams; *361* Bettmann/Corbis; *376* Lee Snider/The Image Works; *377* © Ann Williams; *381* (*bottom left*) Michael Busselle/Corbis, (*top left*) Michael Caby, Musée du Désert, (*bottom right*) Bob Gibbons, Eye Ubiquitous/Corbis; *388* © Ann Williams; *389* © Ann Williams; *397* Jonathan Blair/Corbis; *398* Stephane Ruet/Corbis Sygma; *417* Philip Gould/Corbis; *418* Jack Fields/Corbis; *451* McDuff Everton/Corbis; *452* Mike Southern, Eye Ubiquitous/Corbis; *455* Pascal Parrot/Corbis Sygma; *456* (*clockwise from top right*) Jean Marc Charles/Corbis Sygma, © Ann Williams, Chris Hellier/Corbis; *457* Wolfgang Kaehler; *462* (*top*) Pascal Parrot/Corbis Sygma, (*bottom*) Roger Wood/Corbis; *469* Roger Wood/Corbis; *475* (*top right*) The Purcell Team/Corbis, (*bottom left*) Wolfgang Kaehler, (*bottom right*) Robert Holmes/Corbis; *483* (*top*) Melies/Kobal Collection, (*bottom*) Kobal Collection; *484* (*left*) Prods. Artistes Associes/DA MA/Kobal Collection, (*right*) United Artists/Kobal Collection.

Realia

Page 51 © 2005, Les Éditions Albert René/Goscinny-Uderzo; *92 Histo Magazine; 126* Based on Emmanuel Todd, *The Explanation of Ideology*, Oxford: Basil Blackwell Ltd, 1985, p. v.; *137* National/Citer; *283* l'Université du Québec à Trois Rivières; *220 Le Figaro; 222* adapted from map at www.weatheroffice.com; *264 Le Figaro; 300* «Conditions de vie et les aspirations des Français,» Centre de Recherche pour l'Étude et l'Observation des Conditions de vie, http://www.credoc.asso.fr/ins/aspi.htm (27 July 2005); *307* based on map of the Paris metro, RATP; *383* Adapted from Eugene M. Rasmusson, "Global Climate Change and Variability," Michael Glantz, ed., *Drought and Hunger in Africa*, Cambridge: Cambridge University Press, 1987. Additional data from Nicholson, Sharon E; Some, B; and Kone, B. 2000. "An Analysis of Recent Rainfall Conditions in West Africa, Including the Rainy Seasons of the 1997 El Niño and the 1998 La Niña Years," *Journal of Climate 13:2628–2640; 413* Site national historique de la Résistance en Vercors.

Literature

Page 60 Francoscopie 1997 and *Francoscopie 1999*, Gérard Mermet; *146–147* Adapted from «mode, histoire de la» Encyclopédie Microsoft® Encarta® en ligne 2005. http://fr.encarta.msn.com © 1997-2005 Microsoft Corporation. Tous droits reservés; *192* «Familiale» in *Paroles* by Jacques Prévert. © Éditions Gallimard; *276* «Mon Amant de Saint-Jean» by Émile Carrara and Léon Agel. © 1948 by Les Nouvelles Éditions Méridian. Copyright renewed, international copyright secured. Used by permission. All rights reserved; *324* Photos and text used by permission of Claudette Pelletier Deschênes, daughter of Yolande Dionne. Complete texts and research can be found at: http://www.geocities.com/Heartland/Acres/3561/carmen01.htm. All rights reserved.; *402* «Le partage de la récolte» from *Le conte populaire en Cévennes,* Jean-Noël Pelen, © Éditions Payot et Rivages 1994; *475* Excerpts from *Le gone du Chaâba* de Azouz Begag, © Éditions Seuil 1986, Coll. *Cadre rouge,* 1998, Coll. *Points,* 2005.

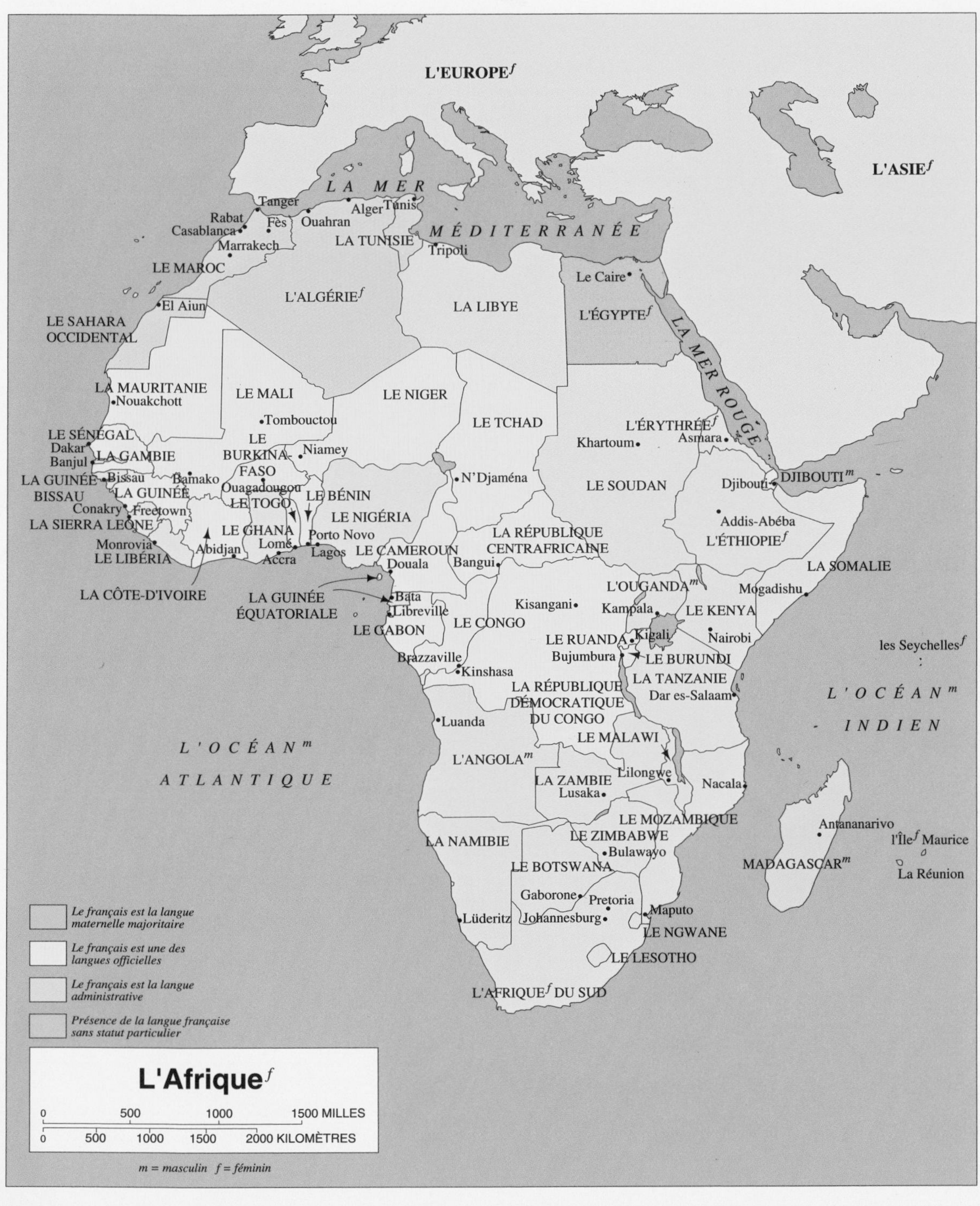
L'EUROPE^f
L'ASIE^f
LA MER MÉDITERRANÉE
LA MER ROUGE
L'OCÉAN^m ATLANTIQUE
L'OCÉAN^m INDIEN
Tanger
Rabat
Casablanca
Fès
Ouahran
Alger
Tunis
Marrakech
LA TUNISIE
Tripoli
LE MAROC
El Aiun
L'ALGÉRIE^f
LA LIBYE
Le Caire
L'ÉGYPTE^f
LE SAHARA OCCIDENTAL
LA MAURITANIE
Nouakchott
LE MALI
LE NIGER
Tombouctou
LE TCHAD
L'ÉRYTHRÉE^f
Asmara
Khartoum
LE SÉNÉGAL
Dakar
Banjul
LA GAMBIE
LE BURKINA-FASO
Niamey
LA GUINÉE-BISSAU
Bissau
Bamako
Ouagadougou
N'Djaména
LE SOUDAN
Djibouti
DJIBOUTI^m
LA GUINÉE
Conakry
Freetown
LA SIERRA LEONE
LE TOGO
LE BÉNIN
LE NIGÉRIA
Addis-Abéba
L'ÉTHIOPIE^f
LE GHANA
Porto Novo
LA RÉPUBLIQUE CENTRAFRICAINE
Monrovia
LE LIBÉRIA
Abidjan
Lomé
Accra
Lagos
LE CAMEROUN
Douala
Bangui
LA SOMALIE
LA CÔTE-D'IVOIRE
LA GUINÉE ÉQUATORIALE
Bata
Libreville
L'OUGANDA^m
Mogadishu
Kisangani
Kampala
LE KENYA
LE GABON
LE CONGO
LE RUANDA
Kigali
Nairobi
les Seychelles^f
Bujumbura
LE BURUNDI
Brazzaville
Kinshasa
LA TANZANIE
LA RÉPUBLIQUE DÉMOCRATIQUE DU CONGO
Dar es-Salaam
Luanda
LE MALAWI
L'ANGOLA^m
Lilongwe
LA ZAMBIE
Lusaka
Nacala
LE MOZAMBIQUE
Antananarivo
LA NAMIBIE
LE ZIMBABWE
Bulawayo
l'Île^f Maurice
MADAGASCAR^m
LE BOTSWANA
La Réunion
Gaborone
Pretoria
Maputo
Lüderitz
Johannesburg
LE NGWANE
LE LESOTHO
L'AFRIQUE^f DU SUD
Le français est la langue maternelle majoritaire
Le français est une des langues officielles
Le français est la langue administrative
Présence de la langue française sans statut particulier
L'Afrique^f
0 500 1000 1500 MILLES
0 500 1000 1500 2000 KILOMÈTRES
m = masculin f = féminin

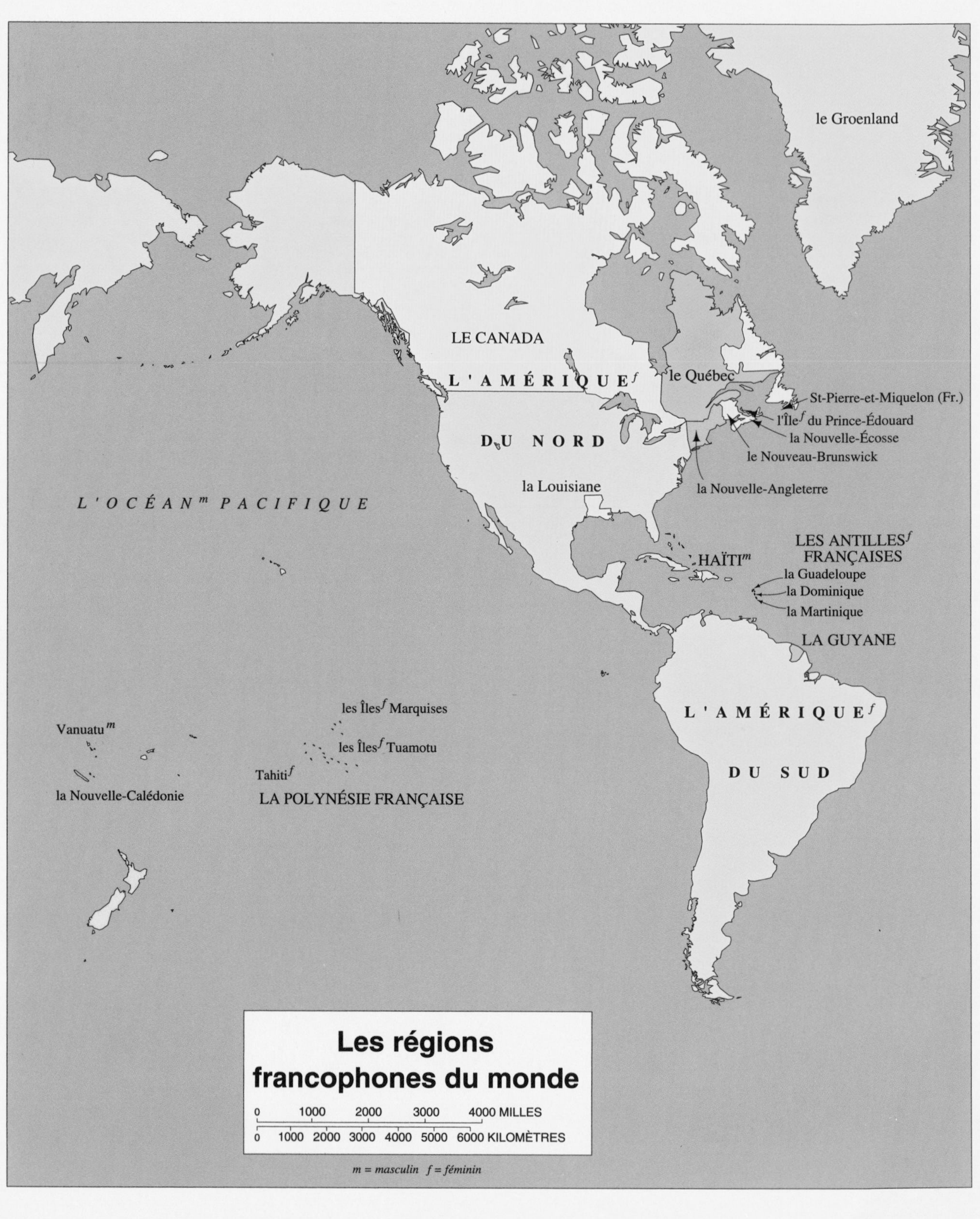
le Groenland
LE CANADA
L'AMÉRIQUE f
DU NORD
le Québec
St-Pierre-et-Miquelon (Fr.)
l'Île f du Prince-Édouard
la Nouvelle-Écosse
le Nouveau-Brunswick
la Louisiane
la Nouvelle-Angleterre
L'OCÉAN m PACIFIQUE
HAÏTI m
LES ANTILLES f FRANÇAISES
la Guadeloupe
la Dominique
la Martinique
LA GUYANE
L'AMÉRIQUE f
DU SUD
les Îles f Marquises
les Îles f Tuamotu
Vanuatu m
Tahiti f
la Nouvelle-Calédonie
LA POLYNÉSIE FRANÇAISE
Les régions francophones du monde
0 1000 2000 3000 4000 MILLES
0 1000 2000 3000 4000 5000 6000 KILOMÈTRES
m = masculin f = féminin